Learning in the Way

For Ian Bennett

*facilitator of adult learning
and Christian vision*

Learning in the Way

Research and Reflection on Adult Christian Education

edited by Jeff Astley

First published in 2000

Gracewing
2 Southern Avenue
Leominster
Herefordshire HR6 0QF

ISBN 0 85244 419 2

Typesetting by
Action Publishing Technology Ltd, Gloucester, GL1 1SP

Printed in England by
Short Run Press Ltd,
Exeter EX2 7LW

Contents

Acknowledgements

The editor wishes to express his thanks for permission to draw on previously published material. Gracewing, for permission to republish, in amended form, some material from the editorial overviews in *Christian Perspectives on Faith Development* (1992), *Critical Perspectives on Christian Education* (1994) and *Theological Perspectives on Christian Formation* (1996). Church House Publishing, for permission to use material from *How Faith Grows* (National Society and Church House Publishing, 1991) and *Tomorrow is Another Country* (Church House Publishing, 1996), both copyright © The Archbishops' Council. Abingdon Press and Professor Jack Seymour, for permission to adapt the chart from Jack Seymour and Donald E. Miller (eds), *Contemporary Approaches to Christian Education* (1982).

Contributors

The Revd Professor Jeff Astley is Director of the North of England Institute for Christian Education and Honorary Professorial Fellow in Practical Theology and Christian Education in the University of Durham.

The Revd Professor Leslie J. Francis is Professor of Practical Theology at the University of Wales, Bangor.

Mrs Meg Orr, formerly a teacher in further education and secondary schools, is now actively involved in adult Christian education in the Diocese of Durham.

Mrs Judith Sadler taught religious education in schools before taking up the post of Children's Work Adviser for the Diocese of Newcastle.

The Revd Mark Savage is Vicar of Bedlington, Northumberland and an Adult Education Course Tutor for the University of Newcastle upon Tyne. He was formerly Adult Education Adviser for the Diocese of Newcastle.

The Revd Roger Walton is Principal of the Wesley Study Centre, Durham. He was formerly Director of the Open Learning Centre of the Methodist Church in England and Wales.

Mrs Carolyn Wilcox is Research Fellow at the North of England Institute for Christian Education.

Preface

In 1988 the General Synod of the Church of England received a report from its Board of Education Working Party entitled *Children in the Way*.[1] This was an inspired title, capturing the ambiguous attitude of the church to its youngest members – who were seen *both* as treading the road of Christian discipleship *and* (tell it not in Gath) as something of a nuisance. They were both 'on the road' and, as we say in my native Lancashire, 'in t' road'.

The church has a similarly ambiguous relationship with adult Christian learners. In his influential paper 'Does the Church Really Want Religious Education?', the American scholar Charles Melchert wrote:

> We should perhaps pay much more attention to adults and adolescents in our education by the church. The virtually exclusive focus of the church's education on children has created the impression that religious education is 'kid stuff', and perhaps even that Christianity is something to be outgrown as one becomes adult.[2]

One gets the impression sometimes, not least from some clergy, that adult Christian education is a dangerous thing, that adult church members are to be protected from it and indeed that ministers themselves need to be protected from exposure to an educated laity. But, as another Christian educationalist has affirmed:

> There are many reasons why our educational ministry, like Jesus' own, must focus on adults. Jesus welcomed the children ... but he chose adults to train as his disciples.
>
> If the church today is to have an impact like that of the early church, it will be because we have rediscovered that focus. A focus on adults. And a focus on discipleship.[3]

It is not, however, my purpose to encourage further polarisation between the concerns of adult Christian educators and those who work with children and young people. Indeed, a feature of this book is the attempt to draw on the widest discussion of religious and Christian education so as to illuminate the problems and possibilities of the formative and critical Christian education of adults. This is unusual in discussions of adult Christian learning, which often arise more from the experience of, and literature on, secular adult education. A great deal of the material in these chapters will therefore be relevant to those involved in the Christian education of children and young people, as well as those whose concerns are restricted to work with adults. Nevertheless, the main focus here is on the adult learner, and on theory and research that is relevant to adult Christian education.

We have tried hard to make the text itself as straightforward as possible. However, the authors and editor have provided full references to the literature in the notes to each chapter, where additional technical issues are also discussed. In this way the book will not only be useful as a general introduction, but should also be of value to those readers who wish to explore the subject in greater depth. For this second group the book may serve as a useful complement to the readers on Christian education that have been published recently by Gracewing, especially:

Jeff Astley and Leslie J. Francis (eds), *Christian Perspectives on Faith Development: A Reader*, Leominster: Gracewing Fowler Wright; Grand Rapids, Mich.: Wm. Eerdmans, 1992;

Jeff Astley and Leslie J. Francis (eds), *Critical Perspectives on Christian Education: A Reader on the Aims*, Principles and Philosophy of Christian Education, Leominster: Gracewing Fowler Wright, 1994;

Jeff Astley, Leslie J. Francis and Colin Crowder (eds), *Theological Perspectives on Christian Formation: A Reader on Theology and Christian Education*, Leominster: Gracewing Fowler Wright; Grand Rapids, Mich.: Wm. Eerdmans, 1996.[4]

Wherever possible, reference has been made to articles as they have been collected in these readers.

This is the second collection of essays produced directly under the auspices of the North of England Institute for Christian Education (NEICE).[5] All the authors have some connection with this ecumenical research institute, either directly as staff members or more remotely as associated Christian educators and researchers.

I should like to express my thanks to all who have helped with the production of this volume: the authors for making their essays available; Evelyn Jackson, Secretary to NEICE, for word-processing (and repeatedly re-processing) the text and preparing it for the printers; and the Management Trustees of NEICE and of the Hild-Bede Trust for their financial support. I know that they would all wish to join with me in dedicating this book, with gratitude and best wishes, to Ian Bennett, formerly Director of Ministry and Training in the Diocese of Newcastle, to mark his retirement as Chairman of NEICE.

Jeff Astley
July 1999

NOTES

[1] General Synod Board of Education, *Children in the Way: New Directions for the Church's Children*, London: National Society/Church House Publishing, 1988.

[2] Charles F. Melchert, 'Does the Church Really Want Religious Education?', *Religious Education*, LXIX, 1, 1974, pp. 12–22, quotation from pp. 20–21. Melchert's title (if not his detailed argument) has provided what has been described as 'one of the most doggedly persistent questions ever raised in contemporary religious education' (Marlene Mayr (ed.), *Does the Church Really Want Religious Education?*, Birmingham, Ala.: Religious Education Press, 1988, p. 7).

[3] Lawrence O. Richards, *A Theology of Christian Education*, Grand Rapids, Mich.: Zondervan, 1975, p. 228.

[4] A further title is in preparation: Jeff Astley and Leslie J. Francis (eds), *Psychological Perspectives on Christian Learning: A Reader on Psychology and Christian Education*.

[5] See also Jeff Astley and David Day (eds), *The Contours of Christian Education*, Great Wakering: McCrimmons, 1992.

1

Aims and Approaches in Christian Education

Jeff Astley

AIMS OF CHRISTIAN EDUCATION

What is Christian Education?

The phrase 'Christian education' has a tendency, which it shares with St Paul, of becoming all things to all people. I want to attempt first of all, therefore, to clarify the range of meanings that have been given to the term, and to define the way in which it is to be used in this book. What is the aim of Christian education?

For some, Christian education means simply *education about Christianity*: that is, the process of learning about and reflecting on Christian scripture, history, beliefs, worship, spirituality, ethical principles and ways of living. Education about Christianity very properly forms a substantial part of religious education in 'county', 'community' or 'state' schools in this country, as well as in many church schools. It is also a proper part of religious studies courses in colleges and universities – sometimes labelled as 'Christian studies' – and is an important complement to the more specifically theological dimensions of courses in 'Christian theology'.[1] A great deal of adult education about Christianity falls under this heading, especially courses offered by further education colleges or adult and continuing education departments of universities.

For others, Christian education labels an *approach to general education* or schooling. It might be described as drawing on a Christian *philosophy of* (in the sense of an aim and understanding of) the function of all education. Those whose interest lies mainly with the church school or college, sometimes called the 'Christian school/ college', often think of Christian education in this sense as something that should happen within its corridors and classrooms right across the range of subjects and activities. Some would even claim that a 'Christian country' should ensure that Christian values and insights undergird, control and permeate the ethos and curriculum even of universities and state schools, as well as of other non-church educational institutions. In the context of adult learning, it is sometimes argued that church-based religious education courses may properly contain secular topics on the grounds that adults 'may experience the meaning of community and the meaning of *agape* in a course on financial planning, and not at all experience these meanings in a discursive study of the gospels'.[2] The focus of such claims is on a *general education* that is based on, and helps to promote, Christian principles, values and experiences.

In this book, however, we shall not say much about these two understandings of Christian education. One reason for this is that our concern is for the church rather than the university, school or general programme of adult education. Another is that – at least for myself, but also for many of the other authors of this book – the preferred definition of the term 'Christian education' is in one sense more limited than those we have just explored, while from another point of view it is much more wide-ranging.

We define Christian education here as *education into Christianity*. On this definition the phrase marks out those *educational processes through which people learn to become Christian and to be more Christian*. Christian education, so defined, results in *Christian learning,* in the sense of the adoption and deepening of Christian beliefs, attitudes and values, and of a person's disposition to act and experience in Christian ways, in addition to changes in other dimensions of the learner's mind, heart and will. So the focus is on Christianity, not general education; but the aim is 'to learn Christianity' and not just to learn about it. Much of it may indeed be described as 'learning Christ' (cf. Ephesians 4:20).

On this broad account, Christian education can include both Christian *evangelism* and Christian *nurture or formation*. As we shall see later, it may also include an induction into the skills and habits of *critical reflection* on the Christian tradition, as people learn to think about and self-critically evaluate their Christian faith. It should also be clear that our definition applies to people right across the age span. Christian education is not just for children; it is also for adolescents, young adults, the middle-aged and the elderly.

This broad definition of Christian education presupposes a broad definition of education, so as to cover a wide range of learning outcomes, as well as a wide range of contexts, methods and processes in and by which people learn. Fundamentally, *learning* is a more or less permanent change in a person brought about by experience (and is therefore to be distinguished from changes in a person's *development* through intellectual or physical maturation). And, of course, learning is not limited to *cognitive* learning: that is, the acquisition of understanding and knowledge. Despite the rhetoric of some adult educators, it is certainly not limited to learning that results from (and in) critical reflection. Our learning also includes the learning of manual and intellectual skills, and of attitudes, values, emotions and dispositions.[3] Others have defined education and learning, and therefore Christian education and Christian learning, more narrowly than this; but in this book we wish to be inclusive rather than exclusive.[4]

We learn all the time, and many of the experiences through which we learn to be Christian as children and as adults 'just happen' to us. They have not been engineered or planned in order that we might learn from them. When people speak of 'education', however, they are usually referring to learning that has been brought about by *teaching*. Hence those activities that fall under the heading of Christian education normally involve some *intentional* activity by a teacher or educator that results in the *facilitation* of Christian learning. This limits the field a little. Nevertheless, the practice of Christian education ranges widely: from formal and explicit occasions (e.g. Sunday School classes and adult Bible study groups) right through to more informal events that give rise to less explicit Christian learning, but which have been structured with an eye to their educational effects (e.g. activities of worship, prayer or meditation; acts of practical ministry and care; even committee meetings and fund-raising events). Christian education is an activity that may be found in a wide variety of contexts; it is not just for the classroom, seminar room or study.

Christian Education, Religious Education, Religious Studies

Education into Christianity, as we have seen, is to be distinguished from education about Christianity. This latter subject is viewed by most educationalists as a proper subject for the publicly-funded educational endeavours of schools and universities. In British schools the subject designated by the term *religious education* (or 'RE')[5] has in recent decades routinely been understood mainly as a 'non-confessional', in the sense of a non-evangelistic and non-nurturing, *study of* the phenomena of Christianity and of other world faiths. As noted above, such 'religious studies' ('RS') courses share many of the same aims as those of departments of religious studies in secular universities. In both schools and colleges they are concerned with developing an empathetic understanding of the religions, and some sort of evaluation of them; they are not aimed at fostering any form of religious commitment. Thus a recent Government publication advises that RE syllabuses in England and Wales 'must not be designed to convert pupils, or to urge a particular religion or religious belief on pupils'.[6] (RE is a compulsory subject of the 'basic curriculum' for all pupils in full-time school education in this country, unless they are withdrawn from studying it at the request of their parents.)[7]

From time to time this rather sharp dividing line between religious nurture and religious education has been challenged.[8] In any case, *school* RE syllabuses often go beyond a purely religious studies approach restricted to learning about and reflecting on religion. Thus many would include within the scope of RE such additional objectives as students (i) 'learning from religion' about themselves and (ii) being encouraged in their own 'search for a faith to live by' – or some other description of a personal quest for meaning and value.[9] Syllabuses also usually recognise that RE should include the further task of developing in pupils certain positive (tolerant) attitudes to religion and to religious believers, as well as promoting the 'spiritual, moral, cultural, mental and physical development of pupils' (a general objective that RE shares with the rest of the curriculum) and preparing them for adult life and society.[10] The legal provision for *school worship* in this country muddies the educational waters even more, for insofar as RE is a non-confessional exploration of religion it is surely in conflict with the requirement that pupils should – unless withdrawn at the request of their parents – engage in worship within the school.[11] Needless to say, *universities* are not expected to extend their students' relationship with religion in these ways.

These debates are not our direct concern. They are helpful, however, in underscoring the contrast between, on the one hand, education into and in religion in the church and, on the other, education about religion in the university or school. In this book we are mainly interested in the distinctive nature of Christian education understood as the church's tasks of Christian evangelism, formation and critical self-reflection. These activities should be clearly distinguished from the education about Christianity that is appropriate in a university or school funded solely by central or local government. 'Christian education', as understood here, is the responsibility of the church; it is no part of the task of the 'common' or 'secular' school or college. (Some further reflection may be appropriate, however, on the work of departments of *Christian theology* in secular universities, and on the task of religious education in *church schools*.)[12]

The Nature of Christianity

In order to define Christian education more closely it is necessary for us to attempt to say what it means for a person to be Christian. This is often the point at which disagreements first arise over the nature of Christian education. These arguments often resolve into (theological) arguments over the nature of Christianity itself. This is itself a topic of considerable significance. But our interest in the discussion is a little more specialised than is that of most Christians, or even most theologians. As Christian educators, we are most concerned with those Christian attributes or characteristics that can be *learned*, either directly or indirectly.

The products of Christian education may be labelled as *Christian learning outcomes*. I attempt to list them below. I should state at the outset that the absence from this list of various theological accounts of, for example, a person's supernatural relationship with God does not mean that such elements are to be ignored. I shall be arguing in the next section that it only indicates that Christian education is a practical subject, and that the Christian educator must concentrate on those results of learning that can be identified in some way and changed by educational processes. Of course, these human attitudes, beliefs, and so on will all be related at one level or another to a person's relationship with God. But as Christian educators we cannot guarantee to deliver or even discover the divine side of that divine-human encounter. We shall have to be content, therefore, to concentrate on what we *can* change. And that means concentrating on the human side, including the effects of human learning.

Our list of Christian learning outcomes ('Christian attributes') might read as follows:[13]

(1) *Christian beliefs-that, understanding and knowledge.* This includes fundamental beliefs about the existence, nature and activity of God and Jesus (both the historical Jesus and the risen, glorified Christ), and theological beliefs about the church, human nature and the world.
(2) *Christian beliefs-in.* This category includes faith and trust in, for example, God, Jesus, salvation or the sacraments. Note that to believe in something is more than believing that it exists or happens – consider what it means 'to believe in Marxism' or 'to believe in baptism'. A 'belief-in' is a 'belief-that' (such as the belief that God exists) that is accompanied by positive evaluations and attitudes of commitment or trust directed towards the object of that belief. It is, if you like, a belief-that 'with attitude', and thus overlaps with the next category.

(3) *Christian attitudes and values.* This covers the attitudes and dispositions of Christian spirituality and 'the Christian virtues'. Examples might include being concerned for others, trustful of and open to God, humble, and so on.

(4) *Christian emotions and feelings.* Examples might include awe, remorse, joy and other 'religious affections'. It is often difficult to distinguish between categories (3) and (4).

(5) *Christian experiences.* These are what some would call 'objective' religious experiences, that is experiences *of* God, Christ or the Spirit and their activities. ('Subjective' experiences, or religious feeling-states, would be included in the previous category.)

(6) *Christian moral actions.* This covers 'Christianity in action', in the sense of *active* love (including the expression of pastoral and prophetic concern), forgiveness and trust, just and honest behaviour, and so on.

(7) *Christian religious actions.* This labels a different type of Christian action, illustrated by such 'explicitly religious' activities as prayer, profession of faith, evangelism, worship and 'church membership' (or other forms of ecclesial involvement).

We should note that attributes of type (5), (6) and (7) cannot be *directly* learned. We can, however, learn the attitudes, dispositions and skills that motivate and enable these experiences and actions. Thus people can learn to be more open to religious experience, and Christian education might develop in the learner tendencies of heart, mind and will to behave in a Christian fashion.

(8) *Christian/theological reflection and criticism.* This category includes those skills and processes of interpretation and evaluation that lead to the activity of 'critical' (i.e. judging, assessing) Christian reflection and theological evaluation. In such 'Christian self-criticism' aspects of the Christian faith are assessed by the Christian learner against certain standards of rationality and of moral and spiritual worth, particularly those that are implicit within the Christian tradition itself. Some would argue that Christian education is not truly 'education' if this learning outcome is neglected. On this view, Christian education is more than just formation or nurture; in the case of adults especially, it should also include some element of *critical Christian education* that leads to '*Christian criticism*' (see pp. 37–40 below).

Learning the Christian Attributes and 'Being Christian'

Some readers may feel uneasy with this analysis. Is there not more to being Christian, as an adult or otherwise, than this? Surely the

Christian attributes are themselves only expressions, or perhaps conditions, of something that is far more fundamental? These are important questions. In order to tackle them properly, I shall have to address some contentious theoretical issues. Some readers may therefore care to move now straight to page 14 or 17, returning to this discussion later.

It seems that there are three main types of candidate for the 'something else' that is said to undergird the Christian attributes.

(i) In the first category we have *the effects of human activity* relating to an individual's identity as a member of the church (and often, therefore, as saved or on the road to salvation). Christians, it might be said, are those who have been baptised with water and the trinitarian name. By such an action their status has been objectively changed. Whatever beliefs, attitudes or actions they adopt or express now or later, they have become Christian 'through baptism'.

(ii) Or the answer might be given instead in terms of *the effects of God's activity* (or that of Christ, or the Holy Spirit). The example of baptism often relates the two, by treating the church's act as effecting a new status that is bestowed by God, or even *as* God's act itself.[14] Others may speak more generally, outside the context of baptism, of the effects of God's grace, or of God's gift of faith, or of the coming of the Spirit. Again, such a change in people may be expressed in their beliefs, attitudes and behaviour, but it is a change that is more fundamental than such expressions.

(iii) A third option speaks of a *relationship with God* (or Christ or the Spirit) as the mark of the true Christian. This is closely related to category (ii), but treats the relationship as more clearly involving both a divine and a human pole. A relationship is something that 'exists' or 'happens' *between* the two parties, even if it is usually described either as something God/Christ/the Spirit does ('looking favourably on us', 'graciously accepting us', 'having his hand on us') or as some change in us ('being in Christ', 'having Jesus in one's heart').

All three types of answer share a common concern for some change that makes people Christian and 'happens to them'. In short, each postulates an *ontological* change: a change in a person's very being. On this view, it might be said, Christians do not necessarily differ from non-Christians in what they *do* (believe, feel, experience, value, think, act), or even in the attitudes, dispositions and so on that they *have*, but at the deeper level of what they *are*. The adjective 'ontological' may be extended to cover those accounts that claim that the difference in a person's being is a matter of her being differently related to God, rather than just changing 'in herself'. In these cases her status is changed but not her substance, or her relationship with God is changed but not her inner being. Yet this sort of change still needs to be distinguished from a change in a person's activity (including their thinking, feeling and believing), which would be a matter of their *function*.

We may note an instructive parallel here with similar ontological/functional debates within Christian theology. The Dutch philosopher Cornelis van Peursen characterised our own age as a period of painful transition from ontological to functional thinking, when 'the nouns of the ontological era become the verbs of the functional era.'[15] In the period of ontological thinking the main issue is *what* something is, but 'in the period of functional thinking, it is *how* something is, how it functions'.[16]

Despite a continuing strong tradition that defends ontological theology,[17] some have come to prefer a theological analysis in terms of function, often indeed of overt, observable functions, and seek to avoid the inevitable mysteriousness of ontological claims. Thus it is sometimes said that Jesus 'is God' because he functions as God: that is, he does the work of God (forgiving, healing, loving, saving); metaphysical questions about natures, being and relations in Christology are by-passed.[18] Similarly, the sacraments are often thought of as sacraments because of their psychological and social effects, rather than on account of some inner, unobservable properties of the 'matter' of the sacrament, or any mysterious changes wrought in the inner being of their recipients. Such a functional sacramental theology is more characteristic of Protestants and liberals than of other Christians, but it is increasingly influential across the board. On this view, baptism effects (creates) a new sociological status in the baptisand. Through baptism she becomes a church member, in terms of her social relationships rather than through any mystical change in her being. She is treated as a member by the church, and the church trusts that eventually she will act as such.[19] There is no suggestion of, and no need for, any 'inner change'. Sociologically, children who are not 'in the church', in the sense of participating in its worship and fellowship, are not in fact usually viewed as *members* of the church, notwithstanding the fact of their having undergone the rite of baptism. So baptism is what it does. (And if it 'doesn't', at least in some sense it 'isn't'!)

Similarly, the elements of bread and wine of the eucharist are seen by many (and not just by Protestants) as 'sacramental' elements on account of the functions they perform and the uses they have, rather than because of their changed substantial nature.[20] The priesthood, too, is more likely nowadays to be interpreted as constituted by priestly functioning, rather than by indelible marks on the soul created by God at ordination. The rhetoric about a priest only having to 'be' and not also to 'do' used to be very popular; but we should be aware how quickly it collapses, for such 'being' can only be identified and distinguished as a species of doing. The same rule applies here: a priest is what a priest does.[21]

To take another example, holy matrimony is often now regarded simply as a public ceremony of mutual promising in which the words and deeds have the 'performative' functions of expressing, promising and helping to generate personal commitment. The older, ontological interpretation of the marriage ceremony, by contrast, pictured it as involving the additional event of the creation of a metaphysical bond (*vinculum*) between husband and wife, a bond that no human power is able to breach. On the functional view, however, marital personal commitments are human behaviour-functions that may fail, and the marriage with them. The relationship, like very many relationships between human beings, is seen solely in terms of the functioning of individuals.[22]

Why has this shift from an ontological to a functional analysis come about? Partly it is a concern to 'spell out' or 'unpack' concepts in a way that makes some practical difference. In theology at least, it is also partly because the modern mind has become very chary of mysterious, inner, unobservable changes. One aspect of the legacy of Logical Positivism[23] is a sense of unease that many feel when confronted by statements about unobservable ontological changes. We may allow (against the Positivists) that such talk does have factual meaning, for the meaning of language is constituted by what it asserts and denies. But the lack of any 'checkability' in these ontological claims renders them suspect and, in a sense, useless. How do we *know* that these changes have happened? Speculation about the 'inner' nature of things is often cut short by such requests for evidence.

These questions multiply. How do we know if this person really is a priest, or 'still married', or a member of the church; whether this is (just) ordinary bread and wine or (also) the body and blood of Christ; whether Jesus is truly the Son of God? Ontological accounts of Christ, the sacraments, priesthood and the church seem suspiciously immune from the risk of the search for evidence. This is one reason why people are less and less interested in them. On functional accounts, on the other hand, there is at least the possibility of knowing whether *a* is *b*, if being *b* is a matter of functioning in a particular way and that functioning finds expression in something that is observable.

In the case of many of the ontological accounts of *what it is to be Christian*, we do not know when and where they apply, except on authority; for the essential changes in a person's being, status or relationship with God are said to be ever mysterious and hidden. Hence the claim that is sometimes voiced that only God really knows who is a Christian. We humans do not, unless there happens to be a correlation between this inner change and some outer, observable sign or precondition of it. On some extreme accounts, if God's action is truly hidden even the Christian herself may not know whether she is a Christian or not.

At one level then, functional theologies simply articulate a workable 'epistemology of religion' (a theory of religious knowing), in that they speak of what can be seen and are agnostic about the metaphysical (ontological) reality that lies beneath the observable effects of sacraments, or the behaviour of priests, or Jesus's activity. But the functional accounts of the liberal theologian are actually more radical than that, for they tend to *define* the nature of sacrament, priest and Christ in terms of their functions.

I must make it clear that the Christian educator and educationalist need not adopt this liberal theological position. I must also point out that I do not wish gratuitously to deny these traditional ontological claims, and acknowledge that I have paid no attention here to the argument that function arises from an underlying ontology. But I do insist that as educators we must recognise that *education is a practical matter*. Learning is defined as a relatively long-lasting change in a person brought about by experience. Such a definition, framed within the context of the practical concerns of education, presupposes that such changes are in principle, and in large part, 'observable'. Admittedly, they are mostly not directly, and sometimes not publicly,[24] observable. Most of them are inferred from, or are presupposed by, what is publicly observable. Some may only be discovered by the introspective activity of the learner (who might then tell other people about them). But in all such cases we, as educators, can know when learning has taken place, at least in principle. There may be other changes in a person: metaphysical, mysterious, 'supernatural', unobservable, ontological changes. But surely Christian educators cannot take those changes into account in the practice – and therefore the theory – of Christian education. Please note that I am *not* arguing that 'only the observable is real'. What I am arguing is that only realities that are observable (in the broad senses outlined above) can be *known* to be real, and that is what matters to the Christian educator who needs to assess her educational practice in terms of its effects.

This is my real justification for the list of Christian attributes outlined above. Christian education requires a definition of being Christian along some such lines; it needs a definition that is of some use to it. And it therefore needs to be able to rely on evidence; it must seek a definition that is 'empirical'. I admit that Christian education, as I have defined it, is not necessarily the same activity as creating citizens of heaven or producing redeemed saints for God, although I am personally sympathetic to a functional theology that tends to equate them. Christian education may not be concerned with 'creating Christians' *in these senses*. Yet those who wish in this way to distinguish radically between 'being Christian', on the one hand, and 'learning Christianity', on the other, should perhaps exercise some caution. They must ask themselves how their account of being Christian can be *used* by evangelists, apologists, nurturers and educators in planning their own work, so that that work may have a Christian point or purpose. Christian educators and evangelists still need to know when someone is (more) Christian. How can they exercise their ministry properly if they do not?

Objecting to Objectives

We are beginning to move from theological to educational concerns. Theologians are not the only ones who may wish to take issue with the approach outlined above. Educationalists might be concerned that what is being presented here is a *behavioural objectives model of Christian learning*, and is therefore open to the criticisms commonly made of such a model (see chapter 7 below). At the heart of the behavioural objectives model is an attempt to clarify the activities of teaching and learning by a specification of observable changes in student behaviour,[25] thus giving educational evaluation something to evaluate.[26] But the model is often dismissed by educationalists as 'an extremely narrow view of the teaching and learning process'. Its critics claim that it is a perspective that is appropriate to 'training' but not 'education', and one that is in any case impracticable (because it would be impossible to specify all the objectives even in one area of learning).[27] Criticism is particularly levelled at those curricula that have *highly specific, short-term* behavioural objectives: for example. that the student must be able to 'describe' something or 'distinguish between' a range of things, or that her essay must 'give critical reasons' for a claim. It is clear both that these are often not the only ways in which a student can show that she possesses the learning outcomes we desire, and that much learning only reveals itself some time after the educational process in which it has been laid down. This is certainly likely to be the case with much Christian education. Further, a great deal of the language of objectives seems to focus on 'performance behaviours', neglecting the less overt activities of thinking, feeling and perceiving. Many examples of 'objectives' teaching do indeed smack of a rather narrow, deterministic, 'measurement-is-everything' view of the art of teaching.[28]

There is value therefore in Elliot Eisner's distinction between *instructional objectives* (that is behavioural objectives – 'forms of behavior whose characteristics are known beforehand') and *expressive objectives*. He writes:

> An expressive objective does not specify the behavior the student is to acquire after having engaged in one or more learning activities. An expressive objective describes an educational encounter ... but it does not specify what from that encounter, situation, problem or task they are to learn.[29]

Although he is writing about schooling, Eisner's words will strike bells for adult educators, who agree that their goals cannot always be precise and that 'there is much that we do, and need to do, without a clear sense of what the objective is'.[30] Expressive objectives give an account of the sort of encounter the teacher should provide for the learner. In a sense, then, they specify the processes of *teaching* (what the teacher and the taught should do within the teaching act), rather than serving as *learning objectives* that specify what is to be learned (what the learner should be able to do after she has been taught). Expressive objectives are couched in language such as 'to visit', 'to interpret', 'to examine and appraise'. They are particularly pertinent to the more open-ended purposes of critical education; whereas instructional objectives fit more closely the 'mastery learning' of formative education (see below, pp. 37–38).

But unless *some* learning objectives are recognised as appropriate and proper outcomes of the educational experiences described by these expressive objectives, and others denied that palm, teachers would not embark on these 'visits' or 'examinations' at all. RE teachers arranging a visit to a mosque intend their children to understand more about Islam and to be more tolerant of religious diversity; they do not intend that they learn more about the taste of beefburgers or become antagonistic to Asian culture. Adult Christian educators similarly intend their planned Bible study to result in growth in *some* particular area of theological understanding, religious attitude or belief. They would not count it a successful educational encounter if all that was learned was an appreciation of the quality of Mrs A's scones and an increased willingness to engage in destructive gossip about the vicar's marriage. At the end of the educational day (which, I agree, is not necessarily on the day itself) we have to come back to specifying some learning outcomes. If we cannot do this, we have perhaps lost all sense of our educational practice having an aim or purpose at all. (And as practical educators we will want those outcomes to be *knowable*, whether through direct observation, from inference from behaviour that is observable, or by introspection.)

We may agree with Lawrence Stenhouse that 'education as induction into knowledge is successful to the extent that it makes the behavioural outcomes of the student unpredictable', for we want learners to learn *how to think*, individually and creatively (and, we might add, Christianly).[31] But this is still an *outcome*, and an outcome of a certain sort. Neither worthwhile knowledge nor higher level cognitive skills are wholly 'indeterminate as to student outcomes'.[32] We know this because we know that certain other outcomes would not be regarded as worthwhile, or even proper. Similarly, while it is true that the sort of adult personal learning that involves insight, transformation of perspective and re-defining of one's self cannot be narrowly specified in advance 'in terms of objectives to be attained or behaviors ... to be performed',[33] yet such broad changes (insight, transformation of perspective, etc.) may themselves properly be designated as 'educational objectives'. And some of them will be 'more Christian' than others. (Despairing about the possibility of meaning, or viewing oneself as beyond moral judgement, are not Christian attributes.) Further, we are surely allowed to specify a *range* of appropriate outcomes that the Christian educator may seek to encourage.

Undoubtedly, one major problem with objectives accounts lies with the sort of learning outcomes that are specified in practice, rather than with the theoretical idea of specifying objectives at all. I trust that the account I have offered above may be defended against these educational criticisms. There is certainly no need to claim that all learning outcomes are changes in *observable* behaviour.[34] Nevertheless, it is important to recognise that although the 'inner', 'hidden' activities of believing, feeling, evaluating, and so on, *may* exist without any outward expression, only rarely do they do so. It is the fact that behavioural expression normally correlates with, and is assumed to correlate with, inner states that allows us to speak of these inner states in others – and indeed in the end to speak of them in ourselves. Modern philosophical work, drawing on Wittgenstein, argues that external behavioural expression is a 'criterion' of inner mental activity. This means that it is part of the way that we conventionally use words that certain outer behaviour is necessarily good evidence for certain mental states. Thus, for example, pain is necessarily identifiable through – although not identical with – pain behaviour; the expression of pain being evidence (but not conclusive evidence) for someone's being in pain.[35]

At the very least, and of more relevance to the educator with her practical concerns, we can only *know* of these 'inner' changes in others when we can observe their concomitant 'outer' manifestations. Thus learning can only be inferred from the observation of changes in behaviour (including verbal behaviour); and teaching can only be assessed on the basis of such observations. Some form of empiricism is thus surely inevitable in education.[36] It would seem to be somewhat bizarre to attempt educational *practice* on any other model. While acknowledging that not all learning outcomes or Christian attributes will 'show' in overt behaviour, I therefore feel justified in claiming that the Christian educator can only properly work with those that do.

A further point may be added here. It is unhelpful to oppose an 'objectives-model' to a 'content-model' of the curriculum, where the latter is regarded as putting the stress on content (usually knowledge or ways of thinking) as worthwhile in itself, while the objectives model is interpreted as viewing content as merely instrumentally useful in creating a desired 'output' in terms of a change in the learner. We certainly need to reflect on what is *intrinsically* good in the content of any educational curriculum, but all that means is that we should reflect on what is intrinsically good in a learner (knowledge, attitudes, values, etc.). The outcome of the learner's learning remains the goal of the educational process.

Further Theological Criticism

Before finally leaving this topic we may briefly consider a rather tamer theological criticism: that being a Christian is not a matter of having *all* the Christian attributes, but is rather constituted by one particular thing – possessing Christian faith, for example, or Christian love. This element may be said to be the 'one thing needful', or to constitute the *essence* of Christianity.

The account given above does not ignore such claims; nor does it exclude their discussion from the outset. By all means let us, as Christians and theologians, argue over the list of Christian attributes – and for the relative importance of some members of that list over others. My only concern would be that one-factor accounts tend to leave important things out of the frame. Multi-factor accounts, however, should not be taken to imply that each element is of equal importance. I have argued elsewhere about the particular importance of the affective and reflective 'Christian attributes'.[37] Such claims are, in broad terms, *theological* claims. Theology is here exercising its quite proper normative function of defining and articulating the nature of the Christian religion.[38] Christian theology will want, and should have, its evaluative say in defining the authentic and valuable Christian attributes that Christian education should promote, as it has its own account (which needs to be related to other accounts) of what constitutes human fulfilment. *Theological evaluation* is intrinsically involved in any account of what it is to be religious. No phenomenological account of the Christian religion can constitute a valid norm for judging whether it is itself *Christian*. That is a theological judgement. It is certainly not an educational judgement based on the social sciences. Although social scientists have far more to teach us than the theologians do about the 'how' of Christian learning, I believe that it is the theologian who retains the ultimate veto in the area of the 'what' of Christian education. But the theologian may also offer a critique, based on the moral and spiritual criteria contained within the Christian tradition, of the acceptability of certain methods of Christian education, for proper educational ends do not justify improper educational means. Adult Christian educators cannot avoid these theological judgements.

Above or Within?

The discussion so far may seem far too thin theologically in another way; for much has been said about human behaviour, but little about the activity of God. One theological issue that quickly raises its head in Christian education is the way in which one thinks of God's rôle in the enterprise.

Most evangelists, and many Christian educators, hold some form of *interventionist* view of God's activity. This allows them not only to speak of God's immanent presence in those laws of individual and social psychology in accordance with which people learn Christian beliefs and ways, but also to recognise as a more decisive feature the existence of particular interventions over, above and beyond such processes. Such a view can lead to the claim that the transcendent God is the *main* Christian educator, with the implication that the only thing that any human being can do is to prepare the ground and hope and pray for divine intervention. What is needed – but is rarely forthcoming – in this discussion is any attempt to work out a link or hinge between the human educator's preparatory ('horizontal') work and

God's decisive ('vertical') activity. James Michael Lee, who is very dismissive of those who found a theory of Christian education on theology rather than the social sciences, criticises any suggestion of a 'blow theory' in Christian education, on the grounds that when the Holy Spirit blows where the Spirit wills it offers us no explanation, predictions or guidance for our own educational activity.[39]

Non-interventionism is an ugly name for the popular theological position that denies, or is very sceptical of, claims about God's anomalous intervention in the processes of nature, including human nature. Its supporters argue that there is little or no rôle for the miraculous in the divine economy. God's involvement in Christian education must therefore be entirely at the level of God's 'primary causation', that is, God's 'uniform enabling of the secondary causes' power to act'.[40] Advocates of this view, if they wish to be consistent, will want to study very seriously the empirical evidence about the processes by which people learn, so as to know how God has so structured these 'secondary causes' in human nature and the world so that people can learn to be Christian.

Of the two, the traditional 'transcendist' or interventionist approach is more orthodox in refusing to limit in advance the activity of God. But does it not limit instead the human contribution to the process of Christian education? What is the point of our working at Christian education, one may wonder, if God's efforts are the only ones that count? A way forward for the more theological perspective would be to describe our human activity as being *sometimes* a necessary condition for Christian learning, whereas God's activity is *always* a necessary condition and may sometimes be sufficient on its own to produce Christian learning. Here is one illustration of how this might work. The task of Christian education includes helping people to understand the Christian concept of God (in an empathetic way). This is an aspect of learning *about* Christianity, which – as we have seen – is also one of the proper tasks of religious studies lecturers in higher education and RE teachers in schools. Such reflection on the Christian concept of God might move the learners to a position where they could receive for themselves a revelation of the transcendent God who is the reality behind that concept. Learning to understand the concept of God first (and thereby, perhaps, even 'being challenged by' or 'falling in love with' it) might for some people be a necessary condition for their being open to receive their own divine revelation–intervention.[41] In this way, human teaching about Christianity might lead to a more divine process of Christian learning.

APPROACHES TO CHRISTIAN EDUCATION

Within the broad definition of the aims of Christian education outlined above, Christians may adopt a variety of approaches to the practical enterprise. A useful attempt to specify approaches to Christian education is to be found in a book edited some years ago by Jack Seymour and Donald Miller.[42] It classifies five different, but overlapping, approaches. The chart on p. 18 below is a simplified and amended version of the summary presented there.[43] It lists these types of Christian education:

- the Faith Community Approach,
- the Critical Christian Education Approach,
- the Faith/Spiritual Development Approach,
- the Liberation Approach, and
- the Interpretation Approach.

I shall now briefly consider each of these approaches in turn.

The Faith Community Approach

The first of these approaches is essentially ecclesial in its concerns. On this view, the primary aim of Christian education is to build up the 'faith community' of the church. Its focus is therefore usually on the worshipping congregation viewed as a body, and on its formation or nurture in the beliefs, values, attitudes, dispositions and life-style of Christianity. The American Episcopalian John Westerhoff is a well-known exponent of this approach. To label it he uses the venerable word 'catechesis', broadening the term to describe 'a process of nurture and conversion' that 'aims to introduce persons into a community of Christian faith with its distinctive values, understandings, and ways'. On Westerhoff's account, this process helps people 'to internalize and adopt the community's faith as their own and to apply that faith to life in the world'.[44] Elsewhere he describes this form of Christian education as 'a pastoral ministry': 'It is a ministry of the Word in which persons are both converted and initiated into, and nurtured and nourished in, an understanding and way of life.' Under this approach, the Christian tradition and culture is seen as being primarily passed on by processes of social formation (sometimes called 'socialisation' or 'enculturation', hence the alternative title of the 'Enculturation Approach'). It is these processes that must be deliberately designed and structured by Christian educators so that learners both 'recall' and 'reconstruct' the church's tradition.[45]

In his more recent writing, Westerhoff distinguishes three inten-

SOME CONTEMPORARY APPROACHES TO CHRISTIAN EDUCATION

	Faith Community	Critical Christian Education	Faith/Spiritual Development	Liberation	Interpretation
Goals:	to build the congregation into a community of mission and ministry, through which people can encounter the faith and learn its life-style	to enable people to understand and critically reflect on Christianity	to enable persons to grow in faith to maturity	to transform the church and persons for liberation, humanisation and social transformation	to connect Christian perspectives and practices to contemporary experiences
View of Teacher:	as a 'priest' for the community	as a facilitator of understanding and evaluation	as a spiritual director or sponsor	as a colleague	as a guide
View of Learner:	individually, as a person struggling to identify with the Christian community; communally, as a congregation seeking to be faithful	as a person struggling to understand the faith and assess it	as a person moving through stages of development to maturity	free and responsible persons and groups, active in the world	as a person seeking to interpret Christianity and experience
Content:	Christian community's faith and life-style	Christian beliefs	Christian faith/human faith/spirituality	critical reflection on life-style in the light of Christian faith	Christian story (tradition) and present experience
Settings for Learning:	community of faith/worship, set within the wider community	formal educational contexts	person's total life/one-to-one discussion	places where Christians are involved in compassion and ministry in the world	person's total life
Key Ideas:	formation/ nurture; enculturation/ socialisation; tradition ('faith transmission')	Christian understanding; evaluation; 'critical openness'	growth/ development; 'faithing'; stages and transitions	freedom; education as political; criticism of tradition	hermeneutics; dialogue; 'faith translation'

Amended from *Contemporary Approaches to Christian Education* by Jack L. Seymour and Donald E. Miller (eds), © 1982 by Abingdon Press tional, systematic and sustained processes that make up catechesis. He describes only one of these as Christian formation. It includes, in addition to shaping people in the community's understanding, character and consciousness ('enculturation'), the outcomes of 'incorporation' or 'induction' and 'apprenticeship'. Westerhoff has now broadened catechesis to include what he calls 'instruction' (transmission of knowledge and skills) and 'education' (a term that he restricts to critical reflection on and prophetic reshaping of Christianity).[46]

Westerhoff's earlier accounts, however, allow that these critical and prophetic dimensions of Christian education may be considered as a *part of* a broader view of Christian formation, because the culture in which Christians are formed includes the radical catalyst of the Christian gospel, which itself critiques and may overturn some of the inherited understandings and practices of Christianity as well as many of those espoused by 'the world'.[47] Transformation then becomes part of formation, and it may be more readily recognised that catechesis does not result – as people often assume – merely in a conserving and therefore conservative Christianity, incapable of changing either the world or the church.

In summary, according to Charles Foster, Christian education 'in the quest for church' involves three actions:[48]

(i)   The first is the binding of the generations (through the community's story), by which the young are gathered into a world-view held by the older generation of adults.

(ii) The second is an appropriation and creation of community tradition, particularly in the 'traditioning' processes of worship, fellowship, mission and the sacramental life. 'The crucial activity' here is 'not so much comprehension as identification. Through ritual, the community celebrates and renews its corporate identity.'

(iii) The third action is the practice of the life-style of the community: 'the repetitive enactment of the actions of Christian community and the trying on of Christian attitudes and perspectives', which leads into a more deliberate instruction in the knowledge, attitudes and behaviour that constitute the community of the church.

Although this Faith Community Approach is most likely to be met in accounts of the Christian education of children and young people, it should be clear that the processes it involves may apply just as much to adult Christian learning. (Adults, after all, are the parents, teachers and church leaders.) Indeed, C. Ellis Nelson agrees that the approach 'starts with adult education', by taking seriously 'the informal direct instruction that goes on constantly within a congregation'.[49]

The Critical Christian Education Approach

Despite my qualifying remarks in the last section, it remains true to say that the Faith Community Approach is often wary of using the language of 'education' and 'criticism', except in its broadest connotations, placing more emphasis on terms such as 'formation', 'nurture' or 'socialisation'. The approach that I have entitled 'Critical Christian Education', however, has no such qualms. Its exponents particularly stress the cognitive dimension of Christianity. They implicitly accept the challenge of the liberal educator that 'real education' should have as its dual focus the understanding *and the critical evaluation* of knowledge-claims. We should note that 'criticism' is a positive term in this approach, even with regard to religion:

> However smooth the passage from birth to adult life, there can be no real personal belief in any depth until it can be called '*my* belief', and this pre-supposes a proper questioning of what has been received. Christian nurture must prepare for this and not try to avoid it.[50]

Even the church's nurturing of Christian beliefs and attitudes must therefore be done in a way that allows for critical reflection or, as some would put it, 'with critical openness'. This phrase is particularly associated with the early work of John Hull, who distances it from mere 'instruction' and even further from 'indoctrination', boldly demanding:

> Are Christians to be conformist, passive acceptors of authority, unable to adapt to crises, too set in the received ways to think creatively? Only a Christian nurtured in critical openness can have characteristics other than these. For those who think (as I do) that this *other* Christian life is essential for the continued vitality and relevance of Christian faith, the problem of how Christian nurture can be like education in possessing critical openness, yet unlike education in intending Christian life and faith, is a central concern.[51]

In a highly influential book on adult Christian education, Hull analyses the pathology of 'the unlearning religious person', particularly the adult who has stopped learning in the religious sphere because it is too painful a task. The only therapy in such cases is a form of Christian learning that involves 'Christian criticism'. This will enable adult learners to construct *self-critical* ideologies (systems of beliefs and values) that will prevent their being trapped in yesterday's inappropriate concerns, causes and beliefs. Hull therefore calls for an adult Christian education that will set people free from 'naive and absolute ideological enclosure' in religion. This demands

> educational procedures which relativize the ideology, not destroying it, but breaking it so that it becomes a more supple and more faithful channel for the saving realities. It is this capacity to faithfully re-ideologize the experience of faith which is the object of the education of faithful adults.[52]

For such adults, the Christian faith will not be a closed, monolithic, unresponsive system of beliefs and values 'once delivered to the saints', but a historical and contemporary shifting deposit of different, contextualised responses to the good news of God. Only critical education can reveal and deliver this faith, according to its advocates.

As we shall see later, some of those who find this position appealing ascribe rather limited aims to it. Christian education is to be defined for them as:

> the process of exploring the church's tradition and self-understanding in such a way that persons can understand, assess, and therefore respond to the truth of the gospel for themselves. It can always be the hope, but never the objective of the teacher that the understanding and the assessment will lead to a response that will transform the person as he or she receives the gift of faith.[53]

I shall take up some of the issues raised by this quotation in the next chapter.

The Faith/Spiritual Development Approach

The word 'develop' is often used in educational circles as a transitive verb that may label any teaching activity with an effect on the learner, as in 'developing his understanding of . . .', 'developing her empathy towards . . .'. At other times, however, the word is used intransitively of a change in a person that is not brought about by learning experiences, but from the pressure of some internal process. In these cases a person 'develops', physically or intellectually, *from the inside* as it were, rather than as a result of outside educational intervention. Such internal development is nevertheless of great significance for educators. This is not only because educators, like pastors, need to know 'where people are'. It is also because it is nowadays usually recognised that teachers can exercise considerable power and responsibility to help or hinder their learners' internal development, not least because cognitive development is a restructuring process which interacts with the educational environment, rather than a simple 'unfolding' maturation.

Thus Christian educators may see themselves as 'sponsors' or 'directors' of a person's moral, spiritual or faith development, to the extent that they provide opportunities and encouragement for religious 'growth'. They do this by helping the other person along the developmental road to a greater maturity, and a more comprehensive and adequate perception of reality, as she changes from within in her ways of thinking, relating to others, judging or valuing.

Many of the accounts of Christian education that proceed along these lines draw heavily on the faith development theory of James Fowler. As this is such a substantial area in itself, I have devoted a separate chapter to it (chapter 6 below). Other advocates of this approach prefer to focus on what they refer to as a 'deepening' of character, through formative educational processes that 'involve a life-long dynamic of centering, decentering, and recentering ourselves in Christ'. Susanne Johnson, who describes spiritual formation as 'the formation of Christian character', identifies worship (and reflection on worship), action towards those in need (and reflection on such action), along with teaching and critical reflection, as the processes that will deliver this 'spiritual development'.[54] Patently, these are all important elements in adult Christian education.

The Liberation Approach

Liberation theology is a major movement in contemporary theological thinking, and 'liberation education' has been very influential in secular education, not least in adult education.[55] It is not surprising, therefore, that some Christian educators have drawn on them both, arguing for a Christian education that is primarily concerned with the actions and way of life ('life-style' or distinctive ethos[56]) of Christians and is therefore in a broad sense *political*. The work of the Brazilian educator Paulo Freire is seminal here, especially his insistence that education should include the discovery by the learners of those political structures that oppress them, rather than being a socialisation into an acceptance of the moral and political *status quo*. Freire criticises what he calls the 'banking' model of education which treats it as a sort of transfer of educational capital in which the teacher '"makes deposits" which the students patiently receive, memorize, and repeat'. By contrast, he advocates a form of education that avoids such domesticating and oppressive processes by encouraging students 'to engage in critical thinking'.[57] 'Education for liberation', he writes, 'is concerned . . . with helping to free human beings from the oppression which strangles them . . . It is therefore political education.'[58]

Such an educational style is 'critical' in a rather different sense from the rational, almost philosophical, critique that is encouraged by many of the advocates of the 'Critical Christian Education' approach outlined above.[59] Here the call is to encourage the learner to move from naivety to a shrewd 'critical consciousness'. This entails a restructuring of how people see their own reality: 'the process of emerging critical reflection whereby people become aware of the historical forces that shape their lives, together with their own, God-given potential freedom and creativity'.[60] This form of criticism is of a more moral and political nature. Thomas H. Groome writes that the political dimension is an inevitable part of all Christian education:

> By what we reclaim from our past heritage or propose for our future, by what we ignore from our past and refuse for our future, Christian religious educators are being political. We have no choice about whether or not Christian education will have political implications. It is inevitably political and our choice is about the direction in which we should shape the future of society by our present engagement as Christians within it.[61]

If 'Faith Community' Christian education allows us to inherit Grandma's furniture (the Christian culture, tradition or way of life), the 'Critical Christian Education' and 'Liberation' approaches encourage us to re-arrange, reconstruct and even throw out much of this inheritance.

The Interpretation Approach

Groome appears more clearly as an exponent of the last of our approaches to Christian education. In reality, all forms of Christian education – and not just liberation education – are concerned to some extent with the 'hermeneutical' task of *interpretation*, for Christian educators routinely work with a tradition ('story', 'vision', 'culture', 'text', 'lifeworld', 'horizon') that has to be re-interpreted by being connected with the present-day world-view or range of vision of the Christian learner. According to Hans-Georg Gadamer, we can only understand any text when there is a 'fusion of horizons' between it and its interpreter, in which 'the text is made to speak through interpretation':

To think historically always involves establishing a connection between those ideas and one's own thinking. To try to eliminate one's own concepts in interpretation is not only impossible, but manifestly absurd. To interpret means precisely to use one's own preconceptions so that the meaning of the text can really be made to speak for us.[62]

This results in a 'circle of understanding', a 'hermeneutical circle' or spiral in which every understanding is grounded in our fore-understanding which is itself changed in this 'true conversation' with the text to become the fore-understanding of a subsequent encounter with tradition. In this interaction we are challenged, criticised and changed by the other, but not absorbed by it. What emerges from the fusion of our horizon with that of the text is something that is contained in neither, but is 'a new creation of understanding'.[63]

If Christian education is understood in this way, the Christian educator – like the scholar – cannot be modelled as a neutral, impersonal channel for the tradition, pouring it into a waiting mould or (to change the analogy) as simply repeating the text and 'transmitting' it like radio signals in an unmodified form to a passive 'receiver'. He or she is rather a *translator* of the tradition, and a translator is an *in-between person* who needs to know two languages, both the language of the tradition and that of the learner, and to interpret the one to the other. (We should recognise that translation is always itself interpretation.[64] Different languages rarely have words that have exactly identical sets of associations and connotations, however 'close in meaning' they may appear to be.)

The teacher is construed on this model as the learner's 'guide', 'facilitator' or 'midwife': 'Theirs is not the task of sharing their encounters with learners in such a way that teachers expect that sharing to be the sum of the learner's experience with the Word. Theirs is the responsibility of bringing each learner into an authentic encounter with that Word.'[65] Here authoritarian transmission, where teachers impose their own understanding on their 'spectator' students, is replaced by an educational encounter that recognises and values the experiences and insights of the learners themselves.[66] And the primary interpreter is, of course, the *learner*. His or her learning task is a new creation of understanding: 'All understanding is always more than the mere recreation of someone else's meaning.'[67] Douglas Wingeier has described the essential function of Christian education as 'faith translation':

For Christians, [their] belief system is shaped by scripture and tradition, and interpreted through the filters of personal experience and rational faculties. This process of rational interpretation of our experience in the light of the root sources of faith in scripture and tradition is what is meant by faith translation. It is a two-way process, involving the development of a belief system, and the assignment of meaning to experience in terms of this growing understanding.[68]

In this approach to Christian education much is therefore made of the notion of a dialogue (or 'dialectic') between the present and the past. For Groome, Christian education properly has a focus on action-reflectively-done ('praxis') and involves a group (hence it is '*shared* praxis') that critically reflects both on its own action and on the Christian tradition. In the dialogue or implicit 'conversation' between (a) the learners' own activity, concerns, history and experience, and (b) the Christian tradition, Christian education can really come alive, as the tradition 'speaks to' and changes the learners and the learners select from, interpret, contribute to *and amend* the tradition.

Groome's plan for effective Christian education is presented as having the following five 'movements':

1. First of all the participants in the group are invited to name their own activity concerning the topic for attention ('present action'). That is, they focus on something they do (or don't do): their present state (what they are doing physically, emotionally, intellectually or spiritually) rather than *someone else's* activities, beliefs or feelings. (Adult Christian learners may sometimes resist this focus on their own experience.)

2. They are then invited to reflect on why they do what they do, and on what is the likely or intended consequences of their actions ('critical reflection').

3. The educator then presents to the group the Christian community's Story concerning the topic at hand and the faith response it invites (the 'Story and its Vision').

4. Next the participants are invited to appropriate the Christian Story to their lives in an interpretative conversation or dialogue with their own stories (a 'dialectic between Story and stories'). Groome poses the central questions for Christian religious education as: 'What does the community's Story mean for (affirm, call in question, invite beyond) our stories, and how do our stories respond to (affirm, recognize limits of, push beyond) the community Story?'

5. Finally, there is an opportunity for the learners to choose a personal faith response for the future, in conversation with the Christian Vision: that is, there is a 'dialectic between the Vision and the participants' visions'.[69]

The emphasis in this approach on collaboration and mutual respect between teacher and learner, and its focus on reflective action and a spirit of critical reflection, reiterate themes that are regarded by many as absolutely central to good practice in adult education in general.[70]

NOTES

[1]   The word 'theology' is used *both* to label a subject-area or field of study (broadly the history and religion of Ancient Israel and the Christian church) that is studied by a variety of disciplines *and* to specify the particular discipline of thought that engages in articulating, systematising and evaluating Christian belief (normally from a perspective within the Christian belief-system).

[2]   Leon McKenzie, *The Religious Education of Adults*, Birmingham, Ala.: Religious Education Press, 1982, p. 134.

[3]   Thus Peter Jarvis, *Adult and Continuing Education: Theory and Practice*, London: Routledge, 1995, pp. 58–59, cf. p. 153.

[4]   See Jeff Astley and David Day (eds), *The Contours of Christian Education*, Great Wakering: McCrimmons, 1992, pp. 13–25 (and contrast Kevin Nichol's chapter, pp. 54–65); Jeff Astley, *The Philosophy of Christian Religious Education*, London: SPCK; Birmingham, Ala.: Religious Education Press, 1994, chs 1 and 3; Jeff Astley and Leslie J. Francis (eds), *Critical Perspectives on Christian Education: a Reader on the Aims, Principles and Philosophy of Christian Education*, Leominster: Gracewing Fowler Wright, 1994, section 1.

[5]   Unfortunately in the United States – where religion is excluded from the curriculum of the state school and college – the phrase 'religious education' is most often used to denote Christian education, nurture or catechesis within the *church*. This different usage is reflected in the titles of many books, much to the confusion of libraries and resources centres in Britain!

[6]   *Circular 1/94: Religious Education and Collective Worship*, London: Department for Education, 1994, p. 15. This restriction does not apply to the voluntary 'church aided' schools.

[7]   This 'right of withdrawal' is somewhat illogical, if RE is a matter of studying and understanding religions and does not involve a pupil being converted to them or nurtured within them. See Terence Copley, *Teaching Religion: Fifty Years of Religious Education in England and Wales*, Exeter: University of Exeter Press, 1997, pp. 206–208.

[8]   For contributions to this debate, see David Day, 'Religious Education Forty Years On: A Permanent Identity Crisis?', *British Journal of Religious Education*, 7, 2, 1985, pp. 55–63; Astley and Francis (eds), *Critical Perspectives on Christian Education*, especially sections 2 and 3; Trevor Cooling, *A Christian Vision for State Education: Reflections on the Theology of Education*, London: SPCK, 1994.

[9]   See, for example, *The Fourth R*, London: National Society/SPCK, 1970, pp. 98–104; Edwin Cox, *Changing Aims in Religious Education*, London: Routledge and Kegan Paul, 1966, pp. 66–70; Michael Grimmitt, *Religious Education and Human Development*, Great Wakering: McCrimmons, 1987, part one; Michael Kincaid, *How to Improve Learning in RE*, London: Hodder & Stoughton, 1991, chs. 4 and 5.

[10]   See the *Education Reform Act 1988*, Section 1(2)(a)(6); *Circular 1/94*, para. 16; and *Model Syllabuses for Religious Education*, London: SCAA, 1994. The

requirement that schools should promote the 'spiritual' development of their pupils is seen by some as placing a question mark against any radical distinction between 'teaching religion' and 'teaching about religion', but most construe 'spiritual' in terms that are not specifically religious.

11 For the debate on school worship, compare and contrast John Hull, *School Worship: An Obituary*, London: SCM, 1975; *The Fourth R*, pp. 129–143; Brenda Watson, *Education and Belief*, Oxford: Blackwell, 1987, ch. 14; Nicholas Edgar Watson, '"Wholly or Mainly . . . Broadly Christian?": Worship, Theology and the Department for Education and Employment', unpublished MA dissertation, University of Durham, 1996; *Collective Worship in Schools*, Abingdon: Culham College Institute, 1996; Adrian Thatcher, 'Educational Arguments for Collective Worship', *Collective Worship (Perspectives 57)*, Exeter: University of Exeter School of Education, 1997, pp. 5–23.

12 On theology in the secular university, see Donald MacKinnon, 'Theology as a Discipline of a Modern University', in Teodor Shanin (ed.), *The Rules of the Game*, London: Tavistock, 1972, pp. 164–174; Stephen W. Sykes, 'The Study of Theology in University and School', in James Barnett (ed.), *Theology at 16+*, London: Epworth, 1984, pp. 132–148; Daniel W. Hardy, 'Theology and the Cultural Reduction of Religion', in Jeff Astley and Leslie J. Francis (eds), *Christian Theology and Religious Education: Connections and Contradictions*, London: SPCK, 1996, pp. 16–37; and the papers by Stephen Toulmin, Edward Farley and Claude Welch, reprinted in Jeff Astley, Leslie J. Francis and Colin Crowder (eds), *Theological Perspectives on Christian Formation: A Reader on Theology and Christian Education*, Leominster: Gracewing Fowler Wright; Grand Rapids, Mich.: Wm. Eerdmans, 1996, section 10. On RE in church schools, see James Arthur, *The Ebbing Tide: Policy and Principles of Catholic Education*, Leominster: Gracewing Fowler Wright, 1995; James Arthur and Simon Gaine, '"Catechesis" and "Religious Education" in Catholic Theory and Practice', in Leslie J. Francis, William K. Kay and William S. Campbell (eds), *Research in Religious Education*, Leominster: Gracewing Fowler Wright; Macon, Georgia: Smyth & Helwys, 1996, pp. 335–357; Mark Chater, 'Different Approaches to Religious Education', in William K. Kay and Leslie J. Francis (eds), *Religion in Education, Volume 1*, Leominster: Gracewing, 1997, pp. 257–288; and Leslie J. Francis and David W. Lankshear (eds), *Christian Perspectives on Church Schools: A Reader*, Leominster: Gracewing Fowler Wright, 1993, *passim*.

13 See Astley, *The Philosophy of Christian Religious Education*, ch. 6 and James Michael Lee, *The Content of Religious Instruction*, Birmingham, Ala.: Religious Education Press, 1985. Empirical research shows that 'what it means for a person to be a Christian' is usually seen as clustering in four dimensions of *public practice, religious belief, personal spirituality and personal morality/relationships*. See, for example, the paper 'What is a Christian', in Astley and Day (eds), *The Contours of Christian Education*, pp. 325–339. For a good summary of the wider literature on the 'dimensions of religion' in the psychology of religion, see Kenneth E. Hyde, *Religion in Childhood and Adolescence: A Comprehensive Review of the Research*, Birmingham, Ala.: Religious Education Press, 1990, Appendix C (despite its title, this book cites much work that is of relevance to adult Christian educators).

14 Such a theological position needs to answer the charge that, on this view, human beings can force God's hand. It may wish, therefore, to retain a place for God's free initiative in offering or withholding grace, despite the human activity of baptising.

15 C. A. van Peursen, 'Man and Reality – The History of Human Thought', *The Student World*, LVI, 1963, reprinted in John Bowden and James Richmond (eds), *A Reader in Contemporary Theology*, London: SCM, 1967 (quotation from p. 119). Van Peursen distinguishes functional thinking from the sort of 'operational thinking' in which realities are *reduced to* the results of certain operations. Such a reductive account may be appropriate in the case of the Intelligent Quotient, but not in the case of the soul or God (pp. 120–122). Functional thinking is therefore *not* the same as 'behaviourism' (see also note 34 below); nor is it to be identified with all the detailed outworkings of *functionalist* schools of thought in anthropology and psychology.

16 *op. cit.*, p. 120.

17 See, for example, Carl E. Braaten and Robert W. Jenson (eds), *Christian Dogmatics*, Philadelphia: Fortress, 1984, *Volume 1*, Sixth Locus: Carl E. Braaten, 'The Person of Jesus Christ', pp. 465–569; *Volume 2*, Ninth Locus: Philip J. Hefner, 'The Church', pp. 179–247; Tenth Locus, Part Two: Robert W. Jenson, 'The Sacraments', pp. 289–389. The majority of writers on Christian education may be said to share some such ontological theological position. A detailed attempt to express this position in educational terms, overagainst what he regards as 'reductionism', is to be found in Robert K. Martin, *The Incarnate Ground of Christian Faith: Toward a Christian Theological Epistemology for the Educational Ministry of the Church*, Lanham, Maryland: University Press of America, 1998.

18 See, for example, John A. T. Robinson, *The Human Face of God*, London: SCM, 1973, pp. 182–185.

19 Cf. Donald M. Baillie, *The Theology of the Sacraments*, New York: Charles Scribner's Sons, 1957, pp. 85–88.

20 Compare, for example, recent usage by Roman Catholics of the terms 'transfinalisation' and 'transignification' in discussions of the traditional doctrine of transubstantiation.

21 Such an account also fits better the notion of the whole church as priest, exercising a ministry that mirrors Israel's relationship to the nations ('the priesthood of all believers'). Compare Hans Küng, *Why Priests?*, trans. J. Cumming, London: Collins, 1972, II and IV. It finds expression too in much of the language of the rites of ordination. Thus the Church of England's *Alternative Service Book* (1980): 'Send down the Holy Spirit upon your servant N for the office and work of a priest in the Church'; 'give to these your servants grace and power to fulfil their ministry'.

22 The obvious counter-example of a human relationship that is seen in ontological (in this case, genetic) terms, is that of being a 'birth' parent. But note how people readily appeal to functional categories even about parenting: 'You have never been a father to me'; 'My foster mother is my real mother'; even 'You are no child of mine'.

23 This was a philosophical movement that rejected as 'factually meaningless' any claims about reality that could not be verified by sense experience.

24 That is, observable by other people.

25 Compare Ralph W. Tyler, *Basic Principles of Curriculum and Instruction*, Chicago: University of Chicago Press, 1949, pp. 46–60.

26 Hilda Taba, *Curriculum Development: Theory and Practice*, New York: Harcourt, Brace and World, 1962, p. 199.

27 Thus Denis Lawton, *An Introduction to Teaching and Learning*, London: Hodder & Stoughton, 1981, p. 116. Cf. Michael MacDonald-Ross, 'Behavioural Objectives – A Critical Review', *Instructional Science*, 2, 1973, pp. 1–52. See

also the criticisms surveyed, and the responses offered, by W. James Popham in his paper 'Probing the Validity of Arguments against Behavioral Goals', in Robert J. Kibler *et al.*, *Objectives for Instruction and Evaluation*, Boston: Allyn and Bacon, 1981, pp. 9–31.

28 Cf. Lawrence Stenhouse, *An Introduction to Curriculum Research and Development*, London: Heinemann, 1975, ch. 6; Hugh Sockett, 'Behavioural Objectives', *London Educational Review*, 2, 3, 1973, pp. 38–45. Note also the comment on the term 'behaviour' in note 34 below.

29 Elliot W. Eisner, 'Instructional and Expressive Educational Objectives', in W. James Popham *et al.* (eds), *Instructional Objectives*, Chicago: Rand McNally, 1969, pp. 15–16.

30 E. W. Eisner, *The Educational Imagination: On the Design and Evaluation of School Programs*, New York: Macmillan, 1985, p. 116.

31 Stenhouse, *op. cit.*, p. 82.

32 *ibid.*, p. 92; cf. Ron Greaves, 'Critical Appraisal of the Justification of Learning Outcome Design in the Subject Area of Religious Studies', *Journal of Beliefs and Values*, 19, 1, 1998, pp. 97–105.

33 Stephen D. Brookfield, *Understanding and Facilitating Adult Learning: A Comprehensive Analysis of Principles and Effective Practices*, Milton Keynes: Open University Press, 1986, p. 213.

34 I must stress again that my analysis is very different from *behaviourism*, and does *not* imply the behaviourist's notorious 'reduction of inner thoughts and feelings to their natural expression in behaviour' (Stuart Hampshire, *Thought and Action*, London: Chatto & Windus, 1959, p. 143). Ralph Tyler, like other psychologists, uses the term 'behaviour' to refer not just to overt behaviour but to '*any* activity of the organism', including 'inner' cognitive or affective processes of thinking, feeling and perceiving. Cf. James Michael Lee, *The Flow of Religious Instruction*, Birmingham, Ala.: Religious Education Press, 1973, p. 297; Lee, *The Content of Religious Instruction*, p. 615. In his later writings Tyler acknowledges that many people have interpreted him incorrectly, as focussing only on 'performance behaviours'. He also admits that it can be seriously restrictive to specify objectives too closely in advance (see Brookfield, *Understanding and Facilitating Adult Learning*, p. 209–210, and literature cited).

35 Wittgenstein writes that 'an "inner process" stands in need of outward criteria' (Ludwig Wittgenstein, *Philosophical Investigations*, trans. G. E. M. Anscombe, Oxford: Blackwell, 1968, part I, para. 580).

36 James Michael Lee makes the additional point that many elements of the content of religious education, e.g. 'faith' and indeed 'religion', are intellectual abstractions or constructs, rather than observable entities and activities. In order to be recognisable and usable, such concepts need to be 'operationalized into demonstrable behaviors which are observable both to the learner and to the religious educator' (but, please note, not reduced to them). Lee, *Content*, p. 615; cf. also Lee, *The Shape of Religious Instruction*, Birmingham, Ala.: Religious Education Press, 1972, pp. 72–74, and his essay in Lee (ed.), *Handbook of Faith*, Birmingham, Ala.: Religious Education Press, 1990, pp. 271–275.

37 See Astley, *The Philosophy of Christian Religious Education*, especially ch. 6.

38 Cf. J. Astley, 'Essay Review', *Religious Education*, 81, 1, 1986, p. 144. Cf. also Lee, *The Shape of Religious Instruction*, pp. 245–246; Lee, 'The Authentic Source of Religious Instruction', in Norma H. Thompson (ed.), *Religious Education and Theology*, Birmingham, Ala.: Religious Education Press, 1982, pp. 181–182.

39 See Lee, *The Flow of Religious Instruction*, chs. 5 and 7. Cf. Ian Knox, *Above or*

Within? The Supernatural in Religious Education, Birmingham, Ala.: Religious Education Press, 1976, ch. V.

40 Maurice Wiles, *God's Action in the World*, London: SCM, 1986, p. 34.

41 See Jeff Astley, 'The Idea of God, the Reality of God, and Religious Education', *Theology*, 84, 698, 1981, pp. 115–120.

42 Jack L. Seymour and Donald E. Miller (eds), *Contemporary Approaches to Christian Education*, Nashville, Tenn.: Abingdon, 1982. See also Jack L. Seymour, 'Contemporary Approaches to Christian Education', reprinted in Astley, Francis and Crowder (eds), *Theological Perspectives on Christian Formation*, pp. 3–13. In Jack L. Seymour and Donald E. Miller (eds), *Theological Approaches to Christian Education* (Nashville, Tenn.: Abingdon, 1990), the 1982 book is described as providing 'a historical description of current approaches, not a philosophical articulation of ideal types', and results in 'sometimes-overlapping metaphors of emerging alternatives in Christian religious education' (ch. 1 and p. 262). See also Jack L. Seymour (ed.), *Mapping Christian Education: Approaches to Congregational Learning*, Nashville, Tenn.: Abingdon, 1997, where these approaches are described as 'alternate filters shaping the field' (p. 15).

43 The 'religious instruction' approach to the teaching of religion was part of Seymour and Miller's original analysis. It is an approach that could be said to include all the other approaches, at least in the version championed by James Michael Lee. For this reason it has been omitted from my version of the chart and from the account that follows. This particular approach is summarised by Lee in his article 'Religious Education and Theology', in Astley, Francis and Crowder (eds), *Theological Perspectives on Christian Formation*, pp. 45–68. I have replaced it with that of 'Critical Christian Education' (which in some ways better represents the account given by Sara Little of 'religious instruction' in her chapter in the *Contemporary Approaches* book).

44 John H. Westerhoff, 'Christian Education as a Theological Discipline', *St Luke's Journal of Theology*, 21, 4, 1978, pp. 280–288.

45 Westerhoff, in John H. Westerhoff and O. C. Edwards (eds), *A Faithful Church: Issues in the History of Catechesis*, Wilton, Connecticut: Morehouse-Barlow, 1981, p. 5. For other advocates of this approach, see Maria Harris, *Fashion Me A People: Curriculum in the Church*, Louisville, Kentucky: Westminster/John Knox Press, 1989; Berard L. Marthaler, *Catechetics in Context*, Huntington, Ind.: Our Sunday Visitor, 1973 and 'Socialization as a Model for Catechetics', reprinted in Michael Warren (ed.), *Sourcebook for Modern Catechetics, Volume 2*, Winona, Minn.: Saint Mary's Press/Christian Brothers Publications, 1997, pp. 120–143; Mary Elizabeth Moore, *Education for Continuity and Change: A New Model for Christian Religious Education*, Nashville, Tenn.: Abingdon, 1983; C. Ellis Nelson, *Where Faith Begins*, Atlanta: John Knox Press, 1967, and his essays 'Is Church Education Something Particular?', reprinted in John H. Westerhoff (ed.), *Who Are We? The Quest for a Religious Education*, Birmingham, Ala.: Religious Education Press, 1978, pp. 193–217 and 'Socialization Revisited', reprinted in Warren (ed.), *op. cit.*, pp. 145–159; Robert T. O'Gorman, 'The Faith Community', in Seymour (ed.), *Mapping Christian Education*, ch. 3; Lawrence O. Richards, 'Experiencing Reality Together', in Thompson (ed.), *Religious Education and Theology*, pp. 198–217; John H. Westerhoff, *Will Our Children Have Faith?*, New York: Seabury Press, 1976; John H. Westerhoff and Gwen Kennedy Neville, *Generation to Generation*, New York: Pilgrim Press, 1979. Compare Kenneth Barker, *Religious Education, Catechesis and Freedom*, Birmingham, Ala.: Religious Education Press, 1981, ch. 5.

46 See Westerhoff, 'Formation, Education, Instruction', reprinted in Astley and Francis (eds), *Critical Perspectives on Christian Education*, pp. 63–66.

47 See Astley, *The Philosophy of Christian Religious Education*, pp. 92–93.

48 Charles R. Foster, 'Education in the Quest for Church', in Seymour and Miller (eds), *Theological Approaches to Christian Education*, pp. 96–98.

49 Nelson, 'Socialization Revisited', p. 153.

50 From the BCC Report, *The Child in the Church*, London: British Council of Churches, 1976, p. 36.

51 John M. Hull, *Studies in Religion and Education*, Lewes: Falmer, 1984, p. 211.

52 John M. Hull, *What Prevents Christian Adults from Learning?*, London: SCM, 1985; Philadelphia: Trinity Press International, 1991, p. 85.

53 From Sara Little's essay in Seymour and Miller (eds), *Contemporary Approaches to Christian Education*, pp. 41–42.

54 Susanne Johnson, 'Education in the Image of God', in Seymour and Miller (eds), *Theological Approaches to Christian Education*, pp. 124–145; cf. Maria Harris and Gabriel Moran, 'Educating Persons', in Seymour (ed.), *Mapping Christian Education*, ch. 4.

55 See David Deshler, 'Radical Adult Education and the Politics of Power', in Peter Jarvis and Nicholas Walters (eds), *Adult Education and Theological Interpretations*, Malabar, Fla.: Krieger, 1993, pp. 273–308.

56 Allen J. Moore (ed.), *Religious Education as Social Transformation*, Birmingham, Ala.: Religious Education Press, 1989, p. 26.

57 Paulo Freire, *The Pedagogy of the Oppressed*, trans. M. B. Ramos, Harmondsworth: Penguin, 1972, pp. 46, 49. Cf. Daniel S. Schipani, *Religious Education Encounters Liberation Theology*, Birmingham, Ala.: Religious Education Press, 1988, p. 15.

58 Paulo Freire, 'Education, Liberation and the Church', reprinted in Astley, Francis and Crowder (eds), *Theological Perspectives on Christian Formation*, p. 172. For a critique of Freire, see John Lockhart, *After Freire: A Continuing Pedagogy*, Manchester: William Temple Foundation, 1997.

59 There are, however, close similarities between these two styles of critical Christian education. On this see Kevin Nichols, 'Education as Liberation', in Dermot A. Lane (ed.), *Religious Education and the Future*, Dublin: Columba, 1986, pp. 143–144. Some educationalists, for example John Hull, seek to promote a form of critical education that draws on the concerns of both these approaches. Hull has increasingly adopted a political critique, developing an educational method from a practical theology that claims that 'the norm of orthodoxy in the kingdom of God is openness to the pain of the world' ('Preface to the American Edition' of *What Prevents Christian Adults from Learning?*, 1991, p. vii).

60 Daniel S. Schipani, 'Education for Social Transformation', in Seymour (ed.), *Mapping Christian Education*, pp. 26–27 (defining 'conscientization').

61 Thomas H. Groome, *Christian Religious Education: Sharing Our Story and Vision*, San Francisco: Harper & Row, 1980, p. 26; see also Groome, 'Christian Education for Freedom: A "Shared-Praxis" Approach', in Padraic O'Hare (ed.), *Foundations of Religious Education*, New York: Paulist Press, 1978, pp. 8–39. For other writing on liberation Christian education, see Grant S. Shockley, 'Liberation Theology, Black Theology, and Religious Education', in Marvin J. Taylor (ed.), *Foundations for Christian Education in an Era of Change*, Nashville, Tenn.: Abingdon, 1976, pp. 80–95; Brian A. Wren, *Education for Justice*, London, SCM, 1977; Olivia Pearl Stokes, 'Black Theology: A Challenge to Religious Education', in Thompson (ed.), *Religious Education and Theology*,

pp. 71–99; Randolph Crump Miller (ed.), *Theologies of Religious Education*, Birmingham, Ala.: Religious Education Press, 1995, chs VIII, XI and XII; Astley, Francis and Crowder (eds), *Theological Perspectives on Christian Formation*, section 5.

62   Hans-Georg Gadamer, *Truth and Method*, trans. and ed. by Garrett Barden and John Cumming, New York: Crossroad, 1982, p. 358. For Gadamer practice comes first, and 'hermeneutics is above all a practice, the art of understanding and of making something understood to someone else'. Hans-Georg Gadamer, 'Reflections on my Philosophical Journey', in L. E. Harn (ed.), *The Philosophy of Hans-Georg Gadamer*, Chicago: Open Court, 1977, pp. 16–17.

63   Gadamer, *Truth and Method*, pp. 347, 419, 530.

64   Gadamer, *Truth and Method*, pp. 349, 486.

65   Trenton R. Ferro, 'The Authority of the Word', in Jarvis and Walters (eds), *Adult Education and Theological Interpretations*, p. 49.

66   A similar point is made in Malcolm Knowles' distinction between the 'andragogue' (teacher of adults), who encourages self-directed learning, and – on a rather limited understanding of this rôle – the teacher of the school child (the 'pedagogue'). See Malcolm S. Knowles, *The Modern Practice of Adult Education: From Pedagogy to Andragogy*, New York: Cambridge Books, 1980; Malcolm S. Knowles and associates, *Andragogy in Action: Applying Modern Principles of Adult Learning*, San Francisco: Jossey-Bass, 1984. For thoughtful critiques of the notion of andragogy, see Brookfield, *Understanding and Facilitating Adult Learning*, ch. 5, especially pp. 120–121 and Jarvis, *Adult and Continuing Education: Theory and Practice*, pp. 90–94, 197–198. Recognising and valuing the learners' own experiences is, of course, an essential part of properly listening to the learner, and taking her or him seriously as a person (see p. 48 below).

67   Gadamer, *Truth and Method*, p. 338.

68   Douglas E. Wingeier, 'Christian Education as Faith Translation', reprinted in Astley and Francis (eds), *Critical Perspectives on Christian Education*, p. 238.

69   Groome, *Christian Religious Education*, ch. 10, quotations from p. 217 and 220. See also Groome, 'Shared Christian Praxis: A Possible Theory/Method of Religious Education', reprinted in Astley and Francis (eds), *Critical Perspectives on Christian Education*, pp. 218–237; Groome, *Sharing Faith: A Comprehensive Approach to Religious Education and Pastoral Ministry*, San Francisco: HarperSanFrancisco, 1991, especially Part II (in this book the dialectic that enables us to appropriate the Christian Vision is moved forward to Movement 4). See also below pp. 81–83. Don Browning views Groome's proposals as close to his own 'revised correlation'/'critical hermeneutical' approach in practical theology, but as more cautious and less truly critical. See Don S. Browning, *A Fundamental Practical Theology: Descriptive and Strategic Proposals*, Minneapolis, Minn.: Fortress, 1989, pp. 215–222. Other advocates of an interpretation approach to Christian education and 'theological reflection' include James D. Whitehead and Evelyn E. Whitehead, *Method in Ministry: Theological Reflection and Christian Ministry*, London: Sheed & Ward, 1997; *Community of Faith: Models and Strategies for Developing Christian Communities*, New York: Seabury, 1982; Charles Winquist, *Practical Hermeneutics: A Revised Agenda for Ministry*, Chico, Cal.: Scholars Press, 1980; Laurie Green, *Let's Do Theology: A Pastoral Cycle Resource Book*, London: Mowbray, 1990; Patricia O'Connell Killen and John de Beer, *The Art of Theological Reflection*, New York: Crossroad, 1995.

70   Brookfield, *Understanding and Facilitating Adult Learning*, pp. 9–11.

2

Dimensions of Christian Education

Jeff Astley

THE VARIABLE ELEMENTS

Analyses such as those given in the last chapter can help us to compare and contrast different approaches to Christian education.[1] One way of doing this is to reflect on the different elements that vary across these different approaches, such as those listed in the first column of the chart on p. 18 above. A longer list of such 'variables' might include the following dimensions of the enterprise of Christian education:

- the particular *goals* stressed,
- the *content* learned – that is, the elements within Christianity that are particularly singled out to be taught,
- the model of the Christian *learner* employed,
- the model of the Christian *educator* ('teacher') employed,
- the rôle of the *tradition* in Christian education,
- the *context* (setting) of Christian education,
- the *curriculum* (learning experiences) that take place in this context, and
- the *processes* and *methods* of Christian education.

Using similar headings, I shall in this chapter analyse the range of approaches that are on offer in adult Christian education. But before doing so I need to acknowledge the danger of any such procedure. This lies in its two-fold temptation. First, the analysis may tempt us to believe that all of these different elements fit together in a framework of logical implication so that, for example, the adoption of one particular Christian education *goal* invariably implies a particular view of the *learner*, a related view of the *teacher*, a particular account of the most important *content* of Christian education and a specific *context* and *method* for Christian education. Now there often is, and more often should be, some such pattern of implication; but we need to retain a certain flexibility with regard to some of these 'variables'. Different approaches can properly accommodate a wider variety of elements than the specification of any 'ideal types' might suggest.[2] Variables, regrettably, can be very variable!

The second temptation of this charting of approaches is closely related to the first. The Christian educator 'on the ground' will often use a number of different approaches as he or she operates, for example, with a number of models of the Christian learner and a variety of educational goals. This is very often quite acceptable, provided that these aims and approaches complement, rather than conflict with, one another. (To avoid any such conflict it may be necessary to modify a particular approach so that it can be used alongside one or more of the others.)

We must always be ready to acknowledge that reality is exceedingly complex, not least in education. Although it is appropriate to simplify matters for the sake of clarity of exposition, we should not be misled into thinking that the clearest chart on the overhead projector always provides the best fit with the real world. Life is often even more messy than our teaching aids ...

GOALS AND CONTENT

Within a general aim for Christian education, different goals may be singled out as particularly significant, and different features of Christianity stressed. We may consider in particular:

- the different elements ('domains') of Christian belief, feeling and activity;
- the distinction between formative and critical Christian education; and
- the significance of the learner's response.

Beliefs, Feelings or Behaviour?

Many attempts to cut up the cake of educational activity distinguish cognitive (thinking), affective (feeling) and volitional (acting) slices.[3] In selecting the content of Christianity that they intend to teach, adult Christian educators may choose to place their emphasis on just one of these: the *belief-component*, the *experience/attitude/emotion-*

component or the *activity-component*. Sometimes such selective attention may be at the expense of the other elements in the Christian life, producing a rather one-sided account of what it is to learn to be Christian. But this need not be so. Many Christian educators, while 'beginning with' one such aspect of the life of faith, go on to relate it to the other aspects, so as to produce what in the end can be a highly integrated approach.

Christian education, like much general education, has traditionally often been regarded as concerned primarily with *cognition*: that is, with the intellectual processes, and resulting mental states, of understanding, belief and knowledge. In such cases Christian education activity has been limited to teaching and learning that engages the mind alone, and takes place through methods and in contexts where mental and intellectual skills and contents can best be developed. This remains a strong focus of concern for adult Christian educators. However, many would criticise such an emphasis as being too 'cool' and intellectual to serve us as an adequate delineation either of Christianity or of Christian education.[4] Some would wish to stress that Christianity is a *religion*, and not just a *theology* or set of beliefs. As a religion, Christianity comprises, in addition to its beliefs, a multi-faceted set of attitudes, emotions and practical behaviours, integrated into a way of life. James Michael Lee writes:

> Religion is a lifestyle activity involving the personally-lived fusion of knowledge, belief, feeling, experience, and practice ... *Religion is basically a way of living* ...[5]

Lee and others adopt what is sometimes describes as a 'holistic' view of religion and of the teaching of religion, in which the cognitive, affective and active (for which he uses the term 'life-style') aspects of religion are recognised as interrelated and interdependent functions of one and the same person.[6]

Conversion

Discussions of Christian education frequently include some reference to the phenomenon of conversion. This is because 'learning to be Christian' is often seen as involving a 'turning' or 'returning' to Christian faith, at least for some people. We should note here that different understandings of the nature of Christianity, and therefore of the content of Christian education, will inevitably lead to differing understandings of the nature of this conversion. Thus those who stress the belief-component of Christianity are likely to envisage conversion as a change in the learner's *beliefs* and *understanding*. For them, evangelism is often seen as including a measured argument for the truth of Christianity (sometimes called Christian 'apologetics'). For other Christian educators, however, conversion begins with a shift of *attitudes and emotions* rather than a change of intellectual conviction. Advocates of this view will naturally see Christian education as primarily concerned with developing the learner's dispositions, feelings and experiences 'in a Christian direction'. A key theme for them might be 'faith': in the sense of our life-orientation and trust. Understood in this way, faith is a fundamental human process which, although it becomes articulated in beliefs, does not begin in the cognitive domain. A further group might want to give primacy to the will in the Christian life, and to focus therefore on the *practice* or '*overt behaviour*' of a Christian, and its provocation or moulding through Christian education. On this account, conversion is primarily understood as a conversion of the will, expressed in different sorts of action. We saw in the last chapter that such a view may be highly activist and sometimes strenuously political. It is likely to reject those accounts of Christian evangelism and nurture that interpret Christian conversion and growth mainly in terms either of beliefs or of feelings, arguing instead that the main purpose of Christian education is to encourage the learner to engage actively in the liberation of the world from hunger, disease, political repression and secular and religious ignorance, by living and promoting human justice and freedom. We shall return to the issue of conversion below.

Understanding and Commitment?
Should the knowledge/belief dimension of the Christian religion be given pre-eminence, as often happens in adult education, Christian education can easily come close in its aims and content to the 'non-confessional' religious education or religious studies of the secular school and university, where the cognitive understanding of Christianity is also the primary goal (see chapter 1 above). For some Christian educators, it is a short step from emphasising the importance of getting people to hold Christian beliefs with understanding, to specifying as the aim of Christian education a more restricted goal that involves *no more than* an understanding of those beliefs.

Thus Charles Melchert has sometimes appeared to argue that understanding is the only proper *educational* goal in the church as well as in the academy. Admittedly, he adopts a broader construal of 'understanding' than do many writers in this area, and recognises the signal importance of the learner understanding the nature of religious experience and religious emotion. Nevertheless, this position comes over as rather a minimalist account of Christian education:

Religious education, insofar as it is true both to education and to religion, will entail helping others to understand in the ways appropriate to religion, ... such ways include not only the traditional academic and intellectual pursuits, but also the more experiential, ineffable and self-transcending ways of understanding appropriate to and characteristic of religion and the religious. I feel compelled to stress, so as to avoid misunderstanding, that helping others to understand the experiential dimensions of religion is not necessarily the same as giving them those experiences or expecting them to be or become committed to that experience or a religion. Educationally what is being sought is understanding.[7]

Such a perspective on Christian education may, in the hands of some, reduce to an account of education *about* Christianity. This, as we have seen, is often regarded as entirely appropriate in 'state' schools, and secular colleges and universities. But it is surely to be distinguished from the aim of education *in* Christianity that is the educational task of the *church*. There is no doubt that the church needs to encourage the study of Christianity (especially among adults) so that it is, at the very least, 'critically examined and intellectually understood'.[8] But the church should expect more than this from its efforts in Christian education.

Among those who lay great stress on the learner's understanding of Christianity, most would add that the Christian educator should (or at least may) hope for the conversion of the learner to the Christian Faith. Yet they too will insist that at least a partial understanding of Christian belief must precede such a conversion, and that we must beware of 'indoctrinatory' methods that produce belief at the expense of the learner's freedom in critical thinking and rational understanding.[9] Those who argue that Christian education *can and should* be *primarily* directed towards developing a commitment to Christianity (or understanding-with-commitment, or 'participant-understanding', of Christianity)[10] may talk about teaching 'towards' or 'for' religious commitment. The intention here is that what is taught and learned are Christian beliefs, values, practices and attitudes that are 'owned' by the learner, rather than *beliefs about* Christian beliefs, practices and attitudes.

Formation or Criticism?

Cutting across this variety of ways of defining the content of Christianity, we may note also a spectrum of emphases on the comparative importance of what may be called *'formative education'* and *'critical education'* in Christian education.[11]

Some approaches to Christian education concentrate on its rôle in passing on the church's values, beliefs and ways – in a word, its 'culture'. This is taught so that it may be internalised by each new generation of children and adults. Such a view lies at the heart of the 'Faith Community Approach' described in the last chapter.[12] This process is often described as some form of cultural formation: 'enculturation' (learning a culture by being brought up in it), 'acculturation' (the additional learning of a new, 'second' culture), 'assimilation' (the learning of a new culture with a loss of one's original culture) or 'biculturalisation' (the blending of two cultures).[13]

This sort of transmissive education may be entitled *formative education*, adopting a broad sense of the noun 'education'. The adjective 'formative' refers here to the formation of a person's beliefs, attitudes, values, dispositions to act, identity and world-view. Formative Christian education is *primarily receptive* of the received self-understanding of the church. Phrases such as 'spiritual formation', 'moral or character formation',[14] 'theological formation' and 'ministerial formation' also utilise this metaphor of moulding or fashioning something into a certain shape or after a certain pattern.[15] Some Christian educators, particularly educators of adults, bridle at the use of this language, as we shall see.[16] But as long as such formation does not disable a person's development towards personal autonomy and critical reflection, it seems to me to be a proper – indeed essential – dimension of *any* education that wishes to call itself Christian. A person's Christian education, after all, should be primarily oriented to her or his *learning to be Christian*, which is largely a matter of being formed in a Christian character.[17]

Other approaches, by contrast, lay far more stress on a *critical education* that encourages a reflective analysis and evaluation of the church's claims, in the light of the learner's own experience and understanding.[18] Critical Christian education is *primarily evaluative* of the church's self-understanding, and therefore in principle less conservatively 'traditional' than formation, when formation is seen simply as passing on a received tradition. This 'Christian criticism' embraces what has been described as the 'deconstruction' of the tradition.[19] As we noted in chapter 1, critical Christian education may be dominated either by a concern for a moral/political/social critique and understanding of Christianity (as interpreted by *liberation educators*), or by the sort of critical Christian education (beloved of *liberal educators*) that stresses rationality and autonomy – that is, 'thinking critically for oneself'. It is in this latter camp that we may place those authors who detect a danger in their colleagues' rhetoric about 'tradition-formation', the 'nurturing of the community of faith' or 'enculturation'. The following quotation from Gabriel Moran, a liberal Catholic commentator on Christian education, illustrates their concerns well:

> The problem is that one might get the impression that the academic, scholarly, and rational have been overemphasized. But it is the academic side that is one of the weakest elements in religious education .... If one had to choose between them, it seems to me obvious that the church has been more successful in providing community/enculturation than in providing schools for studying religion ... what I would also want affirmed is that the church is badly in need of schooling – not the poorly constituted church school of the 19th century but real schools in which religion can be taught/studied (i.e., critically examined and intellectually understood).[20]

This emphasis on (a particular view of) critical education is especially characteristic of British writing on religious education in schools, religious studies in colleges, and adult Christian education in churches. Brenda Watson has challenged the use of the adjective 'critical' on the grounds that it is commonly misunderstood to mean negative, destructive criticism. (She prefers the more positive phrase 'critical affirmation'.)[21] Nevertheless, she joins with other writers in affirming a central place for the critical use of the mind within education in religion:

> In our society which is striving to be an educated one, however superficially, the most signal failure of Christians is their failure to think, and the most serious dereliction of duty is that of not encouraging even the *young* child in a positive search for truth ... [and enabling her] to acquire a basic theological competence with which to make responsible choice.[22]

Clearly this point can be made even more pointedly with regard to an *adult* Christian education for an adult faith, where the learner has moved further from a (relative) dependency towards a (relative) self-directedness.

Although exponents of the socialisation/enculturation theories of Christian education often deny this next point, it is frequently said that such approaches 'do not appear to contain a critical principle whereby religious faith and religious traditions are evaluated, renewed, and revised'.[23] It must be said, however, that most authors acknowledge the importance of both formative and critical elements in Christian education, at least to some degree.[24] We recall that John Westerhoff, a leading exponent of the enculturation approach, has explicitly recognised the necessity for 'critical openness' along with identity-formation in what he calls 'catechesis'.[25] He can therefore advocate a catechesis (broadly equivalent to our notion of Christian education) that includes processes of (i) intentional enculturation and (ii) critical rational reflection. By these means the Christian tradition is *both* maintained, conserved and transmitted, *and* evaluated, changed and reformed.[26] Many indeed argue that *all* education 'involves both socialization (faith formation), by which the basic cultural patterns of a people are appropriated, and faith transformation, where, through dialogue and reflection, our meaning-perspectives are reshaped'.[27] This is not surprising if, as Basil Mitchell has argued, 'faith and criticism are two sides of one coin'. He adds, 'Without faith in an established tradition criticism has nothing to fasten on; without criticism the tradition ceases in the end to have any purchase on reality.'[28] Adult educators must also acknowledge the significance of a proper balance between formative and critical Christian education in the Faith.

Responsive Education?

The above discussion connects with questions about the relative importance that should be given in Christian education to the individual's (or the community's) *response*. The majority of Christian educators recognise the significance of this response by stressing the learner's 'conversion', 'appropriation', 'commitment', 'personal faith', or some such element. But often that is as far as the agreement goes; for the advocates of 'response' differ profoundly as to the acceptable limits within which this response must fall, and the extent to which each generation can and should 're-create' Christianity for itself.

In reading some authors we get a strong sense of Christian education as a matter of passing on the tradition whole, or at least of passing on that element in the received tradition (e.g. the apostolic preaching of the Christ Event) that will evoke the whole of the old tradition anew for the next generation.[29] Other writers, however, especially those who would be happy to be described as 'liberals' rather than as 'traditional' or 'conservative' Christians, disparage this as 'passing on the painting rather than the paintbox'.[30] They argue for a greater rôle and responsibility for the Christian learner herself in remaking the tradition, or responding to the old gospel in new and varied ways. They do not expect each new Christian generation to be identical to the last, pointing out that it lives in a different world of new knowledge, new challenges and different experiences. Today's Christians must have, as it were, their own revelation. Gabriel Moran again:

Each person recommences with fundamental and unpredictable newness the dialogue with God. Just as the Jews of old discovered God in their historical experience, the Christian student of today can discover God only through the experience of his own situation of space, time and community .... I maintain that a theology of revelation demands that the history which the teaching of revelation begins with is always the student's own history.[31]

I have argued elsewhere that a full Christian education needs both educational processes that begin from the tradition ('the past') and those that begin with the learners' present experience.[32]

TRADITION AND EXPERIENCE

There is thus another way of developing this spectrum of responsiveness. The Christian education goals outlined above differ in the emphasis each of them places on the contributions made by the tradition[33] ('that which is handed over') and by the learner's own experience within the practice of Christian education. Westerhoff has memorably analysed different styles of Christian education according to three metaphors or models of teacher-learner interaction. We may adapt and develop his reflections to address this issue.[34]

The 'Production Line Metaphor'

On this view, the teacher does something *to* the learner. She hands on the tradition: the content of the Christian faith derived from the scriptures and the life of the church. Here the learner's part appears to be that of passively receiving that tradition. The educational process thus works like a factory, with the Christian educators as production workers, dealing with an input of raw materials and creating an output of finished products. The goal is 'to transmit efficiently a cultural or religious heritage to the next generation'.[35] The words of the eighteenth-century English philosopher John Locke are often quoted in this context. Locke claimed that, apart from the obvious variety of their personalities, learners (or, at least, children) are all 'as white paper, or wax, to be moulded and fashioned as one pleases'.[36]

Such a transmissive model clearly presents certain difficulties, as its opponents often complain.[37] The underlying metaphor, after all, is impersonal and mechanical. It seems to assume that the learner is entirely passive, and initially wholly unformed. She must take the tradition or leave it; she has nothing to contribute either to her own learning or to the Christian faith itself. So this style of education has often been regarded as a sort of 'symbolic violence': 'invading a person in order to mould and reproduce a person, like everybody else, so that people fit into the machine', by imposing thoughts and ideas that do not necessarily arise from the learner's own questioning.[38] The model is indeed strong on formative Christian education, but does not naturally lead one to look for processes of critical Christian education. It is also a highly deterministic interpretation, taking little account of the *freedom* of the learner or indeed of the teacher. Randolph Crump Miller voices this criticism:

> If we take seriously the meaning of human freedom responding to specific and vague stimuli, both human and divine, we may hope to evoke insights but we cannot determine assembly line results.[39]

The model is also open to the criticisms often levelled against 'market-place values' in general education. As one commentator writes: 'A basic problem with [that] philosophy ... is that it finds it hard to see people except as means to an end, the end being that of consumption. It tends to cheapen the quality of human relationships.'[40] The sole criterion now becomes: Will I (or will my school, college, adult education group or church) 'profit' from this action? 'The work of the teacher or the child is assessed in terms of effectiveness ... how effective is the teacher in turning out the required product, how effective is the child at becoming what society wants him or her to become.'[41] If Christian educators were to adopt a similar attitude to an activity that should be about the facilitation of growth-through-learning not of commodities but of *persons*, similar challenges could be voiced.[42] The approach looks even worse when we focus on the education of adults.[43] There is certainly a danger that in free market thinking moral and religious virtues will become mere second-order principles, which may be over-ridden by the first-order principles of production, consumption and ownership. This will not do, for the ethical must come first – not least in *Christian* education.

Earlier this century the Christian existentialist Gabriel Marcel criticised western educational systems in general as employing an even more extreme version of the 'production line' approach. He castigated this as a 'vessel'-model or 'gramophone record'-model of education, in which the learners have to give back just what they have been given 'unchanged by any mental process'. He wrote that such educational models 'cease to apply in the case where, having explained some idea to a pupil, I ask him to explain it back to me in his own words and if possible with his own illustrations.'[44] The approach he rejected is more-or-less identical to that which Paulo Freire later castigated as the 'banking model' of education,[45] and

Carl Rogers as the 'mug and jug approach'.[46] The alternative educational strategy that Marcel advocated is of course now a commonplace in modern secular education. Although it ensures no more than a beginning to a development of responsiveness in the learner, it is a beginning that already undermines the appropriateness of employing inert or passive metaphors of education *without qualification*, and allows for some critical reflection and personal appropriation on the part of both learners and teachers.

Those who are wedded to a production line model of Christian education must take note of the full range of unfortunate implications that are likely to follow from any uncritical transmission of the Christian faith. Nevertheless, we must acknowledge that the model also has its strengths. It recognises that Christian education does involve some sort of formation, and that that formation is by and into an already existing broadly conceived identity ('nature' or 'form') of Christian being. On this view, tradition is the essential educational content and its passing on the key educational process. I have argued that the phrase 'Christian formation' is used by many in a qualified way that does not carry over all the implications of the underlying metaphor of giving form to unformed matter (as in, for example, the industrial process of moulding metals or plastics). When educators use the word 'formation' to speak of the 'shaping' of attitudes, beliefs, dispositions, and so on – as many Catholic writers routinely do – they are not implying that the learner is entirely without beliefs or attitudes, or even entirely without *religious* beliefs or attitudes of her own. Even the clay on the potter's wheel has its own nature, and learners are not clay. The values and beliefs that are formed through education are, after all, owned by (and therefore aspects of) *persons*. Nor should it be thought that the Christian learner is ever entirely passive and unresponsive when these attributes are being formed in her; that she cannot or does not interact with, co-operate with, or resist, the formative process. All learning is active. We are thinking here only of a *relative passivity*. Indeed, the main point of the language of formation is to underscore the useful distinction that was made earlier between, on the one hand, the adoption or development of Christian attributes (learning outcomes) and, on the other hand, those educational processes that give rise to evaluative ('critical') thinking directed towards those attributes. Clearly, however, the language of formation has to be used with some care, in case it is taken to carry these pejorative connotations of complete passivity and teacher 'manipulation'.[47]

The 'Gardening Metaphor'

On this view, Westerhoff notes, the teacher does something *for* the learner. As a gardener fertilises a rose bush, so the Christian educator applies the Christian tradition to the roots of the Christian learners. Although this metaphor is often used of adult education, it has its more natural home in the education of children and young people. Here Christianity operates – if the simile may be allowed – like manure. It stimulates the plant to develop its own potential and nourishes it so that it may become fully mature. The phrase 'Christian nurture', which is currently influential in debates about religious education in Britain and has been very popular in Christian education discussion in the United States in the past,[48] suggests just such a model. The central image is that of nurturing growth by 'nourishing', even 'suckling', the learner. (The word 'nurture' apparently derives ultimately from the Latin verb *nutrire,* to feed or nourish.) Thus 'nurture is the caring, feeding, supporting and sustaining aspect of religious education'.[49] Education is here still seen as a relationship of dependence, for 'a person could be self-educated but he could not be self-nurtured'.[50] But on this account the learner does have something of her own to contribute. Like the plant, she possesses her own inbuilt genetic pattern that controls her future development.

For some, however, this model gives too lowly a status to tradition, treating it as a mere nutrient or catalyst in a process whose end result is determined by the nature of the plant (the Christian learner) rather than of the fertiliser (the Christian tradition). Other critics argue that it still presents far too deterministic a picture,[51] in that it leaves no room for any significant rôle for an intervening educator, whether human or divine. A third objection is that it underrates the learner. The argument here would be that in the world of the metaphor nutrition has a determinate end-product – the full grown plant or human adult whose pattern of growth is controlled by the DNA within its cells, whereas education should be a much more open-ended process. A related criticism that is often made of the nurture model is that, in fostering commitment and disallowing 'free-wheeling exploration', it produces a Christian education without intellectual rigour, lacking the critical reflection of the confident 'critical learner'. It is the view of many that:

> Some young people who had been used to the loving support of the church in their home locality were singularly unable to cope with the critical stress of, for instance, university life.[52]

In other words, you can sometimes have just too much nurturing ...

Debates about the usefulness of this metaphor of growth also abound in secular education. There Rousseau, with his Romantic notion of natural development (anticipated by Comenius), and Froebel's gardening-model of teaching, have had a considerable influence.[53] Such approaches are undergirded by a view of the learner, and particularly of the child, as naturally good and naturally perfectible, and of education as a matter of allowing the learner's innate potentialities to flower rather than forcing her into a pre-determined mould. This account strongly contrasts with those theological perspectives that emphasise the doctrine of the Fall, with its implication of the necessity for a change in human nature that is more radical than can be provided by natural human development alone.

Growth was an important notion also in the thinking of John Dewey, although as we shall see he interpreted it rather differently. He defined education as a 'continuous process of growth, having as its aim at every stage an added capacity of growth'.[54] But Dewey's insistence that education is not a preparation for future living, but rather a process of living itself,[55] shows that a growth-model for learning need not devalue the learner and her current qualities and experiences by contrasting her unfavourably with a 'Good Time Coming' when the ends of education will be 'achieved'.[56] It is apparent that many Christian educators have disparaged religious education's concern with *children* because of these educators' particular understanding of the implications of a model of growth. But I would agree that those who attempt 'to liquidate children' from the enterprise of Christian education, because of a mistaken understanding of the sense in which Christianity is 'an arrival (adult) religion', appear to be blind to the idea 'of growth as an end to be prized for itself'.[57] Reflection on the Christian education of adults should not ignore the debate about the Christian education of children. This is not just because children grow into adults, but also because discussion of children's education often deals with similar issues both of principle and of practice.

We may finally note that in Quaker circles, where the metaphor of nurture is widely used, the growth of the 'seed' of the Inward Light is not taken to imply any pre-determined growth. There the language is used rather to express our responsibility as Christian educators *non-directively* to tend the garden where the mystery of God's activity will eventually reveal itself:

Growth is from within, is often gradual, unpredictable and mysterious. Friends have not, therefore, been concerned with applying pressure for spiritual decisions which cannot be forced at only one particular time.[58]

The 'Pilgrimage' Metaphor

In the last section I made reference to the work of John Dewey. Dewey, however, was no Romantic educator. His notion of growth rejects the model of unfolding latent powers from within, as much as that of formation from without. In Jim Wilhoit's words, Dewey's child 'is neither a flower which simply needs to unfold, nor raw material which needs to be moulded, but rather a scientist who is seeking to make sense out of the world'.[59] Dewey's pragmatic and instrumentalist view of knowledge, which treats it as something to be used and developed through hypothesis-making and problem-solving, together with his understanding of education as 'a continuing reconstruction of experience',[60] may suggest to us in a Christian context the idea of a learner on a pilgrimage *using* her Christian knowledge.

This, it may be argued, is a particular sort of knowledge. It is *knowledge needed for the journey*, and that means knowledge related to the immediate and prospective tasks of the journey, a knowledge that involves linking the stories and traditions of the community and its respected figures to the windings and uncertainties of the road ahead. In order to be useful learning, appropriate to this new journey, the tradition must be selectively appropriated and critically evaluated; education for the road needs to have this critical component, tradition and experience intersect here.[61] While some would put most of the stress on the learner's own reflections, arguing for a central place for educating the Christian disciple in the skills and character strengths of exploratory thinking and evaluation; others place more emphasis on what can be learned from the road and from those on the road, including the insights inherited from those who have gone before. There must always be a place for this dimension of formative education, alongside the more critical species of Christian education.

Although the pilgrimage model has also been extensively used in relation to the Christian education of children,[62] it is especially apt for modelling adult Christian learning and teaching. In the world of this metaphor the teacher does something *with* the learner, as they both tread the same road on the same journey of exploration, discovery and discipleship. In visualising this we might imagine that both teacher and learner pull behind them a handcart containing the tradition. The teacher utilises the contents of this as they move onwards. She selects, translates and *interprets* the tradition for the learner. Or (better) she helps the learner to do this for herself; for, as we have seen, the learner must relate her *own* present and future experiences to the Christian tradition (which itself is the most potent 'interpreter of experience' for the Christian).

This is a much more personal model than the two others we have explored. There is also more mutuality about it, for the learner as well as the teacher has access to the tradition. Indeed the learner can function as a teacher in her own right: their rôles may be exchanged, as both learner and teacher are co-pilgrims on a common road walking together on a journey of mutual discovery about life, themselves, each other and God.[63] The teacher, on this account, must be ready to act on Montaigne's advice from three centuries ago: 'I would have him listen to his pupil, turn and turn about.'[64]

We may note that this recognition of the learner as a teacher is of immense significance in Christian education, and not just in adult Christian education. It is a common mistake for adult Christians to see children as essentially the recipients of religious education, and themselves as the teachers. The New Testament points in the opposite direction. There we find no explicit references to children simply and straightforwardly being taught; in their place there are two passages where we may be shocked to find that the child is the teacher. The first is the story of the twelve-year-old Jesus and the learned Jewish teachers. It is perhaps rather a suspect example, if only because it is an illustration that ordinary Christians may not feel able to apply to other children. Nevertheless, we may note that Jesus the child is said to be listening and asking questions, and the adults are 'amazed at his understanding *and his answers*'.[65] The child is here both teacher and taught.

The other example is both less ambiguous and more striking: Jesus's act of bringing forward a child as a 'visual aid' for the disciples, to serve as their model of Christian discipleship. Hans-Ruedi Weber writes:

> it is the relationship with Jesus which makes these children representatives of God. As such, they are our teachers. In their objective humility and need, they cry 'mother', 'father', 'Abba', and they stretch out their empty hands. If we want to learn how to receive the Kingdom and how to become God's representatives, we must learn from the child in our midst.[66]

It is important to recognise that the focus of this acted parable is not the child's innocence or intellectual naivety.[67] In my view, the essential point is that children are without status, as the Christian disciple should be, and therefore more likely to accept the kingdom of God in humble dependence. In this way they are like slaves, and the Greek word *pais* may be translated in either way (compare Matt 8:6).[68] Adult educators and adult learners need to acknowledge the true significance of the child in the theology of Christian education; for

Jesus's teaching on this topic is not actually *about* children, it is about the sort of adults we must become for the sake of the kingdom.[69]

If, as many would argue, much Christian learning happens in the context of worship, it may be a major mistake for Christian educators routinely to remove children from the congregation at times of 'adult' worship. This is not just because the children learn from adults what it is to worship and to be Christian; but also because, in a deeper way, the adults can and must learn this from the children.[70] Christian educators, of all educators, need to welcome the claim that the learner can also be a teacher.

The journey metaphor also reminds us that the teacher himself or herself needs to be open to new learning, for who can say what will be around the next corner? All good teachers have at the same time to be good learners; the requirement of empathy with their pupils itself demands it.[71] Craig Dykstra has written of the teachers 'who have really served us' as being those whom we sense know the way, but who were 'willing to wait and see what happens on the journey this time'. He refers to such a teacher along these lines:

> Everything is not all decided in advance, and what happens in my learning will make a difference to her. She is willing to become my equal and to be vulnerable to what takes place. I see in her face that my own learning moves her, and that she is committed to me and my learning over the long haul.[72]

The pilgrimage model we are now considering is likely to appeal most to those Christian educators who inveigh against the church's prevalent 'monological illusion about communication', advocating in its place an interpretative *dialogue* 'in which there is address and response producing a meeting between the meanings the student brings to the educational encounter and the meanings responsibly presented by the teacher'.[73] This results in an appropriate 'balancing of the authority of the teacher with the authority of the learner',[74] which is particularly significant in adult Christian education. This educational *conversation* is a proper facilitation of learning through a 'transactional dialogue' negotiated between educator and learner. The facilitators here are 'not blank ciphers through whom the demands and wishes of learners are uncritically transmitted, but neither are they authoritarian ideologues who prescribe curricula and methods that are to be considered as rigidly fixed and immutable'.[75] As another author notes, 'If teachers have their own projects too much at heart, they cannot be available to the learner.'[76] 'Full listening' is needed for that, and that is a function of 'taking people seriously' and valuing them as ends in themselves.[77]

There is much to be said for the model of the *journey* in the religious life of adults in general, as well as in Christian learning in particular. First of all, the journey is a dynamic and not a static thing. Life and learning are processes. They change us; they move us along. Only the dead do not move. You cannot stay on the Mount of Transfiguration, the Gospels remind us, for even there the road calls us onwards. Secondly, the model of the journey is all-involving: it involves the whole of us. We learn and we teach by movement and music, as well as through words. The cognitive, doctrinal or theological content of the Christian tradition is exceedingly important; but it is not the whole of it and it must be geared into, and express itself through, the other aspects of the Christian life and the other dimensions of our humanness. In particular, theology arises out of worship, and leads us back to worship, for worship is always at the centre of the Christian faith. And worship, perhaps more than anything else, involves the whole of us. Thirdly, the journey of adult Christian education is part of the pilgrimage of Christian discipleship. It is, therefore, no aimless, easy ramble; nor is it merely a matter of *human* journeying. It is not easy, because in Christianity there is much that we can only learn in obedience and commitment and renunciation, and in times of suffering and failure; and those things are never easy. It is not aimless, because the Christian believes that the road is going somewhere, although it may often seem appropriate to add 'God alone knows where'.

Some of these aspects of the present metaphor will appeal particularly to the liberal Christian. I am thinking especially of the themes of open-endedness, process, change and discovery, applied to situations where the learner sets the agenda and decides the journey.[78] But the image of the journey has a more general appeal, and the theologically conservative may also find in it elements that fit his image of Christian learning. Christian pilgrimage may be viewed as an exploration, a 'journey of discovery'; but discovery is not *invention*, and in religion discovery is often viewed as the human pole of God's revelation. Christians search, many will say, because there is something there to be found. Others will add, 'and because they have already been found' and it is in their finding that they are found once again. Basil Mitchell has written:

> After reading ... that religion was most attractive when presented as a search and not as 'peddling answers', I was particularly struck by the overwhelming *affirmations* of Christians. 'The Word was made flesh and dwelt among us and we beheld his glory ...' Here is an answer and not just a search. Yet the emphasis on searching does not seem to be simply a mistake. The meaning of the affirmations cannot be exhausted

by the conceptual formulations of any particular age, so that the church as a whole is constantly trying to understand them afresh; and the individual has to grow gradually into a fuller, but never complete, realisation even of truths which he accepts. Religious education must attempt to convey this idea of the believer as engaged in a search, without suggesting that there are no 'answers'.[79]

Furthermore, both conservative and liberal may presumably agree that this metaphor implies that Christian education is a journey that we do not make alone. At one level this is because no Christian can be totally separate from other believers.[80] Christian truth is not an individual thing. It is given communally to the church and Christians learn it, in part, from one another, and must teach it to one another. Yet at an even more important level, the metaphor hints, no Christian can journey into the faith alone because Christians cannot be alone. It would be a contradiction in terms. Perhaps this is one way of interpreting the claim that there is only one 'Christian educator'.[81] Certainly, at the end, there is only one goal for Christian learning. It is a learning 'in Christ', a learning that is oriented 'to Christ' in its direction and gradient. Christian education as journey is indeed a metaphor of 'openness'; but this may be construed as becoming more open to God and to the contours of the landscape of God, and of *learning Christ in the Way* – 'on the open road'. And that learning is a learning of Christ who *is* the Way, a learning of the road that is Christ.

The figure of the journey is indeed a powerful image for Christian education.

Conversion Yet Again
We should return now to the issue of *conversion*, noting that the metaphor of the journey more easily accommodates this category than do those interpretations of Christian education that model it on the activities of 'gardening' or 'nurture'. The reason for this is that these other views seem to understand the learning of Christianity in a gradualist fashion, treating it as a matter of continual progression or development – of regular 'Christian growth'. But learning Christianity does not always appear to be like that. As with learning more generally, an overturning or transformation may be experienced,[82] as a new fork in the road is chosen and a new direction taken. In many cases this can happen quite dramatically. Conversion has therefore been described as 'a significant sudden transformation of a person's loyalties, pattern of life, and focus of energy'.[83] It is often associated with moving into adulthood, or (in later years) with reconstructing our

image of ourselves within adulthood.

Optimistic, progressivist and evolutionary accounts of Christian learning might be thought to have difficulty in making room for anything more than a very attenuated notion of conversion change. Yet even Christian educators of a liberal and gradualist disposition sometimes stress the need for conversion as a complement to the process they designate as nurture. Hence Westerhoff's claims:

> We cannot gradually educate persons to be Christians, not in this world. Christian faith goes counter to our ordinary understandings and ways. It is hardly possible to grow up in our sort of society and have the eyes and ears of Christian faith. Transformations, reorientations of life, conversions are necessary ...
>
> What the Church's ministry needs is a catechesis which evangelizes and evangelization which catechizes. Nurture and conversion, conversion and nurture, belong together ...
>
> Children and youth are Christians and members of the community of Christian faith by their baptisms. They are to be nurtured in this community's understandings and ways. They are also to be evangelized by God's transforming Word until in their maturity (adulthood) they experience a moment or period of conversion.[84]

These are striking words. But they seem to be in conflict with other approaches to Christian education, for example with the influential 'social-cultural' approach so beloved of liberals and associated with the names of Horace Bushnell and George Albert Coe in the United States.[85] But Bushnell's position was a reaction against a very different view of conversion, and of human nature prior to conversion, than the one that is being appealed to by Westerhoff in the quotations above. In Bushnell's oft-quoted words, 'the true idea of Christian education' is:

> *That the child is to grow up a Christian, and never know himself as being otherwise.*
>
> In other words, the aim, effort, and expectation should be, not, as is commonly assumed, that the child is to grow up in sin, to be converted after he comes to a mature age; but that he is to open on the world as one that is spiritually renewed, not remembering the time when he went through a technical experience, but seeming rather to have loved what is good from his earliest years.[86]

This passage emphasises a close continuity in Christian being and Christian learning between child and adult. Bushnell's rejection of the individualistic and revivalist form of evangelical Christian education, with its insistence on a radical distinction between those who are in Christ and the depraved sinners who had not yet responded to the gospel, expressed his desire that children be brought up 'in conversion' rather than 'for conversion',[87] through the medium of relationships between parents and children that express the discipline of the family.[88] This is how God works, he argued. It is 'the Lord's way of education': the bringing up of children towards responsible adulthood in the 'nurture and admonition' of the Lord (Ephesians 6:4).[89] Westerhoff would surely approve.

Further Comments

Readers will probably think that enough – some might argue more than enough! – has been squeezed out of these metaphors. But the 'unpacking' of metaphorical language, a process that involves reflection on the positive *and negative* characteristics of an analogy,[90] is an important task preliminary to the deployment of such language. It may even be dignified as philosophical work, for language can only be employed in sober argumentation if it can be used in inferences, and inferences cannot be drawn from totally unspecified metaphors or analogies.[91] If such language is to be used in discussions about Christian education, then we must surely make some attempt to specify what it does, and what it does not, *really mean*.

I turn now to some more general issues related to tradition and experience. We have noted that the balance between the church's tradition and the learner's own experience can be tipped in either direction. It is a mistake, however, to interpret all formative education solely as transmissive, didactic, content-centred and 'conservative'; and to recognise critical education alone as creative, experiential, learner-centred and 'liberal'. Critical education passes on a 'tradition' as well, for it transmits a way of thinking and acting and a particular set of ('critical') attitudes and behaviours. This tradition-of-criticism includes, for example, norms of rationality, skills of critical evaluation and the disposition to engage in questioning, all of which are essential to the development or 'formation' of the critical mind, including the Christian (self-critical) mind.[92] Similarly formative education, in pursuing its goal of forming an individual's identity and world-view, may need to evoke new experiences in the learner and encourage her to reflect on her whole life experience.

Thus tradition and experience go together at very many levels. The situation is further blurred by the fact that 'experience' covers such a wide variety of things. All learning, in a sense, is experiential, but the idea of 'experiential learning' is varied and complex.[93] I have used the word 'experience', as do many adult educators, to label the learner's own present and past context, situation and reflections; but there are also narrower, more specifically religious construals of the term. Thus the *charismatic* wishes to help to evoke in his charges, or rather 'to open them up to', their own experiences of the Spirit's power and presence. The *evangelist* may want them to have a conversion experience. The *liturgical* leader may strive to create the best conditions for the evocation of a sense of numinous awe, wonder or 'presence'. A '*school of mysticism*' has a similar end in view: viz. the evocation of a mystical experience. These are *religious experiences* in an explicit sense. We may put alongside them the educational processes and learning outcomes with which other Christian educators work: experiences that they may designate as 'implicitly religious' experiences. I am thinking here of certain feelings of reverence, trust, acceptance, responsibility or compassion, which are outcomes that may be engendered in group work, psychodrama and the like.

To argue for a major place for experience in Christian education, therefore, is to make an ambiguous appeal. Christian educators often agree in interpreting their rôle as 'facilitators of experience', but disagree as to the types of experience that they wish to facilitate. Those who call for more experiential learning of religion need to specify what sort of experience they intend, and the particular sort of learning they expect to precede it and to follow from it.

LEARNERS AND TEACHERS

How do we view ourselves when we take up the task of adult Christian educators or 'facilitators of Christian learning'? We have seen how Christian educators often tend to operate on the basis of metaphors or models drawn from other parts of life. In this section we shall take another look at the range of approaches to Christian education, this time focussing on the models of the teacher (and therefore of the learner) that are associated with them.[94] We should note once more that practical educators in fact often work with several of these teacher-models at the same time. As many of the models are mutually complementary this is usually appropriate. But sometimes there is a tension between these models, and this needs to be recognised by those engaged in Christian education.

The adult Christian educator is often viewed as a sort of *priest*, and Christian education as essentially a community or congregational affair. This chimes in with the 'Faith Community Approach' to Christian education, described in chapter 1 above, which is concerned primarily with building up the church and includes encouraging the *whole* church to function as teacher of Christianity to the world. The 'priestly-Christian-educator' will often be most at home with a Christian education that takes place in the context of the worship of the whole Christian assembly.[95]

The *pastor*-model of the Christian educator is somewhat different. Pastoral work is usually much more of an individual activity: a one-to-one relationship.[96] When Christian education is practised on a pastoral model, the *individual's* growth in faith, belief or Christian behaviour becomes the main target of effort (see the 'Faith/Spiritual Development Approach' in chapter 1). Pastors may see themselves involved in Christian education either as nurturing-gardeners, or as guides and exploring-fellow-pilgrims on a mutual journey of search and discovery (see above). In each case, however, they will recognise their responsibilities for the care of their learners; acknowledging perhaps that Christian education itself is a *pastoral task*, as teaching is a caring relationship.[97]

The above models shade into a view of the Christian educator as *interpreter* (see the 'Interpretation Approach' to Christian education in chapter 1). Such a teacher helps to make the connections between the Christian tradition and the learner's own experience and, like the uprights of a two-rail fence, provides the necessary support for both.[98] The interpreter or 'translator' is the linking person who understands – and perhaps shares – the experiences of the learners, and seeks to develop in them the skills of making *their own* connections. This is a 'pontifical' model, not in any pompous or dogmatic sense but as 'befitting a pontiff' (from the Latin *pontifex*, 'bridge-maker'). Some have interpreted 'the priesthood of the teacher' along similar lines, as offering a bridge between 'received wisdom and the present circumstance', again preferably through the 'ideal hermeneutical vehicle' of an adult education that is respectful of both human experiences and the riches of tradition.[99] (The logic of this understanding of the model seems to suggest that the interpreter-Christian-educator will work best with individuals and small groups.)[100] Wesley Carr's 'consultancy model of ministry' offers a similar picture:

> The word 'consultant' in the proposed model of ministry refers more to the idea of an interpreter than to that of an expert. Such a person ... uses himself as a measure and his commitment is to enable those with whom he is working to understand what is happening and then to take their own authority for acting. . . . A major skill, therefore, is to be able to hold a point of reference which transcends what is immediate without becoming detached from what is happening.

Interestingly, Carr too regards such a model as a 'model of priest-hood'.[101] It may be argued, however, that the person who can best fulfil this interpretative rôle is a 'marginal' figure: an in-betweener who can belong to two different cultures (the church and the world of experience) without being totally identified with either. The educator-as-interpreter may be said to be engaged in the task of *hermeneutical practical theology*. This is a form of reflection which itself develops in interaction with a developing situation that helps people to interpret a situation and engage with it.[102]

One of the other major approaches to Christian education described in the last chapter was the 'Liberation Approach'. This involves the 'conscientization' of the learner: that is, her perception of her social and political context, leading to critical action-reflection and a changed life-style (e.g. by taking action against oppressive elements in the society and culture). On this approach, as we have seen, the teacher operates as a sort of 'colleague' or 'fellow freedom-fighter' in Christian education's struggle to free the learner and the world. Such an analysis relates closely to a view of the Christian educator as a *prophet*,[103] raising the consciousness of her hearers and – through her critique of society and the church – helping to develop their critical faculties. This style of Christian education may find itself in conflict with some of the others: hence the tension often experienced by clergy and ministers who attempt to combine in their own persons elements of both the (disruptive) prophetic- and the (conservative and conserv-ing) pastoral/priestly-Christian-educator; or who seek to minister to a congregation that has been opened up to more prophetic educational influences from others. Yet we may also argue that the critical stance of the prophet is itself a species of concern, just as much as is the pastor's care.[104]

Undoubtedly one of the most popular models of the Christian educator is that of a *preacher* or proclaimer of the gospel.[105] This blanket term, however, covers a range of activities and it may be argued that many preaching styles and approaches have already been referred to under the models of priest, pastor, interpreter and prophet. But there are distinctive theories of Christian education that stress the teacher's authenticity and dedication, or his witnessing and proclaim-ing skills, as significant features of the Christian education process.[106] The Christian educator is here pictured as the herald of the heavenly king, proclaiming the gospel to the learner.[107] This model leads to a very high view of the responsibility and rôle of the Christian educa-tor as a channel for the voice of God.[108] It therefore also carries with it the very real danger of ignoring the human contribution of the reli-gious educator's own voice.

The other traditionally popular model for the Christian educator has been that of the *school-teacher* or *lecturer*. Some have resolutely rejected the 'schooling-instructional' paradigm for Christian education, seeing in it (often unfairly) an undue emphasis on the cognitive and the external aspects of Christianity, a temptation to control and manipulate learners and to predict learning outcomes, or a concentration on the development of critical thinking at the expense of doctrinal or spiritual formation (see the 'Critical Christian Education Approach' in chapter 1).[109] Others would argue that some at least of these emphases and activities have a proper place within adult Christian education, but would deny that they should be viewed as *priorities* for the church, as they might be in more secular forms of education. However, as we have noted, another group has stressed that the church needs to pay particular attention precisely to the cognitive and critical in its religious self-education.[110]

Perhaps all sides should recognise two dangers here. The first is that of confusing 'schooling' (narrowly-conceived) with 'education'. The second danger is that of embracing the wrong sort of professionalisation of Christian education, one that limits its activity to those contexts where the supposedly 'real', that is academic- or schooling-oriented, Christian educators are working. When the church engages in what it most easily and explicitly acknowledges as 'Christian education', whether in Sunday-schools, confirmation/church membership classes or adult groups, the dominant model employed is often still that of the rather old-fashioned sort of school-teacher or lecturer in further or higher education. This sometimes result in a style and content of Christian learning that is inappropriately 'academic', classroom-based and formal.

Taking a more positive view, however, the *teaching model* is entirely appropriate even outside formal academic contexts, provided that it is broadened to cover *all* 'intentional and structured' facilitation of learning, and not just cognitive and academic learning. For some, indeed, this is the only proper view to take of the Christian educator. Thus for Lee, the 'religious instructor' is *literally* a teacher of the Christian religion, but in the wider sense that he or she is defined as a specialist in facilitating Christian learning: that is, encouraging and enabling in a wide variety of ways the wide range of Christian learning outcomes.[111] On this broader view, all the above models and approaches to Christian education may be subsumed under some aspect or another of the category of Christian teaching. But as the teacher's rôle may from time to time share some of the features of a priest, pastor, interpreter, prophet and preacher, we must not understand the designation 'teacher' in too restrictive a manner.[112]

CONTEXT, CURRICULUM AND METHODS

We turn finally to the different views that are held about the most appropriate settings, learning experiences and methods of adult Christian education. This is obviously an enormous field, and in this section we can only touch on some general principles.[113] Further relevant material is to be found in later chapters of this book.

Whichever particular approach to Christian education and model of the Christian educator is adopted, its exponents usually advocate a broad view of these particular variables, arguing that their favoured philosophy of Christian education can operate across a wide spectrum of settings and can utilise a great variety of learning experiences and educational methods. Nevertheless, there will often be a close correlation between certain models and approaches and particular forms of Christian education practice.

Let us look at *context* first of all. Formal education in school and higher education operates at three levels: the individual, the small group and the large group. Thus we find individual teacher-learner interaction throughout school-teaching as well as in university or college tutorials; multiple communication between the educator and a small group (e.g. the set, class or seminar); and educational work that has its setting in a much larger group (e.g. in a large public lecture or a school assembly). Beyond this there are mass communication settings in which very large numbers of students watch a film or listen to radio or TV broadcasts, or indeed read the same text. Clearly the economies of scale that are produced as we increase the audience size for any communication are only bought at the expense of a decrease in 'audience participation', that is of *inter*-communication. This includes both communication within the group and (particularly) communication feedback to the educator. (TV presenters are taught to present themselves as if to the individual in her own home, duping her into believing that 'I'll see you tomorrow night.' In reality, of course, the same image is broadcast in a non-interactive manner to millions of different, isolated, *unobserved* individuals.)

Adult Christian education may utilise a similar range in the size and nature of its learner groups.[114] It is arguable that those who work as 'pastor-Christian-educators' and 'interpreter-Christian-educators' will be most effective with individuals and small groups.[115] 'Priest-Christian-educators', however, may wish to capitalise on the unique experience of the (often inter-generational) large group of the worshipping assembly. Some prophet-Christian-educators may also work best in this situation, or even in wider contexts. Others, however, will prefer a much smaller audience, as did the prophet

Nathan who was at his most effective in a one-to-one relationship with his king.[116] Those engaged in mass communication type Christian education must recognise the educational constraints imposed on them by the lack of feedback and of real fellowship in this medium. They will have little control over, and often little knowledge of, their students' own individual experiences; and however 'interactive' a text or computer program may be there is no *real* dialogue in the sense of a mutual exchange of ideas.[117]

Small groups are often the preferred context for Christian education, and the literature on the needs and problems of group membership and activity is a very useful resource for the Christian educator.[118] It is worth noting that there is some empirical evidence to suggest that group work is more attractive to more extravert personalities, whereas introverts tend to feel less at ease in groups and with learning through discussion, particularly when actively involved themselves. Unfortunately there is also some evidence suggesting that churchgoers tend towards introversion rather than extraversion.[119]

John Westerhoff has suggested that the distinction between 'socialisation' (broadly our 'formative education') and 'education' (broadly 'critical education') may lie in their differing understandings of the learner:

> Might the language of education perceive the learner as an individual who associates with others and forms institutions, and might the language of socialization perceive the learner as a communal being whose identity and growth can only be understood in terms of life in a community which shares a common meaning, vision, authority, rituals, and family-like life together?[120]

Westerhoff envisages as an effective church community ('base community') one that would be 'more like a family than a social institution', but in size as well as 'location' would be positioned somewhere between the family at one extreme, and society and its institutions at the other.[121]

Christian educators may work with groups, both natural and artificial, that have been formed without any reference to the church's Christian education task. Families fall into this category;[122] as do most schools, work places, residential units, hospitals and voluntary groups (of old people, parents, youth, etc.). The expectations and assumptions of groups of this nature will clearly be different from those that have been created deliberately to 'do Christian education'. Such differences need to be taken into account, as 'sector-ministers' and chaplains in such contexts will bear witness.

Christian educators who wish to emphasise one of the three dimensions of Christianity – whether the cognitive, the affective or the active ('life-style') dimensions – may look for settings in which these different educational outcomes are most appropriately pursued. Schools, colleges and adult education classes are likely to suit the 'cognitive-oriented-Christian-educator' best; families, parents' groups and counselling situations are more likely to be the preferred setting for the work of the 'affective-oriented-Christian-educator'; whereas caring agencies and charitable action-groups, youth groups, and political groups will be grist to the mill of the 'conduct-oriented-Christian-educator'.

The learning experiences *(curriculum)* of adult Christian education occupy another broad spectrum, as do its *methods*.[123] These processes of Christian education should be determined by three factors: the goals of the educator, her views of her own rôle, and the setting in which she works. Lectures on the Christian tradition may be appropriate to one such set of variables; an embrace in the context of a strongly affective group meeting or in a situation of worship will best reflect a rather different approach to Christian education. Those who intend to teach beliefs and understanding will inevitably adopt different methods of Christian education from those adopted by teachers whose focus is more on changing attitudes or developing skills.

It is routine to note that the more 'didactic' methods are teacher-centred and content-centred and often pass on the Christian tradition in a highly cognitive way, whereas the more 'experiential' methods are learner-centred and process-centred. The latter species encourages an exploration of the learner's own experience, emotions, attitudes and relationships, rather than focussing on the tradition. Such disparate styles of Christian education practice may be individually appropriate and mutually complementary.[124] But problems can arise when there is a mismatch between particular goals and the methods selected for achieving them. Christian attitudes like trust or charity are not learned best through attending lectures about them; and a better cognitive understanding of the two-nature Christology is not the most likely outcome of an encounter group. Our combination of Christian education variables cannot therefore be allowed to become *too* messy!

Christian educators are sometimes criticised for a certain sort of colonialism, in that they treat everything in the church as an instance of Christian learning. Stanley Hauerwas seems to endorse this position:

> I would contend that everything the church is and does is 'religious education'. Put more strongly, the church does not 'do' religious education at all. Rather, the church *is* a form of education that is religious.[125]

The position might be better represented by the claim that Christian formation (in particular) is not everything that happens in the church, but that it is *a dimension* of everything that happens in the church. We are learning all the time, and the Christian education curriculum is very much like an iceberg. The parts of it that appear clearly above the waves are the experiences that are obviously intended to teach us something: for example, listening to a sermon or talk, reading a study course booklet or engaging in an adult Bible study discussion. Such experiences and activities constitute the *manifest* or *explicit curriculum* of adult Christian learning. But, as with the iceberg, very many of the learning experiences we undergo are hidden from our view, in the sense that we do not immediately recognise them as leading to learning. They constitute the *hidden curriculum* of tacit, implicit, informal and unstructured learning experiences. They do not appear before us with an educational label attached that reads 'this is here to teach you Christianity'. But we learn from them all the same.[126] This hidden curriculum may serve to reinforce, or to work against, the more explicit educational experiences that we undergo: much in the way that our non-verbal communication through our gestures, dress and tone of voice adds to or subtracts from the verbal communication that it accompanies.

Christian educators unquestionably need to reflect on the hidden curriculum that underlies their more obvious attempts to facilitate Christian learning. Often it is as hidden from the teachers as it is from the learners. Educationalists argue that many of our deepest attitudes and values are formed through the hidden curricula embodied in our schools, homes, peer groups, work-places and churches. The church especially needs to recognise that *all the aspects of its life* may be providing learning experiences. All Christians and all Christian activities operate as sources of Christian learning, whether or not they intend or are intended to teach the Faith. The worship, fellowship and sacramental life of the church are particularly potent sources through which adults as well as children learn to be Christian.[127] They should be more openly acknowledged as catalysts of Christian learning, and critically evaluated in this rôle.

It is part of our task as Christian educators to don our wetsuits and plunge into the dark waters to examine this iceberg-below-the-waves that is the hidden curriculum of Christian learning. We ought to assess its dimensions within our own particular church. And we should recognise its effects: noting what it is that people are learning from it. We might then need to set about changing it.

So much of our most significant learning is unconscious. For example, a church whose customs for years have dictated silence in the church prior to its service of worship, the avoidance of personal contact with others in the pews or the sharing of emotion during the service will have difficulty getting its members to engage in a contemporary community celebration.

. . .

We need to look at the total learning experience of people and bring as many aspects of it as possible into our conscious, deliberate, systematic, and sustained efforts. That is what it means to make learning education.[128]

NOTES

1   See also Kieran Scott, 'Three Traditions of Religious Education', reprinted in Jeff Astley and Leslie J. Francis (eds), *Critical Perspectives on Christian Education: A Reader on the Aims, Principles and Philosophy of Christian Education*, Leominster: Gracewing Fowler Wright, 1994, pp. 276–291.

2   See note 42 to chapter 1 above.

3   See, for example, Benjamin S. Bloom *et al. Taxonomy of Educational Objectives: The Classification of Educational Goals, Handbook I: Cognitive Domain*, New York: McKay; London: Longmans, 1956; David R. Krathwohl *et al., Taxonomy of Educational Goals, Handbook II: Affective Domain*, New York: McKay; London: Longmans, 1964; Anita J. Harrow, *Taxonomy of the Psychomotor Domain*, New York: McKay, 1972. We must recognise that such attempts divide up, and abstract from, what is in reality a complex unity.

4   Cf. Nicola Slee, 'Endeavors in a Theology of Adult Education: A Theologian Reflects', in Peter Jarvis and Nicholas Walters (eds), *Adult Education and Theological Interpretations*, Malabar, Fla.: Krieger, 1993, pp. 331–332, and essays cited.

5   James Michael Lee, 'The Authentic Source of Religious Instruction', in Norma H. Thompson (ed.), *Religious Education and Theology*, Birmingham, Ala.: Religious Education Press, 1982, p. 109; see also John H. Westerhoff , *Living the Faith Community*, San Francisco: Harper & Row, 1985, pp. 92–93.

6   See also James Michael Lee, *The Content of Religious Instruction*, Birmingham, Ala.: Religious Education Press, 1985, pp. 131, 141; Arthur Timothy Lines, *Systemic Religious Education*, Birmingham, Ala.: Religious Education Press, 1987.

7   Charles F. Melchert, 'What is Religious Education?', reprinted in Astley and Francis (eds), *Critical Perspectives on Christian Education*, p. 59. For a more nuanced analysis of the relationships between commitment and education in religion, see Melchert's 'The Future of Education: Commitment in Religion and Education', in Gloria Durka and Joanmarie Smith (eds), *Emerging Issues in Religious Education*, New York: Paulist Press, 1976, pp. 88–98, and for a different dimension of his thinking see his *Wise Teaching: Biblical Wisdom and Educational Ministry*, Harrisburg, Penn.: Trinity Press International, 1998, ch. 7.

8   Gabriel Moran, 'Where Now, What Next?', in Padraic O'Hare (ed.), *Foundations of Religious Education*, New York: Paulist Press, 1978, p. 106. Moran does recognise, however, that in the area of religion 'teaching means to show someone a way of life', and that 'the religious form of teaching stands in marked contrast to modern concepts of teaching' understood as rational explanation, dispassionate

before the evidence. He adds: 'No religion could survive on classroom teaching alone.' Gabriel Moran, 'Religious Education', in Mircea Eliade (ed.), *Encyclopedia of Religion*, Vol. 12, New York: Macmillan; London: Collier Macmillan, 1987, p. 322.

9   See the quotation from Sara Little in ch. 1 (p. 21 above). On the thorny question of indoctrination and Christian education, see especially Elmer Thiessen, *Teaching for Commitment: Liberal Education, Indoctrination and Christian Nurture*, Montreal and Kingston: McGill-Queen's University Press; Leominster: Gracewing Fowler Wright, 1993 and Jeff Astley, *The Philosophy of Christian Religious Education*, London: SPCK; Birmingham, Ala.: Religious Education Press, 1994, ch. 4.

10 On the rôle of understanding in both Christian formation and religious education about Christianity, see also Astley, *The Philosophy of Christian Religious Education*, ch. 7 and 'The Place of Understanding in Christian Education and Education about Christianity', in Astley and Francis (eds), *Critical Perspectives on Christian Education*, pp. 105–117.

11 For a detailed working out of this distinction, see Leon McKenzie, *The Religious Education of Adults*, Birmingham, Ala.: Religious Education Press, 1982, pp. 36–37, 64, and Astley, *The Philosophy of Christian Religious Education*, ch. 5.

12 Above pp. 17–20.

13 See John H. Westerhoff, 'Formation, Education, Instruction', reprinted in Astley and Francis (eds), *Critical Perspectives on Christian Education*, p. 67. Similar distinctions are made by sociologists between primary socialisation (learning a social rôle by being raised in a pattern of beliefs and actions), re-socialisation (returning to this pattern) and trans-socialisation (the situation that obtains when those who have not been raised in a particular system come to adopt it).

14 On the rôle played by the passing on of a moral tradition in moral education in general, see Mary Midgley, *Can't We Make Moral Judgements?*, Bristol: Bristol Press, 1991, chs. 6 and 7; David Carr, *Educating the Virtues*, London: Routledge, 1991, ch. 8; Johannes A. van der Ven, *Formation of the Moral Self*, Grand Rapids, Mich.: Wm. Eerdmans, 1998.

15 Etymologically the verb derives from the Latin *formare*, to mould or shape.

16 See below, pp. 41–43.

17 It should be recognised that a great deal of Christian formation in the church is not intentionally engineered or facilitated by any Christian educator, but flows from the 'hidden curriculum' of the church's worship, social fellowship and other activities, often without anyone's intention – or even knowledge (see pp. 60–61 below).

18 Here 'critical' simply points to a judgement, evaluation or assessment based on reflection, and may be either positive or negative; see below.

19 See Leon McKenzie, *Adult Education and Worldview Construction*, Malabar, Fla.: Krieger, 1991, ch. 2.

20 Moran, 'Where Now, What Next', pp. 105–106; see also Gabriel Moran, *Interplay: A Theory of Religion and Education*, Winona, Minnesota: Saint Mary's Press, 1981, pp. 74–78. Compare Walter Kaufmann, *The Faith of a Heretic*, Garden City, N.Y.: Doubleday, 1961, p. 289. Edward Farley criticises Westerhoff's 'call away from schooling and classroom instruction' as disparaging the necessary dimension of *ordered learning*. For Farley, however, this concept appears to include both critical and formative activity, denoting 'self-conscious attempts ... to transmit by means of a sequential process of disciplined didactic activity both the insights and deposits of the past and the methods and modes of

thought and work which enables new insights.' Farley also challenges the view that education means simply any sort of formation, rather than particularly *ordered* learning. See Edward Farley, 'Can Church Education be Theological Education?', reprinted in Astley, Francis and Crowder (eds), *Theological Perspectives on Christian Formation*, especially pp. 35, 42 and 44 (n. 12). See also Meg Orr's essay, ch. 3 below. I should also mention here Moran's plea for 'teaching religion', in his sense of providing learners with 'a language for intelligent discussion and thoughtful ordering of what students already know about religion and what they should know for understanding their world'. Gabriel Moran, *Religious Education as a Second Language*, Birmingham, Ala.: Religious Education Press, 1989, p. 124.

21 Brenda Watson, *et al.*, *Critical Openness*, Oxford: Farmington Institute for Christian Studies, no date, pp. 3, 6–7; Watson, *Education and Belief*, Oxford: Blackwell, 1987, pp. 54–55, 78.

22 Brenda G. Watson, 'The Attractiveness of Christ', *Occasional Papers, 7*, Oxford: Farmington Institute for Christian Studies, no date, p. 2.

23 John L. Elias, *The Foundations and Practice of Adult Religious Education*, Malabar, Fla.: Krieger, 1982, p. 167. Compare also Don S. Browning, *A Fundamental Practical Theology: Descriptive and Strategic Proposals*, Minneapolis, Minn.: Fortress, 1991, p. 217.

24 For example, John H. Westerhoff, *Building God's People in a Materialistic Society*, New York: Seabury Press, 1983, pp. 49–50, 56–57. See also Thomas H. Groome, *Christian Religious Education: Sharing our Story and Vision*, San Francisco: Harper & Row, 1980, pp. 126–127.

25 See above pp. 17–19. Westerhoff extends this analysis to school RE also, where he argues quite properly that, although the emphasis should be on openness, 'the principle of identity maintenance' is also required for a healthy society. See his 'Religious Education and Catechesis', in M. C. Felderhof (ed.), *Religious Education in a Pluralistic Society*, London: Hodder & Stoughton, 1985, p. 57–74.

26 *ibid.*, p. 67. Compare also Westerhoff, *Living the Faith Community*, pp. 85–86.

27 Jack L. Seymour, Margaret Ann Crain and Joseph V. Crockett, *Educating Christians: The Intersection of Meaning, Learning, and Vocation*, Nashville, Tenn.: Abingdon, 1993, p. 53; cf. Astley, *The Philosophy of Christian Religious Education*, pp. 80–86.

28 Basil Mitchell, *Faith and Criticism*, Oxford: Oxford University Press, 1994, p. 88.

29 See Johannes Hofinger, *The Art of Teaching Christian Doctrine*, London: Sands; Notre Dame, Ind.: University of Notre Dame Press, 1962; Josef Andreas Jungmann, *Handing on the Faith*, New York: Herder & Herder, 1962; Harold William Burgess, *An Invitation to Religious Education*, Birmingham, Ala.: Religious Education Press, 1975, ch. II.

30 BCC Report, *The Child in the Church*, London: British Council of Churches, 1976, p. 23.

31 Gabriel Moran, *God Still Speaks*, London: Burns & Oates, 1967 (= *Catechesis as Revelation*, New York: Herder & Herder, 1966), pp. 51, 54. See also Moran, *Design for Religion*, London: Search Press, 1971 and Moran, *Interplay*, ch. 4. Compare also Lewis Joseph Sherrill, *The Gift of Power*, New York: Macmillan, 1955 and Burgess, *An Invitation to Religious Education*, ch. IV.

32 See Jeff Astley, 'Tradition and Experience: Conservative and Liberal Models for Christian Education', in Jeff Astley and David Day (eds), *The Contours of Christian Education*, Great Wakering: McCrimmons, 1992, pp. 41–53.

33 Mary Elizabeth Moore uses the term 'traditioning' for this task of preserving, appropriating (and creating) a community's traditions. See Moore, *Education for Continuity and Change: A New Model for Christian Religious Education*, Nashville, Tenn.: Abingdon, 1983, ch. 3.

34 John H. Westerhoff and O. C. Edwards (eds), *A Faithful Church*, Wilton, Connecticut: Morehouse-Barlow, 1981, pp. 298–301. Westerhoff is not to be held responsible for the rather different use to which I have put his metaphors. Similar Christian education models of 'architecture'/building, 'adventure'/travel and 'agriculture'/gardening are discussed in Ronald T. Habermas, 'Examining Discrepancies in Congregational Perceptions of Life and Faith', *Religious Education*, 85, 3, 1990, pp. 445–454. See also Neil Postman and Charles Weingartner, *Teaching as a Subversive Activity*, Harmondworth: Penguin, 1972, p. 86. Metaphors and 'models' (systematic, extended metaphors) drawn from a familiar situation are often used to illuminate other, less familiar and more mysterious situations and to direct our action appropriately within them. This is a valuable explanatory method which is routinely employed in the sciences, as well as in philosophy and theology.

35 Jim Wilhoit, *Christian Education and the Search for Meaning*, Grand Rapids, Mich.: Baker Book House, 1986, p. 70.

36 John Locke, *Some Thoughts Concerning Education*, reprinted in K. B. Cully (ed.), *Basic Writings in Christian Education*, Philadelphia: Westminster Press, 1960, p. 215.

37 Karl Ernst Nipkow rejects a 'transitive sense' of formation (German *Formung* or *Prägung*) as 'incompatible with the educational and theological foundations' of a proper view of education in religion, while accepting 'an intransitive and reflexive sense' of 'self-formation' (*Selbstbildung*) or critical formation, brought about through an emancipating process of experience and reflection. (He is writing here of schooling, but would be similarly critical of the wrong sort of formation in adult Christian education.) See K. E. Nipkow, 'Pluralism, Theology and Education: A German Perspective', in Jeff Astley and Leslie J. Francis (eds), *Christian Theology and Religious Education: Connections and Contradictions*, London: SPCK, 1996, p. 55.

38 Peter Jarvis, in Jarvis and Walters (eds), *Adult Education and Theological Interpretations*, p. 14. See also Peter Jarvis, *Adult and Continuing Education: Theory and Practice*, London: Routledge, 1995, pp. 143–146.

39 Randolph Crump Miller, 'Continuity and Contrast in the Future of Religious Education', in James Michael Lee (ed.), *The Religious Education We Need*, Birmingham, Ala.: Religious Education Press, 1977, p. 47.

40 Mike Bottery, *The Morality of the School: The Theory and Practice of Values in Education*, London, Cassell, 1990, p. 29.

41 Mike Bottery, *Ethics of Educational Management: Personal, Social and Political Perspectives on School Organization*, London: Cassell, 1992, p. 88.

42 See Jeff Astley, 'Growing into Christ: The Psychology and Politics of Christian Maturity', in Astley and Day (eds), *The Contours of Christian Education*, pp. 307–322 and 'Christian Values and the Management of Schools', in William K. Kay and Leslie J. Francis (eds), *Religion in Education, Volume 2*, Leominster: Gracewing, 1998, pp. 357–386.

43 Cf. Peter Jarvis, *Ethics and Education for Adults in a Late Modern Society*, Leicester: NIACE, 1997, ch. 10.

44 Gabriel Marcel, *The Mystery of Being*, Vol. 1, trans. G. S. Fraser and R. Hague, London: Harvill Press, 1951, p. 20.

45 See above, p. 22.
46 Carl Rogers, *Freedom to Learn for the 80's*, New York: Merrill, 1983, p. 136, 187.
47 Peter Ball uses 'formation' language qualified by 'nurture' and 'pilgrimage' language: 'Formation is about helping a person to develop into shape for which God has given them the potential. In Christian formation the first aim is ... to encourage someone in their search for God, in their meeting with him and in letting their whole life be moulded and changed by that experience. Christian formation is about being transformed into the pattern of Christ.... . It also means valuing the individual personal stories of the people with whom we are travelling as important for themselves and as the scene within which God is at work in his world.' Peter Ball, *Adult Believing: A Guide to the Initiation of Adults*, London: Mowbray, 1988, pp. 18–19.
48 The American theologian Horace Bushnell first published his classic *Christian Nurture* in 1847. He may be thought of as the father-figure of the socialisation/enculturation approach to Christian education. It should be explained, however, that the term 'nurture' has over the years rather shifted in meaning from Bushnell's understanding of it, so that it now refers (often exclusively) to intentional processes of *instruction* effecting Christian learning, rather than – as he intended – the work of God through the less explicit *experiential processes* of the parent-child relationship itself. See Edward Farley, 'The Strange History of Christian Paideia', *Religious Education*, LX, 5, 1965, pp. 339–346; Horace Bushnell, *Christian Nurture*, Grand Rapids, Mich.: Baker Book House, 1979 (reprint of 1861 edition).
49 Lines, *Systemic Religious Education*, p. 10.
50 Iris V. Cully, 'Christian Education: Instruction or Nurture', *Religious Education*, LXII, 3, 1967, p. 259.
51 Wilhoit, *Christian Education and the Search for Meaning*, pp. 62–63.
52 John M. Sutcliffe, *Learning and Teaching Together*, Nutfield: NCEC, 1980, p. 17, cf. p. 44.
53 See John-Jacques Rousseau, *Emile*, trans. Barbara Foxley, London: Dent, 1911 (first published 1780); F. Froebel, *The Education of Man*, trans. W. N. Hailmann, London: Appleton, 1894 (first published 1826); and compare Lawrence Kohlberg and Rochelle Mayer, 'Development as the Aim of Education', *Harvard Education Review*, 42, 1972, pp. 449–496. A similar combination of Romantic, individualistic, learner-centred religious humanism and open-ended educational strategies is characteristic of the classical period of the 'Religious Education Association' in the United States. Compare John H. Westerhoff (ed.), *Who Are We?: The Quest for a Religious Education*, Birmingham, Ala.: Religious Education Press, 1978, *passim*.
54 John Dewey, *Democracy and Education: An Introduction to the Philosophy of Education*, New York: Macmillan, 1916, p. 63.
55 For Dewey, education as growth is its own end: 'Since growth is the characteristic of life, education is all one with growing; it has no end beyond itself' (*op. cit.*, p. 62). Rousseau similarly disapproved of those who saw education merely as a preparation for adult life, and produced 'forced fruit, immature and flavourless' by inverting the natural order that allows children to be children before they can become adults.
56 Compare Alfred North Whitehead: 'You cannot postpone [the mind's] life until you have sharpened it ... whatever powers you are strengthening in the pupil, must be exercised here and now; whatever possibilities of mental life your teach-

ing should impart, must be exhibited here and now. That is the golden rule of education, and a very difficult rule to follow.' A. N. Whitehead, *The Aims of Education*, London: Benn, 1962, p. 9.

57 Lee, *The Content of Religious Instruction*, p. 99.

58 Philip Wragge, 'Religious Society of Friends', in John M. Sutcliffe (ed.), *A Dictionary of Religious Education*, London: SCM, 1984, p. 291.

59 Wilhoit, *Christian Education and the Search for Meaning*, p. 78.

60 John Dewey, 'My Pedagogic Creed', Article III, reprinted in Cully (ed.), *Basic Writings in Christian Education*, p. 318. Cf. Dewey, *Democracy and Education*, pp. 89–93.

61 It is often tempting to take over this tradition, either as a whole or in part, in the state in which it has been received: as undistilled and objectified *products* of the Christian learning of earlier generations – whether as doctrines, practices or documents (including scriptures). But the hermeneutical task of Christian education also includes the identification and re-interpretation of those powerful elements that have in the past undergirded and generated these products: elements that some have identified as 'the wisdom of the elders', or 'the story of those who precede us' on the road.

62 See General Synod Board of Education, *Children in the Way*, London: National Society, 1988, p. 36.

63 Compare Westerhoff, *Living the Faith Community*, p. 93.

64 Michel de Montaigne, *Essays*, I: 26, trans. Geraldine E. Hodgson, *The Teacher's Montaigne*, London: Blackie, 1915, p. 106.

65 Luke 2:47, RSV.

66 Hans-Ruedi Weber, *Jesus and the Children*, Geneva: World Council of Churches, 1979, p. 51; cf. Mk 9:35ff, Mtt 18:1ff.

67 'Jesus never speaks of the innocence of children . . . . He refers rather to the fact that they are modest and unspoiled as compared with adults . . . . The child's littleness, immaturity and need of assistance . . . keep the way open for the fatherly love of God.' Albrecht Oepke, in Gerhard Friedrich Kittel (ed.), *Theological Dictionary of the New Testament*, Vol. V, trans. Geoffrey W. Bromiley, Grand Rapids, Mich.: Eerdmans, 1967, p. 649. See also Stephen Barton, 'Jesus – Friend of Little Children?', in Astley and Day (eds), *The Contours of Christian Education*, pp. 30–40; Ian Stockton, 'Children, Church and Kingdom', *Scottish Journal of Theology*, 36, 1983, pp. 87–97; James Francis, 'Children and Childhood in the New Testament', in Stephen C. Barton (ed.), *The Family in Theological Perspective*, Edinburgh: T. & T. Clark, 1996, pp. 65–85.

68 Apparently the diminutive *paidion* may not.

69 It is, of course, also true that the church has often emphasised its educational work among children *to the exclusion of* the task (at least equally significant) of the adult Christian educator. Cf. Lawrence O. Richards, *A Theology of Christian Education*, Grand Rapids, Mich.: Zondervan, 1975, p. 228.

70 See Judith Sadler's essay, chapter 5 below.

71 Giovanni Gentile stresses that the true teacher learns with the pupil, penetrating the pupil's mind in the process of education: 'the real teacher is within the soul of the pupil, or, better still, the teacher is the pupil himself' (*Reform of Education*, London: Benn, 1923, p. 63).

72 Craig Dykstra, *Vision and Character*, New York: Paulist Press, 1981, p. 104.

73 Reuel L. Howe, 'The Dialogical Foundations for Christian Education', in Marvin J. Taylor (ed.), *An Introduction to Christian Education*, Nashville, Tenn.: Abingdon, 1966, pp. 87–88. Howe advocates the *principle* of dialogue, a principle that may be

applied 'even though there is only one speaker', and thus even by the 'dialogical lecturer who . . . is able to draw his students into an implicit dialogue' with himself (p. 88). See also Howe, *The Miracle of Dialogue*, New York: Seabury, 1963. This position implies that sermons and lectures need 'holes' into which the listener can fit her own concerns, questions and answers. Sam Keen writes that 'the lectures I thought were best, the most logically finished and closed, gave no way to the student to get involved in them. The ones with interstices drew them in, and they become colleagues with me in a wrestling with the mysteries' (from Jim Fowler and Sam Keen, *Life Maps*, Waco, Texas: Winston Press, 1978, p. 158). See also David W. Gilmour, 'Towards a Biblical View of Dialogical Communication', in Ian R. Mears (ed.), *The Knowledge of God: Primitive, Partial or Profound?*, Sydney: Christian Education Publications, 1989, pp. 131–171; Brian A. Wren, *Education for Justice*, London: SCM, 1977, ch. 2. But note that this is only an 'implicit dialogue'. A more explicit dialogical relationship is to be found between a 'mentor' and the student he or she supports, helping the latter to reflect on and learn from his or her practice and experience. See Jarvis, *Ethics and Education for Adults in a Late Modern Society*, pp. 92–96, and Leona M. English, *Mentoring in Religious Education*, Birmingham, Ala.: Religious Education Press, 1998.

74 Howe, 'Dialogical Foundations . . .', p. 93.
75 Stephen D. Brookfield, *Understanding and Facilitating Adult Learning: A Comprehensive Analysis of Principles and Effective Practices*, Milton Keynes: Open University Press, 1986, p. 24.
76 Dudley Plunkett, *Secular and Spiritual Values: Grounds for Hope in Education*, London: Routledge, 1990, p. 133.
77 See Robert Graham, *Taking Each Other Seriously: Experiences in Learning and Teaching*, Durham: Fieldhouse Press/University of Durham School of Education, 1998.
78 Cf. Peter Ball, *Journey into Faith*, London: SPCK, 1988.
79 From Edward Hulmes and Brenda Watson (eds), *Education, Life and Christian Belief*, Oxford: Farmington Institute, no date, p. 25. Compare A. Patrick Purnell, *Our Faith Story*, London: Collins, 1985, pp. 36–37 and *passim* on 'a travelling faith'; also Paul Wignall, 'Patterns in Theology', in Stephen W. Sykes, *The Integrity of Anglicanism*, London and Oxford: Mowbray, 1978, p. 109.
80 See Westerhoff, *Living the Faith Community*, pp. 15, 46.
81 See Nels F. S. Ferré, *A Theology for Christian Education*, Philadelphia: Westminster Press, 1967, pp. 109–112.
82 Cf. Slee, 'Endeavors in a Theology of Adult Education', pp. 332–337.
83 Lewis R. Rambo, 'Psychological Perspectives on Conversion', *Pacific Theological Review*, 13, 2, 1980, p. 22. On the psychology of conversion, see further the same author's article in H. Newton Molony and Samuel Southard (eds), *Handbook of Religious Conversion*, Birmingham, Ala.: Religious Education Press, 1992, and literature cited.
84 John H. Westerhoff, 'Christian Education: Kerygma v. Didache', in John Ferguson (ed.), *Christianity, Society and Education*, London: SPCK, 1981, pp. 192, 194 and Gwen Kennedy Neville and John Westerhoff, *Learning Through Liturgy*, New York: Seabury Press, 1978, p. 147.
85 Cf. Burgess, *An Invitation to Religious Education*, ch. III.
86 Bushnell, *Christian Nurture*, p. 10.
87 *ibid.*, ch. III.
88 See *ibid.*, pp. 30–32 and ch. IV.
89 *ibid.*, p. 9.

90 That is, 'that which it has in common with that for which it stands [and] ... those features which are not shared' (Thomas Fawcett, *The Symbolic Language of Religion*, London: SCM, 1970, p. 55). See also Mary B. Hesse, *Models and Analogies in Science*, London: Sheed & Ward, 1963, pp. 9–10. I treat metaphors here as an extreme case of the analogical use of language. Compare and contrast Janet Martin Soskice, *Metaphor and Religious Language*, Oxford: Clarendon, 1985, and Dan R. Stiver, *The Philosophy of Religious Language*, Oxford: Blackwell, 1996, ch. 6.

91 See Humphrey Palmer, *Analogy*, London and Basingstoke: Macmillan, 1973, especially part 4, and R. J. Kearney, 'Analogical Predication', unpublished D. Phil. thesis, University of Oxford, 1974.

92 See Astley, *The Philosophy of Christian Religious Education*, pp. 84–86.

93 See Jarvis, *Adult and Continuing Education*, pp. 65–67, 97, 136, 148–149.

94 This section is amended from my introductory essay in Astley and Francis (eds), *Critical Perspectives on Christian Education*, pp. 5–9, with permission. Lines offers a different, though overlapping, range of metaphorical typologies. He suggests the images of the Christian educator as parent, coach, scientist, critic, storyteller, artist, visionary, revolutionary, therapist and minister. See Timothy Arthur Lines, *Functional Images of the Religious Educator*, Birmingham, Ala.: Religious Education Press, 1992.

95 Examples of literature reflecting on the theme of worship and Christian education, particularly from Roman Catholic and Anglican sources, include Astley, Francis and Crowder (eds), *Theological Perspectives on Christian Formation*, section 7; Robert L. Browning and Roy A. Reed, *The Sacraments in Religious Education and Liturgy*, Birmingham, Ala.: Religious Education Press, 1985; Duncan B. Forrester, Ian H. MacDonald and Gian Tellini, *Encounter with God: An Introduction to Christian Worship and Practice*, Edinburgh: T. & T. Clark, 1996; Ken Meltz, 'A Program for Affective Liturgy', in Gloria Durka and Joanmarie Smith (eds), *Aesthetic Dimensions of Religious Education*, New York: Paulist Press, 1979, pp. 85–98; Randolph Crump Miller, 'Process Thought, Worship and Religious Education', in *ibid.*, pp. 107–120; Neville and Westerhoff, *Learning Through Liturgy*; Michael Warren, 'Catechesis: An Enriching Category for Religious Education', in M. Warren (ed.), *Sourcebook for Modern Catechetics*, Winona, Minn.: St. Mary's Press, 1983, pp. 379–394; Warren, *Faith, Culture and the Worshiping Community*, Washington D.C.: Pastoral Press, 1993; Warren, 'The Worshiping Assembly: Possible Zone of Cultural Contestation', in M. Warren (ed.), *Sourcebook for Modern Catechetics, Volume 2*, Winona, Minn.: St Mary's Press/Christian Brothers Publications, 1997, pp. 39–52; Louis Weil, 'Facilitating Growth in Faith through Liturgical Worship', in James Michael Lee (ed.), *Handbook of Faith*, Birmingham, Ala.: Religious Education Press, 1990, pp. 203–220; and John H. Westerhoff and William H. Willimon, *Liturgy and Learning through the Life Cycle*, New York: Seabury Press, 1980.

96 Yet the priest-model, with its community emphasis, may also be relevant here – if we agree with the claim that 'the liturgy itself and a congregation's experience of divine worship already functions, even if in a secondary way, as pastoral care'. William H. Willimon, *Worship as Pastoral Care*, Nashville, Tenn.: Abingdon, 1979, p. 48.

97 Compare James W. Fowler, *Stages of Faith*, San Francisco: Harper & Row, 1981, ch. 24; James Michael Lee, *The Shape of Religious Instruction*, Birmingham, Ala.: Religious Education Press, 1971, pp. 251–253; Thomas H. Groome, 'The Spirituality of the Religious Educator', *Religious Education*, 83, 1988, pp. 15–16;

Jeff Astley, 'The Christian Vocation of Teaching and Learning', *The Tufton Review*, 2, 2, 1998, pp. 57–72.

[98] Compare David P. Killen, 'Indigenous Theological Education and Christian Formation', *Insight*, 11, 1984, pp. 3–13, and Patricia O'Connell Killen and John de Beer, *The Art of Theological Reflection*, New York: Crossroad, 1995.

[99] Tony McCaffry, 'The Priesthood of the Teacher – Language and the Teaching of the Word', in Jarvis and Walters (eds), *Adult Education and Theological Interpretations*, pp. 57, 65.

[100] Compare Jack L. Seymour and Carol A. Wehrheim, 'Faith Seeking Understanding: Interpretation as a Task of Christian Education', in Jack L. Seymour and Donald E. Miller (eds), *Contemporary Approaches to Christian Education*, Nashville, Tenn.: Abingdon, 1982, pp. 123–143.

[101] Wesley Carr, *The Priestlike Task*, London: SPCK, 1985, pp. 15, 17.

[102] See also Richard R. Osmer, 'Teaching as Practical Theology', in Jack L. Seymour and Donald E. Miller (eds), *Theological Approaches to Christian Education*, Nashville, Tenn.: Abingdon, 1990, pp. 216–238.

[103] Jack L. Seymour, in Seymour and Miller (eds), *Contemporary Approaches to Christian Education*, pp. 27–28; cf. Allen J. Moore, 'Liberation and the Future of Christian Education', in *ibid*, pp. 103–122 and Paulo Freire's essay in Astley, Francis and Crowder (eds), *Theological Perspectives on Christian Formation*, especially pp. 183–185.

[104] See Donald Evans, *Struggle and Fulfillment: The Inner Dynamics of Religion and Morality*, Cleveland: Collins, 1979, pp. 141–147. Others also regard the essential function of the catechist as being both (in a broader sense) prophetic *and* pastoral: see D. S. Amalorpavadass, 'Catechesis as a Pastoral Task of the Church', in Warren (ed.), *Sourcebook for Modern Catechetics*, pp. 339–360.

[105] It must be stressed that I am here describing preaching as a *model* for (all or most of) Christian education, and not claiming that the activity of *actual preaching* is all or most of what Christian education should be. The same point applies, of course, to each of these models.

[106] Compare the critical account of such theories in James Michael Lee, *The Flow of Religious Instruction*, Birmingham, Ala.: Religious Education Press, 1973, ch. 7.

[107] See Hofinger, *The Art of Teaching Christian Doctrine,* p. 20, compare p. 197, and Joseph Andreas Jungmann, *The Good News Yesterday and Today*, trans. William A. Huesman, New York: Sadlier, 1962, *passim*.

[108] See Karl Barth, *Church Dogmatics, I, 1*, trans. G. W. Bromiley, Edinburgh: T. & T. Clark, 1975, p. 52; cf. Barth, *Church Dogmatics, I, 2*, trans. G. T. Thomson and Harold Knight, Edinburgh: T. & T. Clark, 1956, pp. 802–812.

[109] John H. Westerhoff, *Will Our Children have Faith?*, New York: Seabury Press, 1976, ch. 1; see also Westerhoff, 'A Call to Catechesis', *Living Light*, 14, 3, 1977, pp. 354–358.

[110] See pp. 38–39 and note 20 above.

[111] See Lee, *The Shape of Religious Instruction*, pp. 8, 48–93 and Lee, *The Flow of Religious Instruction*, pp. 196–204, 206–268. For a very wide understanding of the subject-matter content of Christian education, see also Lee, *The Content of Religious Instruction, passim*.

[112] For further discussion of the wide rôle of the teacher in Christian education, see Maria Harris, *Teaching and Religious Imagination: An Essay in the Theology of Teaching*, San Francisco: HarperSanFrancisco, 1987; Sara Little, *To Set One's Heart: Belief and Teaching in the Church*, Atlanta: John Knox Press, 1983; Mary Elizabeth Mullino Moore, *Teaching from the Heart: Theology and Educational*

Method, Harrisburg, Penn.: Trinity Press International, 1998; Richard Robert Osmer, *A Teachable Spirit: Recovering the Teaching Office in the Church*, Louisville, Kentucky: Westminster/John Knox Press, 1990; Richard R. Osmer, 'Teaching as Practical Theology'; Parker J. Palmer, *To Know as We are Known: Education as a Spiritual Journey*, San Francisco: HarperSanFrancisco, 1993; Clark M. Williamson and Ronald J. Allen, *The Teaching Minister*, Louisville, Kentucky: Westminster/John Knox Press, 1991. See also Meg Orr's essay, chapter 3 below.

[113] Adult Christian education will here, naturally and properly, draw on the general literature on adult education. See, for example, Brookfield, *Understanding and Facilitating Adult Learning*; K. Patricia Cross, *Adults as Learners*, London: Jossey-Bass, 1981; C. Daines, J. Daines and B. Graham, *Adult Learning, Adult Teaching*, Nottingham: University of Nottingham, 1992; Jarvis, *Adult and Continuing Education*; Peter Jarvis, John Holford and Colin Griffin, *The Theory and Practice of Learning*, London: Kogan Page, 1998; J. R. Kidd, *How Adults Learn*, New York: Association Press, 1973; Malcolm S. Knowles, *The Modern Practice of Adult Education: From Pedagogy to Andragogy*, New York: Cambridge, 1980; Malcolm S. Knowles, *The Adult Learner: A Neglected Species*, Houston, Texas: Gulf, 1984; M. S. Knowles *et al.*, *Andragogy in Action: Applying Modern Principles of Adult Learning*, San Francisco: Jossey-Bass, 1984; R. Bernard Lovell, *Adult Learning*, New York: Halsted Press; Beckenham: Croom Helm, 1980; M. Osborn, A. Charnley and A. Withnall, *Review of Existing Research in Adult and Continuing Education*, Leicester: NIACE, 1982; Alan Rogers, *Teaching Adults*, Milton Keynes: Open University, 1986; Jennifer Rogers, *Adult Learning*, Milton Keynes: Open University Press, 1989; Peter Sutherland (ed.), *Adult Learning: A Reader*, London: Kogan Page, 1997; M. Tennant, *Psychology and Adult Learning*, London: Routledge, 1988; M. Thorpe, R. Edwards and A. Hanson, *Culture and Processes of Adult Learning*, London: Routledge, 1993; John R. Verduin, Jr., Harry G. Miller and Charles E. Greer, *Adults Teaching Adults: Principles and Strategies*, Austin, Texas: Learning Concepts, 1977.

[114] On this, see Anton Baumohl, *Making Adult Disciples: Learning and Teaching in the Local Church*, London: Scripture Union, 1984, ch. 6; Yvonne Craig, *Learning for Life: A Handbook of Adult Religious Education*, London: Mowbray, 1994, pp. 119–120 and chs 5 and 7 *passim*; Elias, *The Foundations and Practice of Adult Religious Education*, ch. IX; Brian V. Hill, *The Greening of Christian Education*, Homebush West, N.S.W.: Lancer, 1985, ch. 8; Purnell, *Our Faith Story*, part three; Reg Wickett, 'Models of Adult Religious Education', *British Journal of Theological Education*, 4, 1, 1990, pp. 4–16; and R. E. Y. Wickett, *Models of Adult Religious Education Practice*, Birmingham, Ala.: Religious Education Press, 1991.

[115] As the seventeenth-century Jesuit Muzio Vitelleschi strikingly put it, a private talk can penetrate intimately to a pupil's real needs – 'going down to particulars that seem most to meet their wants', and thus working 'more powerfully than many lectures and sermons given in common' (quoted in Thomas Hughes, *Loyola and the Educational System of the Jesuits*, London: Heinemann, 1906, p. 108).

[116] See 2 Sam 12:1–14.

[117] For some challenging insights into the cultural and educational dynamics of the mass media, see Michael Warren, *Communications and Cultural Analysis: A Religious View*, Westport, Connecticut: Bergin & Garvey, 1992.

[118] See, for example, M. L. J. Abercrombie, *Aims and Techniques of Group*

Teaching, London: SRHE, 1974; Cary L. Cooper (ed.), *Theories of Group Processes*, London: Wiley, 1975; A. Paul Hare, *Handbook of Small Group Research*, London: Collier Macmillan, 1976; J. Klein, *Working with Groups*, London: Hutchinson, 1966; G. C. Kemp (ed.), *Perspectives on the Group Process*, Boston, Mass.: Houghton Mifflin, 1964; Margaret Parker, *Leading Groups*, London: Epworth, 1987; Sutherland (ed.), *Adult Learning: A Reader*, section III.

[119] Leslie J. Francis, Jeff Astley, William K. Kay and Marian Carter, 'Is Adult Christian Education mainly for Stable Extraverts?', *Studies in the Education of Adults*, 29, 2, 1997, pp. 191–199.

[120] John H. Westerhoff, 'Catechetics: An Anglican Perspective', in Warren (ed.), *Sourcebook for Modern Catechetics*, p. 433.

[121] Westerhoff, *Living the Faith Community*, pp. 9, 78; cf. also his *The Christian Family*, London, Ontario: Huron College, 1982.

[122] See Jeff Astley, 'The Role of the Family in the Formation and Criticism of Faith', in Barton (ed.), *The Family in Theological Perspective*, pp. 187–202.

[123] For general works on adult Christian education curriculum and methods, see the works already cited in note 114 above, especially Baumohl, *Making Adult Disciples*; Craig. *Learning for Life* and Wickett, *Models of Adult Religious Education Practice*. Other relevant material may be found in Harley Atkinson (ed.), *Handbook of Young Adult Religious Education*, Birmingham, Ala.: Religious Education Press, 1995; Nancy T. Foltz (ed.), *Handbook of Planning in Religious Education*, Birmingham, Ala.: Religious Education Press, 1998; Maria Harris, *Fashion Me a People: Curriculum in the Church*, Louisville, Kentucky: Westminster/John Knox Press, 1989; R. Wade Paschal, *Vital Adult Learning: Choices to Fit Your Church*, ed. Herb Miller, Nashville, Tenn.: Abingdon, 1994; Eugene C. Roehlkepartain, *The Teaching Church: Moving Christian Education to Center Stage*, Nashville, Tenn.: Abingdon, 1993.

[124] See Astley, 'Tradition and Experience: Conservative and Liberal Models for Christian Education'.

[125] Stanley Hauerwas, 'The Gesture of a Truthful Story', reprinted in Astley, Francis and Crowder (eds), *Theological Perspectives on Christian Formation*, p. 97; see also Astley, *The Philosophy of Christian Religious Education*, p. 12, n. 12.

[126] We also receive a message from the 'null curriculum' - that is, from the *absence* in the curriculum of certain issues, facts and voices. Sometimes silence can speak volumes, especially about those things and people that the educator does not take seriously.

[127] On this see, for example, Marianne Sawicki, 'Tradition and Sacramental Education', in Seymour and Miller (eds), *Theological Approaches to Christian Education*, pp. 43–62. Compare Jeff Astley, 'Christian Worship and the Hidden Curriculum of Christian Learning', in Astley and Day (eds), *The Contours of Christian Education*, pp. 141–152, and literature cited.

[128] John H. Westerhoff (ed.), *A Colloquy on Christian Education*, Philadelphia: Pilgrim Press, 1972, pp. 64–65.

3

The Rôle of the Teacher in the Theological Education of the Laity

Meg Orr

This chapter argues that church education for lay people should primarily be *theological education*. I also hope to show here how the teacher is an essential part of church life and growth, and that a practical approach to theology can enable lay people to discover a theology that may be seen as relevant to them and by them.

THE DILEMMA

Edward Farley, writing about North American congregations but offering a challenge for every church, asks:

> How is it that Christian faith, committed as it is to relating faith to reality, world, knowledge, and learning, continues to restrict this effort to its ordained leadership and to withhold it from the laity? Why is it that education in the congregation and for the believer at large is so conceived that it has little to do with the disciplines and rigors of ordered learning? Why is it that *theological* education – ongoing studies in disciplines and skills necessary for the understanding and interpretation of Scripture, doctrines, moral principles and policies, and areas of praxis – is taken to define something needed by Christian clergy but never by Christian laity? In the face of the modern democratisation of education and learning, how is that the church continues to settle for the premodern pattern of educated clergy and uneducated laity and for the almost uncrossable gulf between theological (clergy) education and church education?[1]

Farley's questions need to be put to and asked by Christian educators working in our churches today. Has the church lost its teaching office and its teaching rôle?

Before we look at the place of the teacher in the church today, we might read again Ephesians 4:11f: 'And his gifts were that some should be apostles, some prophets, some evangelists, some pastors and teachers for the equipment of the saints for the work of ministry, for building up the body of Christ.' The grace gifts are here spelled out in terms of the church's ministries. The construction of the phrase 'pastors and teachers', with one definite article covering both words, suggests that the two functions were shared by the same individual, or at least group. These would be local congregational leaders in charge of established churches that had been brought into existence by the preaching of the apostles and others. In verse 12 the bestowal of Christ's gifts of ministry has a specific purpose in view, viz. that all God's people may be equipped to offer their own gift of service in the world. Through the complementary functions both of a regular ministry, ordained and appointed by the head of the church, *and* of the 'rank and file' of that church, Christ's body may be edified.[2]

In the New Testament church the task of teaching was probably most concerned with passing on the traditions of the life and teaching of Jesus, and with catechetical instruction of new converts. In this way teachers played an indispensable part in the building up of a strong Christian community. But we recall that James 3:1 discourages too many of his readers from becoming teachers, because of the responsibility they bore: 'You know that we teachers shall be judged more severely.' We may ask whether a sense of this high responsibility prevents people from seeking a teaching ministry in the church today.

THE TEACHER TODAY

To some adult Christian educators, talk of the teacher and of the rôle of the teacher is unfashionable and even distasteful. It connotes an authoritarian attitude, redolent of heavily didactic procedures and with overtones of schooling. We are often told that for too long the church has understood education, and particularly religious education, as a transmissive exercise of imparting information to the ignorant. Nowadays the teacher must recognise that she is rather to be a facilitator, enabler or resource person. 'We don't teach, we enable people to learn.'[3] 'Enabling' is seen as an educational concept that fits in well with an educational approach which places *learning* at the centre, rather than teaching.

But this contrast is too sharply drawn. Surely teaching is all about *how* we enable and facilitate,[4] and those activities draw heavily upon the personal skills of the teacher. While there may be some truth in the claim about the widespread use of dangerously authoritarian and didactic procedures in both secular and religious education in the past, I believe that in its application to the church today it is no more than a myth. While some would say that the churches are too much like schools, my criticism (like Farley's) is rather that the institutions are not similar enough. Gabriel Moran similarly argues that the church is badly in need of schooling: 'real schools in which religion can be taught/studied (i.e. critically examined and intellectually under-stood)'.[5] If we persist in reminding lay people how awful their schooldays have been, as do some adult Christian educators, they will go on believing that teachers and teaching should be given a wide berth. This myth too should be laid to rest, simply by our refusing to speak in such negative terms. In any case, many adults will remember at least some teachers with profound gratitude and affection. We need, surely, to learn to speak more boldly about the *positive value of teaching*. And we need to speak not only of the joys of learning, and the discovery of learning, but also about the joys of an education that is above all the 'education of desire', which is to 'teach desire to desire, to desire better, to desire more, and above all to desire in a different way'.[6]

What Kind of Teacher?

Martin Buber's understanding of the teacher is a healthy corrective to a fashionable – and depressingly negative – interpretation of teaching. He reminds us that there was a time when there neither was, nor needed to be, any specific calling of educator or teacher. Yet teaching took place. There was instead a master, a philosopher or a coppersmith whose journeymen and apprentices lived with him, and learned by being allowed to share in what he had to teach them of his handicraft or brainwork. These persons 'learned, without noticing that they did, the mystery of personal life: they received the spirit'.[7] There is more to this than just learning facts or skills. Can it be described as catching the 'spark of life', and as sharing that which is held sacred, holy and precious? Is it a meeting of our need, as the Augustinian nuns say, for 'someone to whom we can relate with our human experience ... who shows us the way to find our true selves ... who goes before us in the stupendous and arduous ways of God'?[8] This sort of learning can mean a never-ending discovery of meeting with oneself, through and in the joy of meeting with others.

The master-mentor remains a proper model for the teacher. On this model the educator, if he has to act consciously must do it 'as though he did not'. According to Buber, there is 'influence' here but there must be no hint of 'interference'. The educator then finds himself in the midst of need by being a bit deeper in it, in the midst of service by being a little higher up – a status which he 'invokes without words'. Buber thus directs our thinking to the majesty and mystery surrounding the relationship of teacher and learner, and it is precisely at this point that the teacher as enabler or facilitator is required. Derek Webster points out that unless teachers have themselves pondered the mystery of their own being, they are unlikely to convey 'a fragment of that mystery', 'that spiritual existential' which surrounds all being.[9]

Theology arises out of, and in turn encourages, an orientation to transcendent mystery; hence theology is a spiritual discipline touching upon the very centre of human life.[10] Basil Yeaxlee's pioneering work on adult education, written in 1925, views education itself as a spiritual activity. He recognises that the human person is a finite spirit participating in the life of the Infinite and of the universe. The starting point of Yeaxlee's philosophy of adult education includes assumptions about persons and personalities subsumed under the notion of 'the spirit of man'. His philosophy is theistic, stressing the unity of man, nature and God. Here the spiritual nature of human persons within the context of society and the state forms the basis for a theory of education as a spiritual activity that has as its goal the development of spiritual values.[11] On this account, the teacher is to develop minds and spirits that are sensitive to spiritual values in the world. Only where this view prevails will education be alive.

Douglas Cleverley Ford reminds us, in a tone heavy with irony, that everyone knows that 'teaching with authority is "out"'. And so, presumably, is the text about Jesus, 'They were astounded at his teaching, for, unlike the doctors of law, he taught with a note of authority.' Yet he also points out that Jesus applied no sanctions, no coercion, no imposed syllabus. So where did his authority lie? Clearly, the authority of Jesus was personal.[12] What Jesus said needed no external authority to bring it home to his hearers. It needed no authorisation, for it was self-authenticating. It was self-authenticating in that it was heard because it was always an answer, an answer to questions that his pupils themselves raised and which he by his person provoked. Thus could Jesus the master, the model, act and teach as though he did not. He influenced but did not interfere. He invoked without words his servant rôle, which paradoxically became that of the master-teacher.

What Kind of Teaching?

> We meet awkwardly.
> I invite you to walk.
> I find you dancing.[13]

This piece of haiku provides an example of a way of talking about and approaching teaching, and a way of teaching theology, that is all too rare: the way of the imagination. Maria Harris draws on the religious imagination as a vision for teaching. Although techniques and procedures and skills are needed for a proper understanding of teaching, these do not lie at its heart. The heart of teaching, Harris says, is imagination. She believes that the activity of teaching, when viewed as a religiously imaginative act, is able 'to save and redeem'.[14] She quotes Paul Ricoeur as one who is also persuaded of the importance of imagination: 'the imagination is par excellence, the instituting and constituting of what is humanly possible; in imagining possibilities, human beings act as prophets of their own existence'.[15] This is a philosophy that begins not with technique, but with the majesty and mystery involved in teaching; and it is a philosophy that acknowledges these things in every person's imagination. The teacher of adults in a church-based setting has much to learn from Harris about the nature of the teaching act, and about the attitude towards one's own person in the teaching rôle.

If teaching as mystery is a work of the imagination, we must bring to teaching an attitude similar to that which we bring to art. Such an attitude implies a readiness on the part of the teacher to see what is there and to let what is there speak, rather than adopting a stance of incessant activity in which teachers are agents, doers and performers. Such a philosophy of teaching is reminiscent of Simone Weil's argument that there is a special way of 'waiting upon truth, setting our hearts upon it, yet not allowing ourselves to go in search of it'.[16] This is a way of waiting, of 'giving attention', that lies at the heart both of education and of religion.

The first moment in teaching when it is seen as a work of religious imagination is contemplation. Teaching must give rise to the contemplative moment which involves the learner seeing the teacher as a Thou, and the teacher seeing the learner as a Thou. This requires stopping, taking time, and the wide-awakeness necessary to take in the personhood(s) involved.[17] The teacher must consciously prepare and create a mood of contemplation by using the language of self-awareness and of calm, and so engendering a time to imagine. The words of William Blake highlight such an awareness:

I know that this world is a world of Imagination and Vision. I see every thing I paint in this world, but every body does not see alike. To the eyes of a miser a guinea is far more beautiful than the sun, and a bag worn with the use of money has more beautiful proportions than a vine filled with grapes. The tree which moves some to tears of joy is in the eyes of others only a green thing which stands in the way. . . . As a man is, so he sees.[18]

Contemplation helps us realise that our subject-matter is also a Thou, and that it evokes our love. Harris points out that a 'creative dynamic' exists in the subject-matter: that there is an energy and excitement all of its own waiting to be experienced there. If this is so, then neither the teacher of theology nor those whom she teaches have to do it all, for the subject-matter is itself a partner in the teaching process. If teaching theology in a contemplative mode can put us in touch with the heart of our emotions, wherein 'lie the deepest patterns of human meaning',[19] then such teaching should always encourage creative imagination – embracing, enhancing, strengthening and inspiring our souls.

THEOLOGY

'Many people see theology as something of a handicap, complicating simple faith and piety, certainly not good for the punters, and at best the curious interest of a few rarefied souls.'[20] But theology is a necessary part of Christian life. It is the process by which we discover what God is saying to us, as we become more aware of ourselves and our world and think things through in the light of the Christian tradition.

If theology is indispensable, it should not be seen as a luxury for adult lay people. The church as a whole needs to look to the critical and reflective activity of ordinary believers, not only because they have kept the central questions of theology alive, but also because they themselves are at the forefront of the church's mission and ministry. Stephen Neill made this point, albeit in a less gender-free way than we now expect, in the early 1960s: 'If the Church is ever again to penetrate this alienated world and claim it in the name of Christ, its only resources are in its convinced and converted laymen. There are vast areas, geographical and spiritual, which the ordained minister can hardly penetrate; the laymen are already there and are there every day.'[21]

Theology, I would claim, is not an esoteric subject, intelligible only to a select group of people. But neither is it just a psychological description of what our basic convictions happen to be. It claims to be concerned with what *ought to be* the basic convictions of every person. If we believe the claim that human words can be used, however indirectly, to point to the truth about God, then lay people should be encouraged to explore and discover what *they* mean by God, however falteringly that understanding may be, so that their theology may be both broadened and deepened. God is present to us all, even to those of us who have few ideas about him, and we all need a theology which helps us discover more about God's nature and purpose in our lives.

What Kind of Theology?

Christian theology can help us look at our life from the perspective of faith in God. We should do our theology in the context of the whole of life, reflecting on our present experience in the light of the Christian tradition (that is, the witness to Jesus in the Bible and subsequent Christian experience), and discovering how the two can relate to each other and to what God is asking of us here and now.

This is in effect a *practical theology*: a theology which is not primarily the application of theology to practice, but is about living and thinking theologically in and through the circumstances of our life. This is a theology that is not so much applied as *discovered*. Whatever is the given with which theology works, it must be 'grist to the mill' of our lives. We discover what theology is as it thus emerges in the midst of our experience.

However, most clergy and laity simply do not engage in this sort of contextual theology, partly because the Christian faith is assumed to be about *religion* and not about *life*. Certainly, learning to live the faith *theologically*, 'with the name of God on our lips, the concept of God in our minds, the image of God in our hearts',[22] is not something that is handed to us on a plate. We have to work for it. But the teacher must refrain from launching into theology without first winning its starting point in the lives of the learners. Accomplishing that task will depend greatly on the *craft* of the teacher: a craft that includes enabling adult lay people to be 'at ease' with theology and then, by way of the imagination, to seek to forge the links between theology and our capacity to live theologically.

All of this should be a matter of deep concern to the churches. But are the churches listening?

What Kind of Theological Education?

Edward Farley proposes a way of doing theology that should not only be acceptable to existing theological institutions, but which is also relevant to – indeed essential for – the growth and life of the whole church. It is a theological vision that is concerned with encouraging, enhancing and inspiring us both as the people of God and as individual persons. Farley's thinking on this topic is complex and elusive, but worth investigating none the less.

The first distinctively Christian use of the term 'theology', one we have now largely lost, was simply our knowledge of God: a 'cognitive disposition' in which the self-disclosing God is grasped and revealed. In this sense theology is what the Christian faith is all about, for knowledge of God and salvation coincide. Such a theology cannot be anything but practical. It is for the sake of God, but that means it is for God's appointed salvific ends for human beings. On this view, theology is a *habitus* (habit) of the human soul, a term that labels an experiential dimension constituting and shaping the self.[23] This may lead to, but is more fundamental than, the idea of theology as the *scholarly discipline* of investigation and reflection: that is, theology 'as a science'.

Fundamentally, theology should never take the form of abstract impersonal knowledge. It is, rather, knowledge with life very much caught up in it. This knowledge, this habitus or disposition of the soul, has *wisdom* as its primary characteristic, and is an integral part of Christian living. Clearly, such wisdom can be promoted, deepened and extended by human study and argument. Yet Farley's way of theological knowing is more than thinking: it is thinking taken up into a way of being – with body, mind and soul integrated into one. This, he says, is a proper goal not only of ministerial training, but for every Christian lay person in the church. It is a theology for all. The notion of theology as habitus is not easy to grasp partly because this usage has long been absent from the Christian community, its churches and its schools. It should be restored.

The life of the lay person, no less than that of the professional church leader, calls for the response, interpretation and understanding that is theology. Theology arises in the critical and reflective activity of the individual believer. Theology and theological study should also originate communally, in the church. Farley argues, and this is critical to his thinking, that church education should be theological education in the full and rigorous sense of *ordered learning*. Ordered learning refers to 'self-conscious attempts, usually in a corporate setting, to transmit by means of a sequential process of discipline and didactic activity both the insights and deposits of the past and the methods and modes of thought and work which enable new insights'.[24]

Farley complains that there is little by way of an accumulation of knowledge or skill built into the educational programmes of the churches today. Education in this full sense also needs to be restored in the church. Church education as theological education cannot avoid a rigorous study of theology's subject-matter, the Christian faith. Nor, he argues, can this be reduced to Bible study; Christianity's whole historical movement must be included. Farley's programme for church education would therefore include a historical knowledge of, and ability to interpret, the whole range of Christian stories, literatures and traditions. It would also include a self-conscious exercise of what Bernard Lonergan calls *dialectic*, the encounter with the tradition that is a matter of meeting persons, 'appreciating the values they represent, criticizing their defects, and allowing one's living to be challenged at its very roots by their words and by their deeds'.[25] This is the process that will provide the open-minded with the occasion to ask themselves some basic questions: 'questions, first, about others but eventually, even about themselves'.[26]

Farley wonders whether there is not something about the nature of faith that requires of the community of faith a greater seriousness about ordered learning. In attempting an answer he raises two issues: the relationship between faith and reality (truth), and the relationship between faith and theology (wisdom). Truth, like deceit, is a posture of the heart; wisdom likewise refers to a matter of the heart, which is the very centre and depth of human being. Wisdom is constituted by awe, fear and knowledge of the Lord. It is not simply a matter of cleverness or the retention of information, it is a matter of learning how to live before God. Truth and wisdom are therefore matters of redemption.

Farley sees ordered learning as intrinsic to faith itself, and theology as necessary for our understanding of this process. The reason for this is that faith is more than emotion or feeling, it includes a type of knowledge. It is a practical knowledge with the character of wisdom, because it has to do with living before God and making sense of one's life before God. He argues that the wisdom of faith has a certain natural structure, oriented towards reality and grounded in history, community and tradition; and thus that faith involves ordered learning, in the sense that it is oriented to disciplined efforts to equip the believer to interpret reality. And the reason why theology as reflective wisdom is needed is that existence in the world before God is not an utterly spontaneous pre-reflective matter, but is self-consciously *interpretative*.

But when the churches began to treat education as the total formative process in which faith originates and is nurtured, education lost its usual ordinary sense. Ordered learning was then no longer the primary meaning of education. It was no longer about teachers, students (learners) and sequential, cumulative learning. In much of the theory and practice of Christian formation the essential ingredients of ordered learning are now missing. Thus there is no starting point and no finishing point, and the teacher as theological educator is no longer someone with special training. The result of all this is that 'the monumental education failure of the church' is rendered invisible at the level of its laity and congregations.[27]

Farley contends that the *clericalisation of theology* is so much in the air we breathe in the church that it is very difficult to imagine a time when things were any different. Clericalisation has so influenced education in Protestant churches and their seminaries that education in the churches, whatever it is, simply cannot be seen as the study of theology. His conclusion is that these churches have not seriously considered the viability of *theological education as church education*. If it is now to be restructured as theological education, something of the structure of theology itself will have to be incorporated into the church's educational programme. This is present in the wider church today, however, only in sporadic and occasional ways. We need to escape from the dominance of this 'clerical paradigm' for theological education. And, according to Farley, we need educators 'on the church staff' who are *theologian-teachers*.[28]

Thomas Groome also believes that if theology is ever to be practical it will have to be taught differently. Theology, he writes, 'should arise from the faith of a community reflected on in light of the [Christian] Story/Vision and not from a group of scholars isolated from the community to reflect on the community's behalf'.[29] On the usual theory-to-practice paradigm, theology is either done *for* the people or *to* the people. Theology *by* the people seems often to have been forgotten. Neither the lived faith of the community, nor its historical context within its social, cultural and political realities, is taken seriously in our usual approaches to doing and teaching theology. We tend to train people to do theology in their heads but not on their feet. This does not prepare people in Farley's habitus of doing theology. But it is essential that we form pastoral ministers in the habitus of theology in the church, and the same is true of teachers and of all lay people.

We need to acknowledge the fact that people have a natural tendency and capacity to speak their own word about God, and we need to stop seeing this as something very difficult that only specialists do – or can do. Nevertheless, while all may have a natural capacity for the divine ('by nature we are lured to the transcendent', it has been said), most people in our churches need more than divine help to get them moving and exploring and reflecting theologically in a meaningful way.

Groome believes he has something to contribute to this task. For some years he has been advocating an approach to Christian religious education which he calls 'shared praxis'. Praxis is action that is reflectively done, or reflection in action. In Groome's epistemology it is only in being reflectively done that knowledge is known; knowledge is not knowledge until it is done. 'It enables us to become creators of our reality and not merely creatures produced by it.'[30] This is not the sole solution, but it is one attempt to give a working description to the notion of doing theology.

Groome draws heavily upon the Critical Theorists who broaden and reaffirm the importance of the concept of praxis in its reflective and active mode. They believe that a shared praxis approach can encourage people to discover confidence and skills, experiences and ideas, and to learn to be able to share them. The concept of praxis is also frequently found in Christian discourse. Liberation theologians especially have 'spearheaded its return to our consciousness, along with a rediscovered awareness that the word and the work of Christ are events of freedom for us'.[31]

Groome believes that the Christian educators' concern with theology is unique because of the particular interest we bring to it: to enable ourselves and others to encounter Christ and the Spirit, to enter into communion with the Father and one another, and to interpret and live our lives in the light of God's word. In Christian education God's word is made present, and we come to speak our own word in a response that is seen in the lives that we live. Groome claims that all this is best served and promoted by a praxis method of doing Christian education.

Using some of the practical insights developed in north-east England, through the North East Ordination Course's[32] 'Life and Work' Project and the Cleveland 'Theology and Change' Project, I shall now try to illustrate and broaden the procedure Groome proposes for creating a theological understanding of ourselves.

Praxis in Theology

Groome's approach begins with a focus on the present 'activities, aspirations, feelings, needs, hopes, beliefs, anxieties, etc.' of the participants.[33] It is important to begin by recognising a key historical or faith life issue, as it is reflected in one's own life praxis. This enables us to establish the question, Who are we?, as we live our lives and relate to one another and the world. This first stage encourages people to think about their own 'operating understanding' of who they are, which is not so much their theory about themselves and others, but a matter of their praxis (reflective-action). This leads on to a second stage where students engage in the activities of critical reasoning, analytic memory and creative imagination focussed on 'my everyday understanding of myself as a person' (while adopting a hermeneutic of suspicion that never simply presumes 'that's the way it is'). In short, it is coming to see how one's membership in certain social, political, economic and cultural environments has shaped one's present accepted practice or customs. An exercise in creative imagination then invites the participants to image and create new possibilities beyond their present praxis, leading to an imagining of what is not yet but might be. By bringing reason, memory and imagination to reflect critically on their own present action, learners can in this way come to express and critique their own stories and visions. The recurrent questions throughout this stage are, 'Who, what, has influenced our understanding of ourselves? What are its consequences? Is there anything we would want to change?'

The *Theology and Change Project* begins with a situation analysis using a printed questionnaire, devised by the Urban Theology Unit in Sheffield. The aim is to get to know who you are, your world around you, your place (local work place, with conversations about your feelings about it), and your church (facts, figures, leadership, activities and relationship to other world faiths). The exercise looks objectively at your present situation and how you fit in or don't fit in (your operating understanding of yourself), by checking your own perceptions, involvement, judgements and prejudices against those of other people (hence the questionnaire should be worked on with a partner or in a group).[34]

The *Life and Work Project* requires students to explore a particular question, issue or topic within their own working or daily experience, and to identify its pastoral, theological, ethical, or personal implications. The discovery of the best kinds of questions to ask is an important part of the process. An example of a specific topic is given as: 'Confessions of a Mother Inferior: the search for value and self esteem'. Some directions and guidance are also provided, e.g. (a) describe the experience briefly – tell the story, outline the situation; (b) ask what rôles you were conscious of – at the time, now, after some thought; (c) ask what changes were involved for you – e.g. useful-superfluous, sick-whole, calm-anxious; (d) ask how these were confronted, avoided, resolved; (e) ask what was the cost to you and to the others involved.[35]

We turn next, in Groome's approach and in the methodology of these two projects, to an encounter with the Christian 'Story' and 'Vision' and the promise it has for our lives. This further stage is an invitation to decision and response to a new or renewed praxis which can lead to a decision for overt action or to a variety of other responses. The *Theology and Change Project* focusses on personal reflections, and the aim is to gain an honest understanding of your own present beliefs and how they relate to your present life and situation. Some questions to be asked might be, 'What do I believe now?', 'How does this influence my life, and how does my life influence my beliefs' and 'How are my beliefs nourished by the Bible and Christian tradition?' These questions encourage people to take stock of what they actually believe, rather than what they think they ought to believe. Rôle-play, and using a Bible story in a contemporary situation, all help to make the right connections. The 'Life Experience and Christian Storehouse' section looks at how the Christian tradition grows out of lived experience and uses diagrams to discover patterns of meaning. (Participants on the course are also encouraged to draw their own patterns.) The overall aim is to look critically at how God is involved in our present experience and decide our response to this involvement. It poses questions such as, 'How have you changed/grown in your understanding of yourself and God, through your work topic and subsequent learning from it, (a) as a human being, (b) as a Christian, (c) as a minister or as a lay member of your church?'

The Cleveland *Theology and Change Project* invites participants to explore various ways of doing mission, looking at a biblical example, a historical example and a contemporary example. As words cannot grasp the full meaning of the term 'mission', students are told that it is important to take the words they choose only as a starting point and allow them to be changed during the process. Everyone is encouraged to look at the practical possibilities and problems of a particular situation with regard to their action within it.

Both these approaches to doing theology are appealing. Essentially they represent a way of doing theology that depends on *the art of asking the right questions*, thus giving tremendous scope to *teachers* in the churches. Using such approaches, the teacher invites the learners into a journey of discovery. It is a journey that in some ways has already been made, but it is also a journey that still is to be made. And because teaching theology is more about waiting and wanting God to be discovered, rather than already wearing him on our sleeves (or T-shirts), the journey includes learning to live and cope with the unexpected around the next bend of the road.

But more is demanded of the teacher even than this. For her rôle in the process is to help the adult learner to be caught up by the *spirit of theology*: by its very life, where knowledge and the heart come together, so that theology becomes, in Farley's sense, a way of knowing and of being and of loving and of living. Is this not a preparation of our hearts and minds before God? Is it not also an acknowledgement of all that we are and all we are meant to be?

Is this what theology means to us, as learners and teachers? Are we drawn by the very dynamics of theology itself, and the delights that it holds, so that when we participate in theology it becomes a part of our life's blood, our *raison d'être* and our eternal hope? If this were so for us all, we would all share in a common theology and all be caught up in a common questioning.

Most Christians are not called to grapple with academic theology. However, we are all called to enter into this spirit of theology, and we may do this best by releasing our imagination, our curiosity, our searching and yearning, our insights and our hopes. These are the elements that can truly give voice to the people of God.

THE LAITY

In the Anglican report *All are Called*, the working party wished to affirm very strongly certain biblical and theological insights about the rôle of the laity within the whole church of Jesus Christ. Among other things, it stressed that all human beings are made in the image of God, therefore all are called to become the people of God: the church servants and ministers and citizens of the kingdom, a new humanity in Jesus Christ. There is, however, little in the report on the education and strengthening of lay people as persons. But it is precisely this that will enable lay people to give full expression to their humanness, to become a new humanity in Jesus.

In his contribution to the report, Tony Dyson acknowledges that much consideration has been given to the ordained ministry, its organisation and its theology, while the laity – who make up by far the larger part of the church – have not debated their identity and purpose in anything like the same detail. Dyson writes, 'despite rhetoric to the contrary, the laity often seem to have been theologically out of sight and out of mind'.[36] So we are left with a strong affirmation of a calling to a lay Christian rôle on the one hand, and an abysmal neglect of a person's unique calling and the importance of a personal theology on the other. The question of call that is crucial here is not one about a vocation to some special and particular rôle in the life of the church, but rather a calling to explore those existential questions that are raised by the educational processes proposed by Farley and Groome: questions about *what it means to be a person*, in particular a Christian person. This includes knowing the difference between naming oneself and being named by others; being a subject that matters; and having a personal consciousness that enables and equips one to step into the church and out into the world.

Francis Dewar's work may be helpful here.[37] Dewar believes that there is a deep confusion in the church's life between a calling to a rôle and a person's unique calling. He offers a threefold understanding of the nature of vocation. There is first the vocation to be a Christian, to be a follower of Christ. Then there is the calling to a rôle that is essentially defined by others, which most people, apart perhaps from the clergy, would not recognise as a calling from God. But there is also the unique vocation which potentially is for everyone. This can be a task or activity engaged in for the love of it, by which others may be enriched or released. It is something you do as a freely-chosen expression of your nature and energy, something that expresses the unique essence of yourself that God calls out from you; it is not something that is defined or required by others. The teacher in the church is in a unique position to encourage, enhance and inspire lay people to live out their personhood and their own unique personal calling. There is much that needs to be done in this area of adult theological education.

'To Desire More, to Desire Better, to Desire in a Different Way?'

This chapter has been concerned with the recovery of a lost dimension in church education: namely a mature Christian education, which is a theological education, whereby teacher and lay person can become part of the liberating work which church education so desperately needs. A pre-requisite for any form of commitment is a sense of personal identity. A church education which is theological education can provide the means whereby a lay person discovers her own identity and learns to name herself as one who makes up the people of God. We should consider all this to be a natural process. We should live with, and teach with, high expectations of meeting flourishing, capable and far-sighted adult lay people in the church. And we should, as teachers, delight in their learning and in their ministry of showing *us* the way also.

Theology is the people's understanding of its own *raison d'être*. Without such an understanding there is not a people, only an uncertain drifting, spineless mass of human beings. If faith seeks understanding then it needs theology, a lay theology. And if lay theology is to be restored it needs an educated laity. Lay education, when it is theological education, should foster the curious interest of every member of the church. Only then can we all fully share what we have all discovered, heard and understood. If we believe theology to be liberating, then we must capture the hearts and minds of lay members of the church with all the inventiveness possible, so that they too may experience the joy of discovering a theology that is *theirs*.

Adult lay theological education does happen. Often it involves lay people as teachers as well as learners. All kinds of people are involved in helping others to learn in our churches, often in very informal ways. It seems to me that what they learn, how they learn, why they learn, is largely unknown to conventional theological institutions. If lay people are to involve themselves in teaching theology in the ways proposed here, not only do they need to be taught theology themselves (which often they are not), they also require practical guidance and training – which they are very unlikely to receive. Yet if we subscribe to Farley's view that church education should be ordered, sequential, cumulative learning, then we must recognise that it requires of the whole church some *resourceful* way of entering into genuine dialogue with all those who teach in our churches. This includes teaching and training these lay teachers and helping *them* to organise, structure and evaluate their teaching and its resources.

The expertise of teachers and trainers is badly needed in our churches, not just as an occasional back-up service but in continuing partnership with other ministers, and with an awareness that this is really how things are meant to be. For the sake of lay Christian education, should we ask for more interest in and more involvement from our teacher-theologians? Should we ask for a better understanding and a better awareness of their ministry from our parish priests and ministers? Should we ask for new perspectives and new insights about this enterprise from our bishops and church leaders? And is the time now not long overdue for churches to create properly-funded *lay teaching and training centres*, and other lively lay educational enterprises, if we are to truly believe in and honour the learning people of God?

NOTES

[1] E. Farley, 'Can Church Education be Theological Education?', in his *The Fragility of Knowledge: Theological Education in the Church and University*, Philadelphia: Fortress Press, 1988, p. 85. This chapter is reprinted in Jeff Astley, Leslie J. Francis and Colin Crowder (eds), *Theological Perspectives on Christian Formation: A Reader on Theology and Christian Education*, Leominster:

Gracewing Fowler Wright; Grand Rapids, Mich.: Eerdmans, 1996 (the quotation is from p. 31).

2   Cf. D. Guthrie *et al.* (ed.), *The New Bible Commentary Revised*, Leicester: Inter-Varsity Press, 1970, p. 1116.

3   D. Goodbourn, 'Theological Training for Christian Education', *Education in Church Today*, 5, Summer 1991, p. 8.

4   For a balanced view of adult educators as facilitators, which criticises 'ceding control for defining learning goals entirely to learners', see S. D. Brookfield, *Understanding and Facilitating Adult Learning*, Milton Keynes: Open University Press, 1986, pp. 62–63, 83–89, 123–146.

5   G. Moran, 'Where Now, What Next', in P. O'Hare (ed.), *Foundations of Religious Education*, New York: Paulist Press, 1978, p. 106.

6   E. P. Thompson, *William Morris: Romantic to Revolutionary*, London: Merlin, 1977, p. 791, cited by Peter Jarvis in P. Jarvis and N. Walters (eds), *Adult Education and Theological Interpretations*, Malabar, Fla.: Krieger, 1993, p. 319.

7   M. Buber, 'Education', in *Between Man and Man*, trans. R. G. Smith, London: Kegan Paul, 1947, p. 90.

8   M. Guerrini, O.S.A, *Late Have I Loved You*, Slough: St Paul Publications, 1986, p. 5.

9   D. Webster, 'A Spiritual Dimension for Education?', *Theology*, 88, 721, 1985, pp. 11–21.

10   J. Macquarrie, 'Why Theology?', in E. Hulmes and B. Watson (eds), *Religious Studies and Public Examinations*, Oxford: Farmington Institute for Christian Studies, 1980, p. 36.

11   B. A. Yeaxlee, *Spiritual Values in Adult Education: A Study of a Neglected Aspect*, two volumes, London: Oxford University Press, 1925. See J. Elias, 'Basil Yeaxlee: Educator of Adult Spirituality', *British Journal of Religious Education*, 7, 3, 1985, pp. 104–111.

12   D. W. C. Ford, 'The Teacher's Ultimate Authority', in Hulmes and Watson (eds), *Religious Studies and Public Examinations*, pp. 73–76.

13   Haiku by Bill Maroon, quoted in Maria Harris, *Teaching and Religious Imagination: An Essay in the Theology of Teaching*, San Francisco: HarperSanFrancisco, 1987, p. 23.

14   Harris, *Teaching and Religious Imagination*, p. 3.

15   P. Ricoeur, 'The Image of God and the Epic of Man', in *History and Truth*, Evanston, Illinois: Northwestern University Press, 1965, p. 127, quoted in Harris, *Teaching and Religious Imagination*, p. 3.

16   S. Weil, *Waiting on God*, trans. E. Craufurd, London: Collins, 1959, pp. 72–73.

17   Harris, *Teaching and Religious Imagination*, p. 26.

18   W. Blake, from a letter to the Revd Dr J. Trusler (23 August 1799), in G. Keynes (ed.), *Poetry and Prose of William Blake*, London: Nonesuch, 1961, p. 835.

19   K. Nichols, 'Feeling and Form in Worship', in J. Astley and D. Day (eds), *The Contours of Christian Education*, Great Wakering, Essex: McCrimmons, 1992, p. 128. See also his *Refracting the Light: Learning the Languages of Faith*, Dublin: Lindisfarne Books, 1997.

20   E. Templeton, personal communication.

21   S. Neill, *The Layman in Christian History*, London: SCM, 1963, p. 22.

22   J. Astley, *Learning to Live Theologically*, Durham: North of England Institute for Christian Education, 1990, p. 5.

23   See E. Farley, *Theologia: The Fragmentation and Unity of Theological Education*, Philadelphia: Fortress Press, 1983, ch. 2.

24 Farley, *The Fragility of Knowledge*, p. 98 (in Astley, Francis and Crowder (eds), *Theological Perspectives on Christian Formation*, p. 42).

25 B. J. F. Lonergan, S.J., *Method in Theology*, London: Darton, Longman & Todd, 1973, p. 247.

26 *ibid.*, p. 253.

27 Farley, *The Fragility of Knowledge*, p. 99 (in *Theological Perspectives on Christian Formation*, p. 43).

28 *loc. cit.*

29 T. H. Groome, *Christian Religious Education: Sharing Our Story and Vision*, San Francisco: Harper and Row, 1980, p. 229.

30 T. H. Groome, 'Christian Education for Freedom: A "Shared Praxis" Approach', in O'Hare (ed.), *Foundations of Religious Education*, p. 23.

31 T. Groome, 'Shared Christian Praxis: A Possible Theory/Method of Religious Education', reprinted in J. Astley and L. J. Francis (eds), *Critical Perspectives on Christian Education: A Reader on the Aims, Principles and Philosophy of Christian Education*, Leominster: Gracewing Fowler Wright, 1994, p. 218.

32 Now sometimes known as the 'North East Oecumenical Course'.

33 Groome, 'Shared Christian Praxis', p. 233.

34 M. Kane (ed.), *Theology and Change*, Durham: Respond! and Durham Diocesan Board of Education, 1992.

35 *Life and Work Project*, Durham: North East Ordination Course, 1994, pp. 18–19.

36 A. Dyson, 'Clericalism, Church and Laity', in *All are Called: Towards a Theology of the Laity*, London: Church Information Office/General Synod Board of Education Report, 1985, p. 13.

37 F. Dewar, 'Consider Your Call', *Theology*, 88, 726, 1985, p. 462.

4

Assessment in Adult Christian Education

Roger L. Walton

If we want to discover the truth about an educational system we must look into its assessment procedures. What student qualities and achievements are actively valued and rewarded by the system? ... To what extent are the hopes and ideals, aims and objectives ... truly perceived? ... The answers to these questions are to be found in what the system requires students to do in order to survive and prosper. The spirit and style of student assessment defines the *de facto* curriculum. (Rowntree, 1987: 1)

INTRODUCTION

The question of the place of assessment in adult Christian education has been raised by the explosion of interest in educational accreditation generally during the 1990s. Where formerly many church-sponsored programmes of education and training were related to vocational or personal interest, for which external validation or accreditation were considered unnecessary or inappropriate, now it is difficult to find a course which does not have some kind of recognised credit attached to it (or at least a submission for validation pending).[1]

As quality assurance and control processes are of major interest to accrediting bodies, many adult Christian education course leaders and managers are busy refining the learning outcomes or exit competencies of their courses, and introducing or scrutinising more closely existing assessment procedures. It is timely therefore to ask certain questions about assessment in the realm of Christian education, particularly as it affects adults. Before simply getting caught up in the issues of assessment methods and management, Christian course providers ought to ask questions about the nature and practice of assessment in relation to the basic aims of their courses and the aims of Christian education in general. In other words, we need to probe whether assessment is a necessary but burdensome requirement to satisfy external bodies and assure participants of the quality and usability of the course, or if it provides additional, useful tools for Christian teaching and learning. We need to ask: 'What kinds of assessment are compatible with Christian values?', 'Are there assessment methods which can tell us anything about a person's developing Christian commitment and maturity?', and, not least, 'Are there assessment techniques that will further a person's learning and Christian growth?'

Other writers have hinted that such an exploration ought to be undertaken. Astley and Day, for example, write:

'Assessment' is not necessarily the product of utilitarian educational systems, whittling square pegs down to fit round holes. But the ends of Christian education must be congruent with the ends of Christianity . . . (Astley and Day, 1992: 21)

Brian Hill (1993) has explored some of these questions in relation to Christian education in the school setting. However, to my knowledge little has been written about these issues in the context of adult Christian education. The aim of this chapter, therefore, is to explore the rôle of assessment in relation to adult Christian education programmes, and to identify elements that should be considered in any attempt to use assessment to make judgements about Christian commitment and maturity.

The Scope and Structure of the Chapter

The focus of this chapter is adult Christian courses or structured development schemes sponsored by the churches or Christian agencies. The use of the word *adult* means that we are seeking to exclude from the discussion school-based religious education, concentrating rather on Christian education which is offered to those of post-school age. We can assume that these participants choose to seek Christian education for themselves either for vocational or personal interest reasons. The use of the terms *course* or *structured development scheme* is again to confine the study to a manageable area. There is a great deal of informal, incidental and loosely structured education and learning within the churches which is worthy of exploration, and for which the study of the rôle of assessment might be beneficial. This terrain is, however, too vast for consideration here. The best we can hope to achieve is to comment on the areas where structured educational activities are formally organised and to reflect on possible implications for other aspects of Christian learning. Finally, the word *Christian* will need more detailed examination later, but at this point it is taken to mean that the education provider and the courses have as an implicit aim the development of a better understanding and practice of Christian faith.

The structure of the chapter is broadly in four sections. First, we shall look at what is meant by assessment and explore a Christian perspective on the issue. Second, we shall look at some features emerging from the discourse about assessment which may prove interesting to Christian educators. In the third section we shall examine some developments in adult Christian education that relate to the issue and suggest some ways of tackling assessment. Finally, we will offer two case studies that help us to see the creative use of certain aspects of assessment in Christian education. The conclusion will then reflect on implications for the structure of assessment both in adult Christian courses and for Christian education in general.

THE NATURE OF ASSESSMENT

Assessment has been defined as 'processes of getting information and communicating it to people so that they can make judgements and decisions' (Desforges, 1989: 9). This information might be for the student, the teacher or for wider society. For the student, assessment might yield data that can be used to reinforce learning, correct error, measure progress or achievement and predict future learning. For the teacher or tutor, it may help to monitor the pace of work set and measure the effectiveness of the curriculum process. For society, assessment can provide a way of reporting achievement, estimating aptitude for new learning or potential for responsibility, or providing a student character reference. It may also have secondary functions, such as to provide data for accountability or indeed political control, to motivate students and teachers, and even as a disciplinary tool. Clearly, some of these purposes of assessment may well be in conflict with others.

Assessment is a controversial subject. Where stakes are high, such as in GCSE examinations or the publication of league tables of student examination results by schools, the clash between political and educational agendas over assessment is particularly intense. Cohen, Manion and Morrison (1996: 367) note the vast political dimension to the subject of assessment in the UK since the 1960s. Typically, educationalists fear that the desire to produce data that is easy to compile, compare and communicate to the public pushes education towards tests that are capable of statistical analysis and less expensive in terms of resources. Educationalists themselves prefer assessment methods that harness the skills of the teacher, are more suited to the assessment task, are a better measure of a student's achievement and, most importantly, can be utilised effectively for ongoing learning and teaching. Inevitably, the interpretation of research on assessment becomes emotionally and politically charged.

In the world of Christian education, the subject of assessment is also surrounded by conflicting views and emotions. Because assessment in schools has in some cases been deeply damaging to self-confidence, for example to many who 'failed' their 11+ examination, Christians have sometimes been cautious about assessment in order to avoid the same loss of self-esteem. Indeed the church has often needed to help people rebuild confidence to counter the effects of such experiences. On the other hand, those offering themselves to the church for certain kinds of ministry or training (ordained or lay) have been assessed, often with the assessment criteria either hidden or operating at subjective levels and therefore invisible to candidates. Even in the field of religious education in schools, we find ambivalence about whether the subject is capable of assessment through conventional methods.

For these reasons, it may be helpful to look in some detail at Christian attitudes to assessment.

CHRISTIAN PERSPECTIVES ON ASSESSMENT

A good starting point for this discussion is Brian Hill's article 'Is Assessment Compatible with Agape' (Hill, 1993; cf. Hill, 1994, 1997). In this paper Hill is trying to grapple with assessment as it is being experienced in schools from the point of view of a Christian value system. While Hill's concerns are for children within a state education system, and for Christian teachers faced with using assessment in their work, his theological perspective has a wider relevance. He offers a number of 'key doctrines' that should influence the teacher's attitude to assessment.

Hill accepts that assessment is compatible with the biblical theme of judgement, pointing out that the concepts of judgement and measurement run throughout the Scriptures. 'Reality testing and having a true estimate of oneself are constantly enjoined upon believers.' Assessment may serve a purpose in such reality testing, saving people from self-delusion and enabling them to take personal responsibility. The theme of judgement, however, is balanced in Scripture by a love that forgives and encourages and does not sacrifice the individual to the collective. Other theological values demand of us a certain caution in dealing with assessment (especially in a charged political climate). Hill argues that 'nothing has higher priority than individual human consciousness' (cf. Ps 8 and Matt 18:1–7). He fears that the political and national 'interests' that are apparent in many current assessment schemes may suppress such individuality. In this context Christians ought to resist the tendency to place curriculum and standardised assessment schemes higher than the development of individual self-esteem and personal strengths.

Hill argues further that there is a Christian view of the nature of the learner. On this view God gives to human beings the capacity to reason, create, choose and enter into dialogue with one another. This is a special kind of freedom which allows us to make choices, and assumes that God holds people responsible for the choices they make. Hence Hill is against 'assessment models which treat children as bundles of conditioned responses, or mere memory tanks', but by implication he is in favour of systems that facilitate self-consciousness about one's capacity to act responsibly in the world. Finally, Hill stresses 'the worth of the self'. Christians should be foremost in respecting and strengthening the self-esteem of students, through affir-mation of their worth as persons. Lack of self-respect is damaging in the extreme; people who have no love or respect for themselves are unlikely to be able to love others (Lk 10:27). Therefore assessment must not mean a 'litany of constant denigration' which diminishes the learner's self-respect and capacity to love and respect others.

One detects in Hill's arguments a certain fear that the state system's concerns with some approaches to assessment (perhaps those that will yield school league tables) threatens to undermine Christian values in teaching, learning and citizenship. The political need to be seen to be 'raising standards', and thus increasing pressure on schools to perform well in high stakes assessment, is a bulldozer which could damage the individual self-respect and development of many children. This is an appropriate Christian concern, but may result in a distortedly cautious and even negative view of assessment. It may be that Hill is mainly addressing the politically-driven agenda on assessment, and so gives little attention to some of the new and alternative approaches and methods that might promote some of the Christian values he outlines. For example, Hill makes little reference to the developments in self and peer assessment which would meet his concern 'to give to learners the opportunity to review their own learning'.

From our point of view, all Hill's points are valuable. The concept of reality testing has to be set alongside the ideas of the development of human consciousness, self-esteem and personal responsibility. It is possible, however, to add to or develop these theological perspectives in three ways. First, the New Testament supports the idea of a person discovering his or her gifts and using their strengths for the service of others. This emerges through self-awareness and dialogue. Ephesians 4 argues that the discovery and use of gifts is through 'speaking the truth in love', which must at least resonate with the concept of assessment for self-knowledge. Assessment may therefore serve to help people identify strengths and use them. Second, the Christian church has a sense of mission and is obliged to test its own thinking and action against the challenge of the kingdom of God, both in the development of personal characteristics such as compassion, empathy and a commitment to justice, and in the testing of its action in the light of the needs of the world (Matt 25). This requires honest personal as well as corporate appraisal. Finally, Derek Rowntree's (1987) point that assessment is to some extent 'an attempt to know that person', is a deeply Christian concept. The idea of knowing and being known at an intimate level (Hebrew *yada'*) is a constant theme in the Judeo-Christian tradition and represents the ultimate goal of God's purposes for humankind. The kind of knowing we must have in mind here is a personal encounter which enlivens and enriches.[2]

We may say therefore that there is much about the concept and practice of assessment that could both represent and promote Christian values. It would be naive, however, to think that these values are to the fore in much that passes for assessment in the educational world, and equally naive to imagine that assessment systems managed by Christian churches and agencies are always based on these values. Looking for good practice in assessment should concern Christian course providers more than it does. For this reason also it is important to pay attention to the discourse about assessment.

THE DISCOURSE ABOUT ASSESSMENT

Gipps (1994) charts the history of assessment through three stages: psychometrics, educational measurement and educational assessment. The approaches to assessment that correspond with each of these paradigm shifts has its own set of limitations and strengths. The earliest form of testing, *psychometrics*, flowed from those theories of intelligence where intelligence was conceived of as innate and fixed. As the tests to measure intelligence were often limited in dimensionality, they were capable of high reliability and standardisation. Participants could be compared easily using statistical methods and so the tests were mostly norm-referenced.[3] These tests, however, proved to be extremely limited in measuring complex multi-dimensional skills, as well as having the effect of labelling some students intelligent and others not, and thus possibly limiting future learning.

From the early 1960s the idea of *educational measurement* began to emerge with Glaser's concept of criterion-referenced assessment (Glaser, 1963). Essentially, this is a matter of measuring a person's ability by reference to a set of predetermined, carefully prescribed criteria. Its strengths were immediately apparent. The aim of this kind of assessment was to measure individual achievement and assess competence rather than intelligence. With criterion-referenced assessment it would be possible to structure education so that learners could clearly understand what they were aiming at, and there would be no reason for more people not to succeed. Assessment could take place in more natural conditions and would provide diagnostic data to improve the individual's learning. This form of assessment was oriented towards effective learning and teaching and for success in demonstrating achievement.

In practice, however, criterion-referenced assessment became very difficult to implement. One reason for this was that it depended upon highly detailed specifications of the elements of a competence, which often proved to be unworkable. It is one thing to define a competence in a given subject in broad terms such as 'ability to organise the systematic collection and ordering of information', but the details of what this means in terms of the sources of information, the level of sophistication assumed, the degree of critical engagement with the sources, the technological (IT) resources involved etc., need extensive and detailed specification. Moreover, if there is to be any comparison of achievement between students, particularly in different places, in addition to the specification of these items, extensive information is required about the context and the tutor-support given. This can quickly and easily run into pages and pages of specification, and thus make the assessment extremely difficult to carry out. As Gipps puts it:

> In order to meet the requirement for strict criterion-referenced assessment, criteria need to be specified in fine detail; however, this leads to over-specification and a focus on narrow, tightly defined objectives. (Gipps, 1994: 93)[4]

The problem at the heart of this difficulty is one of reliability versus validity. *Reliability* refers to the extent to which a similar result would be obtained if the assessment were to be repeated. It addresses one aspect of our need to have confidence in the results of assessment. *Validity* is that aspect of assessment that relates how well the result reflects the skill, knowledge or attitudes that it was designed to assess. The two are clearly related, but it is sometimes difficult to have both high reliability and high validity. To increase one aspect may decrease the other. To illustrate, Harlen cites the example of standardised reading:

> For example, a standardised reading test has high reliability when children are required to read isolated words free of context. The results, however, are a less valid assessment of how well children read when using context to help them, an ability which can be tested by a more realistic (but less reliable) reading task. (Harlen, 1994: 12)

When psychometric testing was the main approach to assessment, the narrow and limited focus of intelligence tests meant that reliability was high. Criterion-referenced assessment, on the other hand, was probably never intended to be used for comparison of achievement on a large or national scale. Its great promise was the possibility of assessing people in their learning or work *context*, rather than through the artificiality of intelligence tests which were predominantly of a paper-and-pencil type and purposely removed from the context of learning or work. Validity can arguably be enhanced by the performance-in-context nature of criterion-referenced assessment, but reliability may be reduced. In any assessment, it is argued, validity and reliability can never both be 100 per cent;[5] but in the case of criterion-referenced assessment the intricate and detailed specification needed to achieve high reliability renders the assessment unmanageable.

Various attempts to modify criterion-referenced assessment and other emerging approaches have yielded what Gipps describes as *educational assessment*. The emphasis here is on assessing performance – an assessment of the learner's ability to use previously acquired knowledge to solve novel problems. Like criterion-referenced assessment, educational assessment involves some specified criteria, including cognitive demands, performance standards and context quality, but also draws heavily on the professional ability of teachers and assessors. This latter dimension is increasingly recognised as addressing the weakness of criterion-referenced assessment, namely the consistency or reliability of the assessment. It is argued that where professionals are trained in assessment and are also in a continuing conversation over standards, a shared understanding emerges: what Wiliam (1996) calls 'internalised notions of levelness'.

In one sense this is not new. In higher education and in many fields of expertise standards are set and maintained by communities of scholarship in conversation. This is consistent with the widely accepted notion of knowledge as construct (Habermas, 1987) wherein both individuals and communities are in dialogue about what constitutes knowledge. It is within this dialogue and consensus that the achievements of students can be judged, and thus it is not only appropriate but necessary that a community of scholarship, interpretation and practice should be a vital part of the assessment process. With a highly trained profession in conversation about assessment it is possible to move from a mathematical model of reliability with its inevitable narrowing of the scope of the assessment, to new criteria for quality in educational assessment such as dependability, which is assured through the community of practice in dialogue, and transferability (rather than generalisation), which can be assured through curriculum fidelity and careful context descriptions.

Another strand in recent developments has been the emergence of *ipsative* or *self-assessment* methods. Since the mid 1970s there has been a growing interest in the rôle of self-assessment at all levels of education and professional development (Agyris and Schön, 1974; Israelite, 1983; Rogers, 1983; Heron, 1974, 1981, 1988; Boud, 1995; Kramp and Humphreys, 1993; Taylor and Marienau, 1993), together with experimentation and research involving students in assessing their own work in a wide range of areas, for example in foreign language learning (Oskarsson, 1980), student writing (Butler, 1982) and engineering education (Cowan, 1975, 1988).

Advocates argue that this is not simply another technique for assessment but has more far-reaching outcomes in terms of the equipping and enabling of self-directed learners. Well constructed self-assessment has the potential for prompting deep approaches to learning, encouraging students to take responsibility for their own learning both in their current course and beyond in their professional life (Boud, 1995: 24–47). To achieve this, however, one must not only involve students in marking exercises but engage them in discussing and determining the criteria for assessment.

> Self-assessment means more than students grading their own work; it means involving them in the process of determining what is good work in any given situation. It requires them to consider what are the characteristics of, say, a good essay or practical report and to apply this to their own work. (Boud, 1995: 12)

This is a form of empowerment and, in the most sophisticated forms of self-assessment, the criteria developed in the dialogue between students and staff may alter the teaching and structure of the course from that point onwards.[6] Perhaps unsurprisingly the notion has the support of many adult education writers who have built their understanding of adult education around the concept of the self-directed learner (see, for example, Knowles, 1984; Brookfield, 1986, 1987; and Jarvis, 1983: 115 and 224).

Closely associated, though distinct, is the development of *peer assessment*. This is where student peers are involved in grading or in giving feedback to the student for self-assessment purposes. Whilst the literature suggests that this needs careful preparation and a structure to ensure that the feedback (and/or grading) is given and received constructively, the work of Smith and Hatton (1993) suggests that students develop their learning to greater depth when they discuss their work with a peer as distinct from a discussion with an expert or tutor.

Whilst these developments have their enthusiasts, they also face critics. Some have argued that it may be irresponsible for teachers or tutors to abdicate the responsibility for assessment to students. Students may see the teacher or tutor's rôle as primarily one of assessing and resent this work being given to them, especially if one of the motives for introducing self-assessment is to reduce the work load of staff burdened with increasing class or lecture sizes. Student/teacher discussion aimed at establishing criteria for assessment may take a significant amount of time – time that ought perhaps to be given to teaching the subject-matter of the course. Moreover, if there is a genuine openness about determining the criteria, what guarantees are there that the criteria are acceptable within the subject discipline at the appropriate level? Finally, collusion and cheating can occur if the system is not carefully structured, and in some cases peer assessment can be damaging rather than confidence building.

Both these areas are in relatively early stages of development. Though forms of peer and self-assessment are present in primary, secondary and tertiary education, many aspects still need to be explored. Research to date has overwhelmingly concentrated on whether or not the students' rating of themselves (or their peers) is higher, lower or close to their assessment by the teaching staff. The evidence does not yield a clear answer.[7] Reports, however, consistently show that students value self-assessment highly, especially where it forms part of the overall assessment and contributes to the final mark. The majority of those participating feel that the process is engaging and contributes significantly to their current and future learning, as well as increasing their self-esteem and confidence.

In summary, we can say that the debates and experimentation on

assessment in recent years have yielded three developments of significance. First, since the introduction of criterion-referenced assessment
there has been a strong emphasis on clearly articulated learning
outcomes and assessment criteria which can be understood, worked
towards and used to reinforce learning. This has also generated a
variety of ways of collecting data for assessment, such as portfolios
and observation in concrete tasks, as well as via written work and
conversation. Second, there is an increasing emphasis on the professional community as a vital part of the assessment process. This
'community in dialogue' saves criterion-referenced assessment from
overwhelming bureaucracy and endless specification, thus allowing its
strengths for personal achievement and development to be utilised.
Third, self and peer assessment have emerged as a major new force
in the work of assessment.

ASSESSMENT IN ADULT CHRISTIAN EDUCATION

There are some developments in the world of adult Christian education which are worthy of attention for this discussion. They not only
denote tendencies in Christian education practice but also provide
some tentative suggestions for the use of assessment in adult Christian
education. These are:

(a)   the defining of outcomes for Christian education,
(b)   the use of instruments to measure growth in Christian values and
      attitudes,
(c)   the development of courses and schemes which use self and peer
      assessment,
(d)   the emergence of a self-conscious Christian education commu-
      nity.

The Defining of Outcomes for Christian Education

Attempting to define Christian educational outcomes takes us back to
the debate about what we mean by Christian education. Earlier we
opted for a definition of Christian education as education aiming to
develop a better understanding and practice of Christian faith. This is
by no means the only definition of Christian education (See, e.g.,
Groome, 1980; Hull, 1984; Astley and Day, 1992), but it is one with
sufficient support to relate to a significant discourse and is appropriate to the context of church-sponsored adult education.[8]
   It is one thing to define Christian education, it is quite another to

translate this into specific educational outcomes and to attempt to assess whether these outcomes have been achieved. Some indeed would argue that certain Christian characteristics are so inward or 'spiritual' that they are not capable of being measured and it may even be a (sinful) presumption to try. It is certainly easier to find explicit outcomes of Christian courses concerned with historical-critical skills, or (more recently) in competency terms that focus on performing functions (e.g. leading public worship), than in term of attitudes, values or moral actions. These latter behaviours may in fact carry the more distinctively Christian nature of the education, but they are rarely defined or assessed. The North American religious education-alist J. M. Lee (1973, 1996) has argued against the view that Christian education outcomes cannot be defined and measured. He suggests that the Christian-ness of a person can be discerned through observing a person's cognitive, affective and life-style behaviours and, following Mager (1962), argues that through a careful threefold process of (1) identifying terminal behaviour, (2) defining the conditions under which the behaviour can be predicted or expected to occur, and (3) specifying the criteria of acceptable performance, it is possible to determine and measure Christian education outcomes.

On this side of the Atlantic, Astley has done much to delineate what this process, more aptly named 'Christian formation', means in terms of beliefs, attitudes, values or dispositions (Astley and Day, 1992; Astley, 1994; Astley and Francis, 1994; Astley, Francis and Crowder, 1996). He has attempted to outline a taxonomy of the Christian attributes that Christian education will seek to develop in an individual.[9] This work is a vital first step in developing appropriate Christian outcomes for specific courses. It is unclear whether these or any similar range of attributes have been considered or explored in the construction of particular course outcomes. (There is an interesting research project here.) Certainly, Astley does not suggest how these attributes might be assessed, and we have not been able to locate any serious action or research in developing the necessary assessment processes. Thus we can only discuss some aspects of his proposal and suggest some ways forward.[10]

Clearly, one of the key problems in relation to Astley's taxonomy of attributes is that of measuring attributes in the affective domain. As long ago as 1964, Benjamin Bloom and his co-workers recognised the difficulties of defining and measuring this domain, and even the rather limited taxonomy they produced has been widely disputed (Krathwohl *et al.*, 1964). Emotions, feelings, attitudes and values are all located in or entangled with the affective realm. Holmberg (1989: 42) has argued that it is particularly important to be explicit about intended outcomes in the affective domain because of the sensitivities surrounding it, yet consistently this area presents problems for assessment. In 1983 the Assessment of Performance Unit gave up its attempts to identify and propose assessment methods for aesthetic development as unmanageable, settling instead for the less demanding description of artistic development, which can be located more easily within a variety of skills or competencies (e.g. handling skills, skills of discourse, artistic appraisals, etc.: APU, 1983). The same problems occur in values education. There have been a number of attempts in recent times to initiate discussion about values education (e.g. the 1996 SCAA consultation on values in education and the community) but consistently these become problematic at the assessment stage. Halliday notes the problems of values in competency-based education:

> For example, honesty does not seem to be at all amenable to criterion referencing. We may wonder about the number of occasions on which someone has to be honest before they meet the criterion of honesty. (Halliday, 1995: 134)

This slightly tongue-in-cheek comment highlights the problems of certain approaches to assessment when faced with the affective and life-style domains. Criterion-referenced assessment is clearly the wrong tool for the assessment of values, as it is probably impossible to define performance criteria against which to make judgements.

Nevertheless, the attempt to define appropriate Christian outcomes has begun, however hesitatingly, and this may allow us to address creatively the issues of assessment in adult Christian education.

The Use of Instruments to Measure Growth in Christian Values and Attitudes

Another development is in the arena of personality tests. It is common now in many clergy training programmes to use Myers-Briggs personality tests for developing self-understanding and reflection on ministry. Increasingly Honey and Mumford's work on learning styles (Honey, 1994; Mumford, 1982 and 1986) is also used to help course participants to become aware of their own preferred learning style, its implication for their own learning and the ways they may facilitate other people's learning.[11] Both these reveal, to some extent, attitudes, values and personality traits and these can be used to promote reflective practice through discussion and personal profiling. James Fowler's work on faith development (Fowler, 1981) has also stimulated attempts to define and use growth in affective as well as cognitive dimensions of faith.[12]

In North America much more work has been done on instruments to measure religious orientation, spiritual well-being and maturity, and faith development (Sappington and Wilson, 1991; Hill and Hood, 1999). The data, often collected through questionnaire and interviews, relates to inner motivations, feelings, attitudes and the basis for personal or group actions. It is not easy to say why these have not been used more extensively in the UK. Perhaps the cultural assumptions are substantially different, or perhaps there has been a fear of this type of psychometric testing and its associated labelling. The new climate associated with the Myers-Briggs and Honey and Mumford tests, however, suggests that students enter into these explorations freely, curious to know about themselves and debate the findings. It is likely that some of these inventories, indexes and Christian life assessment scales will prove on detailed investigation to be limited and inappropriate, but others may form the basis for discussion and, linked with self-assessment techniques, may allow assessment of the affective domain.

The Use of Self and Peer Assessment

There is evidence that self and peer assessment are proving very useful to churches and Christian education institutions. The two case studies cited at the end of this chapter both make substantial use of self and peer assessment, one for appraisal, the other for measuring individual growth in a Christian education programme. In both cases the method enables both the personal goals of the individual and the broader aims of the local or national church to be combined and measured very effectively.

Self and peer assessment may be, as one writer put it, 'ideas whose time has come' (Knight, 1995: 20). The rapidly extending relevant literature and widespread experimentation confirms considerable interest at all levels of the education system. Its particular strengths seem to be in preparing students to be self-directed learners, in the nurturing of meta-cognitive skills and in encouraging discussion about the nature of knowledge and the criteria for assessment. In this power sharing context, it is possible for a number of dialogues to take place: dialogue concerning personal learning goals and course objectives; dialogue on group criteria for success in relation to an individual's criteria; dialogue with (and within) the community of scholarship that relates to the field of study.

It is probable that self-assessment will not replace all other forms of assessment. Rather, one can imagine it operating alongside a variety of assessment processes, and becoming increasingly recognised as part of the formal assessment system. In many ways this will allow self-assessment to contribute its strengths without asking it to attempt to do work that it will never be able to do. In allowing the personal agenda of students to become more active in the assessment process, it will also mean that personal values, attitudes, and even feelings can be discussed with integrity, and through discussion become incorporated into the ongoing self-assessment process. It is not difficult to imagine personal profiles and portfolios that include life-style reflection, reasons for ethical decisions, etc.[13]

The Emergence of a Self-conscious Christian Education Community

The suggestions above imply much experimentation and risk taking. If developed, they may take some time to reach maturity and arrive at any well tested processes and robust standards for assessing Christian educational outcomes. We would do well to encourage a conversation within the community of teaching and learning in which sharing of practices is common and a vigorous debate about their strengths, weaknesses and achievements undertaken. It is interesting to note that in the article on values education quoted above (Halliday, 1995), the author argues that the way forward is in an explicit recognition of 'the meta-values that guide the development' and which 'do not exist apart from the tradition but as an unformalised part of it'. In other words, without a continuing conversation about the key values within the Christian community and its educational programmes there can be no genuine values education. The mechanism exists for such a debate within church education structures. A separate structure for 'theological education' has been growing up over recent years (ACATE)[14] which cuts across lay and ordained, full-time, part-time and leisure time Christian education provision. This is the place for the continuing dialogue, and ACATE might be encouraged to do more to promote this conversation.

TWO CASE STUDIES OF ASSESSMENT

The following two case studies illustrate, I think, the beginning of developments of new patterns of assessment in Christian adult education.

'Training for Learning and Service'

This course was developed originally by the Church of Scotland but runs now under the Scottish Churches Open College. It is for lay people and is broadly geared towards developing Christian disciple-ship and service. The course is in two parts: a foundation course which takes eighteen months, followed by practical ministry modules which are chosen by participants to build on their foundation work.

Assessment in the foundation course is through two parallel systems. All students have to undertake an 'assessment of personal and spiritual development'; only those who are registered for certain ministries (e.g. lay preaching) or who wish to obtain the Certificate in Higher Education in Church Studies are required to take the 'intellectual development' assessment which is through a series of marked assignments. Making the personal and spiritual development assessment an obligatory part of the course conveys certain values about assessment independent of the certificated assessment. Moreover, the opening statement of the *Guide to Personal Assessments (1996/97)* states:

> 'Assessment' in TLS is not for our benefit but for yours. It is to help you monitor your own growth and learning, so you can judge for your-self how well you are meeting your aims in taking the course.

This valuing of the participant's own learning goals is, however, not allowed to nurture a wholly individualistic approach. The system requires that any person entering the course has both a district tutor (responsible for running the district group meetings) and a personal support group from the local church or locality. Both are involved with the participant throughout the course, and each has a part to play in the personal assessment process.

The purpose of the assessment is stated as:

(a) to help the student monitor his or her progress through the course,
(b) to develop in the student self-critical and analytical abilities, designed to enable continuing deeper ability to evaluate his or her own work long after the course is over, and
(c) to enable course managers to keep track of the extent to which students are meeting the basic requirements of the course.

Three times in the course the student is prompted by the regional organiser to complete a self-assessment form. The student is asked to give forms to both the district tutor and the support group who are asked to complete these, commenting on the person's development since the beginning of the course (or since the last assessment) and suggesting personal goals for the student to consider. The forms are returned to the student and discussed with him or her before the student completes and submits the self-assessment to the organiser. The students are required to use three criteria against which to measure themselves:

(a)   their own learning goals, set after discussion with the support group and in the light of the nature of the course,
(b)   the learning outcomes of the modules they have undertaken, as outlined in the module descriptors, and
(c)   fulfilment of the required procedures of the course, as stated in the student handbook.

The self-assessment submission itself is in two parts: Part 1 is a simple report on his or her fulfilment of course requirements (attendance at district groups, etc.); Part 2 is a more reflective account of the person's learning goals, response to the comments of the support group and district tutor, and a specification of measurable targets to be achieved by the next assessment. A Certificate of Satisfactory Progress is issued by the organiser on receipt and, unless there is cause for concern (in which case an interview is arranged), the assessment is reviewed as part of the next self-assessment.

This approach to assessment carries some of the features for which we have argued. First, the self-assessment is deliberately aimed at the development of analytical and critical skills in the student for use in the course and beyond it. Second, it allows for a variety of personal learning goals. The feedback from, and discussion with, the tutor and support group ensures that dialogue takes place and the assessment and learning goals are earthed both in the tutor's knowledge of the person's participation in the course meetings and in the local context. The course providers have also managed to incorporate the self-assessment with the formal intellectual assessment, in as much as Napier University, the validating body, will not award the Certificate of Higher Education in Church Studies unless all the personal assessments have been completed. Although they do not inspect the self-assessment submission, this is nevertheless essential to the formal validation. Whilst there is little evidence of the discussion of general assessment criteria for the modules, and it is not clear how the organisers ensure consistency in the self-assessment submissions, this is manifestly a course which uses a sophisticated self-assessment process for the strengthening of Christian education outcomes.

Accompanied Self-Appraisal

The second case study is a scheme introduced by the British Methodist Church for the appraisal of ordained ministers. It is included here as a structure for personal development rather than a formal course, and as such offers slightly different perspectives on assessment.

The scheme, approved by the Methodist Church in 1993, is a

supported self-appraisal scheme and is compulsory for all ordained ministers. Rather than a hierarchical appraisal structure, the appraisal is in the hands of the minister with the help of a trained 'accompanist' and feedback from various colleagues, church members and others with whom the minister works. The aim of the scheme is to contribute to 'a life-long process of reflection and routine development' by providing:

(a) places of safety for them as public people to talk openly,
(b) opportunity to find, recover and maintain a sense of direction, and
(c) a process whereby ministers can check out their goals and vision within a context of their daily work.

There is no reference to identifying or addressing training or educational needs, but these may also be outcomes of the process.

The scheme has five stages:

Stage 1: Through a district structure the self-appraiser (SA) is linked to an accompanist. Both are briefed on the process by the district officer. The SA then prepares a fact sheet about his or her situation, experience and work.

Stage 2: The accompanist and SA meet to establish a relationship and to clarify the fact sheet information. The SA is invited to offer personal reflections on his/her ministry in the last twelve months, and to identify both the specific areas of work to be considered and a list of relevant people to be invited to give feedback. The SA will also agree a method of proceeding and a timetable. The agreed syllabus, times and strategies are written down as a reminder for both as to what is being attempted.

Stage 3: The SA seeks information and opinion on specified areas of work and records the responses, together with his/her own reactions.

Stage 4: The SA presents and discusses his/her responses to the findings in order to determine what has been learned from the process, and writes down any goals, personal development needs, etc., for the next twelve months. (This may be discussed further with appropriate people in the circuit.) Dates are fixed for any future meeting(s).

Stage 5: Evaluation of the process takes place, with any appropriate feedback to the district officer.

The scheme is another example of self-assessment in dialogue with others. Again it gives control to the participants both in deciding which areas of work or competence to explore, and in determining personal development goals. The feedback encourages reality testing and ensures that appraisal is related to daily work and working relationships, as well as prompting personal reflection on reactions and responses to the views of others. It also allows the minister to determine the assessment criteria in discussion with the accompanist, and initiates goal-setting processes that can be reviewed after twelve months. The openness of the content means that it is equally possible to focus on life-style, emotional development or pastoral ministry. It should promote ongoing self-assessment skills and thus contribute significantly to the development of the minister as a self-directed learner. Whether it has sufficient safeguards within it for a dialogue about the church's goals over against the minister's personal agenda cannot be fully analysed here, and in any case the scheme developers see this as one part of a larger scheme of life-long learning and development in which various elements contribute different components. It is for us another example of assessment (albeit named 'appraisal') which seeks to develop people in a Christian direction.

CONCLUSIONS

We have identified an important area of debate. The interface between the emerging self-conscious world of adult Christian education and the complex and developing sphere of educational assessment is a little researched field. A good deal of work needs to take place on the explicit and implicit outcomes of Christian education programmes and how these are being assessed (if at all). Equally the new research on self and peer assessment may find that Christian education programmes offer insights into how these can be applied to the affective domain. Clearly, Christian courses and development schemes need to work substantially in this domain, and may therefore initiate and experiment in ways that other educational courses as yet do not explore.

We have suggested some ways forward for the assessment of adult Christian education. Both the use of personality tests and portfolios as tools for developing dialogue, and reflection on values, attitudes and emotional development, need experimental research. Data needs to be collected on the use of self and peer assessment in Christian education courses. Finally, a debate needs to take place about the rôle of the Christian education community in creating, debating and identifying practices and standards in assessment.[15]

NOTES

1   Degree and other higher education courses in theology have always carried the validation of the awarding university or HE college, but recently programmes for voluntary youth workers, lay readers, local preachers and Sunday School teachers have been submitted for accreditation through various channels. At the time of writing, many dioceses are seeking accreditation or validation of lay training courses. Nationally developed ecumenical programmes such as *Spectrum* (for youth workers), *Kaleidoscope* (for voluntary workers with children) and *Faith & Worship* (the Methodist training course for local preachers) now have formal accreditation.

2   As Birenbaum (1995) notes, the Latin root of the word 'assessment' is *assidere* meaning 'to sit alongside'. This contrasts strongly with the Latin root of the word 'test', *testum*, which means to examine the purity of a metal. Where assessment genuinely develops human understanding of the self or another, without manipulation or exploitation, it may be a human encounter that reflects the highest in human consciousness and something of the divine purpose.

3   *Norm-referenced* assessment indicates how good a person is in relation to others (as, for example, 'in the top 20% of exam results'). *Criterion-referenced* assessment measures an individual's performance against specific criteria, which are independent of the performance of others (as in a driving test).

4   Compare Popham (1994) and Wiliam (1996).

5   Harlen (1994) notes that the consequence of this is that assessment can never be 'accurate' in the way that word is used in the context of measurement in the physical world.

6   Cowan (1988) and Edwards (1989) both describe in detail their own changed rôles as teachers/tutors in particular courses where self-assessment was introduced.

7   In some situations students seem to mark lower than staff, in others' higher. The factors in the situations causing these differences are not clear. There is some evidence, however, that the more able students tend to mark themselves lower, whereas the less able mark themselves higher than do their teachers. For a full discussion of the research, see Boud and Falchikov (1995).

8   Astley and Day list five different uses of the term 'Christian education', building on Hull's earlier work. They recognise that many writers in the field use the term in a confessional sense that 'covers any and every (structured) learning experience that gives rise to the adoption or deepening of a person's Christian beliefs, attitudes, values, or dispositions to act and experience "in a Christian way"' (1992: 17).

9   Astley's eight attributes are: 1. Christian beliefs-that; 2. Christian beliefs-in; 3. Christian attitudes and values; 4. Christian emotions and feelings; 5. Christian experiences; 6. Christian moral actions; 7. Christian religious actions; 8. Christian or theological reflection and criticism. (Astley, 1994: ch. 6; see above pp. 5–6.) He argues that this is a complete or ideal list. That is, it represents the full range of attributes that the fully Christian educated person has learned or possesses. Whilst he recognises that some will not learn or possess certain elements (e.g. the mentally disabled may be limited in their beliefs, and not everyone will develop critical skills), he nevertheless argues that Christians will generally learn and develop in all these areas. Thus Christian education will address all these attributes in its nurturing of Christians. The order of the list is not meant to indicate either an order for Christian education nor a hierarchy of attributes, as his later argument shows. Interestingly, Astley goes on to argue that the education of the Christian emotions is the primary and all-important focus of Christian education.

[10] See also chapter 1 above.
[11] See also chapter 7 below.
[12] See also chapter 6 below.
[13] Self and peer assessment is not new to the Christian church. Boud (1995) argues that it has its roots in the Judeo-Christian tradition of confession. One might add to this the Puritan patterns of prophesying, the Methodist class meetings and the rules of membership of the Iona community, all of which were structured for self and peer assessment on spiritual development, Christian life-style and ministry. The approach is a recurring practice in Christianity. Self-assessment may well allow a greater exploration of Christian educational outcomes in courses than has been previously possible.
[14] ACATE = The Association of Centres of Adult Theological Education.
[15] Whatever the outcomes of this research, it is as well to remind ourselves of the opening paragraphs of Rowntree (1987). We need to ask *ourselves*, What does the assessment system of adult Christian education say about Christianity?

REFERENCES

Agyris, C. and Schön, D. (1974), *Theory in Practice: Increasing Professional Effectiveness*, San Francisco: Jossey-Bass.

APU (1983), *Aesthetic Development*, London: Assessment of Performance Unit.

Astley, J. (1994), *The Philosophy of Christian Religious Education*, Birmingham, Ala.: Religious Education Press.

Astley, J. and Day, D. (eds) (1992), *The Contours of Christian Education*, Great Wakering: McCrimmons.

Astley, J. and Francis, L. J. (eds) (1994), *Critical Perspectives on Christian Education*, Leominster: Gracewing Fowler Wright.

Astley, J. and Francis, L. J. (eds) (1996), *Christian Theology and Religious Education*, London: SPCK.

Astley, J., Francis, L. J. and Crowder, C. (eds) (1996), *Theological Perspectives on Christian Formation*, Leominster: Gracewing Fowler Wright; Grand Rapids, Mich.: Eerdmans.

Birenbaum, M. and Dochy, F. J. R. C. (eds) (1995), *Alternatives in Assessment of Achievements: Learning Processes and Prior Knowledge*, London: Kluwer.

Bloom, B. (1956), *Taxonomy of Educational Objectives: Book 1, Cognitive Domain*, London: Longmans.

Boud, D. (ed.) (1988), *Developing Student Autonomy in Learning* (2nd edition), London: Kogan Page.

Boud, D. *et al.* (1995), *Enhancing Learning through Self Assessment*, London: Kogan Page.

Boud, D. and Falchikov, N. (1995), 'What does Research tell us about Self Assessment?', in Boud *et al.* (1995), pp. 155–166.

Brookfield, S. (1986), *Understanding and Facilitating Adult Learning*, Milton Keynes: Open University Press.

Brookfield, S. (1987), *Developing Critical Thinkers*, Milton Keynes: Open University Press.

Butler, S. (1982), 'Assessing the Journal: An Exercise in Self Evaluation', *English Quarterly*, 14, 4, pp. 75–83.

Cohen, L., Manion, L. and Morrison, K. (1996), *A Guide to Teaching Practice*

(4th ed.), London and New York: Routledge.

Cowan, J. (1975), 'The Ability to Appraise One's Own Work', *Higher Education Bulletin*, 3, pp. 127–128.

Cowan, J. (1988), 'Struggling with Student Self-Assessment', in Boud (ed.) (1988), pp. 192–210.

Desforges, C. (1989), *Testing and Assessment*, London: Cassell.

Edwards, R. M. (1989), 'An Experiment in Student Self-Assessment', *British Journal of Educational Technology*, 20, 1, pp. 4–20.

Fowler, J. W. (1981), *Stages of Faith*, San Francisco: Harper and Row.

Gipps, C. (1994), *Beyond Testing*, London: Falmer.

Glaser, R. (1963), 'Instructional Technology and the Measurement of Learning Outcomes: Some Questions', *American Psychologist*, 18, pp. 519–521.

Groome, T. H. (1980), *Christian Religious Education*, San Francisco: Harper and Row.

Habermas, J. (1987), *Knowledge and Human Interests*, trans. J. Shapiro, London: Polity Press. First published in German in 1968 by Suhrkamp Verlag.

Halliday, J. (1995), 'Assessment, Competence and Values', *Curriculum*, 16, 2, pp. 130–138.

Harlen, W. (ed.) (1994), *Enhancing Quality in Assessment*, BERA, London: Chapman.

Heron, J. (1974), *The Concept of the Peer Learning Community*, Guildford: University of Surrey.

Heron, J. (1981), 'Self and Peer Assessment', in T. Boydell and M. Pedler (eds), *Management Self-Development: Concepts and Practices*, Aldershot: Gower, pp. 111–128.

Heron, J. (1988), 'Assessment Revisited', in Boud (ed.) (1988), pp. 77–90.

Hill, Brian V. (1993), 'Is Assessment Compatible with Agape?', *Spectrum*, 25, 1, pp. 39–56.

Hill, Brian V. (1994), 'May we Assess Religious Development at School?', *Spectrum*, 26, 2, pp. 125–139.

Hill, Brian V. (1997), 'Evaluation and Assessment: The Tail that Wags the Dog?', in J. Shortt and T. Cooling (eds), *Agenda for Educational Change*, Leicester: Apollos, pp. 132–147.

Hill, Peter C. and Hood, Ralph W. (eds) (1999), *Measures of Religiosity*, Birmingham Ala.: Religious Education Press.

Holmberg, B. (1989), *Theory and Practice of Distance Education*, London: Routledge.

Honey, P. (1994), 'Styles of Learning', in A. Mumford (ed.), *Handbook of Management Development*, Aldershot: Gower, pp. 101–111.

Hull, J. M. (1984), *Studies in Religion and Education*, Lewes: Falmer.

Israelite, L. (1983), 'Adult Student Self Evaluation', *Performance and Instruction Journal*, 22, 5, pp. 15–16.

Jarvis, P. (1983), *Adult and Continuing Education: Theory and Practice*, London: Croom Helm.

Knight, P. (1995), *Assessment for Learning in Higher Education,* London: Kogan Page.

Knowles, M. S. (1984), *Andragogy in Action*, San Francisco: Jossey-Bass.

Kramp, M. K. and Humphreys, W. L. (1993), 'Narrative, Self Assessment and the Reflective Learner', *College Teaching,* 41, 3, pp. 83–88.

Krathwohl, D. R., Bloom, B. and Masia, B. B. (1964), *Taxonomy of Educational Objectives: Book 2, Affective Domain*, London: Longmans.

Lee, J. M. (1973), *The Flow of Religious Instruction*, Birmingham, Ala.: Religious Education Press.

Lee, J. M. (1996), 'Religious Education and Theology', in J. Astley, L. J. Francis and C. Crowder (eds) (1996), pp. 45–68.

Mager, R. M. (1962), *Preparing Instructional Objectives*, Palo Alto, Calif.: Fearson.

Mumford, A. (1982), 'Learning Styles and Learning Skills', *Journal of Management Development*, 1, 2, pp. 55–65.

Mumford, A. (1986), 'The Influence of Learning Styles on Learning', *Training and Development*, 13, 1, pp. 7–9.

Oskarsson, M. (1980), *Approaches to Self Assessment in Foreign Language Learning*, Oxford: Pergamon.

Popham, W. J. (1994), 'The Instructional Consequences of Criterion-Referenced Clarity', *Educational Measurement: Issues and Practice*, 13, 4, pp. 15–18, 30.

Rogers, C. R. (1983), *Freedom to Learn for the 80s,* Columbus, Ohio: Charles Merrill.

Rowntree, D. (1987), *Assessing Students: How Do We Know Them?*, London: Kogan Page.

Sappington, D. and Wilson, F. R. (1991), 'Towards an Assessment of Spiritual Maturity: A Critique of Measurement Tools', *Christian Education Journal*, 12, 3, pp. 46–48.

Smith, D. L. and Hatton, N. (1993), 'Reflection in Teacher Education: a Study in Progress', *Education Research and Perspectives*, 20, 1, pp. 13–23.

Smith, D. L. and Hatton, N. (1993), 'Reflection in Teacher Education: A Study in Progress', *Education Research and Perspectives*, 20, 1, pp. 13–23.

Taylor, K. and Marienau, C. (1993), 'Self Assessment: A Source for Individual and Organisational Learning', *Contemporary Education*, 64, 3, pp. 166–169.

Wiliam, D. (1996), 'Standards in Examinations: A Matter of Trust?', *The Curriculum Journal*, 7, 3, pp. 293–306.

5

Learning Together: All-Age Learning in the Church

Judith Sadler

INTRODUCTION

In an urban parish, at a church where the congregation was small and predominantly elderly, three young teenagers wanted to be confirmed. Some preparation was called for. The leaders of what would become an ongoing learning group believed that it would be a much more interesting and fruitful experience if its membership was of mixed ages. To this end they invited a boy of eleven years, an older teenager, a woman in her twenties, another in her thirties, and a third in her sixties, to join the teenagers.

The meetings were informal and the methods of study varied; there was always a lot of discussion. The oldest woman admitted to a lack of confidence at the outset: she was shy, but happy to listen. After some months she was asked if she thought the meetings were of particular value because of their inter-generational nature. 'Oh yes,' she replied, without hesitation. 'It's wonderful. These young people ask questions which I have never been able to ask. I have learned a great deal ... I have found that I am able to talk and join in ... and, by their example, I have learned a terrific amount.'

The older teenager, on being asked the same question, was equally enthusiastic. She thought that there was a freedom within the group that was something to do with the mixture of ages. In addition, she felt that having an older person present meant that there would be less likelihood of their forgetting tradition and that past events would be kept alive 'in some way'.

*   *   *

Since the publication of the report *Children In The Way* in 1988, all-age learning has become a significant feature of education in the Church of England.[1] The warm reception given to the report and the endorsement of many of its recommendations have encouraged an increased number of events and learning programmes specifically designed to provide opportunities for people of different ages to learn with and from one another.[2]

Such a positive response is not unique to the Anglican Church. In 1995 the report *Unfinished Business* was produced by the British Council of Churches' Consultative Group on Ministry among Children. This ecumenical publication also promotes all-age learning, exhorting all churches 'to create more appropriate models of faith-sharing amongst people of different ages'.[3] It includes all-age activities in its examples of good practice, and repeatedly makes reference to the importance of children's contributions to the faith journey of the whole church.[4]

The apparent popularity of 'all-age' or 'inter-generational' learning within the church has implications for all concerned with Christian education, as well as for church leaders and theologians. Interest in all-age has been awakened not only among those with a concern for the place of children within Christian faith communities, but also among those who recognise that inter-generational concerns might lead to surprising shifts of power and authority, changing teaching styles, and different ways of operating as a church. I believe that it is therefore of signal importance for *adult* Christian education.

Widening Perspectives

Faith as a term need not be restricted to the religious dimension of life. Although faith is usually regarded as a matter of cognition which has social, moral and affective consequences, James Fowler and his colleagues would argue that such aspects are not simply consequential, but part of the faithing process itself.[5] Faithing encompasses all that a person is, and all the ways that a person responds to the myriad of experiences that touch his or her life. Despite Fowler's repeated claims that these other aspects feature significantly in faithing, he is still criticised for over-emphasising the cognitive dimension of faith.[6] Such criticism has raised the question of additional dimensions which may be regarded as essential components in the structuring of life's experiences. Thus, in addition to the factors identified by Fowler, other commentators have also identified the elements of trust, volition, perception, humour, fear and awe.[7] If the definition of faith is widened in this way, its aspects become more easily recognisable in an even wider variety of people, including children. This can only serve to open up new opportunities and reveal new resources for learning within faith communities.

Barriers to learning may be broken down when all ages are brought together and learning is designed for individuals within a group who are at different stages of development. One of the most useful insights of faith development theory is that people of the *same age* might be at *different stages* (and, of course, that people of different ages might be at the same stage). Educationalists display an unrealistic perception of what is being learned if they assume, for example, that a particular learning programme designed for abstract-thinking adults is appropriate for all adults and inappropriate for all children. Likewise, much is lost when it is assumed that adults cannot learn with and from those younger than themselves.

The Child in Us

Such a realisation may challenge a community even further. To recognise that faith development varies from person to person, despite physical maturation or chronological age, and that such development is multi-faceted, demands that value be given to all. It may also help us to recognise that characteristics of childhood are to be valued, and that not to do so might distort or inhibit their development. In developmental schemes the characteristics of one stage are often said to be taken up and amended in the next. Like the concentric annual rings of the tree trunk, the adult stage encompasses the tighter circles of both the youth and the child 'within'.[8] Having been encouraged to 'grow out of', rather than to develop, such characteristics as directness, vulnerability or desire for knowledge, many adults might now benefit from recapturing the values of such apparently child-like attributes. There are theological implications here for a faith community whose God, it might be argued, is partly characterised by analogous dimensions of character.

THE FAITH COMMUNITY AND ALL-AGE LEARNING

Like any education, Christian education is an intentional process of learning. The Christian faith community holds dear its own 'centres of value', 'images of power' and 'master stories', which constitute the 'content' of faith on Fowler's analysis. Every church community conveys the content of its faith through its worshipping, social and educational activities. The *whole* life of the church, therefore, is significant in relation to what is learned by its members. This *forma-*

tion is crucial to the faith community, whose primary rôle is that of conveying the faith story. Much of this formative educational activity may properly take place in an inter-generational context. But educationalists also look to a dynamic process which involves reflection upon experience, criticism, new insights, new action and thus a *changing* tradition. Christian education is therefore about both formation and *self-criticism*. Can all-age education also play a significant part in enabling proper critical education to take place?

Jeff Astley argues that formative education, without too much emphasis on the critical element, may be all that is required by some who are within the faith community.[9] Certainly the church will and should include those who cannot cope with the application of a critical approach (and perhaps also those who may not *want* to deal with the consequences of such an approach). These may include not only very young children, but also those adults who are still within early faith stages, for whom a safe and reassuring environment in which they feel they belong is essential to their faithing processes. On the other hand, there are those – and this surely includes the majority of adults – for whom a questioning, critical approach is vital as they work out their own relationship with God.

Those who are in the earliest stages of religious development particularly need to be involved in the life of the community. This is, first, because they need to feel secure and, secondly, to prepare them for when they are ready to grapple with the more critical approach that is so essential to a healthy church. But their presence may also remind people who are themselves in the process of struggling with questions, of the sure foundation upon which the community is built. This reassurance relates to the gift that is sometimes referred to as 'simple faith'. This dimension should not be misunderstood. Adults often fear the risk of learning because it is something which (they think) they have long since left behind, and because the very idea of it may evoke insecurity and fear of change.[10] To learn and worship with children can be encouraging and reassuring partly because children are people who usually *do* relish new learning. The children's lack of fear of learning, their openness and their confidence can serve as a reminder to others of the *fundamental safety* of a process that includes the honourable aims of a full – and therefore critical – education, *within the context* of a faith that is itself based upon trust and hope.

The Significance of Alternative Media

The increased variety and richness of learning and faithing that is made possible by harnessing the potential contributions of *all* members of the Christian community is of considerable significance. In particular, effective all-age work involves moving away from too much reliance on texts. The power wielded by the written word in the churches is often seriously under-estimated, particularly by those who benefit from that power. It is difficult for a church that relies almost entirely on the high literacy of the majority of its members to learn from those who are less literate. And church life is *so* wordy. Consider all those books of worship, those educational materials, Synodical documents and doctrine reports! The emphasis upon the written word at the expense of other media may well restrict the ways in which *adults* learn about the work of God in the world. All-age events have the potential of making alternative media available to greater numbers of people. There learning will take place, and beliefs will be expressed effectively, through dance, drama, art, music, clay-modelling, games, and so on. There prayer may take the form of movement, as well as words, and can find expression in light, shape, pictures and even smells. A variety of senses will be involved: the sight that is crucial to the icon-painter and the flower-arranger; the hearing that is so important to the musician; the touch that guides the clay-worker and the dancer. None of these activities requires an ability to read and write, but nor do such activities exclude those who rely more on their literacy skills to understand God and express their beliefs.

The experience of all-age learning and worship quickly reveals that the use of these other media is not to be seen simply as a concession to the less literate. Rather, they provide the church with new ways of expressing what it knows of God. As those who are less literate are encouraged and affirmed in these ways to take their rightful place within the faith community, and to use the variety of opportunities available to them to express their own religious commitment, so the more literate adults can be opened to new ways of knowing and affirming the divine.

The Pragmatic Value of All-Age Learning Programmes

Any new learning should be challenging and stimulating. Increasing age, as well as negative memories of earlier educational experiences, often lead individuals to avoid such challenge and stimulation. As mentioned above, the attractiveness of all-age events and programmes can be exploited as a non-threatening opportunity to introduce learning experiences that can be shared with younger people, who ostensibly need adult co-operation and support. Older participants appear not only to enjoy this supportive rôle, they are also frequently surprised to discover that they have learned something new, some-times from their younger colleagues in the faith.[11]

A further advantage of all-age learning is that it can cater for *families* who wish to spend time together, rather than being dispersed. Likewise in worship: many families prefer to worship together and appreciate all-age services for this reason. All-age also removes some of the pressure on small congregations to provide 'leaders', for lead-ership becomes much more of a shared responsibility when learning is taking place in and from a wider group of people. Small congrega-tions may only have small numbers within particular age groups; to bring these age groups together not only reduces the need to organise several worship and learning groups, it also enhances the sense of community for all.

Political Implications

All-age is a self-perpetuating phenomenon. My experience is that when programmes are effectively implemented many participants find such value in them that they seek more opportunities to learn together. In such contexts the church might even find a new direction. When adults genuinely seek to learn with and from younger, and apparently less experienced, members of the community, they are not only surprised to gain new skills, confidence, attitudes and sources of authority, they also come to recognise the value of the opinions that are held by those who have traditionally been regarded as having views of lesser worth. Such perceived worth-lessness rests in power-lessness, and this has implications for those communities who regard a high sense of self-worth as an essential element within faith. It is with this in mind that all-age events might be regarded as a means of bringing about a shift in power towards previously under-valued groups of people. Such a shift is expressed when children become involved in decision-making, not as a gimmick or token gesture, but as a natural and valued democratic progression.[12] Once children have been given value and authority in learning situations, it may soon become an accepted assumption that they should be referred to within the wider and more long-term life of the community. This is one way in which we can bestow value on young people in terms of their future membership of the church. Those who are the 'Church of Tomorrow' must have their membership of today valued and affirmed in order that they may become effective adults within *their* faith community of the future.

WIDENING THE CIRCLE: THE SYMBOLISM OF ALL-AGE

The impression is often given that authority for doctrine and worship in the church lies in a very particular arena of knowledge and experience, far removed from the experience and meaning-making of the majority of worshippers, not to mention those on the edge or even outside church life. In the Church of England, for example, the locus of such authority is the House of Bishops and the Liturgical and Doctrine Commissions of General Synod. Despite recent changes to their gender balance, such groups remain predominantly male, clerical and/or academic, and of course adult, whereas all churches mainly comprise women and children[13] and naturally are predominately 'lay' in every sense. This is not to say that male academics and clerics are only sensitive to the needs and views of their own or similar groups within the church. However, the message which the church has given in the past by appointing people only from such particular strands of society to these important commissions is clear: male academics and clerics are those best qualified to advise on belief and liturgy.

Many welcome this, claiming that theology is a body of knowledge best articulated and passed down through the generations by recognised guardians of the faith and reflected upon by authorised and accredited thinkers, i.e. the priests and theologians of the church. Yet most would also wish to recognise that revelation is ongoing, manifests itself in the unpredictable, and occurs throughout all creation. All-age contexts can illustrate how God is revealed and reflected upon by a much wider range of people and throughout the whole of creation. Just as adults and children can genuinely learn together about God, so may many others who are not necessarily peers, nor of the same age, gender or educational and social background. The symbolism is clear: the faith is for the whole people of God. And the symbolism can be extended. Just as children can become teachers of adults within the all-age experience, so might the older generations at least *listen to* the wisdom of the young in the rest of church life. (Possibly even in questions of doctrine; and especially, perhaps, on liturgical questions.) Adults are seen as representing power and authority; all-age learning is symbolic of a shift in that power and authority. An appreciation of such a wider perspective on God brings with it a wider recognition of the range of meaning and value within the church. The scope of theology itself may even widen, perhaps becoming as wide and unpredictable as the range of people for whom God, revealed through Jesus, is of ultimate importance.

Of course, the extent to which the symbolism of all-age can be drawn out depends upon who is deemed to be among the marginalised and less powerful, which in turn will depend on the society within which we live, and how conscious we are of its injustices. All Christians have a responsibility to take all people seriously. Wherever faith communities are located, an open, listening, valuing attitude to the beliefs and worship preferences of others is essential. Richer people, whether or not they have known poverty, cannot *fully* identify with the poor; one gender cannot *fully* appreciate how it is to be the other; adults, although all have been children, cannot know *from the inside* the experience of modern childhood; white people cannot *really* know what it is to be black. In a word, those who are not marginalised need to learn from those who are. They may thus discover and appreciate different perspectives on God, the church and worship. The all-age experience is symbolic of this widening of perspective.

A THEOLOGY OF ALL-AGE?

Theology has been described as 'a process of thinking in which each person reflects on their experience of life and how this relates to God'.[14] Margaret Kane suggests that participation in this process has to be available to all people: everyone should be encouraged to work out God's relationship with themselves and the world of their experience. If theology is restricted to a very specific group of people, who work it out on behalf of everyone else in the church, it can easily become stagnant and deformed.[15]

Children, to varying degrees, are marginalised in churches as much as in society as a whole. It has been argued, however, that even quite young children are perfectly capable of doing theology. Whilst *reflective* thinking is not easily regarded as a universal characteristic of childhood, there is no reason to underestimate the theology that is expressed in child-like concrete thinking processes.[16] The thinking of young children is mainly restricted to what they hear and see. They work out their image of God on this basis. For example, one child who was told that God wasn't a 'human bean' decided that he must therefore be a butter bean! But she imagined that this bean was 'big, bright, sparkly and warm'. For a while that was her – very positive – image of God. She had reflected in her concrete terms and thus engaged in some simple theology. Was this wholly without value?

The theology of young children exists in their *experiencing* and *imaging*, and is expressed in their behaviour. Careful observation quickly reveals that a tiny baby expresses in her behaviour degrees of trust and security based on her experience of nourishment, comfort, constancy, warmth and affection. The secure and assured infant can therefore 'teach' a theology of *security and assurance* to those who are aware of what she offers them. Other age groups offer different lessons. Toddlers and infants are fascinated by what goes on around them, they seek to label God and associate God with magical qualities and absolute power. They have many questions to ask about God, but their theology may best be described as one of *novelty, reassurance and confidence*. Among older children there exists more of a need to find out what is 'true' and 'right', to establish patterns and to make sense of what is presented to them. Their theology might be represented as one of *energy, justice and discovery*. Their questions, protests and challenges also form an essential part of their meaning-making, and of their quest to relate their own experiences to the things that are of God. From them we too can learn to question and root out answers from the tradition. In such ways all ages can contribute to our own (adult) theological reflection.

It has been pointed out that children express their theology primarily by way of their behaviour. Adults, with their relatively sophisticated means of articulating what they believe, may be dismissive of this, but it is crucial to any understanding of children's theology to appreciate that their understanding and questioning of God is not restricted in its expression to words alone. Although verbal questioning certainly represents one way in which young children reach out for understanding, such enquiries inevitably themselves spring from the child's predominant mode of discovery *through action*. This may be seen even in simple behaviour involving sensory experience and physical movement in which, though questions may not be voiced, they are often implicit.[17] Are *adults* always so very different? Many adults in many congregations have an implicit, enacted, unarticulated theology, not unlike that of a child. It needs to be taken more seriously.

CONCLUSION

Those adults who have discovered helpful and enriching expressions of belief within an all-age context have learned wider and richer ways of knowing God. 'Maturity' is often inhibited when people are pressured into growing out of, rather than being encouraged in, those child-like characteristics that may be proper to Christian disciples. With this in mind, adults can benefit not only by learning about children's theology, but also by seizing the opportunity to acknowledge – even to re-capture – some of these characteristics of child-like faith within themselves that remain appropriate in the believing adult. Meanwhile the children benefit by having such characteristics affirmed by the adults around them.

All-age has the potential to be radical. The radical nature of this educational approach might be traced back to Jesus using the child as a metaphor for the kingdom of God, when he urges his hearers to 'become like a child'.[18] It requires an enormous shift for most of us to look to those who symbolise the least significant members of society and to see them as authorities for our own discipleship.

If all-age learning does bring about a deeper understanding of the Christian faith and its implications, then the church as a whole faces an uncomfortable journey. Perhaps this explains in part the resistance to the process which, on the one hand, presents exciting opportunities, but on the other, threatens long-standing traditions and expectations of authority and power. It is perhaps worth noting that the reference from Mark 10:13–16, which is often used to give biblical authority to all-age activities, reinforces the notion that all-age must begin with the needs of *all* people, and not exclusively with the needs of children. There is a child, it seems, within everyone – and it is those child-like qualities which all-age would aim to retain or recapture. Such an approach, in which the faith story is lived out in the life of the *whole* community, should enable *all* the members of the church to accept their responsibility to fulfil their own potential, and to play a full part in what is essentially a process of transformation within and for the world. Thus may the church live out its rôle as the body of Christ, co-operating with God in God's creative purpose for all.

NOTES

1   General Synod Board of Education, *Children in the Way*, London: National Society/Church House Publishing, 1988.
2   In the Anglican Diocese of Newcastle, as in many English dioceses, there has been a consistently high response to all-age events and resource meetings. In New Zealand the interest is such that the New Zealand Anglican Prayer Book provides supplementary material relating to all-age worship.
3   Consultative Group on Ministry among Children, *Unfinished Business*, London: CCBI Publications, 1995, p. 22.
4   An increasing quantity of material for use in all-age learning and worship situations is becoming available in church bookshops: e.g. Peter Privett, *Signposts*, London: National Society, 1993; Susan Sayers, *Come and See*, Bury St Edmunds: Kevin Mayhew, 1990; Sharon Swain, *The Sermon Slot*, London: SPCK, 1992; Ruth Tiller, *Keeping the Feast*, Bury St Edmunds: Kevin Mayhew, 1995; Susan Sayers, *Living Stones*, Bury St Edmunds: Kevin Mayhew, 1997; Hamish Bruce

and Diana Murrie, *Worship Through the Christian Year*, London: National Society/Church House Publishing, 1997; Stuart Thomas, *Come to the Feast*, Bury St Edmunds: Kevin Mayhew, 1997.

5 See chapter 6 below.

6 Cf. Sharon Daloz Parks, 'The North American Critique of James Fowler's Theory of Faith Development', in James W. Fowler, Karl Ernst Nipkow and Friedrich Schweitzer (eds), *Stages of Faith and Religious Development*, London: SCM, 1991, p. 106.

7 Parks, *loc. cit.*

8 John H. Westerhoff, III, *Will Our Children Have Faith?*, New York: Seabury, 1976, pp. 90–91.

9 Jeff Astley, *The Philosophy of Christian Religious Education*, Birmingham, Ala.: Religious Education Press; London: SPCK, 1994, p. 87.

10 John Hull, *What Prevents Christian Adults from Learning?*, London: SCM, 1985, p. 37.

11 In a survey carried out by the author, organisers of all-age events identified the following as learning outcomes of such events *for the adults* present: an appreciation of active learning, experiences of new ways of worship, a new awareness of the needs of others, new social skills, increased tolerance, becoming aware of different expressions of belief, developing listening skills, learning story-telling techniques, and an awareness of the effectiveness of different media of Christian communication.

12 A parish known to the author, with a small congregation and an increasing emphasis upon all-age learning and worship, included young people from the age of ten years and upwards in a decision-making process affecting the future life of the whole church community. The author's survey, referred to in the previous note, indicated that 46% of respondents believed that all-age had led to greater involvement in decision-making on the part of all age groups within their church, at least 'to some extent'. In the Diocese of New South Wales, Australia, children have been invited to make a contribution at Synod.

13 Peter Brierley, *Prospects for the Nineties: All England*, London: Marc Europe, 1991, p. 39.

14 Margaret Kane, *What Kind of God?*, London: SCM, 1986, p. 81.

15 *ibid.*, p. 120.

16 John Hull, *God-Talk with Young Children*, Birmingham: CREDAR, 1991, p. 11.

17 Violet Madge, *Children in Search of Meaning*, London: SCM, 1965, p. 19.

18 Cf. Mark 10:15; Hans Ruedi Weber, *Jesus and the Children*, Geneva: World Council of Churches, 1979, pp. 22–29. Weber suggests that the metaphor of the child, while it may refer to child-like characteristics of humility, obedience and dependence, points more to the way the child receives the kingdom: her willingness to receive, indeed to claim, what she thinks is hers. Such is the confidence of a person who knows that God's grace is given freely. (Compare, pp. 47–48 above.)

6

Insights from Faith Development Theory and Research

Jeff Astley

'Faith development' is a controversial phrase which refers to a controversial theory. The term is associated with the work of James Fowler and his associates in the United States, first at Harvard University and later at Emory University, Atlanta. His theory has been developed, adapted, applied, criticised and generally debated now for over two decades.[1]

FAITH IN FOCUS

Faith development theory is controversial for three main reasons. First, it greatly broadens our usual idea of faith. For Fowler, *faith is universal*. He argues that we all 'believe in' – that is trust, relate to, 'find' and 'make' meaning in – something or someone. Faith isn't just for the religious.

> *Faith* has to do with the making, maintenance, and transformation of human meaning. It is a mode of knowing and being. In faith, we shape our lives in relation to more or less comprehensive convictions or assumptions about reality. Faith composes a felt sense of the world as having character, pattern and unity.[2]

'The opposite of faith', Fowler writes, 'is not doubt. Rather, the opposite of faith is nihilism': that is, the inability to describe *anything* in which one believes 'and despair about the possibility of even negative meaning'.[3] Fowler's research is a study of *human faith*, a generic term labelling our believing in and relating to whatever is 'ultimate' for us. It is to be understood as:

the composing or interpreting of an ultimate environment *and* as a way-of-being-in-relation to it. [It] must be seen as a central aspect of a person's life orientation. Faith is a primary motivating power in the journey of the self. It plays a central role in shaping the responses a person will make in and against the force-field of his or her life. Faith, then, is a core element in one's character or personality.[4]

For Fowler, religious faith differs from other forms of faith in having specifically religious objects or contents. In his terminology, these are *religious* 'centres of value' and 'images of power' in which we believe, and *religious* 'master stories' by which we live our lives.[5] But we all have something in which or someone in whom we believe; some object of our 'worth-ship'; some acknowledged influential powers; some life-directing narrative or myth of who we are and should be, and of what 'life is all about'. Conversion is a change in these contents of faith, which comes about as and when we come to focus our faith on different 'gods'.

Secondly, Fowler's theory is contentious in concentrating on *the form, rather than the content of faith*. This seems perverse to many. Most religious, and indeed most non-religious, people are interested in *what* people believe and *what* they believe in. They are concerned, then, with the content of faith. Fowler, on the other hand, has as his focus of research the ways in which we have faith, the *how* of faith. He argues that this form of faith can be viewed under a number of interrelated dimensions. They are listed below, and include such elements as the way we reason, the way we make moral judgements, the way we rely on authorities for our faith, our view of symbols, and the way we hold our experience and beliefs together. These aspects of faith are sometimes described as 'windows into faith'. This is a useful metaphor, for different windows will always give us different, partial views into a building; while some of the contents of the building may remain forever out of sight of observers, even though they peer in through all its windows.

The third main area of controversy is Fowler's claim that *the form of faith develops*. Again, details of this development are to be found below. Drawing on various studies of cognitive development, and broadening them, Fowler argues that the way we hold our faith can pass through up to six stages. At each stage we 'faith' differently. ('Faithing' is perhaps a proper word to coin in this context, for the logic of faith is that of a verb rather than a noun; it is an activity, something we *do*.) As we move from one stage to another we often suffer the trauma of losing a familiar way of being in faith before we can take up a new way of composing meaning and enter into a new balanced relationship ('equilibrium') between our patterns of thinking, relating and valuing, and the world of our experience. This scheme of faith development draws on evidence from several hundred in-depth interviews that Fowler and others have done with children, young people and adults right across the age range.

It should be noted at the outset that some researchers are sceptical both of the empirical support for the theory and of its theological, educational and psychological presuppositions, whereas others are more enthusiastic.[6] Many educators and pastors accept that Fowler's faith stages 'chime in' with the experience they have had of the development of adults, youth and children in their charge. Many others claim to recognise in Fowler's scheme a process through which they themselves have moved. The theory has therefore been applied to pastoral counselling, to work with congregations and families, and to ministry with the mentally handicapped, in addition to educational work with students, young people and adults of all ages.[7]

Before filling in the details of faith development theory, I will offer two examples of ways in which the theory can help to illuminate our understanding of and relationship with other people.

How is it that we, as adults and particularly as parents, so often cannot 'get through' to adolescents: that they seem to be in another world from us? The situation may partly be explained by the fact that they believe in different things, of course. But faith development theory suggests that it may also be because the way they believe is so different from our own. Although most adolescents are able to think perfectly logically and abstractly, many of them have not yet started to 'think for themselves' and to reflect on their own world-views. It is always difficult to converse with people in a certain place if they do not know why they are there, or even *that* they are there. Most adolescents, and indeed many adults, are at Fowler's Faith Stage 3. At this stage they hardly know how or that they are in faith, or where their faith comes from. They operate a form of 'tacit meaning-making' which is blind to itself. It is like the implicit knowledge we have that enables us to recognise other people's faces or to ride a bicycle, while being quite unable to explain how we are doing it. The parent or teacher of adolescents and young adults needs to know that at the present moment many of her charges simply cannot recognise where their values and beliefs come from, or how they have created their world-views. (And at this stage getting such people to concentrate on 'how they are doing the riding' may only result in their falling off their bikes.) Imagine that you are at this stage. It is a period when our ideologies can *only* operate 'not in front of our eyes but from behind our backs', to appropriate a phrase from John Hull.[8] This is what Stage 3 faith is like.

Here is another area where faith development theory can offer some illumination: Christian disagreements. Stephen Sykes has argued that disagreement is endemic in the church. He writes: 'Conflict in Christianity is not accidental or occasional, but intrinsic and chronic ... Diversity ... is the norm for Christianity.'[9] Even a cursory review of church history will provide illustrative data to support this interpretation. Now faith development theory can offer us a useful commentary on at least some forms of this theological or religious disagreement. Its main insight is this. Those who have moved through several faith stages can appreciate the positions they have left, but it is simply not possible for them to imagine what things are like much ahead of their current standpoint. Life, in this respect, *is* like a journey. We know the countryside we have passed through, but we cannot yet recognise what lies ahead. 'It does not yet appear what we shall be.' Thus – as the report *How Faith Grows* puts it – 'some controversial figures in the church may be better able to understand their opponents' positions than those opponents can understand the people *they* oppose'.[10] In particular, those in the early stages of faith development (and I do not refer just to adolescents and young adults here, as we shall see) can often appreciate only one viewpoint; whereas those at later stages have a more open and wider sympathy, accommodating a variety of views. This is surely a mark of what we ordinarily describe as a move to a 'more mature' form of faith. Faith development theory can help us to acknowledge more easily this rather galling situation of one-sided incomprehension, and perhaps to live with it more patiently.

Before considering Fowler's theory in greater detail, we should reflect on one particular question that is often raised about it. Does this account offer a neutral *description* of how people actually develop, or a *prescription* of how they ought to develop? Fowler claims that people could be mystically alive at Stage 1, and spiritual saints from Stage 3. No stage is more 'worthy' than another (certainly not *religiously*-speaking). He argues that the stages are not stages of faithfulness or virtue, and insists that each stage is 'appropriate' for the person who has equilibrated at it. Yet he also writes that later stages in faith development theory involve 'genuine growth toward wider and more accurate response to God, and toward more consistently humane care for other human beings'.[11] Development is a good thing, then, if only for this reason.[12] In particular, the later stages are 'more comprehensive and adequate' than earlier stages:[13] they give a wider perspective on life and on other people, and they are more adequate in meeting the demands and perceptions of the new experiences that people tend to have later in life.

This is especially true of Stage 6, although Fowler admits that this stage, like the endpoints of most developmental theories, expresses *philosophical* – and I think *theological* – commitments and traditions. He describes them as 'grounding values and visions' that 'cannot be ... empirically established as most developed, most true, or most adequate by strictly value-free procedures of inquiry'. That is to say, empirical research of an entirely open-ended form cannot establish 'the normative qualities of the most developed stage', for these derive from 'some faith vision of the excellence to which humans are called and for which we are potentiated'.[14]

But we must constantly remind ourselves that any stage may be regarded as Christian (if it has a Christian content). Further, it is a mistake to attempt to rush people through the stages. Fowler writes:

> Other things being equal, persons should be supported and encouraged to continue to engage the issues of their lives and vocations in such ways that development will be a likely result. Pastoral care will seek to involve them in disciplines and action, in struggles and reflection, that will keep their faith and vocations responsive to the ongoing call of God. But we must remember that developmental stage transition is a complex and often protracted affair. Transitions cannot and should not be rushed. Development takes time. Much of our concern in pastoral care has to do with helping persons extend the operations of a given stage to the full range of their experiences and interactions.[15]

Nevertheless, development progressively provides new structures of understanding and meaning-making that are more able to cope with the complex reality that *adults* experience. There are implications here for adult Christian educators. To quote from *How Faith Grows*:

> It is only when people are 'trapped' in a faith stage that they have partly otherwise 'outgrown' (for example in their way of thinking), or when they have precociously 'advanced' beyond their actual psychological and social maturity, that the pastor or educator should step in to help them work on those aspects of their faithing that are out of step with the rest of their meaning-making.[16] Faith, says Fowler, is like a shawl (of meaning) that we knit and wrap around ourselves. It is not the job of the pastor or educator to slash at this with a knife or rip it from a person's shoulders. But sometimes the shawl starts to unravel of its own accord. And then we should step in to help: not by darning up the loose ends, but by rolling up the wool, standing by the wearer in his naked-ness, and then encouraging him to knit a new shawl for himself.
>
> On the other hand we should not insulate people from reality (as they begin to perceive it anew), or try to keep people at a faith stage which psychologically they are outgrowing ... There is always the danger that

a person will 'over defend existing faith structures by screening out and "not knowing" dissonant data'.[17] It is new experience that often leads to faith stage change, as and when the existing structures can no longer accommodate it. This causes a situation of conflict in which a person's faith is thrown off balance. Its form needs to change to restore some sort of equilibrium and with it a sense of 'coping'.[18]

Faith Aspects

As has already been indicated, the target of Fowler's work is the form of faith or *faith-as-a-process*. (However, Fowler does not discount the importance of the content of a person's faith, and the inevitable inter-action between form and content.) In analysing the form of faith, Fowler discerns several aspects or elements within it. These aspects are:

- our reasoning (the way we think),
- our perspective-taking (our ability to adopt another's perspective),
- our moral judging (the way we make judgements about moral situations),
- our social awareness (where and how we set the limits to our 'community of faith'),
- our relation to authority (where and how we find the authorities on which we rely),
- our forming of a world-view (our way of 'holding it all together'), and
- our relation to symbols (our understanding of, and response to, symbols).

Fowler analyses all his faith stages in terms of these seven aspects. At each developmental stage a person's faith will exemplify a particular form of reasoning, of perspective-taking, of moral decision-making, etc. Fowler writes that 'to be "in" a given stage of faith means to have a characteristic way of finding and giving meaning to everyday life'. It is to have a world-view, 'with a particular "take" on things'.[19] The transition from one faith stage to another is marked by a change in one or more of these aspects of faith, as they mutate to the form that is more characteristic of a later stage. It is only when all the other faith aspects have changed in a similar way that the person can be said to have moved fully to the next stage.

The aspects of faith analysed by Fowler largely comprise *cognitive* skills and competencies, and are thus related to thinking, knowing and understanding. But a number also focus on relationships and the nature of the self. These latter aspects are more *affective* (related to feeling) than the others. Fowler recognises that the human process that he sometimes calls 'faith-knowing' has its affective side too. Faith for Fowler is basically a holistic concept involving the whole person – feeling, valuation and volition included. Although the cognitive dimension usually dominates his account of faith, Fowler is interested in the development of this whole complex of 'structures or patterns of thinking, valuing, committing and believing' that makes up a person's faithing.[20] He thus often writes of faith's 'logic of conviction' as something that is broader than the 'logic of rational certainty' of mere cognition.

Each of these aspects of faith can change. One of the most significant of these changes is the change in our reasoning processes, our 'form of logic'. As we mature intellectually we become more capable of – or at least more willing to engage in – abstract thought. Our thinking is then less tied to concrete, particular experiences. As we continue to develop we may move into Faith Stage 4 where our reasoning powers are more fully released, and we really start to 'think for ourselves'. Adult Christian education can now take off. But at this stage we are often very dogmatic and defensive in our employment of our new, autonomous thinking, and that can pose new problems for Christian reflection and communication. Later we may change further, so that we become more willing to acknowledge tensions and paradoxes in our world-view, and more open to the outlooks and convictions of others. All these cognitive shifts have knock-on effects on our moral thinking and our ability to adopt the perspectives of other people, and on other, more affective, aspects of our meaning-making.

FAITH STAGES

From the many interviews they have carried out, Fowler and his associates claim to have discovered six stages or styles of faith through which people may develop. I say 'may', because although some might argue that the pattern of progress is the same for everyone, everywhere (Fowler does not go so far as to claim this himself), many of us do not get very far in our faith development. And hardly anyone is at Stage 6! (Fowler quips that it is puzzling that this is the stage his lecture audiences are *really* interested in, despite the fact that so few experience it. He knows, of course, that we are bound to be fascinated by a stage that is the extrapolated 'end point' towards which our own development appears to be moving.)

As we have already noted, for Fowler conversion is a change in the contents of faith. It is a matter of believing in different things.[21] Others, however, have identified the transition from one stage to another as itself a sort of conversion. We might think of this as a conversion in the form of faith, a 'structural change' that is a type of identity-formation in which someone discovers who she really is. This sort of conversion unifies and integrates the self, particularly in adolescence and middle-age. V. Bailey Gillespie has called it 'religious-identity-conversion'.[22] When form-change and content-change go together (and Fowler recognises that either may precipitate the other[23]), we may indeed have 'a re-orientation of a person's entire life'.[24]

In each stage there is a degree of stability in 'the ways one holds, understands, and takes responsibility for living one's faith'.[25] But the stages alternate with the periods of transition described earlier, which are in many ways of equal significance to the faith stages themselves. These transitions may occur when the equilibrium of a given stage is upset by personal crises or novel experiences, disclosures and challenges that threaten the limits of the person's existing faith patterns and structuring of experience. Faith development often results from such situations. But internal developmental forces, by transforming one aspect of faith so that it 'runs ahead' of other aspects, also contribute to a loss of stage stability, with the result that our faithing becomes more shaky and insecure.

The faith stages[26] are complex integrated structures of understanding, interpreting, valuing and relating. They are thought of as (i) *invariant* and (ii) *hierarchical*. These terms mean that (i) the sequence of stages always occur in a fixed order and no one 'misses out' a stage,[27] and that (ii) each stage builds on it predecessors, in the sense of incorporating the capacities that developed during earlier stages. Cognitive stage development theory, particularly the work of Piaget, has been much criticised, especially for underestimating the reasoning powers of young children and the influence of environmental pressures (for instance through education).[28] In my view, however, the broad pattern of Fowler's schema can survive most of these criticisms, particularly in his account of the stages of adult faith.

In the section that follows I have used the titles for the faith stages that we adopted in *How Faith Grows*. Fowler's own, sometimes rather jaw-breaking, terminology is printed in square brackets.[29] Although our concern in this book is mainly with adults, it is important to rehearse the whole sequence of stages that lead to, and in a developmental sense may be said to 'make up', adult faith.

Stage 0: Nursed Faith or Foundation Faith [Primal Faith]

Age: *0–4 approximately*

This is not so much a stage as a 'pre-stage', which is not really open to empirical investigation. The foundations for faith are here laid down in the early experiences of being picked up and nursed, when trust is first formed. This nursing 'is a real and vital part of any sort of nurture that we might dare to call "Christian"... We are loved into knowing and feeling, as we are loved into being.'[30]

Stage 1: Chaotic Faith or Unordered Faith or Impressionistic Faith [Intuitive-Projective Faith]

Age: *3/4–7/8 approximately*

At this stage the child's relatively uninhibited imagination yields a chaos of powerful images. As thinking is intuitive and episodic, reality is perceived as a scrap-book of impressions as yet not much ordered logically. It is another feature of this stage that symbols are viewed magically, and are treated as being what they represent. The powerful symbols of Christian experience, tradition and liturgy can contribute deep and lasting images in this stage of faith. Hence it may be that young children who are excluded from experiencing ritual and sacrament alongside adult Christians, on the grounds that 'they don't yet understand', are being cut off from a vital form of nourishment. Dependable, structured parenting continues to be crucial at this stage.

Stage 2: Ordering Faith [Mythic-Literal Faith]

Age: *6/7–11/12 approximately, and some adults*

At this stage the individual's power to think, to unify experience and to trace patterns of cause and effect enables her to order her experience. Story-telling is important at this stage, including telling the story of the Christian community to which the child or adult belongs. 'True stories' are now distinguished from others; but we are always 'in' the story rather than 'outside' it, and have no viewpoint from which to compare and criticise stories. People at this stage are very much 'belongers'. (We may recall how junior school aged children are so keen to belong to some club or group; and how their self-image is to a large extent constituted by such belonging.) By this stage individuals have achieved a measure of simple, concrete perspective-taking, overcoming the egocentricity of the smaller child.

Stage 3: Conforming Faith [Synthetic-Conventional Faith]

Age: *11/12–17/18 approximately, and many adults*
(It is worth noting that, according to Fowler's research, over a quarter of adults over the age of thirty are at this faith stage.) The ability to think abstractly has fully developed by now, and there is a new capacity for (mutual, interpersonal) perspective-taking, as the adolescent or adult begins to see herself as others see her. Interpersonal relationships are now very significant. What her peers think and say is regarded as particularly important. But the same is true of other 'significant others', including parents, teachers – and sometimes church leaders. However rebellious we may view ourselves to be, at this stage we are actually little (or, if adult, big) conformists. 'It is a time of going with a particular faith-current, or faith-crowd.'[31] The ability to reason in a new and more powerful way, which is a significant feature of the stage, provides Christian educators with exciting opportunities for more abstract teaching and discussion. The scope of this remains limited, however, because the circle of people to whom we relate still does so much to provide our meaning-making, and we are largely unaware of that process. Those who are at this stage are not yet able adequately to reflect on their beliefs and values, or the way in which these are held. Thus when our views are challenged we may respond very defensively, without really knowing why.

Stage 4: Choosing Faith or Either/Or Faith [Individuative-Reflective Faith]

Age: *from approximately 17/18 onwards, or for others from their 30s or 40s onwards (but note that a substantial proportion of the adult population never reach this stage)*
The transition to Stage 4 can be long and traumatic, taking many years of struggle. Christian educators need to be particularly sensitive here, allowing people space to grow out of Stage 3 'faithing' into this new way of meaning-making. At Stage 4 I am able to take a 'third person' perspective from which to evaluate my own beliefs and relationships, as I distance myself from my previous value-system. Now 'I can no longer tolerate having my faith at second-hand. I must know who I am for myself, when I am not being defined by my relationships with other people.'[32] Beliefs and values which previously were rather unexamined can now be deliberately adopted. For the first time we explicitly and consciously take charge of, and accept responsibility for, our commitments, evaluations and world-view. At this stage faith can become one's own.

The 'certainties' of the individual who is at Faith Stage 4 arise from and contribute to his or her new-found autonomy and maturity. Most Christian educators would applaud such changes, as the beginning of a truly 'adult faith'. But there are also dangers here, including the danger of 'an arid over-intellectualism, ... a conceited autonomy',[33] and an unrealistic sense of independence. There is also a tendency in Stage 4 to caricature the faith of others in order to justify one's own truth, and an over-simplifying 'either/or' determination to create a *tidy* faith. This may result in our collapsing the inevitable paradoxes and tensions within our belief-system.

Stage 5: Balanced Faith or Inclusive Faith or Both/And Faith [Conjunctive Faith]

Age: *rare before the age of 30*
Many adults are content with their Stage 4 faithing, but others eventually find that their compulsion to resolve these tensions and to strive for clarification is becoming a psychological burden. Such people may be moving towards a fifth stage of faith which is characterised by a much greater openness to, and mutuality with, other world-views and perspectives. This faith stage is a marked development from the more rigid concerns for definition and conceptual clarity that are so characteristic of Stage 4.

Stage 5 faith is thus a more balanced and inclusive style of faith. It may be regarded as a *reworking* of Stage 4's unity, tidiness and coherence, and shows a more porous, 'dialectical' or 'dialogical' way of knowing that keeps in tension the paradoxes and polarities of faith, allowing us to live with ambiguity in our meaning-system. Those at Stage 5 are truly – but discriminatingly – *open* to other people and their viewpoints; they recognise that truth is too complex and many-sided for it to be adequately delineated from any one perspective. 'The person at Stage 5 is willing to engage the other and to be changed by the other in a way that was not possible from the posture of Stage 4.'[34] Such people also recognise that reason needs to be supplemented by other ways of knowing reality (especially intuition), and that our instruments of coherence and clarity are just too blunt to work the raw materials of faith adequately. The capacity for self-criticism, self-questioning and self-doubt develops more strongly as people move into Stage 5. Interestingly, Fowler claims that the individual's transition between Stage 4 and Stage 5 recapitulates the development in the history of ideas from the ideals of Enlightenment rationality, espoused in the eighteenth-century 'Age of Reason', to the less tidy and more plural multi-perspectival post-Enlightenment modes of consciousness that characterise today's 'postmodernity'.[35]

At this stage, then, the unity and coherence of our Stage 4 faith is beginning to fade. The new stage that may emerge from it can result from our coping with failure and/or our living with the consequences of earlier decisions. It is often characterised by a new humility and a fuller recognition of our inevitable *inter*dependence.

Stage 6: Selfless Faith [Universalizing Faith]

Age: *usually only in later life; a very rare stage (and something of a theoretical extrapolation from Stage 5)*
This way of being in faith is essentially a relinquishing and transcending of the self. 'Stage 6 people ... go out to transform [the] world. And they often die in the attempt.'[36]

GROWING UP IN FAITH

So James Fowler's researches into human 'faith' or 'meaning-making' claim to show that individuals develop over time, through a sequence of stages, in the ways in which they understand, value and interpret that which they take to be ultimate, whether that be religious or not. In this section I want to concentrate on some rather more familiar adult and near-adult *life stages*, and to pick up some of the claims that Fowler's faith development theory makes about them.

Adolescence

Faith development research suggests that the majority of teenagers are at Stage 3 on Fowler's scheme. We should note, however, that a proportion (over 12%) are still in transition from Stage 2, and nearly 4% are still actually *at* Stage 2. Stage 3 is marked both by the ability to think abstractly and by a new capacity for mutual, interpersonal perspective-taking. That sounds good. But Fowler's stage of 'Synthetic-Conventional Faith' is labelled above as the stage of *Conforming Faith*. Sharon Parks describes the adolescent as living 'under the tyranny of the "they"', and writes of the task of late adolescence as the development of a self-identity and self-aware responsibility that has the power to counter this powerful psychological subjugation.[37]

Those who are at this stage are sometimes said to be 'embedded' in their faith outlook, in the sense that they are not yet able to reflect on their own beliefs and values. Thus, although the circle of people we relate to at this stage does so much to provide our meaning-making, we are largely unaware of that process. To quote Fowler:

> While beliefs and values are deeply felt, they typically are tacitly held – the person 'dwells' in them and the meaning world they mediate. But there has not been occasion to reflectively step outside them to examine them explicitly or systematically. At Stage 3 a person has an 'ideology', a more or less consistent clustering of values and beliefs, but he/she has not objectified it for examination, and in a sense is unaware of having it.[38]

It is this feature that partly explains the phenomenon that we noted earlier in this chapter: the difficulty of reasoning with young people about the views they have and the influences that others hold over them. And the same applies to those *adults* who remain in Stage 3.

Young Adulthood

We have noted that many adults may be described as being at Stage 3 throughout their lives. Others, however, do change. By the time that they have reached the 21 to 30 age-group, less than 18% are still at Stage 3, with the great majority in transition to or stabilising at Stage 4. This transition to Faith Stage 4, which itself may take several years, is often entered into in late adolescence. But for many it will come later, as a mid-life transition. It is a change that involves my distancing myself from the others who have been so significant to me before, so as to discover who I am and what I really believe *for myself*. Stage 4 (Fowler's stage of 'Individuative-Reflective Faith'; in our terminology, *Choosing Faith*) is therefore marked by a double development:

> The self, previously sustained in its identity and faith compositions by an interpersonal circle of significant others, now claims an identity no longer defined by the composite of one's rôles or meanings to others. To sustain that new identity it composes a meaning frame conscious of its own boundaries and inner-connections, and aware of its self as a 'world-view'. [39]

For many, this transition to Stage 4 will seem to be a loss of faith, but it is in fact – like all faith stage transitions – only *a loss of one way of being in faith*, in order to take on a very different way. Nevertheless, the development of a more autonomous, self-reflective faith can be the most traumatic of the transitions. Significantly, Parks distinguishes two distinct stages within Fowler's Stage 4. The first of these is a (post-adolescent) young adult stage of wary and tentative 'probing commitment' that develops before the more fully 'adult' faith stage is reached.[40]

The move from Stage 3 to Stage 4 often involves a literal, or at least a psychological, 'leaving home', as I withdraw to a vantage-point from which I feel that I can make my own decisions in a way appropriate to my new-found sense of autonomy. I can only move to Stage 4 by stepping out of my faith current and away from the faith crowd 'to choose a world-view for myself'. I may later return, as it were, to the bosom of my faith-family or faith-church; but even when I do I shall never be the same again. That would be like trying to recapture a first innocence. What I believe is now at last what *I* believe. I have after all, *chosen* to be here – and that makes all the difference.

Mature Adulthood

As we have seen, some adults will later change even further as they enter the mid-life Stage 5 (Fowler's 'Conjunctive Faith'; our *Both/And Faith*). Only in the 30–40 age group do we find a substantial proportion in this faith stage (although people at Stage 5 make up only about 15% of the whole age group of interviewees over 30). Recall that Stage 5 subjects are more 'open' and responsive to other people and their world-views than they were at Stage 4. They are also less concerned with doctrinal orthodoxy, and they are not continually demythologising – or translating into doctrinal beliefs – the symbol systems of religion.

Experience has often given development a helping hand here, and Fowler describes those who are at this stage as knowing 'the sacrament of defeat and the reality of irrevocable commitments and acts'.[41] Thinking more generally about the dynamics of life and faith around the age of thirty, Henry Simmons writes of this as 'a time of crisis and growth'. He adds the challenge: 'We must stop keeping the experience of adulthood a secret.'[42] The person at Fowler's Stage 5, we noted, is more realistic and humble in her cognitions and affections than she was before, having developed a perspective that recognises meaning and truth as many-faceted and likely to be found in unexpected places.

Readers should note how difficult it can be for a Stage 5 person to flourish within the fellowship of the church. Christian educators and pastors will recognise that adults at this stage have a viewpoint that is more complex and inclusive than hitherto. Church leaders should also acknowledge this: 'Too often the Church fears Stage 5 learners because they are difficult to control, pigeon-hole or understand.'[43] In those congregations or denominations where people's main concerns are for conceptual clarity and the resolution of all intellectual and moral tensions (as at Stage 4), or for obedience to clerical authority-figures from which lay people are expected to receive their own world-view (as at Stage 3), the individual who is at Stage 5 is a real threat. Much of the history of Christianity, including perhaps its earliest years, may be interpreting in part as a series of conflicts between Stage 5 (and indeed Stage 6) perspectives, overagainst those Christians who possessed rather more circumscribed ways of being in faith.

FAITH, SEX AND MATURITY

Women have often been rather suspicious of Fowler's faith development scheme. One main reason has been that Fowler's Faith Stage 4, with its stress on 'autonomy' and 'distancing' oneself from other viewpoints, often sounds like a peculiarly masculine way of being in faith. Karen DeNicola has complained that 'persons who fail to blend reason and feeling – specifically, persons who rely solely on rational certainty – can too easily be scored at Stage 4, while persons who emphasize feeling can too easily be scored at Stage 3'.[44] This is not in fact, she thinks, a gender bias, but more of a bias towards thinking and intellect, with a consequent underplaying of the emotions. Such a scoring bias would explain why more men than women 'advance' (and advance earlier) to Stage 4.[45]

Fowler himself acknowledges the force of such criticisms. In his Foreword to *Christian Perspectives on Faith Development*, he draws on the influential publication *Women's Ways of Knowing*:[46]

> Though Belenky and her co-authors do not claim to have offered a stage theory of women's development, the styles of knowing they describe parallel in some significant ways the development stages of William Perry, Lawrence Kohlberg, and our own. Roughly corresponding to our synthetic-conventional stage, they describe a style of knowing they call 'subjective' knowing. Approximating our individuative-reflective stage they describe a style of 'procedural' knowing. Key for our interests is their distinction between two different ways of developing procedural knowing. On the one hand, there is the 'separate' variant, the development of reflective and critical awareness and testing of one's knowing through objectifying the known and distancing oneself from emotional involvement with. This style is resonant with the Cartesian subject-object distinction and with Enlightenment ideals of objective rationality.

On the other hand, Belenky and her co-authors identify a movement into procedural knowing which proceeds by a style they call 'connected' knowing. This is a knowing 'in rapport', a knowing that proceeds toward self-awareness and critical reflection through and by way of participation, relation, and the disciplining of subjectivity through dialogue and reflection. My suggestion is that in describing the movement from the synthetic-conventional to the individuative-reflective stage we [i.e. faith development researchers] have highlighted the 'separate' style of critical reflection and differentiation and have muted the 'connected' pattern. In not fully developing the latter, I believe we have underscored some of our female subjects, and likely, overscored some of our male subjects as well.[47]

It should be emphasised again that we are dealing here not so much with gender differences as with different developmental stages and faith styles that we may perhaps label *'feminine' (connected knowing)* and *'masculine' (separate knowing)*, as long as we recognise that many men may take the 'feminine' route and vice-versa (i.e. 'feminine' is not the same as 'female').[48] The two ways of knowing are different routes into a full Stage 4 perspective which can incorporate and use both. The argument here is *not* that Stage 4 is mainly for men or solely for cool, objective, 'separate' intellectuals, and is therefore not available to those whose knowing and faithing remains more subjective, 'connected' and relationship-oriented (as they are in many females). Rather, two different pathways exist that lead to the same stage of self-conscious, reflective (Stage 4) faith.

This account of the matter is close to the description Gabriel Moran gives of a truly Christian and human notion of 'maturity' and 'adulthood'. This is Moran's image of a synthesising of opposites, which involves the integration of very different elements.[49] Children and adolescents can be one-sided, but adult maturity demands balance and wholeness, and a holding together of what might otherwise fly apart. Moran recognises three areas that demand such integration: the rational and the non-rational, dependence and independence, and life and death.

There is little doubt that Fowler's Stage 5 fits such a more balanced and integrated (and integrating) notion of adulthood, at least in some respects.[50] Certainly it is a stage of faithing at which the more intuitive and non-verbal functions of the self (controlled in many people by the right lobe of the brain) are combined again with the (left lobe) rational, verbal and intellectual activities. Certainly too, it is the stage for older adults who have learned the 'wisdom of time' (Sam Keen), have begun to face the inevitability of their own death, and have come fully to acknowledge the relatively fleeting and contingent nature of human relationships, hopes and successes. Stage 5 would also appear to be a time of recognition of the *inter*dependence of our relationships, as opposed to the sometimes dangerously *in*dependent cognition of Stage 4, and the (inevitably) more 'immature' dependence of the earlier stages. Stage 5 offers itself, therefore, as a candidate for recognition as a more authentically human – and Christian – notion of adulthood, and therefore of (this particular view of) maturity. On such an analysis, it is of considerable significance for the adult Christian educator.

NOTES

[1]   For an overview of faith development theory and its critics, see Jeff Astley *et al.*, *How Faith Grows: Faith Development and Christian Education*, London: National Society and Church House Publishing, 1991, from which parts of this chapter are drawn, with permission.

[2]   James W. Fowler, 'Faith and the Structuring of Meaning', in J. W. Fowler and A. Vergote (eds), *Toward Moral and Religious Maturity*, Morristown, N.J.: Silver Burdett, 1980, p. 53.

[3]   James W. Fowler, *Stages of Faith: The Psychology of Human Development and the Quest for Meaning*, San Francisco: Harper & Row, 1981 (republished 1995), p. 31. Where the concept is thus construed as 'a system of convictions which defines for us what is of value, good, and real', faith 'has been described as the same as a meaning-perspective'. Jack L. Seymour, Margaret Ann Crain and Joseph V. Crockett, *Educating Christians: The Intersection of Meaning, Learning and Vocation*, Nashville, Tenn.: Abingdon, 1993, p. 49.

[4]   James Fowler and Sam Keen, *Life Maps: Conversations on the Journey of Faith*, ed. Jerome Berryman, Minneapolis, Minn.: Winston Press, 1978, p. 25.

[5]   Fowler, *Stages of Faith*, pp. 276–277.

[6]   For a taste of the debate, see Kenneth Stokes (ed.), *Faith Development in the Adult Life Cycle*, Chicago: W. H. Sadlier, 1982; Craig Dykstra and Sharon Parks (eds), *Faith Development and Fowler*, Birmingham, Ala.: Religious Education Press, 1986; Jeff Astley *et al.*, *How Faith Grows*, ch. 3; John Snarey, 'Faith Development, Moral Development and Nontheistic Judaism: A Construct Validity Study', in W. M. Kurtines and J. L. Gewirtz (eds), *Handbook of Moral Behavior and Development, Vol. 2: Research*, Hillsdale, N.J.: Erlbaum, 1991, pp. 279–305; Jeff Astley and Leslie J. Francis (eds), *Christian Perspectives on Faith Development: A Reader*, Leominster: Gracewing Fowler Wright; Grand Rapids, Mich.: Eerdmans, 1992; James W. Fowler, Karl Ernst Nipkow and Friedrich Schweitzer (eds), *Stages of Faith and Religious Development: Implications for Church, Education and Society*, London: SCM, 1992; Nicola M. Slee, 'Further on from Fowler: Post-Fowler Faith Development Research', in Leslie J. Francis, William K. Kay and William S. Campbell (eds), *Research in Religious Education*, Leominster: Gracewing Fowler Wright; Macon, Georgia: Smyth and Helwys, 1996, pp. 88–91.

[7]   See James W. Fowler, *Becoming Adult, Becoming Christian*, San Francisco: Harper & Row, 1984; Sharon Parks, *The Critical Years: The Young Adult Search for a Faith to Live By*, San Francisco: Harper & Row, 1986; James W. Fowler,

Faith Development and Pastoral Care, Philadelphia: Fortress, 1987; Astley and Francis (eds), *Christian Perspectives on Faith Development*, sections 7 and 8.

[8] John M. Hull, *What Prevents Christian Adults from Learning?*, London: SCM, 1985, p. 67.

[9] Stephen W. Sykes, *The Identity of Christianity*, London: SPCK, 1984, p. 52.

[10] Astley *et al.*, *How Faith Grows*, p. 68–69.

[11] Fowler, 'Faith and the Structuring of Meaning', pp. 82–83.

[12] See Fowler, *Faith Development and Pastoral Care*, pp. 80–81.

[13] Fowler, *Stages of Faith*, p. 101.

[14] Fowler, 'The Vocation of Faith Development Theory', in Fowler, Nipkow and Schweitzer (eds), *Stages of Faith and Religious Development*, pp. 35–36.

[15] Fowler, *Faith Development and Pastoral Care*, pp. 80–81.

[16] Fowler, *Stages of Faith*, p. 114. See also Bradley Courtenay, 'Personhood – Personal and Faith Development', in Peter Jarvis and Nicholas Walters (eds), *Adult Education and Theological Interpretations*, Malabar, Fla.: Krieger, 1993, pp. 164–167.

[17] Fowler, 'Faith and the Structuring of Meaning', p. 67. Cf. Hull, *op. cit.*, ch. 3.

[18] *How Faith Grows*, pp. 40–41.

[19] James W. Fowler, *Faithful Change: The Personal and Public Challenges of Postmodern Life*, Nashville, Tenn.: Abingdon, 1996, p. 68.

[20] James W. Fowler, 'Faith Development Theory and the Aims of Religious Socialization', in Gloria Durka and Joanmarie Smith (eds), *Emerging Issues in Religious Education*, New York: Paulist Press, 1976, p. 200.

[21] Fowler, *Stages of Faith*, p. 281; *Becoming Adult, Becoming Christian*, p. 95.

[22] V. B. Gillespie, *Religious Conversion and Personal Identity*, Birmingham, Ala.: Religious Education Press, 1979, p. 126; cf. Walter Conn, *Christian Conversion: A Developmental Interpretation of Autonomy and Surrender*, New York: Paulist Press, 1986, pp. 31, 208–210.

[23] See Fowler, *Stages of Faith*, pp. 285–286.

[24] *How Faith Grows*, p. 17.

[25] Fowler, *Faithful Change*, p. 68.

[26] The faith stages are modelled on and develop the cognitive stages argued for by Jean Piaget and Lawrence Kohlberg (his 'stages of moral judgement').

[27] It is usually assumed that there is no regression back down the stages either, except presumably in cases of senility or as a result of gross psychological trauma.

[28] See Margaret Donaldson, *Children's Minds*, London, HarperCollins, 1978; Jeff Astley and William K. Kay, 'Piaget and Fowler', in William K. Kay and Leslie J. Francis (eds), *Religion in Education: 2*, Leominster: Gracewing, 1998, pp. 162–165. The individualistic orientation of Piaget's work is criticised by 'social constructivist' theories that place more emphasis on the interaction of the individual with his/her social context and the rôle of language in development (see L. S. Vygotsky, *Thought and Language*, Cambridge, Mass.: MIT Press; V. John-Steiner and H. Mahn, 'Sociocultural Approaches to Learning and Development: A Vygotskyan Framework', *Educational Psychologist*, 31, 1996, pp. 191–206).

[29] This summary is largely drawn from my introductory essay in Astley and Francis (eds), *Christian Perspectives on Faith Development*, pp. xx-xxii, and from material in *How Faith Grows*, with permission.

[30] *How Faith Grows*, p. 19.

[31] *How Faith Grows*, p. 25.

[32] *How Faith Grows*, p. 27.

[33] *How Faith Grows*, p. 28.

[34] Romney M. Moseley, David Jarvis and James W. Fowler, *Manual for Faith Development Research*, Atlanta, Georgia: Center for Faith Development, 1986 edition, p. 155; 1993 edition, p. 60.

[35] James W. Fowler, 'The Enlightenment and Faith Development Theory', in Astley and Francis (eds), *Christian Perspectives on Faith Development*, pp. 15–28; Fowler, *Faithful Change*, pp. 172–176. Compare Walter James and Brian Russell, 'How has Post-Modernism Changed Education?', in *Tomorrow is Another Country: Post-Modernism and Christian Education*, London: General Synod Board of Education, 1996, pp. 26–33.

[36] *How Faith Grows*, p. 34.

[37] Parks, *The Critical Years*, p. 76; cf. Jeff Astley and Nick Wills, 'Adolescent "Faith" and its Development', *Youth and Policy: The Journal of Critical Analysis*, 65, 1999, pp. 60–71.

[38] James W. Fowler, 'Perspectives on the Family from the Standpoint of Faith Development Theory', in Astley and Francis (eds), *Christian Perspectives on Faith Development*, p. 334.

[39] Fowler, 'Perspectives on the Family . . .', p. 335.

[40] Parks, *The Critical Years*, ch. 5.

[41] Fowler, 'Faith and the Structuring of Meaning', p. 73.

[42] Henry C. Simmons, 'Human Development: Some Conditions for Adult Faith at Age Thirty', reprinted in John L. Elias (ed.), *Religious Education in Adulthood*, New Haven, Conn.: Religious Education Association, 1992, p. 18.

[43] *How Faith Grows*, p. 32.

[44] Karen Boyd DeNicola, 'Formal Operation Thinking, Stage 4, and Practical Knowing', unpublished paper, 1992, p. 1. This is reprinted as an appendix to the second edition of the *Manual for Faith Development Research*, 1993.

[45] See also Slee, 'Further on from Fowler: Post-Fowler Faith Development Research'.

[46] Mary Field Belenky, Blythe McVicker Clinchy, Nancy Rule Goldberger and Jill Mattuck Tarule, *Women's Ways of Knowing: The Development of Self, Voice and Mind,* New York: Basic Books, 1986, ch. 6.

[47] James W. Fowler, 'Foreword', in Astley and Francis (eds), *Christian Perspectives on Faith Development*, p. xiii. Fowler actually uses the adjectives 'separative' and 'connective'.

[48] See Leslie J. Francis and Carolyn Wilcox, 'Religion and Gender Orientation', *Personality and Individual Differences*, 20, 1996, pp. 119–121; Leslie J. Francis, 'The Psychology of Gender Differences in Religion: A Review of Empirical Research', *Religion*, 27, 1997, pp. 81–96; Belenky *et al.* write that 'separate and connected knowing are not gender specific. The two modes may be gender-related: It is possible that more women than men tip toward connected knowing and more men than women toward separate knowing.' Belenky *et al.*, *Women's Ways of Knowing*, pp. 102–103.

[49] Gabriel Moran, *Education toward Adulthood*, New York: Paulist Press, 1979, pp. 28–34. Cf. Jeff Astley, 'Growing into Christ: The Psychology and Politics of Christian Maturity', in Jeff Astley and David Day (eds), *The Contours of Christian Education*, Great Wakering: McCrimmons, 1992, pp. 307–322.

[50] See Fowler, *Becoming Adult, Becoming Christian*, p. 65.

7

Adult Learning and the Churches

Mark D. J. Savage

SPURS AND BARRIERS TO LEARNING IN THE CHURCH

There was an indignant outcry, mostly from some of the older members of the congregation. 'What's he thinking of, suggesting that we need educating? We don't need educating!'

All I wanted to say is that Lent is too busy a time to start up adult education groups. I wished to put down a marker for other adult educational opportunities, as and when time allowed, later in the year. But my rather unexceptional little article in the parish magazine clearly touched a raw nerve. I was forced to think again, or at least to realise that I should steer well clear of the word 'education'. Perhaps it was associated with too many memories of a school life that was for many stultifying and oppressive, rather than exciting and liberating. Perhaps it was simply not understood.

But it is not just the word 'education' that is difficult. The very idea of learning in the context of the church can be threatening and subversive. It is possible to give different names to the process of adult learning, but the deeper issue remains that adults learn best when they perceive the need to do so. Situations in which the need to learn is recognised are not always the situations that we, as educators, choose. No one would welcome, for example, the need to cope with the implications, practical and emotional, that follow the death of a loved one. Sometimes, in an emergency and out of necessity, we learn fast. A life crisis may spur us to make new connections between life and faith. There are often many questions at such a time, but in less stressful situations the resistance to learning is frequently considerable. Many people, for much of the time, do not perceive their need to learn about their faith, nor of discovering new ways of putting that faith into action.

Over the last quarter of a century, adult learning in the churches was prompted by the increasing involvement of the laity in the ministry and decision-making processes of the church, at both local and wider levels. The need to know led to Bible study groups, 'Bishop's Certificates' in theology, courses in pastoral formation and training for elders. The ecumenical movement prompted a flurry of Lent courses, many involving local radio (which then declined again in the 1990s as the need to meet – and the novelty of meeting – seemed to become less pressing, or as the way forward for church unity became less clear). For others, the need to learn was spurred on by changes in the wider society that demonstrated the exciting opportunities for self-awareness and development made possible by experientially-based, human-relations training.

Those Whose Needs Have Not Been Met

Throughout this time, very many other Christians have remained untouched and unmoved by such events and opportunities. Having never been encouraged before to be more aware of the church's changing patterns of ministry and belief, perhaps they found it almost impossible to imagine how a process called 'education' could in any way help them to lead better, happier or more fulfilled lives. Many had in fact learned that for them faith and learning should not mix. Others had learned different, rather painful, lessons about the church's lack of interest in their private struggles to relate what they heard on Sundays to what went on during the rest of the week. They also learned to cope with this negative learning, and to establish their own integrity as adults. It is hardly surprising that such people should be somewhat distrustful of a church which, having shown little interest in their needs before, now seems to threaten those hard-won integrities and, perhaps, seeks to impose something new and foreign. Many adult Christians do not see the need to be threatened and exposed in this way.

The purpose of this chapter is to summarise some of the ways in which adults learn, and to say something about the provision for adult learners made by churches in Britain. It cannot be a comprehensive survey. It is more of a snapshot, distorted by the personal viewpoint of this particular photographer of the scene at the end of the 1990s.

ADULTS AS LEARNERS

Adulthood, Ageing and Experience

There is an increasingly impressive body of evidence to show that, until the physical and/or mental decline of extreme old age arrives, there are very few physiological barriers to learning, although 'I'm too old to learn that' is an attitudinal problem that is not always easily overcome. Perhaps the most significant and striking difference between children and adults as learners is the sheer amount of life experience that adults bring with them to their learning. Indeed, it is not so much that adults bring their experience with them; they *are* their experience (Weil, 1989).

Much of the store of knowledge that adults have accumulated from experience is the result of 'everyday learning': information gleaned often semi-consciously from other people, the television and a myriad of other informal sources. We are continually bombarded from all sides with information that has to be sifted, accepted, rejected or ignored. 'Learning projects' that arise from this process may be haphazard, but they are almost always targeted towards a concrete situation and are often to do with solving a problem. For example, some years ago I found the rapid growth of a curious mould in my cellar rather worrying. I set out to find out what it was and what I should do about it. As a result, I now know quite a lot about dry rot. I have also formed some strong opinions about the need to ventilate cool, damp rooms, and about the need to take preventative measures before problems get out of hand.

My newly formed opinions are fairly typical of the products of a kind of reflection that is engaged in by all adults in their everyday learning. The ability to theorise in this way has both its strengths and its weaknesses. We need established attitudes and beliefs in order to help us cope with new situations and ideas, but they may also prevent us from taking new information and perspectives sufficiently seriously. We may then resist a new set of facts ('there may be Salmonella bacteria in uncooked eggs, but I've eaten home-made mayonnaise for years without coming to any harm') or even a new set of attitudes, as John Hull has illustrated by his description of an anti-Semitic white Christian who was nonplussed to discover that Jesus was an Asiatic Jew (Hull, 1991). As one author has put it: 'the past experience of adults affects their current learning, sometimes serving as an enhancement, sometimes as a hindrance' (Brookfield, 1986: 31).

Experiential Learning

The recognition of the significance of everyday learning adds weight to theories of 'experiential learning'. David A. Kolb has provided the most influential account, but he acknowledges a debt to earlier writers, especially Lewin, Dewey and Piaget. He offers as his summary definition of learning: 'learning is the process whereby knowledge is created through the transformation of experience'. He suggests that there are several distinctive characteristics of experiential learning:

(i)   Learning is best conceived as a process, not in terms of outcomes. The underlying assumption here is that ideas are not fixed but are continually formed and re-formed through experience. Kolb distrusts learning objectives if they are no longer open to change through experience.[1]

(ii) Learning is a continuous process grounded in experience. That is to say, all learning is a kind of re-learning, in that no one enters learning with a blank mind or without strongly-held ideas.

(iii) The process of learning requires the resolution of conflicts between dialectically opposed modes of adaptation to the world. Thus learning demands change. These 'dialectically opposed modes' are variously described. One example is the conflict between observation and action (Lewin), another is the process of accommodating ideas to the external world in contrast to assimilating experience into existing ways of thinking (Piaget).

(iv) Learning is a holistic process of adaptation to the world. It is the way in which people integrate their thinking, feeling, perceiving and behaving. It happens always and everywhere.

(v)   Learning involves transactions between the person and the environment. This is illustrated by two different ways of understanding 'experience'. One is internal and subjective (e.g. 'happiness'), the other is external and objective (e.g. 'I have driven down this road dozens of times'). The two kinds of experience are interrelated in complex ways (I may not always find that it makes me happy to drive down that road).

(vi) Learning is the process of creating knowledge. Learning is the result of the transaction between refined or social knowledge and personal knowledge or common sense (Kolb, 1984).[2]

The Learning Cycle

The notion of a learning cycle was also developed by Kolb (see Kolb and Fry, 1975). In this cycle – or continuous spiral – concrete experience leads to observation and reflection, then to more abstract generalisation and conceptualisation, and from there to the testing of concepts in new situations, which itself gives rise to further experience. Peter Jarvis has criticised this as an oversimple description of the learning processes, and proposed a more complex pathway (Jarvis, 1995: 69–71). Nevertheless, some version of this cycle from experience through reflection/review, conclusion, testing/planning, and then back to experience, is commonly appealed to in adult education.

The process is closely similar to the so-called 'pastoral cycle' within liberation thinking and practical theology, with its movement from the starting point of experience, through exploration, reflection and action, and then back (or on) to experience again (see Ballard and Pritchard, 1996).

It is arguable that at each stage in the cycle impediments to learning may arise. One publication lists the following among the feelings that impede learning:

- fear of failure and making mistakes,
- fear of ridicule,
- lack of self-confidence,
- feeling short of time and irritated with slow progress of learning,
- being out of sympathy with rational reflection,
- feeling reluctant to commit oneself to action;
- feeling irritated by the need for specificity and precision.

The authors add 'perhaps the emotion that does the most damage to the learning process, at all stages in the cycle, is the feeling of complacency', which lulls people into a false sense of security about the need for reflection and for recognising change (Honey and Mumford, 1989: section 7, p. 4).

Learning Styles

Kolb clearly recognised that not every adult learns in the same way. He identified four basic 'learning styles': the problem-solving 'convergent' learning style, the imaginative 'divergent' learning style, the theoretical model-building 'assimilative' learning style and the adaptive, pragmatic 'accommodative' learning style. This analysis has been found to correlate to some extent with the Myers-Briggs Type Indicator of Personality (MBTI).[3]

Peter Honey and Alan Mumford also argue for four different learning styles (Mumford, 1982; Honey and Mumford, 1986, 1992; cf. Craig, 1994: ch. 4) which they call 'activist', 'theorist', 'pragmatist'

and 'reflector'. Nobody adopts one style to the complete exclusion of
the other three, and a dominance or preference in one does not imply
an inability to operate in another. Nevertheless, a link may be drawn
between each preferred learning style and the methods by which
people learn. For example, *activists* value variety and learn best when
they can move quite quickly from activity to activity. They are flexible and open-minded, but they tend not to respond well to the kind of
learning that involves a great deal of routine and repetition. In learning, as in life, they may act without thinking and take unnecessary
risks. *Theorists*, on the other hand, tend to be highly disciplined and
enjoy learning that allows them to pay attention to detail. They are
rational and objective, and good at asking probing questions. But they
are less comfortable with ambiguity or uncertainty, and with statements based on feeling or intuition. *Reflectors* are thoughtful people
who bring care and thoroughness to their learning. They have a good
ability to listen and to assimilate information, but they do not like to
be rushed and may frequently be over-cautious. They are not often
very forthcoming in discussion. *Pragmatists* (the strongest preference
among people doing managerial and professional tasks in UK industry) are businesslike and realistic people, who love to try things out
in practice. They are 'down to earth' women and men, who may be
bored by long theoretical discussions and frustrated by anything that
does not seem to have an obvious application.

Theorists, naturally enough, may show themselves ill at ease with
activists. On the other hand, activists may become quickly frustrated
by the theorists' concerns – as may pragmatists – and equally irritated
by the reflectors' reluctance to launch into an activity. Reflectors may
be hurt by the pragmatist's concern for completing a task, rather than
attending to people's needs.

Such diverse and sometimes conflicting preferences can have a
powerful effect in a group of adults trying to learn together. An
awareness of the learning styles within a group can be an invaluable
aid to ensuring that learning is effective, both by enabling the teacher
to devise strategies that are more likely to engage the majority of
learners, and also by enabling the members to understand why other
people may or may not find certain approaches exciting or engaging.
Individuals can be encouraged to pursue a strategy that will strengthen
those learning styles which, left to themselves, they would prefer not
to adopt. Teachers also need to be aware that their own *teaching style*
is likely to be strongly influenced by their own preferred learning
style.

Factors that Help or Block Adult Learning

Taking a more positive line, ten significant factors that help adults to learn are summarised by Yvonne Craig using the mnemonic REVE-LATION (Craig, 1994: ch. 3; cf. Jarvis, 1995: 50-53, 102-106). They are:

Relevance: Adult learners need to see the point of doing something.
  (As in the case of my urgent need to solve the problem of dry rot in the cellar.)
Experience: Adults learn best when experience is used to earth and illuminate practice.
  (For example, a group of baptism visitors gained far more from a short course on the theology of baptism than did those adults who were not part of such a practical group. The baptism visitors could see how different theologies might affect what they said and did when they visited a family.)
Variety: Adult learners value a variety of opportunities, methods and commitment to match a variety of needs.
  (Every learner's circumstances are different and need to be respected.)
Enjoyment: Learning that is fun usually proves to be effective. A comfortable environment helps too.
  (A long lecture in a cold, draughty church hall, to an audience seated on hard wooden chairs, needs to be quite exceptional if it is to be remembered for anything other than being a taste of purgatory.)
Learning skills: Adults often need particular help to acquire learning skills.
  (Simple study skills – such as how to search a library index, and how to plan an essay – can be huge barriers to learning if they are not properly dealt with.)
Acceptance: People learn best when they start from a place of security.
  (The resistance to learning expressed by so many church people is often rooted in a fear of being humiliated and in not being taken seriously as adults.)
Tutoring skills: Tutors need to practise what they preach.
  (Craig reminds us that the tutor who takes an hour and fifty minutes to say that the best attention span for adults is twenty minutes really does exist somewhere!)
Individual differences: Individual needs must be met and individual progress affirmed.
  (We need to take time to encourage and give appropriate feedback to each adult learner.)

Opportunities: Learning is reinforced when opportunities to practise what has been learned are available.
(And, conversely, learning that cannot be put into practice often leads either to immense frustration or to a disinclination to engage in further learning.)

Nurture: The chance to nurture and teach others is itself a valuable learning experience.
(How often is it said that the best way to learn something is to have to teach it? There are also many other benefits to be gained from being active as an educator in a learning community, with the support and encouragement of other people.)

As well as the mismatch of certain learning styles, there are a number of other blocks which may prevent adults from learning. This is the subject of a major and very influential study by John Hull entitled *What Prevents Christian Adults from Learning?* (Hull, 1991). More generally, adults fail to learn when they lack confidence, are scared of failure, are not respected by a teacher or tutor, or when they find themselves without peer or group support.

It is clear from the above, and from our experience of the nature of 'everyday learning', that adults do not always need or wish to learn *in groups*. While some prefer a very formal setting within a large group or class, and others enjoy the interaction possible within a small group, there are yet others who much prefer to learn alone. The development of information technology has helped here, but it has also presented providers of learning with the challenge of adapting the learning process to an increasingly complex array of learning situations.

Much of what has been said so far assumes that learning is, or should be 'learner-centred', that adults learn best when they take control of their own learning. Perhaps too much has been made of the dichotomy between 'traditional' and 'experiential' poles in Christian education; but the anxieties of those who feel threatened by the challenge to relate the Christian faith to their everyday world have their roots partly in the chasm that has wrongly been allowed to open between the two extremes. As Jeff Astley has pointed out, the church has sometimes been so seduced by the need to give people access to the 'Christian paintbox' that it has deliberately ignored the value of looking at existing examples of great Christian art. A balanced Christian education needs *both* educational experiences that begin with reflections on, and explorations of, our own experience, *and also* educational experiences that give a more complete account of Christian tradition articulated from its own point of view (Astley,

1992 and chapter 2 above). If this balance is properly maintained, it should provide sufficient safety to begin to ease a way to new learning for those who are disabled by a negative and damaging experience of education, or an overly objective understanding of faith.

THE CHURCHES' RESPONSE

A Brief History: From Lent Groups to Post-Modernism

A great deal of adult Christian learning takes place in relatively informal, often self-help, groups. Except for those situations in which a suitably qualified lay person or member of the clergy assumes the rôle of theologian, most of these groups do not depend on a teacher who is a subject specialist in the way that might be the norm in a WEA or university extra-mural class. The group might have formed initially primarily to offer friendship, or to pray, or to study the Bible. But the reasons for people coming together may not always be clear.

In the case of both informal and formal groups, those who participate will have several different, individual reasons for their continuing involvement. A wide variety of reasons for participation is by no means peculiar to self-help groups. A close colleague, an archaeologist of international reputation, taught extra-mural groups of adult students for over thirty years. To his dismay, some faces remained the same from his first class to the very last. Some kept coming because they valued the quality of the few new insights that they gained each year, even though the bulk of the material they studied was by then enormously familiar. Many others came because they found friendship in the class. Others kept coming because after a while they simply could not imagine any other way to spend a Tuesday morning. There are lessons here for adult Christian educators!

Formal groups may be gathered in response to the need to relate faith to everyday life or to address a particular issue. In the Roman Catholic Church, the rise of the catechetical movement in the early 1960s, especially following Vatican II, prompted many parents to learn in response to their need to answer their children's questions. New access to the Bible was a spur for many others. In the Church of England, the opening out of church government to involve lay people helped to create a need for a better informed and more theologically articulate laity.

The Ecumenical Movement has also in recent decades created a great deal of enthusiasm for people learning together across denominational boundaries, culminating in the mid 1980s with a series of national Lent courses, which were very widely followed in the build-up to the 'Called to be One' process. Even before then, large numbers of people participated in locally-based ecumenical Lent courses, often run in partnership with local radio stations (as with the 1983 Lent course by Radio Kent, which involved 20,000 listeners: see Hiscox, 1986). Not all the radio-linked courses were successful, however, in part because of the difficulty of reconciling the broadcasters' concerns for 'good radio' and the educators' desire to promote effective learning.

In many churches the growth of the concept of shared ministry, whether out of conviction or as a result of the decline in numbers of the clergy, led to a huge growth in training packages designed to equip lay people to carry out tasks that had previously been the main preserve of the ordained. In addition, ordination training itself was forced to change through the requirement to develop part-time courses designed to train mature people, many of whom would serve as non-stipendiary ministers while continuing in full-time secular employment.

During the 1980s the traditional adult education providers (including the WEA and the universities) were joined in the educational market-place by many other bodies, including the church colleges. New funding arrangements for further and higher education in the 1990s further complicated the picture, with a swing away from liberal adult education towards accredited courses. This, in turn, led to moves to accredit prior learning and to a 'portfolio approach' to training. *Portfolio-based training* seeks to establish an agreed and highly sophisticated list of competencies, knowledge and even attitudes that are seen to be appropriate to particular tasks or responsibilities. It has been pioneered most effectively in the Church of England by the Diocese of Oxford, and has now begun to exercise a strong appeal amongst many other providers of ministerial training, partly because it enables a training programme to be constructed that takes account of different needs and different levels of achievement, yet all within an agreed syllabus, and partly because it has helped to enable providers better to target precious resources to the points of greatest need.

A major new development bridging formal and non-formal learning has been the upsurge of interest in distance and open learning programmes. In the United Kingdom much pioneering work was done by the Open University, which continues to set the standard for good practice. Distance learning now forms a major part of the provision for adult Christian learning offered by many colleges, including a partnership between the Church of England Board of Education and the Anglican Church Colleges that offers both the 'Exploring Faith: Theology for Life' programme, which can lead to a certificate in adult learning and theology or ministry, and a certificate/diploma/higher degree course on adult education with theological reflection. Specifically theological education is available in distance-learning form through a range of other courses, including the 'Education for Ministry' programme of the University of the South, Tennessee, which is now well-established in the UK (while this does not actually focus on any particular ministry, it does provide a rigorous theological training for lay people).

Styles of Adult Education

Something of the diversity of educational provision within the churches, and of the thinking that accompanies this, is portrayed in the chart below. This is adapted from the description of 'six styles of education' – or 'lenses through which to look at and assess educational practice' – in the publication *Tomorrow is Another Country*. There have been many attempts, over twenty years or more, to categorise approaches to education within the church context, and this account samples that literature.[4]

The six styles are neither comprehensive nor mutually exclusive, but are sketches, almost caricatures, of the range of educational provision to be found within the churches today. Indeed any such attempt to define models inevitably risks some degree of distortion. 'Dogmatic education' here implies a particular and narrow understanding of revealed truth. In this, the 'main problem' – sin – is coloured by a particular theology of revelation (as expounded by Karl Barth) which insists that fallen human beings have no capacity of their own to attain authentic religious knowledge, and no contribution to make to their own understanding of God. More liberal theologies take more seriously the learner's own reasoning, understanding and life experience. Such accounts are therefore more sympathetic to the 'progressive', 'humanistic' or 'radical' approaches to adult education (Saddington, 1992: 47; cf. Elias, 1982: ch. VI).

Notions of 'liberal education' are also open to a range of interpretation and disagreement. Jeff Astley comments:

> The approach of 'liberal education' has not fared well in recent discussion in adult Christian education. *Tomorrow is Another Country* characterises liberal educators as viewing the learner in terms of 'a container to be filled' (Cundy, 1996: 36). The general picture of liberal education presented there appears to be that of a didactic teacher who promotes a

Six Styles of Education

	sees main problem as	sees rôle of educator as	sees knowledge as	employs descriptive metaphor of	recognises as a key value	sees the educated person as
Liberal	ignorance	one who transmits	wisdom	'initiation'	reason	knowledgeable
Progressive	social change	guide	judgement and ability to act	'problem-solving'	democracy	responsible
Humanist	meaninglessness	one who supports	wholeness	'growth'	acceptance	integrated
Technological	need for production and efficiency	instructor	performance	'moulding'	efficiency	competent
Radical	oppression	one who 'conscientizes'	praxis (reflective thought and action)	'empowerment'	freedom	liberated
Dogmatic	sin and disobedience	one who proclaims	revealed truth	'feeding'	faithfulness	obedient

After Elias, Saddington, Craig and Green etc.:
see particularly *Tomorrow is Another Country: Post-Modernism and Christian Education, 1996, pp. 36–40*

content-led, transmissive initiation into knowledge. But the liberal tradition is not just about 'mere transmission or absorption of factual knowledge'. It also embraces the development of wisdom, of moral, spiritual and aesthetic values, and especially of the exercise of 'the skills necessary for critical judgement' (Saddington, 1992: 38–39). For John Henry Newman, the great exponent of liberal education, this is a matter not of 'mere knowledge' but of the 'cultivation of the intellect, as such' – that is, of the discipline of thought – so as 'to open the mind, to correct it, to refine it' (Newman, 1899: discourse V). The ultimate goal of teachers in the tradition of liberal education is that 'students become original or creative' (Elias and Merriam, 1980: 31). Furthermore, Saddington himself recognises that some writers see the progressive tradition as a strand within a (broader) liberal education that involves more than just the cultivation of the intellect. Perhaps the word 'liberal' should not be too quickly dismissed as an inappropriately rational, transmissive (or even elitist) adjective to apply to adult Christian education. (Astley, 1999: 4)

THE REALITY ON THE GROUND

Case Study 1: A Parish Learning Project

An exposure to a huge range of resources does not guarantee that a learning community will emerge that is significantly different from what exists in those churches that do not have that advantage. The simple lesson is that it takes a great deal of time to change the *culture of learning*, and that if a community or the individuals within it have not come to recognise that they have a *need* to learn, even the most lavish resources will not help much of themselves. For example, at the completion of one parish-based project extended interviews were carried out with about twenty-five of the people who had participated. Although almost everyone was quick to praise the project, and to express an appreciation for all the hard work that had been exercised on their behalf, there was little sense of *ownership* of it. It remained 'on their behalf' – something done for them. The notion of self-help in learning, or of taking responsibility for one's own learning, was still foreign to them. The culture of dependence on (ordained) authority had not been greatly disturbed. There remained a considerable gap between the attitudes and opinions discovered and brought to life so vividly by that project, and the opportunities for learning that take those findings seriously. 'Off-the-peg' courses, though enjoyed by those who participated at the time, seemed to encourage only shallow roots in the soil of further learning.

These criticisms serve to emphasise one of the more intractable barriers to learning: a barrier that would be found in any similar context. This is further illustrated by the fact that, in addition to the project proper, occasional training courses also took place in the same parish. One of these trained members of a group to act as baptismal visitors. This seemed to be quite effective, but mostly in that it met the *institution's* need rather than the particular needs of those adults who took part in the training. Again, we may find a warning here for those who seek to provide adult Christian education.

Case Study 2: 'Exploration in Faith' and 'Living Faith'

Between 1984 and 1988, over five hundred people in the Diocese of Newcastle took part in a two year long foundation course entitled 'Exploration in Faith'. The whole programme consisted of half a dozen units, each of six meetings. Some of the groups were earthed in particular communities, but the majority had a more eclectic membership. The ability of course members to carry on with and manage their own learning at the end of the programme would certainly count as an indicator of its success, but this outcome was not easy to measure. The fear of creating an inappropriate dependency meant that groups were encouraged not to continue, but rather to move on to other things. Undoubtedly there were many individuals who were grateful for the spur to learning given by the course. Some, for example, went on to train as Readers as a result. And, of course, the kind of knowledge and resources for knowledge acquired through the study of such highly-structured, content-based courses remain available to the individuals who participated. As a support for their continuing, everyday learning, such courses should never be under-valued.

There was much about 'Exploration in Faith' that was excellent. But there were some (mainly tutors, but also some learners) who expressed a frustration that the course did not meet their group's needs with sufficient sensitivity. They felt that the style was too tutor-dominated, and slanted too much towards traditional rather than experiential learning. At the end of the course an evaluation was carried out by the North of England Institute for Christian Education by means of a lengthy and probing questionnaire. This revealed that the majority of learners had enjoyed and benefited from the course and found it to be at the right level. But warning bells were sounded by the discovery that the course members who responded to the survey (42% of the entire student body) were predominantly women (79% of the sample), aged 50 or over (65% of the sample), and had been formally educated beyond the age of sixteen. Partly in response to this, and in order to try and attract a broader audience, a new course ('Living Faith') was launched in 1992. This had a far smaller take-up than its predecessor. The resource materials on this course were designed to be more flexible and to be managed much more according to local needs, and all the groups were encouraged to be community-based rather than eclectic. One key aim was to help learners to gain confidence and to take responsibility for their own learning.

Both courses made considerable demands on their participants to gather data, and to think and reflect outside the group sessions. Where these demands were taken up and met by the participants, the level of commitment and of ownership was noticeably greater. For this reason, 'Living Faith' was designed to take a step away from a structured content-based *programme*, and a step towards a structured learning *process* in which the success or failure of the course depended much more on the material brought by the group. This was a calculated risk, but one which was felt to be essential if the key aims of the course were to be met.

Tutor training and support had always been one of the strong features of 'Exploration in Faith', and was central to the success of 'Living Faith' also. In the later course, at the conclusion of an 'access unit' (a very welcome innovation which not only gave the group a 'taste' of the course but also, more importantly, enabled them to form as a group), the tutor and the group were asked to draw up a contract. This allowed groups to follow their own track through the units on offer and to determine the length of their own course (as no accreditation was involved, each group could do as little or as much as it wished). Continuous evaluation was built into the new course, as the responsibility of each learning group itself. In some cases increased confidence and theological articulateness were striking and welcome outcomes; but we found that the rôle of the tutor was as important as ever, and the culture of dependence remained frustratingly deeply-rooted.

The abiding lesson from both courses has been that no materials, however excellent, count for much without a skilled tutor, able to interpret and adapt them to a particular group's needs and context. But this produces a tension: the more excellent the tutor, the greater is the danger of creating dependence on her. It requires rare skills in the tutor to enable a group as a whole (even more than particular individuals within it) to move on and to take full responsibility for its own learning.

But here lies another tension. Perhaps there has been too great a concentration by church educators on the *group*, and too many expec-

tations placed on its success or failure, rather than focussing on the
needs of the individuals who comprise it. Group learning is attractive
because it seems to show a commitment to community life rather than
to individualism. In addition, peer groups are well-known to be a key
factor in the provision of effective support for learning. By contrast,
the portfolio approach to training, distance learning courses, the
possibilities afforded by information technology and the dominant
culture of accreditation all tend to emphasise *individuals* and their
special needs. Both theology and education are challenged to respond
to the issues raised by these different approaches.

POSTSCRIPT

However clear may be our understanding of how adults learn, we
must acknowledge that the routes to learning are almost as varied as
the learners themselves. There appears to be a considerable gap
between everyday learning, where the individual is more than
prepared to manage his or her own learning, and those more formal
learning situations where educational providers offer packages in the
hope (albeit well-researched and well-intentioned) of meeting needs.
The church is often caught in an uncomfortable place where people's
expectations of formal learning situations still tend towards traditional
forms, so that courses which make other assumptions about the learning process are regarded with suspicion.

Adult learning is now entering a new culture which is pulling in two
quite different directions. One places the emphasis on technology, and
on the acquisition of transferable and measurable skills that must be
accredited (and which often form part of a portfolio designed to enable
the individual to compete in the market-place). The other embraces
the messiness of postmodernity; it is less rational and tidy, more open-
ended, and delights in blurred boundaries.

Perhaps it is hardly surprising that so many adult learners, unsettled by a world so radically different from the one in which they grew
up, look to the church as a haven of stability and predictability. It is
also little wonder that some find the whole idea of the church's enthusiasm for education deeply disturbing.

NOTES

[1]   A vigorous debate about the principles and place of learning objectives has
engaged a number of educationalists (see chs. 1 and 4 above). E. W. Eisner, one

of the leading critics of educational objectives, claims that the outcomes of learn-ing are too variable to predict and quantify. In the arts, for example, behaviour may result that is a surprise to both learner and teacher alike (see Curzon, 1990 for a summary of the discussion). There is also a debate about the nature and inter-relationship of 'product content' and 'process content' in education, which relates to the distinction made by the philosopher Gilbert Ryle between 'knowing that' and 'knowing how' (Ryle, 1949: ch. II).

2   For a broader discussion of the variety of types of learning from experience, see Jarvis, Holford and Griffin (1998: ch. 6).

3   Kolb, 1984: ch. 4. The MBTI (Briggs Myers, 1993) is now widely used in church circles. It is based on Jung's psychological types of extravert-introvert (whether our preferred focus is on our outer or our inner world), sensing-intuition (our preferred mode of perceiving: focussing on facts/skills or using imagination/inspi-ration), thinking-feeling (our preferred mode of decision-making or judgement) and judging-perceiving (whether our preferred approach to life is planned/organ-ised judgement or open/flexible perception). Personality will clearly affect preferred learning style, in particular:

> if the best learning is to happen, thinking types must pursue logical order; feeling types must follow their hearts; sensing types must strive to engage their senses in the mastery of practical skills; and intuitive types must follow whatever inspires.
>
> (Lawrence, 1982: 17)

4   Harold Burgess (1975) was one of the first to analyse different approaches to reli-gious education, under the headings of aim, content, teacher, student, environment and evaluation, with reference to leading (mostly North American) writers on Christian education. A similar task was attempted by Seymour and Miller (1982) – see chapters 1 and 2 above. The list in *Tomorrow is Another Country* (Cundy, 1996) is adapted from Craig (1994), who in turn adapted it from the work of J. A. Saddington of the University of Cape Town, South Africa (Saddington, 1992). Earlier typologies of general adult education are offered by Elias and Merriam (1980) and Elias (1982: ch. VI): viz. liberal, progressive, behaviourist (or social-ization-behaviouristic), humanistic and radical (or socio-political). Cf. also Wickett (1991). Cultural context doubtless has some influence on such typologies.

REFERENCES

Astley, J. (1992), 'Tradition and Experience: Conservative and Liberal Models for Christian Education', in J. Astley and D. Day (eds), *The Contours of Christian Education*, Great Wakering: McCrimmons, ch. 3.

Astley, J. (1999), 'Some Reflections on the Ethics of Adult Christian Education', Durham: NEICE.

Ballard, P. and Pritchard, J. (1996), *Practical Theology in Action: Christian Thinking in the Service of the Church and Society*, London: SPCK.

Briggs Myers, I. (1993), *Gifts Differing: Understanding Personality Type*, Palo Alto, Calif.: CPP Books.

Brookfield, S. D. (1986), *Understanding and Facilitating Adult Learning*, Milton Keynes: Open University Press.

Burgess, H. W. (1975), *An Invitation to Religious Education*, Birmingham, Ala.:

Religious Education Press.

Craig, Y. (1994), *Learning for Life: A Handbook of Adult Religious Education*, London: Mowbray.

Cundy, I. *et al.* (1996), *Tomorrow is Another Country: Post-Modernism and Christian Education*, London: Board of Education of the General Synod of the Church of England (GS Misc 467).

Curzon, L. B. (1990), 'Teaching in Further Education, An Outline of Principles and Practice,' in part reprinted in Thorpe, Edwards and Hanson (1993), ch. 15.

Elias, J. L. (1982), *The Foundations and Practice of Adult Religious Education*, Malabar, Fla.: Krieger.

Elias, J. L. and Merriam, S. (1980), *Philosophical Foundations of Adult Education*, Malabar, Fla.: Krieger.

Hiscox, R. (1986), *Eager to Learn: A Review of Christian Adult Learning Materials*, London: Advisory Council for the Church's Ministry.

Honey, P. and Mumford, A. (1986, 1992), *The Manual of Learning Styles*, Maidenhead: Peter Honey.

Honey, P. and Mumford, A. (1989), *The Manual of Learning Opportunities*, Maidenhead: Peter Honey.

Hull, J. M. (1991), *What Prevents Christian Adults from Learning?*, New York: Trinity Press International.

Jarvis, P. (1995), *Adult and Continuing Education: Theory and Practice*, London: Routledge.

Jarvis, P., Holford, J. and Griffin, C. (1998), *The Theory and Practice of Learning*, London: Kogan Page.

Kolb, D. A. (1984), *Experiential Learning: Experience as the Source of Learning and Development*, Englewood Cliffs, N. J.: Prentice-Hall.

Kolb, D. A. and Fry, R. (1975), 'Towards an Applied Theory of Experiential Learning', in C. L. Cooper (ed.), *Theories of Group Processes*, London: Wiley, ch. 3.

Lawrence, G. (1982), *People Types and Tiger Stripes: A Practical Guide to Learning Styles*, Gainesville, Fla.: Center for Applications of Psychological Type.

Lee, J. M. (1985), *The Content of Religious Instruction*, Birmingham, Ala.: Religious Education Press.

Mumford, A. (1982), 'Learning Style and Learning Skills', *Journal of Management Development*, 1, 2, pp. 55–65.

Newman, J. H. (1899), *The Idea of a University*, London: Longmans, Green.

Ryle, G. (1949), *The Concept of Mind*, London: Penguin.

Saddington, J. A. (1992), 'Learner Experience: A Rich Resource for Learning', in J. Mulligan and P. Griffin (eds), *Empowerment through Experiential Learning*, London: Kogan Page, ch. 2.

Seymour, J. L. and Miller, D. E. (eds) (1982), *Contemporary Approaches to Christian Education*, Nashville, Tenn.: Abingdon.

Thorpe, M., Edwards, R. and Hanson, A. (eds) (1993), *Culture and Processes of Adult Learning*, London: Routledge/The Open University Press.

Weil, S. W. (1989), 'Access: Towards Education or Miseducation? Adults Imagine the Future', in Thorpe, Edwards and Hanson (1993), ch. 10.

Wickett, R. E. Y. (1991), *Models of Adult Religious Education Practice*, Birmingham, Ala.: Religious Education Press.

8

The Pews Talk Back: The Church Congregation Survey

Leslie J. Francis

INTRODUCTION

A great deal of Christian education continues to take part within the context of Sunday services. Across the denominations only a minority of adult Christians currently attend mid-week house groups, Bible study sessions and discussion meetings, or participate in other forms of Christian learning. The disadvantage faced by clergy and Christian educators in the context of worship and liturgy is the lack of opportunity to hear the people sitting in the pews talk back. In the absence of such feedback, those involved in promoting Christian learning within this context have little formal opportunity to test their working assumptions about the beliefs, needs and backgrounds of those who attend church. The Church Congregation Survey was designed to meet this need and to provide a mechanism for the pews to talk back.

The aim of the present chapter is to describe the rationale underpinning the Church Congregation Survey and to illustrate how the instrument was set to work in one town where the Anglican, Methodist, Roman Catholic and United Reformed Church all agreed to listen to the voices of their church attenders on one specific Sunday. No claims are made here about how representative this survey is for the churches generally. It should be clear, however, how valuable such data can be for informing the work of adult Christian education in a given context, for a specific group of churchgoers with their particular attitudes, beliefs and concerns.

THE CHURCH CONGREGATION SURVEY

The Church Congregation Survey is a small self-completion booklet which was designed after extensive consultation with clergy and Christian educators in order to reflect the range of their practical concerns. The survey instrument comprises three parts.

The first part of the survey instrument contains 28 multiple choice questions. These question are concerned with key pieces of background information (like age and sex), information about current religious practice (like frequency of church attendance and personal prayer) and information about contact with other churches. In each case the respondent simply needs to tick a box.

The second part of the survey instrument contains 132 questions about beliefs, values, and attitudes. Each question is offered for response on a five point Likert-type scale. The five possible responses offered are 'agree strongly', 'agree', 'not certain', 'disagree' and 'disagree strongly'. In each case the respondent simply needs to circle one of these categories. The 132 questions in this section are intended to provide information about fifteen different areas altogether. These areas explore churchgoers' motivations for churchgoing, their sense of belonging to their church, the strengths and weaknesses which they perceive in their church, the agenda which they feel their church should promote for the future, their personal involvement in church activities, their self-perceptions of their growth and learning in the Christian faith, the sources of spiritual help which they find beneficial, their awareness of religious experience, the extent to which they are open to change in their churches, their preferences for traditional and for modern worship, the extent to which they hold traditional Christian beliefs, what they believe about the Bible, their commitment to the social gospel, their view of the churches' involvement in politics and matters of social concern, and their commitment to co-operation between the denominations. Data from eleven of these areas of concern are reported here.

The third part of the survey instrument presents the abbreviated form of the Revised Eysenck Personality Questionnaire as developed by Francis, Brown and Philipchalk.[1] This instrument proposes brief six item measures of the three major dimensions of personality known as extraversion, neuroticism and psychoticism. It also proposes a six item lie scale. Each item is assessed on a dichotomous response. In each case the respondent simply needs to circle either 'yes' or 'no'. The present chapter does not have space to present the findings from this third part of the Church Congregation Survey.

Data Collection

The Church Congregation Survey was set to work by the clergy ministering in a town centre area of a middle-sized town in the North of England. The town centre included four churches, one Anglican, one Methodist, one Roman Catholic and one United Reformed Church. Each of these churches agreed to invite all the attenders at their services on one designated Sunday to complete a copy of the Church Congregation Survey. The response was good and seems in line with the average attendances at these four churches. The weakness in the study is that the clergy did not keep a note of the number of people who refused to participate in the study.

The Roman Catholic church held three services. The first on Saturday evening produced 48 completed copies of the questionnaire, while the two Sunday morning services at 9.00 and 10.30 produced 67 and 62 copies respectively, making a total of 177 respondents. The Anglican church held two services. The morning service at 10.30 produced 85 completed copies of the questionnaire, while the evening service at 6.30 produced a further 23 copies, making a total of 108 respondents. The Methodist church held one service which produced 75 completed copies of the questionnaire. The United Reformed Church also held one service which produced 47 completed copies of the questionnaire. The whole survey, therefore, involved 409 churchgoers.

Throughout the following analysis this town centre area will be referred to by the fictitious name of Market Astey (no relation – Ed.).

Who Attends Church?

It is a well established fact from many surveys that churches generally attract two women for every one man. Market Astey was no exception to this general trend. Here 64% of churchgoers were women, with some slight variation between the denominations: 55% in the URC, 62% in the Anglican, 64% in the Roman Catholic and 73% in the Methodist.

It is also generally the case that church congregations tend to attract older people. Here in Market Astey two in every five churchgoers (40%) are aged sixty or over. There are important variations between the denominations. In the Methodist church 59% are aged sixty or over, compared with 51% in the URC, 34% in the Catholic and 31% in the Anglican church.

Six out of every ten churchgoers in Market Astey (61%) are married, 13% are widowed and 4% are divorced. The remaining 22%

are single people who have never been married. Marital status varies somewhat from denomination to denomination. While 9% of Anglicans and 9% of Catholics are widowed, the proportion rises to 24% among the Methodists and 26% among the URCs.

One out of every eight churchgoers in Market Astey (13%) are graduates. This figure includes 10% of the URCs, 10% of the Anglicans, 13% of the Methodists and 14% of the Catholics.

How Long have they been Attending?

In established areas churches tend to build up stable congregations which retain a core membership over many years. Overall in Market Astey between two-fifths and one-half (44%) of the churchgoers had been attending the same place of worship for more than twenty years. Again there is interesting variation between the denominations. In the Methodist church 57% had been attending for more than twenty years, compared with 46% in the Catholic, 45% in the URC and 32% in the Anglican church.

A similar variation occurs in the ability of different churches to recruit new members. In Market Astey as a whole, just 22% of the present congregation had been recruited within the past five years. While the Anglican church had recruited 37% of the congregation during this period, the comparable figures stood at 24% for the URC, 16% for the Catholics and 9% for the Methodists.

Where do the Churchgoers Live?

The vast majority of churchgoers in Market Astey (97%) live within a two mile radius of the church which they attend. This is the case for 99% of the Catholics, 96% of the Methodists, 94% of the Anglicans and 94% of the URCs.

Over a third of the churchgoers (36%) have lived at or near their present address in Market Astey for more than twenty years, while a further 21% have done so for between eleven and twenty years.

About one in six churchgoers in Market Astey (17%) live on their own. This is the case for 10% of Anglicans, 11% of Catholics, 27% of URCs and 31% of Methodists.

The vast majority of churchgoers in Market Astey live in owner-occupied housing (92%). There is little difference between the denominations on this matter.

What do the Churchgoers do for a Living?

Only three out of every ten (29%) churchgoers in Market Astey is in full-time paid employment, with a further 9% in part-time paid employment. The largest category of churchgoers (33%) describe themselves as retired people. Then 16% describe themselves as within the category of housewife, househusband or home maker. A further 11% are in full-time education. The remaining 2% of churchgoers are unemployed.

The employment status of churchgoers varies considerably from denomination to denomination in Market Astey. For example, the retired constitute 23% of the Anglicans, 29% of the Catholics, 47% of the Methodists and 47% of the URCs. Those in full-time paid employment constitute 20% of the Methodists, 27% of the URCs, 29% of the Anglicans and 33% of the Catholics.

Of those churchgoers in full-time or part-time employment, the majority (85%) are engaged in non-manual occupations. In this respect there is very little difference among the four denominations.

Denominational Identity

It cannot be assumed that all churchgoers are currently attending the denomination into which they were confirmed or admitted to adult membership, although this was clearly the case for the majority of churchgoers in Market Astey. Nonetheless, among those attending the Catholic church, 2% had been confirmed as Anglicans and 1% had been admitted to membership of the Methodist church. Among those attending the Methodist church, 4% had been Anglicans and 3% Presbyterians or Congregationalists. Among those attending the Anglican church, 5% had been Catholics and 2% Methodists. Among those attending the United Reformed Church 4% had been Catholic, 6% Methodists and 23% Anglicans.

Many of the churchgoers in Market Astey had experience of the other denominations during the past year. Of the Anglican churchgoers, 51% had attended the Methodist church, 45% the URC and 29% the Catholic church. Of the Methodist churchgoers, 33% had attended the Anglican church, 16% the URC and 12% the Catholic church. Of the URC churchgoers, 26% had attended the Methodist church, 24% the Anglican and 10% the Catholic church. Of the Catholic churchgoers, 27% had attended the Anglican church, 20% the URC and 18% the Methodist church.

Why this Church?

The majority of churchgoers in Market Astey are attending their present church for one of three main reasons: they were first brought there by their parents, it is their nearest church, or it is the nearest church of their denomination. These three reasons account for the attendance of 90% of the Catholics, 64% of the Methodists, 64% of the Anglicans, and 63% of the URC.

By way of comparison, other reasons for attending this specific church account for comparatively few of the worshippers. Thus 7% first came because friends invited them, 5% because they belonged to one of the organisations, 4% because their children came first, 2% because the clergy visited them, and 2% because they attended a special service, wedding or funeral.

Personal Commitment

The majority of churches tend still to work most with committed regular churchgoers. The majority of churchgoers in Market Astey tend to attend service at least once a week (87%), with a further 8% attending at least once every other week. The pattern varies somewhat from denomination to denomination. Weekly churchgoers account for 95% of the Catholics, 90% of the Methodists, 86% of the URCs and 70% of the Anglicans.

A committed pattern of daily prayer cannot be assumed among churchgoers. In Market Astey a pattern of daily prayer is practised by 69% of the Methodists, 67% of the URCs, 62% of the Anglicans and 60% of the Catholics. At the other end of the spectrum, personal prayer is practised less than once a week by 16% of the URCs, 21% of the Catholics, 25% of the Methodists and 26% of the Anglicans.

The discipline of daily Bible reading is practised in Market Astey by 32% of the Methodists, 23% of the URCs, 20% of the Anglicans and 6% of the Catholics. At the other end of the spectrum, the Bible is never read at home by 38% of the Catholics, 19% of the Anglicans, 19% of the URCs and 5% of the Methodists.

The discipline of grace before meals is observed on a daily basis by 20% of the URCs, 16% of the Catholics, 11% of the Methodists and 4% of the Anglicans. A much higher proportion of churchgoers never thinks of saying grace before meals. This is the case for 50% of the Anglicans, 41% of the Catholics, 37% of the URCs and 24% of the Methodists.

Personal Participation

Churchgoers are participating in some form of social activity by the very act of coming out to attend church services. In addition to attending services, the majority (64%) of churchgoers in Market Astey are also involved in some form of church group or organization, such as choirs, committees and house groups. While 40% of churchgoers are involved in one or two activities of this nature in the course of a year, a further 16% are involved in three, four or five groups and 8% are involved in six or more groups in the course of a year.

Participation in church groups or organisations varies considerably from denomination to denomination. While only 7% of Methodists are involved in no group during the course of a year, the proportions rise to 33% among Anglicans, 39% among URCs and 50% among Catholics.

Churchgoers also tend to be involved in other non-church groups or organisations operating within the wider local community. In Market Astey nearly three-quarters of the churchgoers (72%) have participated in at least one non-church group or organisation during the past year. Participation in non-church activities has involved three or more different groups for 28% of the Methodists, 27% of the Anglicans, 24% of the Catholics and 10% of the URCs.

Motivation for Churchgoing

The Church Congregation Survey included ten items to explore churchgoers' motivations for continuing to attend the church where they worship, with respondents being permitted to choose more than one reason. Taking all four congregations in Market Astey together, the following picture emerged.

Four out of every five worshippers made the points that they attended their particular church because the word of God was preached there (83%), because they feel at home there (82%), and because they enjoy the worship (79%). Between one-half and two-thirds of the worshippers said that they attended their particular church because they liked the people (64%), because the members seem spiritually alive (53%), and because they like the minister or priest (49%). One-third say that they attended their particular church because they grew up there (31%). One-fifth attended because they love the building (20%). One in seven attended because their children enjoyed the activities there (15%). Just one in twenty-five attended because they could not travel to another church.

Table one demonstrates that there are some important variations between the motivations of those who attend the different denominations.

Table 1   Motivations for Churchgoing

	Cath %	Angl %	Meth %	URC %
I attend this church because the Word of God is preached here	87	76	84	85
I attend this church because I enjoy the worship	78	75	89	77
I attend this church because I grew up in it	38	26	25	26
I attend this church because the members seem spiritually alive	51	48	61	57
I attend this church because I like the minister/priest	43	53	47	69
I attend this church because I feel at home here	78	74	92	94
I attend this church because I like the people	55	65	76	75
I attend this church because my children enjoy its activities	17	16	10	15
I attend this church because I love the building	14	30	23	19
I attend this church because I cannot travel to another	4	7	1	4

Roman Catholics are more inclined than members of other denominations to attend their church because they grew up in it. On the other hand, Roman Catholics are less inclined than members of other denominations to attend their church because they like the priest, because they like the building, or because they like the people.

Anglicans are more inclined than members of other denominations to attend their church because they like the minister or because they like the building. On the other hand, Anglicans are less inclined than members of other denominations to attend their church because they feel the Word of God is preached there, because the members seem spiritually alive, or even because they like the worship or feel at home there.

Methodists are more inclined than members of other denominations to attend their church because they like the worship, because the members seem spiritually alive, because they feel at home there, or because they like the people. On the other hand, Methodists are less inclined than members of other denominations to attend their particular church because they grew up in it or because their children enjoy its activities.

Members of the United Reformed Church are more inclined than members of the other denominations to attend their church because they like the minister, because they feel at home there and because they like the people. On the other hand, there are no motivations which members of the United Reformed Church are less likely to cite than members of other denominations.

A Sense of Belonging

The Church Congregation Survey included nine items to explore churchgoers' sense of belonging to the church where they worship, again allowing multiple responses. Taking all four congregations in Market Astey together, the following picture emerged.

Nearly nine out of every ten churchgoers in Market Astey said that they had a strong sense of belonging to their church (88%). Half of them were being drawn into even closer commitment and said that they were coming to their church more regularly than had previously been the case (51%).

Between four and five churchgoers in every ten see their church as an important centre for social contact and for personal support. Thus, 47% claim that their church is important for their social life, and 45% say that they often turn to fellow members of their church when they need help. At the same time, these figures clearly show that by no means all churchgoers feel that their church is a major centre for social support. As many as one in three say that their relationships are fairly superficial within their church. While the majority of church-goers (89%) say that they like meeting other people when they go to church, a significant minority (8%) are clear that they do not wish to talk with other people when they go to church.

Other indices of a sense of belonging are reflected by the statistics that 30% of churchgoers often invite other people to come to their church. A similar proportion (28%) feel that they can influence their church's decisions.

Table two demonstrates that there are some important variations between the sense of belonging of those who attend different denominations.

Roman Catholics are more inclined than members of other denominations to feel that their relationships are fairly superficial within their church, and to express the view that they do not wish to talk with other people when they go to church. At the same time, Roman Catholics are less inclined than members of other denominations to feel that their church is important for their social life or to turn to fellow members of their church when they need help. They are also less inclined to feel that they can influence their church's decisions. They are less inclined to invite other people to come to their church.

Table 2   A Sense of Belonging

	Cath %	Angl %	Meth %	URC %
I feel a strong sense of belonging to this church	89	81	95	94
This church is important for my social life	38	43	69	51
My relationships are fairly superficial within this church	38	36	25	17
I can influence the church's decisions	21	28	33	43
I often invite other people to come to this church	22	34	36	38
I turn to fellow members of this church when I need help	37	39	67	55
I am coming to this church more regularly nowadays	50	56	47	53
I like meeting other people when I go to church	83	94	96	93
I do not wish to talk with other people when I go to church	13	3	8	4

Anglicans are less inclined than members of other denominations to feel a strong sense of belonging to their church. In contrast with members of the Free Churches, they share with the Catholics a lower estimation of the rôle of the church in their social life and of the rôle of fellow members of their church when they need help.

Methodists place a particularly high emphasis on a sense of belonging. Methodists score higher than any other denominational group with respect to regarding their church as important for their social life and turning to fellow members of their church when they need help. Methodists score above average on liking to meet other people when they go to church, on often inviting other people to come to their church, and on feeling that they can influence the decisions of their church.

Members of the United Reformed Church place a particularly high value on involvement in the life of their church. They are much more likely than members of the other denominations to feel that they can influence their church's decisions. They are much less likely than members of the other denominations to feel that their relationships are superficial within their church. Members of the United Reformed Church score well above average in regarding their church as important for their social life, in turning to fellow members of their church when they need help, and in inviting other people to come to their church.

Strengths and Weaknesses

The Church Congregation Survey included nine items to explore churchgoers' perceptions of the strengths and weaknesses of the church where they worship. Taking all four congregations in Market Astey together, the following picture emerged.

The clear majority of churchgoers in Market Astey feel drawn nearer to God through the worship of their church (84%). For 71% the preaching draws them nearer to God, for 68% it is the ritual, and for 61% it is the music. Three out of every five churchgoers in Market Astey are conscious that members of their church care deeply for one another (61%).

Looking to the less positive aspects of church life, churchgoers in Market Astey are generally reluctant to find fault with their church. The biggest problem identified concerns the difficulty which newcomers may experience in integrating with church life. One in four churchgoers (25%) say that it is not easy for newcomers in their church.

A small, but nonetheless important minority of churchgoers feel that their church is making too many demands on their time (5%) or on their money (4%). One in ten churchgoers (9%) feel that the Sunday worship of their church is boring. As many as one in seven churchgoers reported that they were aware of considerable conflict in their church (14%).

Table three demonstrates that there are some important variations between the perceptions of those who attend the different denominations.

The Roman Catholics are more inclined than members of other denominations to feel drawn nearer to God through the ritual of their church. On the other hand, Catholics are less inclined than members of the Free Churches to feel drawn nearer to God through the preaching of their church.

Generally the Anglicans are the least satisfied with their church. The Anglicans are less inclined than members of other denominations to feel drawn nearer to God through the worship of their church, including the preaching and the music. The Anglicans are more inclined than members of other denominations to feel that the Sunday worship of their church is boring and that their church does not make things easy for newcomers. The Anglicans are also much more aware of considerable conflict within their church than is the case among members of other denominations. The Anglicans are less likely than members of other denominations to feel that members of their church care deeply for one another.

Table 3 Strengths and Weaknesses

	Cath %	Angl %	Meth %	URC %
I am drawn nearer to God through the music of this church	65	55	59	68
I am drawn nearer to God through the preaching of this church	70	64	81	73
I am drawn nearer to God through the worship of this church	83	79	92	82
I am drawn nearer to God through the ritual of this church	75	69	60	53
Members of this church care deeply for one another	58	44	80	83
I am aware of considerable conflict in this church	10	35	4	0
The church makes too many demands on my time	2	5	9	4
This church makes too many demands on my money	5	7	1	2
Sunday worship in this church is boring	11	14	4	0
It is not easy for newcomers in this church	25	32	17	20

Worship and preaching are very important to the Methodists. The Methodists are more inclined than members of other denominations to say that they are drawn nearer to God through the worship of their church and through the preaching of their church. They are more inclined than Anglicans and Roman Catholics to feel that the members of their church care deeply for one another. They are disinclined to think that the Sunday worship of their church is boring or that it may be difficult for newcomers to feel at home in their services.

Members of the United Reformed Church place a higher value on music in worship than members of other denominations, while at the same time placing a lower value on ritual in worship. In some ways members of the United Reformed Church seem to consider themselves as belonging to the ideal congregation, where members of the church care deeply for one another. None of them is aware of conflict within this church. None of them considers that the Sunday worship of this church is ever boring.

Growth and Learning

The Church Congregation Survey included ten items to explore churchgoers' perceptions of their growth and learning in the Christian faith. Taking all four congregations in Market Astey together, the following picture emerged.

Two out of every three churchgoers feel that they are continuing to grow in their Christian faith (67%). Nonetheless, more churchgoers remain hungry for further opportunities to develop their faith than feel that such opportunities are not needed. Thus, 55% of churchgoers say that they would welcome more opportunities to learn about Christianity, compared with 15% who say that they would not welcome such opportunities.

As part of a learning community, 44% of churchgoers feel that they are competent to explain their faith to other people. On the other hand, 21% of churchgoers say that they do not feel competent to explain their faith to other people, while the remaining 35% feel uncertain about their level of competence in this area.

The major source of church-related literature read by churchgoers is locally produced material. Three out of every four churchgoers say that they often read local church magazines or pamphlets (73%), compared with 36% who often read national church newspapers, 35% who often read religious books, and 33% who often read Bible reading notes.

For the majority of churchgoers, their Christian faith influences the way they live. Thus 83% say their Christian faith influences their attitude towards other people, and 77% say their Christian faith influences important decisions in life.

While the majority of people who remain churchgoers clearly feel that they are making some progress in the Christian life, an important minority feel that things are going the other way. Nearly one in every five churchgoers say that nowadays they feel less close to God than they used to (18%).

Table four demonstrates that there are some important variations in perceptions of growth and learning between those who attend different denominations.

Roman Catholics are much more likely than members of other denominations to feel that they are competent to explain their faith to other people. Of all the denominations, Roman Catholics are the most likely to read a national church newspaper and the least likely to read Bible reading notes. Of all the denominations, Roman Catholics are the most likely to say that nowadays they feel less close to God than they used to.

Anglicans are less likely than average to feel competent to explain

Table 4 Growth and Learning

	Cath %	Angl %	Meth %	URC %
I am growing in my Christian faith	60	69	68	64
I feel competent to explain my faith to other people	52	37	37	40
I would welcome more opportunities to learn about Christianity	56	61	51	47
I often read local church magazines or pamphlets	74	69	69	81
I often read religious books	36	31	43	30
I often read Bible reading notes	27	31	44	43
I often read national church newspapers	46	24	40	21
My Christian faith influences my important decisions in life	76	73	84	76
My Christian faith influences my attitude towards other people	84	78	92	82
Nowadays I feel less close to God than I used to	23	14	16	15

their faith to other people. Anglicans are also less likely than average to read religious books or to read a national church newspaper. Anglicans are also less likely than average to feel that their Christian faith influences their attitude toward other people or affects the important decisions in their life. Although they are the churchgoers who feel least secure in their faith, Anglicans are also the ones who are most likely to welcome more opportunities to learn about Christianity.

Like Anglicans, Methodists are comparatively unsure about their competence to explain their faith to other people. Unlike Anglicans, however, Methodists show an above average uptake to read religious books, Bible reading notes and a national church newspaper. Methodists are the most likely of any denominational group to feel that their faith touches the whole of life by influencing their attitudes towards other people and by affecting the important decisions in their lives.

Members of the United Reformed Church are avid readers of local church bulletins and are much more likely to study Bible reading notes than is the case among Anglicans and Catholics. On the other hand, they show a below average interest in religious books and the national church press. While members of the United Reformed Church display much less confidence than Roman Catholics in their ability to explain their faith to others, they are also much less likely than Roman Catholics to welcome more opportunities to learn about their faith.

Sources of Spiritual Help

The Church Congregation Survey included eight items to explore churchgoers' perceptions of how helpful they find various aspects of the Christian life. Taking all four congregations in Market Astey together, the following picture emerged.

Overall, the aspect of church services found helpful by the largest number of churchgoers was silence. Indeed four in every five churchgoers said that they find periods of silence in services helpful (80%), compared with 71% who find listening to sermons helpful. The proportion falls to 56% of churchgoers who find ritual in services helpful.

Churchgoers are much more likely to find the public reading of Scripture helpful than to benefit from other forms of Bible study. Thus 73% of churchgoers said that they find hearing the Bible read in church helpful, compared with 49% who find reading the Bible by themselves helpful and 32% who find Bible study groups helpful.

For the majority of churchgoers prayer is seen as a highly personal and private activity. Only 32% of churchgoers said that they find prayer groups helpful, compared with 84% who find praying by themselves helpful.

Table five demonstrates that there are some important differences in the sources of spiritual help valued by members of the different denominations.

Roman Catholics are clearly people influenced by the drama of worship more than by the word. Roman Catholics are much more likely than members of other denominations to derive help from ritual and from periods of silence in services. At the same time Roman Catholics are much less likely than members of other denominations to derive help from hearing the Bible read in church or from listening to sermons. Roman Catholics are also less likely to find reading the Bible by themselves helpful.

Anglicans emerge as the least prayerful of the denominations. Of the four denominational groups the Anglicans record the lowest response for deriving help both from praying by themselves and from participating in prayer groups. Anglicans also record the lowest response for deriving help from periods of silence in services. As far as Scripture is concerned, Anglicans occupy a midway position

Table 5   Sources of Spiritual Help

	Cath %	Angl %	Meth %	URC %
I find hearing the Bible read in church helpful	65	76	87	77
I find reading the Bible by myself helpful	37	49	72	62
I find Bible study groups helpful	27	30	37	33
I find prayer groups helpful	32	27	33	36
I find praying by myself helpful	85	79	85	87
I find periods of silence helpful in services	86	70	80	81
I find ritual helpful in services	71	64	24	28
I find listening to sermons helpful	64	72	83	72

between the Roman Catholics and members of the Free Churches. They derive more help from hearing the Bible read in church, reading the Bible by themselves, or attending Bible study groups than is the case among Roman Catholics, but less help from these activities than is the case among members of the Methodist Church and the United Reformed Church.

Methodists are clearly people of the book. In comparison with the other three denominational groups, the Methodists are more likely to find help from hearing the Bible read in church, from reading the Bible by themselves, and from attending Bible study groups. As people of the book Methodists are also people of the word. In comparison with the other three denominational groups, the Methodists are more likely to find help from listening to sermons. Together with their emphasis on the word, Methodists reject the ritual and ceremony of worship. In comparison with the other three denominational groups, the Methodists are least likely to find help from ritual in services.

In many ways members of the United Reformed Church adopt a similar profile of preferences to that adopted by the Methodists. The profile is simply slightly less clear or less extreme among the United Reformed Church members.

Religious Experience

The Church Congregation Survey included nine items to explore churchgoers' religious experience within a broad understanding of that concept. Taking all four congregations in Market Astey together, the following picture emerged.

Many churchgoers are more confident about speaking of their experience of God the Father than speaking of their experience of the third member of the Trinity. While three-quarters of the churchgoers recognise themselves as conscious of God's guidance in their daily life (77%), the proportion falls to two-thirds who recognise that the Holy Spirit helps them in their daily life (68%).

About one in five churchgoers speak in terms of having experienced a religious conversion (19%). One in ten churchgoers would describe themselves as 'born again Christians', and 13% consider that their faith has been positively influenced by the charismatic movement. Almost one in ten churchgoers have experienced glossolalia, being moved to pray or speak in a language unknown to them (8%).

About three out of every five churchgoers is conscious of being part of the wider Christian family, feeling close to other Christians living locally (56%), living in this country (62%) or living throughout the world (62%).

Table six demonstrates that there are some important variations in the ways in which members of the different denominations assess their religious experiences.

The Roman Catholics are clearly more likely to reject language like 'born again Christians', but they are just as open as members of the other denominations to being influenced positively by the charismatic movement or to speaking in tongues.

The Anglicans are people who are less likely than members of other denominations to be aware of the Holy Spirit helping them in their daily life. Anglicans are also less likely than members of other denominations to be conscious of being part of a worldwide fellowship. Anglicans are less likely to feel close to other Christians living in this country or living throughout the world.

Traditionally the Methodists are a 'holy people'. In this survey they are more likely than members of other denominations to be conscious of God's guidance in their daily life and to feel that the Holy Spirit helps them in their daily life. The Methodists are more likely than members of other denominations to be conscious of being part of a worldwide fellowship. Methodists are more likely to feel close to other Christians living locally, living in this country, and living throughout the world.

The most important feature in this section to characterise the members of the United Reformed Church concerns the way in which their distinctive religious experience separates them from other local Christians. On the one hand, members of the United Reformed Church display a higher than average awareness of feeling close to other Christians living in this country and throughout the world. On

Table 6   Religious Experience

	Cath %	Angl %	Meth %	URC %
I am conscious of God's guidance in my daily life	75	73	83	81
The Holy Spirit helps me in my daily life	72	60	75	62
I have experienced a religious conversion	19	18	17	21
My faith has been influenced positively by the charismatic movement	14	12	9	15
I have felt moved to pray or speak in a language unknown to me	10	8	5	4
I describe myself as a 'born again Christian'	5	8	19	15
I feel close to other Christians living locally	54	55	68	49
I feel close to other Christians living in this country	64	54	68	66
I feel close to other Christians throughout the world	61	57	68	67

the other hand, members of the United Reformed Church are less likely than members of other denominations to feel close to other Christians living locally.

Open to Change

The Church Congregation Survey included nine items to explore churchgoers' perceptions of the various changes being faced by the church today. Taking all four congregations in Market Astey together, the following picture emerged.

The practice of the remarriage of divorced people in church now clearly has the support of the majority of churchgoers, with 57% in favour, 15% against, and 28% undecided. The practice of lay people leading worship is less clearly decided, with 50% in favour, 20% against and 30% undecided.

A significant minority of churchgoers still feel uncomfortable with women leading worship. Thus, 18% disagree with women leading worship, compared with 57% in favour. Similarly, 25% disagree with the ordination of women to the priesthood, compared with 56% in favour. While the majority of churchgoers know where they stand on the rôle of women in the leadership of worship, they are much less decided about the use of inclusive language in church services. Thus,

53% say that they have not made up their mind on this issue, compared with 32% in favour and 15% against.

In the area of Christian initiation only a minority of churchgoers consider that churches should not baptise babies (7%) or that churches should only baptise babies of regular churchgoers (11%). Open baptism of infants remains the norm favoured by the people in the pews. One in every two churchgoers feel that eight-year-olds should be welcome to receive communion (51%).

The question of tithing splits churchgoers into three groups of nearly equal size. One-third agree that Christians should give at least five percent of their income to the church (33%). Just over a third disagree with this view (37%). Just under a third have not made up their minds (30%).

Table seven demonstrates that there are some important variations between the different denominations on these often controversial issues.

Table 7   Open to Change

	Cath %	Angl %	Meth %	URC %
I am in favour of lay leadership of worship	39	39	71	85
I am in favour of using inclusive language in church services	36	36	23	20
I am in favour of the ordination of women to the priesthood	31	69	80	83
I am in favour of female leadership of worship	38	61	81	80
Divorced people should be allowed to be remarried in church	40	60	79	79
Churches should not baptise babies	8	5	5	15
Churches should only baptise babies of regular churchgoers	14	7	12	11
Churchgoing eight-year-olds should be welcome to receive communion	80	33	24	28
Christians should give at least five percent of their income to the church	35	25	35	38

Compared with the other denominations, Roman Catholics show much less enthusiasm for women to be involved in the leadership of worship or for women to be ordained to the priesthood. Along with Anglicans, Roman Catholics show much less enthusiasm than members of the Free Churches for lay leadership or worship. Roman

Catholics are more inclined than members of other denominations to take a hard line against the remarriage of divorced people in church. In accordance with their general practice, Roman Catholics are much more likely than members of other denominations to welcome church-going eight-year-olds to communion.

Anglicans are less likely than members of other denominations to think that Christians should give at least five percent of their income to the church. Anglicans show more support than Roman Catholics for female leadership of worship and for the ordination of women, but less support for these issues than members of the Free Churches. Similarly, Anglicans show more support than Roman Catholics for the remarriage of divorced people in church, but less support for this than members of the Free Churches.

On many of these issues there is much in common between members of the Methodist and United Reformed Church, in clear contrast with Anglicans and Roman Catholics. The Free Churches are much more in favour of lay leadership of worship and of the full involvement of women in leading worship and in ministry. The Free Churches are more liberal in their attitude toward the remarriage of divorced people in church. On the other hand, members of the Free Churches are less in favour of using inclusive language in church services, compared with Anglicans and Roman Catholics. The one issue on which the members of the United Reformed Church stand apart from the Methodists concerns their even greater enthusiasm for lay leadership of worship.

The Tenets of Faith

The Church Congregation Survey included nine items to test the extent to which churchgoers today hold to the traditional tenets of Christian belief. Taking all four congregations in Market Astey together, the following picture emerged.

It cannot be taken for granted that everyone who attends church is secure in his or her faith in God. While 95% of the churchgoers in Market Astey could say with confidence that they believed in God and in Jesus Christ, the remaining 5% were not so sure. In other words, one in every twenty churchgoers preferred to call themselves agnostics who were, in one sense or another, seeking faith rather than celebrating faith through their attendance at church.

Churchgoers are generally less sure of their faith in the third person of the Trinity. While 86% of churchgoers confessed belief in the Holy Spirit, 13% remained uncertain and 1% denied belief. Traditional beliefs about Jesus are held by around seven churchgoers in every ten.

Thus 73% believe that Jesus physically rose from the dead and 72% believe in the virgin birth of Jesus. Looked at from the opposite perspective, the physical resurrection is denied by 6% and the virgin birth by 8%. Four-fifths of churchgoers believe in life after death (78%). Two-thirds believe heaven is a real place (64%), but only one third believe hell is a real place (32%).

The exclusivity of the Christian faith is maintained by four or five churchgoers out of every ten. The view that Christianity is the only true religion is accepted by 44%, but rejected by 31%. The remaining 25% are undecided.

Table eight demonstrates the extent to which orthodoxy in belief varies between those who attend the different denominations.

Table 8 The Tenets of Faith

	Cath %	Angl %	Meth %	URC %
I believe in God	96	92	97	92
I believe in Jesus Christ	96	93	97	94
I believe in the Holy Spirit	91	82	88	77
I believe in life after death	83	72	84	66
I believe that Jesus physically rose from the dead	81	63	73	64
I believe in the virgin birth of Jesus	83	61	65	64
Heaven is a real place	72	58	56	57
Hell is a real place	40	28	23	30
Christianity is the only true religion	53	40	33	38

Roman Catholics clearly emerge as the most orthodox believers in Market Astey. Roman Catholics are more likely than members of other denominations to express belief in the Holy Spirit, in the virgin birth and in the physical resurrection of Jesus, and in heaven and hell as real places. Roman Catholics are also more likely than members of other denominations to take the view that Christianity is the only true religion.

Overall, Anglicans are less orthodox in their beliefs than Roman Catholics. In Anglican congregations there is a higher proportion of people who are uncertain about their faith in God, Jesus and the Holy Spirit. Anglicans are less inclined to believe in the virgin birth and physical resurrection of Jesus. Anglicans are less inclined to believe in heaven and hell as real places.

Just as there are sharp contrasts between the Anglicans and Roman Catholics, so there are between the members of the Methodist and United Reformed Church. The Methodists are more firmly committed to a traditional pattern of beliefs than the members of the United Reformed Church.

Of all the denominations, Methodists are most clear in their rejection of hell as a real place. Of all the denominations, members of the United Reformed Church are least clear in their belief in life after death.

Believing the Bible

The Church Congregation Survey included six items specifically designed to test churchgoers' beliefs about the Bible. Taking all four congregations in Market Astey together, the following picture emerged.

Overall, only one in every six churchgoers believes in the inerrancy of Scripture, with 17% agreeing that the Bible is completely true without any error. On the other hand, 45% reject this statement and 38% are not clear what to believe. Two out of every five churchgoers take a creationist view, with 41% agreeing that God made the world in six days and rested on the seventh. On the other hand, 26% reject this statement and 33% are not clear what to believe. The majority of churchgoers take a literal and factually historical view of the gospel stories of the miracles of Jesus, believing that Jesus really healed lepers (77%), that Jesus really turned water into wine (61%), that Jesus really walked on water (55%) and that Jesus really fed 5,000 people with five loaves and two fishes (54%).

Table nine demonstrates that there are some important variations in beliefs about the Bible between those who attend the different denominations.

Overall, the Roman Catholics held the most fundamentalist view of Scripture. A higher percentage of Roman Catholics than of other denominations believe that Jesus really healed lepers, turned water into wine, walked on water, and fed the five thousand. A higher percentage of Roman Catholics than of other denominations believe that God made the world in six days and rested on the seventh.

Overall, the Anglicans held the most liberal view of Scripture. A lower percentage of Anglicans than of other denominations agreed with the statement that the Bible is completely true, without any error.

While members of the United Reformed Church are more likely to claim belief in the inerrancy of Scripture than the Methodists, the rest of the statistics show that it is the Methodists who are more likely to believe what they read.

Table 9   Believing the Bible

	Cath %	Angl %	Meth %	URC %
The Bible is completely true, without any error	20	12	15	21
Jesus really turned water into wine	70	51	60	57
Jesus really healed lepers	82	73	80	66
Jesus really fed 5,000 people with five loaves and two fishes	62	44	53	49
Jesus really walked on water	65	46	49	49
God made the world in six days and rested on the seventh	49	34	39	32

The Social Gospel

The Church Congregation Survey included nine items to explore churchgoers' priorities in connection with the social gospel. Taking all four congregations in Market Astey together, the following picture emerged.

There is no doubt in churchgoers' minds that churches should be actively involved helping those in need. At the same time there is a fairly clear set of priorities as to which needs should be higher on the agenda. More than nine out of every ten churchgoers feel that churches should be in business to help the lonely (97%), the handicapped (93%) and the elderly (92%). There is less sympathy, however, for other areas of need. The proportions fall to around three-quarters of churchgoers who feel that churches should help alcoholics (77%), AIDS sufferers (75%), drug addicts (75%), one-parent families (75%), ethnic minorities (73%) and the unemployed (72%).

Table ten demonstrates how the social gospel is interpreted differently by those who attend different denominations.

Overall, Roman Catholics emerge as the group most committed to the social gospel in Market Astey. While the priorities of the Roman Catholics follow the general trend, each issue receives a slightly higher vote than is the case among other denominations.

Overall, Anglicans emerge as slightly less committed to the social gospel than the average churchgoer in Market Astey. In particular they show somewhat less concern for AIDS sufferers and for drug addicts.

Methodists are people who show empathy for the churches' work among the lonely, the handicapped and the elderly. They show much

Table 10   The Social Gospel

	Cath %	Angl %	Meth %	URC %
Churches should help the lonely	97	97	99	96
Churches should help the handicapped	96	90	92	94
Churches should help the elderly	93	88	92	96
Churches should help alcoholics	81	75	68	85
Churches should help AIDS sufferers	80	69	61	87
Churches should help drug addicts	78	70	67	85
Churches should help ethnic minorities	76	70	69	72
Churches should help one-parent families	76	75	64	87
Churches should help the unemployed	73	69	64	84

less concern, however, for alcoholics, AIDS sufferers, drug addicts, ethnic minorities, one-parent families and the unemployed.

It is the members of the United Reformed Church who show the highest level of concern, compared with the other denominations, that churches should work among alcoholics, AIDS sufferers, drug addicts, one-parent families and the unemployed. However, their particular emphasis on the social gospel does not extend so far with regard to helping ethnic minorities.

Political and Social Concerns

The Church Congregation Survey included six items to explore the extent to which churchgoers considered that churches should be actively involved in political and social matters. Taking all four congregations in Market Astey together, the following picture emerged.

Around three-quarters of churchgoers are clear that there is a positive rôle for the churches in family issues. Thus, 77% of churchgoers maintain that churches should be actively involved in marriage guidance. Almost as much importance is given to educational and social issues, with 71% maintaining that churches should be involved in educational issues, and 71% maintaining that churches should be involved in social issues.

Churchgoers are generally less certain about the churches' involvement in environmental issues. Thus, 60% maintain that churches should be involved in environmental issues and 55% maintain that churches should be involved in green issues.

There is much less commitment to the churches' involvement in politics. Faced with the claim that churches should be actively involved in political issues, 33% of churchgoers are in favour, 41% are against, and 26% are undecided.

Table eleven demonstrates that there are some important variations in attitudes towards these areas by those who attend different denominations.

Table 11   Political and Social Concerns

	Cath %	Angl %	Meth %	URC %
Churches should be actively involved in political issues	37	26	25	43
Churches should be actively involved in environmental issues	56	64	57	71
Churches should be actively involved in educational issues	76	69	53	80
Churches should be actively involved in social issues	71	72	68	75
Churches should be actively involved in marriage guidance	83	76	67	75
Churches should be actively involved in green issues	52	60	48	62

Roman Catholics display an above average concern for the churches' involvement in marriage guidance and in educational issues.

Anglicans display an above average concern for the churches' involvement in environmental and green issues. Anglicans also display an above average reluctance to permit religion to mix with politics.

Methodists display the overall lowest level of concern for the churches to be involved in political and social issues. In particular they are much less concerned than members of other denominations that churches should be involved in educational issues.

By way of contrast, members of the United Reformed Church display the overall highest level of concern for the churches to be involved in political and social issues. This is the case regarding educational, social, environmental and green issues. Members of the United Reformed Church are less concerned than Roman Catholics with the issue of marriage guidance.

POSTSCRIPT

The churches in Market Astey employed the findings from the Church Congregation Survey in order to evaluate their current programmes of Christian education and to assess the ways in which they could profitably co-operate in learning together and the ways in which such co-operation would prove to be unrealistic or unhelpful. Others may find it equally valuable as a piece of research to aid their reflection on adult Christian education strategies.

The Church Congregation Survey is now available for other local churches or groups of churches to use in their own situation. Those who are interested in exploring this opportunity further are invited to contact the Revd Professor Jeff Astley, Director of the North of England Institute for Christian Education in Durham, for further details.

NOTE

[1]   The abbreviated form of the Revised Eysenck Personality Questionnaire is described fully in L. J. Francis, L. B. Brown and R. Philipchalk, 'The Development of an Abbreviated Form of the Revised Eysenck Personality Questionnaire (EPQR-A): Its Use among Students in England, Canada, the USA and Australia', *Personality and Individual Differences*, 13, 1992, pp. 443–449. A number of studies are beginning to demonstrate the importance of personality theory for helping to understand the preferences displayed by different churchgoers. Examples of such studies are provided by L. J. Francis and J. Martineau, *Rural Praise*, Leominster: Gracewing Fowler Wright, 1996, and by L. J. Francis, J. Astley, W. K. Kay and M. Carter, 'Is Adult Christian Education Mainly for Stable Extraverts?', *Studies in the Education of Adults*, 29, 1997, pp. 191–199.

Appendix

Finding Out for Yourself: DIY Surveys

Carolyn Wilcox

All honest attempts to study a problem systematically or to add to our knowledge of a problem may be regarded as research.[1]

INTRODUCTION

Those with a responsibility for Christian education may wish to find out more for themselves about the adult learners committed to their charge, for education always needs to begin where people are. The empirical research that informs many of the essays in this book is based on *survey work* with adults, both churchgoers and non-church-goers. This is a very effective method of 'listening to the learners', in a careful and ordered manner.

Before embarking on any piece of research, it is vital to ask and answer three pertinent questions:

1. What do I need to know ? (Asking *why* I need to know it can also be helpful.)
2. What is the best way to collect the information?
3. When the information has been collected, what am I going to do with it?

Using the answers to these questions, a statement of aims and objectives may be written. Then, before the project is taken any further, it should be discussed with colleagues, and anyone else who might be able to offer advice or information. If sufficient enthusiasm and energy remain after all this, the study may be planned in more detail. If, on the other hand, enthusiasm has evaporated, then a good deal of time and effort has been saved. *All research needs careful planning.*

WHAT IS A SURVEY?

A survey is a useful way of collecting information from a large number of people in a relatively short space of time. This can be achieved using techniques such as questionnaires and interviews. The aim of a survey is to obtain information which when analysed allows patterns within the data to be discerned and comparisons made. The data produced by a survey can be used to test certain hypotheses, but cannot be used to establish cause/effect relationships.

Representative Samples

The national census, which takes place every 10 years, aims to cover 100% of the population of Great Britain, but few surveys are so ambitious. If your population is fairly small, as might be the case for a church congregation or school, then it is possible to use the whole population. If, however, your population size is much greater than say 300, it will probably be necessary to use a *representative sample*. For example, instead of surveying everyone living in a rural county, it would be more economical to chose a typical village as a sample of the population of the county. Provided that the sample is truly representative, the findings may be presented as typical of the population as a whole. But is it representative? How you select your sample depends very much on the characteristics of your population. If your population is large and contains subgroups – such as different age groups, men and women, black and white and so on – it is first necessary to decide what proportion of the population each of the subgroups represents. This will determine how many from each subgroup should be included in the sample. It is often better to ignore natural groups (such as villages) in favour of a selected representative sampling across the wider population.

Example
Population size 350, which may be broken down *in terms of age* as follows:

under 18	18–30 yrs	31–45 yrs	46–60 yrs	60+ yrs
50	60	100	100	40

This may be expressed graphically, in a 'pie chart':

Age groups in population

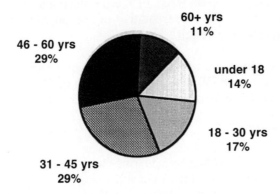

The population may be 'broken down *by sex*' (as social scientists sometimes wittily put it) into further subgroups:

	under 18	18–30 yrs	31–45 yrs	46–60 yrs	60+ yrs
Female:	30	40	70	60	20
Male:	20	20	30	40	20

This may also be expressed graphically, this time in a 'bar chart':

What is clear from this (purely fictitious) population is that if only one of the age groups was surveyed, or the same number sampled from each of the groups, then the findings would be unlikely to be representative of the population as a whole. In order to avoid this, the researcher should decide on the size of sample, say 150, and then work out how many to take from each subgroup, so that their proportions in the sample mimic those of the parent population.

To produce a sample representative of the population given in the example above would require :

Twenty-two respondents *under 18*, made up of 13 *girls* and 9 *boys*
Twenty-four in the 18–30 age group, made up of 16 *women* and 8 *men*
Forty-three 31–45 year olds, made up of 30 *women* and 13 *men*
Forty-three 46–60 year olds, made up of 26 *women* and 17 *men*
Eighteen over 60's, made up of 9 *men* and 9 *women*

These figures are rounded up, bearing in mind that 0.5 (or any fraction) of a person is difficult to consult!

Respondents should be selected, at random if possible, from the electoral roll or any other appropriate list. Random selection can be achieved in several ways, for example by picking every third (or 2nd, or *nth*) name until enough participants have been selected.

Homogeneous Populations

If the target population is fairly homogeneous and has no obvious subgroups then participants may be selected, again *at random*, from whatever list has been chosen. Selecting at random is important for research, because it helps reduce any bias that might be introduced by the person selecting the sample. It is easy to get the answers you want by asking the people you know will give that answer. And it is very easy to do this unconsciously.

Volunteers

Asking for volunteers has both advantages and disadvantages. The main advantage is that a person who volunteers to do something is more likely to complete the task. The main disadvantage is that people who volunteer are different from those who don't, and this may reduce the representative nature of the sample. *A representative sample is the ideal situation*, in real life things are often far from ideal but the aim should be to get as close to this situation as possible.

SURVEY DESIGN AND ADMINISTRATION

Having completed the preliminary planning stage, decided that a survey is the appropriate method for gathering the information required, identified the target population and selected a sample, the next step is to decide whether a questionnaire survey or an interview survey will best suit the purposes of the research.

Questionnaires

> The world is full of well-meaning people who believe that anyone who can write plain English and has a modicum of common sense can produce a good questionnaire.[2]

Unfortunately, although common sense and the ability to write plain English are very helpful, they are not enough. The design stage of any questionnaire requires that careful thought be given to:

1. selecting question type,
2. framing the questions,
3. designing and determining layout of the questionnaire,
4. piloting the forms bearing the questionnaire.

All these steps should take place before a single form is given out to the representative sample. They are all time-consuming, but in the long run they will save a great deal of time and effort, and should ensure that your findings are useful.[3] Next comes:

5. distribution and return of the forms, and finally,
6. analysis of responses once the forms have been completed.

Having decided what information is required by the research, it is imperative that you work out carefully the exact questions for the questionnaire.

Types of Question

There are two major categories of question: *verbal or open* and *structured or closed*.

Verbal or Open Questions

> *I'd like you to look back, and tell me your main impressions of your time at school.*

Questions like this leave respondents free to answer in their own words and can produce useful information. However, analysis of responses to this type of question can be a problem and may require some sort of 'content analysis'.[4]

Structured or Closed Questions

More structured questions will not present so many problems at the analysis stage because they limit the reply to a fixed set of responses. They do, however, require careful planning. Structured questions may use one of a number of formats:

☐ A list of items is offered, any number of which may be selected – e.g. a list of qualifications. Care needs to be taken to ensure an *adequate* list of items is given.

☐ The response is only one of a given set of categories, this format is often used for identifying ages (e.g. 21–35 yrs, etc.). Again care is required to ensure that all possible categories are included ('other, please specify' can overcome this, but should be used sparingly).

☐ The respondent is asked to place items in order of rank, e.g. some types of competition make use of this format by asking people to place characteristics of cars, such as safety, comfort, reliability, etc., in order of importance.

☐ The response is a number (exact or approximate) giving the amount of some characteristic, e.g. height, salary, exact age.

Guidelines for Framing Questions

There are three golden rules to follow, *the three S's*. The aim is to achieve questions which are :

 short long questions are difficult to follow and may cause confusion.

 simple so that the questions can be understood by a wide range of people. (Avoid technical terms or terms which may mean different things to different people.)

 single each question should only ask one thing at a time, not e.g. 'Do you pray and attend church?'

Other Pitfalls

Avoid questions which may bias responses by:

- making use of emotive language, e.g. 'Do you think that single mothers should be allowed to scrounge off the tax payer?'
- pressuring people into agreeing, e.g. 'Experts agree that men are less tolerant; what do you think?' If experts agree, who is the respondent to disagree?
- asking leading questions, e.g. 'Do you not agree that parents should have the right to have a say in their children's education?' It may be difficult for parents to say 'No' in response to this statement.
- making assumptions about the respondent, e.g. 'Which Sunday School does your child attend?' makes several assumptions: that the respondent has a child, that there is only one such child, and that the child attends Sunday School.
- asking for information of a very personal nature. Such questions should only be asked if absolutely necessary, and should be very carefully worded in order to avoid offending respondents and losing their co-operation. The best position for questions of a personal nature is towards the end of the questionnaire.
- making other presumptions, e.g. 'Does your employment make adequate provision for maternity/paternity leave?' makes two presumptions: first that leave should be given, and secondly that this should apply to fathers as well as mothers. The question is thus rendered invalid.
- asking for information that the respondent is unlikely to have (or may have to search to find out), as this may well cause the respondent to abandon the whole questionnaire.

Design and Layout

Recipients of questionnaires need to be encouraged to read and to answer your questions. Presentation plays a very important rôle in achieving this aim; anything which looks untidy or confusing may be filed in the bin!

Here are *some simple guidelines:*

- Questionnaires should be typed or printed.
- Instructions should be clear.
- Questions should be well spaced out.
- Response boxes should be kept large enough, in line, and to

the right of the page. This will make both writing in them and extracting information from them much easier.

- Take care over the order of questions. Start with straightforward easy-to-answer questions, before moving on to the more complex topics. Leave sensitive issues until later in the questionnaire.
- Avoid the risk of response bias (that is, the respondent getting set in a pattern of ticking all the boxes in the same way without thinking), by varying the way responses have to be made.
- If you intend to use a computer for analysis, leave space at the right of the sheet for coding.

'Piloting the Instrument'

This may, at first glance, seem like a waste of time, but many irritating hitches can be avoided by asking a small group of friends or colleagues to run through the form for you. They will give you an idea of how long it takes to complete and should pinpoint any unclear instructions or difficult questions. It may also be instructive to ask for any other general comments they may have about the questionnaire.

Distribution of Questionnaires

Before distributing your questionnaires, you need to give careful thought to how you are going to introduce your survey to participants. You need to state, briefly, the purpose of the questionnaire and what you intend doing with the information gathered. Respondents often feel reassured if a guarantee of anonymity and/or confidentiality is given, but before promising either decide what you mean by the terms. Do you mean that there will be no way of identifying individual respondents or that only specific people will see the returns? Do you mean that the report will be published but no names mentioned, or that only certain people will see the report? You need to be sure of what you are offering and to make this clear to your respondents.[5]

Ideally the questionnaire should be given to the respondent personally. Then explanations can be given, queries dealt with and in some cases questionnaires may be completed on the spot. Co-operation is much improved if personal contact has been established. Alternatively, colleagues and friends could help with distribution, but they would need careful briefing if they are to explain the questionnaire or a carefully-worded covering letter needs to be given out.

Failing this, forms will need to be sent through the post. A carefully-worded letter of explanation and a self-addressed reply envelope (stamped if the form is to be returned by post) should be included with the questionnaire.

However forms are distributed, it is important to decide on a return date. Experience has shown that it is unwise to allow too long, two weeks is a reasonable time for completion. Specify the precise day and date rather than just a vague 'please return in two weeks'. Giving the day and the date helps to jog some people's memories. Having said that, people differ in their responses to such requests, and in the case of other respondents giving them a precise return date could be to invite them to keep the questionnaires on their desks until that date, and then to throw them away because it is now 'too late'. The choice is yours!

Interviews

Responses to items on a questionnaire have to be taken at face value, but an interview can allow a response to be developed and clarified, which may be a considerable advantage. The major disadvantage of using interviews is that they are very time consuming, which makes them expensive. The interviewer's influence on the way in which a participant responds is an additional factor that needs to be taken into consideration. In an effort to control and minimise these inter-personal variables, it is important that interviewers receive some training in listening skills, non-verbal communication and natural questioning techniques.

Interviews may take a variety of forms. They can in fact be completely *structured*, which is very like presenting a questionnaire face-to-face. The interviewer follows a carefully laid out series of closed questions with answers pre-coded. This means that information gathered from different people can be compared, and the procedure for developing this type of interview is the same as that just discussed for the development of questionnaires. For first time interviewers, the structured interview is probably the best option. However, the technique is not flexible and this means that answers will be limited and possibly incomplete.

Some of these problems may be overcome by using a *structured open-ended* interview format. The open-ended questions are carefully planned in advance, with all respondents being asked the same questions but answering in their own words. The drawbacks of this technique involve problems associated with recording and coding responses. The advantages lie in the flexibility to follow up and clarify responses and in the richness of the data gathered.

It may be helpful to use a tape recorder to record responses. Should this method be chosen it is vital to get the participant's permission first and to allow time (and money) for transcribing the data after the interview.

For someone skilled in the art of interviewing, it is possible to be even less formal and just use prompts to guide the respondent through an area of interest, or even to adopt a completely informal approach and let the respondent determine the direction taken by the interview. These methods are adopted by researchers interested in gathering wholly qualitative data and are unlikely to be appropriate in small studies.

PROCESSING THE DATA

Recording the Information

In a questionnaire survey, once the questionnaires have been completed and returned the investigator will be faced with a pile of forms full of information. To be of any use, this information must now be organised by transferring it to summary sheets (which should, ideally, have been prepared at the same time as the questionnaire). The exact layout of a summary sheet is up to the investigator, but the example shown below demonstrates one way of setting it out.

Respondent	Age Group 1 2 3 4 5 6 7	Sex M F	Question 1 yes no	Question 2 1 2 3 4 5
1	1	1	1	1
2	1	1	1	1
3	1	1	1	1
4	1	1	1	1

The first column is for the respondent's name or (better still) number, the second column might be for information about age group, the third records the sex of the respondent, and so on until all the information from each form has been recorded.

Questions with open-ended answers need processing rather differently. Probably the best approach in this case is to record each answer word for word on separate, cross-referenced, sheets of paper.

Scales of Measurement

It is important to realise that there are different types of data, different *scales of measurement*. The type of data you have collected will determine the method of analysis which can be used.

Nominal scales

Nominal scales are the simplest, and arise when categories with no numerical significance are used. For example, an item on a questionnaire may ask for a 'yes' or 'no' response. To aid coding, numbers may be attached to these, as in this example:

response:	Anglican	Baptist	Methodist
code :	1	2	3

This is called the 'coding frame'

These numbers (the codes) are completely arbitrary and are merely ways of labelling categories. *Remember, they have no numerical significance.*

Ordinal scales

Ordinal scales arise where items are rated or ranked. Such a coding frame might be:

disagree strongly	disagree	neutral	agree	agree strongly
1	2	3	4	5

In this instance, the higher the category chosen the greater the strength of agreement, thus the responses may be put *in order* from highest to lowest. Ranks in the armed forces give rise to an ordinal scale, since a private has the lowest status, a sergeant is 'higher', and so on. Ordinal scales distinguish order but tell you nothing about the distance between the points on the scale. (They tell you that 1 is less than 2 but not by how much.)

Interval scales

Interval scales are more sophisticated again. Exam marks, IQ scores and other measures of performance are usually regarded as following an interval scale. On such a scale, scores are not only placed in order but, as equal intervals represent equal amounts, it is also possible to use the size of the difference between individuals for comparison purposes. However, no marking system on a performance test can measure the full range of ability (full marks on a test does not mean that you know all there is to know about a subject). Thus if A scores 75 marks, B 45 marks and C 15 marks, it is not possible to say that A is five times more proficient than C, because the test examines only a selected area of the subject. But it is possible to say that, with regard to the test questions, A knows as much more than B as B knows more than C.

Ratio scales

Ratio scales are the highest order of measurement. Age, height, salary and so on follow ratio scales. As with interval scales, equal differences represent equal amounts, but unlike interval scales absolute measurements are valid. Thus it may be said that a person of 50 has lived for twice as long as a person of 25, or that someone earning £10,000 a year earns half as much as someone earning £20,000. This property is unique to the ratio scale of measurement.

Methods of Analysis

There are many ways in which data may be analysed, too many to be covered comprehensively within the scope of this appendix. However, it is possible to look at two basic techniques that might be useful.

1.   Describing the data using *graphs, tables* and *descriptive statistics.*
2.   Simple *content analysis* for the open questions.

Graphs and Tables

Let us assume that the first question of your survey asks,

  Do you think church services are too long?   Yes/No

The summary sheet indicates that 50 people said 'yes' and 50 people said 'no'. On closer examination it is discovered that it is mainly younger people who think services are too long. How may this be shown clearly? A table or a simple bar chart shows clearly the frequencies for each age group. (Because the sample is of 100 respondents, the number in each category corresponds with the *percentage*, which is usually the preferred figure to display.)

Table   Services too long?

Age group	Yes	No	Total
12–18 years old	15	5	20
19–30 years old	4	1	5
31–45 years old	12	8	20
46–55 years old	10	10	20
56 years or more	4	31	35
	45	55	100

Bar Chart

If the question is rephrased slightly it becomes the statement: *I think church services are too long*, and responses that fit an ordinal scale may be invited:

Table   Services too long?

disagree strongly	disagree	neutral	agree	agree strongly
25	20	15	15	25

This time I have used a simple pie chart that gives the number of people choosing each option as a percentage of the total sample. (It is up to the investigator to decide whether to use graphs and/or tables to display the results.)

Pie Chart

Some Descriptive Statistics

Statistical information is the *numerical* data gathered during *quantitative* research. It would be overwhelming, to say the least, to be presented with each individual score for every question. Rather, what is expected in a report of any research is a summary of any major trends and differences. This may be achieved by means of statistical analysis. As the term suggests, descriptive statistics provide a means of describing group data. Such statistics include:

- *measures of central tendency* or *averages* (the value which is most typical of the group); and
- *measures of dispersion* or *spread* (how much or how little the group tends to vary around this central or typical value).

There are many statistics books that explain how these measures may be determined. What follows is a brief description of the types of measures which may be appropriate. For further information on calculation you will need to refer to a more specialised text.[6]

Measures of Central Tendency

There are three measures of central tendency commonly used: the mode, median and mean.

The mode is the most frequently occurring value, or in the case of grouped data, the modal class is the one which has the highest frequency. For example:

12 – 18 yrs	*19 – 30 yrs*	*31 – 45 yrs*	*46 – 55 yrs*	*56+ yrs*
20	5	20	20	35

In this example the modal group for age would be 56+ years. This is a very simple measure and can be used even where a variable is measured on the nominal scale. The mode does not take into account the exact values of each item, and it may not be very useful for relatively small sets of values where there are several modes – e.g. 1, 1, 2, 3, 3, 4, 4, 5, 6, 6, 7, 8, 9 (multiple modes: 1, 3, 4 and 6).

The median is the middle value when the data are listed in order, with as many values 'above' it as there are 'below'. If there are an odd number of values, as in the following example, the median is the mid value – in this case 15:

25, 23, **15**, 12, 11

By definition, a median can only exist for data that can be placed in order, i.e. variables that follow ordinal, interval or ratio scales. The median does not take into account the exact value of each item, and if values are few it may not be representative (thus for the data 2, 3, 5, 98, 112 the median would be 5).

The arithmetic mean, or simply 'the mean', is the measure that people usually think of when they talk about averages. The mean can only be used for variables measured on the interval or ratio scale. The arithmetic mean is the sum of values divided by the number of cases. To take an example, a group of ten parishioners have each given as their ideal for the duration of a particular service of worship (in minutes) 60, 60, 60, 45, **40**, **40**, 40, 40, 35, 35. These figures added together give 455, so the mean would be 45.5 mins. Note that the most frequent value (or mode) is 40 and the middle value (or median) is also 40. (In this example there are an even number of values, so the median is calculated by adding the two central values and dividing them by two.)

Example
A sample of 30 congregation members were asked to indicate how long they felt a church service should last. They provided the following responses: 10, 10, 10, 10, 10, 10, 20, 35, 35, 40, 40, 40, 40, 45, **45**, **50**, 50, 60, 60, 60, 60, 60, 60, 60, 60, 60, 90, 90, 120, 360 (*service time in minutes*).

- The modal (most common) value for this sequence of values is 60 minutes.
- The median (mid value) is 47.5 minutes (45 + 50 divided by 2).
- The mean is 56.7 minutes (1700 divided by 30).

We may ask why these 'typical' values in this example are so different. One way of understanding why this should be involves looking at the 'spread' or dispersion of the answers given by the participants in the study.

Measures of Dispersion

Measures of central tendency give the most typical value, but tell nothing about the distribution or spread of all the values. Measures of dispersion describe and quantify the *variability* within a set of data: that is, how much or how little the rest of the values tend to vary around the central or typical value. Measures of dispersion, if presented along with the measures of central tendency, help to summarise a set of data better by giving a description of the spread of the data around this value.

The three most commonly used measures of dispersion are: range, semi-interquartile range, and standard deviation. There are many statistics books which explain how measures of dispersion may be calculated and it is not intended here to go into the details of their determination. Suffice it to say that *the range*, the simplest measure of dispersion, is rather crude but may be useful when the data are evenly spread and there are no extreme values. The range has the advantage of being easy to calculate but it has a number of disadvantages. In particular it is easily distorted by extreme values and provides no information about the grouping of values around the typical value (or mean). If a set of data has a small number of extreme values the range gives a very misleading picture of the spread of the data. (In our example the range is 351 minutes.)

If the *median* is used as the measure of central tendency, then the ***semi-interquartile range*** is the most appropriate measure of dispersion. The semi-interquartile range concentrates on the distance between the two values which cut off the bottom and top 25% of scores, known as the lower and upper quartile respectively. The semi-interquartile range, although it is representative of the central values, still takes no account of extreme values and once again the result may not give a very accurate indication of the spread of responses. (In our example the upper quartile is 60, the lower quartile is 40. The semi-interquartile range is $\frac{1}{2}(60-40) = 10$.)

Where the *mean* is used, the ***standard deviation*** is the most appropriate measure of dispersion. This statistic takes into account all the values in the set. The larger the value of the standard deviation the greater the spread of responses around the mean. (In our example the standard deviation is 129·1.)

Content Analysis

Analysis of any open-ended questions that are used as part of a questionnaire or interview requires the use of content analysis, a technique developed for quantifying descriptive (or 'qualitative') material. Originally content analysis was devised as a specific method for sampling and analysing messages from the media, literature, famous people's speeches, or war time propaganda.

Step 1

The first thing you, as the researcher, must do is to become very familiar with the material which has been collected. This familiarity will enable you to decide on the *coding units* into which the material is to be categorised. For example, in a survey that asks adults about their view of God these units might be :

- words, e.g. gender-related words, such as 'Father', 'Mother' etc.;
- themes, e.g. judgement, forgiveness, creativity;
- time and space – the time and space devoted in each answer to particular themes, such as those given above.

In other areas (e.g. views of church services), a useful unit might be:

- items, e.g. parts of the service, building etc.

Step 2

Once these coding units have been decided upon and defined clearly, so that a system for categorising occurrences can be written down, then the data can be analysed in several ways:

- by *counting*: the number of units in each category might be counted, for example counting how many times the word 'Father' appears, this would provide nominal data;
- by *ranking*: for example responses to a question about attitude to religion could be ranked in terms of how positive they are, providing ordinal data;
- by *rating*: for example items could be scored for how much space has been devoted to each category, again providing ordinal data.

Ideally the *coding* should be done by people who have not been involved in conducting the research, thus removing any risk of researcher bias interfering with the results. This is not always possible but, to check that the coding scheme is accurate and reliable, it is important to ask someone who has not been involved in the research to code the responses using the pre-determined scheme. If the two coders disagree to any great extent then the coding units will require further thought and tighter definition.

CONCLUSION

The aim of this appendix has been to give a brief overview of research methodology. I hope that it will have provided some hints about conducting your own research. Considerable emphasis has been placed on the need for careful thought, planning and consultation *before* embarking on any field work. This is because, in general, the more detailed the preliminary work, the more useful the data are likely to be.

The *bibliography* at the end of this chapter contains some suggestions for further reading about survey methods, and some texts that include data relating to churchgoers in the United Kingdom and religious data about the general population. Before that, however, there is a *specimen questionnaire* which provides some examples showing how open and closed questions may be laid out.

SPECIMEN QUESTIONNAIRE

[Some specimen questions taken from a recent survey. The small figures in square brackets next to each question are included to assist in preparing the data for analysis.]

> Please circle only one number for each question
> unless requested otherwise

1.1. Are you male or female?

Female	 2	[1]
Male	 1	

1.2. To which age group do you belong?

20–29	 1	
30–39	 2	
40–49	 3	[2]
50–59	 4	
60–69	 5	
70–79	 6	
over 79	 7	

1.3. How long have you been attending your present church?

Less than 1 year	 1	
1–5 years	 2	[3]
6–10 years	 3	
More than 10 years	 4	

1.4. How would you best describe the location of the parish?

Rural	 1	
Semi-rural	 2	
Small town	 3	[4]
Suburban	 4	
Urban	 5	
Inner City	 6	
Other	 7	
Please specify	....	

1.5. Which term(s) best describe the predominant churchmanship of the parish? (You may circle **more than one** number.)

Anglo-Catholic	 1	
Low church	 2	[5–11]
Evangelical	 3	
Charismatic	 4	
Broad	 5	
Liberal	 6	
Other	 7	
Please specify	....	

For the next three questions, indicate your response by circling the number next to **the view closest to your own**. Please give the first answer which comes naturally to you; don't spend too long pondering over each question.

2.11. Baptism of infants is important.

Agree strongly	....	5
Agree	....	4
Uncertain	....	3	[12]
Disagree	....	2
Disagree strongly	....	1

2.12. A child becomes a full member of the Church through baptism.

Agree strongly	....	5
Agree	....	4
Uncertain	....	3	[13]
Disagree	....	2
Disagree strongly	....	1

2.13. Any child who is baptised should be entitled to receive at the Eucharist.

Agree strongly	....	5
Agree	....	4
Uncertain	....	3	[14]
Disagree	....	2
Disagree strongly	....	1

2.14. Baptism is important because:

. . . .

. . . .

NOTES

[1] Theodorson and Theodorson, 1969: 347.
[2] Oppenheim, 1992: 1.
[3] See p. 196 for a description of the summary sheets which should also be prepared during the design stage.
[4] See pp. 203–204 for a discussion of content analysis.
[5] 'Anonymity' in this context means that there are no means of identifying respondents, whereas 'confidentiality' is usually understood as a commitment not to identify individual respondents in any reports, verbal or written, based on the data collected.
[6] See, for example Heyes, 1993.

BIBLIOGRAPHY

This section includes books mentioned in the text, together with other books and articles that may be helpful either for further study of survey techniques or for examining data about churchgoing and non-churchgoing adults and their beliefs and values.

Abrams, Mark *et al.* (1985), *Values and Social Change in Britain*, Basingstoke: Macmillan.

Astley, Jeff and Day, David (eds) (1992), *The Contours of Christian Education*, Great Wakering: McCrimmons, part three.

Bailey, Kenneth D. (1982), *Methods of Social Research*, 2nd. edition, New York: The Free Press. (Although this is a textbook, it is very readable and provides clear explanations of the major methods used in social research.)

Bell, Judith (1987), *Doing Your Research Project: A Guide for First Time Researchers in Education and Social Science*, Milton Keynes: Open University Press. (This is an excellent little book which covers all you need to know about conducting your own research.)

Brierley, Peter (1991), *'Christian England': What the 1989 English Church Census Reveals*, London: MARC Europe.

Brierley, Peter (ed.) (1991), *Prospects for the Nineties: All England*, London: MARC Europe.

Brierley, Peter (1994), *Christianity by Numbers: Problems of Christian Data, Reactions of People, the Value of Christian Statistics*, London: Christian Research.

Brierley, Peter (ed.) (1999), *Religious Trends No. 2, 2000/01*, London: Christian Research/HarperCollins*Religious*. (Includes updates of statistics covering topics such as church attendance, church membership etc., across denominations and across the country.)

Bruce, Steve (1995), *Religion in Modern Britain*, Oxford: Oxford University Press.

Bryman, A. and Cramer, D. (1992), *Quantitative Data Analysis for Social Scientists*, London: Routledge.

Burgess, R. G. (ed.) (1989), *The Ethics of Educational Research*, New York: Falmer.

Buckler, Guy (1998), *Planning to Learn: Adult Christian Education in the Local Church*, ed. Jeff Astley, Leominster: Gracewing.

Buckler, Guy and Astley, Jeff (1992),'Learning and Believing in an Urban Parish', in Astley and Day (1992), ch. 26. (Includes data gathered by the research procedures described in Buckler, 1998.)

Church of Scotland Board of Social Responsibility (1987), *Lifestyle Survey*, Edinburgh: Quorum Press.

Coolican, Hugh (1990), *Research Methods and Statistics in Psychology*, London: Hodder and Stoughton. (Coolican covers the methods and statistics used in psychological research in a very accessible way. This is a useful book for investigating descriptive statistics further.)

Davie, Grace (1994), *Religion in Britain since 1945: Believing without Belonging*, Oxford: Blackwell.

Fisher, Elizabeth; Astley, Jeff and Wilcox, Carolyn (1992), 'A Survey of Bible Reading Practices and Attitudes to the Bible among Anglican Congregations', in Astley and Day (1992), ch. 25.

Francis, Leslie J.; Wilcox, Carolyn and Astley, Jeff (1992), 'What is a Christian? Investigating the Understanding of 16- to 19-year-olds', in Astley and Day (1992), ch. 22.

Gill, Robin (1999), *Churchgoing and Christian Ethics*, Cambridge: Cambridge University Press.

Gill, Robin; Hadaway, C. Kirk; Marler, Penny Long (1998), 'Is Religious Belief Declining in Britain?', *Journal for the Scientific Study of Religion*, 37, 3, 1998, pp. 507–516.

Griffin, Tom (ed.) (1990), *Social Trends 20*, London: HMSO. (See particularly chapter 11, pp. 165–168, relating to participation in the life of the community.)

Heyes, Steve (1993), *Starting Statistics in Psychology and Education: A Student Handbook*, London: Weidenfield. (A small, inexpensive paperback book which gives basic instructions for calculating measures of central tendency and dispersion.)

Hughes, J. (1990), *The Philosophy of Social Research*, 2nd edition, London: Longman.

Jackson, W. Carroll; Dudley, Carl S. and McKinney, William (eds) (1986), *Handbook for Congregational Studies*, Nashville, Tenn.: Abingdon.

Jowell, Roger; Witherspoon, Sharon and Brook, Lindsay (eds) (1990), *British Social Attitudes: The 7th Report*, Aldershot: Gower. (Provides some fascinating information and insights; pp. 184–190 looks at religion in Northern Ireland.)

Jowell, Roger; Curtice, John; Park, Alison; Brook, Lindsay; Thomson, Katerina and Bryson, Caroline (eds) (1998), *British and European Social Attitudes: The 15th Report*, Aldershot: Ashgate.

Kay, William K. and Francis, Leslie, J. (1996), *Drift from the Churches*, Cardiff: University of Wales Press. (A major review of data on attitude toward Christianity during childhood and adolescence, but with relevance for work with adults.)

Kay, William K. (1997), 'Belief in God in Great Britain 1945–1996: Moving the Scenery behind Classroom RE', *British Journal of Religious Education*, 20, 1, pp. 28–41. (A recent article which provides both a summary of figures relating to belief in God in Britain over the past fifty years and some useful references.)

Krarup, Helen (1982), *Conventional Religion and Common Religion in Leeds: Interview Schedule, Basic Frequencies by Question*, Leeds: University of Leeds (The raw data from a major survey of believing in the general population.)

Maunder, W.F. (ed.) (1986), 'Religion', *Reviews of United Kingdom Statistical Sources*, Vol. XX, Oxford: Pergamon. (This volume contains many facts and figures relating to religions in the UK, based on surveys conducted in the early 1980s.)

Oppenheim, A. N. (1992), *Questionnaire Design, Interviewing and Attitude Measurement*, London: Pinter. (*The* book on the design and administration of questionnaires and interviews.)

Patton, Michael Quinn (1987), *How to Use Qualitative Methods in Evaluation*, Newbury Park: Sage. (Discusses content analysis in some detail, see pp. 149–164.)

Rendle, Gilbert R. (1998), 'Assessing the Needs of a Congregation', in Nancy T. Foltz (ed.), *Handbook of Planning in Religious Education*, Birmingham, Ala.: Religious Education Press, ch. 5.

Richter, Philip and Francis, Leslie J. (1998), *Gone But Not Forgotten: Church Leaving and Returning*, London: Darton, Longman and Todd. (Data about those who leave the church.)

Svennevig, M. *et al.* (1988), *Godwatching: Viewers, Religion and Television*, London: John Libbey.

Theodorson, G. A. and Theodorson, A. G. (1969), *A Modern Dictionary of Sociology*, New York: Crowell.

Wraight, H. and Brierley, P. (1999), *UK Christian Handbook*, 2000/01, Millennium Edition, London: Christian Research and HarperCollins*Religious*.

Index of Subjects

Index of Names

CULTURE AND SOCIETY IN THE STUART RESTORATION

CULTURE AND SOCIETY IN THE STUART RESTORATION

Literature, Drama, History

EDITED BY

GERALD MACLEAN

Wayne State University, Detroit

CAMBRIDGE
UNIVERSITY PRESS

Published by the Press Syndicate of the University of Cambridge
The Pitt Building, Trumpington Street, Cambridge, CB2 1RP
40 West 20th Street, New York, NY 10011-4211, USA
10 Stamford Road, Oakleigh, Melbourne 3166, Australia

First published 1995

A catalogue record for this book is available from the British Library

Library of Congress cataloguing in publication data

Culture and society in the Stuart Restoration / edited by Gerald MacLean.
p.   cm.
Includes index.
ISBN 0 521 41605 1 (hardback) ISBN 0 521 47566 X (paperback)
1. English literature – Early modern, 1500–1700 – History and criticism. 2. Literature and
society – Great Britain – History – 18th century. 3. Great Britain – History – Restoration,
1660–1688. 4. Great Britain – Civilization – 17th Century.   I. MacLean, Gerald M.,
1952– .
PR437.L55   1995
942.06′6–dc20   94-19821   CIP

ISBN 0 521 41605 1 hardback
ISBN 0 521 47566 X paperback

Transferred to digital printing 2005

Contents

Notes on contributors

MOIRA FERGUSON is the James E. Ryan Chair in English and Women's Literature at the University of Nebraska-Lincoln. Her recent publications include *Subject to Others: British Women Writers and Colonial Slavery 1670–1834* (1992), *Colonial and Gender Relations from Mary Wollstonecraft to Jamaica Kincaid* (1993), and *The Hart Sisters: Early African-Caribbean Writers, Evangelicals, Radicals* (1993).

BRIDGET HILL is the author of *The Republican Virago: The Life and Times of Catharine Macaulay, Historian* (1992). With Christopher Hill she has recently completed an article on "Catharine Macaulay's *History* and her 'Catalogue of Tracts'." Her current work is on eighteenth-century domestic servants.

ELAINE HOBBY is Reader in Women's Studies at the Department of English and Drama, Loughborough University, where she has worked, very happily, since 1988. She began researching seventeenth-century women's writings in 1978, in direct response to being told, when a postgraduate student, that "there weren't any women then." The author of *Virtue of Necessity: English Women's Writing, 1649–1688* (1988) and numerous articles and chapters, she is currently working on a book about seventeenth-century women's sexuality.

ROBERT ILIFFE is presently at the Institute of Historical Research in the University of London and has published a number of articles on the history of science in the seventeenth and eighteenth centuries. He is currently completing a book on the construction of scientific instruments and the London instrument-making trade between 1550 and 1760.

N. H. KEEBLE is a Reader in English Studies at the University of Stirling. His publications, which are chiefly in the area of English cultural history of the early modern period, include studies of *Richard Baxter: Puritan Man of Letters* (1982) and *The Literary Culture of Nonconformity in Later Seventeenth-century England* (1987), editions of Richard Baxter's *Autobiography* (1974), *The Pilgrim's Progress* (1984) and tercentenary essays on Bunyan (1988), a two-volume *Calendar of the Correspondence of Richard Baxter* (1991) edited with Geoffrey F. Nuttall, and an anthology, *The Cultural Identity of Seventeenth-Century Woman: A Reader* (1994). He is currently editing Lucy Hutchinson's *Memoirs of the Life of Colonel Hutchinson* for Everyman's Library.

GERALD MACLEAN is Associate Professor of English at Wayne State University, Detroit. He has edited the 1677 English translation of François Poullain De la Barre's *The Woman as Good as the Man: Or, The Equality of Both Sexes* (1988). He is the author of *Time's Witness: Historical Representation in English Poetry, 1603–1660* (1990), and is the co-author with Donna Landry of *Materialist Feminisms* (1993). He is currently striving to complete a historical edition of the English poems published in 1660 commemorating the Stuart Restoration.

NANCY KLEIN MAGUIRE is Scholar-in-Residence at the Folger Shakespeare Library in Washington, D.C. She is the author of *Regicide and Restoration: English Tragicomedy, 1660–1671* (1992) and has contributed essays on the relationship of theatre and politics to *The Journal of British Studies, English Literary Renaissance,* and *The Appropriation of Shakespeare: Post-Renaissance Reconstructions of the Works and the Myth* (1991). She is the editor of *Renaissance Tragicomedy: Explorations in Genre and Politics* (1987), and is currently working on Anglo-French relations during the reign of Charles II.

JOHN PATRICK MONTAÑO is Assistant Professor of History at the University of Delaware. His book, *Courting the Moderates: Ideology, Consensus, and Politics in the Reign of Charles II* is forthcoming from Routledge, Chapman and Hall. At present he is engaged upon a study of privateering and government finance in the later seventeenth century.

STEVEN C. A. PINCUS is Assistant Professor of History at the University of Chicago. His book *Protestantism and Patriotism: Ideologies and the Making of English Foreign Policy 1650–1668* is forthcoming from Cambridge University Press. He has written a number of articles on later Stuart political culture, and is currently finishing a book on the rhetoric of universal monarchy 1559–1720 for Yale University Press.

JAMES GRANTHAM TURNER is Professor of English at the University of California, Berkeley. He has edited *Politics, Poetics and Hermeneutics in Milton's Prose* (1990) with David Loewenstein, and *Sexuality and Gender in Early Modern Europe: Institutions, Texts, Images* (1993), both from Cambridge University Press. He is the author of *The Politics of Landscape: Rural Scenery and Society in English Poetry, 1630–1660* (1979), and numerous articles on 17th- and 18th-century culture. *One Flesh: Paradisal Marriage and Sexual Relations in the Age of Milton* (1987) has just been reissued in a Clarendon Paperback edition by Oxford University Press.

ANDREW R. WALKLING is Assistant Professor of History at St. Olaf College, Minnesota, and has a number of articles dealing with Restoration Court culture forthcoming in musicological journals. He is currently completing a book on the role of the royal court in the politics of the 1670s and 1680s, focusing on Charles II's self-representation as a "baroque" monarch through his patronage of music and theater.

BLAIR WORDEN is Fellow and Tutor in Modern History at St. Edmund Hall, Oxford. His publications include *The Rump Parliament 1649–1653* (1974), an edition of Edmund Ludlow's *A Voice from the Watch Tower* (1978), and a series of essays on the political, religious and intellectual history of early modern England.

STEVEN N. ZWICKER is Professor of English at Washington University, St. Louis. He has written on Marvell, Milton, and Dryden, including: *Dryden's Political Poetry: The Typology of King and Nation* (1972), *Politics and Language in Dryden's Poetry: The Arts of Disguise* (1984), *Lines of Authority: Politics and English Literary Culture, 1649–1689* (1993), and has co-edited *Politics of Discourse: The Literature and History of Seventeenth-century England* (1987).

Acknowledgments

Chapter 11 first appeared in Moira Ferguson, *Subject to Others: British Women Writers and Colonial Slavery, 1670–1834* (New York and London, 1992), pp. 51–67, and is reprinted with permission from Routledge, Chapman and Hall, Inc., New York.

The page from the manuscript of Pepys's diary for 9 February 1668, is reproduced on p. 97 with the generous permission of the Master and Fellows, Magdalene College, Cambridge.

My thanks to Kevin Taylor for supporting the project since its inception, and to Michael Cordner and the other (anonymous) readers at Cambridge University Press. I drafted the initial proposal and solicited contributions during the autumn of 1989 while at the Center for Seventeenth- and Eighteenth-Century Studies at the William Andrews Clark Library of UCLA, with fellowship support from funds supplied by the National Endowment for the Humanities. For early conversations and advice, my thanks to Leo Braudy, John Brewer, Tim Keirns, Alan Roper, Susan Staves, Simon Shaffer, and Simon Varey. For general advice and critically informed encouragement at various times, I am also grateful to Iain Boal, Peter Borsay, Tim Harris, John Henry, Christopher Hill, Michael Hunter, Ronald Hutton, Don McKenzie, Michael McKeon, Frank Melton, Annabel Patterson, Stephen Pumphrey, Paul Seaward, Nigel Smith, and Sir Roy Strong. Special thanks to Donna Landry, David Loewenstein, Nancy Maguire, Arthur Marotti, John Reed, Charles Stivale, James Turner, Joseph Ward, Harold Weber, and Steve Zwicker, for reading and commenting on various drafts of the Introduction. Research funds from the office of the Vice President for Research at Wayne State University helped defray costs of preparing the manuscript. Jo Dulan once again took time away from her own research to help keyboard the chapters, for which I am particularly, however inadequately, grateful.

Abbreviations and note on the text

Place of publication for printed works is London unless otherwise stated. Spelling and punctuation in quotations from seventeenth- and eighteenth-century works follow the original except in the chapter by Blair Worden. Dates are given Old Style, but with the year regarded as starting on 1 January.

Abbreviated references to works frequently cited in single chapters are indicated in footnotes following the first reference. Footnote references to works frequently cited in two or more chapters are given according to the following abbreviations.

Burnet, *History*	Gilbert Burnet, *History of His Own Time*, 2nd ed. 6 vols. (Oxford, 1833).
CJ	*Journals of the House of Commons*
Clarendon, *History*	Edward Hyde, Earl of Clarendon, *The History of the Rebellion and Civil War in England*, ed. W. Dunn Macray, 6 vols. (Oxford, 1888). Rpt. 1958.
Crowne, *Works*	*The Dramatic Works of John Crowne*, ed. James Maidment and W. H. Logan, 4 vols. (Edinburgh, 1874).
CSPD	*Calendar of State Papers, Domestic*
CSPV	*Calendar of State Papers, Venetian*
DNB	*Dictionary of National Biography*
Dryden, *Poems*	*The Poems and Fables of John Dryden*, ed. James Kinsley, 4 vols. (Oxford, 1958). Rpt. 1961.

EHR	·*English Historical Review*
Grey, *Debates*	Anchitell Grey, ed., *Debates of the House of Commons From the Year 1667 to the Year 1694*, 10 vols. (1763).
Haley, *Shaftesbury*	K. H. D. Haley, *The First Earl of Shaftesbury* (Oxford, 1968).
Harris, *London Crowds*	Tim Harris, *London Crowds in the Reign of Charles II: Propaganda and Politics from the Restoration Until the Exclusion Crisis* (Oxford, 1985).
Harris, *et al.*, *Politics of Religion*	Tim Harris, Paul Seaward, and Mark Goldie, eds., *The Politics of Religion in Restoration England* (Oxford, 1990).
Hill, *Milton*	Christopher Hill, *Milton and the English Revolution* (1977).
Hill, *Experience of Defeat*	Christopher Hill, *The Experience of Defeat: Milton and Some Contemporaries* (1984).
Hobby, *Virtue of Necessity*	Elaine Hobby, *Virtue of Necessity: English Women's Writing, 1649–1688* (1988).
HLQ	*Huntington Library Quarterly*
Hutton, *Restoration*	Ronald Hutton, *The Restoration: A Political and Religious History of England and Wales 1658–1667* (Oxford, 1985).
Hutton, *Charles the Second*	Ronald Hutton, *Charles the Second, King of England, Scotland, and Ireland*, (Oxford, 1989).
Jose, *Ideas of the Restoration*	Nicolas Jose, *Ideas of The Restoration in English Literature, 1660–71* (Cambridge, Mass., 1984).
LJ	*Journals of the House of Lords*
Ludlow, "Voyce"	Edmund Ludlow, "A Voyce from the Watch Tower,"

	Bodleian Library, MS Eng. hist. c. 487.
Ludlow, *Voyce*	Edmund Ludlow, *A Voyce from the Watch Tower 1660–1662*, ed. A. B. Worden, Royal Historical Society, 4th ser., 21 (1978).
Masson, *Life of Milton*	David Masson, *The Life of John Milton*, 7 vols. (Cambridge, 1859–94).
Milton, *Poems*	*The Poems of John Milton*, ed. John Carey and Alastair Fowler (1968).
Milton, *Prose*	*The Complete Prose Works of John Milton*, ed. D. M. Wolfe *et al.*, 8 vols. (New Haven, 1953–82).
OED	*Oxford English Dictionary*
Pepys	*The Diary of Samuel Pepys*, ed. R. C. Latham and W. C. Matthews, 11 vols. (Los Angeles and Berkeley, 1970–83).
PMLA	*Publications of the Modern Language Association of America.*
POAS	*Poems on Affairs of State*, ed. George de Forest Lord *et al.*, 7 vols. (New Haven, 1963–75).
Scott, *Sidney*	Jonathan Scott, *Algernon Sidney and the Restoration Crisis 1677–1683* (Cambridge, 1991).
Stone, *Family*	Lawrence Stone, *The Family, Sex and Marriage in England, 1500–1800* (1977).
Zwicker, *Politics and Language*	Steven N. Zwicker, *Politics and Language in Dryden's Poetry: The Arts of Disguise* (Princeton, 1984).

Introduction

CHAPTER I

Literature, culture, and society in Restoration England

Gerald MacLean

I

What we mean when we talk about the Stuart Restoration might at first seem clear enough. But like similar terms used to indicate both a specific historical event and a period, "Restoration" has been used in different ways for different purposes and has different meanings in different contexts. Most often, the Restoration appears simply as a date that marks the beginning or ending of some other period. Marking either the final exhaustion of the "Renaissance," or the start of the long eighteenth century, the Restoration is frequently conceived as simply an adjacency. When studied as a political event, the Restoration can refer to those circumstances that made necessary and possible a return to monarchical government, and so primarily designates those events and negotiations of 1658–60 surrounding and immediately following Charles's return.[1] But political historians have also taken a longer view and regard the Restoration as an uneasy, brief settlement within longer-term political negotiations among Crown, Parliament, Church, and people, the struggles over which continue through the Revolution of 1688 to reverberate well into the eighteenth century and beyond.[2]

For social and cultural historians, the years following the Restoration constitute a period of contending activities and attitudes, ways of thinking, feeling, and behaving, that cannot entirely be accounted for in terms of the attempted political settlement of 1660.

---

[1] See, for example, Godfrey Davies, *The Restoration of Charles II, 1658–1660* (San Marino, Calif., 1955), and Hutton, *Restoration*.

[2] See J. R. Jones, ed., *The Restored Monarchy, 1660–1688* (1979), Introduction; Paul Seaward, *The Cavalier Parliament and the Reconstruction of the Old Regime, 1661–1667* (Cambridge, 1986), and "The Restoration, 1660–1688," in Blair Worden, ed., *Stuart England* (Oxford, 1991) pp. 147–55; and Tim Harris, *Politics Under the Later Stuarts: Party Conflict in a Divided Society 1660–1715* (1993).

It has long been clear that the nation which summoned Charles back in 1660 differed considerably from the realm over which his father had once attempted to rule. The traditional scholarly emphasis on the self-consciously neo-classical style in conversation, theatrical staging, music, oil-portraiture, and clothing, initially introduced by members of Charles's Court to London and thence to the nation at large, has shifted toward study of those continuing forms of resistance, dissent, and control, of contending political and religious languages and practices, that were inherited from the 1640s and 1650s.[3] The king's return was accompanied by various constitutional and social changes that might appear to indicate a general return to conditions prevailing before the civil wars, but the Restoration was, as Tim Harris puts it, "a deeply contradictory affair, the product of an already divided society."[4] Church courts were reopened, some sequestered estates were given back, Court censorship returned. With monarchy came the return of the House of Lords, of bishops, tithing, the licensing of clergymen, and attempts to legislate religious uniformity. Women, though granted certain novel freedoms like that of professional acting, often found themselves again subjected to gender codes that they had been busily undoing during the revolutionary decades.[5]

---

[3] See Harris, *London Crowds*; Peter Borsay, *The English Urban Renaissance: Culture and Society in the Provincial Town, 1660–1770* (Oxford, 1989); Andrew Colby, *Central Government and the Localities: Hampshire, 1649–1689* (Cambridge, 1987); David Underdown, *Revel, Riot, and Rebellion: Popular Politics and Culture in England, 1603–1660* (Oxford, 1985); Jonathan Scott, *Algernon Sidney and the English Republic, 1623–1677* (Cambridge, 1988), and *Algernon Sidney and the Restoration Crisis, 1677–1683* (Cambridge, 1991); Richard L. Greaves, *Deliver Us From Evil: The Radical Underground in Britain, 1660–1663* (New York, 1986); N. H. Keeble, *The Literary Culture of Nonconformity in Later Seventeenth-Century England* (Leicester, 1987); Nigel Smith, *Perfection Proclaimed: Language and Literature in English Radical Religion* (Oxford, 1989); David Cressy, *Bonfires and Bells: National Memory and the Protestant Calendar in Elizabethan and Stuart England* (1989); and John Spurr, *The Restoration Church of England, 1646–1689* (New Haven, 1991). In a useful review article, "Reconstructing the Restoration," *Journal of British Studies* 29: 4 (1990): 393–401, Victor L. Slater concludes that "the Restoration reconstruction was a vital turning point" (p. 401).   [4] Harris, *Politics*, p. 26.

[5] See Hobby, *Virtue of Necessity*. Despite considerable interest in women writers of the Restoration period, there is still no detailed social and cultural history of how the Restoration affected women's lives. On women writers, see also Janet Todd, *The Sign of Angellica: Women, Writing and Fiction, 1660–1800* (1989); Jane Spencer, *The Rise of the Woman Novelist: From Aphra Behn to Jane Austen* (Oxford, 1986); Elspeth Graham, Hilary Hinds, Elaine Hobby, and Helen Wilcox, eds., *Her Own Life: Autobiographical Writings by Seventeenth-Century Englishwomen* (1989). Roger Thompson's *Women in Stuart England and America: A Comparative Study* (1974) can still prove useful, but in the category of general histories has been superseded by Antonia Fraser's *The Weaker Vessel* (1984). See also important new specialized work such as Susan Amussen, *An Ordered Society: Gender and Class in Early Modern*

What recent scholarship has been making increasingly clear is that not all of these measures were similarly successful or long-lived. Public theaters were back in business, the publishing trade flourished, often in defiance of government controls, and women continued to write and to publish.[6] Religious dissent by no means came to an end; despite evidence of initial support for a return to the Anglican liturgy, widespread absenteeism and Nonconformity bedeviled attempts to impose an established state Church.[7] With England's continuing growth as a commercial nation, expansion overseas in search of resources and new markets led to conflicts with other powers, and brought about increased contacts with, and colonization of, Asia, Africa, and the "New World." Questions of national identity and difference, of what it meant to be English or British or both, could be framed in terms of international trade and imperial ambition that operated independently of loyalty to the Crown.[8] For political, social and cultural historians, the Restoration constitutes a complex intersection of changing practices and ideas that are central to our understanding of early-modern Britain, and what was to pass for civility in much of the modern world.

Of course, for literary historians, the Restoration has usually appeared to be a rather more literary phenomenon. Treated as contextual background to the literature, the years following Charles's

England (Oxford, 1988), and Susan Cahn, *Industry of Devotion: The Transformation of Women's Work in England, 1500–1660* (New York, 1987).

[6] For the public theaters, see Nancy Klein Maguire, *Regicide and Restoration: English Tragicomedy, 1660–1671* (Cambridge, 1992), pp. 102–37. On the continuing activities of the radical press, see Greaves, *Deliver Us*, pp. 207–25. On publications by women writers before and after the Restoration, see Patricia Crawford, "Women's Published Writings 1600–1700," in Mary Prior, ed., *Women in English Society 1500–1800* (1985), pp. 211–82. Kathryn Shevelow, *Women and Print Culture: The Construction of Femininity in the Early Periodical* (1989) provides a useful neo-Foucauldian take on how English periodicals published between 1690 and 1760 helped construct the discursive figure "woman."

[7] Geoffrey Holmes writes of "the sheer confusion of practice at parish level," in his recent *The Making of a Great Power: Late Stuart and Early Georgian Britain* (1993), p. 40; and see Spurr, *Restoration Church*, p. xvii, and Cressy, *Bonfires*, pp. 48–49. For a summary of recent scholarship, see Tim Harris, "Introduction: Revising the Restoration," in Harris, *et al.*, *Politics of Religion*, pp. 1–28; on absenteeism, see pp. 17–18. See also J. A. I. Champion, *The Pillars of Priestcraft Shaken: The Church of England and its Enemies, 1660–1730* (Cambridge, 1992).

[8] See Holmes, *Great Power*, pp. 93–105; Brian Levack, *The Formation of the British State: England, Scotland and the Union 1603–1707* (Oxford, 1987); Peter Earle, *The Making of the English Middle Class: Business, Society and Family Life in London 1660–1730* (1989); and, more generally, Benedict Anderson, *Imagined Communities: Reflections on the Origin and Spread of Nationalism* (1983). And see Cressy's argument throughout *Bonfires*, that the peculiarity of "the calendar in seventeenth-century England ... was based on, and gave expression to, a mythic and patriotic sense of national identity" (p. xi).

return provide seemingly self-evident examples of how the disciplinary distinction between "literature" and "history" arises both inevitably and inexorably. The traditional literary-historian's version is a familiar one. In 1660, after a period of bloody civil unrest during which arms flourished and arts withered, the king returned. Now that the "Puritan" revolution was over, everyone wanted peace and order: satire flourished to translate disruptive anger and hostility into either companionable irony and innuendo or partisan indignation, the public theaters reopened (with women actors) to entertain an urban public, poets started writing in heroic couplets that structurally replicated principles of social order and civic harmony, and the novel figuring the rise of the bourgeois self began its problematic emergence as the dominant literary genre.

In various forms, this pragmatic version of events as background to literature has encouraged what we might call a division of textual or archival labor. To literary scholars belongs the study of the works of Samuel Butler, Andrew Marvell, John Bunyan, John Dryden, the Earl of Rochester, Daniel Defoe, William Congreve, William Wycherley, and Aphra Behn; to historians the study of the lives and works of Charles, Clarendon, Shaftesbury, Samuel Pepys, Gilbert Burnet, John Locke, Isaac Newton, and Robert Hooke, together with all the Court records, Parliamentary debates, parish registers, and other published and unpublished archival materials. Yet this division of the archive, to the extent that it has helped to shape the way generations of scholars have set about understanding the period, corresponds more readily to the subsequent development of academic disciplines than it does to Restoration beliefs or practices. And it has recently begun to show signs of breaking up, to the advantage of all concerned.

Scholars of Restoration literature have traditionally acknowledged the importance of historical context, in part, no doubt, because of this literature's highly developed engagement with the history of its own times. But if it is difficult to imagine reading *Absalom and Achitophel* without some understanding of the high politics of the time, the literary critic's use of historical background to explain topical references in Restoration literary texts has often depended upon and served to reinforce the archival and disciplinary distinction between literature and history. To read a literary text as referring in some precise way to otherwise knowable historical events is one way of demonstrating how the literary and the historical differ categorically:

here is the literary text, and here are the historical events to which it refers and which make available some of its specific resonances. Sometimes the evidence seems intractable, but the grounding distinction remains clear. Earl Miner, for example, reports a number of places where Dryden "has been supposed to have related historical fact, although the only evidence derives solely from what he wrote."[9] Even when it contains little or nothing relevant, the archive of historical information can nevertheless be supposed to offer necessary and independent evidence confirming a text's claim to accurate historical documentation, as well as reinforcing its literary status. Literature, Miner assumes, is not history; a formulation that would have made sense in Restoration Britain, but not perhaps in quite the same ways it does today.

To paraphrase Miner, both literature and the Restoration seem to require greater attention than has been given to what people were writing about literature in the seventeenth century, and to the relationship of literature to other cultural activities.[10] When Miner writes that "critics and poets during the Restoration hold to a concept of literature that was dignified, grand, and perhaps even exorbitant in its claims,"[11] we might wonder if "poetry" – or better yet "poesy" – would not be more appropriate than "literature." For our current academic understanding of the ways "literature" differs from "history" can come dangerously close to misreplicating the neo-classical, and largely rhetorical, distinction between "poesy" and "history" still being discussed by critics and poets following the Restoration. At that time, the question involved the differing formal, generic and compositional practices appropriate to treating different subject-matter in a particular national language; this is the thematics of Dryden's important preface to *Annus Mirabilis* (1667), and it underlies many of his concerns in *Of Dramatic Poesy* (1668), both of which imaginatively frame their discussion of literary concerns within the nationalistic enterprise of naval supremacy. Although "poesy" or "poetry" had started becoming restricted to signifying metrical composition rather than prose from the middle of the seventeenth century – most notably in the exchange between Hobbes and Davenant over the latter's *Gondibert* (1650) – "literature" did not become associated with specifically imaginative writing, as opposed

[9] Earl Miner, "The Restoration: Age of Faith, Age of Satire," in Antony Coleman and Antony Hammond, eds., *Poetry and Drama, 1570–1700* (1981), pp. 90–109; this passage p. 108.   [10] *Ibid.*, p. 90.   [11] *Ibid.*, p. 98.

to historical or scientific writing, until much later. Poetry, after all, was commonly written on historical themes. If it meant anything at all to Dryden and his contemporaries, then, distinguishing "literature" from "history" would have meant marking the general differences between writing and past events. Not until long after 1660 did "literature" start assuming the imaginative and fictional specificity formerly indicated by "poesy."

In *Keywords*, Raymond Williams reminds us that "as late as" Dr. Johnson, the principal meaning of "literature" continued to be "polite learning through reading,"[12] a usage corresponding more closely to our notions of literacy than to the material objects of imaginative writing. The association between reading and skilled knowledge is given a specifically practical turn by the single instance of the term in Shakespeare's works, where it appears in the significant context of a scene that parodies Renaissance learning in the cause of arousing patriotic sentiment across striking national and social differences. In the midst of the battle of Agincourt, Act 4 scene 7 of *Henry V* opens with Fluellen's horrified discovery that the French have slaughtered the unarmed baggage-boys back at the British camp. The Englishman Gower assures him that Henry's command to kill any captured French soldiers is a noble and just revenge, causing the Welsh soldier to launch into his memorable panegyric of their king, in dialect, which nevertheless displays a very specific kind of historical learning and understanding of rhetorical form by humorously elaborating an extended Plutarchan parallel between the lives and achievements of Henry and Alexander the Great, one that makes much of topographical similarities between Macedonia and Wales. Ever keen to display his reading in the chronicles of British history, Fluellen is soon able, when the king enters, to remind Henry himself of his Welsh ancestry. Thus it is in the accent of Fluellen, this scion of learning and spokesman for what might be called an ethnically divided, yet resolutely "national" history, that we hear Shakespeare's only use of any form of "literature," when Fluellen assures Henry that "Gower is a good captain, and is good knowledge, and literatured in the wars" (4.7.153–54).

This basic sense of being literatured as being well read and well versed in something of national significance, a personal condition

---

[12] Raymond Williams, *Keywords: A Vocabulary of Culture and Society*, (1976; rev. ed. New York, 1983), p. 184.

entailing the acquisition by reading of cultural skills and knowledges, also informs Johnson's terse definition in the *Dictionary* – "Learning; skill in letters."[13] In his *Life of Cowley* (1779), Johnson later praised his subject's "pregnancy of imagination and elegance of language" as the conditions which "have deservedly set him high in the ranks of literature," a shift from the personal condition to include the objective sense of "literary work or production."[14] Williams associates this emergence of literature as "a practice and a profession of writing" with the seventeenth-century shift in literary production from patronage to commercial publishing, but he also notes that literature nevertheless retained its traditional emphasis on "the whole body of books and writing" produced by a national language well into the nineteenth century.[15] By this time its Shakespearian contexts had become its contents. The *OED* cites a typical usage of 1857 that marks the association with national identity as definitive: "Literature, when it is a healthy and unforced state, is simply the form in which the knowledge of a country is registered."

This general development, from the personal qualities and cultural condition of being well-read, to the objective range of material texts, accompanied by the socially evaluative and nationalistic connotations of great books by great English men, places the history of the concept of "literature" centrally amidst the development of a precise critical vocabulary suited to making these very distinctions. For the emergence of this critical language, with all its social and cultural implications, we are largely indebted to the efforts of Dryden, to whom literature meant the production of writings in English, whether on historical or imaginative topics. Before 1660, there had been little general concern over questions of the national literature as such. But by the time Dryden died at the end of the century, literary history had become a key component of a nationalist cultural enterprise. Various literary texts, and even entire genres, had served nationalistic purposes before, but the development of a specifically national literature, one which could look backward into its own past in order to trace its origins and progress from a distinguished body of vernacular writing: this development took on new and distinct importance as a public discipline of knowledge. In short, the Restoration period saw the development and dispersal of a soph-

---

[13] Samuel Johnson, *A Dictionary of the English Language*, 4th ed. (1770); cited in Williams, *Keywords*, p. 185.   [14] Cited *OED* 2.   [15] Williams, *Keywords*, p. 185.

isticated critical vocabulary suited to the needs of a great national literature, one with a distinguished history that was eagerly being written, and with a future that was no less eagerly being projected. The theatrical success of attempts to improve Shakespeare's plays indicates something of this historical shuttle between continuously revised pasts and projected futures in the construction of a national literature.

A central aim of the present book is to restore the contemporary senses of "literature" to the literatures produced, in English, during the period following the return of monarchy. The increasingly emphatic understanding of literature as a key to national identity situates Restoration literary activity as a whole within the broader social and cultural developments of the modern era. Consequently, this book adopts a historicized sense of literature that includes scientific, economic, religious and political texts, as well as the conditions of, and constraints upon, their production and reception.

II

When Charles arrived in England, literature was already thoroughly politicized in ways that would have been unthinkable at his grandfather's Court.[16] During the 1640s and 1650s, writers, printers, and booksellers had become confidently aware of the special intimacy enjoyed between literature and politics, and had grown accustomed to assuming the freedom and authority to comment in public upon the personal lives and policies of national leaders in the hopes of guiding opinion and, thereby, the course of events. This self-authorizing freedom, of using print to challenge and even ridicule political leaders, was a direct and irreversible inheritance from the revolutionary decades. It can be traced back at least to the collapse of censorship in 1641 and the immediate appearance of the oppositional and insurgent writing that led people to take up arms against the traditional authority of the Crown, Lords, and Bishops.[17]

---

[16] See Jonathan Goldberg, *James I and the Politics of Literature* (Baltimore, 1983); Graham Parry, *The Golden Age Restor'd: The Culture of the Stuart Court, 1603–42* (Manchester, 1981). See also Kevin Sharpe, *Criticism and Complaint: The Politics of Literature in the England of Charles I* (Cambridge, 1987). For a recent assessment of how Restoration England inherited a literary culture that had been transformed by the 1640s and 1650s, see Thomas Corns, *Uncloister'd Virtue: English Political Literature, 1640–1660* (Oxford, 1992), pp. 294–308.

[17] See Christopher Hill, "The Restoration and Literature," in *A Nation of Change and Novelty: Radical Politics, Religion and Literature in Seventeenth-Century England* (1990), pp. 218–43; and

After 1641, subsequent attempts at censorship by no means stopped writers from attacking authority; the threat of possible prosecution rather redirected the languages of irreverence and protest by challenging writers to continue adopting imaginative forms of coding and disguise.[18] Criticizing royal policy obliquely by mocking powerful Court favorites or royal advisers – such as the attacks on the Duke of Buckingham in the 1620s, and Archbishop Laud and the Earl of Strafford in the early 1640s – gives way to bolder and more direct forms of criticism during the revolutionary decades, including personal attacks on the king. Satiric character assassinations of royal persons and powerful governmental leaders continue after the Restoration: in the anti-Rump satires of 1659–60, in the work of writers as different as Behn, Samuel Butler, Milton, Marvell, and Rochester, and even in the muted ironies of Dryden's portrayal of Charles in *Absalom and Achitophel*.

Restoration literature is characteristically political not only because it commonly addresses social and political issues with an irreverent attitude toward established authority, but also because of the ways in which reading and writing had made public debate increasingly central to the political experience of ordinary people living through the social and cultural changes of the 1640s and 1650s. Attacks on political authority published during the early years of the Civil War both accompanied and encouraged widespread public debates on other questions of received authority, most notably those formerly regulated by the established Church, such as biblical interpretation, baptism, communion, and marriage. For two decades and in unprecedented numbers, works of religious and theological controversy, moral tracts, biblical commentaries, sermons, and works of prophecy, often expressing not simply anti-prelatical but even heretical ideas, found their way into print and into the conversations, attitudes, and expectations of an increasingly critical reading public.[19] In 1661 one commentator warned: "The liberty of the late

Gerald M. MacLean, *Time's Witness: Historical Representation in English Poetry, 1603–1660* (Madison, 1990), pp. 64–126.

[18] See Zwicker, *Politics and Language*; Margaret Doody, *The Daring Muse: Augustan Poetry Reconsidered* (Cambridge, 1985); Annabel Patterson, *Censorship and Interpretation: The Conditions of Writing and Reading in Early Modern England* (Madison, 1984); and most recently, Lois Potter, *Secret Rites and Secret Writing: Royalist Literature, 1641–1660* (Cambridge, 1989).

[19] See Paul S. Seaver, *The Puritan Lectureships: The Politics of Religious Dissent, 1560–1662* (Stanford, 1970), and *Wallington's World: A Puritan Artisan in Seventeenth-Century London* (Stanford, 1985). It is a shame that Nehemiah Wallington, upon whose writings Seaver's

times gave men so much light, and diffused it so universally amongst the people, that they ... are become so good judges of what they hear that the clergy ought to be very wary before they go about to impose upon their understandings, which are grown less humble than they were in former times."[20] Although the return of the king brought with it the return of bishops, tithing, and the licensing of clergymen authorized to preach and interpret the Bible, the authority of the Church of England never fully recovered from the effects of two decades during which "ordinary men and women became accustomed to liberty of debate and liberty of printing."[21]

These decades of public irreverence toward traditional political and religious authority also involved widespread questioning of established gender codes. Legally defined only in relation to men, as daughters or wives, women from all walks of life evidently found that the cultural climate of the 1640s and 1650s was conducive to speaking and writing both as women and as socially responsible agents. Some women found themselves with little or no choice. Changes in civil administration meant that women could now be called upon to testify before the newly instituted county committees, often against former social superiors.[22] Some women found themselves forced into print by the need to defend themselves, their actions, and their reputations. In 1653, Hester Shaw claimed that she wrote to defend herself against charges of "immodesty" which, if left unanswered, would have ruined not simply her personal reputation but also her ability to continue making a living as a professional midwife.[23] But for the most part, the women who entered public discourse did so in order to insist that their social and political agency be recognized as legitimate. During the Civil War, women of all ranks assumed increasing responsibility for domestic, social, and economic activities as men went off to fight and sometimes die. As Elaine Hobby

marvelous case-study of artisanal literacy is based, did not survive the Restoration. On literacy and print in the period, see also Natascha Würzbach, *The Rise of the English Street Ballad, 1550–1650*, trans. Gayna Walls (Cambridge, 1990); Tessa Watt, *Cheap Print and Popular Piety 1550–1640* (Cambridge, 1991); Bernard Capp, *Astrology and the Popular Press: English Almanacs 1500–1800* (1979); Margaret Spufford, *Small Books and Pleasant Histories: Popular Fiction and its Readership in Seventeenth-Century England* (Athens, Ga., 1981); Smith, *Perfection Proclaimed*, and *Literature and Revolution in England 1640–1660* (New Haven, Conn., 1994); Christopher Hill, Barry Reay, and William Lamont, *The World of the Muggletonians* (1983); and Barry Reay, ed., *Popular Culture in Seventeenth-Century England* (New York, 1985).
[20] Cited by Spurr, *Restoration Church*, p. 219.
[21] Hill, *Change and Novelty*, p. 219; and see Champion, *Pillars*.
[22] Graham, *et al.*, eds., *Her Own Life*, p. 12.   [23] Hobby, *Virtue of Necessity*, pp. 9–10.

observes, "the challenges being made to the status quo involved new freedoms and activities for women."[24]

During the 1640s and 1650s, women from all sides of the political spectrum started to petition Parliament on matters ranging from personal grievances over property settlements to trade regulations, poor relief, and the conduct of criminal trials. The women petitioners insistently asserted the right of women to speak out on public matters and to expect that what they had to say would influence government policy since "we have a very equal share and interest with men in the Commonwealth."[25] During the same period, other women spoke out publicly on social and political issues in the form of prophecy, sometimes writing and publishing their views.[26] As Patricia Crawford has shown in her analysis of women's published writings in English for the entire century, women wrote for publication during the 1640s in unprecedented numbers, and continued to do so after 1660. Although the actual numbers of women writing for publication remained relatively small, by the end of the century women had "gained a sense of their own developing literary tradition ... By 1700 it was no longer a wonder that a woman should write for publication."[27]

III

The relative freedom enjoyed by the press during the 1640s and 1650s meant that, by 1660, literature had established its own irreversible authority as a socially constitutive field of public activity. The return of monarchy was, in part, accomplished through large scale social reorganization that required a great deal of cultural work, including the writing and production of texts of all sorts. So crucial had the commercial press become by 1660 that, during the months immediately preceding and following Charles's return, all manner of commemorative and celebratory publications appeared which set about giving symbolic and cultural meaning to the social and

---

[24] *Ibid.*, p. 11.
[25] *England's Moderate Messenger* (1649), cited by Ann Marie McEntee, "'The [Un]Civill-Sisterhood of Oranges and Lemons': Female Petitioners and Demonstrators, 1642–53," in James Holstun, ed., *Pamphlet Wars: Prose in the English Revolution* (1992), pp. 92–111, this passage p. 98. See also Hobby, *Virtue of Necessity*, pp. 13–17; Patricia Higgins, "The Reactions of Women, with Special Reference to Women Petitioners," in Brian Manning, ed., *Politics, Religion and the English Civil War* (1973), pp. 179–97.
[26] See Phyllis Mack, "Women as Prophets during the English Civil War," *Feminist Studies* 8: 1 (Spring 1982): 19–47.   [27] Crawford, "Women's Published Writings," pp. 231.

political changes in British life.[28] The return to monarchy was the first time that the commercial press in Britain played so direct and central a role in establishing the terms of a national political settlement. There had, of course, been previous occasions when the press had flexed its political muscles in opposition: we might think of the Marprelate controversies of the late 1580s, or the insurgent pamphleteering of the early 1640s.[29] But the Restoration was the first time that the commercial press played so massive a part in helping to bring in and legitimate a new government, and in so doing, helped to define and set conditions for the terms of the political settlement. By 1660 the social agency of the press had produced an irreverent, secularizing, commercial, literary culture that had already captured much of the political high ground once claimed by the authorized discourse of the established Church.

Literary production was a major cultural ingredient of the king's return. Writers and printers produced an unprecedented number of celebratory publications in a wide variety of kinds – formal poems, sermons, prose characters, ballads, closet dramas and masques, histories, scientific treatises, biographies and autobiographies, romances and histories, translations of Virgil, and even a cookbook. For writers seeking to legitimate Charles's accession during the early spring and summer of 1660, the tasks included accounting for the recent past, interpreting the startling events making up the present, and constructing a desirable future that only monarchy could guarantee.

Robert May's *The Accomplisht Cook, Or The Art and Mystery of Cookery*, which appeared in May 1660, provides an intriguing palimpsest of literary strategies and cultural concerns common to the revisionary historiography of Stuart propaganda.[30] In part, May's text exemplifies a favorite method for dealing with the social effects of

[28] See Carolyn Edie, "Right Rejoicing: Sermons on the Occasion of the Stuart Restoration, 1660," *Bulletin of the John Rylands Library* 62 (1979–80): 61–86, and "News From Abroad: Advice to the People of England on the Eve of the Stuart Restoration," *Bulletin of the John Rylands Library* 76 (1984): 382–407; Gerald M. MacLean, "An Edition of Poems on the Restoration," *Restoration* 11 (1987): 117–21, and *Time's Witness*, pp. 256–67; and see Jonathan Sawday, "Re-Writing a Revolution: History, Symbol, and Text in the Restoration," *The Seventeenth Century* 7: 2 (1992): 171–99.

[29] See Christopher Hill, "From Marprelate to the Levellers," in *Collected Essays Volume One: Writing and Revolution in 17th Century England* (Brighton, 1985), pp. 75–95.

[30] George Thomason dated his copy sometime in May; see George Fortescue, ed., *Catalogue of the Pamphlets, Books, Newspapers, and Manuscripts Relating to the Civil War, The Commonwealth, and Restoration, Collected by George Thomason, 1641–1661*, 2 vols. (1908), 2: 315, entry E.1741. For more on May, see Elaine Hobby's essay in this volume.

the previous two decades, which was to suggest that they could be forgotten now that the king's return promised a return to the good old days. Following a dedicatory epistle, an address "To the Master Cooks," and a brief narrative describing the author's life in service to various Royalist families, a section entitled "Triumphs and Trophies in Cookery, to be used at Festival Times," seeks to achieve a nostalgic cancellation of the past two decades by describing the kind of celebratory festivity and conspicuous consumption to be enjoyed by loyal Englishmen now that monarchy has been restored. The section provides a curiously detailed account of how to stage-manage a banquet that would be suitable for the new age precisely because, according to May's claim at least, it promises to revive social forms and practices that "were formerly the delight of the Nobility, before good House-keeping had left *England*, and the Sword really acted that which was oneley counterfeited in such honest and laudable Exercises as these."[31] What are these honest entertainments to be retrieved from the aristocratic past?

First of all, the would-be cook is instructed to manufacture a paste-board model of a ship, complete with bamboo cannons on each side which are to be linked by "such holes and trains of powder that they may all take fire," and to place it at one end of a banquet table on a "great Charger" filled with "salt" and studded with "egg-shells full of sweet water." For the other end of the table, "at a distance from the Ship to fire at each other," the reader is invited to imagine manufacturing a castle, also complete with bamboo cannons on all sides, and similarly surrounded by water-filled egg shells. Between these, and also surrounded by egg shells filled with "rose-water," is to be placed a model of a stag "with a broad arrow in the side of him, and his body filled with claret wine."[32]

What is already abundantly evident from these instructions is that the "accomplisht" cook is conceived of as no mere producer of tasty food and wholesome drink, but as a highly skilled craftsman and pyrotechnician with the authority to produce symbolic interpretations of political history. May's cook is obviously an advocate, if not entrepreneur, of conspicuous consumption.[33] Everything that May

---

[31] Robert May, *The Accomplisht Cook, Or the Art and Mystery of Cookery* (1660), sig. [A8].
[32] *Ibid.*, sig. [A7v].
[33] Among studies of the development of consumerism in early-modern Britain that have appeared since the ground-breaking study, *The Birth of a Consumer Society: The Commercialization of Eighteenth-Century England* (1982) by Neil McKendrick, John Brewer, and J. H.

instructs him to make (and May's accomplished cook is unquestionably male) is designed to be wasted. Even the two huge pies, to be
made from "course" pastry and placed on either side of the stag, are
not for eating: "in one of which let there be some live Frogs, in the
other live Birds."[34]

Once this inedible collation has been arranged before a suitable
assembly, May instructs: "before you fire the trains of powder, order
it so that some of the Ladies may be perswaded to pluck the Arrow
out of the Stag, then will the Claret wine follow as blood running out
of a wound." Since May doesn't specify who, if anyone, is permitted
or likely to drink the claret, we might presume that, like the sacrificial
blood of royal stags and martyrs, it too must be seen to be wasted.
"This being done," May continues, "with admiration to the
beholders, after some short pawse, fire the traine of the Castle ... then
fire the trains of one side of the Ship as in a battle." Once the ship and
castle have been turned around and all the cannons have been fired,
other elements of the festivity come rapidly into play, not so much
recalling the formal Court entertainments of Charles I and Henrietta
Maria as anticipating the pleasure-seeking values and attitudes of the
Restoration Court:

This done, to sweeten the stinck of the powder, the Ladies take the egg shells
full of sweet waters and throw them at each other. All dangers being seemed
over, by this time you may suppose they will desire to see what is in the pies;
where lifting first the lid off one pie, out skips some Frogs, which makes the
Ladies to skip and shreek; next after the other pie, whence comes out the
Birds; who by a natural instinct flying at the light, will put out the candles;
so that what with the flying Birds, and skipping Frogs; the one above, the
other beneath, will cause much delight and pleasure to the whole company:
at length the candles are lighted, and a Banquet brought in, the musick
sounds, and every one with much delight and content rehearses their actions
in the former passages. These were formerly the delights of the Nobility ...[35]

The final sentence, which has already been quoted, ends the entire
section entitled "Triumphs and Trophies." I have broken it off here
in order to draw attention to how the section ends; not only does May

Plumb, see especially Lorna Weatherill, *Consumer Behavior and Material Culture in Britain,
1660–1770* (Cambridge, 1988), and Carole Shammas, *The Pre-Industrial Consumer in England
and America* (Oxford, 1990).

[34] May, *Accomplisht Cook*, sig. [A7v]. For recent work on consumerism, see Joseph P. Ward,
"Reinterpreting the Consumer Revolution," *Journal of British Studies* 29:4 (1990): 408–14.

[35] May, *Accomplisht Cook*, sig. [A8].

reinvent aristocratic desire and pleasure, but he does so in order to foreclose on the revolutionary decades by linking the Restoration present directly to the pre-revolutionary past. May's text imaginatively invokes the social upheavals of the 1640s and 1650s, but only in order to displace and then cancel their social meaning. In the scene described, the participants are imagined as having a delightful time symbolically reproducing a "counterfeit" of the years separating them from a time of "good House-keeping," an activity specifically designed to produce sociability by providing everyone with memories of a shared experience to talk about while food is being served. The fantasy of victorious sociable consumption figures doubly here, both as nostalgia for, and as itself an essential component of, the past aristocratic pleasures to which May seems keen his readers should want to return. Constructing political authority by characterizing a desirable past now being recovered through recreation and identification, this textual fantasy links past and present by making imaginatively available that delight at rehearsing triumphs formerly enjoyed by the "Nobility."

It is hardly surprising that May advises his cook to "order it so that some of the Ladies may be perswaded" to start things going, since the entire "exercise" figuratively thematizes the return of aristocratic male domination over unruly women. Following the unsettling noise of cannon and the smell of gunpowder, direct male control begins to recede and decorum disappears. Once the guns have been discharged, the impresario in command of the entertainments withdraws, like a providential dramaturge, to permit the predictable: "the Ladies take the egg shells..." In such circumstances, it seems, ladies can be trusted to behave in certain ways, causing the world to turn upside down.[36] The reader is invited to imagine ladies throwing egg shells about the place and drenching themselves and each other until "all dangers being seemed over, by this time you may suppose" that female curiosity will bring social chaos, mayhem, and darkness. May's fantasy displaces the possibility of female authority, ridiculing and trivializing female agency by representing women voyeuristically

---

[36] Nearly a generation later, things seem not to have altered greatly. On 27 March 1683, Francis Gwyn writes to the Earl of Conway: "The King came hither about 4 yesterday afternoon and the whole Court and had hardly recovered the fright they were put into by the fire at Newmarket, especially the ladies, who were all in great confusion," *CSPD*, p. 136. My thanks to Nancy Klein Maguire for this reference. On the popular seventeenth-century taste for noise and pyrotechnic displays, see Cressy, *Bonfires*, pp. 80–90, especially pp. 88–89.

as objects of the male gaze, as spectacles and animal bodies. All those women shrieking and skipping about in their wet clothing amongst the terrified frogs and panicked birds, "the one above, the other beneath": in producing this fantasy of the cook's power, May casually alludes to the key tenet of hermetic philosophy, reminding us that his general project in writing *The Accomplisht Cook* is to insist on and protect the professionalized status of the "Art" and "Mystery" of cookery. And as was sometimes the case with traditional guild mysteries, the powerful knowledges and skills required of the cook seem to have been a male preserve; at least May addresses his book "to all honest well intending Men of our Profession."[37]

May's aristocratic and eroticized fantasy of absolute subjective male power indicates how triumphant male heterosexuality could figuratively be used to contain the "uncertainty at the heart of the Restoration."[38] Like other writers celebrating the king's return in 1660, May evidently realized that literary production was itself a socially constitutive activity in which gender and sexuality provided necessary terms for imaginatively negotiating the return of royal authority and canceling the effects of the previous two decades. Jonathan Sawday has recently examined how, throughout the spring and summer of 1660, "the Restoration itself" came to be "transformed into a marriage ceremony with Charles in the role of the bridegroom, and England in the role of the bride – an iconography which carries with it triumphal scriptural echoes."[39] That same year, in *Vota, Non Bella*, Ralph Astell varies the formula, transforming the Restoration not into a wedding, but into Britain's successful delivery of a king after twelve years of agonized labor pains.[40] These metaphors of marriage and childbirth figure doubly, representing the Restoration as the return of legitimate male authority over key moments in the reproduction of social life, while also legitimating that return as itself the necessary consequence of the patriarchal narrative of dynastic succession.

---

[37] May, *Accomplisht Cook*, sig. A4. May's work is in a long line of cookery books written by men for women; see Susanne W. Hull, *Chaste, Silent, and Obedient: English Books for Women, 1475–1640* (San Marino, Calif., 1982); Hobby, *Virtue of Necessity*, pp. 169–71.

[38] Jose, *Ideas of the Restoration*, p. 29.   [39] Sawday, "Re-Writing a Revolution," p. 181.

[40] The title page reads: [border design] / **VOTA, / NON BELLA.** / [line] / NeW-CastLe's / HeartIe GratULatIon / TO HER / SaCreD SoVeraIgn / KIng CharLes The SeConD; / ON / HIs noW-GlorIoUs RestaUratIon / To HIs BIrth-rIght-PoWer. / [line] / By Ralph Astell, M. A. / [line] / *Gateshead*, Printed by *Stephen Bulkley*, 1660. I have quoted from the copy in the British Library, shelfmark G 18923.

Writers who supported the king's return in the early months of
1660 set about revising national history, and in doing so produced a
variety of often self-contradictory accounts through which to explain
away the interruption in monarchical succession. By no means
univocal, the literary discourse of the king's return was highly
opportunistic in its use of historical evidence and explanation. But
those producing it were surely in general agreement that they were
authorized to use the public press in this way. For Ralph Astell, the
agency of literary culture is central to the formation of the new nation
state. In Astell's poem, the scene of Britain's agonized lying-in and
final delivery is framed within a national literary contest being
conducted by female muses, complete with discussions of literary
decorum, poetic form, and the contingencies of regional difference.
Thematically, the poem focuses throughout on questions of literary
authority; who is authorized to interpret and represent recent
events? what is a proper poetic response to the king's return? In
pursuing these questions, the poem warns that the political promise
of national unity signified by the king's rebirth can only be made
good in the terms provided by a national literary culture; it depends
upon the appearance of a poet capable of resolving regional and
cultural differences.

Uncle and tutor to Mary Astell, the pioneering English feminist,[41]
Ralph Astell was evidently much concerned with questions of gender
and sexual difference, and in particular with women's education and
the roles women played in the construction of a national literary
culture. Published in Gateshead, just across the river Tyne from
Newcastle, where Ralph Astell lived, his poetic celebration of the
king's return is one of the very few poems written and published
during 1660 from a regional perspective.[42] It is spoken by the female
personification of Newcastle, who calls herself a "black Northern
Lass" and begins by humbly daring herself to join in "the glistering
Train / Of *Britain's* fairest Nymphs" (lines 13–14), those muses who
are currently busy inspiring poets to celebrate the king's return. She
describes for the king how, in London, those "Southern Ladies" first

[41] See Bridget Hill, ed., *The First English Feminist: 'Reflections Upon Marriage' and Other Writings
by Mary Astell*, (Aldershot, Hants., 1986); and the useful biographical study by Ruth Perry,
The Celebrated Mary Astell: An Early English Feminist (Chicago, 1986) which contains
interesting details about uncle Ralph.
[42] On Newcastle, see Roger Howell, *Newcastle-upon-Tyne in the Puritan Revolution* (Oxford, 1967),
and David Levine and Keith Wrightson, *The Making of an Industrial Society: Whickham,
1560–1765* (Oxford, 1991).

lay their "High-born Strains of Poetry" at his feet, then imagines his
rebirth amidst the ashes left behind once these dazzling and flashy
ephemera have done their job:

> Nay, Phoenix-like (me thinks) I see them bring
> *Arabian* Spices on their nimble Wing,
> And build a Pile; which on your New-birth-day
> Kindly aspected by Your Solar Ray,
> Becomes a Royall Bon fire, in whose flashes
> They gloriously expire; yet 'midst those Ashes
> A Seed is couch'd; which, influenc'd by You,
> A self-born Phoenix yearly doth renew.   (lines 27–34)

Humility, it seems, is partly a guise by means of which competitive
literary production comes to figure regional difference and poetic
authority. Imaginatively setting fire to the poetic tributes being
published in London is a bold move, but it enables Astell to establish
textual production as a prior condition of the king's magical return
and rebirth. It also clears the scene for Newcastle to offer her own
version of recent events, which describes startling regional and
cultural differences that will only be resolved by the appearance of a
national literary culture.[43]

In Newcastle's version of events, the king may have returned but
the nation remains socially divided, not only by region but also by
language and culture, as illustrated by Newcastle's own irreverence
toward the manners and poetry of the Court. Unlike those fair-
skinned southerners whose flashy performances blaze aromatically,
coal-faced Newcastle insists on the humble origins of her own plain
style, since humility is both a condition of her ability to tell the truth
and evidence of her loyalty:

> Whilst I, black Northern Lass, from *Kedar's* Tents
> Approach your Court with no such Fragrant Scents:
> Nor can I Greet You in a Golden Strain,
> Whose finest Metall runs through a Cole Vein...   (lines 35–38)

Newcastle later recalls that her loyalty to the king, which fills her
honest heart with language of joy at his return, is not a hidden secret
but a matter of public record (lines 81–88). After reminding us of her

---

[43] See Borsay, *Urban Renaissance*, pp. 311–20.

known loyalty to the Stuarts throughout the Civil Wars and Protectorate, Newcastle castigates the outward displays of poetic loyalty being produced not only in London, but also Oxford and Cambridge, by recalling how the muses in those cities had inspired poets to praise Cromwell:

> Recant your fawning *Protectorian* Notes,
> And to an higher Key skrew up your Throats,
> Your warbling Tongues re-tune, let her be shent
> Who to that bloudy Tyrant durst present
> Her (*Olive Branch of Peace*:) may that soul crime
> Hereafter ne'r attaint her Nobler Rhyme!
> Our *CHARLES* is born again! your Fancies fearse,
> And once more measure His Genethliack Verse. (lines 189–96)

Poems on the births of kings provide language in which differences temporarily seem to disappear and nations can be imagined to exist.[44] In this account, questions of literary discourse silently replace even the king himself as the key to national identity; the national unity promised by the king's return is in large part a cultural matter of appropriate poetic form. Rather than a wedding ceremony, Astell imagines a grotesquely overdue birth that could only be brought to term when Monck, the providentially ordained man-midwife, arrives from the North "t'obstetricate" (lines 197–239). Britain is delivered of her king, and the celebrations can begin.

In the excitement of the occasion, Newcastle feels free to sing her own brief stanza of loyal joy. Insistently, this song returns to the politics of literary form, and the need for a poetic resolution to the regional and cultural differences still threatening national unity. Literary change figures a new political settlement. George Monck has transformed the legendary tale of rescue by St. George into national history (lines 287–92), so what is needed now is an English poet capable of filling up the empty cultural spaces which prevent national unity:

> Oh, for a *Virgil* now! whose *Skilfull* Quill
> With new *Georgicks* might our Country fill. (lines 293–94)

After this last dig at the failures of Court panegyric to achieve what the occasion demands, Newcastle retreats from the public arena into provincial retirement, utterance gives way to admiration, and the

---

[44] See Anderson, *Imagined Communities*, p. 132.

poem closes with a self-deprecatory fantasy of pastoral otium
regionalized amongst the coal smuts:

> Unto my smutchy Cell I will retire,
> And what I cannot utter, there admire.
>   I'le sit me down, and wonder how You made
> (O're-come at *Wor'ster*...   (lines 300–03)

Astell finally depoliticizes this female figure for literary agency,
showing her leaving behind the activities of public life for the
pleasures of retirement and imagination; just like many a cavalier.
The general celebration at the king's return requires textual
production on a huge and popular scale, but as soon as it is over,
poets should not presume to make policy. The provinces will no
doubt cease to figure in or matter very much to the new courtly
culture. And, by extension, might we not also gather that women
should retire from public life? Newcastle withdraws, however, only
after characterizing the cultural crisis at the heart of the Restoration
settlement as the need for a national literature.

IV

The celebratory writings produced in 1660 do not necessarily provide
a reliable guide to Restoration literature as a whole. Astell's poem
reminds us, for example, that neo-classical panegyric poetry proved
to have only a short-lived revival during the early months of Charles's
return to English soil; within a very short time, even the poet laureate
would be writing satirically. In 1660, however, Dryden's vision in
Astraea Redux – "Our Nation with united Int'rest blest / Not now
content to poize, shall sway the rest" – employs panegyric in order to
offer advice.[45] Charles has been brought in to rule, not a realm, but
a nation. According to this view of things, the key to national unity
will be an aggressive foreign policy that will promote an expansion of
trade. Conspicuously absent from Dryden's political program with
which his panegyric ends, is any role for an established Church. By
1660, a secular and sometimes irreverent literary culture had come to
adjudicate and regulate many aspects of social life formerly the
domain of the Church. For two decades and more, religious discourse
had provided terms in which social and regional differences had
become matters of political dissent and national division. And it

---

[45] Dryden, *Poems*, lines 296–97. See Gerald M. MacLean, "Poetry as History: The
Argumentative Design of Dryden's *Astraea Redux*," *Restoration* 4 (1980): 54–64.

continued to do so in the partisan disputes which followed the Restoration. Yet in subsequent decades, literary culture contested traditional Church authority in the formation of both personal and national identities.[46] The chapters in this book identify and examine different ways in which various literary forms and genres were employed during the decades following the Stuart Restoration to establish a claim upon the national identity.

The relicensing of the public theaters in London after 1660 was a signal event in the literary culture of the nation. The politics of drama in Restoration London, however, extend beyond the theaters onto the streets, as John Montaño recalls in his detailed examination of the scripts by John Ogilby, John Tatham, and Thomas Jordan used for public ceremonies such as the coronation and the Lord Mayor's Shows of the 1670s. Royal and civic pageantry of this sort, and the whole iconographical tradition of ostentatious public performance and display which gave it substance, had fallen out of favor long ago. They were revived and articulated at the Restoration, Montaño argues, in order "to consolidate belief in a national consensus supporting the restored monarchy." Although contributing to what Montaño calls "the ideology of consensus," the Lord Mayor's Shows failed to survive the fragmentation of London politics by the end of the century.

Another dramatic genre that was revived at the Restoration, the Court masque, did not long survive its revival intact; its dominant features were largely transposed into public opera and, as Nancy Klein Maguire has recently argued, the rhymed heroic play.[47] But Christopher Hill and others have underestimated the political significance of the masques composed after 1660, as Andrew Walkling argues here in his study of Nahum Tate and Henry Purcell's *Dido and Aeneas*.[48] This masque, Walkling shows, requires carefully detailed historical analysis if its political nuances are to be fully understood since, like other Court masques, it serves "as both commentary and critique" upon specific political controversies.

Turning to the public theater in her chapter here, Nancy Klein Maguire also analyzes topical political allusions in order to examine

---

[46] See Harris, *Politics*; Spurr, *Restoration Church*; and Richard W. F. Kroll, *The Material Word: Literate Culture in the Restoration and Early Eighteenth Century* (Baltimore, 1991).

[47] See Maguire, *Regicide and Restoration*, pp. 83–101.

[48] "The masque, with all its facile magical solutions to all problems, and the panegyrics to royalty which accompanied the divine right of kings, could no more survive the 1640s than could tragedy," writes Hill in *Change and Novelty*, p. 234.

the ways John Crowne adapted Shakespeare's *Henry VI* plays in his response to the "problem of being a 'Tory' during the religious and political crisis of 1678–83." Such was the authority of dramatic literature in the years following the Restoration that playwrights used adaptations of earlier plays to analyze current events. In the historical installation of a national literature, Shakespeare provided Crowne with a safe position from which he could loyally criticize royal persons and policies.

Fascination with daily events in the personal lives of the royal family was not uniformly critical, entirely irreverent, or even always satirical. James Turner reminds us that the sight of the king's dog defecating could make even Samuel Pepys, that loyal servant of Oliver Cromwell who became a dedicated fan of the royals, briefly reflect in a republican fashion "that a King and all that belong to him are but just as others are." Yet for Pepys, Turner argues, this momentary sense of physical community encouraged him to imitate Charles, to construct and live through a personal fantasy of what it meant to inhabit the king's body and be a royal person, someone whose private life was predicated on public gossip and the constant thrill of possibly impending public exposure. Turner reads Pepys's coded accounts of various sexual exploits and fantasies not as evidence of Pepys's guilty need for privacy but as deliberate strategies of public being. "However private the experience," Turner points out, "it is still couched in a language that reveals the social formation of Pepys's consciousness and implies the scrutiny (and applause) of an audience." For Pepys, authorship creates that implicit audience.

If both writing and the return of a profligate king authorized Pepys to carry on in the ways he tells us he did, Milton and other well-known republicans experienced the king's return as the occasion for confronting quite different problems of authority and authorship. Blair Worden examines responses to the failure of the English republic in writings by Edmund Ludlow, Algernon Sidney, and Sir Henry Vane in order to cast fresh light on the political ambiguities of Milton's *Samson Agonistes*. Worden shows how Milton's language constantly rings with idiomatic usages that place his closet drama firmly inside republican discourse after the Restoration, one filled with tropes of betrayal and resistance. Suggesting that *Samson Agonistes* was composed close to publication date, Worden sees authorship providing Milton with a means of struggling to live when to do so involved actively serving a God who seemed to have deserted both him and the good old cause. "If," Worden speculates, Milton wrote the central section of *Paradise Lost* "amidst the national catastrophe and personal danger and affliction of 1660, then the achievement, like Samson's, is one to defy human calculation."

Milton was one of the few republicans to survive the experience of defeat and live long enough to write about that experience at length and in differing forms. After *Paradise Lost*, Milton's status as the greatest living poet of his generation meant that he soon found himself, like Shakespeare, being assigned a place in the emerging national literature. And he also found his epic being rewritten for the Restoration stage, by none other than John Dryden. Steven Zwicker rereads the encounter between Milton and Dryden amidst the shifting fortunes of literary authority after the king returned, "from what might have been Milton's point of view" in order "to suggest why Dryden might have made Milton nervous, where in Milton's work the anxiety might be confronted, and how it might have shaped his masterpiece *Paradise Regained*."

For the new men of science, like Isaac Newton, the anxieties over publication and literary authority were also especially acute. In part, it was argued that this was because the scientific claim upon the truth of what one wrote could easily be compromised were one's writings accepted as truth simply on the basis of the author's reputation. The new literary culture of Restoration England soon demanded celebrities from among its greatest scientists, and Newton the iconoclast found himself cast as the great man, an idol of his disciples. Robert Iliffe examines Newton's struggle to maintain control not only over the publication of the *Principia*, but also over his public reputation, going on to "demonstrate how he controlled accounts of the meaning of the *Principia* by selectively allowing access to himself and to his private notes."

For women writers too, publication could work in complex and contradictory ways, offering an honest means of intellectually satisfying employment at the same time that it exposed the female author to public ridicule, contempt, and exploitation. Elaine Hobby shows how the market for domestic manuals and cookbooks led an unscrupulous bookseller and hack writer to issue *The Gentlewoman's Companion* as if it had been written by Hannah Wolley. Examining this best-selling work in the contexts of Wolley's life and writings, Hobby argues that while "Wolley's books do not, of course, give us an unmediated access to the 'truth' of a woman's life," they nevertheless challenge "the stereotypes offered through Restoration comedies" of how the middling sort of English women could gain access to social agency through writing.

For aristocratic women, writing offered a different sort of social empowerment and a different genre from the domestic conduct books which Hannah Wolley wrote to make a living. N. H. Keeble argues that for Anne, Lady Halkett as for Ann, Lady Fanshawe, the conventions governing the writing of loyalist memoir, those "testimonies of loyalty and obedience to prince and to husband," could provide opportunities for political and cultural disobedience. Deprived of their husbands during the wars, aristocratic women had learned how to "act on the public stage independently of men," and so they plotted their memoirs "as a series of challenging adventures, casting their authors in the role of dynamic and initiating protagonists, rather than repining and lonely wives."

If Royalist women wrote memoirs in order to challenge dominant gender ideologies, Quaker women preached and wrote in order to retain some degree of the institutional control they had exercised over the Society of Friends during the 1640s and 1650s, but which George Fox's quietist accommodation to the Restoration had brought to an end. Moira Ferguson examines the writings of Quaker women who "fought to hold their own and ... refused to be bound by the new conservative politics," especially Fox's "pro-slavery accommodations." Although not entirely free from complicity in cultural imperialism, Alice Curwen, Elizabeth Hooton, and Joan Vokins were among the first to articulate an emancipationist agenda in English. As a result of their efforts, Ferguson points out, "the Quaker position on slavery changed qualitatively as they became the first unified group of British men and women to demand abolition and emancipation."

Slavery was not the only controversial issue arising from Britain's increasing centrality in world trade during the years following the Restoration. The commercial press provided plenty of material to feed what Steven Pincus calls the "native and lively popular discussion about European affairs in England throughout the later seventeenth century," a discussion that, he observes, "always connected domestic and foreign concerns" and that "turned on the proper identification of the universal monarch." Royalists wrote in support of the third Anglo-Dutch war of 1672–74, insisting that the republican Dutch were seeking universal dominion. Against this claim, Pincus argues, "English radicals proclaimed with a united voice that universal monarchy was in fact the sole aim and purpose of French policy." Pincus reads the published debates to show how reports of events eventually disproved Royalist claims, causing public opinion to turn against the war – but not before "English moderates shifted their foreign policy orientation... because they were well aware that the struggle for European mastery had begun."

For Britain, and so perhaps for Europe and the world, that struggle resulted in the events of 1688–89, when a foreign but Protestant king acceded to the throne. Had he lived this long, Milton might not have been satisfied with a constitutional monarch, even in preference to a Catholic one. But the "Glorious Revolution" showed how the radical and republican ideals of the 1640s and 1650s continued to influence the political debates shaping Britain's future as an imperial nation. This book ends with Bridget Hill's study of how, written with the hindsight of a century, Catharine Macaulay's history of the second half of the seventeenth century "not only influenced English radicalism profoundly but also contributed substantially to American and French revolutionary ideology." Like other radical thinkers of the 1760s who were critical of the inadequacies of the 1688–89 settlement, Macaulay called for "a fundamental reform of the whole system of representation involving not only a more equable distribution of seats, but an extension of the franchise and secret ballot." The Restoration might have put an end to the English republican experiment, but it could not put an end to those competing traditions of radical and republican thought that English men and women had become accustomed to seeing debated in print since the 1640s. Although religious differences helped shape partisan disputes, social identities, and political allegiances after the Restoration, ecclesiastical authority gave way before the secular authority of a literary culture geared to the demands of a developing commercial and imperial nation.

PART I

Drama and politics

CHAPTER 2

The quest for consensus: the Lord Mayor's Day Shows in the 1670s

John Patrick Montaño

Civic pageantry had enjoyed a long and distinguished career throughout Europe by 1660. The tradition of street pageantry was an old one, incorporating emblematic imagery, both verbal and visual, with a long ancestry of political service. It had proved an effective means for cities, magnates, guilds, and mayors to demonstrate their wealth and influence. In England, civic spectacles had such an immense popularity among Londoners that James I had relied on the drawing power of the Lord Mayor's Day Show to rob his nemesis Sir Walter Raleigh of the constituency for his final performance. Raleigh had asked for a delay of a few days to prepare for his execution, "but was refused, and it was determined to carry out the execution on the following morning, 29 October 1618. That was the day of the Lord Mayor's Pageant, which would be sure to draw a large crowd to the east end of London, and thus, it was hoped, deprive the actor of an audience."[1] The popularity of these entertainments may have had as much to do with the free handouts provided by the various guilds as it did with the spectacles and themes of the pageant. However, beyond this possibility for free advertising and the occasion to parade the guilds' immense wealth, there were ideological overtones as well. Indeed, once Charles II began attending the Lord Mayor's Show regularly after 1671, these pageants began to promote government propaganda directly.

I shall argue that the Lord Mayor's Day Shows were designed to bring an oral and emblematic version of government policy onto the streets for the ideological consumption of the London populace. The

I wish to express my gratitude to John Brewer and to Megan Reid for their support and assistance in the preparation of this chapter. The research was made possible by a grant from the William Andrews Clark Memorial Library.

[1] Stephen J. Greenblatt, *Sir Walter Raleigh: The Renaissance Man and His Roles* (New Haven, 1973), p. 7.

reason for this was a desire to consolidate belief in a national consensus supporting the restored monarchy. By participating in civic pageantry, the government of the 1670s revealed its interest in using all forms of culture – both elite and popular – to propagate the ideology of consensus. Beyond a simple prescription of political philosophy, civic pageants allowed the Court to illustrate for the nation how peace, prosperity, and order were all inextricably linked with the restoration of monarchy.[2]

I THE NEED FOR CULTURAL CONSENSUS

The English people had learned much from the Civil War besides the relatively simple lesson that monarchs could be executed. For twenty years the political elite had experienced what a fracturing of their dominant culture meant. The triumphant supporters of the old order were keenly aware that the many-headed monster created in 1641 was still very much at large in 1660. With the exception of a very few diehard republicans and chiliasts, the nation's social and political elite sought to re-establish their traditional unanimity and were determined to dominate political debate. They recognized that Charles I's neglect of popular politics after 1640 had allowed his opponents to undermine the conventional belief in an indisputable consensus in support of the king. Once Charles I had lost control of the City and had raised his standard at Nottingham, people were forced into choosing sides. It was this unprecedented choice – and the resulting civil war – that first exemplified the lack of consensus.

Accordingly, the restored government needed to demonstrate that unity, concord, and prosperity were the results of monarchy. To prove this they relied on the received wisdom that traditional harmony had been destroyed by a small cadre of ambitious conspirators who had hoodwinked much of the nation into abandoning their allegiance. Many had been beguiled, and, it was argued, most of the deluded naturally came from the ranks of the multitude. The facility with which the zealous hypocrites had exploited the rabble was an ideological trope after 1660. This was not a

---

[2] For important recent studies of social and political life in London both before and after 1688 that offer interpretations sometimes different from my own, see Harris, *London Crowds*, and Gary S. De Krey, *A Fractured Society: London Politics in the First Age of Party 1688–1715* (Oxford, 1985), "London Radicals and Revolutionary Politics, 1765–1683," in Harris, *et al.*, *Politics of Religion*, pp. 133–62, "Political Radicalism in London after the Glorious Revolution," *Journal of Modern History* 55 (1983): 584–617.

commonplace in Anglican sermons and Royalist panegyric alone. This unholy alliance of ambition, conspiracy, and providential design which allowed the wicked to prosper is an explanation which runs throughout Clarendon's *History*, government propaganda, and civic pageantry of the 1660s and 1670s. Implicit in this line of reasoning are two important points: if the design of providence was "very visible, in infatuating the people ... into all the perverse actions of folly and madness," it was equally apparent in the sudden, miraculous, and peaceful restoration of monarchy.[3] Secondly, if consensual politics were abandoned again, every faction might vie for the affections and loyalty of the readily bedazzled populace – and it was avoiding this sort of insecurity and division which generated consensus in 1660.

In the context of the late troubles it is apparent why Court ideology juxtaposed obedience to rebellion, loyalty to faction, duty to ambition, reason to passion, and moderation to extremism. Once all these positions had become conflated in government propaganda to support the return of monarchy, the attractions of Court ideology were apparent to those united by a distaste for disorder, army rule, and radicalism in any form. Clarendon hoped to capitalize on this disenchantment and fear in re-establishing political unity.

This strategy was manifested in seemingly contradictory policies: on the one hand the government tried to limit "tumultuous petitioning,"[4] prohibit conventicles, control the number of printing presses, and silence its opponents through the Licensing Act and the watchfulness of a Surveyor of the Press. Conversely, the government of Charles II acknowledged the importance of popular support by its attention to carefully crafted pageants and spectacles. The more criticism aimed at undermining the consensus in support of monarchy, the greater the need for an accessible civic pageantry to propagate the consensual ideology of the Court.

In order to prevent a return to the strife of the past nineteen years, the government led by Clarendon immediately set about appropriating every possible authorizing language and imagery in an attempt to create the sort of inclusive consensus essential to maintaining its power and authority. The government had demonstrated in the Act of Indemnity and Oblivion its understanding that "the first condition of political quiescence was cleansing the political

---

[3] Clarendon, *History*, 1: 1.   [4] 13 Car. II, c. 5.

vocabulary; the second was altering and forgetting the past; the third was the reestablishment of civic themes to which all men might adhere, themes of wide ideological appeal: the defense of liberty, the right of property, and religion by law established."[5] The prescription of these common values can be seen in the outpouring of the revivified Anglicans' paeans to monarchy, hierarchy, loyalty, and obedience, the poetical panegyrics to the king, and the coronation ceremony itself, which was designed to illustrate to one and all – literate and illiterate – the many advantages of monarchy. The role of this ceremony in successfully educating and captivating the spectators was crucial. Clarendon recalls in his *Life* how he and the king agreed:

That the novelties and new inventions, with which the kingdom had been so much intoxicated for so many years together, might be discountenanced and discredited in the eyes of the people, for the folly and want of state thereof; his majesty had directed the records and old formularies should be examined, and thereupon all things should be prepared, and all forms accustomed be used, that might add lustre and splendor to the solemnity.[6]

Indeed, even before the king's arrival, theorists were arguing that the "idea of the possibility of a republic without king and lords had never entered the minds of Englishmen from the time of the Heptarchy downwards. Men were born with the idea of a king in their heads as camels with indurations on their knees."[7] But, rather than rely on any innate consensus about the monarchy, the government provided a civic pageant which would set the tone for all subsequent displays of the Court's consensual ideology.

In May 1660, Charles II had proceeded to London amidst cheering crowds and a deluge of loyal petitions and declarations from mayors, towns, and ministers along his route. However, these haphazard examples of loyalty were nothing compared to the carefully prepared entry of the sovereign the day before his coronation less than a year later. The only comparable displays in the last century would have been the coronations of James I and Elizabeth. The coronation pageant for James had been delayed and attendance limited by an outbreak of the plague, while that for Elizabeth had taken place over 100 years before. In 1625 the plague intervened once again, this time portentously causing the festivities

---

[5] Zwicker, *Politics and Language*, p. 10.
[6] Edward Hyde, Earl of Clarendon, *The Life*, 2 vols. (Oxford, 1827), 2: 10.
[7] Cited in Carolyn A. Edie, "The Popular Idea of Monarchy on the Eve of the Stuart Restoration," *HLQ* 39 (1976): 343–73; this passage p. 346.

for the coronation of Charles I to be canceled. According to Eric Halfpenny, in the thirty-five years which followed, "the Commonwealth had come and gone, and a generation had grown up to whom the full panoply of regal pomp was unknown." More significantly, for most people, "their first glimpse of the returning monarch was as he threaded the narrow streets on that bright April morning, the principal character in a pageant whose brilliance outshone all else within living memory."[8] Fully convinced of the need for popular support, the restored government was not about to miss its first opportunity to portray the advantages and propriety of monarchy.

II OGILBY'S CORONATION PAGEANT, 1661

It was only in February 1661 that the City fathers were notified of the king's intentions to make a progress through London the day before his coronation. For this occasion John Ogilby was appointed to dazzle the audience attending the king's passage through the City with images of traditional virtues and the rewards of concord, loyalty, obedience, and monarchy. By the time of the king's return, "Ogilby's royalist sympathies and associations were sufficiently well known to earn him the prestigious commission of organizing an appropriate spectacle for the royal entry."[9] In addition, Ogilby had presented the king with a beautiful Bible on the day he stepped ashore at Dover, and this must have guaranteed royal support for his employment in 1661. This instance of Restoration propaganda – Ogilby's *Entertainment* – demonstrates the way in which biblical and classical allusions were combined to provide "metaphors linking the golden age with Eden, chaos and satanic rebellion with the Flood and terrestrial insurrections."[10] The reopening of the theaters and the outburst of panegyric poetry began the celebration of the king's return and were central to the creation of the images of monarchy. Drawing on a multitude of allusions from the torrent of literature from 1660 as well as previous royal entries to European cities, Ogilby helped to formulate the belief in the return of an Augustan golden age. Furthermore, "the public displays shared the desire of printed

---

[8] Eric Halfpenny, "The Citie's Loyalty Display'd," *Guildhall Miscellany* 10 (1959): 19–35; this passage p. 19.
[9] Ronald Knowles, Introduction to *The Entertainment of His Most Excellent Majestie Charles II* (New York, 1988), p. 11. [10] *Ibid.*, p. 39.

panegyric to praise the event while also determining what form the renewed nation should take. Like the writers, the organizers of pageantry sought to inspire in their audiences an exalted sensation of wonder. "[11] This public theater was crucial in expressing the values of the Court; it was one method of transmitting the message which required no formal literacy, for pageantry by its very nature was the most socially and artistically inclusive form of discourse. The procession from one setting or monument to the next provided a series of "set changes" which proved exceedingly advantageous in endowing the pageants with a unified theme which substituted for a plot. This scenic design in turn dictated a unity of thematic content which resulted in a type of sermon or "an illustrated lecture in dramatic form on government and political philosophy."[12]

As Charles and his retinue progressed from the Tower to Whitehall, the king took part in a political drama in four acts. According to the program sold to the spectators, after "the glorious Restauration of the Sovereign to His Throne, and of us His Subjects to our Laws, Liberties, and Religion, after a dismal Night of Usurpation, and Oppression," England decided to imitate "the antient *Romanes*, who, at the return of their Emperours, erected *Arches* of Marble."[13] Relying on timber rather than marble, London erected four arches in the streets – an arrangement followed in many future pageants during Charles's reign. At each arch, a dramatic interlude was performed, linking Charles with the verbal and visual qualities represented.

Ogilby mobilized familiar Augustan tropes. The fascination with Imperial Rome was not new to England in 1660, but the similarities between the lives of Charles II and Augustus were readily apparent to Restoration panegyrists. According to Ronald Knowles, "political Augustanism lies in the effective conflation of the *Aeneid*, book six, the *Fourth Eclogue*, the first and fourth *Georgic* and contemporary English history."[14] And who better suited to the task of organizing the king's entry than a recent translator of Virgil – John Ogilby. The extent to which these texts had been used to describe the king's return has been demonstrated by Knowles and Howard Erskine-Hill, and is revealed in Dryden's *Astraea Redux* of June 1660:

---

[11] Jose, *Ideas of the Restoration*, p. 120.
[12] Glynne Wickham, *Early English Stages*, 2 vols. (1963), 2: 59.
[13] John Ogilby, *Relation of His Majestie's Entertainment Passing ... To His CORONATION* (1661), p. 1.   [14] Knowles, *Entertainment*, p. 20.

Our Nation with united Int'rest blest
Not now content to poize, shall sway the rest.

...

Oh Happy Age! Oh times like those alone
By Fate reserv'd for great *Augustus* Throne!
When the joint growth of Armes and Arts foreshew
The World and Monarch, and that Monarch *You*.[15]

Ogilby's use of Augustan tropes of naval superiority, Concord and Plenty, demonstrates what had, by 1662, become a general claim: that Charles's return inaugurated a golden age in English history, one that included a flourishing of the arts under wise and wealthy patrons – with a modern Virgil, Horace, and Polybius immortalizing the monarch and nation. More significantly, the pageantry did not imply that the king would simply graft Roman virtues onto the royal oak. Such slogans as "UNITAS," "PATER PATRIAE," and "MENS OMNIBUS UNA" were meant to indicate that the king's return was dependent on the concurrence of the people. While extolling Charles as a new Augustus who restores peace, plenty, and justice, the panegyrics and pageantry were also implying that the obedience, unity, and consensus of the nation were integral to his survival.

III CONSENSUS AND CABAL, 1662–1668

Within a year of the king's return one can find a definite trend in the values and ideals being expressed in the writings of those patronized by the Court. Despite considerable variety, Court ideologues emphasized the need for a religious and political consensus which was authorized by tradition, Aristotelian moderation, the lessons of history, and the power of scripture. These common themes appeared in publications as diverse as the carefully designed heroic dramas, polemics against Nonconformity, sermons on obedience, official newsletters, speeches from the throne, and Proclamations. Also, once a year, on the Lord Mayor's Day, the City of London reaffirmed its loyalty by sponsoring a procession past a series of arches displaying civic virtues.

Besides obvious affiliations with the stage and opera,[16] the mayoral pageants were didactic, employing historical settings not unlike those

---

[15] Dryden, *Poems* 1:23–24. See Knowles, *Entertainment*, pp. 18–19; Howard Erskine-Hill, *The Augustan Idea in English Literature* (1983), pp. 209–11, 248–49, 328–29.
[16] See L. J. Morrissey, "English Street Theatre: 1655–1708," *Costerus* 4 (1975): 105–38.

in the heroic plays so popular at the commercial theaters. Yet pageantry's "distinctive affiliation was with the contemporary panegyric, political pamphleteering and propagandistic display."[17] The outdoor staging of this theater was an essential point of contact with those officially excluded from the political nation. Since these mobile plays contained little or no plot, the dramatic burden fell on the theme. And in line with the newly emerging tradition of Restoration Court culture – from Clarendon's propaganda in exile, to formal panegyric, to the coronation itself – the most persistent theme developed by the Lord Mayor's pageants was the need for a political and religious consensus. The results of this consensus were demonstrated rhetorically by the use of a common literary tradition which supplied a series of concatenated themes. The rhetoricians' duty to embellish and amplify meant that classical thought, English tradition, scripture, and history – both ancient and contemporary – could be used to associate consensus with an Augustan golden age.

But the need for consensus was not only a matter of cultural representation; it was also a crucial term in political disputes and events of the time. The history of the Lord Mayor's Shows reflects both the links and divisions between culture and politics at this time. While the earlier Stuarts were attracted to the exclusivity of the masque, public pageants like the Lord Mayor's Shows came to supplant spectacles that had previously been intended as entertainment for the monarch alone. Although the Shows of the 1630s increasingly emphasized the distinction between the City and the Court, they were nonetheless too theatrical for Commonwealth taste, and with the outbreak of war both the pageantry and the theaters were discontinued. A single pageant was displayed in 1655, followed by two in 1656. In 1657 the Skinner's Guild chose John Tatham to compose a Show which resurrected the traditional form with customary scenic motifs designed to evoke the City and the Livery Companies. Indeed, the Companies were sufficiently pleased with his efforts to grant Tatham "a position tantamount to that of official City poet" and, from 1657 until 1664, civic pageants and Lord Mayor's Shows were composed by Tatham.[18]

There is evidence for the king attending the Lord Mayor's Show in 1661, and both the king and City were undoubtedly eager to

[17] Jose, *Ideas of the Restoration*, p. 120.
[18] Kenneth Richards, "The Restoration Pageants of John Tatham," in Kenneth Richards and David Mayer, eds., *Western Popular Theatre*, (1977), pp. 49–73, this passage p. 62.

demonstrate the restoration of political consensus after 1660. This emphasis on consensus remained standard fare in civic entertainments which, throughout Charles's reign, followed the thematic lead of his coronation. From the moment he stepped ashore at Dover, "Charles II took full opportunity to exploit by personal appearance and celebratory display the popularity of his return."[19] The obvious advantages of demonstrating the return of political consensus through public performance can be seen throughout the monarchy-inspired pageantry of 1660–62. These displays by Tatham and Ogilby each celebrated the rejection of puritanical rule, the revival of trade and prosperity, and the restoration of unity and concord. Clearly, the Augustan golden age promised something for everyone.

There were some, however, who felt that the lustre of the king's return was no guarantee of London's continued loyalty. Although the Corporation Act of 1662 was unconcerned with cultural consensus, this legislation did allow royal commissioners to "displace" members of Liveried Companies.[20] The unintended consequence of this legislation was a Court-approved City government responsible for organizing civic entertainments. Consequently, different Companies relied on the same City poet year after year to preserve cultural and political conventions. In 1663 and 1664, Tatham returned to the theme of commercial prosperity, but the Great Fire both impoverished the City and destroyed the pageants and figures used in the Shows, terminating the pageantry for six years. By the time it was revived, the ministry had changed and Tatham had died.

While the miraculous return of the king in 1660 helped sustain the cultural consensus, a more explicit strategy for political union emanated from the Cavalier Parliament, which in addition to reconstructing the old regime, attempted to formalize the return to consensus through the legislation unfairly known as the Clarendon Code.[21] Their method concentrated on silencing Nonconformists and excluding them from political participation. As a result, many of these high flyers eventually forsook Clarendon for appearing soft on Nonconformity. After the Plague, the Great Fire, and the humiliation

---

[19] *Ibid.*, p. 51.

[20] For an example, see Baron Heath, *Some Account of the Worshipful Company of Grocers*, 3rd ed. (1869), p. 121.

[21] The Commons' desire for a more divisive settlement than that favored by the king is examined in Paul Seaward, *The Cavalier Parliament and the Reconstruction of the Old Regime, 1661–1667* (Cambridge, 1989), pp. 35–70, 162–95.

in the Medway had resulted in Clarendon's banishment, the new ministers chose to abandon Cavalier uniformity for a more comprehensive political position. The Cabal, that group of ministers who replaced the domineering Chancellor, persuaded Charles that a silent majority actually existed which favored toleration. To their way of thinking, a less rigid religious settlement would lead to a large majority in the Commons – a majority whose gratitude to the king would be communicated through a hefty parliamentary grant for the impoverished Court.

Embracing this advice from the Cabal, Charles sought the support of Nonconformists of all stripes, trusting that strict Anglicans had no alternative to supporting his policies. After 1668 the repressive aspects of the Clarendon Code were softened, the Triple Alliance signed, and restrictions on the press relaxed. Just as suddenly in 1670, Charles signed the Treaty of Dover with the French. Both Nonconformists and allies of the Church were horrified by this alliance with the leaders of militant Catholicism, and some already suspected that there were additional secret articles. Fanning the flames of these religious and diplomatic concerns was the political apprehension bred by the Duke of York's refusal to attend Anglican service. With the heir to the throne an advocate of popery and an administration consisting of a Catholic Treasurer in Clifford, a Royalist Secretary in Arlington, the champion of Nonconformity in Buckingham, a former Cromwellian in Ashley Cooper, and a wild card in Lauderdale, any pronouncement about consensus in this period would appear absurd. While the Cabal's inability to present a unified position did cause a fragmentation of both policy and diplomacy, the impending war with the Dutch necessitated a return to a strategic consensus at home. In 1671, one way to play the patriotic card – and to squelch fifth-column activity among Nonconformists opposed to war with their Dutch fellow-travelers – was to appropriate the pageantry of the Lord Mayor's Day for government purposes.

IV THOMAS JORDAN'S LORD MAYOR SHOWS, 1671–1673

1671 marks the debut of Thomas Jordan as City poet. An ardent Royalist during the 1640s, Jordan had resurfaced in the spring of 1660 writing a number of broadsides and dramatic speeches supporting Monck's actions. After the Restoration he wrote several dramatic speeches for various City guilds and numerous prologues and epilogues for the stage. His aptitude for both loyalty and ephemeral verse, and his friendship with Tatham, must have convinced the Guildhall leaders that he was the man to replace Tatham when the Lord Mayor's Show returned in 1671.[22] Owing to the heavy losses from the fire, the Guilds wished both to limit expenditures on the Shows and to centralize control over the poet and craftsmen.[23] As a result, conventionality and repetition were preferred to novelty and invention, assuring Jordan of employment until 1684. Similarly, Jordan's dependence on commonplaces made certain that the Shows would perpetuate the Augustan themes associated with the king's return.[24]

Much like the two theaters of Restoration London, these renewed "civic ridings...continued to be political and moral lessons in support of established, stable government."[25] Rather than follow the Renaissance tradition of offering "mirrors for magistrates" in these entertainments, Jordan directed most of his advice to the spectators. Not surprisingly, the speeches and allegorical settings in Jordan's first Show for 1671 fitted nicely with the Court's renewed interest in consensus. The restored alliance between the Court and the City meant that the erosion of the consensus associated with the king's return required them to increase the intensity of their pleas for unity and concord. Jordan went beyond simply describing the benefits of consensus to prescribing it as both an ethical and social virtue. At the same time, attacks on those opposed to concord play an increasingly prominent role.

The opening speech has Orpheus, "the Hieroglyphick of good Government," relate how he originally brought harmony to the warring animals in nature. Jordan's title, *London's Resurrection to Joy and Triumph*, associates the rebuilding of London and its return to prosperity with the revival of civic entertainments. By linking Peace with Plenty, and Consent with good Government, Jordan demonstrates fealty to official themes used by Dryden, now the Poet Laureate, and Ogilby in his coronation pageant.

> By the sweet power of his [Orpheus's] hand,
> Reduc'd their salvage Natures, made 'um stand

[22] See *DNB*; Charles Knight, ed., *London*, 7 vols. (1843), 6: 154–55. On Jordan's remuneration, see L. J. Morrisey, "Theatrical Records of the London Guilds, 1655–1708," *Theatre Notebook* 29: 3 (1975): 99–113, especially pp. 101–04.   [23] *Ibid.*, pp. 101, 106.

[24] Richards, "Restoration Pageants," p. 55.

[25] Morrisey, "Theatrical Records," p. 100.

> Listen, attend, and with their active paws
> Dance and conform their feet to **Musicks Laws**.
> Such is the power of **Concord**, and **Consent**,
> The very soul of humane Government.
>
>   ...
>
>   We hope y'are one
> That will restore our long lost Union.
> 'Twill make us **Rich**, and **Righteous**, and please **God**,
> Firm to our Friends, fierce to our Foes abroad.
> **Union** breeds **Peace**, and Plenty in a Land;
> But Cities self-divided **Cannot stand**.[26]

Harmony, the precondition of any ordered and stable polity, brings about concord which, as was already axiomatic, in turn, ensures prosperity.

By encouraging a return to union and consent, the pageant also warned what would happen if unity were renounced. If the point were not clear enough from the previous allegory, the extent to which the prosperity of London was linked to monarchic loyalty was reiterated in a droll. As evidence of the revived union of interests between the City and the Crown, a final scene introduced a figure called Oliver Faction. After Oliver exults in the joys of faction, a loyal trio denounces the memories of the 1640s, and "Citizen" insists Oliver Faction will fool no one in the City because

> Their hearts now with faith and reality
> Are united so much unto Loyalty,
> Love, true Religion and Royalty,
> They to the Sovereign power do fix.[27]

Amidst fears of the imminent third Dutch war, one would expect this civic pageant to feature loyalty, unity, and Anglicanism. As the threat of conspiracy and division grew, the need for persuasive examples of concord increased. Jordan, determined to keep his pageantry relevant, turned from distant history to a more recent instance, representing consensus as the surest barricade against the divisiveness and chaos which once begat the upheaval and military tyranny of Cromwell and the republic.

After 1671, what is most striking is Jordan's willingness to combine topicality with allegorical tropes. In 1672, six months into the third Dutch war, Charles attended the Show for Sir Robert Hanson. At the

---

[26] Thomas Jordan, *London's Resurrection to Joy and Triumph* (1671), pp. 4–5.
[27] *Ibid.*, p. 17.

Guildhall he was joined by "his brother, the duke of Monmouth, Prince Rupert, the Archbishop of Canterbury, [and] all the bishops present in London."[28] Whether it seemed the king was tilting toward Catholicism, Nonconformity, or absolutism, his appearance with the Anglican hierarchy was surely a straightforward response to religious fears arising from the Declaration of Indulgence. With this unmistakable example of the monarch's fidelity to the Anglican Church, it was left to Jordan to remind the nation of the dangers of abandoning allegiance to the king.

The growing criticism of the government during 1672 compelled Jordan to generate harrowing images and examples of the consequences of a return to faction.[29] Significantly, on the pageant intended to celebrate Hanson's Company, Jordan again asserted the common interests of the City, the Company, the mayor and the king in enforcing the laws. In a speech by Apollo, a figure traditionally associated with the Grocers, he insists that the first victim of those subverting civic tranquility will be:

> Justice, whose true Use is
> To right the wronged, and suppress Abuses.

Conversely, history has shown that:

> Without Justice, all the World would be
> A Den of Dragon like Deformitie:
> Usurping Guilt would on the Weak prevail,
> And injured Innocence rot in Jail.

Furthermore, Justice is depicted as a buffer against sedition as well as a buttress for commercial prosperity and civil unity:

> May no Rebellious Seeds-men sow Discord
> Twixt Whitehall Scepter, and the Guildhall Sword:
> May Peace, Truth, Trade, Plenty and Content
> Make all men Bless'd under your Government.[30]

The emphasis on "private treachery" directly addresses a growing concern that the flourishing of seditious news disbursed by the Dutch might be successfully inspiring personal ambition and faction among certain Englishmen to supplant the rule of law with private interest. Jordan unearths the roots of this design in a song entitled "The

[28] Thomas Jordan, *London Triumphant, or the City in Jollity and Splendour* (1672), p. 12.
[29] See K. H. D. Haley, *William of Orange and the English Opposition 1672–1674* (Oxford, 1952), pp. 77ff. [30] Jordan, *London Triumphant*, pp. 8–11.

Discontented Cavalier." Here Jordan employs the past to help explain topical issues. Sung by the "City Musick" after dinner, it declares that:

> Times are well changed, but Crimes are the same;
> Nothing is right
> To the minds that delight
> In Reformation;
> Pride and Ambition are Cocks of the Game
>
> ...
>
> The Politician
> Calls Ambition
> By the name of Honour
>
> ...
>
> He that hatcheth Treason
> In a merry season
> Is a Fellow void of love and reason.[31]

The references to treason and irrationality make it clear that Jordan and the City were determined to use the Show for attacking those opposed to the established authorities in Church and State. In the years to come, the modulations in tone were entirely dependent on the political situation.

The imputation of greed and madness to the king's opponents would be used repeatedly in future Shows. One reason for this was the increasingly marked distinction between those supporting consensus and the rebels who rejected it. In March 1673, Parliament brought about the withdrawal of the king's Indulgence, and passed a Test Act which would drive the Treasurer and the heir to the throne from office, would institute a return to Anglican uniformity, and would fuel increasing opposition to the war. The result was the disappearance of the Cabal and the emergence of a new advisor, Sir Thomas Osborne, a man determined to recapture the moderate majority who longed for the stability and prosperity promised by Augustan imagery.

V DANBY, 1674–1678

Within a year of the Treaty of Westminster, Osborne, now Earl of Danby, was firmly established as the king's most influential advisor. The most adept minister at gauging the pulse of the Anglican moderates who longed for consensus, Danby set about regaining the

---

[31] *Ibid.*, p. 16.

Such thinly veiled threats provided warning that consensus was now of sufficient political value to be enforced – not just culturally prescribed. Moreover, in the next session of Parliament, Danby attempted to legislate all non-Anglicans out of the political process by introducing a new Test Bill for those holding any office. The Test proposed was an oath never to attempt to alter the government in Church or State as presently established. Had this Bill become law, political consensus would have been constitutionally achieved for those allowed to participate.

Although Danby's Test failed thanks to a legal squabble over precedence between the two Houses, it was apparent that the Treasurer sought to conflate justice with obedience and loyalty with acceptance of established authorities in Church and State. In the five years before his fall from power, two issues emerged to threaten Danby's authority and to dominate the political discourse. On the one hand, the open Catholicism of the king's brother and heir presumptive brought religion and the succession to the fore of public concern. Related to these concerns was the fear of absolute government. Not only were popery and arbitrary government inextricably linked in people's minds, but the customs windfall of the prosperous 1670s, the subsidies from Louis XIV, and Danby's fiscal retrenchment allowed Charles to "live of his own." Despite centuries of demanding financial responsibility, many government opponents were horrified by the king's ability to survive for years at a time without summoning Parliament. Fears of another personal rule and repeated invocations of the growth of popery and arbitrary government led Jordan to develop a variety of justifications for adhering to the political consensus which had yielded so many benefits since 1660.

In 1675, with the failed Test fresh in people's minds, the Lord Mayor's Show for that year, *The Triumph of London … [for] the truly Noble Pattern of Prudence and Loyalty Sir Joseph Sheldon …*, opened with a speech by Triumph which reiterated all the virtues considered essential to an ordered state:

> The Influence with which you are indu'd
> Are Prudence, Justice, Temperance, Fortitude.
>
> [points to them]
> To match with these, four bright Beams more are sent ye,
> Piety, Peace, with Purity and Plenty.[36]

[36] Jordan, *Triumph of London*, p. 11.

allegiance of this central group by reshaping royal policies to entice the predominant moderate bloc in Parliament. Steven Zwicker has noted how Danby recognized the Cavalier belief that, "in the center stood the common good, the ancient constitution with its balance of parliamentary privilege and kingly prerogative." From 1673 to 1678, Danby "made a special effort to fix his identity with the true protestant faith and with the assertion and maintenance of the laws and liberties of his subjects, a code established in 1660, and repeatedly invoked by Charles."[32] The Lord Treasurer quickly moved to improve the administration of the revenue, break with the French, ally with the Church hierarchy, and initiate the protection of commerce.[33] Even his arrangement of the match between William of Orange and Princess Mary was done with an eye toward public display. A key aspect of this quest for consensus was making the king's moderation, Anglicanism, and frugality known to the people.

At the beginning of Danby's ascendancy, the Lord Mayor's Show provided a good example of the close relation between the City leaders and the Court. The new mayor was the Maecenas of the Goldsmiths, Robert Vyner. His election was no doubt meant to indicate the Goldsmiths' continuing importance and prosperity following the Stop of the Exchequer in 1672. Furthermore, the continuing negotiations for an alliance of the Danby and Vyner families illustrates the intimacy between the leaders in London and Westminster.[34] Although the familiar figures of Justice and Prosperity appear, Jordan introduces an assertive tone in describing Court policy. Indeed, the confidence of the government can be seen in the overt claim that the rod of discipline ought to be wielded with determination by the mayor:

> You'll oftener use the Ballance than the Sword;
> ... though without dispute,
> When properly provok'd they're both acute,
> And at all times shall serviceable be,
> To the KING, the City, and your Companie.[35]

---

[32] Zwicker, *Politics and Language*, p. 10.
[33] See British Library, Add. MSS, 28042, fos. 15, 17; two memoranda to the king from October 1673 in which Danby spells out his policies for promoting the "Protestant interest both at home and abroad," for suffering "no dimunition nor imbelzelment of the revenue," and for governing Parliament "by the rules sett down."
[34] See David Allen, "Bridget Hyde and Lord Treasurer Danby's Alliance with Lord Mayor Vyner," *Guildhall Studies in London History* 2: 1 (1975): 1–22.
[35] Thomas Jordan, *The Goldsmiths Jubilee: or, Londons Triumphs* (1674), p. 9.

To complement this consensual litany, Jordan attacked the litigious tactics which Shaftesbury had used to defeat statutory consensus: "Suits which the Clients so wear out in slavery, / Whilst the Pleader makes Conscience a Cloak for his knavery."[37] If there were a knave in the legal pack, Shaftesbury – thanks to his legal defeat of Danby's Test – would surely have been identified as the "Pleader."[38]

As the fear of the succession and popery grew, Jordan looked to sustain support for monarchy by drawing on the very real consensus about the evils of the Commonwealth. This strategy can be found in his 1676 pageant, *London's Triumphs*, which presented Government and utilized many of the arguments found in Dryden's *Aureng-Zebe*, a play revived before the Court on 29 May of that year.[39] Both the loyalty and passive obedience exemplified by Aureng-Zebe and the recollection of the Protectorate were used by Jordan to promote political consensus.

The "fierce spirits" who wished to alter the hereditary succession were like all other historical characters who had deprived men of their rights under the pretense of preserving their liberty. Jordan has Government advise the new Lord Mayor to brandish the just power of legal authority:

> Correct these Knaves, who by false force and might,
> Would Hector modest men out of their Right...
> Purge this fair City from such foul Pollution,
> The laws are good, put them in Execution
> If Malefactors be not kept in aw, [sic]
> Lust, Theft, and Murder will become Law.[40]

Here the pageant goes beyond describing the merits of justice and union. Under the guise of instructing the Mayor, it calls for a crackdown on men like Sir Thomas Player and Thomas Papillon who were polluting City politics.

The repercussions from ignoring such examples were revealed by a subsequent scene in which a rustic setting representing Plenty and the joys of rural life was transformed by the entrance of a group of "mad Frolick Shepherds" who were dancing out of time with the

---

[37] *Ibid.*, p. 21.
[38] For the best account of Shaftesbury's use of Shirley v. Fagg to divide the Houses and force a prorogation, see Haley, *Shaftesbury*, pp. 372–402.
[39] See L. A. Beaurline, ed., *John Dryden: Four Tragedies* (Chicago, 1967), pp. 108–09.
[40] Jordan, *London's Triumphs*, p. 7.

accompanying music. Once again, Jordan relies on the collective
memory of the Interregnum as a period of destruction, tyranny, and
poverty. Indeed, stage directions indicate that the actors should
demonstrate their dementia "with many ridiculous gestures, which
the worst [sic] it is done, the better it pleases, being intended for a
description of Disorder, and an Elaborate Expression of Confusion."[41]

During the later months of 1676 and through the following year,
the increased vigilance recommended by Jordan, combined with the
moderate policies of Danby and the Court, contributed to a steady
improvement in support for the government. While both propaganda
and patronage were increasing the numbers and power of the Court
party in Parliament, consensus seemed a real possibility.[42] In his
Dedication to the Lord Mayor, Sir Francis Chaplin, in 1677, Jordan
even claimed that a form of consensus had raised Chaplin to the
magistracy, insisting that "Providence, Prudence, Prosperity, Popular Affection, Due Election, and Royal Conformation" had made
him mayor. In addition, this consensus granted him a "dignity...
which representeth Royal Authority, as Sovereignty is the Image of
a Deity."[43]

Throughout the time that Jordan was presenting images of
moderation and political agreement, he was also developing cau-
tionary images concerning those spurning consensus. As moderation
gained widespread acceptance under Danby, those rejecting it were
increasingly portrayed as extremists. The irrationality inherent in
disdaining the mixed monarchy of England as well as the centrist
liturgy of the Anglican Church was sometimes used to justify
excluding such nonconformity from the protection of the law.[44] This
principle for exclusion provided an additional mode for Jordan's
Shows. As early as 1672 Jordan had written that anyone who
"hatcheth Treason... Is a Fellow void of love and reason."[45] In 1676
Jordan's figure of Tamberlaine warned the mayor about fanatics
who would prove "As hard to be reduc'd as the Great Turk."[46]

[41] *Ibid.*, p. 14.
[42] See Hutton, *Charles the Second*, pp. 320–80; J. R. Jones, *Charles II: Royal Politician* (Oxford, 1989), pp. 108–34; Andrew Browning, "Parties and Party Organization in the Reign of Charles II," *Transactions of the Royal Historical Society*, 4th series, 30 (1945): 21–36.
[43] Jordan, *Londons Triumphs Illustrated* (1677), p. i.
[44] The most ardent proponent of this position was Samuel Parker; see his *A Discourse of Ecclesiastical Politie* (1670).   [45] Jordan, *London Triumphant*, p. 16.
[46] Jordan, *London's Triumphs*, p. 10.

Again, in 1677, Jordan conflated disobedience and lunacy in a song performed for the king, the bishops, and the Prince of Orange:

> ... since Forty and One
> Such things have been done
> Will make the next Ages to wonder...
> New Bedlam must not
> Be ever forgot,
> Of Lunaticks we have such a plenty,
> That I dare engage
> In the succeeding age
> The chambers will never be empty.[47]

The Lord Mayor's Show, along with Danby's government, relied on the idea of consensus to represent all those opposed to established authority as either insane or treacherous. If the Lord Treasurer could combine consensus and obedience with his growing "party" in Parliament, then he had a real chance to end the conflict between Crown and Parliament. Unfortunately for Danby, his dream of executive control of the legislature was shattered in the autumn of 1678 when the Popish Plot and Montagu's revelations about French subsidies confirmed many in their fears of a conspiracy to destroy the ancient constitution.

VI THE EXCLUSION CRISIS, 1678

Faced with what was to prove the most divisive event in Charles II's reign, Jordan fell back on the themes of loyalty and union. The new mayor, James Edwards, was admonished to "provoke all persons under Your Government to be **regular and obedient**."[48] On the day of the Show, 29 October, the Parliament had known of the plot against the king's life for one week. In an attempt to profit from this threat, Jordan presented *The Fortress of Government*, a pageant which reiterated the bond between religion and obedience:

> The adamantine rock 'tis built upon
> Merits the name of true religion.
> The walls are make of Union, and well known
> To be intire; Truth is the cornerstone.
> The battlements are Concord.[49]

---

[47] Jordan, *Londons Triumphs Illustrated*, p. 19.
[48] Jordan, *The Triumphs of London* (1678), p. iv. [49] *Ibid.*, p. 4.

The disintegration of union would readmit faction into politics, so to preserve the established forms in Church and State, people must realize that just government relies upon union, constancy, concord – consensus.

Lest anyone miss the point, Jordan explained his purposes:

> And though this fort, thus arm'd and top'd by Glory,
> Is but a model built by Allegory,
> The moral's pertinent, and pregnant too,
> It intimates your government and you:
> Without these virtues which are here set forth,
> A magistrate will want much of his worth.
> Rebellion, fraud, whoredom, and felonie,
> In short time will grow greater than he.[50]

Without the virtues "here set forth" the country seemed again destined for rebellion. Using a representative cross-section of the population in the figures of a soldier, a citizen, and a West Countryman, Jordan clearly states that the deterioration of consensus was caused by irrational and irreligious people who cared only for themselves:

> SWAB. Want of amity
>   Breeds calamity,
>   We are too much divided;
>   By atheistick persons too
>   Religion is derided.
> SELF. With arguments as light as air,
> SWAB. Opinions got in Reason's chair...
> CRAB. The new-vound lights have spoil'd our zights,
>   And caus'd this disagreeing.[51]

As a final clarification of the model and allegory of the fort, the Show for 1678 ends with the stylistic device of a Chorus which claims:

> Since union and concord bring plenty and peace,
> And amity is the kind cause of increase;
> Let love from division our fancys release,
> And all our dissentions ever shall cease.[52]

But the Chorus which concluded the pageant in 1678 suggested a social and political harmony which hardly existed.

Like any successful propaganda, the Lord Mayor's Shows of the 1670s had to present images that would appeal to the spectators.

[50] *Ibid.*, pp. 6–7.   [51] *Ibid.*, p. 18.   [52] *Ibid.*, pp. 18–19.

With the Commonwealth still a tangible memory, concord and union remained the most alluring themes in the political discourse. Teamed with commonplace Augustan tropes, these themes can be found in all forms of legally published material in the 1670s. Furthermore, as the policies of the Earl of Danby continued to reflect the foreign, domestic, and religious views of the political moderates, the consensual ideology of the pageantry helped create an increasing number of adherents for the Court. The revival of the Lord Mayor's Show from 1671 on provided a forum for propagating images of consensus, and thanks to Charles's regular attendance from 1671–78, they offered an animated expression of the concord between government and people.

As Danby's majority in both Houses grew in the late 1670s – and opponents like Shaftesbury and Buckingham spent long periods in the Tower – the quest for consensus and the marginalization of all those outside it increased. Not only were the Crown and Parliament beginning to march in step, the consensual policies and propaganda emanating from the Court had the support of a growing majority of the political nation. By the same token, however, the Earl of Danby's accountability for this propaganda also contributed to his downfall. Once he was shown to be in the pocket of Louis XIV, and his moderation exposed as a blind for subverting the ancient constitution, he lost his majorities and his freedom. The desperation of his opponents by 1678 may explain why Shaftesbury and his allies championed the falsehoods and distortions of Titus Oates. By embracing the epithet of Whigs, they not only distinguished themselves from the Tories, but shattered the Court ideology's assertion of consensus. Not surprisingly, at the height of the Exclusion Crisis, the pageantry of the Lord Mayor's Day was countered by lavish pope-burnings sponsored by the Whigs on 5 November as both sides sought to demonstrate their support among the populace.

After Thomas Jordan's death in 1685, the fractured society of City politics meant that the Show never again had a consistent author or theme. Indeed, after 1688, the celebrations of Protestantism on the 5th and 17th of November supplanted the Lord Mayor's Day as civic spectacles, and despite the participation of Elkanah Settle, the pageantry was discontinued after 1708.

CHAPTER 3

Politics and the Restoration masque: the case of Dido and Aeneas

Andrew R. Walkling

Our understanding of the relationship between politics and literature in early-modern England has increased significantly in recent years, and we are now seeing the beginnings of a full investigation into the ways in which much of the literature – particularly the drama – of Restoration England was explicitly political, both in its conception and in its rhetoric.[1] Yet despite this growing interest in the political nature of Restoration literature, little attention has been devoted to the politics of the Restoration masque. As we now know from the work of Kevin Sharpe, Martin Butler, and others, the masque as it existed before the outbreak of the Civil War was a highly politicized form, in which these ostensibly most panegyrical of dramatic texts commonly engaged in political controversy, sometimes offering criticism of royal policy.[2] Not surprisingly, the same holds true of Restoration masques which, like their Jacobean and Caroline counterparts, were addressed primarily to members of the political and social elite, and sought to advise that audience about important contemporary issues. Similarly, the power and influence wielded by those who attended masques at both the pre- and post-Civil War English Courts dictated that the author adopt an aesthetics of

I would like to thank Gary De Krey, Carol V. Kaske, Lynn Laufenberg, Gerald MacLean, Nancy Klein Maguire, Jessica Waldoff, James Winn, and Neal Zaslaw for their comments and suggestions on this essay.

[1] While this approach to Restoration literature began three decades ago with John Loftis's *The Politics of Drama in Augustan England* (Oxford, 1963), it has only begun to come into its own since the mid-1980s. A significant example of this work is Zwicker, *Politics and Language*. See also Richard Ashcraft and Alan Roper, *Politics as Reflected in Literature: Papers Presented at a Clark Library Seminar 24 January 1987* (Los Angeles, 1989). A well-traversed area of Restoration political interpretation is the debate over Thomas Otway's *Venice Preserv'd*; for a summary, see Phillip Harth, "Political Interpretations of Venice Preserv'd," *Modern Philology* 85 (1987–88): 345–62.

[2] See Kevin Sharpe, *Criticism and Compliment: The Politics of Literature in the England of Charles I* (Cambridge, 1987), especially Chapter 5, and Martin Butler, "Politics and the Masque: The Triumph of Peace," *The Seventeenth Century* 2 (1988): 117–41.

dissimulation in order to avoid running foul of the censor or, which would be worse, losing Court patronage.

Yet during the Restoration, the strategies by which political messages were both concealed from and revealed to their audience became far more elaborate and complex than in earlier reigns. This complexity, coupled with the fragmentary and ill-defined nature of the genre, and the limited amount of surviving evidence regarding the dates and performances of most of these works, may account for the lack of scholarly attention devoted to Restoration masques.[3] Moreover, since many of the most controversial political arguments would be concealed or circumscribed within texts that are of a highly formulaic and encomiastic nature, we can see why, on the one hand, the Restoration masque has been largely overlooked as a political medium, and on the other, why a fuller examination of this form is essential to our understanding of the social functioning of Court culture in the later seventeenth century.

The aim of this essay is to demonstrate the value for both literary and historical studies of understanding how Restoration masques expressed covert political statements. By recognizing this genre as surreptitiously political, literary critics can gain a greater sense of how dramatic literature commented upon and interacted with politics in Restoration courtly circles, an understanding already being achieved for the public theaters by a number of recent studies. At the same time, historians of Restoration culture and society can benefit from an increased understanding of the place of literature within that society, particularly at its points of contact with those who held the reins of power. By exploring how authors of Restoration Court masques assumed the role of commentator upon contemporary issues, I hope to indicate for literary critics and historians alike the benefits of a symbiotic critical inquiry into Restoration culture which draws upon both areas of study. After briefly outlining a hermeneutical framework for interpreting Restoration masques from a political standpoint, I will apply that interpretive paradigm to a specific, and notable, case – Nahum Tate and Henry Purcell's *Dido and Aeneas*.

The search for a hermeneutic of Restoration drama requires the assessment of two important but conflicting models for understanding

---

[3] But see Curtis A. Price, "Political Allegory in Late-Seventeenth-Century English Opera," in Nigel Fortune, ed., *Music and Theatre: Essays in Honour of Winton Dean* (Cambridge, 1987), pp. 1–29.

topical allusion and political commentary in seventeenth-century literature. The first, advanced by John M. Wallace,[4] argues that Restoration readers sought to extract general precepts from what they read, and that the "meaning" of a given text had to be sufficiently fragmentary and obscure in its conception to allow for a spectrum of interpretation based on the resonances generated by the work in different readers. This hermeneutical model stresses creative inference on the part of readers, rather than controlled authorial implication. Wallace argues that to expect one-to-one correspondences in Restoration literature between characters in a poem or on the stage and real-life figures in contemporary politics is to ignore broader aspects of Restoration poetic or dramatic allegory, in which the desire to address fundamental aspects of the culture, rather than a specific issue, is paramount.

The problem with this approach is that to search for general precepts is to overlook the powerfully emblematic nature of much Restoration literature, particularly its tragic and encomiastic drama. Restoration readers were often expected to read works à clef; on occasion printers even provided a "key" that assisted in the decoding of concealed meaning. Moreover, the selective use of state censorship in a few celebrated instances related to theatrical productions, such as the forbidding of Dryden and Lee's The Duke of Guise in 1682,[5] demonstrates that the authorities were aware of and sensitive to the political applications that could be drawn from dramatic productions, both by inference and by implication.

A second model, outlined by Annabel Patterson in Censorship and Interpretation,[6] addresses these problems while attending to the admittedly limited number of cases in which government censors actually did intervene in the process of literary dissemination, or in which a specific political interpretation of a text has come down to us in the correspondence or marginalia left behind by an informed Restoration reader. Working with a variety of texts from throughout the seventeenth century, Patterson describes a system of "functional

[4] "Dryden and History: A Problem in Allegorical Reading," ELH 36 (1969): 265–90, and "'Examples Are Best Precepts': Readers and Meanings in Seventeenth-Century Poetry," Critical Inquiry 1 (1974–75): 273–90.

[5] See also Annabel Patterson, "The Country Gentleman: Howard, Marvell, and Dryden in the Theater of Politics," Studies in English Literature 25 (1985): 491–509.

[6] Patterson's Censorship and Interpretation: The Conditions of Writing and Reading in Early Modern England (Madison, 1984), has recently been reissued "with a new introduction" which has the effect of altering all subsequent references in the text by eight pages.

ambiguity," in which a delicate balance was struck between the creators and the interpreters of texts, and between the differing types of authority that each wielded. In the case of texts in which political references can be inferred, Patterson argues, the author's intentional "encoding" of a particular political message must be regarded as an important element of the work's "meaning." "Functional ambiguity" is a kind of equivocation, injected into a text by its creator and implicitly accepted by his audience, that engaged the interpretive impulse of the reader, or viewer, by provoking an attempt to "discover" the meaning, while at the same time retaining enough ambiguity to allow room for maneuver should the issue of the author's intentions be broached publicly. By this means the work was able to navigate the treacherous path of official censorship.

My analysis of the Restoration masque starts from Patterson's theoretical assumptions about intention and reception. When a text invites us to notice specific correspondences or a system of topical allusions, looking for general precepts and a multiplicity of interpretations becomes unhelpful and obstructive to a clear understanding of how the text interacts with its audience and with the circumstances under which it was written. Even so, an author's intended meaning was itself subject to modifications and misreadings which could lead to interpretations that carried a valid contemporary resonance never anticipated by the author. While my goal in this essay is to "unpack" the allegory of *Dido and Aeneas* in order to reveal a compelling pattern of specific political allusion, I will also suggest how ambiguity persists, even in a text in which contemporary references are clearly identifiable, and how changing political circumstances can be seen to affect the reception of a work's meaning.

Like Jacobean and Caroline masques, those of the Restoration were susceptible to political interpretation. None the less, the Restoration masque departs from the structure and conventions of its early seventeenth century forerunners, and demands a specific interpretive approach. The growth in popularity of the *roman à clef* during the 1640s and 1650s, a period in which covert writing developed new forms,[7] greatly affected the shape that much Restoration political allegory would take: *Absalom and Achitophel* is only the most well known of a host of examples of unambiguously

[7] See Lois Potter, *Secret Rites and Secret Writing: Royalist Literature, 1641–1660* (Cambridge, 1989).

polemical works in which the reader was expected to "decode" the meaning by applying a simple key.[8] In the case of Restoration masques the pattern of concealment is equally systematic, yet far more sophisticated. While direct one-to-one correspondences continue, the masque establishes a complex of differing types of allegorization, a multi-tiered representational structure which allows for the allegorical portrayal both of actual political personages, such as the king, and of institutions or corporate bodies, such as England or the Church, by characters on stage. In addition, certain interest groups within Restoration society – Papists, Nonconformists, Whig or Tory partisans – are represented by solo-chorus combinations, in which the chorus leader serves as spokesperson for the group's collective opinions and positions. The chorus itself dramatizes the group's aggregate quality, responding with statements that affirm a conventional perception of its character – Papists are evil, partisans love carnage. The allegorical framework of the masque provides a common forum for these different levels of political commentary. The locus of their intersection, the masque itself, thus permits a kind of political commentary unachievable in other dramatic genres, one in which different allegorical modes interact.

Writers of Restoration Court masques commonly signalled their covert intentions by creatively adapting classical sources, ostensibly in line with contemporary tastes. In the process of reworking classical narrative into Restoration masque, authors would introduce new elements or change some key aspect of the original. A literate Restoration spectator or reader, familiar with the source, was expected to observe these changes easily, and would be compelled to ponder how such alterations invited a contemporary political application. In *Dido and Aeneas*, Tate left several explicit clues, at least one of which is well known to modern audiences – the "Weyward Sisters," Tate's *Macbeth*-inspired sorceresses. By introducing the Witches into the masque, Tate displaces the prevalent role of fate in Virgil's *Aeneid*: the story of Aeneas's abandonment of Dido is debased from an heroic epic of fate and its precedence over human desires and actions to a miserable tale of human folly, misunderstanding, and good intentions gone awry. In addition to lowering Virgil's epic,

---

[8] These keys began to appear in print shortly after *Absalom and Achitophel* was first published; see Zwicker, *Politics and Language*, p. 57 on marginalia to contemporary copies of the poem, and his more recent study, *Lines of Authority: Politics and English Literary Culture, 1649–1689* (Ithaca, New York, 1993), p. 6.

Tate alters the familiar chronology of the story: where in Virgil, the storm which sends the characters fleeing back to town provides the opportunity for Dido and Aeneas to retire to a cave and consummate their relationship, in the masque the consummation has already taken place, and the storm is simply another malicious disruption conjured up by the Witches.

Dido's death-scene is another point of departure: while gruesome onstage slaughter was by no means common practice in Restoration masques and operas, Dido's fate at the end of Tate's masque is left conspicuously unclear. The stage directions and the chorus both refer to "her tomb," and she herself tells her confidante Belinda that "death invades me" (3.58),[9] yet there is no explicit textual instruction that she die. This is a far cry from Virgil's epic, in which Dido stabs herself with a dagger while sitting atop a funeral pyre made from her marriage-bed and the accoutrements of war Aeneas has left behind. There are other, less striking differences between the two versions of the story,[10] yet all of them contribute to the process by which classical myth becomes Restoration political allegory.

The politics of a given masque is, initially, a function of the work's date and of its first production. Yet in the case of *Dido and Aeneas*, we know nothing definite about the masque's composition or its earliest performances.[11] Until very recently, *Dido* was thought to have been written for, and first performed at, a girls' boarding school at Chelsea run by the dancing-master Josias Priest, probably in 1689. Recent evidence, however, suggests that *Dido* may actually be a Court masque dating from the reign of James II, and that the 1689 boarding school production was not the work's first performance.[12] Unfortunately, while this new conception of the performance history of *Dido* seems entirely plausible, given what we know about the circumstances of other Restoration masques, the evidence itself is

[9] All quotations from Curtis Price, ed., *Dido and Aeneas: An Opera* (New York, 1986), pp. 63–79. Italics in the stage directions are reversed. Where I disagree with Price's choice of copy-text, I have made my own emendations in parentheses.

[10] For example, Hugh M. Lee points out that "whereas Dido is more the pursuer in the *Aeneid*, in the opera it is Aeneas; the Queen in contrast is the pursued and makes a more dignified impression than her raging counterpart of the poem;" see "Purcell's *Dido and Aneas* [sic]: Aeneas as Romantic Hero," *Vergilius* 23 [1977]: 21–29, this passage p. 25. Lee's article provides the best comparison of Tate's redaction with Virgil's original.

[11] The most comprehensive discussion of *Dido* and the problems it presents can be found in Price's edition.

[12] The impetus for this reconsideration was the publication of Richard Luckett, "A New Source for 'Venus and Adonis,'" *The Musical Times* 130 (1989): 76–79.

only inferential, and any attempt to date the hypothetical Court production (and thus the masque's composition) more accurately than "1689 or earlier" must still be considered speculative.[13]

Nevertheless, a political reading of Tate's text can both clarify and obscure the issue of dating. The series of events chronicled in the first and second Acts of the masque suggest a *terminus a quo* of approximately 1687, when James II's policies were widely perceived to be leading toward a breakdown of constitutional order in England. Yet in Act 3, when a suggestively similar breakdown occurs, it is less clear to which historical occasion the masque is referring. Both James II and William III were regarded – sometimes by the same people – as having upset the nation's ancient constitutional structures, and thus *Dido and Aeneas* can be shown to function as a timely political allegory both before and after the "Glorious" Revolution of 1688.

Either way, *Dido and Aeneas* presents a history of the process by which James II's pro-Catholic policies had alienated his subjects and appeared to be threatening the destruction of England's constitution and the rule of law. The masque investigates and comments upon this political situation through a searching psychological examination of the relationship between the lovers Aeneas and Dido which provides an allegorical commentary on James's policies in England. This is achieved by means of a system of allegorization whose basis is the multi-leveled representational structure discussed above, and which also draws upon certain conventions of the *roman à clef* genre: here, Aeneas can be read as James, while Dido can be seen to represent England. Moreover, the love-relationship acted out on stage between the two characters offers significantly idealized conceptions of a king's relationship to his realm and vice versa. Aeneas's love for Dido follows early-modern commonplaces of a king who is both lover and spouse of his people. Dido's love for Aeneas, on the other hand, suggests a more directly topical relationship, one which is central to the masque's allegory: as Dido loves Aeneas, so England recognizes James as her rightful king, a notion that implicitly rejects Whig attempts to impose alternative heirs on Charles II during the Exclusion Crisis of 1679–81.

---

[13] Bruce Wood and Andrew Pinnock have recently attempted to assign *Dido* to 1684 on the basis of musical and textual concordances in "'Unscarr'd by turning times'?: The dating of Purcell's *Dido and Aeneas*," *Early Music* 20 (1992): 372–90; their assertions, however, are not entirely convincing; see my "'The dating of Purcell's *Dido and Aeneas*'?: A reply to Bruce Wood and Andrew Pinnock," *Early Music* 22 (August 1994): 469–81.

Tate's version of the sequence of events in which Dido and Aeneas come together, and eventually part, gives shape to a central theme of the masque: the disruptive power of bad counsel. Every major character either gives or gets advice at some point in the masque, and in every case that advice not only turns out to be ill conceived, but also leads in some way to the story's tragic end. The most obvious example is the speech of the Sorceress's "Spirit" to Aeneas, ordering him to leave at once for Rome, to which I will return. Another important instance of bad counsel occurs in Act I when Belinda encourages Dido to accept Aeneas despite the Queen's strong reservations. Belinda admonishes Dido, "Fear no danger to ensue, / The hero loves as well as you" (1.35–36), advice that, while it may reflect an accurate superficial reading of the demeanor of Dido's suitor, does not take into account the serious flaws hidden beneath Aeneas's heroic exterior. Even Dido herself is guilty of dispensing bad counsel when, in the final scene, she turns on Aeneas despite his obvious hesitation and commands him to leave her, an injunction that will have repercussions for the allegorical meaning of the last Act. Finally, there is the case of the First Sailor, a character whose admonition to his comrades seems to provide a moment of comic relief from the otherwise sombre mood of the last Act:

> Take a bouze short leave of your nymphs on the shore,
>   And silence their mourning
>   With vows of returning,
> But never intending to visit them more.   (3.3–6)

Yet if we take into account a recently advanced suggestion, made on the basis of an examination of theater records, that the First Sailor and the Sorceress may share a single stage persona,[14] the Sailor's apparently frivolous advice acquires a far more sinister quality, and infects even this lighthearted scene with an air of foreboding. In each of these examples, bad counsel can be shown to lead directly to the departure of Aeneas from Carthage and to Dido's resultant death.

In order to understand how the representation of James II and England as Aeneas and Dido, combined with the underlying issue of bad counsel, allegorizes the political events of the 1680s, it is necessary to look more closely at the characters of the hero and heroine of the masque. Aeneas has a surprisingly limited dramatic role: he is

---

[14] Curtis Price and Irena Cholij, "Dido's Bass Sorceress," *The Musical Times* 127 (1986): 615–18.

assigned no arias, singing almost exclusively in recitative. Yet of all the characters in Dido, his personality is most searchingly examined. The picture that results is decidedly unflattering: one commentator has referred to Tate and Purcell's Aeneas as "a complete booby";[15] another calls him "a meandering oaf."[16] While Aeneas does appear to be genuinely distraught at having to abandon his queen at the behest of the Witches, his handling of the situation is singularly unheroic. After the sham Mercury has dispensed his supposed divine injunction, a moment when some circumspection might be in order, Aeneas blusters, almost comically, "Jove's commands shall be obeyed / Tonight our anchors shall be weighed" (2.59–60); yet when firmness is called for in his subsequent encounter with Dido, he vacillates pathetically. This incongruous conjunction of stubbornness and indecision is the very set of character traits that was commonly attributed to James II, whose brief and ultimately disastrous reign is a study in political ineptitude and miscalculation, combined with dogmatic rigidity and an irrational reliance on ministers and favorites who did not have the best interests of the Crown at heart.[17] In the case of both Aeneas and James II, susceptibility to bad counsel is a function of this combination of elements.

In contrast to Aeneas, the character of Dido exemplifies personal, civic, and political virtue. Dido's initial fear and hesitation in the first Act, and her final sorrow and despair in the last, are treated as the main dramatic and musical themes in the work. Her heroism, in part, suggests a national steadfastness, the ability of the English to adapt to adverse circumstances. But her deep sorrow, particularly throughout the first Act, indicates a darker side to the events being depicted in the masque. Like England during the Exclusion Crisis, when even James's supporters expressed concern that his Catholicism could bring ruin on the nation, Dido is torn between her love for Aeneas and the knowledge that he is fated to abandon her in pursuit of his larger goal of founding Rome. The significance of this particular locale in a Restoration context must not be overlooked: like Aeneas, James II's own future appeared to hold a kind of founding of Rome, that is, of the Rome-in-England represented by a restoration of the

---

[15] Joseph Kerman, *Opera as Drama* (Berkeley, 1988), p. 43.
[16] David Z. Kushner, "Henry Purcell's 'Dido and Aeneas': An Analytical Discussion," *The American Music Teacher* 21/1 (September/October 1971): 25–28, this passage p. 28.
[17] For a characterization of James, see John Miller, *James II: A Study in Kingship* (Hove, 1978), pp. 121–24 and 240–42.

Catholic Church. In this context, Dido's statement to Belinda, "Peace and I are strangers grown" (1.11), powerfully recalls England's political turmoil during the years 1679–81.

The first Act of *Dido and Aeneas* plays out the chronology of the period from the late 1670s to James's accession in 1685. The scene opens with Dido's sorrow and indecision over her conflicting feelings about Aeneas, a sentiment which is quickly countered by Belinda, who attempts to play up the hero's merits. The discussion that ensues recalls the issues and circumstances of the Exclusion Crisis: just as James was forced to sit by, in temporary exile, while the nation deliberated his future, so Dido and her advisors debate in Aeneas's absence whether or not the queen should openly confess her love for him. The discussion between Dido, Belinda, and the Second Woman treats several facets of the popular view of James. The first portrays him as a military and political hero, invoking his career as Lord High Admiral during the Second and Third Dutch Wars and as a leading figure at Charles II's Court. Dido asks:

> Whence could so much virtue spring,
> What storms, what battles did he sing[?]
> Anchises' valour mix'd with Venus' charms,
> How soft in peace, and yet how fierce in arms. (1.22–25)

By the mid-1680s, however, the image of James as conquering hero held by his sympathizers came to be supplanted by another, when many in England began to consider that he had suffered unjustly at the hands of his opponents. Writing in September 1688, Viscount Lonsdale recalled that while some were still strongly opposed to James, even after he had succeeded to the throne,

yet a ffar greater number had then no such apprehensions, who were composed of those who had been ffollowers of his ffortune into Fflanders and Scotland, which journies looking like a kind of banishment, and his danger of being lost in the Glocester, made the usuall operation in the minds of English men, pittie ffor the afflicted.[18]

Lonsdale further noted that:

ffrom men's attempting to exclude him, they att this juncture of time made him their darling; no more was his religion terrible, his magnanimous courage and the hardships he had undergone, were the discours of all men.[19]

---

[18] John Lord Viscount Lonsdale, *Memoir of the Reign of James II*, (York, 1808), pp. 2–3.
[19] *Ibid.*, p. 3.

This sentiment is reflected in the rejoinders of Belinda and the Second Woman to Dido's remarks about Aeneas, and in Dido's own response to them:

> BELINDA. A tale so strong and full of woe,
>   Might melt the rocks as well as you.
> 2ND WOMAN. What stubborn heart unmoved could see,
>   Such distress, such pi(e)ty[?]
> DIDO. Mine with storms of care oppress'd,
>   Is taught to pity the distress'd.
>   Mean wretches(') grief can touch,
>   So soft so sensible my breast,
>   But ah! I fear, I pity his too much. (1.26–34)

This last remark by Dido, expressing concern that her attraction to and sympathy for Aeneas could overcome her better judgment, gains an ominous significance once Aeneas has finally come onstage. The hero declares his love, an action which reflects James's desire to be England's king. Dido, however, is apprehensive: her response to Aeneas, "Fate forbids what you pursue" (1.45), represents the view that James's position as heir to the throne and his Roman Catholicism were mutually incompatible. However, the Trojan hero has a ready answer to her challenge:

> Aeneas has no fate but you.
> Let Dido smile, and I'll defy
> The feeble stroke of Destiny. (1.46–48)

This passage is strikingly reminiscent of James's own response in 1685 to the charge that once he became king, his policies would inevitably tend toward popery and absolutism. In a speech to his privy council, made on the day he ascended the throne, James asserted that

I have been reported to be a Man for Arbitrary Power, but that is not the onely Story has been made of Me; And I shall make it My Endeavor to Preserve this Government both in Church and State as it is now by Law Established.[20]

Thus James's own defiance of what was perceived to be his "destiny" served to assuage the fears of many of his subjects, and James was accepted as king, just as Aeneas is finally accepted by Dido, with general rejoicing.

---

[20] *London Gazette* 2006 (5–9 February 1685), verso (italics reversed).

The celebratory mood conjured up at the end of the first Act occasions a brief moment of respite from the gravity of the rest of the masque, and this easing of tension (although interrupted in the drama itself by the Witches' scene) is carried over into the second scene of Act 2, the Grove scene. Taken together, the two scenes of Act 2 imaginatively reconstruct crucial events from shortly after James's accession to the throne until the moment when the crisis brought about by the king's pursuit of arbitrary policies began to grip the nation. Dido plays almost no part in the Grove scene, although she remains on stage throughout most of it. Aeneas, on the other hand, has a significant role. Whereas in the first Act, we only know of Aeneas's heroism because others describe it, here he displays it for all to see:

> Behold upon my bending spear,
> A monster's head stands bleeding,
> With tushes far exceeding
> Those did Venus' huntsman tear. (2.41–44)

Much has been made of the phallic and sexual imagery of this passage, and its apparent effect on Dido, as she nervously warns of the impending storm conjured up by the Witches.[21] More interesting for a political reading of the masque is the reference to "Venus' huntsman," Adonis, an apparent bow to John Blow's Court masque *Venus and Adonis*, from which Purcell and Tate are believed to have derived much of their inspiration for Dido. If *Venus and Adonis* is read politically, the boar who kills Adonis clearly represents the factional and partisan strife that threatened the stability of Charles II's rule during the years of and immediately following the Exclusion Crisis.[22]

Yet Charles II, unlike the shepherd who represented him in Blow's masque, was not actually laid low by this "monster." Rather, the boar in *Venus* serves as a warning of the potential for grave harm caused by the Whig–Tory struggle of the early 1680s. In *Dido*, however, Aeneas is at pains to point out that this boar – "With tushes far exceeding" – is much more dangerous than that which confronted Adonis, and that he, unlike Adonis, has managed to defeat the menace. Indeed, James II did encounter a far more serious threat to his authority than the party conflicts of his brother's reign: this came in the form of the Western Rebellion of 1685, led by the Duke

---

[21] See, for example, Curtis Price, "*Dido and Aeneas* in Context," in Price, ed., *Dido and Aeneas*, pp. 3–41, especially p. 22.
[22] See my "*Venus and Adonis*: the Politics of Consensus," forthcoming.

of Monmouth, Charles II's eldest bastard son. Having landed in the West Country on 11 June, Monmouth proclaimed himself king, accusing his uncle of having murdered Charles II in order to gain the throne, and led an insurrection which was supposed to spark a nationwide uprising against James. Nonetheless, like Aeneas in the masque, James was easily able to defeat this challenge to his power. The rebellion was crushed in short order, and Monmouth was captured and, like Aeneas's boar, beheaded.

This important event could arguably be called the first and last great victory of James II's reign, for a few months after the defeat of Monmouth's rebellion James became embroiled in a controversy with Parliament over his employment of Catholic officers in the army. The dispute led to a standoff, and to the prorogation (and eventual dissolution) of the Parliament, the last one to meet during the reign. This series of events represented the first stage in James's resort to the use of arbitrary power in order to advance the position of the Catholic Church in England, and the process is chronicled in *Dido and Aeneas*, in which the boar episode is followed immediately by the arrival of the storm conjured up by the Witches, sending the assembled company fleeing for the shelter of the palace. Only Aeneas remains behind, at the behest of the Witches' "trusty elf" who, posing as Mercury, informs Aeneas that the gods have commanded him to depart at once for Rome.

How, then, do the Witches signify in the political allegory of *Dido and Aeneas*? What motive do Tate's "enchantresses" have for playing their fatal ruse on the Trojan prince? One answer can be found in Tate's use of a commonplace in Restoration drama, the use of witches to represent Papists.[23] This device features prominently in Sir William Davenant's 1660s adaptation of *Macbeth* and its 1673 revival, as well as in Thomas Shadwell's Popish Plot farce *The Lancashire Witches* (1682). In *Dido*, many of the statements made by the Witches, both in Act 2, Scene 1, and at the beginning of Act 3, are designed to reflect a prototypical Restoration view of what Papists did and thought. "Harm's our delight and mischief all our skill" (2.8) sing the Witches at one point, and "Destruction('s) our delight, delight our greatest sorrow" (3.18) a maxim that, reinforced by their gleeful "ho ho ho"s, excludes the possibility of even a modicum of scruples. Many at the time were of the opinion that the Papists only wished to

[23] See Steven E. Plank, "'And Now About the Cauldron Sing': Music and the Supernatural on the Restoration Stage," *Early Music* 18 (1990): 392–407.

destroy England in order to satisfy their own blood-lust. Similarly, Tate's Witches seem to have no clear motivation for their hatred of Dido, except that she is "in prosperous state" (2.10), while their determination to "storm her lover on the ocean" (3.15) after he has unwittingly helped them to carry out their plan suggests that what most strongly motivates the Sorceress and her hags is a taste for gratuitous violence.

If we accept the association of the Witches with Restoration Papists, and consider their role in the masque as a substitution for Virgil's emphasis on fate, Tate's employment of the theme of bad counsel comes into sharp focus. Aeneas's encounter with the bogus Mercury at the end of the second Act presents a powerful validation of both the dramatic theme and the political message of the masque. In his unquestioning acceptance of the alleged divine injunction, Aeneas appears as a weak and undiscerning anti-hero, and thus James is allegorically attacked for following the advice of the increasingly exclusive circle of Catholic extremists with whom he surrounded himself at Court.

It is these Papist advisers, the masque asserts, who have led astray a well-intentioned hero-monarch by playing upon his greatest weakness, his susceptibility to bad counsel. This view is reflected in the abundance of literature produced during the "Glorious" Revolution which, in the words of Steven Zwicker, "attempt[ed] to shuffle James beneath the cover of wicked advisers and evil Jesuits."[24] In its initial stages, the "Glorious" Revolution did not seek the overthrow of James II, but rather the removal of his popish advisers and the securing of the Anglican Church and English constitutional liberties. As one broadside issued in late 1688 declared:

the King by his several Declarations, since his Accession to the Crown, had promised to protect the Protestant Religion; which Repeated Promises (it's believed) he had more exactly perform'd, had he not been otherwise drawn aside by Evil Councellors.[25]

And in his own declaration justifying his invasion of England, William of Orange explained that:

---

[24] Steven N. Zwicker, "Representing the Revolution: Politics and High Culture in 1688," in Eveline Cruickshanks, ed., *By Force or By Default?: The Revolution of 1688–89* (Edinburgh, 1989), pp. 109–34, this passage p. 131.

[25] *A Rare a Show: or England's Betrayers Expos'd, in a Catalogue of the several Persons exempted by his Highness the Prince of Orange; to be brought to Account, before the next ensuing Parliament* ([London?], 1688).

wee have thought fit to goe over to England, and to Carry over with us a force, sufficient by the blessing of God, to defend us from the Violence of those Evill Councellours.[26]

These statements express a contemporary opinion that James was not solely responsible for the policies that had brought his kingdom to the brink of disaster. Rather, his error was in allowing himself to become the unwitting tool of wicked and self-serving advisers whose true aims were the subjection of England to the yoke of popery.

Like James, Aeneas has been duped into a course of action that cannot be in his own interests or those of his lover. Yet he accepts the Witches' advice unhesitatingly, and the last Act of *Dido and Aeneas* spins out the devastating result. With this final descent into tragedy and despair, however, the politics of the masque's conclusion become less clear. The final confrontation between Aeneas and Dido reads like an exercise in cross-purposes. When Aeneas announces that he is going to depart, Dido accuses him of being a hypocrite and shedding crocodile tears. But when he changes his mind and decides to stay after all, Dido orders him out of her sight, a command that Aeneas obeys without even a word of farewell. Having thus displayed her pride and fortitude, Dido realizes she cannot go on without him, and after singing her famous lament, she dies.

The problem with this confused series of dramatic events is that it obscures the question of culpability raised in earlier scenes. It is clear that the Witches are the chief evildoers in the drama, and that Aeneas's weakness of character plays an equally important role in the masque's tragic outcome. Here, however, Dido is also given a part of the blame for Aeneas's departure and thus for her own demise, while Aeneas receives what might almost be called a sympathetic treatment. He does offer to remain behind, to "Offend the gods, and love obey" (3.42), and it is only at Dido's insistence that he finally leaves. Yet Dido's love for Aeneas remains so strong, even after her petulant outburst, that (as she tells Belinda), "Death must come when he is gone" (3.52). The fact that Dido's love for Aeneas persists, even after he has abandoned her, serves as a pointed assertion of the principle that a king's legitimacy can never be negated, even by evil deeds or weakness of character. This perspective on Aeneas's actions reflects the attitude of many in England during the late 1680s who asserted

---

[26] *The Declaration of His Highnes William Henry ... Of the Reasons Inducing him, to appear in Armes in the Kingdome of England ...* (The Hague, 1688), p. 7.

the inalienability of James II's right to rule, but who were at the same time alarmed by his use of arbitrary methods to achieve his proselytizing goals. Prominent among those who held this belief were many English Roman Catholics, including the recent convert John Dryden.[27] As the career and writings of Dryden indicate, however, what had existed before 1688 as a sense of anger at James for having subverted the constitution in the pursuit of his policies became, in the wake of the "Glorious" Revolution, a profound disillusionment with what was perceived as an equally anti-constitutional solution to the problem.

This concern with anti-constitutional actions informs the final Act of *Dido and Aeneas*. Yet within this framework the masque's denouement functions equally well as a political commentary whether *Dido* is taken to refer to events before the 1688–89 Revolution or after it. In both cases, Dido's "death" (left intentionally ambiguous because England cannot truly "die") can be read as a response to the breakdown of the rule of law which resulted from arbitrary acts on the part of the monarch. If the masque is dated 1687 or 1688, that breakdown is the consequence of James's increasingly pro-Catholic policies and his abandonment of his promises to the nation, represented allegorically by Aeneas's departure to found Rome. Dido's continuing love for him serves as a reminder that he is still king, despite his having shattered the bonds of trust between monarch and people, and her death indicates the extent to which the nation had been devastated by James's actions. If, on the other hand, we date *Dido and Aeneas* to 1689, the breakdown of constitutional principles that the masque addresses is the result of William of Orange's assumption of the throne after the "Glorious" Revolution, an event no less calamitous to supporters of divine-right monarchy than James's own invasions of the rights of his subjects. Dido's command to Aeneas to leave her, despite the prince's wish to stay, can be seen to represent James's physical flight from the country, while her continuing love for Aeneas expresses the view that James was still England's legitimate king, despite William's illegal usurp-

---

[27] See Louis I. Bredvold, *The Intellectual Milieu of John Dryden: Studies in Some Aspects of Seventeenth-Century Thought* (Ann Arbor, 1934; rpt. 1956), pp. 164–84 (Appendix D: "English Catholic Opinion in the Reign of James II"). Bredvold demonstrates that many English Catholics who had, despite official persecution, managed to live and worship freely under Charles II were deeply concerned that James's ill-advised actions might lead to a powerful backlash against them.

ation, an event whose disastrous consequences are allegorized in Dido's expressions of despair, and in her death.[28]

The bifurcation of meaning in the final events of *Dido and Aeneas* presents an interesting commentary on the contingency of historicist readings. While it is possible to identify many specific political references in Restoration literary texts, those texts are also subject to a kind of indeterminacy, an illustration of the ways in which interpretation was conditioned by the strategies of concealment to which seventeenth-century authors resorted. It would, of course, be gratifying to unearth a document that would allow us to assign an exact date to the original production of *Dido and Aeneas* or, for that matter, to discover more biographical information on Nahum Tate and his political affiliations in the late 1680s, about which we know very little.[29] Yet even if this were to occur, we would still not be able to tell the whole story of *Dido* as a contemporary political document. The masque's reception by its audiences (both at Court and at the girls' boarding school at Chelsea) was necessarily conditioned by the subtle shading of meaning it continued to take on as events in the late 1680s progressed.

As this examination of *Dido and Aeneas* indicates, a politically-informed approach to Restoration masque helps to shed light on how drama functioned as both commentary and critique in a society whose expression was circumscribed by the mechanisms of official censorship. The Court drama of seventeenth-century England was indeed a "masque," behind which concealment and revelation coexisted in a state of dynamic tension, seeking both to obscure and to "discover" political meaning to its royal and courtly audience. The case of *Dido and Aeneas* demonstrates the reciprocity of literary

---

[28] Interestingly, some new evidence suggests that this latter interpretation may have been applied at the performance at Priest's boarding school, which is known to have taken place in 1689, shortly after William and Mary's assumption of the royal title. Mark Goldie has discovered a letter which notes that Priest "hath lately had an opera, which I'me sure hath done him a great injurey; & ye Parents of ye Childern not satisfied with so Publick a show." This letter, written to the wife of a prominent Whig MP, suggests that the negative reading of the "Glorious" Revolution presented in the masque may have been picked up by some members of the audience, a situation which would have put Priest in a very awkward position politically. See Mark Goldie, "The Earliest Notice of Purcell's *Dido and Aeneas*," *Early Music* 20 (1992): 392–400.

[29] Although Tate became Poet Laureate in 1692, there is reason to believe that his sympathies lay with the Tories as late as 1688–89. See for example [William Crofts], *The Deliverance. A Poem: To the Prince of Orange* (1689), p. 8, in which Tate is reviled along with Settle, D'Urfey, and Dryden, presumably because of his authorship of the second part of *Absalom and Achitophel*.

and historical meaning within this form: the masque documents its historical environment at the same time that it shows how that environment was itself a determinant of textual reading and interpretation. Moreover, it illustrates the way in which a symbiosis of literary and historical inquiry contributes to our understanding of the workings of political discourse in the Restoration.

CHAPTER 4

Factionary politics: John Crowne's Henry VI

Nancy Klein Maguire

... so he have but a Priest at one end of the Play,
and a Faction at 'tother end of the Pit, it shall
be fam'd for an excellent piece.

That he shall know both Parties, now he Glories;
By Hisses th' *Whiggs*, and by their Claps the *Tories*.
Thomas Durfey, Sir Barnaby Whigg (1681)[1]

John Crowne's two-part adaptation of Shakespeare's *Henry VI* trilogy[2] uncovers the problem of being a "Tory" during the religious and political crisis of 1678–83. Scholars consider Crowne a political fence-sitter, like John Dryden, yet Crowne's *The Misery of Civil-War. A Tragedy* (1680) and *Henry the Sixth, The First Part. With the Murder of Humphry Duke of Gloucester* (1681) suggest that Crowne rather illustrates the fluidity of party identity, particularly the shifting attitudes toward succession. Perhaps genuinely ambivalent about religious and constitutional issues, Crowne appears to choose legitimacy, the Stuart right to the throne, in the first adaptation but equivocates about the advisability of a Catholic king in the second. In sharp contrast to other party literature, Crowne's adaptations portray both Whig and Tory sympathies. Crowne's indecisive drama thus encodes the faction-ridden ambivalence of 1678–83 even better

I began work on this paper during a 1990 National Endowment for the Humanities seminar chaired by Annabel Patterson at Breadloaf, Vermont, and through the courtesy of Middlebury College, Vermont, continued work on the project the following summer. For comments on various drafts, I wish to thank Kent Cartwright, Mark Goldie, Gary Hamilton, Robert D. Hume, Ronald Hutton, J. P. Kenyon, Arthur F. Kinney, Phyllis Rackin, David Harris Sacks, and A. H. Scouten.

[1] Thomas Durfey, *Sir Barnaby Whigg: Or, No Wit like a Womans* (1681), sigs. A3r, A4r.
[2] Aside from Arthur Franklin White's *John Crowne: His Life and Dramatic Works* (Cleveland, 1922), the fullest literary treatment of the *Henry VI* adaptations is Matthew H. Wikander's *The Play of Truth & State: Historical Drama from Shakespeare to Brecht* (Baltimore, 1986), pp. 113–14.

than, for example, the blatantly Tory satire of Thomas Otway's more familiar *Venice Preserv'd* (1682).

In part, certainly, Crowne was consciously "trimming," changing parties to follow political shifts, but he and his contemporaries were also struggling to balance political and religious agendas, muddling through to fundamental party tenets. Stratified interest groups or factions, which shifted with quicksilver volatility, preceded the familiar two-party structure; to some extent, therefore, political classifications are not constructive for 1678–83. "Whig" and "Tory" referred to fluctuating – if polarized – beliefs rather than to institutionalized structures.[3] Indeed, except for the pro-French and pro-Catholic king and the heir apparent, distinguishing Whigs from Tories is difficult. To oversimplify, if pushed to a succession choice, "Whigs" would choose Protestantism, "Tories" legitimacy. Most Englishmen occupied the fluctuating middle ground situated between these extremes. The issue to some extent was fence-sitting, but, in part, fence-sitting encoded the shifts in political climate. As Jonathan Scott puts it, "as events transformed the situation, so they frequently transformed the behaviour and immediate objects of those individuals involved."[4] By 1682–83, for example, no one dared hint at the exclusion of James, yet in 1678–79, no one had dared speak out against the apocryphal Popish Plot.

In September 1678, Titus Oates, a disreputable minister, revealed the purported plot to poison the king. Putting the pro-Catholic faction in a bind, Oates's revelations ignited smouldering issues, bringing "a new and terrifying immediacy to the problem of the catholic succession."[5] As Crowne put it:

> The *Romish Beast* has fear'd her from her Wits,
> And thrown her in her old Convulsion Fits.
> The same she had many Year's since, 'tis said.[6]

---

[3] Historians currently debate the "Whig/Tory" question. Until the challenge of Jonathan Scott's *Algernon Sidney and the Restoration Crisis 1677–1683* (Cambridge, 1991), J. R. Jones's interpretation, *The First Whigs: The Politics of the Exclusion Crisis, 1678–1683* (1961) was the standard text. For a discussion of the religious nature of party structures, see Mark Goldie, "Danby, The Bishops and the Whigs," in Harris, *et al.*, *Politics of Religion*, pp. 75–105, especially pp. 79–81. The most recent contributions to the debate are made by Gary S. De Krey, Tim Harris, James Rosenheim, Richard L. Greaves, and Jonathan Scott in a special issue of *Albion* entitled "Order and Authority in Restoration England," 25:4 (Winter, 1993).   [4] Scott, *Sidney*, p. 24.   [5] Harris, *London Crowds*, p. 96.

[6] Since they are omitted from Crowne, *Works*, I quote both the *Henry* plays from the first London editions, citing the first adaptation "*M*" and the second "*H*." The present quotation is, thus, *H*, sig. κ3v.

Dreading a French universal monarchy, most of the political spectrum feared the implications of the intersection of the Duke of York's conversion to Catholicism in 1669 (publicized in 1676 by James's refusal to attend Easter communion) with the apparent invincibility of Louis XIV, the "supreme popish bogeyman."[7] The murder, allegedly by Catholics, in October 1678, of Sir Edmund Berry Godfrey, the chief magistrate before whom Oates had sworn a deposition detailing the plot, inflamed the already explosive crisis. In the midst of their attack on Thomas Osborne, the Earl of Danby and Lord Treasurer, the House of Commons hurriedly started the movement toward exclusion "not sparing in their discourses to reflect on the Duke [of York] in plain terms, even to wish that never such a curse may befall the nation as to have a Popish prince."[8] The Commons introduced the first Exclusion Bill on 15 May 1679. On 11 November 1680, about six months before the opening of Crowne's *Henry the Sixth*, they passed the second Exclusion Bill.

Crowne's politically ambivalent adaptations reveal some of the issues at stake, and, in a sense, since the vast middle ground agreed on the desirability of a Protestant successor, reconcile rather than polarize. Struggling to balance the issues of legitimacy and anti-Catholicism, Crowne's politics lined up with those of Danby, the leader of the Court party, who tried to resolve the Tory dilemma by limiting James's power.[9] Although Crowne could not afford to say everything, Danby's politics allowed him to say a great deal, and Danby's anti-exclusionist but also anti-French and anti-Catholic politics served as a model for Crowne's adaptations. Like Danby, Crowne tried to connect Toryism with anti-Catholicism, even competing with the Whigs' large-scale Pope-burning processions. Torn between conscious political prudence and his own partly unconscious political sympathies, Crowne's position was undeniably delicate. Two different factors were at stake: the nature of Toryism and Crowne's own need to trim.

Close scrutiny of Crowne's *Henry VI* plays suggests a quagmire of conflicting motives. Especially during the box-office slump of

---

[7] John Kenyon, *The Popish Plot* (New York, 1972), p. 15; and see p. 32 for the dates of James's conversion and abandonment of Anglican services.

[8] *Historical Manuscripts Commission, Ormonde Papers*, 12 November 1678, 4: 470; hereafter "*HMC, Ormonde.*"

[9] See Goldie, "Danby," pp. 84–90. For a general history of anti-popery, see Peter Lake, "Anti-popery: the Structure of a Prejudice," in Richard Cust and Ann Hughes, eds., *Conflict in Early Stuart England: Studies in Religion and Politics, 1603–1642* (1989), pp. 72–106.

1678–83, Crowne needed royal patronage – which required royal forbearance for his father's oppositional politics. Only a year before Charles's coronation, Crowne's radical republican father had welcomed the regicides Edward Whalley and William Goffe to Boston, Massachusetts; earlier, in 1656, Oliver Cromwell had rewarded the senior Crowne with a large tract of land in Nova Scotia. The playwright ruefully recognized that the 1667 surrender of Nova Scotia to the French "fixt me in a dependence" upon Charles's Court, "for I could have compensation no where else."[10] Since anything which threatened Charles's power weakened Crowne's prospects, economic necessity forced Crowne into a desperate and inevitably irresolute Royalism. Yet "Since his first aim was to make a living, he... followed the taste of his public with an eye to the ultimate returns."[11] Thus Crowne's dilemma was that economic necessity, as well as his own political ambivalence, forced him to please a waveringly bipartisan audience.

In five plays written between 1678 and 1683, Crowne shrewdly and frequently alludes to the religious and political crisis. In his oft cited, anti-Whig *City Politiques*, written in early 1682, he even caricatures prominent oppositional figures and replicates Crown evidence in the trial of Anthony Ashley Cooper, first Earl of Shaftesbury. Yet before the defeat of Parliamentary exclusion in 1681, Crowne was more cautious. An ambivalent Tory, and perhaps a constitutional monarchist, Crowne camouflaged his trimming tactics by disguising his oppositional views, perhaps even from himself at times, in adaptations of Shakespeare.

I TRIMMING SHAKESPEARE

Shakespeare's thickly valent plays suited the ambiguity of the Restoration crisis. Turning to Shakespeare for profit and safety, hedging playwrights could safely discuss the succession while asserting divine-right kingship. Indeed, of the twenty-three Shakespearean plays staged in London theaters between 1660 and 1700, ten were adapted between 1678 and 1683. In *The Ingratitude of a Commonwealth*, adapted from *Coriolanus*, Nahum Tate explains, "what ever the Superstructure prove, it was my good fortune to build upon

---

[10] Crowne, *Works*, 4: 19.   [11] White, *John Crowne*, p. 196.

a Rock.''[12] Hiding behind this rock, playwrights could criticize Charles and James with nearly complete safety. Many malleable playwrights depending on patronage hid behind Shakespeare, but, with a murky family history, the uneasy Crowne had particular need of Shakespearean cover.

Imitating Shakespeare, who himself had appropriated fifteenth-century English history to comment on Elizabeth's reign,[13] Crowne played off Shakespeare's *2–3 Henry VI*, taking snippets from *I Henry VI* and *The Tragedy of Richard the Third*,[14] in order to comment on the Restoration crisis. While occasionally copying Shakespeare's text verbatim, for the most part Crowne modifies Shakespeare's already apt plot and themes. The civil wars between the Lancastrians and Yorkists, of course, immediately resonated with the terrifying prospect of a repetition of 1642–47, as did the scenes of fathers and sons killing each other. In another double-layered historical parallel, Shakespeare's French Catholic Queen Margaret re-echoed fears of the French and of Catholicism. Most crucially, *3 Henry VI* ends with the king's brother Richard plotting to take the throne. Yet Crowne refashions Shakespeare's text to reverberate even more with the climate of 1678–83. While Shakespeare manipulated his sources to create Jack Cade, Crowne identifies the notorious Cade with Oates. Or again, while Shakespeare departed from his sources to bring Margaret and Eleanor into the same epoch, Crowne accentuates

---

[12] N[ahum] Tate, *The Ingratitude of a Common-wealth: Or, The Fall of Caius Martius Coriolanus* (1682), sig. A2r.

[13] Shakespeare particularly used the collective histories conflated under the names of Edward Hall and Raphael Holinshed. For Shakespeare's historical sources in the first tetralogy, see Annabel Patterson, *Shakespeare and the Popular Voice* (Oxford, 1989), pp. 32–51. For a full discussion of Shakespeare's history plays, see Phyllis Rackin's excellent *Stages of History: Shakespeare's English Chronicles* (Ithaca, New York, 1990).

[14] Shakespeare's *Henry VI* trilogy begins with the death of Henry V, then moves to the French rebellion and the ensuing war of the roses. While the English burn Joan of Arc at the stake, Suffolk brings Margaret of Anjou on stage as a prisoner, then decides to marry her to Henry VI. *2 Henry VI* opens with Margaret's arrival in England. Led by Gloucester's Cardinal uncle, jealous peers challenge his power and succeed in entrapping Gloucester's wife Eleanor and murdering him. After engineering the Jack Cade revolt, York claims the throne; following the resultant battle, Henry's party flees. *3 Henry VI* begins with York discussing issues of legitimacy while claiming the throne. At the end of the debate, Henry entails his crown to York's heirs. Following Hall, who characterizes Margaret as a "manly woman," Shakespeare's Margaret then takes over the army to regain the succession for her son. After Margaret and Clifford kill York, the king-maker Warwick enthrones York's eldest son Edward. In the game of monarchical musical chairs, Warwick reverts to Henry's side when Edward dishonors him by marrying Lady Elizabeth Grey. Henry once more regains the throne, but in the last Act, Edmund's brother Richard murders Henry and his son. The trilogy ends with Edward again in power but with Richard plotting to overthrow him.

their quarrels. Less subtly, Crowne adds new characters, scenes, and a major subplot as well as making various production adaptations.[15] While retaining Shakespeare's addition of Lady Grey, for instance, Crowne also gives Edward a new mistress, featuring her in four new scenes.[16]

Some of Crowne's modifications even attempt to influence the outcome of the crisis. Purportedly restaging Shakespeare's trilogy to promote another Duke of York's claim to the throne, Crowne, possibly inescapably, allowed opposition voices in both adaptations. His equivocal audience could thus interpret his double-edged adaptations as either Whig or Tory propaganda. The reader consistently has the sensation of seeing double. Do the plays offer a critique of Royalist policy during the Popish Plot, or do they merely record its events? Rather than creating sharply defined and exclusive parallels, Crowne filtered out and recorded topical situations and sentiments which the audience could apply according to their awareness or predilection. At times, Crowne camouflages his commentary by inserting new scenes and lines within Shakespeare's original speeches. At other times, he disinforms by shifting his parallels: for example, Crowne's "Glocester" [sic] could alternately suggest James, Danby, or even Charles II, and "Lady Elianor" [sic] glances at both Charles's victimized Catholic Queen and his popular Protestant mistress Nell Gwyn. Even though using imprecise parallels, Crowne encourages several character identifications; he seems to have gone to some lengths, for example, to depict Edward and Margaret as Whiggish portraits of Charles and his French Catholic mistress, Louise de Kéroualle, Duchess of Portsmouth, the "whore" whose "pocky bum / So powerful is of late, / ... / It rules both Church and State."[17] Crowne also provides parallels for the débâcle of the rigged Popish-Plot trials whose ultimate defendants were James and Queen Catherine. Between November 1678, and July 1679, Lord Chief Justice Sir William Scroggs had tried and executed thirteen priests and laymen on the testimony of patently suborned witnesses. Yet on 18 July 1679, Scroggs (a Danby appointee and

---

[15] To accommodate further the new political and theatrical arrangements, Crowne reshuffled scenes, made visual what Shakespeare narrated, divided long speeches, added spectacle – including a breeches part for Lady Grey – and dropped some characters, speeches, and scenes.

[16] *Richard III*, 3.7.5, perhaps suggested the new mistress. All references to Shakespeare's plays are to the Pelican edition.   [17] "A Satire," in *POAS*, 2: 291.

prerogative man) acquitted Queen Catherine's Catholic physician, Sir George Wakeman, in what the entire political spectrum considered a Tory sell-out.[18]

II A POET'S BUSINESS

The playwright Thomas Durfey claimed that "in this Age 'tis not a Poets Merit, but his Party that must do his busines," and Crowne's business involved his party directly.[19] In *The Misery of Civil-War*, written before February 1680, Crowne adapted the second and third parts of Shakespeare's *Henry VI* in order to underscore his own declared anti-exclusion position while strengthening a box-office overpowered by the theater of politics. Besides beginning and concluding *The Misery of Civil-War* with a Royalist prologue and epilogue, Crowne adds a major scene featuring the ghost of Richard II. After identifying himself to Henry VI, Richard summarizes the punishment visited on the Lancastrian usurpers and explicitly warns the usurping exclusionists:

> When e're Oh! *England*,
> Thou hast a mind to see thy Cities fir'd,
> Thy people slaughter'd, and thy Country desolate,
> Send all the dirty Traytours in the Kingdom
> To climb the Royal Rights, and Throne invade,
> Then a high road for vast destruction's made.   (*M*, sig. K2v)

A spirit "clad in a white Robe" then enters and lectures to Henry, as well as to the 1680 House of Commons, on the nature of the English monarchy:

> The Crown of *England* is not made of Clay
> The Common people, so can ne're be crumbled
> Into the dirt, 'tis not compos'd if [*sic*] it:
> Nor made of Iron, the Sword, so cannot rust;
> But of unmingled solid lasting Gold,
> Of Antient Rights, and 'tis the gift of Heav'n.   (*M*, sig.K2v)

Because the right of kings is both ancient and divine, the ghost prophesies that "torn will be his sacrilegious hand" who "dares

---

[18] See J. P. Kenyon, "The Acquittal of Sir George Wakeman: 18 July 1679," *Historical Journal* 14:4 (1971): 693–708.   [19] Durfey, *Sir Barnaby Whigg*, sig. A3r.

presumptuously pretend a Right" (*M*, sig. K2v). After much more self-promotional sermonizing, Crowne ends this hedging play with yet another assertion of the divine right of kings:

> A Monarch's Right is an unshaken Rock,
> Nor storms of War nor time can wear away,
> And Wracks those Pirates that come there for prey. (*M*, sig. 4r)

Having safely established his legitimist position, Crowne turns to pleasing a wider audience, playing directly to the inherent drama of the Popish Plot. The title page to the 1594 quarto of Shakespeare's *2 Henry VI* designates the play as "The First Part of the Contention betwixt the two famous Houses of Yorke and Lancaster, with the death of the good Duke Humphry ... with the notable Rebellion of *Iack Cade*; *And the Duke of Yorkes first claime unto the Crowne.*" Custom-tailoring Shakespeare's trilogy, Crowne saves the murder of the good Duke Humphrey for his second adaptation and opens *The Misery of Civil-War* with Jack Cade, Shakespeare's Titus Oates and then in the middle of the second Act moves from Shakespeare's Cade scene (*2 Henry VI*, Act 4) to *3 Henry VI*. Crowne told Charles II "that he plotted slowly and awkwardly,"[20] and, since the première of the play took place before February 1680, Crowne probably started writing soon after Oates's revelations became public.

In *City Politiques*, Crowne would demolish the Whiggish Oates in the character of Doctor Panchy,[21] but in 1680 the outcome of the succession crisis was unclear, and Crowne proceeds more cautiously, clearly aware of the danger of publicly impugning exclusion. Hiding behind Shakespeare in his denigration of Oates, Crowne focuses on the Popish Plot trials. Fleshing out Cade's cronies who repeatedly insist on hanging lawyers,[22] Crowne harps on suborning witnesses and on the degeneracy of the aristocracy. When asked whether he should "not spare the Lords that are our friends," Cade cannily answers, "No Lord is our Friend, you Fool, they meerly chouse us" (*M*, sig. B2v). Oates's fabricated "evidence" brought people to

---

[20] [John] Dennis, *Original Letters Familiar, Moral and Critical*, 2 vols. (1721), 1: sig. E2r.

[21] A manuscript newsletter dated 20 January 1683, reports: "Dᵣ Oates pfectly represented ... the papist plott Egregiously Rediculed" in "Newdigate Newsletters," 15 August 1682, Folger shelfmark LC 1327; transcribed by John Harold Wilson in "Theatre Notes from the Newdigate Newsletters," *Theatre Notebook* 15 (Spring 1961): 81.

[22] Cade's cronies "love hanging, there's / Never any hanging, but I leave my Stall to go see it" (*M*, sig. B1v). Crowne multiplies Shakespeare's "let's kill all the lawyers" (*2 Henry VI*, 4.2.70) into five more specific invitations to hang lawyers.

execution, and Crowne's Cade claims that "my mouth shall be the Law" (*M*, sig. B4r).[23] Reprimanding his father for negotiating with the disreputable Cade/Oates mob, the young Lord Clifford disgustedly recognizes that "The King must barter for his Crowne with Rascals" (*M*, sig. B4v). The audience recognized, of course, that Charles "must barter for his Crowne" with Shaftesbury and Oates's supporters in the House of Commons – as well as bartering for his playwright John Crowne.

During the reign of William and Mary, Crowne safely bragged, "in what I wrote for the Court, I spar'd not their tampering with knavish lawyers, magistrates, and Irish evidence."[24] Crowne clearly alludes to the trial of Wakeman, yet in 1680 the Tories in the audience could apply legal gerrymandering to the Whigs' use of suborned witnesses. Subornation flourished. An Irish witness, in fact, boasted that he "could have as many witnesses as he pleased from Ireland to forswear themselves for *2s. 6d.* each."[25] False "evidence" terrified Englishmen who recognized, as Gloucester did, that "I shall not want false Witness to condemn me."[26] Crowne perhaps recalled the convoluted and suborned "evidence" marshalled against the Tory actor Matthew Medbourne, a member of Crowne's company who had acted in at least two of his plays, and a crony of Oates.

Philipps swears a certain woman brought to him by Mrs. Medbourne offered him money to swear that Oates offered him money to bring witnesses against Medburne.[27]

Enriching the historical record, Crowne records the sentiments of fearful jurists who acquiesced in unjust judgments: "Why shou'd I stay for proofs of what I know?" (*H*, sig. G4r). Sir Henry Coventry notes "the people being so affrighted and incensed at this plot that there is hardly patience anywhere to hear the least defence in the behalf of anybody when accused."[28]

---

[23] Crowne appears to have conflated several of Shakespeare's lines: the Butcher's, "that the laws of England may come out of your mouth," Cade's "My mouth shall be the parliament of England (*2 Henry VI*, 4.7.5–6, 12–13), and Edward's "my will shall stand for law" (*3 Henry VI*, 4.1.50).   [24] Crowne, *Works*, 4: 19.

[25] Narcissus Luttrell, *A Brief Relation of State Affairs*, 6 vols. (Oxford, 1857), 1: 90.

[26] When Crowne repeats, paraphrases, or echoes Shakespeare's text, I include the Shakespearean source parenthetically. Thus, this citation is from *2 Henry VI*, 3.1.168 which Crowne borrows in *H*, sig. G2v.   [27] *CSPD*, 1679–80, 7 February 1679, p. 69.

[28] *HMC, Ormonde*, 26 November 1678, 4: 245.

After the Cade business (and a modified version of *2 Henry VI*, Act 5), Crowne moves to Shakespeare's succession debate in *3 Henry VI*, Act 1, adding a speech in which York delineates the line of succession between his three sons, "Three goodly Pillars" (*M*, sig. D4r). Tory polemicists neurotically revived the Caroline mythology, and Crowne probably refers to the succession of Charles I's three sons, Charles, James, and Henry (died in 1660). Yet Crowne still temporizes, delaying commitment to the Stuarts by imitating the Whiggish satires which underscored Charles II's "adulteries and promiscuous scatterings."[29] Crowne, in fact, transmogrifies Edward into a gross womanizer.[30] His courtiers, for example, rail: "there's a Woman: / Oh! we are ruin'd! for I will be damn'd, / If he has not been with her all this Night" (*M*, sig. F3r). (Ironically, of course, the Whig hero Monmouth resulted from such activity.) Crowne uses his new female character, the Lady Elianor Butler, to belabour Charles's sexual infidelities: she angrily comments, "No one Woman merit's Your Love, so you divide it among all" and tells Edward's new wife, Lady Grey: "his love in which thou think'st thee happy, / 'Tis like a Green-land-Summer, short and hot, / And whilst it lasts 'tis day, all smiling day" (*M*, sigs. D3r, H4r). In an audience-pleasing move, Crowne adds a major subplot in which Warwick, Edward's ambassador to France, attempts to seduce Lady Grey; the more knowledgeable members of the audience, of course, could apply the subplot to the embarrassing 1678 affair between Charles's mistress Barbara Palmer, Lady Castlemaine, and Ralph Montagu, the English ambassador to France.

Crowne also joins the opposition in his critique of, in Ronald Hutton's words, "the unofficial royal family."[31] Paraphrasing Shakespeare, Edward acknowledges, "I have Children too, though I'm a Batchelour" (*3 Henry VI*, 3.2.103–04; *M*, sig. H2v), and Crowne increases interest in royal children by giving Lady Grey "Many poor young Orphans" instead of Shakespeare's three children (*3 Henry VI*, 3.2.29; *M*, sig. H1v). One of the taxpayers' grievances was that Charles ennobled at least eleven of his thirty-odd

---

29 Anon., "A Letter to a Person of Honour concerning the King's disavowing the having been married to the Duke of Monmoth's Mother," in [John Lord Somers], *A Collection of Scarce and Valuable Tracts*, 2nd edn., ed. Walter Scott, 13 vols. (1812), 8: 202. Ronald Hutton notes that "The King's sexual habits continued to create a mixture of disgust and ribaldry, and to sap confidence in the government in general" (Hutton, *Charles the Second*, p. 338).

30 Shakespeare suggests Edward's wantonness in 3 *Henry VI*, 1.4.74, 2.1.42, 3.2.129, and in *Richard III*, 3.5.75, 80–84.   31 Hutton, *Charles the Second*, p. 337, for example.

illegitimate children, providing them with royal accoutrements.[32] An opposition pamphlet explicitly complained

> This making of bastards great,
> And Duchessing every whore,
> The surplus and Treasury cheat.[33]

Lady Grey knowingly and shrewdly requests "their Father's Lands" for the "poor Orphans" (*M*, sig. H2r). Flaunting the prevailing and provocative issue of royal bigamy, and perhaps supporting the attempt to legitimize Charles's eldest son, James Scott, the Duke of Monmouth, Crowne adds a pseudo-marriage intimated in Shakespeare's *Richard III* (3.7.5). Crowne's Richard comments, "let the King mean while finish his marriage... I'm told he has another Wife" and schemes "The King once dead, I'll Bastardize his Children" (*Richard III*, 3.5.75; *M*, sig. H3v).

London playwrights, as well as pamphleteers, "expected not only to gain financial reward, but to influence events."[34] The pro-Stuart faction insistently tried to preserve the myth of the holy martyr, Charles I, and Crowne adds new lines to accent the historiography. Edward, like Charles II, claims his kingship from his murdered father: "Who, now my Fathers murdered, am your King," and Richard asks a familiar post-1649 question: "And do you thus revenge our Fathers blood" (*M*, sig. F3v). Crowne perhaps suggests that if the Stuarts act properly and follow Danby's anti-Catholic and anti-French agenda, England could still be saved. The prop of a centering mythology, of course, depends on the succession of James and the uneasy triumph of legitimacy over religion.

III PARTY BUSINESS

Both the need to shore up the Court party by associating Tories with anti-French and anti-Catholic policies and Crowne's financial need to please a Protestant audience motivate his adaptation of Shakespeare's *2 Henry VI*. In the prologue to *Henry the Sixth, The First Part With the Murder of Humphry, Duke of Gloucester* (Spring? 1681), Crowne

---

[32] As early as 31 October 1673, Lord Cavendish had explicitly complained in the House of Commons that the money "we have given is turned to raising of families, and not paying the King's debts"; see Grey, *Debates*, 2: 200. For a list of Charles's ennobled children, see *POAS*, 3: 478–79, lines 1–2.   [33] "Old Rowley the King," in *POAS*, 3: 479–80.
[34] Haley, *Shaftesbury*, p. 498.

promises "A little Vineger against the *Pope*" (*H*, sig. A2r). Later, in the published dedication, he more explicitly describes the play as "no indifferent Satyre upon the most pompous fortunate and potent Folly, that ever reigned over the minds of men, called Popery"; he proudly claims: "To expose these Follies to the People is the business of this Play" (*H*, sig. A4r). Advocating a strong anti-French policy, Crowne delivers a Scroggs-like tirade against French Catholicism: "What appears too ridiculous here for the mouth of a Stage-fool, in a Country no less polished then *France*, is recommended to the Faith and Devotion of no less a Prince then the *Dauphin*" (*H*, sig. A4r). Attacking the pro-French Court faction, Crowne complains that:

> my Father, and by consequence my self, his Heir, was stript long since (by the advice of some ill great Men, who sacrifice both private and publick Interest to their own) of the Moity of a Province so considerable, the *French Crown* thought it worth contending for, many Years. And if that fortunate Kingdom strove for it, you may imagine they got it. (*H*, sigs. A4r-v)

While lambasting French Catholicism for personal, financial, and political reasons, Crowne, like Danby, tries to protect himself from charges of being pro-exclusion by appearing to support James. Always hedging, Crowne even dedicated *Henry the Sixth* to the father of James's favorite mistress.[35] Nonetheless, in Crowne's words, "ere it liv'd long, it was stifled by command."[36] Even Shakespeare could not provide cover against the pro-Catholic, pro-French, Court faction.

The popular Pope-burning processions of 1679, 1680, and 1681, began with a bellman crying "in a loud doleful Voice, *Remember Justice* Godfrey," followed by "A dead Bloody Corps, representing Sir *Edm Ber Godf*," which "is carried on horseback, supported by a Jesuit behind, who hath a Bloody Dagger in his Hand."[37] Linking anti-Catholicism with his (and Danby's) version of ambivalent Toryism, Crowne's major coup in adapting *2 Henry VI* exploits the furore over Godfrey's murder.[38] Disingenuously complaining that

[35] James created Sir Charles Sedley's daughter Countess of Dorchester; Sedley claimed to have reciprocated by supporting William of Orange, thereby making James's daughter a queen.

[36] Crowne, *Works*, 4: 19.

[37] *The Solemn Mock = Procession: Or the Tryal & Execution of the Pope and His Ministers* (1680), sig. A3r.

[38] A 1679 broadside dedicated to Shaftesbury, "an Eminent Promoter of the Protestant Interest," even shows Godfrey as "the Kingdom's Martyr"; see "England's Grand Memorial" (1679), broadside, described in *Catalogue of Prints and Drawings in the British Museum*, Division 1 (1870), pp. 603–04. Parliament incessantly worried about the crime; see, for example, *LJ*, *CJ*, and Grey, *Debates*, from the opening of Parliament on 21 October 1678, *passim*.

Shakespeare "has hudled up the Murder of Duke *Humphrey*, as if he had been guilty of [it] himself, and was afraid to shew how it was done" (*H*, sig. A3v), Crowne opportunely centers *Henry the Sixth* on the murder of "the good Duke Humphrey," conveniently strangled, as Godfrey was. The informer Miles Prance asserted that a priest instigated the murder of Godfrey, and, of course, Shakespeare's Cardinal organized the murder of Glocester. With one eye on the box-office and the other on the events of the past months, Crowne hides behind Shakespeare to launch a vicious attack on popery.

In Crowne's hands, Shakespeare's history play becomes a Tory Pope-burning. Crowne's dedication at once forces the reader to connect the murders of Godfrey and Glocester with popery: "there is not a Tool us'd in the murder of Duke *Humphry* in this Play, but what is taken out of their own Church Armory, nor a word put into the mouth of the *Cardinal* and his foolish Instruments, but what first dropt from the Heads that adorn their own Church Battlements" (*H*, sig. A3v). Complaining that Shakespeare's Cardinal "is duller then ever Priest was" (*H*, sig. A3v) Crowne makes his Cardinal more Jesuitical and more vicious, thus identifying himself with what Mark Goldie calls "the passionate renewal of anti-prelatical politics."[39]

According to a Frenchman then resident in London, "The name of 'Jesuit' is hated above all else – even by priests both secular and regular, and by the Catholic layfolk as well, because it is said that the Jesuits have caused this raging storm." Indeed, the Pope-burning procession of 1680 claimed that "A Iesuit can do nothing but whats ill."[40] Miming the popular and despised Jesuit stereotype, Crowne's Cardinal scorns other religious orders; referring to the "miracle" at St. Albans' shrine, he exposes his superior Jesuitical knowledge of Papist tricks:

> I will be hang'd, if this be not some damn'd cheat
> Plaid by the Fryars: I who wait at the Altar,
> Know well what tricks are plaid behind the Altar. (*H*, sig. D3v)

Confident of his own superiority, he decides to "face this fable with my Scarlet" (*H*, sig. D4r) – in popular opinion, of course, the Jesuits

---

[39] Goldie, "Danby," p. 81.

[40] [John Warner], *The History of the English Persecution of Catholics and the Presbyterian Plot*, Catholic Record Society, vols. 47 and 48, ed. T. A. Birrell (1953), 47: 214; *The Solemn Mock Procession of the Pope, Cardinals, Iesuits, Fryers, Nuns, &c.*, (1680) broadside; see *Catalogue of Prints*, 1: 636.

had already brazenly "faced" the Popish Plot. Many Englishmen believed that the Pope encouraged the murder of non-Catholics,[41] and Crowne's Cardinal advises his fellow conspirators:

> This Murder then is one of Heaven's back Stairs.
> Kill him, his Blood will oyl the Churches Keys,
> That you shall choose what Room in Heaven you please.
>
> (*H*, sig. G4v)

Heartening the hesitant murderers with promises of heavenly as well as financial reward, the Cardinal assures them that "stopping of a Heretick's Windpipe, / Is stopping a wide Leak sprung in the Church" (*H*, sig. H2r). The third murderer stubbornly argues about whether "the Church is infallible," and, after the Cardinal repents Gloucester's murder, all three murderers mock "Oh! gallant, brave Infallibility" (*H*, sigs. H3r, I4r). Crowne perhaps imitates the 1679 Pope-burning procession in which the devil left "his *Infallibility-ship* in the lurch."[42] Instead of finding the Duke dead in bed, he is discovered "dead in a Chair" (*2 Henry VI*, 3.2.29; *H*, sig. I1r), perhaps evoking the ride of Godfrey's corpse in a sedan chair. Using a popular theatrical effect (also used, of course, in *Richard III*, as well as in the Pope-burning processions), the ghost of Duke Humphrey unnerves the guilty Cardinal.

"Perkin Warbeck *alias* the duke of Monmouth"[43] was one of the exclusionist candidates for the throne, and although Charles did not allow anyone to criticize his favorite son,[44] Crowne emphasizes the Cardinal's illegitimacy, and, at times, encourages the anti-exclusionists to compare Monmouth with the Cardinal. In spite of the repeated attempts by the exclusionists to document a marriage between Monmouth's mother and Charles, Crowne's Cardinal, who has the arrogance of Monmouth, admits: "at my making it seems did want / Some Holy Ceremonies." He expostulates, "I'm that the Rude Ill-manar'd Law calls Bastard" (*H*, sig. D1r). Possibly referring

---

[41] The 1679 Pope-burning procession featured a priest "giving *Pardons* very Plentifully to all those that should *Murder* Protestants, and Proclaiming it *Meritorious*"; see *Londons Defiance to Rome, A Perfect Narrative* (1679), sig. A1v.   [42] *Ibid.*, sig. A2v.

[43] Anthony à Wood, *The Life and Times of Anthony Wood*, ed. Andrew Clark, 5 vols. (Oxford, 1891–1900), 2: 462.

[44] In July 1682, Charles II banned Dryden and Nathanial Lee's collaborative *The Duke of Guise* for satirizing Monmouth. In August 1682, the Lord Chamberlain went so far as to have Aphra Behn brought into custody for allegorizing Monmouth's "Rebelling 'gainst a King and Father," epilogue to anon., *Romulus and Hersilia; Or, the Sabine War* (1683), sig. I4r. For custody order see "Newdigate Newsletters," 15 August 1682, Folger shelfmark LC 1261; transcribed by Wilson in "Theatre Notes," p. 81.

to a 1680–81 treatise written for Monmouth attacking the laws
disinheriting bastards,[45] the Cardinal bitterly resents that "the Law
has thrust me from Succession / To the great Temporal Glories of My
Father" (*H*, sig. D1r). Emphasizing his Cardinal uncle's monarchical
ambition, Henry VI (borrowing sentiments from Shakespeare's
Exeter) recalls that Henry V, "from depth of Knowledg, not from
Prophesie, / Said, That if e're you were a Cardinal. / You'd make
your Cap vye with your Prince's Crowne" (*I Henry VI*, 5.1.31–33; *H*,
sig. F4v). Accenting the unpriestly nature of the Cardinal, as well as
his identification with the quarrelsome soldier Monmouth, Salisbury
asserts, again borrowing from Shakespeare:

> I have seen the Cardinal demean himself
> More like a Soldier than a Priest; he'l often
> Swear like a Ruffian, quarrel like a Hector,
> Trample on all, as he were Lord of all.
> (*2 Henry VI*, 1.1.183–86; *H*, sig. B2v)

Exclusionist pamphlets emphasized the religious nature of James,
and in a new speech, the Cardinal reflects that:

> The King and I ought to change Offices,
> He is more fit to be a Priest than I,
> And I'm more fit to be a King than he.   (*H*, sig. D3v)

In the context of the exclusion debates, the Tory element in the
audience could easily identify the saintly king and scheming Cardinal
with James and Monmouth.

In generating mistrust of Monmouth, Crowne also encourages the
anti-exclusionists to imply support for James. Glancing at both James
and Danby, Crowne's treatment of the heir-apparent Glocester
invites the audience to reassess the need for a stronger royal authority
and to reconsider Danby's impeachment. A weak king and jealous
peers caused Glocester's loss of power, and throughout *Henry the
Sixth*, Crowne considers Danby's predicament in 1679. Now in league
with Shaftesbury and the French ambassador Paul Barrillon
d'Armoncourt, Montagu divulged letters from Danby to Louis XIV
(authorized by Charles II) to the House of Commons; in the letters,
in the words of the Commons, Danby "was merchandizing for
Peace" with Louis at the same time that he asked Parliament for

---

[45] William Lawrence, *Marriage by the Morall Law of God Vindicated*, and *The Right of Primogeniture,
In Succession to the Kingdoms of England, Scotland, and Ireland* (1680, 1681). I am indebted to
Mark Goldie for the reference.

money to "engage in an actual War against *France*."[46] An enraged
Commons demanded Danby's impeachment on 19 December 1678.
Charles responded on 22 March 1679, by pardoning Danby and
loading him with money and honors.[47] Nonetheless, the Lords sent
Danby to the Tower on 16 April 1679,[48] where he remained until
1684.

IV PARTY HEDGING

Following Shakespeare closely, Crowne allows the audience to focus
either on the villainous nature of the Shakespearean attackers or on
the opposition's censure of the loyal Gloucester/Danby. The audience knew, of course, of Danby's French correspondence, and
York/Shaftesbury accuses Gloucester of false dealing with the
French. Trying to blame Gloucester for the entire French fiasco,
York tells Henry:

> He squeez'd the *English* Purses till Blood
> followed,
> Upon pretence to pay your Troops in *France* ...
> Then by not sending any of that Money;
> He starv'd your Troops, and almost lost you *France*.
> (*H*, sig. F4v).

Danby managed Parliament, in part, by means of bribes, and York
stresses: "you took Bribes from *France*, / And being Protector, staid
the Souldiers Pay, / By means whereby all *France* is almost lost" (*2
Henry VI*, 3.1.104–06; *H*, sig. G1v).[49] Neatly echoing the Commons'
charge that Danby "traiterously encroached to himself Regal
Power,"[50] Suffolk accuses Gloucester:

> Since you were King, (As who is King but you)
> The Common-wealth has daily run to ruine.
> The Dauphin seiz'd our Provinces in *France*,
> And you our Liberties and Honors here.
> (*2 Henry VI*, 1.3.121–25; *H*, sig. C3r)

Yet, circumspectly safeguarding his Royalist posture, Crowne
amplifies "Let me be blessed for the peace I make / Against this
proud Protector with my sword" (*2 Henry VI*, 2.1.35–36) to a ten-line

---

[46] Grey, *Debates*, 7: 5; see also Hutton, *Charles the Second*, pp. 364–65, and Kenyon, *Popish Plot*, pp. 130–31.   [47] For details, see Hutton, *Charles the Second*, p. 369.
[48] *LJ*, 13: 521; *CJ*, 9: 597.
[49] Many English politicians accepted bribes from France, including the Whig martyr Algernon Sidney.   [50] *CJ*, 9: 561.

defensive response to Danby's impeachment. The audience could have applied the entire speech to the equivocating House of Commons who knew that, in Hutton's words, "Charles himself was completely responsible for this disaster."[51] Crowne's wily Cardinal asks:

> Good Heaven, what Arts has the Protector us'd
> To charm you, Sir, that you can see all Loyalty
> In him who means you hurt? and none in us;
> Who shew our Loyal Zeal to guard you from him?
> Were it but one of us that shewed this Zeal,
> It might be thought an Envy to his Greatness,
> And a design to get into his Office:
> But since we all unite our Accusations,
> We can have no design but Loyalty,
> Since all of us cannot be Lord Protectors.   (H, sig. D3r)

Crowne also adds new lines to comment on Charles's position, making a crucial observation on the impeachment of Danby as well as on the Popish Plot. Charles did not conceal his belief that Oates was "tampered withal" and that Oates's crony William Bedloe "was tampered withal,"[52] and Henry says:

> There's mischief in this Business, I discern it;
> The Common People have been tamper'd with,
> To try how they will like a change of Princes;
> And to make way for it, my right is question'd,
> And my good Lord Protector sent away from me.
>
>   (H, sig. E4v)

Well aware of the falsity of the charges against Danby, Charles, like Henry, complains "These Winds and Waves beat on my Lord Protector, / Because he is a Rock that Guards my Coast" and recognizes: "they scarce know what to accuse him of / And yet Arrest him, now I find e'm out" (H, sigs. D3r, G2r). According to Sir William Temple, "the Dutchess of *Portsmouth* and Earl of *Sunderland* were joyn'd with the Duke of *Monmouth* and Earl of *Shaftesbury* in the design of his [Danby's] ruine,"[53] and, closely paraphrasing Shakespeare, Henry/Charles realizes: "these great Lords, and *Margaret* your Queen, / Do seek subversion of your harmless life, / And I your King want power to save you from e'm" (*2 Henry VI*, 3.1.207–08, 219; H, sig. G2v).

---

[51] Hutton, *Charles the Second*, p. 365.
[52] HMC, *Ormonde*, 4: 481; see also Burnet, *History*, 2: 161.
[53] *The Works of Sir William Temple*, 2 vols. (1720), 1: sig. 3P4v.

Crowne's most blatant audience-pandering appears in his revision of Margaret. Even though carefully and conspicuously omitting mention of Joan of Arc (admittedly from *1 Henry VI*), the rabidly anti-French and anti-Catholic Crowne covertly incites opinion against the French Catholic Portsmouth, and, of course, against Charles and James. The only major female role in Shakespeare's history plays, the French, Catholic, and adulterous Margaret already resembles Portsmouth, and Crowne increases the potential identification. Fleshed out in the first adaptation, Margaret becomes even more powerful, bloody, and ambitious in the second, insisting "Now I shall be a Queen" (*H*, sig. c2v).[54]

Crowne gives Margaret a new speech ironically commenting on Portsmouth's (and Catherine's) relationship to the King and perhaps snickering at his domestic arrangements.

> Indeed the Marriage 'tween the King and me
> Is but a strange one; for to speak the truth
> I'm Wedded to the Throne more than to him
>
>   ...
>
> Heaven is the King's spacious Seraglio.   (*H*, sig. c1v)

In spite of Crowne's financial need to support the Stuarts, his treatment of Margaret suggests that he, like many Englishmen, deplored Charles's domestic arrangements. Englishmen were well aware of "the King's spacious Seraglio," and many would agree that Margaret/Portsmouth was "Wedded to the Throne." If in Shakespeare's *Henry VI*, Margaret directs events, Crowne points toward Portsmouth. Amplifying Margaret's adulterous scenes with Suffolk, Crowne makes Margaret/Portsmouth a political power-figure leagued with "her damn'd Minion, Trayterous *Suffolk*" (*H*, sig. B4v), probably Robert Spencer, Earl of Sunderland, then Secretary of State. Broadly paraphrasing Shakespeare, Crowne's Suffolk promises that "*England* at the Queen's command shall be"; Portsmouth/Margaret responds, "I'le Govern that, and thou shalt govern me" (*1 Henry VI*, 5.5.107–08; *H*, sig. c2v).

Reflecting the moral disorder of the Court, and echoing an opposition pamphlet referring to Charles's "two queens,"[55] Crowne gives his audience portraits of both Charles's "wives," glancing at Catherine in the greatly enlarged character of Elianor, the wife of

---

[54] Compare Shakespeare's "am I a queen in title and in style" and "Why, now is Henry king, and Margaret queen" (*2 Henry VI*, 1.3.46; 2.3.39.).

[55] "Old Rowley the King," in *POAS*, 3: 482.

Glocester. Crowne may have believed, or knew the audience wanted to believe, that Elianor's sentiments were those of Catherine. Perhaps echoing popular speculation, Oates claimed that he heard the Queen say "That she would no longer bear these affronts she had, but be revenged for the violation of her bed."[56] Using the Shakespearean squabbles between Elianor and Margaret, Crowne glances at the perceived relationship between Portsmouth and Catherine (as well as at the notorious quarrels between Portsmouth and Nell Gwyn). Motivated in Crowne's adaptation by hatred of Margaret more than ambition, Elianor frequently vents her loathing: "I'em Enemy to nothing but the Queen" and "I must hate the Queen in spite of me" (*H*, sig. B4r). Even during her penance, Elianor refers to "that vile Woman, who abhors us all" (*H*, sig. F2v). In a lengthy new speech, Elianor expresses the feelings that many Englishmen attributed to Catherine. Elianor rants:

> I must confess I mortally abhor,
> And scorn that Woman, which is now my Queen.
> Oh! hateful thought! she! she! my Queen – a Vassal
> Of *France* subdu'd by us into a Province;
> And she a Beggar in that Conquer'd Province,
> Become the Queen, and Mistress of her Conquerors;
> I the first Woman of Victorious *England*,
> Bow to the last of low dejected *France*?   (*H*, sig. B3v)

Crowne perhaps puts his own sentiments about Portsmouth into her mouth: "What shou'd be done to her who is that Curse? / Let her not live, or rather let her live, / But live no Queen" (*H*, sig. B3v).

V MONARCHICAL BUSINESS

In Blair Worden's words, the succession question "crystallised the fundamental constitutional issue of the seventeenth century. Did the power of kings come from above, by divine right, or from below, by the consent of the people?"[57] In spite of his insistent legitimist position, Crowne's treatment of Charles/Henry and Danby/Glocester suggests that skillful party management rather than divine right empowers kings. Charles, like Gloucester, could not protect his wife during the Popish Plot threat. Imaging Charles's powerlessness, Edward comments: "Both the fair Kingdom, and the

---

[56] *HMC, Ormonde*, new series, 4: 480.
[57] Blair Worden, "Despairing Radicals," *London Review of Books* (25 June 1992): 17.

fair Queen lye / Sick of the impotence of a Weak King" (*M*, sig. c2v). Charles himself complained that "he found everybody more afraid to displease the Parliament than him," and in the autumn of 1681, he protested: "It is a hard case that I am the last man to have law and justice in the whole nation."[58] Petulantly echoing Charles's complaints, Margaret/Portsmouth grumbles, "The King's the only Subject in the Kingdom / He obeys all, and no one obeys him" (*H*, sig. clv).

Although closer to the original Shakespeare than *Misery of Civil-War*, *Henry the Sixth* criticizes Charles more directly, especially his pro-French and pro-Catholic tendencies. In a completely new speech, the Cardinal indicts Charles (and perhaps Danby)[59] while damning Portsmouth:

> He who was Govern'd by so ill a Woman,
> Is very unfit to be the Kingdoms Governor;
> She was his Counsellor, the Devil hers;
> Conjecture then what his Designs must be.   (*H*, sig. E3v)

The House of Commons clearly suspected Charles's "Designs." In 1679, a member of the House worried "Though we gave Money to be rid of our fears of *France*, yet I find that, as long as we give Money, the fears of *France* will be suggested." Another member explicitly advised: "Purge yourselves... from the *French* at *Whitehall*, and there is no danger of them out of *France*."[60]

To appease the House of Commons, in spring 1679, Charles offered to place limitations on the succession, as well as to reform the Privy Council, and, paraphrasing Shakespeare, *Henry the Sixth* ends with Henry promising the rebels to "mend my Government, for I confess, / *England* may yet Curse my unfortunate Reign" (*2 Henry VI*, 4.9.48–49; *H*, sig. K3r). Crowne ironically gives his own final anti-exclusion comment to Margaret/Portsmouth:

> yield not, Sir, to Rebels.
> Royalty like great Beauty, must be chaste,
> Rogues will have all, if once they get a taste.   (*H*, sig. K3r)

The Popish Plot died back in the spring and summer of 1680, and for various reasons, legitimacy and the anxiety over repeating 1641 allowed Charles to defuse the Exclusion Bill. In March of 1681,

---

[58] *CSPD*, 1679–80, 24 January 1679, p. 52; *Memoirs of Sir John Reresby*, ed. Andrew Browning (Glasgow, 1936), p. 234.
[59] *DNB* refers to Danby's "alleged dependence on his wife."
[60] Grey, *Debates*, 7: 109, 110.

Charles II effectively destroyed Parliamentary exclusion by dis-
solving the Oxford Parliament. Yet the dissolution did not stop the
fear of a Catholic king.

VI JAMES II

As John Miller has shown at length,[61] the hatred and fear of
Catholicism went very deep, and though conforming outwardly,
many faltering Tories expressed their concerns covertly. The accession of James II in 1685 forced Crowne to go under cover with his
anti-Popery, but his most vituperative satire on Catholicism, *The
English Friar* (mid-March 1690), dramatized the Catholic excesses of
James's reign. The womanizing Father Finica boldly personates
Edward Petre, James's Jesuit Privy Councillor, and the prologue to
The English Friar claims that the author "does make bold a farce to
shew, / Priests made and acted here some months ago; / They turn'd
to farce the Court, the Church, the Laws." Crowne mocks those "so
mad, they'd give up England's glory, / Only to keep the wretched
name of Tory."[62] Although Crowne's anti-James sentiment does not
dominate his *Henry VI* plays, it seeps through. The Pope-burning
processions featured placards proclaiming "*We Protestants in Masquerade usher in Popery,*"[63] and Crowne could be one of those Royalists
who "in Masquerade usher in exclusion."

Close readings of these ostensibly anti-exclusion plays uncover
reservations about a Catholic king. Hedging his bets in every
direction, the sometime Royalist hides behind Shakespeare's plot and
"the plot" to advance a cautious and subdued proposal to exclude
James. Crowne's Elianor suggests: "'Tis more disloyalty / T'impose
a Crown upon Religious *Henry*, / Than 'tis to Usurp one from
another King" (*H*, sig. B3r). Again stressing James's religious
convictions, she asks "Is it ill / To the good Pious King, to take from
him / A heavy Weight that presses him to Earth" (*H*, sig. B3r).
Borrowing Shakespeare's "brazen images" phrase (*2 Henry VI*,
1.3.58), Crowne's Suffolk describes the religious but ineffective
Henry:

> He comes from kissing Brazen Images,
> And Bones, and Sculs of Saints, that were more cold
> When they were living, than you'l be when dead. (*H*, sig. F1v)

---

[61] John Miller, *Popery and Politics in England, 1660–1688* (Cambridge, 1973).
[62] Crowne, *Works*, 4: 27.   [63] *The Solemn Mock = Procession*, sig. A3v.

Again and again, propagandists emphasized James's religious nature, and Crowne perhaps mocks a religious king, questioning his political effectiveness.

Although legitimacy wins out, Crowne voices the opposition, allowing various characters to speak against the theory of divine-right succession. Young Lord Clifford, for example, oddly poses the hypothesis: "Say, the King's Grand-father Murther'd his King / And damn'd his Soul for it, what's that to thee?" (*M*, sig. c3r). Margaret asks the pious and fearful Henry, "What if your Grand-father murder'd his King? / Must you take Physick for his sicknesses?" (*M*, sig. ılv). The king-maker Warwick imitates Dryden's king-maker Almanzor in *The Conquest of Granada*, but Warwick also owes something to the opportunistic Sunderland. Much later, when he heard that William might abdicate, Sunderland commented that the tall Earl of Pembroke "would be a good stick of wood, out of which to form a king,"[64] and Warwick brags in new lines, "When e're I went to work to make a King, I ne're yet fail'd, whatever stuff I had" (*M*, sig. ı4r). Allowing voices which depict a kingship dependent on shrewd politics and cunning party management, rather than on divine right, Crowne reveals his flexible alliances. Closely paraphrasing Shakespeare in a double-edged power-play, the king-maker Sunderland/Warwick promises, "The Day is coming, when the Earl of *Warwick* / Shall make the Duke of *York* the King of *England*" (*2 Henry VI*, 2.2.88–89; *H*, sig. E2v).

In many ways a typical ambivalent Tory, Crowne serves as a barometer for Tory integrity as well as for party flexibility. Writing eighteen politically diverse plays, Crowne survived as a playwright during three regimes. Perhaps in 1680–81, Crowne imagined that James might abdicate in favor of the devoutly Anglican Princess Mary, Crowne's one-time patroness,[65] and already married to a Protestant prince. Shortly before the production of *Henry the Sixth*, Nahum Tate offered a similar solution, letting King Lear retire so that Kent and Cordelia could rule.[66] Like other politically ambivalent but sensitive and sensible courtiers, such as Danby, Portsmouth, Dryden, and Tate, Crowne survived the factionary politics of the late seventeenth century by shifting allegiances while

---

[64] Burnet, *History*, 4: 362n.

[65] As early as 1674, Crowne wrote a masque, *Calisto*, for Princess Mary.

[66] See my "Nahum Tate's *King Lear*: 'The king's blest restoration,'" in Jean I. Marsden, ed., *The Appropriation of Shakespeare: Post-Renaissance Reconstructions of the Works and the Myths* (1991), pp. 29–42, especially p. 39.

carefully hedging his bets. Even though he situated himself all over the political spectrum, in John Genest's words, Crowne's "career of loyalty" was consistent.[67]

---

[67] [John Genest], *Some Account of the English Stage from the Restoration in* 1660 *to* 1830, 10 vols. (Bath, 1832), 1: 124.

PART II

Authorship and authority

CHAPTER 5

Pepys and the private parts of monarchy

James Grantham Turner

On the morning of Sunday 9 February 1668, Samuel Pepys appears to have been in two places at once: "Up, and at my chamber all the morning and the office, doing business and also reading a little of *L'escolle des Filles.*" His entanglement with this quintessential libertine text – "a mighty lewd book, but yet not amiss for a sober man once to read over to inform himself in the villainy of the world" – had begun four weeks before in a more public setting, a respectable bookshop in the Strand. He discovered it to be "the most bawdy, lewd book that I ever saw, rather worse than *putana errante* – that I was ashamed of reading it."[1] Nevertheless, on 8 February he returned to "that idle, roguish book, *L'escolle des Filles*; which I have bought in plain binding (avoiding the buying of it better bound)," and on the following Lord's Day he took his pleasure of it in full, starting in the morning while simultaneously doing "business" in the office, and finishing it in his chamber that night. "After I had done it, I burned it, that it might not be among my books to my shame."

Understandably, this *Escole des Filles* passage has become a sacred text of the "History of Private Life"; though this paper will argue that the construction of sexuality, under a priapic monarch, breaks down the dichotomy of private and public, we should begin by recognizing the layers of secrecy that screen the episode from view. For Keith Thomas it is the *ne plus ultra* of private experience, combining sex (which all cultures conceal in some way) with the solitary enjoyment of a printed book.[2] Francis Barker finds in it not

---

[1] Pepys, 13 January 1668; John Martin the bookseller had been joint printer to the Royal Society since 1663. It should be pointed out that Pepys's "chamber" and his "office" were in the same building.

[2] "Behind Closed Doors," *New York Review of Books* (9 November 1989): 18: "Here, if anywhere, is truly private experience." Thomas is here citing Roger Chartier's contribution to vol. 3 of *Historie de la vie privée, De la Renaissance aux Lumières*, ed. Chartier, trans. Arthur Goldhammer as *A History of Private Life III. Passions of the Renaissance* (1989), pp. 143–44. This

only a paradigmatic example of a "tremulous" and "private" bourgeois attitude to the body and the self, but also "perhaps... the typical structure of all bourgeois discourse."[3] Barker makes several happy discoveries in his close reading of the text: that Pepys dissociates himself by using the third person ("sober man") but then relocates himself "in the villainy of the world"; that his description of a musical gathering, which separates the morning and evening pornography-sessions, is itself shot through with signs of guilt ("I must confess") and hints of an erotic subtext (the energetic "Mr. Tempest" who "understands everything at first sight"); that Pepys's parenthetical mention of childbirth and smallpox shows his mind still running on the troublesome associations of sex. But Barker unfortunately uses a twice-bowdlerized text, a selection made for schoolchildren from the prudish Victorian edition; his larger thesis thus collapses, hinging as it does on "the guilty sexuality which the passage takes such pains to speak."[4] Pepys actually glorifies sensuous delight throughout the diary, in staged debates between "business" and "pleasure" often won by the latter, and in this very place he records that *L'Escole des Filles* "did hazer my prick para stand all the while, and una vez to decharger."[5]

The diary *is* private in many ways, of course, and the sexual references *are* embedded even more deeply than the rest of the text. In the passage describing his arousal Pepys's grammar places his sex in a double wrapper, a parenthetical "but" clause nesting inside another "but" clause. Then it is encoded, first by the shorthand, then by the lingua franca of European vocabulary, and then by the schoolboyish habit of adding nonsense-syllables to certain words, turning *pleasure* into "plelesonure," *belly* into "benleri," and *did* (perhaps significantly) into "dild"; when Pepys's pen came to record

translation restores Pepys's own text (the French version [p. 144] obscured most of the stylistic effects discussed in this section, including the split between office and chamber) but preserves certain errors: the author of *La Puttana Errante* is still given as Aretino, and Mrs. Pepys's maiden name as Marchand.

[3] Francis Barker, *The Tremulous Private Body: Essays in Subjection* (1984), p. 6. Barker's close reading appears on pp. 3–9, and is then alluded to throughout the book.

[4] Barker, *Tremulous Private Body*, p. 62.

[5] Pepys, 9 February 1668. Barker's textual blunder has been noted by Gerald MacLean in his Introduction to François Poullain de la Barre's *The Woman as Good as the Man: Or, The Equality of Both Sexes*, trans. A. L., 1677, (Detroit, 1988), p. 50 n. 48, and by Donald F. McKenzie in his 1989 Lyell Lectures in Bibliography at the University of Oxford, where he also points out that Pepys's shorthand (*pace* Barker) is not a difficult one (text kindly communicated by Professor McKenzie). The bowdlerized version is restored in Robert Latham's *The Shorter Pepys* (Berkeley and Los Angeles, 1985), incidentally.

Figure 1. Extract from Samuel Pepys's diary for 9 February 1668.

his adventures with *L'Escole* it wrote, not the bold "prick," but the bashful "primick."[6] Yet it would be a mistake to regard this simply as "denial" or suppression. However private the experience, it is still couched in a language that reveals the social formation of Pepys's consciousness and implies the scrutiny (and applause) of an audience. Pepys's codes are quite penetrable, the French and Spanish words being particularly transparent. As Fig. 1 shows clearly, the key words "L'escholle des Filles" and "decharger" are written in longhand, and blaze forth from the page of shorthand. Rather than concealing, Pepys's polyglottism adds color and worldly sophistication, injecting

[6] William Matthews, editor of the only full version of the diary, omitted this garbling from his published text and gave only one full specimen of it, in his note to 31 May 1667. I am grateful to Dr. Richard Luckett, Pepys Librarian, Magdalene College, Cambridge, for advice on the transcription of certain shorthand passages, and to the Master and Fellows of Magdalene for supplying a photograph of the *Escole des Filles* entry (Fig. 1).

a self-conscious and performative tone into the private space of the diary. Here as elsewhere, his linguistic codes bring Court culture and European geography into the microcosm of the body: treating the delicate subject of his (French) wife's vaginal ulcer, he locates it "in the lip of her *chose*"; chatting intimately about the sexual goings-on at Court, both Pepys and Lord Sandwich speak in French – a move that increases the glamour of the gossip and at the same time protects the servants from the scandalous attitudes of their rulers (2 August and 7 October 1660). In his libertine novel *Les Bijoux indiscrets* Diderot slips into English to describe the sexual assaults of a coarse but vigorous sea captain. Conversely, the clerk of the Royal Navy uses Mediterranean languages to describe the warmer regions of his body. He does not deny his sex, as Barker insists, but dresses it up, with a *baguette* under its arm and a little sombrero on its head.

To read the *Escole* episode as a scene of concealment, then, gives only half the truth. And it is equally unconvincing to read it as a scene of unrelieved "bourgeois" guilt. Pepys admits "shame" at the thought of being posthumously exposed as the owner of this "idle, roguish book" or reading it openly in the bookshop, but his language is only half-condemnatory. "Idle" is a stern word from a man of business, but it could also suggest the fashionable vacuity of the Court Wits, who fascinated him deeply. "Roguish" may refer to real wrongdoing, but it easily softens into indulgence, especially when applied to a discourse or performance – a bawdy tale told by a waterman on a "pleasant mooneshine night" or a comedy by Etherege (seen two days before he bought *L'Escole*), condemned as "a silly dull thing, *though* there was something very roguish and witty" (emphasis added).[7] Pepys's phrase could have been spoken in the back seat of a coach, with a friendly slap; contrast the judicial language used to condemn *L'Escole des Filles* in France, where both author and text are sentenced to burning for being "against the honour of God and the Church, and quite contrary to good morals and Christian discipline," or in England, where the bookseller is indicted for publishing a "nequissimum scandalosum vitiosum et illicitum librum," horribly corrupting the young male subjects of Charles II.[8]

---

[7] Cf. Pepys, 3 November 1662, 28 October 1667; 6 December 1660, 21 March 1664, 6 February 1668.

[8] *L'Escole des Filles* (1655), ed. Pascal Pia (Paris, 1969), pp. 177, 199; Greater London Record Office, Middlesex Session Roll MJ/SR 1582 (1680).

Though Pepys's encounter with *L'Escole* clearly takes place amidst trouble and tension, his sexual practices and attitudes refuse to fit into the neat polarities of private and public, repression and acceptance. It is absurd to say that he "loathed" the body – his problems come rather from seeing the world exclusively *as* body, to be measured, bought, fondled, and stroked – yet he does feel anxiety at the thought that his indulgences might be exposed. He was clearly fascinated by the steamy domestic fornication of *L'Escole des Filles*, which erupted in his mind after his wife hired a new and attractive "fille" from "the school at Bow."[9] But he himself was more of a Puttana Errante, wandering out into the teeming, random, bawdy life of the city rather than shrinking back into a "private" sphere. His sexual activity was largely picaresque, performed in coaches, boats, churches, taverns, and odd corners of the office. He would shuttle back and forth across London several times a day to lie with his carpenter's wife, glimpse an actress's breast, feel a neighbour's thigh, or lure a servant-maid to the street behind his garden, where he might "tocar sus mamelles con mi mano and su cosa with mi cosa" for a shilling.[10] Pepys would have been surprised to learn, from Barker, that he had "banished" sex to a "secluded domain ... a silent bedroom"; his marriage-bed was for him one of the least sexual areas of London.

The priapic passages of the diary reveal, in fact, not intrapsychic pressures but professional and national troubles. Disaster had overwhelmed the navy in 1667 when the Dutch entered the Medway and fired the ill-equipped fleet, and Pepys himself was under investigation for his handling of prize-money. His fling with *L'Escole* is surrounded by entries that reveal his profound fear of "miscarriage" and his need to "perfect my Narrative" before the hearing; safe sex, or sex in the form of narrative, would provide an obvious escape.[11] He goes straight from a consultation with Captain Cocke (likewise called to account for prize-money) to buy *L'Escole*, and we

---

[9] For Pepys's erotic obsession with the "little girl" Deborah Willett, and his use of the French word "fille," see 20 May, 24, 27, and 30 September 1667.

[10] Pepys, 6 May 1668 (other instances are too many to cite); after this fondling scene at "our back entry" Pepys goes innocently indoors "to put up things ... for my wife," including "a very fine salmon-pie."

[11] Pepys, 5–15 February 1668. The entry for 6 February shows the same split into "business" time and "pleasure" time that we saw in the reading of *L'Escole*: "to the office, where a while busy; my head not being free of my trouble about my prize business, I home to bed. This evening coming home I did put my hand under the coats of Mercer, and did touch her thigh" etc. For an exploration of temporality in Pepys, see Stuart Sherman, "Pepys and the Mobile Medium of the Diary" (manuscript communicated by Professor Sherman).

can speculate that to "decharger" over a wicked text kept his mind off the possibility of being discharged for keeping bad books. His fear of disease was equally well founded. The recent smallpox epidemic had reached as far as the royal family, the Great Plague was scarcely two years over, and the spread of syphilis was inextricably associated with both. The threat of sexual disease may have been particularly vivid for Pepys, since the traumatic episode in 1664 when he had to examine the genitals of his own brother, dying in rambling lunacy, for evidence that might quash the damaging rumor that the fatal illness was the pox (13–15 March).

The association of eroticism and contagion is sometimes concealed in Pepys's text, but it can also be declared explicitly; Barker is wrong to assume that the "bourgeois" subject inevitably conceals such matters. When Pepys "took two or three wanton turns about the idle places" of Drury Lane to see the prostitutes, and reports "no satisfaction, but a great fear of the plague among them," his slippery language leaves it unclear whether it is he or the whores who experience fear and trouble, and what kind of "plague" he expects among them (14 March 1666). At the height of the Great Plague, however, he spells out the connection in this lyrical narration of an erotic dream:

Up by 4 a-clock, and walked to Greenwich, where called at Captain Cockes and to his chamber, he being in bed – where something put my last night's dream into my head, which I think is the best that ever was dreamed – which was, that I had my Lady Castlemayne in my armes and was admitted to use all the dalliance I desired with her, and then dreamed that this could not be awake but that it was only a dream. But that since it was a dream and that I took so much real pleasure in it, what a happy thing it would be, if when we are in our graves (as Shakespeere resembles it), we could dream, and dream but such dreams as this – that then we should not need to be so fearful of death as we are this plague-time.[12]

---

[12] Pepys, 15 August 1665 (see *OED* "resemble" v^1 3 for Pepys's usage); this echo of the "To be or not to be" speech may be the first recorded use of *Hamlet* in private meditation. E. Pearlman relates this dream to other sexual encounters, and to the simultaneous exaltation and debasement of women in the figure of Lady Castlemaine, in "Pepys and Lady Castlemaine," *Restoration* 7 (1983): 43–53, and in a "Reply" to a rejoinder, *Restoration* 9 (1985): 37–38; Pearlman does not explore the homoerotic frame of the narration, however. Pepys seems to have attached the name "Cocke" to the only prostitute who seriously tempted him (Pepys, 29 July 1664), and the "something" that recalled his dream could be explained by comparing another episode cited by Pearlman to show Mrs. Pepys's jealousy: "I do often find that in my dreams she doth lay her hand upon my cockerel to observe what she can" (Pepys, 7 February 1669). Does he dream that she puts her hand on his "cockerel" to learn its secret, or does she really do it?

Pepys may deflect the homoerotic implications of finding himself at dawn in the bedroom of "Captain Cock," feeling "something" that reminded him of a sexual dream; but he is quite frank about his desire for the king's mistress and the direct connection between such imaginings and the terror of the Plague.

Given her virtually unprecedented prominence as Royal Mistress – a role that confounds not only the public-private dichotomy but also the status-hierarchy of "public" women and countesses – it seems inevitable that Pepys's erotic obsessions should focus on Lady Castlemaine and take a voyeuristic and pictorial form. (I refer, of course, to Barbara Palmer, née Villiers, later Duchess of Cleveland.) He always encounters her in culturally-charged spaces associated with the Court, and he does his best to turn his inner world into just such a space. He first sees Castlemaine in the Royal Chapel at Whitehall, talking "very wantonly" with the Duke of York "through the hangings that part the King's closet and the closet where the ladies sit," and a visual version of this paradigmatic drama is enacted every time Pepys's gaze crosses the social and physical distance that parts him from "my Lady Castlemayne, whom I do heartily adore." Communication "through the hangings" was achieved two years later: "in the privy Garden saw the finest smocks and linen petticoats of my Lady Castlemaynes, laced with rich lace at the bottomes, that ever I saw; and did me good to look upon them." (The suspended sentence-structure and lyrical phrasing re-enacts his pleasure in an almost Proustian way.) He would spy her from the pit of the theater or from the roof of the Banqueting House ("over against us"), and on these occasions "glutted myself with looking on her." Attending the Catholic High Mass at St. James's, he watched "my Castlemayne [sic], who looks prettily in her night-clothes," and "did make myself to do la cosa by mere imagination ... and with my eyes open, which I never did before – and God forgive me for it, it being in the chapel."[13]

Meanwhile, both before and after his dream of Castlemaine, Pepys worked hard to possess her through the medium of the *image*. In

---

[13] Pepys, 14 October 1660; 5 February, 21 May and 23 August 1662; 20 July 1664; 24 December 1667. Pepys does not say that he watched Lady Castlemaine as he ejaculated in chapel, but admits rather vaguely that he was "mirando a jolie mosa [i.e., *moza*]"; contrast the more specific entry on 3 May 1668: "to church again where I did please myself con mes ojos shut in futar in conceit the hook-nosed young lady, a merchant's daughter, in the upper pew" – a remarkable exercise in social and spatial "placing."

1662, at the studio of the Court Painter Sir Peter Lely, he "saw the
so much by me desired picture of my Lady Castlemayne, which is a
most blessed picture and that I must have a copy of"; four years later
he buys several copies of her engraved portrait and proceeds to apply
fixative, sending one to be "varnished" and framed, and "pasting"
another onto a mount – after a busy morning in the office fondling a
client's breasts "so as to make mi mismo espender with great
pleasure."[14] He learned earlier that Castlemaine "hath all the tricks
of Aretin that are to be practised to give pleasure" (15 May 1663),
and at some point he acquires and reads *La Puttana Errante*, the work
– then thought to be by Aretino himself, and frequently bound with
erotic prints – in which the thirty-six "postures" were most readily
available.[15] When he says that in his dream he "was admitted to use
all the dalliance I desired with her," we can be sure that he means
"all the tricks of Aretin," the *figures Veneris* as imagined by the
collector of prints and consumer of pornography. His first critical
response to *L'Escole des Filles*, as we saw, was to draw it into this chain
of association by placing it in relation to the postures of "Aretino":
the French text is "rather worse than *putana errante*."

If sexual "figures" were disturbing as well as fascinating for Pepys,
it was not on account of his "bourgeois" hatred of sexuality *per se*, but
because they were inextricably connected to the troubles of England
under Charles II. The monarch's sexuality is never wholly private,
and the subject's responses are inevitably shaped by political reality:
Archbishop Laud dreamed that "the Duke of Buckingham seemed to
me to ascend into my bed, where he carried himselfe with much love
towards me," and the Restoration naval official dreams of the Royal
Mistress in what Halifax called "the immediate Hours of her
Ministry."[16] The vicarious pleasure that Pepys derived from the lusty

---

[14] Pepys, 20 October 1662, 1 and 21 December 1666, 8 May 1667.

[15] After listening avidly to a conversation about buggery on 1 July 1663, Pepys confessed that
"I do not to this day know what is the meaning of this sin, nor which is the agent nor which
the patient"; he must have read *La Puttana Errante* after that date, since the Italian text gives
ample information about anal intercourse (admittedly heterosexual).

[16] George Savile, Marquis of Halifax, *Complete Works*, ed. Walter Raleigh (Oxford, 1912), p.
193; Laud's diary entry for 21 August 1625 ("Ea nocte in somnis visus est mihi Dux
Buckinghamiae in lectum meum ascendere, ubi multo erga me amore se gessit"), in *Works*,
ed. James Bliss, 3 vols. (Oxford, 1853), 3: 170, translated by William Prynne in *A Breviate
of the Life of William Laud* (1644), p. 6. The Primate adds the detail that "many seemed to
me to enter the Chamber, who did see this," which to the modern reader suggests a
Kafkaesque anxiety about sexual transgression. But Laud may have recorded this as
evidence of his pride in the friendship of an important man; Prynne later published this

king – he admits to feeling delighted that Charles continues to visit
Lady Castlemaine after his marriage (Pepys, 6 July 1661) – could not
be separated from his revulsion at the flouting of social rules, his
horror at the king's weakness in council and appalling misman-
agement of public affairs, and his near certainty (shared by many
commentators including John Evelyn) that the nation was on the
brink of collapse because its governor was "only governed by his
lust" (Pepys, 29 July 1667).

Conventional portraits of the "easy" and "indulgent" king fail to
convey how deeply his sexual behavior violated the norms of the
society he ruled, and how vehemently he forced his pleasures into
public view. His intention to install Lady Castlemaine in the queen's
entourage, thus flaunting his illicit sexuality in the face of the world
and publicly humiliating his bride only a month after their marriage,
was carried out with all the zeal and determination of Oliver
Cromwell at the battle of Naseby: he invokes "Almighty God" to his
aid, and solemnly swears "I wish I may be unhappy in this world and
in the world to come, if I faile in the least degree what I have
resolved."[17] Pepys expressed abhorrence at Charles's frequent
pardoning of friends who had committed gross indecency, violence,
and murder, and his diary records many instances of royal transgression; during one visit to Newmarket, Pepys believed, a girl
actually leaped to her death to escape the royal embrace.[18] Yet the
Crown could, paradoxically, launch savage attacks on those who
spread prurient gossip or joked about the royal mistresses. Henry
Killigrew junior was first banished from Court – for speculating

---

dream to influence the Archbishop's trial, showing him too favorably inclined to the
absolutist Duke, but he never hints at an Alcibiadic love affair.

[17] Letter to Clarendon, *c.* June 1662, cited in Godfrey Davies, "Charles II in 1660," *HLQ* 19
(1955–56): 268. Ronald Hutton, noting Charles's expressions of happiness in the days after
his wedding night, remarks dryly that "this adds colour to the belief of Charles's apologists
that his next move, to install Barbara as his bride's Lady of the Bedchamber, was motivated
solely by the need to reward yet another loyal subject for more than usually important past
services," Hutton, *Charles the Second*, p. 187.

[18] Pepys, 18 July 1668; cf. 22 and 25 February 1662, 1 July 1663, 23, and 26 October 1668 for
various incidents involving Dorset, Sedley, and the king's "horrid" connivance at, and
participation in, their transgressions. For the Duke of Buckingham's violence and the king's
pardon for murder, see Christine Phipps, ed., *Buckingham, Public and Private Man: The Prose,
Poems and Commonplace Book of George Villiers, Second Duke of Buckingham (1628–1687)* (1985),
pp. 15–16, 31, 50; Pepys, 17 January, 5–6 February, 15 May 1668, 19 May 1669; Anna
Clare Bryson, "Concepts of Civility in England c. 1560–1685," Oxford D. Phil. dissertation
(1984), p. 340. It is only fair to point out that this condoning of sexual offenses did not cease
with the Stuarts; George II pardoned Colonel Charteris for rape.

about Lady Castlemaine's youthful masturbation – and later
wounded in nine places, and left for dead, for claiming to have slept
with the Duke of Buckingham's mistress.[19] (Pepys was lucky that only
his heart "aked" after his bawdy conversation with Killigrew.)
When Sir John Coventry proposed a tax on playhouses and asked, in
the Commons, "whether did the king's pleasure lie among the men
or the women that acted," the king (already the father of ten
acknowledged bastards by five different mothers) grew concerned
that gossip about his Court Amours might become fashionable; this
was in 1670, after a decade in which, as we learn from Pepys, his
private parts had been in everybody's mouth. The unruly Member
was thus properly defaced: following the king's orders, twenty-five
armed men from Monmouth's guard ambushed him outside his
lodgings, "threw him down, and with a Knife cut off almost all the
End of his Nose."[20] The anointed sovereign, already commander of
a judicial system that could "deface" his subjects by branding the
cheek and mutilating the nose and ears, here chooses to exercise his
royal power like a bully from the London underworld.

This arbitrary mix of hedonism and repression generated confusion, social tension, and hostility toward displays of libertinism.
Even in the afterglow of the Restoration, Pepys sensed "no content or
satisfaccion anywhere in any one sort of people" (Pepys, 31 August
1661). The most striking expression of this unrest was the brothel-
storming apprentice riot of 1668, which threatened to engulf "the
great bawdy-house at White hall," but it can be felt in smaller
incidents provoked by Pepys's own attempts at dalliance. When he
fondles a woman in a tavern, an angry passer-by smashes the window
with a stone. When he starts to grope another woman in church, she
takes out a set of pins "to prick me if I should touch her again."[21]

When the royal family penetrate the "hangings" of class and

---

[19] Pepys, 21 October 1666, 19 May 1669, and cf. 30 May 1668 (talking about sexual
adventures with a group of Wits including Henry Killigrew junior, he records that "their
mad bawdy talk did make my heart ake").

[20] Andrew Marvell, *The Poems and Letters of Andrew Marvell*, ed. H. M. Margoliouth, 3rd ed.
rev. Pierre Legouis with E. E. Duncan-Jones, 2 vols. (Oxford, 1971), 2: 321, see also 2: 125,
2: 135, 2: 325; Burnet, *History*, 1: 495–97. Coventry was responding to the king's assertion
that "the players were the king's servants, and a part of his pleasure," consequently exempt
from jurisdiction and taxation; as Burnet notes, the king's violent actions took place in a
context of fear that he was about to establish an absolutist rule in emulation of his cousin and
paymaster Louis XIV. Charles's bastards are conveniently listed in G. E. Cokayne, *The
Complete Peerage*, ed. Vicary Gibbs et al., (1926), 6: Appendix F.

[21] Pepys, 29 June 1663, 18 August 1667.

morality with their "wanton talk" and sexual adventures, and when the bureaucrat imitates their lewdness behind a *cordon sanitaire* of secrecy, a conceptual channel opens up between zones of license widely separated by social status. The subcultures of whoredom and the "superculture" of the Court exchange features; Whitehall can be perceived as a "great bawdy-house," and the brothel as a little Court. As Peter Stallybrass and Allon White observe, "the Restoration Court projected a collective image of living in ironic and even defiant incompatibility with its inherited forms of public representation... The Court was both classical and grotesque, both regal and foolish, high and low."[22] Stratification is at once confused and reinforced, the partitions of class are at once penetrated and confirmed, by the Court's "wanton talk" and obscene writing, drunken brawling, riot, injury, outrage, insolence, duelling, ruffianly assaults, window-smashing, and wife-snatching – a general state of warfare, both verbal and physical, in which sexuality and disease are the weapons.

Conversation on sexual matters – itself a form of prurient transgression that Evelyn found deeply shocking, and that the worldly Samuel Butler compared to cunnilingus – is now inextricably tied to anxiety about affairs of state. In 1663, for example, Pepys discourses with Sir Thomas Crew "upon the unhappy posture of things at this time; that the King doth mind nothing but pleasure and hates the very sight or thoughts of business; that my Lady Castlemayne rules him." It is in this context that he learns about the "tricks of Aretin" – evidence of her commanding position – and about the anatomical reason for the Sovereign's exclusive devotion to "pleasure, in which he is too able, having a large ———." Pepys's pen cannot quite set down the royal organ in his native English, forming a dash instead, but the thought finds an outlet in a Romance language: "that which is the unhappiness is that, as the Italian proverb says, *Cazzo dritto non vuolt consiglio.*"[23] The political scene becomes a "posture," a *cazzaria*,

22 Peter Stallybrass and Allon White, *The Poetics and Politics of Transgression* (Ithaca, New York, 1986), pp. 101–02.

23 Pepys, 15 May 1663. Evelyn warns his son the day before his wedding to avoid "uncomely and filthy expressions in your most seacret communications and familiarities" (letter to John Evelyn, junior, [1679], numbered 1526, in Evelyn family papers currently on deposit in the Library of Christ Church, Oxford; I am grateful to John Wing, librarian of Christ Church, for permission to examine this manuscript, parts of which have been transcribed in W. G. Hiscock, *John Evelyn and his Family Circle* [1955], pp. 122–23). Cf. Samuel Butler, *Characters and Passages from Notebooks*, ed. A. R. Waller (Cambridge, 1908), p. 193 (the ribald

a pornographic episode which proves the primick has a mind of its own.

The historiography of the Restoration generally sets aside the question of sexuality in the monarch and his officials, in effect upholding the fundamental distinction between the serious public sphere and private realm of pleasure, irrelevant to the conduct of "business." Lawrence Stone, for example, interprets Pepys's sexual behavior as an escape, release, or distraction from the pressures of the office.[24] On the contrary, these pressures themselves *took a sexual form.* The worse goes the naval war with Holland, the more Charles is observed to fool with his mistresses, so that by 1667 Pepys, the model subject, feels contaminated by the presence of his monarch: in Whitehall garden, scene of much ardent gazing, he sees "the King (whom I have not had any desire to see since the Dutch came upon the coast first at Sheerness, for shame that I should see him, or he me methinks, after such a dishonour)" and immediately afterwards is astonished to see Lady Castlemaine, supposedly separated from the royal lover she has "ruled" to such disastrous effect. Pepys's parenthetical sentence-structure tries to part the political and the sexual again, but in terms that reveal their connection: because of the proximity of the mistress that both men "desire to see," Charles becomes an *object* of shame as well as a source of guilt, a walking Count Cazzo "so weak in his passion that he dare not" leave the duchess, as well as a great monarch incensed at his subject's miscarriages. The king's openly displayed priapism made it difficult to separate him into "two bodies," and mingled the public realm of political authority with the private emotions aroused by illicit sexuality: jealousy, excitement, furtive identification, and shame. Too naked and too close, the desire provoked by the sexual object – the royal *maîtresse en titre*, the pornographic image, perhaps even the monarch himself – becomes disruptive and embarrassing. The ambivalence experienced here in the royal presence is re-enacted, I suggest, in the scene with *L'Escole des Filles*: he resolves to buy it in plain wrapper and burn it the moment after enjoyment, "that it may not *stand* in the list of books, nor among them, to disgrace *them* if it

---

"plays an After-game of Letchery with his Tongue much worse than that which the *Cunnilingi* used among the old Romans").

[24] Stone, *Family,* p. 555; Stone does recognize, in contrast, that sex and business were completely interconnected when it came to dealing with *subordinates* – a point made more forcefully by Pearlman in "Pepys," and "Reply."

should be found" (emphasis added); the brazen text would "disgrace" Pepys's other books if it were to appear, like Lady Castlemaine, in full-dress binding and "titled."[25]

The Restoration may well mark the emergence of a new political and social order, a "new ensemble of what can only be described as power relations," as Barker puts it; but it did not take the form that Barker claims.[26] Far from involving "guilty secrecy" about sexuality and "the disappearance of the body from public view," this revolutionary change involved the social display of a once-private libertinism, the merging of Aretino's postures with the "posture of things at this time." Charles attempted to assert his power *both* by flaunting his illicit sexuality *and* by forcing his subjects to speak as if they had seen nothing; the concept of concealment, like the dichotomy of public and private, is inadequate to describe this strategy – reproduced on a smaller scale in Pepys's rash-yet-timid, invisible-yet-conspicuous eroticism. The spectacle of cultivated rudeness was only acted out by a small minority, but it affected the whole society. For a figure like Pepys – thoroughly "middle class" and yet dependent on the Court for his livelihood, status, and manners – the relation between the political and the personal grew more complex. The boundaries of public and private were not merely shifting, but becoming more *permeable*, like the "hangings" which are supposed to separate but which actually permit "wanton talk." The priapism of the king and the Duke of York enhances their glamour and sanctions Pepys's own looser morality, but at the same time the royal charisma is itself dissipated by their public acknowledgment of the private parts, associated with negligence, laxness, and irresponsibility. The mingling of sex and power at Whitehall was emulated by hurried gropings and ejaculations in Seething Lane; Pepys's extra-marital emissions always took place with subordinates and frequently involved what one critic calls, accurately if severely, "an indecent abuse of authority" – the granting of a contract or petition in exchange for sexual opportunities.[27] Nevertheless, Pepys

[25] Pepys, 29 July and 10 September 1667, 8 February 1668; cf. 15 February 1668 (six days after reading *L'Escole*) for an exhausting evening spent "titling," i.e., labelling the spines of, newly-bound books. [26] Barker, *Tremulous Private Body*, pp. 11, 14.

[27] Pearlman, "Reply," p. 37. Stone recounts the same examples in an altogether more indulgent tone in *Family*, pp. 555–59; he mentions, for example, that Pepys "toyed for hours" with Mrs. Pennington, a social equal, whereas Pearlman points out (quite rightly) that Pepys was hypocritically shocked that "a lady" would permit his hand on her breast – a vivid example of the double standard and the blame of women for sexual responses incited by men; Pearlman, "Pepys," pp. 44–45.

shows a remarkable ability to dissociate himself from the sins he was copying in miniature, lamenting the "luxury and looseness of the times" shortly after thrusting his finger into the ship's carpenter's wife, reporting with approval a fierce sermon that compared the king to David and Bathsheba while at the same time thinking of using his administrative office to move his mistress's husband around the country, precisely as David did with Bathsheba's husband.[28]

Royal libertinism could be interpreted both as an "effeminate" slackness and as a masculine declaration of power and privilege, an implicit but unmistakable equation of sovereign authority with phallic vigor. This mingling of the personal and the political had one obvious shortcoming; it allowed any waning of erotic energy to be read as a weakening of authority – a connection which the Court satirists, and Dryden's Achitophel, exploit to the full:

> His Scepter and his Prick are of a Length...
> His Crowne and Codds have both one date,
> For as these fall, so falls the State.[29]

On the other hand, it may have initiated the sentimental identification with the royal family that has erupted intermittently, and kept them on the throne, ever since. On the eve of the Restoration, Pepys was delighted to see a royal spaniel defecate because it made him "think that a King and all that belong to him are but just as others are" (Pepys, 25 May 1660); he may have felt the same mixture of distaste, amusement, and creaturely solidarity when contemplating other forms of looseness.

The king's evident submission to Lady Castlemaine and reputed sexual failures, projected onto the large screen of anxious-prurient gossip, could spread contempt for royal power, but could also encourage his subjects to be less embarrassed by the feebler aspects of their own sexuality. If Charles is perceived to be at the mercy of a terrifying female power – a libertine Lady Macbeth who threatens to "dash the brains of it out before the King's face" when he refuses to acknowledge her latest bastard – then the Navy Clerk need worry less

---

[28] E.g. Pepys, 20 and 21 February 1665, 3 and 29 July 1667. In 2 Samuel 11 David brings Uriah the Hittite back to Jerusalem as a cover for Bathsheba's pregnancy, and then sends him away to a dangerous battle-front; Pepys wants to bring Samuel Martin home from his posting in Scotland when Mrs. Martin fears she is pregnant.

[29] Rochester, *The Poems of John Wilmot, Earl of Rochester*, ed. Keith Walker (Oxford, 1984), p. 74; Bror Danielsson and David M. Vieth, eds., *The Gyldenstolpe Manuscript Miscellany* (Stockholm, 1967), p. 302 ("The Looking-Glass"); compare *Absalom and Achitophel*, line 710 (the king "Is grown in *Bathsheba*'s Embraces old").

about "miscarriages" at the office and domestic quarrelling at home. If he learns (from conversation with the Treasurer of the Navy himself) that Charles "is at the command of any woman like a slave," and "cannot command himself in the presence of a woman he likes" – a typical conflation of sexual and political language – then it may be easier to accept his own inability "to command myself in the pleasures of my eye."[30] If "the King's greatest pleasure hath been with his fingers, being able to do no more" during the Dutch crisis, then Pepys need not feel bad about "discharging" himself over *L'Escole des Filles*, or failing to make love to his wife – as the diary admits – during the "half-year" that the British Navy reached its lowest point in recorded history.[31]

In the conventional reading of "bourgeois" experience, the private sphere of the home is isolated from the larger pressures of society, whether it is seen as a crucible of guilt and repression or as a shelter from the heartless forces of Court corruption and "business." But Pepys's household clearly resembles the larger world dominated by the Court in its unstable mingling of politics and personal emotion. The central concept in his condemnation of Charles is at once political and moral – he cannot *command* himself – and the same concept lies at the heart of Pepys's gender-relations, both with his wife and with his servants. When her dancing lessons distract Elizabeth from "her business," introducing her to "other sweets besides pleasing of me," he writes explicitly that "I fear, without great discretion, I shall go near to lose too my command over her." He fears the other household members who had witnessed Elizabeth's fury at Pepys's jealousy and his inability to school or tame her, using the revealing phrase "the rest of the world" for the small group of servants gathered round the dining-room table (Pepys, 21 May 1663). However narrow the domestic space (office, bedroom, library shelf) it is always filled with the rest of the world. However intimate or private the relationship, it is always *institutional*. Even the urge to read *L'Escole des Filles*, analyzed in this paper as the product of Court and Office, grows out of the politics of the household. On 12 January 1668, Elizabeth St. Michel Pepys raged against her lack of "money and liberty," the very issues that convulsed the political nation. Next day Pepys rushes to the bookshop in search of "the French book

[30] Pepys, 25 April 1666, 27 July 1667; in the same conversation with Carteret, Pepys learns that Charles "this day delivers himself up to this [man] and the next to that, to the ruin of himself and business." [31] Pepys, 30 July and 2 August 1667.

which I did think to have had for my wife to translate." Translating a sophisticated but subtly didactic French text – the "School" for young women like herself – would provide her with intellectual stimulus and productive self-esteem without the danger his jealous mind most feared: a priapic intruder, idle, roguish yet irresistible, exerting a sovereign power to seduce.

CHAPTER 6

Milton, Samson Agonistes, *and the Restoration*

Blair Worden

I

Milton's *Samson Agonistes* raises in an unusually stark form the question how far a work of imaginative literature can or should be understood in terms of the historical background to its composition. From William Godwin to David Masson to Christopher Hill, a succession of historians and of historically minded critics has supposed that Samson's predicament corresponds to Milton's experience of the Restoration, and to the struggle of the blind poet to come to terms with the defeat of the Puritan cause.[1] To that view, some distinguished literary critics have taken profound exception. E. M. Krouse argued that "any attempt... to make political allegory the heart of this poem is indefensible." Barbara Lewalski has maintained that there is "no basis for reading the play as political allegory of any kind," and that the "echoes" of Restoration politics which have been detected "are merely the contemporary reverberation of a universal paradigm recurring throughout history." W. R. Parker's biography of Milton not only declined to recognize any "personal" or "political allusions" in *Samson Agonistes*, but concluded, on stylistic grounds, that the poem was written not after the Restoration but well before it – though that view seems to have lost such favor as it once enjoyed.[2]

Which is the greater, the exasperation of historians when literary critics dismiss the historical context, or the indignation of literary

---

[1] William Godwin, *Lives of Edward and John Philips* (1815), pp. 84–85; Masson, *Life of Milton*, 6: 670–78; Hill, *Milton*, pp. 428–48, 481–86, and Hill, *Experience of Defeat*, pp. 310–19.

[2] E. M. Krouse, *Milton's Samson and the Christian Tradition* (Princeton, 1949), p. 93; Barbara Lewalski, "*Samson Agonistes* and the 'Tragedy' of the Apocalypse," *PMLA* 85 (1970): 1050–62, passage cited p. 1061; W. R. Parker, *Milton. A Biography*, 2 vols. (Oxford, 1968), 1: 313–22, 2: 903–17, especially p. 907. No one, I imagine, would question the possibility that Milton had planned a poem on Samson, perhaps drafted one, before 1660.

critics when historians are blind to the literary one? At issue, as
always in the discussion of local allusions in a work that transcends its
time, is the relationship of a writer's imagination to the world around
him. I am with the historians (even if not with their every word). Of
course, historians face temptations. *Samson Agonistes* is not a *pièce à clef*,
even if, as I shall indicate, it projects some carefully drawn parallels
between then and now. Being a triumph of imagination, it mirrors a
far wider range of experience than Milton's own, which is why the
greatness of the poem has been evident to countless readers who know
little or nothing of the seventeenth century. Yet literary critics face
temptations too. I do not think Milton would have been impressed by
the argument that because the poem conforms to the rules of
Sophoclean tragedy, or because it belongs to high traditions of
biblical typology, it cannot have been animated by the poet's
personal and political experience. In any case the location of formal
and typological patterns in the poem, which have been held to give
it its coherence, has not convinced all critics. *Samson Agonistes* remains
a puzzling poem, and Samson a puzzling hero. I believe that the
puzzles diminish when we relate the work, more fully than has yet
been done, to the Restoration, and when we explore more thoroughly
the correspondences that link Samson to Milton and to the cause for
which he stood.

To assist the comparison, I shall set poetry beside prose. I shall
place *Samson Agonistes* alongside the writings of Roundhead politicians
of the 1660s, and particularly of three of them: Edmund Ludlow,
Algernon Sidney, and Sir Henry Vane. All three were "commonwealthmen" or republicans. All were prominent in the government
of Britain under the Commonwealth of 1649–53; all broke with
Cromwell upon what they called his "usurpation" of 1653; all
proclaimed allegiance to that "good old cause" which they held
Cromwell to have betrayed, and whose "language" Milton tells us
that he "speaks" in *The Ready and Easy Way* in early 1660.[3] All of
them turned to the biblical example which Milton likewise selected to
explain England's apostasy of that year: the nation chose "a captain
back to Egypt."[4]

First there is the regicide Edmund Ludlow, who fled to Switzerland

---

[3] Milton, *Prose*, 7: 387, 7: 462.
[4] *Ibid.*, 7: 463; Ludlow, *Voyce*, pp. 115, 150; Algernon Sidney, "Court Maxims, Discussed and
Refelled," Warwickshire Record Office, p. 203; *The Tryal of Sir Henry Vane, Kt.* (1662), p.
117.

in 1660 and there composed an enormous manuscript autobiography, "A Voyce from the Watch Tower."[5] In it he strove to confront the calamity of the Restoration and to explain it, as he sought to explain everything, in terms of God's providence. To him, the Puritan Revolution had seemed a decisive stage in the divine scheme of history, in which God's chosen people, His "saints," would purge and purify Church and State and perhaps prepare the world for the second coming. In 1660 those hopes were shattered: "all things," as Ludlow observed, "running counter to what the providences of the Lord had led to for twenty years past." Now God was pleased "to make them the tail, who before were the head," and His people were forced to "bow down that their enemies may go over them."[6] No less than Samson's "restless thoughts" do Ludlow's meditations "present / Times past, what once I was, and what am now."[7] No less than Samson is Ludlow's cause "the glory late of Israel, now the grief" (line 179). Ludlow discovers what Milton's Chorus, addressing God, tells of His way with "such as thou hast solemnly elected":

> thou oft
> Amidst their height of noon,
> Changest thy countenance, and thy hand with no regard
> Of highest favours past
> From thee on them, or them to thee of service. (lines 678, 682–85).

Like Samson, Ludlow knows that the defeat of God's cause owes nothing to its enemies – to the Philistines in Samson's time, to the Cavaliers in Ludlow's – and everything to the sinfulness which God punishes in His servants.[8] Like Samson, Ludlow has to absorb the lesson of divine humiliation. And like Samson, he has to learn how to keep faith with – in Ludlow's words – God's "seemingly dead and buried cause."[9]

My second figure is another exile of the 1660s, Algernon Sidney, who would be executed in 1683 for his alleged complicity in the Rye House Plot. In the mid-1660s he attacked the restored monarchy in a treatise – never published – entitled "Court Maxims, Discussed and Refelled." No two seventeenth-century republicans are closer in

---

[5] Only the portion from 1660 has been found: it is Bodleian Library, MS Eng. hist. c. 487, hereafter "Ludlow, 'Voyce'." A section of it has been edited by me in Ludlow, *Voyce.*

[6] Ludlow, *Voyce,* p. 123.

[7] Milton, *Poems,* lines 19–22. Subsequent line references are given parenthetically.

[8] Ludlow, *Voyce,* pp. 149, 200.   [9] Ludlow, "Voyce," p. 1111.

their ideas than Sidney and Milton. Like the Milton of the prose works, Sidney sees "liberty" as the natural ally of "discipline," of "frugality," "industry," "temperance," "sobriety," "honesty poverty," and regards "tyranny" as the natural ally of "licence" and of "luxury." With Milton, Sidney grasps "how firm a union there is between idolatry and tyranny."[10] When Milton's Chorus regrets that "nations grown corrupt" prefer "bondage with ease" to "strenuous liberty" (lines 268, 270–71), we remember *Eikonoklastes*, where Milton notes that the English, "with a besotted and degenerate baseness of spirit," have proved "not fit for that liberty which they cried out and bellowed for," and are "running their own heads into the yoke of bondage."[11] Sidney for his part laments that in 1660 a "free and gallant nation" could not "be contented until we returned again into ... bondage."[12]

My third figure, Sir Henry Vane, thought "no nation truly free that is in bondage to corruption."[13] His chaplain George Sykes, meditating on Vane's death, indicated that the English, by "a most irrational yielding up ourselves into captivity" in 1660, had "set up the basest of men," the Cavaliers, "over them ... that are in bondage to the same inferior lusts with themselves."[14] Vane was executed by the restored government in 1662, and a number of writings by and about him were quickly released after his death. Sykes, urging their importance on the nation, acknowledged that to some readers Vane seemed to write "as but cloudily or not at all making out what he speaks of."[15] It was an understatement. Yet Vane was a major influence on his many followers. In Ludlow and Sidney he inspired something like hero-worship. To Ludlow he was "this choice martyr of Christ."[16] Sidney wrote a memoir of Vane, emphasizing his "frugality," "industry," and "discipline,"[17] and ruled that "the nation ... had not another man equal to him in virtue, prudence, courage, industry, reputation and godliness."[18]

---

[10] Sidney, "Court Maxims," pp. 13, 178, 180, 198; Algernon Sidney, *Discourses concerning Government*, ed. Thomas G. West (Indianapolis, 1990), pp. 164–65, 184, 254, 350.
[11] Milton, *Prose*, 3: 344, 488, 581.   [12] Sidney, "Court Maxims," pp. 54, 203.
[13] *A Needful Corrective or Ballance in Popular Government* (1659), p. 7. This pamphlet, though probably written by Vane, may have been composed by a different author with Vane's "advice or approbation": see Austin Woolrych, "The Good Old Cause and the Fall of the Protectorate," *Cambridge Historical Journal* 13 (1957): 133–61, at p. 153.
[14] George Sykes, *The Life and Death of Sir Henry Vane, Kt.* (1662), p. 23.
[15] *Ibid.*, p. 130.   [16] Ludlow, *Voyce*, p. 313.
[17] It is printed in Violet A. Rowe, *Sir Henry Vane the Younger* (1970), pp. 275–83.
[18] Sidney, "Court Maxims," p. 188.

Milton had praised Vane, for his brave and almost solitary struggle in Parliament for the separation of Church from State, in a sonnet of 1652, which was first published in George Sykes's biography of Vane ten years later.[19] Sykes is alert to the contemporary relevance of the Samson story. He refers to it on his opening page. Later, and more suggestively, he writes that Vane "has more advantaged a good CAUSE and condemned a bad one, done his honest countrymen more service and his enemies more disservice, by his death (as Samson served the Philistines) than before in all his life, though that also were very considerable."[20] Vane, and Milton's Samson, have much in common, so much that one is bound to suspect that Milton knew the writings by and about Vane and that they made an imprint on the poem. The point is not critical. Men who spoke "the language of the good old cause" were likely to relate common experiences in a common vocabulary. At all events, the common experiences of Vane and Samson are plentiful. Samson is destined to be Israel's "deliverer" (lines 38–39, 274, 1214, 1270): Vane, in Sykes's words, is "this English Joseph and deliverer."[21] Samson – like Abdiel, the transparently autobiographical creation of *Paradise Lost* – fights "single" in God's service (line 1111): Vane maintains that God did "single me out to the defence and justification of his cause," and declares himself willing "to stand single in the witness I am to give to this glorious cause."[22] The Philistines "put out" Samson's "eyes" (lines 33, 1103, 1160): Vane's chaplain protests at the determination of the restored regime "to put out the eyes of all the good people of England."[23] Samson, despairing at his impotence and his affliction, thinks his "race of glory run" (line 597): Vane, his "race of action being run" after his fall from power, subsequently endured his "suffering scene."[24] Milton's Samson is revived by "secret refreshings" of the spirit (line 665): for Vane, "secret dew" nourishes the "inward man" under the persecution of the Restoration.[25] Where Samson's sin has broken his military prowess, in Vane's mind "our sins have been the cause that our counsels, our forces, our wit, our conquests, and ourselves have been destructive to ourselves."[26]

Shortly before his imprisonment in October 1660, the month of the first executions among the regicides, Vane delivered a sermon to his

---

[19] Sykes, *Life of Vane,* pp. 93–94.   [20] *Ibid.,* p. 119.   [21] *Ibid.,* p. 121.

[22] *The Substance of what Sir Henry Vane Intended to have Spoken upon the Scaffold on Tower Hill* (1662), p. 3; *Tryal,* p. 62.   [23] Sykes, *Life of Vane,* pp. 138, 142.   [24] *Ibid.,* p. 105.

[25] Sir Henry Vane, *Two Treatises* (1662), p. 2.   [26] *Tryal,* p. 120.

family which focused on another Old Testament figure whose career had exposed the failings of the Israelites: Baruch, the "choice and dear servant of the Lord that on proof and trial had showed himself very courageous and bold in the service of God."[27] Milton's Samson experiences "humours black" and "black mortification" (lines 600, 622): Vane recalls the "black and dismal prospect" that confronted Baruch, and fears "that the like... may be brought to pass in our days." Milton's Samson, once so privileged in his closeness to God, is tormented by "restless thoughts" (line 19): Vane's Baruch, "after all the experience he had had of God... could find no rest at all in any way... no visible support or help." Yet Vane, like Samson, would find a renewed purpose in death. Preparing for his execution, he was "certain" that "this cause shall have its resurrection in my death."[28] Milton's Chorus assures us at the end that the benevolence of God's providence has become evident "in the close" (line 1748): Sykes, in his conclusion, assures the persecuted godly that God "will send deliverance in the close."[29]

Parallels between biblical and contemporary experience belonged to the everyday vocabulary of Puritan politics. To write a poem about Samson was unavoidably to invite comparisons with contemporary events. In the Old Testament, the Puritan saints discovered the figurative models that made sense of their own time. "Our case hath been parallel" to that of the Israelites, explained Vane's disciple Henry Stubbe in 1659, "and we may therein read the grounds of our confidence that through a resemblance of events the same providence operateth now in us which did of old, and we expect the same issue."[30] Or as Milton's Chorus has it, "God hath wrought things as incredible / For his people of old; what hinders now?" (lines 1532–33).[31] Biblical parallels were not always so reassuring.

[27] Victoria and Albert Museum, Forster MS. 48. D. 4: (Vane's sermons), pp. 1–3.

[28] Vane, *Two Treatises*, pp. 79–80. Vane knew that the execution would occur "as upon a public theatre," and saw his death as belonging to the "last act" or "spectacle" of a divine scheme of history (*Tryal*, p. 89; *Substance of what Sir Henry Vane Intended*, p. 1; Vane, *Two Treatises*, pp. 54–55). Jose, *Ideas of the Restoration*, chapter 8, emphasizes the resemblances between the Philistine temple and the Restoration playhouse.

[29] Sykes, *Life of Vane*, p. 143.

[30] Henry Stubbe, *Malice Rebuked* (1659), p. 4. See also Blair Worden, "Providence and Politics in Cromwellian England," *Past and Present* 109 (1985): 55–99, especially p. 89.

[31] John Barkstead, one of the regicides executed in 1662, compared the suffering saints of the Restoration with the Nazarites (whom Samson represented). *The Speeches, Discourses and Prayers of Col. John Barkstead, Col. John Okey, and Mr. Miles Corbet* (1662), octavo edition, p. 27.

England's "condition" at the Restoration, explained Vane, "held much resemblance with that of the Jews" when they provoked God by establishing a monarchy, "and we deserve as well to be rejected as they were."[32] Sidney drew the same parallel – but was glad to recall that, even in the Israelites' self-inflicted adversity, God (as in the Samson story) did not desert them: He "kept a lamp still burning in the house of David."[33] The Puritan imagination was especially struck by Old Testament stories which (like the Samson story) involved obliterative punishment from heaven. Vane was imprisoned by Cromwell in 1656 after blaming the recent humiliation of Cromwell's hitherto invincible forces, which had been crushed by the Spaniards in the Caribbean, on the hypocrisy and ambition behind the creation of the Protectorate. Vane had compared those failings with the sin of Achan, whose embezzlement had rendered Joshua's hitherto invincible forces as helpless as Dalila's wiles had rendered Samson, and had exposed them to devastating defeat.[34] In Ludlow's autobiography Charles I is described as "the Achan that troubled Israel."[35] Milton, who thought of writing a tragedy about Achan,[36] in 1659 compared the Cromwellians among the officers of the New Model Army as "the Achan among them."[37]

The Old Testament God was a God of battle and of honour. Samson is wretched to think of the "dishonour" which his impotence has brought upon his God and the "honour" it has given to Dagon (lines 449–52). The saints of the Restoration were equally conscious of having brought "dishonour" on God by their failure.[38] In the civil war battles as in the Samson story, the outcome determined "whose God is God" (line 1176). In Milton's poem

> all the contest is now
> 'Twixt God and Dagon; Dagon hath presumed,
> Me overthrown, to enter lists with God,
> His deity comparing and preferring
> Before the God of Abraham.   (lines 461–65)

---

[32] *Tryal*, pp. 119–20.   [33] Sidney, "Court Maxims," pp. 36, 200.

[34] Blair Worden, "Oliver Cromwell and the Sin of Achan," in Derek Beales and Geoffrey Best, eds., *History, Society and the Churches. Essays in Honour of Owen Chadwick* (Cambridge, 1985), pp. 125–45, see pp. 136–39.   [35] Ludlow, *Voyce*, p. 200.

[36] Milton, *Prose*, 8: 555.   [37] Milton, *Prose*, 7: 328.

[38] See e.g. *Speeches*, p. 84. The condemned regicides were as anxious as Samson to "honour" and not "dishonour" God by the manner of their deaths (H. G. Tibbutt, "Colonel John Okey 1606–1682," *Bedfordshire Historical Record Society* 35 [1955]: 145, 150), for they were as conscious as Samson that "death to life is crown or shame" (line 1579).

In the civil wars, both sides repeatedly "appealed" to God to declare for their cause in battle.[39] The Roundhead victory at Cheriton in 1644, declared a Puritan preacher before Parliament, "was a victory after a mutual appeal to God": "the enemy's word was, *God is for us.* Our word was, *God is with us*"; so "the Lord seemed to decide the great doubt, and to resolve the question which side was right; whose cause was His."[40] In 1649 the Commonwealth declared that "the great God of battle," by "a continued series of providences and wonders," had "determined very much in favour of the Parliament."[41] Yet in 1660 the Puritans were as vulnerable to Royalist mockery as is Samson to the taunts of Harapha. "The court of heaven," crowed the Royalist clergyman Gilbert Ironside in that year, "hath been solicited this many years *pro* and *con* ... and now let the world judge whose prayers have been heard."[42] God's verdict on Parliament's behalf, conceded Vane, had been "made void" by the sins of His people.[43]

In the eyes of the commonwealthmen, the restored monarchy is what Dagon is in Milton's poem, an "idol" (lines 13, 441, 453, 456, 1297, 1358, 1364, 1378). At the Restoration, lamented Sidney, "we set up an idol and dance about it;"[44] Ludlow was horrified to observe the nation's "great zeal to the idol that was set up;"[45] England's "most successfully acquired liberty," bemoaned Vane's chaplain, was being "swallowed up again into downright heathenish idolatry."[46] Like Milton's Philistines, the Englishmen of the Restoration, an "idolatrous rout amidst their wine" (line 443), were "Drunk with idolatry, drunk with wine" (line 1670). *Paradise Lost* tells us that in 1660 Milton, while "with dangers compassed round," heard "the barbarous dissonance / Of Bacchus and his revellers" (*PL* 7: 27–33); Sidney noticed that at the Restoration "the rites of Bacchus" were "publicly celebrated" by "wicked idolaters;"[47] Ludlow, like Milton hiding in London, contrived to be "an eye and ear witness" of the drunken revelry of the king's return, when

the debauched party through London manifested great joy that now they were in a way of enjoying their lusts without control. And I observed a

[39] Worden, "Providence and Politics," pp. 81–82.
[40] Obadiah Sedgwick, *A Thanksgiving-Sermon* (1644), p. 81.
[41] *The Parliamentary or Constitutional History of England*, 21 vols. (1751–62), 19: 68, 19: 177.
[42] Gilbert Ironside, *A Sermon Preached at Dorchester* (1660), p. 13.   [43] *Tryal*, p. 119.
[44] Sidney, "Court Maxims," p. 203.
[45] Ludlow, *Voyce*, p. 170; see also pp. 122, 204, and Ludlow, "Voyce," pp. 1131, 1150, 1154.
[46] Sykes, *Life of Vane*, p. 130.   [47] Sidney, "Court Maxims," p. 194.

vintner, who set out a hogshead of wine, making those drink the king's health who passed by, which they did upon their knees till they lost the use of their legs. (Ludlow, *Voyce*, pp. 118, 158)

Ludlow's movements in the spring and summer of 1660 are vividly recorded in his autobiography. For five months he evidently moved back and forth among many houses, a number of them in Holborn, bolting doors, checking escape-routes, venturing out only at night, hoping for a moonless sky, hiding in alleys or behind boards when potential enemies passed by.[48] Other regicides who sought to conceal themselves were less fortunate, and went to their deaths; but the serjeant-at-arms had to inform the Commons that Ludlow was "not to be found,"[49] just as the official proclamation against Milton admitted that, by "obscuring himself," he had thwarted the government's intention to try him for treason.[50] Through a network of faithful friends and kinswomen in Holborn, Ludlow was able to keep in touch with other regicides nearby.[51] While Parliament debated the Act of Pardon, and decided which regicides and Cromwellians to punish, he and his friends confronted urgent decisions. Should they give themselves up, and rely on the spirit of clemency promised in the Declaration of Breda? Or should they stay in hiding until the government's intentions toward the regicides became clear?

Like Ludlow, Milton hid in London for several months. His plight that summer, "In darkness, and with dangers compassed round," must have been desperate – as desperate in its way as Samson's, who tells the Chorus "How many evils have enclosed me round" (line 194).[52] At last, in or around September, Milton felt it safe to reappear. Yet even then he chose to move to Holborn, where the Dissenting network would doubtless have been able to help him escape if, as must have seemed all too possible, the threat to his life was renewed.[53] Only once the Act of Pardon had passed the seals did he move to more comfortable surroundings.[54]

His survival, like that of other advocates of regicide, depended on clemency from Parliament. We can watch Ludlow seeking that

---

[48] Ludlow, *Voyce*, especially pp. 114, 119, 150–51, 158, 169, 178, 182–83, 188–90.
[49] *Ibid.*, p. 186.   [50] Parker, *Milton*, 2: 573.   [51] Ludlow, *Voyce*, pp. 150, 176, 178.
[52] Like Samson (line 8), Ludlow suffered from the want of "air" in his confinement: Ludlow, *Voyce*, p. 183. Parker's vividly imagined account of Milton's experience in hiding (*Milton*, 1: 567ff.) will ring true to readers of Ludlow's autobiography.
[53] For that network see also *Speeches*, p. 23.   [54] Parker, *Milton*, 1: 574, 1: 577, 2: 1089.

clemency and calculating its likelihood. Thanks to the memoirs of
Lucy Hutchinson we can also watch her husband, the regicide
colonel, who "lay very private in the town" until the Act of Pardon
was passed,[55] confronting the same quandary. Intermediaries for
Ludlow and Hutchinson ceaselessly lobbied members of both houses,
just as intermediaries did on behalf of Milton, among them Andrew
Marvell, who "made a considerable party for him," and who was
one of the "many good friends to intercede for him."[56] Such
exertions help us to understand the large presence in Milton's poem
of a theme which owes nothing to biblical or literary tradition: the
efforts of Samson's father, Manoa, to secure Samson's release through
the payment of ransom. Just as Manoa, by "solicitation," has
"attempted one by one the lords" (lines 488, 1457), so Ludlow
records that "my father Oldsworth" – his father-in-law – approached "the Lords" and "solicited many of them" to get Ludlow
spared.[57] Mrs. Hutchinson, fighting to save her husband, "made it
her business to solicit all her friends for his safety," and persuaded an
ally in the Commons to "solicit all his friends" too.[58] Three figures
who appear to have aided Milton's bid for clemency – Monck's ally
William Morice, Arthur Annesley, and Lady Ranelagh[59] – all tried
to help Ludlow too.[60] In Ludlow's and Lucy Hutchinson's accounts,
some MPs, high-flying Anglicans among them, responded to pleas for
leniency with bitter vindictiveness, others with personal oppor-
tunism, others still with heart-warming magnanimity.[61] The stories
told by those authors are strikingly similar to Manoa's:

> Some much averse I found and wondrous harsh,
> Contemptuous, proud, set on revenge and spite;
> That part most reverenced Dagon and his priests,
> Others more moderate seeming, but their aim
> Private reward, for which both god and state
> They easily would set to sale, a third
> More generous far and civil, who confessed
> They had enough revenged, having reduced
> Their foe to misery beneath their fears.   (lines 1461–69)

After his arrest, Milton sued successfully for a pardon, an act of
submission that cost heavy gaolers' fees and, we can only suppose,

---

[55] Lucy Hutchinson, *Memoirs of the Life of Colonel Hutchinson*, ed. James Sutherland (1973), p.
231.   [56] Helen Darbishire, ed., *The Early Lives of Milton* (1932), pp. 74, 177.
[57] Ludlow, *Voyce*, p. 165.   [58] Hutchinson, *Memoirs*, pp. 229, 232.
[59] Parker, *Milton*, 1: 571–72.   [60] Ludlow, *Voyce*, pp. 119, 165, 166.
[61] *Ibid.*, pp. 125, 165–66, 180; Hutchinson, *Memoirs*, pp. 230–33.

some anguish of spirit.[62] Manoa confronts Samson with a similar dilemma. Samson longs only to die, and meanwhile to "expiate, if possible, my crime" through servitude and imprisonment (line 490, cf. line 1263). Manoa retorts that "self-preservation bids" his son to use the "means" that might bring him release and safety (lines 505–16). Samson asks how, released, he could be "useful" and "serve / My nation" (lines 564–65). Manoa by contrast is sure that God purposes to "use" Samson "further yet in some great service" (line 1498).

The debate between Samson and Manoa corresponds closely to the debate among the regicides in the Restoration. In 1662 Vane, like Samson declaring a longing for death, "might have had an opportunity of escaping," or have avoided his fate "by policy," but felt "unable to decline that which was come upon him." "Friends" urged him "to make some submission to the king," but when some of them spoke of "giving some thousands of pounds for his life," he said, "If a thousand farthings would gain it, he would not do it."[63] The regicide Thomas Harrison, before his execution in 1660, was equally firm. He took no steps to avoid arrest, being so certain "of his duty to seal the truth" of the "cause which the Lord had honoured him to be an instrument in" that "he was not free to withdraw himself out of his house for the saving of his life, as apprehending his doing so would be a turning of his back upon the cause of God."[64] If Vane and Harrison take Samson's line, Ludlow follows Manoa's. Ludlow believed it his duty to use all possible "means" for his own "preservation," so that he might remain useful "for the serving of his generation."[65] Colonel Hutchinson, having initially resolved to give himself up, was persuaded by his wife that God had "singled him out for preservation," and thereafter "would often say the Lord had not thus eminently preserved him for nothing, but that he was yet kept for some eminent service" in God's cause.[66]

Would Milton in 1660 be "kept" for the "eminent service" of his greatest poetry, on which he had recently embarked? Longing to be

---

[62] Parker, *Milton,* 1 : 576. The payment of fees or sweeteners was a necessity for other regicides too: Ludlow, *Voyce,* pp. 164, 174–75; Hutchinson, *Memoirs,* p. 232. Hints that regicides might be able to save their lives through bribery – see *Speeches,* p.21; *Tryal,* p. 81; R. H. C. Catterall, "Sir George Downing and the Regicides," *American Historical Review* 17 (1912): 268–89, p. 282 – perhaps correspond to the offer of "magnanimity" by some Philistine lords "if some convenient ransom were proposed" (lines 1470–71).   [63] *Tryal,* pp. 77, 81.

[64] Ludlow, *Voyce,* p. 126; with which compare Milton, *Prose,* 6: 605.

[65] Ludlow, *Voyce,* pp. 108, 169, 182, 302, 305, 312.

[66] Hutchinson, *Memoirs,* pp. 229, 234.

"of use" to God and country, he dreaded, like Samson, to be
"useless." "That one talent which is death to hide" had been
"lodged with me useless."[67] In 1666 he hoped "not" to "be useless,
whatever duty remains for me to carry out in this life."[68] Samson
dreads to be, in useless idleness, "to visitants a gaze" (line 567):
Milton after 1660, John Aubrey tells us, was "visited much," "more
than he did desire."[69]

II

Ludlow tells how the sweeping tide of Royalist emotion in 1660
caused "my heart to ache"; Sidney tells how it generated "the
anguish of my spirit, broken through the abundance of my sorrow";[70]
Samson speaks of "the anguish of my soul" (lines 458, 600). In
October 1660 sleds carrying condemned regicides to Tyburn passed
close to Milton's house in Holborn. Two years later Vane and three
other regicides would likewise be carried to execution. To the
commonwealthmen and to the saints, those deaths were judicial
murders, which mocked elementary principles and procedures of
justice. Sidney, indignant at the conduct of the "tribunals," saw a
parallel in the Old Testament murder of Naboth, and observed that
"the men of Belial, false witnesses and corrupt judges," had been
"the pillars upon which that monarchy stood." But Sidney did not
despair, for he remembered that the "pillars" had fallen when "God
raised up an avenger" to overthrow Naboth's persecutors.[71] There
were other atrocities (as the godly saw them) to endure. In 1660 the
corpses of regicides who had already been buried, among them
Milton's friend and hero John Bradshaw, were ripped up and
exposed to public derision on poles at Tyburn. Commonwealthmen
who were spared in 1660 soon found themselves in prison on suspicion
of conspiracy, among them Robert Overton, another friend and hero
of Milton,[72] who as Ludlow records was "barbarously treated."[73]
The prisoners experienced miserable conditions in their dungeons,
where some died (among them Colonel Hutchinson, who had been
arrested after his pardon) and others were broken in body and mind
(among them the republican theorist James Harrington, who at the

---

[67] Sonnet XVI.
[68] J. Milton French, ed., *The Life Records of John Milton*, 5 vols. (New Brunswick, 1949–58), 4:
425.   [69] Darbishire, *Early Lives*, p. 6.
[70] Ludlow, *Voyce*, p. 123; Sidney, "Court Maxims," p. 203.
[71] Sidney, "Court Maxims," pp. 194, 37, 137.   [72] Milton, *Prose*, 4(1.): 676.
[73] Ludlow, "Voyce," p. 962.

Restoration is said to have hidden in the house of Milton's friend the printer William Dugard.)[74] God's chosen were afflicted in Restoration England as in *Samson Agonistes*, where the Lord

> Oft leav'st them to the hostile sword
> Of heathen and profane, their carcases
> To dogs and fowls a prey, or else captived:
> Or to the unjust tribunals, under change of times,
>
> ...
>
> If these they scape, perhaps in poverty
> With sickness and disease thou bow'st them down.
>
> (lines 692–95, 697–98)

Ludlow repeatedly describes the saints of the Restoration as "prey" and their persecutors as "birds" or "beasts of prey."[75] The three regicides executed in April 1662 proclaimed that their cause would survive "when the fowls have eaten of our vile bodies."[76]

Among the afflictions visited on the elect, notes the Chorus, is the "condemnation of the ungrateful multitude" (line 696). Samson is "sung and proverbed for a fool / In every street" (lines 203–04). On the king's return, says Lucy Hutchinson, "every ballad singer sung up and down the streets ribald rhymes made in reproach of the late Commonwealth and all those worthies that therein endeavoured the people's freedom and happiness."[77] Samson's enemies come to "stare" at his "affliction" (lines 112–13): in 1660, according to Lucy Hutchinson, a gloating Colonel Monck came with his wife to Lambeth House, where the regicides were being held, and "caused them to be brought down, only to stare at them; which was such a barbarism for that man who had betrayed so many poor men to death and misery ... to glut his bloody eyes with beholding them in their bondage, as no story can parallel the inhumanity."[78] When in May the regicide John Desborough was brought into captivity he was jeered by boys lining the streets and chanting "Fanatic, fanatic!"[79] Milton himself, like Samson, had to endure in full measure his "foes' derision" (line 366). Pamphlets rejoiced in the overthrow of the writer whose boasts of Puritan triumph and whose scorn of the defeated Royalists had been noised across Europe. A placard described his blindness as a punishment for writing the tracts which

---

[74] Parker, *Milton*, 1: 568, 973.

[75] Ludlow, *Voyce*, pp. 124, 151, 195; Ludlow, "Voyce," pp. 1052, 1063, 1082, 1192, 1197.

[76] *Speeches*, p. 41.   [77] Hutchinson, *Memoirs*, p. 227.   [78] *Ibid.*, p. 232.

[79] Richard L. Greaves, *Deliver Us From Evil: The Radical Underground in Britain, 1660–1663* (New York, 1986), p. 30.

Parliament now ordered to be burned[80] – just as Samson's enemies
say "How well / Are come upon him his deserts" (lines 204–05).
Soon after 1660 there would become fashionable "not only the
jeering of godliness and godly men, but the histrionical acting of the
zeal and affection" of godly ministers "by way of mockery and
derision upon stageplays." The regicides condemned in April 1662,
who feared to seem to "die like fools," had to suffer at their
executions the taunts of a Lord and a courtier, "by way of derision."[81]

Those regicides – John Barkstead, Miles Corbet, and John Okey –
had fled to the Continent in 1660. They owed their deaths to the
subtle and ruthless coup of George Downing, Okey's former chaplain.
Downing, who had been Cromwell's agent in Holland in the 1650s
and was Charles II's in the 1660s, lured the exiles to Delft, kidnapped
them, and sent them to England. By his cunning and bullying he
secured the complicity of the Dutch government, which was
traditionally committed to sheltering political exiles but which, like
the Royalist party, had fought a bitter war with the godly of
England.[82] The saints would never forgive the Dutch treachery of
1662 in yielding up the regicides. There is a striking similarity
between Downing's tactics toward the Dutch and the methods used
toward Dalila by the Philistines, who, she reports,

> came in person,
> Solicited, commanded, threatened, urged,
> Adjured by all the bonds of civil duty
> And of religion, pressed how just it was,
> How honourable, how glorious to entrap
> A common enemy, who had destroyed
> Such numbers of our nation.   (lines 851–57)

Samson tells Dalila that "If aught against my life / Thy country
sought of thee, it sought unjustly, / Against the law of nature, law of
nations" (lines 888–90): Ludlow records that the regicides were
seized in Holland contrary to all "laws ... of nature or nations."[83]

Ludlow writes of the "lust and rage" with which the Cavaliers
pursued their "prey" among the saints and regicides;[84] Sidney of the
"lust and rage" of Charles II against men "who had been the most
worthy and successful instruments in our deliverance";[85] Vane of the

---

[80] Parker, *Milton*, 1: 568–69, 571.   [81] *Speeches*, pp. 6, 10, 24.

[82] Catterall, "Sir George Downing," remains the best account of this episode.

[83] Ludlow, *Voyce*, pp. 297–98. Here as elsewhere Ludlow reproduces words from the
martyrological pamphlet literature published in England during 1660–62 and sent out to
him in Switzerland.   [84] *Ibid.*, p. 150.   [85] Sidney, "Court Maxims," p. 203.

"rage and indignation of the world and powers of it" against the victims of the Restoration.[86] In *The Ready and Easy Way* Milton had noticed "how open and unbounded" was "the insolence and rage" of the Royalists.[87] The Chorus tells the same story: the "violent men" who "support / Tyrannic power" are "raging to pursue/ The righteous and all such as honour truth" (lines 1273-76). Happily, in the Restoration as in the poem, God will avenge His servant. Just as Samson's triumph brings down Dagon's temple "Upon the heads" of the Philistines (line 1652, cf. line 1589), so Vane's chaplain predicts that the "mischief" of the Royalists "shall return upon their own heads,"[88] Ludlow that God "will certainly ... bring down vengeance upon their heads."[89] Ludlow and Vane subscribed to the saintly commonplace of the 1660s, that "the blood of the saints ... cries out for vengeance." God, claimed Vane, "hath the weapons of vengeance in readiness."[90] Those weapons would be deployed, the saints knew, when the Royalists, by glorying in their wickedness and in blood, had filled up the measure of their iniquity.[91] Sidney says that the Royalists are "ripening themselves for destruction";[92] Ludlow that God's anger will culminate in the "destruction of His enemies";[93] Milton's Semichorus that the Philistines "Unweetingly importuned / Their own destruction" (lines 1680-81). Like the Philistines, the Royalists were so foolish as to "resist" God's "uncontrollable intent" (lines 1753-54). For the saints knew that although God, for His own purposes, may sometimes prosper the wicked, He does so only for a season. Samson is confident that Dagon will be humiliated "ere long" (line 468), an assertion welcomed by Manoa as a "prophecy," "for God, / Nothing more certain, will not long defer / To vindicate the glory of his name" (lines 473-75). Just so is Vane's chaplain sure that God will overthrow the Cavaliers "ere long";[94] just so does Sidney proclaim that God "will not long delay his appointed vengeance";[95] just so does Ludlow await the approaching hour when God will act "for the vindicating of His honour."[96]

In that expectation Ludlow records the "continued prodigies"[97] that the saints were so eager to detect in the 1660s and to interpret as

[86] Vane, *Two Treatises,* p. 2.   [87] Milton, *Prose,* 7: 463.
[88] Sykes, *Life of Vane,* p. 138. See Psalm 7. 16.   [89] Ludlow, *Voyce,* p. 208.
[90] Vane, *Two Treatises,* p. 2.
[91] Ludlow, *Voyce,* p. 143, and Ludlow "Voyce," pp. 1079, 1136; Sidney, "Court Maxims," pp. 78, 195, 200.   [92] *Ibid.,* p. 78.   [93] Ludlow, *Voyce,* p. 127.
[94] Sykes, *Life of Vane,* p. 109.   [95] Sidney, "Court Maxims," p. 195.
[96] Ludlow, *Voyce,* p. 115.   [97] *Ibid.,* p. 294.

evidence of divine wrath upon their enemies. He is particularly struck
by a prodigy which ruined the dinner held in Westminster Hall on
the evening of Charles II's coronation, that "superstitious ceremony," as Ludlow calls it, "of anointing their idol." Ludlow is
always repelled by the "feasting and carousing" of Charles II's
Court.[98] In *Samson Agonistes* the Philistines, on the day of their
destruction, "their hearts" filled "with mirth, high cheer, and
wine," "turned" to their "sports" (lines 1613–14). Amidst the
merriment of Charles II's dinner, the courtiers indulge the taste for
entertainment by (as Ludlow informs us) "riders" which they share
with Milton's Philistines (line 1324). "The champion Mr.
Dimmock," Ludlow reports, "armed *de cap à pied*, enters on
horseback, challenging to fight with any person who should deny
Charles Stuart to be lawful king of England," an invitation
comparable with Harapha's challenge to Samson. The sequel has its
resemblances too. As in Milton's poem, so in Restoration England,
God finds ways to make His purposes apparent, at least to those
willing to comprehend them. In Milton's poem, the "deliverance" of
the Israelites is accomplished when the roof falls on the Philistines'
heads "with burst of thunder" (line 1651). Charles II's dinner,
reports Ludlow:

was not half ended, before this mock king was enforced to rise and run away
to Whitehall, by reason of the unheard-of thunder, lightning, and rain;
which though his own flatterers profanely applied to the greatening of their
solemnity, as if heaven itself expressed its joy thereat by the discharge of their
cannon, yet others, more understanding in the dispensations of the Lord,
supposed it rather a testimony from heaven against the wickedness of those
that would not only that he should rule over them, but were willing to make
them a captain to lead them into Egyptian bondage; from which the Lord
by his providence plainly spake his desire to have delivered them.[99]

III

Samson's "dreadful" and "dearly-bought revenge" (lines 1591,
1660) appeases God's "wrath" toward the Philistines (line 1683) and
His "ire" toward Samson (line 520). Milton's writings had always
displayed an appetite for vengeance.[100] Yet we cannot reach the
"understanding" of God's "dispensations" which Ludlow urges

[98] Ludlow, "Voyce," p. 1271.
[99] Ludlow, *Voyce*, pp. 286–87; see also p. 294, and Ludlow "Voyce," pp. 1237, 1260–61, 1387.
[100] See Hugh Trevor-Roper, "Milton in Politics," in *Catholics, Anglicans and Puritans* (1987),
pp. 231–82, p. 280.

merely by examining His punishment of His enemies. We need to grasp the benevolence of His intentions toward His afflicted ones. That benevolence can be hard to credit, as Samson finds. In *Paradise Lost* Milton sought to "assert eternal providence, and justify the ways of God to men." There he wanted to refute the Calvinist dogma which turns the Fall into an act of divine tyranny, and to demonstrate the justice and the wonder of God's scheme of salvation. In *Samson Agonistes*, too, Milton insists, with his Chorus, that "Just are the ways of God, / And justifiable to men" (lines 293–94). This time he seeks to demonstrate the benevolence of providence amidst the sufferings of His servants in Restoration England. Milton addresses those "who doubt his ways not just" (line 300). Samson doubts, or is on the edge of doubting. He struggles not to "call in doubt / Divine prediction" (lines 43–44), or to "quarrel with the will / Of highest dispensation, which herein / Haply had ends above my reach to know" (lines 60–62). Yet the "hornets" of Samson's "restless thoughts" "rush upon" him (lines 19–21). "Why" and "wherefore," he asks, did God select him for "great exploits," for the deliverance of his nation, only to cast him into deepest humiliation and despair (lines 23, 30–32, 85)? Samson's "sense of heaven's desertion" (line 632) leaves him outside "the list of them that hope" (line 647).

It is, in Puritan terms, a terrible statement. To despair of God's providence is to despair of the faith which alone can save us. "To murmur against God's verdict, and resist his doom," Vane reminded himself as he surveyed the cataclysm of the Restoration, "is to become adversaries to God, and to betray our country."[101] Yet in one respect, at least, Samson has grasped more than his advisers. The Chorus, and Manoa, think that Samson's punishment exceeds the crime (lines 368–72, 691), but Samson warns his father to "Appoint not heavenly disposition," for "Nothing of all these evils hath befallen me / But justly; I myself have brought them on, / Sole author I, sole cause" (lines 372–75). Vane and other regicides accepted that God had punished them "justly."[102] Samson traces his trespass, and his subsequent failure to deliver his people, to his "impotence of mind, in body strong" (line 52). He has failed because he lacks "wisdom" or "virtue" proportionate to his "strength" (lines 54, 173). Milton had earlier levelled the same charge against the English people to explain their inability to grasp the opportunity

---

[101] *Tryal*, p. 119; cf. Worden, "Providence and Politics," p. 79.
[102] *Tryal*, p. 120; *Speeches*, pp. 68, 84.

for liberty which the heroic victories of the civil war had handed to them.[103] Ludlow concurred: God "put a prize into our hands, which had we wisdom we might have made a wonderful improvement of."[104]

The saints of the Restoration must come to terms with their past and with their failures and, like Samson, "Repent the sin" (line 504, cf. line 1376).[105] Milton had long questioned the "fitness" of the English for godly reformation, and had concluded that they were "fitter to be led back into their own servitude."[106] Ludlow too had decided that the nation "seemed not to be fitted for that glorious work."[107] Yet, unlike Samson, Ludlow is "in the list of them that hope." For, he writes, "when God hath humbled a people and fitted them for himself," when He has "purified" them in "the furnace of affliction," "making them willing to be abused for him, He will certainly lift them up and bring them to honour."[108] Samson, lifted up, at the last restores "honour" to Israel (line 1715).

The saints, like the "saints" in *Samson Agonistes* (line 1288), will be "delivered." The verb "deliver" runs through the saintly literature of the Restoration as it runs through Milton's poem. But the saints will need one virtue above all: patience, the quality of those who, like Milton, "only stand and wait." Samson's blindness, thinks the Chorus, is likely to "number" him with "those / Whom patience finally must crown" (lines 1295–96). Patience is

> more oft the exercise
> Of saints, the trial of their fortitude,
> Making them each his own deliverer,
> And victor over all
> That tyranny or fortune can inflict.   (lines 1287–91)

Ludlow repeatedly tells his kindred spirits that "this is the day of the patience of the Lord and his saints."[109] Vane's advice to the saints recalls the experience of Milton's Samson: they must be "patiently waiting till God's time come wherein He will open the prison doors, either by death, or some other way."[110]

---

[103] Milton, *Prose*, 5: 449–51; Blair Worden, "Milton's Republicanism and the Tyranny of Heaven," in Gisela Bock, Quentin Skinner and Maurizio Viroli, eds., *Machiavelli and Republicanism* (Cambridge, 1990), pp. 225–45, especially pp. 233–35.

[104] Ludlow, *Voyce*, p. 307, cf. p. 248.   [105] See *Tryal*, pp. 119–20; *Speeches*, p. 68.

[106] Milton, *Prose*, 3: 581.   [107] Ludlow, *Voyce*, p. 149.

[108] *Ibid.*, pp. 11, 115, and Ludlow, "Voyce," p. 1082.

[109] Ludlow, *Voyce*, pp. 11–12, and Ludlow, "Voyce," p. 1019. See also Milton, *Prose*, 6: 662–63.   [110] Vane, *Two Treatises*, p. 98.

The duty of the saints to "wait upon God," in "a waiting posture," was well known to Puritans. To attune oneself to God's timetable was an essential step in the saint's submission to His sovereignty. He must learn – as Samson does – to act in the Lord's time, not man's.[111] Ludlow, wondering how the saints could or should seek to bring down the restored regime, asks God to "give us wisdom to know when to go forward and when to stand still." He recommends a middle course, so that "by making haste we may not strengthen the hand of the enemy, nor by standing still neglect the opportunity He puts into our hands, but that, being on our watch tower, and living by faith, we may see our duty so plainly, that when the Lord's time is come we may" – like Samson at the last – "up and be doing."[112]

Some saints and commonwealthmen thought that the hour of "deliverance" was "very near," that it would come "in a very little time," in "but a little moment." At other times they acknowledged that it "was not yet come," that God "seems to permit the scales to continue," that "the Lord's people seem as yet unworthy" of deliverance, and that consequently "there is more of the bitter cup" of divine punishment left "behind for his people to drink of."[113] Yet was such speculation about the divine timetable legitimate? One "sin" of the godly of the Puritan Revolution had been to presume too much upon providence, to pry into its secrets, into those "ends" that may be "above" Samson's "reach to know." *Samson Agonistes* confounds every human calculation that is made in it, and exposes man's "ever-failing trust / In mortal strength" (lines 348–49). The Puritan God emphasizes His sovereignty by the suddenness and unexpectedness of His mercies. Oliver Cromwell thought God's dispensations best "when they have not been forecast, but sudden providences."[114] Vane thought that the "revival" of God's cause would be "sudden,"[115] as it is in Milton's poem.

God's sovereignty is demonstrated in other ways too. Ludlow, writing about the fate of the regicides, remarks on the Lord's tendency "to show His prerogative, and that He can when he pleaseth work by unlikely, yea contrary means."[116] The God of *Samson Agonistes* has an inseparable adjunct of prerogative, the authority to

---

[111] Worden, "Providence and Politics," pp. 64–66.   [112] Ludlow, *Voyce,* pp. 309–10.

[113] See e.g., *ibid.,* p. 11, and Ludlow, "Voyce," pp. 1139, 1260. Samson "bitterly hast ... paid, and still art paying" (line 432).   [114] Worden, "Providence and Politics," p. 92.

[115] *Substance of what Sir Henry Vane Intended,* pp. 5–6.   [116] Ludlow, *Voyce,* p. 295.

"dispense" with His own laws (line 314), a privilege which explains His decision to wed Samson to a Philistine. The Chorus rebukes men who

> would confine the Interminable,
> And tie him to his own prescript,
> Who made our laws to bind us, not himself,
> And hath full right to exempt
> Whomso it pleases him by choice
> From national obstriction.   (lines 307–12)

God likes to dispense with all the rules that lead men to award glory to themselves rather than to Him. In the battles of the English civil wars He would pointedly place His followers at an initial dis-advantage, to prove that the ensuing victory was His alone. Thus during the battle of Dunbar in 1650, when defeat stared Cromwell's army in the face, God did what in Milton's poem He does with Samson: He "stepped out of heaven to raise those who were even as dead, and to judge His adversaries."[117] In the poem it is God who "Puts invincible might" into "the hands of" the "deliverer," and whose intervention enables the "oppressed" to overcome men who "rage" against the "righteous" who "honour truth" (lines 1269–71, 1276). It was upon His elect that the Puritan God bestowed such privileges. The contrast drawn by the Chorus between God's "even" distribution of "providence" in the usual exercise of His sovereignty, and His "various" or "contrarious" handling of "such as thou hast solemnly elected" (lines 668–71, 678), corresponds to a conventional Puritan distinction between the "general" providence which rules mankind at large and the "special" providence that watches over the elect.[118] Samson experiences extremities of fortune because God "hath of his special favour," "Under his special eye," raised him as Israel's "deliverer" (lines 273–74, 636). The extremities experienced by the Puritan saints were explained in the same way.

But what would the saints and commonwealthmen of Restoration England contribute to their own deliverance? There were those, Algernon Sidney among them, who argued for armed resistance. On the same side was the Dissenting minister Nicholas Lockyer, who claimed that "there wants but the jawbone of an ass" to overthrow the Restoration monarchy.[119] Yet the main thrust of saintly literature after 1660 warns against resistance, and advises the godly to "sit

---

[117] Worden, "Providence and Politics," pp. 68–69.   [118] *Ibid.*, p. 60.
[119] Ludlow, "Voyce," p. 1079. See Milton, *Prose*, 1: 859.

still" or "stand still," to "make not haste", not to "resist" or use unlawful "means."[120] The saints, thought Vane, should steer clear of "popular tumults," "conspiracies," and "insurrection."[121] Vane, and Ludlow in his more resigned moods, believe what Samson in his despair has concluded. Samson thinks that his own role as divine instrument is past, that "the strife / With me hath end," that God will now fight Dagon not through human intermediaries but directly (lines 460–67). Vane agrees. He judges that God has resolved "to take the business into His own hands, and to put forth the power of His wrath by heavenly instruments, forasmuch as earthly ones (as you have seen) have proved ineffectual." So we must "depend upon God for the avenging of His people, even when all human ability to perform it is vanished." The saints, having failed in the world, should be "retiring into the life of your head and root, the life that is hid with Christ in God."[122] For Ludlow, too, "the weapons which the Lord hath appointed for the destruction of Antichrist" are now "not carnal but spiritual."[123]

Yet Samson is proved wrong. God turns to His chosen instrument once more, for the act that will give meaning to his whole life. There would, of course, be no warrant for taking Milton's *dénouement* to be a program or argument for political action in the 1660s. We would have as much or as little justification for thinking of it as an escapist fantasy. The one calculation we can safely make is that calculation is impotent. We may hope or believe that God, in some unpredictable way, will deliver us, through us, but He will do so only when we have surrendered our own presumptions and learned to wait upon Him.

Yet if *Samson Agonistes* is no call to resistance, it is far from ruling resistance out. Samson's terrorist raids on his Philistine masters, we learn, were "just" (line 237). He scorns a political obedience that would "displease / God for the fear of man" (lines 1373–74). Dalila, maintains Samson, owed no obedience to her "country" when it was governed by "an impious crew / Of men conspiring to uphold their state / By worse than hostile deeds" (lines 891–93), a description close to those given by Ludlow and Sidney of what they took to be the usurping regime of the 1660s – and reminiscent of Milton's description of Samson in the *First Defence* as a rebel against "his

[120] See e.g., Ludlow, *Voyce,* p. 79; Ludlow, "Voyce," pp. 1049, 1211; Sykes, *Life of Vane,* p. 117; Vane, *Two Treatises,* pp. 3, 92; Tibbutt, "John Okey," pp. 160–61.
[121] Sykes, *Life of Vane,* pp. 112–13.　　　[122] Vane, *Two Treatises,* pp. 2–3.
[123] Ludlow, "Voyce," p. 1248.

country's tyrants," whom Samson had a duty to slay even though the majority of his fellow-citizens "did not balk at slavery."[124] Some critics have believed that the Samson of the poem is presented with a series of "temptations" which foreshadow the meek suffering of Christ in *Paradise Regained*. But the temptation which Samson resists, if temptation it is, is to turn the other cheek. Harapha offers less a temptation than a provocation. In rising to it, Samson becomes his old self.

The poem addresses the issue of resistance from another angle too. Milton had long been interested in the Protestant tradition which argued that, while in normal circumstances the only legitimate acts of resistance against monarchy are those sanctioned by inferior magistrates, a special dispensation might be claimed by a private individual who has a special call from God – and who thus ceases to be "private."[125] Samson, as he indignantly tells Harapha, has been "no private but a person raised / With strength sufficient and command from heaven / To free my country" (lines 1211–13). He identifies the moments to fulfill God's role for him from "intimate impulse" (line 223), from "Divine impulsion prompting" (lines 422), from the "rousing motions in me" (lines 1382) by which he is "persuaded inwardly that this was from God" ("Argument," lines 72–73). His position corresponds to an antinomian streak in the saints, which is to be found even among those of them who professed to be horrified by antinomianism. Edmund Ludlow, whom we have seen questioning Thomas Harrison's decision to give himself up as a sacrifice in 1660, nonetheless suspended judgment, on the ground that Harrison had been moved by "a more than ordinary impulse of spirit."[126] Later Ludlow faced a similar dilemma in appraising the action of a Frenchman who, without premeditation, had run his sword through a "Romish priest" in Paris while the priest was celebrating mass. Though troubled by the breach of law and of conventional morality, Ludlow was impressed by the assassin's testimony that he had acted "as moved in his spirit" to "bear that witness against the idolatry." Even under the terrors of execution,

---

[124] Milton, *Prose*, 4(1.): 402.

[125] Martin Dzelzainis, *John Milton. Political Writings* (Cambridge, 1991), pp. xiii–xv. But under the Commonwealth, at least, the argument had troubled Milton. Dzelzainis emphasizes Milton's informed disagreement with it in 1649. In the first *Defence* (Milton, *Prose*, 4(1.): 402) Milton perhaps still had doubts, for he was then apparently uncertain whether Samson's destruction of the temple had been "prompted by God or by his own valour."

[126] Ludlow, *Voyce*, p. 126.

records Ludlow, the assassin "continued fixed in his testimony, rejoicing that the Lord honoured him to die as a martyr for His cause." So "I dare not judge the person, not knowing what extraordinary call he had" from heaven.[127]

IV

Samson is much closer to Milton and to Milton's cause in the poem than in its sources. Samson, "himself an army" (line 346), whose "locks, / That of a nation armed the strength contained" (lines 1493–94), is in part the poet, in part the cause for which the New Model Army had fought. Milton's relationship to the fellow members of his cause is admittedly a problem. By 1660 he looks to have become a party of one. Yet whatever mistakes he took his colleagues to have made, the regicide had been, for him, a "glorious and heroic deed," a "Matchless deed,"[128] instigated by an army which, no less than Samson, had been "matchless in might" (line 178). Why had so glorious a cause collapsed?

In apportioning the blame – Samson's or England's – the poem makes a clear distinction. In the Bible, Samson is a judge, a ruler of Israel. Milton's version sets Samson apart from Israel's rulers, in a passage which establishes parallels between then and now. Blame, explains Samson, must be identified on two separate levels. That the Israelites remain in servitude is a "fault I take not on me, but transfer / On Israel's governors and heads of tribes" (lines 241–42). In 1660, the ruling Parliament brought back the exiled regime and resolved to prosecute the regicides, who had to decide on what terms, if any, to give themselves up. How similar is Parliament's conduct to that of the "men of Judah" in the poem who "beset [Samson] round" and entice him to surrender "on some conditions" before they yield him as a "prey" to the Philistines who have "Entered Judea." Just as the commonwealthmen had yearned in early 1660 for an armed rising that would prevent the Restoration, so Samson observes that Israel would still be free "Had Judah that day joined, or one whole tribe" (lines 251–65). Instead the Israelites surrender Samson "As a league-breaker" (lines 1184, 1189, 1209), just as the Presbyterians who proceeded against the regicides in 1660 took the vilest offence of their victims to have been their breach of the Solemn League and

<hr/>

[127] Ludlow, "Voyce," pp. 1248–49.   [128] Milton, *Prose,* 3: 212, 344.

Covenant. Israel's governors, in repudiating Samson, spurned the "great acts which God had done" through him, spurned the "Deliverance offered," and "persisted deaf" (lines 243–49). How often had Milton urged England's rulers to seize the opportunity for "deliverance," and how deaf those rulers had been.

Yet, as well as the fault of Israel's governors, there is, more centrally to the story and to its concerns, Samson's fault: the fault of a man "Designed," as Milton knew himself to be, "for great exploits" (line 32). Like Samson, the saints of the Restoration must look into their own hearts, and ask Samson's terrible question: "what if all foretold" – all the apocalyptic prophecies to which Milton and others had so confidently subscribed in 1641–2 – "Had been fulfilled but through mine own default" (lines 44–45)?

In dedication to God's service, Milton, like Samson, "grew up" "Abstemious" (line 637). In the Puritan Revolution he suspended his poetic ambitions for the greater part of two decades, in the hope of guiding the nation, through his prose, toward deliverance and reformation. The careers both of Samson and of Milton illustrate the tendency of "nations grown corrupt..."

> to despise, or envy, or suspect
> Whom God hath of his special favour raised
> As their deliverer; if he [the deliverer] aught begin,
> How frequent to desert him, and at last
> To heap ingratitude on worthiest deeds?   (lines 268, 272–76)

"Corruption," in Samson's mind and in the minds of Milton and his fellow commonwealthmen, is indissolubly associated with "effeminacy," which enthrones passion over reason in the sovereignty of the soul. Like Samson, the English of the Restoration are "Effeminately vanquished" (line 562). Like Samson, too, they have been "Ensnared" (line 365): ensnared above all by George Monck, whose announcement as he moved south that he intended to restore only the Rump, not the king, outwitted the godly as cunningly and decisively as Dalila's "peal of words" "vanquished" Samson (line 235).

Milton in the spring of 1660 had proposed that Monck be made king.[129] Should he not have known better? Had he not, like Samson, been "warned by oft experience" (line 382)? After all, he had been deceived before. In 1653–54, unlike Ludlow or Sidney or Vane,

---

[129] *Ibid.*, 8: 203, 482. The saints were bitterly conscious of their weakness in having succumbed to another verbal deception too, the promise of clemency in the Declaration of Breda: see Hutchinson, *Memoirs*, p. 234; *Tryal*, p. 119.

unlike Bradshaw or Overton, he had supported Cromwell's usurpation. By 1659 he had more than learned his lesson. Now the
Protectorate seemed to him to have been a "scandalous night of
interruption."[130] Had his service under it been for him what Samson's
"former" and degenerate "servitude" had been: "ignoble, /
Unmanly, ignominious, infamous, / True slavery" (lines 416–18)?

   We can only speculate. Yet speculation can have its value. Did
"restless thoughts" "rush upon" Milton in the Restoration? Did he,
like Samson, experience a "sense of heaven's desertion", "As one
past hope" (line 120), and feel "cast ... off as never known" by a
God who

>   to those cruel enemies,
> Whom I by his appointment had provoked,
> Left me all helpless with the irreparable loss
> Of sight, reserved alike to be repeated
> The subject of their cruelty, or scorn?   (lines 641–46)

When Milton had considered (perhaps in 1652) how his light was
spent, he had been tempted to "murmur" against providence.
"Patience" had quelled that incipient protest – but for how long? In
the sonnet "Upon his Blindness" (perhaps written around 1655) he
reflected again on the providence that had afflicted him. This time he
seemed more confident: he was able to "argue not / Against heaven's
hand or will" because his "conscience" assured him that he had
become blind through writing "in liberty's defence." But what use
could such a reflection be in 1660, when his writings in liberty's
defence were derided or burned?

   Yet if there may be a parallel of despair, there may also be a
parallel of hope. Samson's wait upon God has its correspondence in
Milton's literary life. In Milton's "late spring," we remember, "no
bud or blossom showeth," "And inward ripeness doth much less
appear."[131] In *The Reason of Church Government* in 1642 he registers,
like Samson, God's gift of an impulse of the spirit: "an inward
prompting" which has informed the poet of immortal gifts to serve
God and country.[132] Yet in the Puritan Revolution he is left to "stand
and wait." Eventually, "beginning late" (*PL*, 9.26), he writes
Paradise Lost, and justifies the ways of God to men. If he really writes
its central section amidst the national catastrophe and personal

---

[130] Milton, *Prose*, 7: 274; Austin Woolrych, "Milton and Cromwell: 'A Short but Scandalous
Night of Interruption,'" in M. Lieb and J. T. Shawcross, eds., *Achievements of the Left Hand*
(Boston, 1977), pp. 185–218.   [131] Sonnett VII.   [132] Milton, *Prose*, 1: 810.

danger and affliction of 1660, then the achievement, like Samson's, is one to defy human calculation. Samson's locks have grown again. Like Samson, Milton proves not to be "useless":

> And which is best and happiest yet, all this
> With God not parted from him, as was feared,
> But favouring and assisting to the end.   (lines 1718–20)[133]

---

[133] I have claimed that *Samson Agonistes* was written after the Restoration. It was first published, together with *Paradise Regained*, in 1670–01. If I am right in detecting the influence of the trials of regicides in 1662, and of the literature which followed those trials, in the poem, then it cannot have been written before that year. There are no lines which seem to me to demand to be explained with reference to events later than 1662 (although some critics have detected allusions to the Anglo-Dutch war of 1665–67). But we could not properly argue that the poem must have been written immediately or shortly after the events which are so forcefully present in it.

CHAPTER 7

Milton, Dryden, and the politics of literary controversy

Steven N. Zwicker

I

Questions of influence – of imitation and adaptation, of pedagogy and admiration – exercise a steady interest for students of literary relations; they seem especially appropriate when posed to relations among writers who were contemporaries, perhaps acquaintances or friends, intimates or collaborators: Eliot and Pound, Ford and Conrad, Coleridge and Wordsworth, Swift and Pope, Milton and Dryden. But recent work on the relations between authors and among texts has so complicated our notion of influence that the word itself seems slightly worn. Indeed, the idea of influence has come to imply models of acquisition and contest that subsume and all but exclude imitation and admiration. Without denying the older language I want here to consider "contest" as the shadow under which negotiations between Milton and Dryden took place, to suggest that while adaptation and admiration describe aspects of Dryden's encounter with Milton – surely admiration inflects the lines that Dryden wrote for the frontispiece portrait of the 1688 *Paradise Lost*[1] – it was contestation, perhaps envy and denial, that rather more powerfully determined Milton's response to Dryden.

Notions of literary dominance and strong writing, perhaps even literary histories of a slightly Whiggish cast,[2] have so long determined

---

[1] "Three Poets, in three distant Ages born, / Greece, Italy, and England did adorn. / The First in loftiness of thought Surpass'd; / The Next in Majesty; in both the Last. / The force of Nature cou'd no farther goe: / To make a Third she joynd the former two"; Dryden, *Poems*, 2:540. Hugh Macdonald, *John Dryden: A Bibliography of Early Editions* (Oxford, 1939), p. 48, notes that the epigram was first published anonymously and that Dryden's name was attached when the epigram was reprinted in *Miscellany Poems* in 1716.

[2] Richard Garnett and Edmund Gosse's *English Literature, An Illustrated Record*, 4 vols. (1903–06) is fairly typical of the Whiggish mode: "A writer like Dryden, responsible for the movement of literature in the years immediately succeeding the Restoration, had a grave

our reading of relations between Milton and Dryden that it takes a special effort to imagine the possibility of literary anxiety moving in more than one direction. We are ready enough to concede the political anxiety that Milton felt after 25 May 1660, and we have become increasingly attentive to the ways in which political anxiety and resistance are written into *Paradise Lost*.[3] But having acknowledged Milton's political quietism and his necessary revision of the politics of election after 1660, we often assume that Milton swept the literary field, that the massive self-confidence of the opening lines of *Paradise Lost*, the poem's manifest ambition and majesty, determined the poet's dominance over the whole of later seventeenth-century literary endeavor. The immediate reception and subsequent printing history of *Paradise Lost* deny such accounts of literary relations in these decades; and yet knowing how the story would eventually be told, we find it difficult to keep that knowledge at bay. Biographical sketches only confirm the familiar contours of the story. In such accounts the protagonist is an aging republican beached on the shores of an alien culture, writing poetry that casts into doubt the very premise of Stuart Court culture; the antagonist is the ambitious new man, aiming at success and sinecure from that Court, but nervously acknowledging while sidestepping the master's great achievement. What better confirms the model than Dryden's, shall we say ridiculous, adaptation of *Paradise Lost* as a rhymed heroic drama?

This story is a staple of our literary histories; it has been told often, and always to the same effect. In its sharpest renditions not only are we led to discover the diminution of epic into opera, but Milton's spiritual grandeur and generic ambitions are made everywhere to reflect on the laureate's servitude, his partisan allegories and satires, his fulsome prefaces, his timeserving odes and panegyrics. Such accounts present an anxious Dryden trying to maneuver bits of Milton into strategic corners of his own verse, and *Paradise Lost* is made to hover luminously, or perhaps ominously, over Dryden's

---

task before him. He was face to face with a bankruptcy; he had to float a new concern on the spot where the old had sunken. That uniformity of manner, that lack of salient and picturesque individuality, which annoy the hasty reader, were really unavoidable. Dryden and Tillotson, Locke and Otway, with their solicitude for lucidity of language, rigidity of form, and closeness of reasoning, were laying anew the foundations upon which literature might once more be built;" 3: 174.

[3] Hill, *Milton* was crucial to this revaluation, but see as well, among a number of more recent works: Hill, *Experience of Defeat*; Andrew Milner, *John Milton and the English Revolution* (1981); and Mary Ann Radzinowicz, "The Politics of *Paradise Lost*," in Kevin Sharpe and Steven Zwicker, eds., *Politics of Discourse* (Berkeley and Los Angeles, 1987), pp. 204–29.

whole career, the monument that blocked his own epic ambitions. In the renditions of Dryden's visit to Milton, we are asked to look on as the blind sage politely but contemptuously allows the eager neophyte – now in fact aged forty-one and both laureate and historiographer royal – "to tagge his verses."[4] Nor is the story an invention of our time; at its origin we might be surprised to find Dryden himself: "This Man Cuts us All Out," or so Jonathan Richardson reported of Dryden's response to *Paradise Lost*.[5]

If this were the only construction to be made of their relations, the story would hardly be worth another recitation; perhaps a detail or two might be adjusted, another citing of *Paradise Lost* might be added to our store of borrowings and allusions.[6] But without reconceiving the outlines of the story, without adjusting the model to allow contestation and ambivalence running in both directions, it is familiar enough to forbid retelling. What I propose is to reconceive the story by narrating it, at first, from what might have been Milton's point of view. Like the familiar version of their relations, this is a story of influence and anxiety; it begins, however, with Milton's nerves. And the anxiety of influence, since it has been told of Dryden, I want to attribute to Milton, to suggest why Dryden might have made Milton nervous, where in Milton's work the anxiety might be confronted, and how it might have shaped his masterpiece *Paradise Regained*. For I want to suggest that *Paradise Regained* is a response to something other and more formidable than Thomas Ellwood's "Thou hast said much here of Paradise Lost, but what hast thou to say of Paradise Found?"[7] Milton not only orchestrated a variety of sacred themes, rewriting the Book of Job and the Gospels, but he also wished to engage, to question, and to controvert the formidable literary challenge posed by the new drama and the astonishing career of its foremost apologist, theorist, and practitioner, John Dryden. Milton shaped his brief epic as an answer to and a repudiation of the heroic drama: its rhyming couplets, its bombast and cant, its

---

[4] The story originates with Aubrey; see Helen Darbishire, ed., *The Early Lives of Milton* (1932), p. 7; and commentary by Morris Freedman, "Dryden's 'Memorable Visit' to Milton," *HLQ* 18 (1955): 99–108. Earl Miner also reviews the biographical and literary encounters, "Dryden's Admired Acquaintance, Mr. Milton," *Milton Studies*, ed. B. Rajan, 11 (1978): 3–27.

[5] J. Richardson, *Explanatory Notes and Remarks on Milton's "Paradise Lost"* (1734), pp. cxix–cxx.

[6] See, for example, David Hopkins, "Dryden's 'Baucis and Philemon' and *Paradise Lost*," *Notes and Queries* ns 29 (1982): 503–4, or Edward Sichi, Jr., "'A Crowd of Little Poets': Dryden's Use of Milton's Serpent in His *Aeneid*, II," *American Notes and Queries* 2 (1989): 94–97. [7] Masson, *Life of Milton*, 6: 496.

aristocratic code of virtue and honor, its spectacle and rhetoric, its scenes and stage machines, its exotic lands and erotic intrigues, its warring heroes and virgin queens, its exaltation of passion and elevation of empire. Milton conceived *Paradise Regained* as a drama in the form of an epic in order to display "deeds / Above heroic," while demonstrating what literary mode might best accommodate spiritual fortitude, what style might best express heroic virtue, and how heroic colloquy ought truly to sound. I want, that is, to readjust the story of literary relations in the late 1660s to allow the contestative force of *Paradise Regained* – its challenge to the form, style, and ethos of the heroic drama, to the theoretical defense of the form, and to Dryden's astonishing career as the central protagonist of a new literary culture, one that brought him commercial and critical success beyond anything that Milton had experienced or could now hope to achieve.

II

Of Milton's anxieties over the new drama and its defense, there can be no doubt.[8] It would be wrong to suggest that Milton had lost control over the tone of his headnote to *Paradise Lost*, but surely his remarks on rhyme have an odd and urgent ring;[9] and if Milton was defensive in 1668 as he prepared the remarks on blank verse and rhyme, it was with some reason.[10] Who among the English, Italian, or French epic poets had used blank verse? All had chosen rhyme. But consider Milton's language at the start of the note – "rhyme being no necessary adjunct or true ornament of poem or good verse, in longer works especially, but the invention of a barbarous age, to set off wretched matter and lame metre" – and observe the proud political gesture at the close, where Milton argues *Paradise Lost* as epic of "ancient liberty" and explicates that powerful term by glossing rhyme as "troublesome and modern bondage."[11] The extraordinary

---

[8] Morris Freedman in "Dryden's 'Memorable Visit'" first made this argument; see as well Jackson I. Cope, "*Paradise Regained*: Inner Ritual," *Milton Studies* 1 ed. James D. Simmonds (1969): 53–54. Cope alone among Milton critics proposes that *Paradise Regained* might be read as a response to the heroic drama.

[9] See the discussion of rhyme and republicanism in the 1668 headnote to *Paradise Lost* in David Norbrook's review of *The Faber Book of Political Verse*, ed. Tom Paulin, *London Review of Books* 8: 10 (3 July 1986), p. 7, and the subsequent exchange of letters between Norbrook and Craig Raine on this theme, *ibid.* 8: 12, 8: 13, 8: 15, 8: 16, 8: 20, 8: 22, and 9: 1.

[10] See William Riley Parker, *Milton: A Biography*, 2 vols. (Oxford, 1968), 2: 1108, n. 29.

[11] Milton, *Poems*, pp. 456–57.

combativeness of the headnote not only signals a sensitivity to genre and form but suggests as well that Milton had hold of a large cultural project in his repudiation of rhyme. Rhyme was a key term in the delineation of that project, but it was only one term. For what Milton attempts in the diffuse epic of 1667 and the brief epic of 1671 is a full definition and demonstration of heroic action and the literary forms best suited to its enactment and display.

In the prefatory note on verse, *Paradise Lost* is explicitly pitched into contest with classical and continental models, and yet more pointedly, it is positioned against a very powerful and articulate literary world identified by the discourse on rhyme.[12] But it is more than tone that surprises in the headnote; it is also the presence of the drama. In mapping the critical terrain for *Paradise Lost* we might well have expected Spenser, the Fletchers, Davenant, or Cowley, but Milton's concentration on rhyme, that key term in the defense of the new drama, reveals a particular and peculiar alignment, not with English epic poetry but with English blank verse tragedy. The odd skewing came about not because *Paradise Lost* is a blank verse *tragedy*, but because the poem is positioned in relation to its own literary culture, that of the mid- and late-1660s. The primary contexts that Milton summoned for *Paradise Lost* are scripture and classical poetry; but the inventions of a barbarous age also comprise a setting for *Paradise Lost*, one rather fractiously admitted by the headnote on verse.

The companion piece to the 1668 note on verse is the preface to the first issue of *Paradise Regained and Samson Agonistes* (1671). Although the note prefaces *Samson Agonistes*, it signals for the whole volume Milton's continuing engagement with the heroic drama: "This is mentioned to vindicate tragedy from the small esteem, or rather infamy, which in the account of many it undergoes at this day with other common interludes; happening through the poet's error of intermixing comic stuff with tragic sadness and gravity; or introducing trivial and vulgar persons, which by all judicious hath been counted absurd; and brought in without discretion, corruptly to gratify the people. And though ancient tragedy use no prologue, yet using sometimes in case of self-defence, or explanation, that which

---

[12] On the debate and its literary context see Arthur C. Kirsch, *Dryden's Heroic Drama* (Princeton, 1965), pp. 22–33; Eric Rothstein, *Restoration Tragedy* (Madison, 1967), pp. 29–40; and Robert D. Hume, *The Development of English Drama in the Late Seventeenth Century* (Oxford, 1976), pp. 172–73.

Martial calls an epistle; in behalf of this tragedy coming forth after the ancient manner, much different from what among us passes for best, thus much beforehand may be epistled ... "[13] What is then epistled is the modeling of verse and stanza on classical and Italian examples and some fairly routine remarks on the unities. *Paradise Regained* lacks a preface, but the 1668 preface to *Paradise Lost* and the note for *Samson Agonistes* function on behalf of *Paradise Regained*, announcing the presence of the heroic drama as a continuous literary context for Milton's late work.

The development of a new dramatic genre and, more generally, the reinvigoration of the stage dominated the production of literature and literary theory in the 1660s. The polemical verse of the mid-1660s predicts the genius of satire for the whole of Restoration culture, but for writers in the 1660s, the dominant form was the heroic drama. It was practiced, imitated, praised, defended, defined, and finally and ironically canonized in Buckingham's *Rehearsal*. Although the form was loosely identified with a group of aristocrats and courtiers – Sir Robert Howard, Sir William Davenant, and the Earl of Orrery – its hero was John Dryden. It was Dryden who theorized the form in a series of works beginning with *An Essay of Dramatic Poesy* (1668) and culminating in *An Essay of Heroic Plays* (1672), and it was Dryden whose work was most completely identified with the new drama through theatrical production and publication: *The Indian Queen* (1664/65); *The Indian Emperor* (1665/67); *Tyrannick Love; or, The Royal Martyr* (1669/70); *The Conquest of Granada* (1670/72); and *Aureng-Zebe* (1675/76).

It may be difficult from our distance to appreciate the impact of the heroic drama on courtly and popular culture in the first decade of the Restoration, but it is not difficult to imagine Milton's sensitivity to the new form. His interest in dramatic forms and themes was longstanding;[14] *Comus* and *Samson* witness the early and late public engagement and experimentation with theatrical forms, but the Trinity College manuscript in which Milton records schemes for the theater is also crucial. Thought to date from the early 1640s, the manuscript discovers Milton thinking on Old Testament tragedies, on New Testament theater, and on a number of British and Scottish topics. Milton identifies scriptural and national themes, but the notes

[13] Milton, *Poems*, p. 344.
[14] See John G. Demaray, *Milton's Theatrical Epic* (Cambridge, Mass., 1980), chapter 2, "Inconstant Theatrical Designs."

also display a vivid theatrical imagination: the severities of Greek choric tragedy but also a theater rather more luxurious in its deployment of scenes and machines – angels girt with flame; the burning and destruction of cities and temples; slaughter, battle, and mayhem; witchcraft and ghosts. The Trinity manuscript also reveals Milton's interest in theatrical music and song, hymns, masques, dances, and allegories. His heroes are drawn after the examples of God's servants; but Milton also imagines a rather more spectacular theater, centered in murder, lust, and mayhem, and figuring not only the defeat of tyrants and martyrdom of Christians, but as well scenes of usurpation, seduction, and betrayal.

Some of the dramas have biblical settings, but others are set in monasteries and nunneries, battlefields and castles where Milton imagines his casts in combat and intrigue, in revelry and in adulterous union. His heroes are warrior kings and princes; his heroines, noble ladies and ravished virgins; but we also see whores and concubines, and whole armies of Saxons, Angles, Northumbrians, and Danes. Milton drew from a number of sources, from Bede, Geoffrey of Monmouth, Holinshed, and Speed, as well as from myth and sacred history. But the shorthand multiplicity of these notes looks less like a considered plan for a historical drama than sketches for an epic theater. Although the settings do not quite rival the exotic realms of the Restoration epic theater, distance and antiquity are clear effects in Milton's notes; so too is the epic dimension of Milton's theater: love and honor are prominent among his themes, and heroic action is the aim of theatrical representation.

Here is Milton musing on epic theater set in Alfred's reign: "A Heroicall Poem may be founded somwhere in Alfreds reigne. especially at his issuing out of Edelingsey on the Danes. whose actions are wel like those of Ulysses."[15] Tragedy on the Greek model is among Milton's preoccupations, but just as clearly epic drama is another, a theater that would compact diffuse action, heighten the themes of virtue and honor, alternate and redeem love with combat. Such had been Milton's notions for an epic theater in the early 1640s; and such a theater was preeminent among the aims of the heroic drama as it was shaped by Dryden in theory and practice in the first decade of the Restoration. How else, then, could Milton have responded but with intense curiosity and competitiveness when a

[15] *The Works of John Milton*, ed. Frank A. Patterson *et al.*, 18 vols. (New York, 1938), 18: 243.

form suddenly appeared in the mid-1660s which claimed to do exactly what had preoccupied him in the 1640s and toward which he had made his own notes and plans? It is the very engagement signaled in the prefaces to *Paradise Lost* and *Samson Agonistes*, and in the construction of that heroic drama cast as brief epic, exploring and redefining the themes of love and empire, the nature of glory, the uses of wealth and wisdom, observing the unities, spare in style and severe in manner, which Milton published in 1671 under the name of *Paradise Regained*.

By the rather slow standards of literary evolution, the heroic drama looks like an instantaneous creation; but it was not produced full blown from Dryden's imagination. Dryden's theorizing of the genre began with the defense of rhyme for the stage in the dedication to *The Rival Ladies* (1664): rhyme offers the advantages of rapidity, grace, point, sweetness, and beauty; it "bounds and circumscribes the fancy"; without rhyme the imagination grows luxuriant.[16] The arguments are developed in *An Essay of Dramatic Poesy* (1668), but even in the dedication to *The Rival Ladies* the strength of the defense is surprising. What it lacks in 1664 is the assertion of a new dramatic idiom; and that comes with the *Essay*, the last quarter of which is devoted to a debate over the rival literary claims of rhyme and blank verse. Dryden's management of the argument in favor of rhyme is well known, as is the rivalry here begun with Sir Robert Howard which, throughout the 1660s, takes rhyme as its overt subject. For our immediate purposes, however, it is the connection that Dryden makes between rhyme and the *new* literary mode that presents the most sensitive issue, for that explicit declaration of modernity brings us to what must have been the pressure point for Milton.

In contending with that age of giants – Jonson, Fletcher, and Shakespeare – Dryden stakes his claim with the moderns: "either not to write at all, or to attempt some other way. There is no bays to be expected in their walks: *tentanda via est, qua me quoque possum tollere humo*."[17] The tag from Virgil might well remind the reader that Dryden's is an informed radicalism, but the flag of novelty, argued out of a rather melodramatic literary desperation, flies high over this literary camp: "We acknowledge them our fathers in wit; but they have ruined their estates themselves, before they came to their

---

[16] *Essays of John Dryden*, ed. W. P. Ker, 2 vols. (Oxford, 1900), 1: 8.
[17] *Essay of Dramatic Poesy*, ibid., 1: 99.

children's hands. There is scarce an humour, a character, or any kind of plot, which they have not blown upon. All comes sullied or wasted to us: and were they to entertain this age, they could not make so plenteous treatments out of such decayed fortunes."[18] Arguing that heroic rhyme – the way of "writing in verse they have only left free to us" – is the "noblest kind of modern verse,"[19] Dryden puts into direct contest rhyme and blank verse, a mode "too low for a poem, nay more, for a paper of verses; but if too low for an ordinary sonnet, how much more for Tragedy, which is by Aristotle, in the dispute betwixt the epic poesy and the dramatic, for many reasons he there alleges, ranked above it?"[20]

It would have been difficult to invent a literary program more galling to Milton in the mid-1660s than the one sketched here with its aggressive modernism, elevation of drama above epic, fluent alignment with Latin literary culture, celebration of Court taste, and attack on blank verse. I suspect that Milton was galled as well by the casual elegance of the prose, a style that was clearly not native to his talent. But more than the elegant and knowing manner of the *Essay*, it is the program of rhymed heroic drama, here first enunciated, that must at once have angered Milton and caused a sense of despair. Of course, Milton had had some experience as the prophet of lost causes; he composed and published *The Readie and Easie Way* just weeks before Charles Stuart's restoration. Dryden's theorizing of the new drama together with its triumph on the London stage created another circumstance in which Milton must have felt that he was pitching his tent in a whirlwind.[21] How else are we to understand the banked fury and contempt of the prefatory note to *Paradise Lost*? But Milton's encounter with the heroic drama was hardly over when he had added the angry note on verse to his epic. The encounter had a deeper and more lasting form in the poems of 1671: in the repudiatory challenges of the note prefatory to *Samson*, in the choric forms and gestures of the drama, and, I think, most intriguingly and most subtly in the brief epic. It is almost as if Milton anticipated in *Paradise Regained* the formula Dryden would achieve in the *Essay of Heroic Plays*: "an heroic play ought to be an imitation, in little, of an heroic

[18] *Ibid.*, 1:99.   [19] *Ibid.*, 1:99–101.   [20] *Ibid.*, 1:101.
[21] I owe this figure to Barbara K. Lewalski's foreword to "The Political and Religious Tracts of 1659–1660," in J. Max Patrick *et al.*, eds., *The Prose of John Milton* (New York, 1967), p. 439: "Trying to cope with the English political crisis of 1659–60 was for the Puritans like trying to tame a whirlwind."

poem."[22] That imitation in little – compact, "no time was then / For long indulgence to ... fears or grief" (*PR* 1.109–10),[23] observant of the unities, redefining love and valor – is *Paradise Regained*.

III

Milton's brief epic has not had an easy or an appreciative critical history. Its identity as sequel to *Paradise Lost* contributes to the difficulty – as literary project it seems in no way sequential to the diffuse epic – but *Paradise Regained* presents barriers in ways quite independent of its relation to *Paradise Lost*. It is not brevity that presents the problems; rather it is the poem's severity that has been at the heart of resistance. Despite critical appreciation of its variety of figurative speech, the levels and patterning of Milton's rhetoric, the poem's metrical subtlety, *Paradise Regained* remains so insistently and programmatically fixed in the plain style that defenses of the poem's art seem almost votive exercises in special pleading. To rescue the stylistic program of *Paradise Regained* by stressing its rhetorical flair and figurative richness seems wholly to miss the contestative energy of this poem, a program that begins to come clear when we observe the style conjoined to that other striking feature of the epic, its dramatic force. The poem is more than three-quarters dramatic colloquy, and nothing in the literary models that have been adduced for the brief epic – from Sannazaro and Marino to Aylett or Fletcher – prepares us for the poem as drama.[24] *Paradise Regained* does not simply fall into dramatic colloquy or occasionally deploy the unities: the poem is designed for their display, it engages in the most central concerns of drama as they had been debated from Aristotle's *Poetics* through Sidney's *Defence of Poesy*, and as they were once again under scrutiny in the lively critical forum that fostered the creation of the heroic drama.

Paradise Lost makes brilliant use of soliloquy and colloquy, but we do not for a moment doubt its epic character. This is hardly the case with *Paradise Regained*: its technical features so clearly suggest the drama that some have argued the poem's origins as a drama

---

[22] Dryden, *Essays*, 1: 150.

[23] Book and line references to *Paradise Regained* (*PR*) are given parenthetically from Milton, *Poems*.

[24] Barbara K. Lewalski reviews the models in *Milton's Brief Epic* (Providence, 1966), "Part 1: The Genre."

originally written near the time of the Trinity manuscript.[25] Despite the density of colloquy, the thrust of the point and counterpoint in the temptations, the poem as drama is framed by a narrative voice that balances one set of generic imperatives against another. Part of the effect is the familiar Miltonic mixture of genres, though the generic interplay in *Paradise Regained* is narrower and sharper than in *Paradise Lost*.[26] In *Paradise Regained* the center of generic mixture is drama and epic with occasional adversion to pastoral. Yet the density of the dramatic effect is overwhelming. No one had asked permission to dramatize *Paradise Regained*, but it would have been less daunting than the task Dryden assumed in *The State of Innocence*. Not only had Milton created soliloquy and dialogue; he very nearly provided copy text for production. A small cast and unities of time, action, and – by means of Satan's optic skill – place suggest the technical and aesthetic requirements of the stage more exactly than they accommodate the models of brief epic.

The poem begins with generic signals: the allusions to *Paradise Lost*, to Virgil and Spenser, give certain definition at the outset. Yet the modesty of the invocation and Milton's immediate qualifying of the epic cast of poem and hero – "obscure, / Unmarked, unknown" (*PR* 1.24–25) and "deeds / Above heroic, though in secret done" (*PR* 1.14–15) – not only remind us of Milton's earlier contest with epic heroism but anticipate the unfolding temptations which argue, with great clarity, that while epic may be the formal genre, the poem intends to subject the genre to severe scrutiny, to formal challenge and moral redefinition. So much we have come to expect from Milton, but the redefinition of epic is so radical here that the formal composition of the poem seems almost wholly to deny epic expectations. Combat and empire are the familiar idioms of epic poetry, even when they are subsumed in and spiritualized by the vast design of *Paradise Lost*; but this brief epic insists on static denial, on inwardness, submission, and patience, on perseverance, "humiliation and strong sufferance" (*PR* 1.160), on poverty and solitude as epic conditions and attributes. Here simplicity defeats cunning; plain style subverts guile and double sense; weakness overcomes a martial foe. The encounter is heroic; from Satan's perspective the contest is epic battle. But Christ's idiom is meditative; his weapons are

---

[25] See John T. Shawcross, *Paradise Regain'd* (Pittsburgh, 1988), pp. 17–28.
[26] On generic mixture in Milton's poetry, see Barbara K. Lewalski, *"Paradise Lost" and the Rhetoric of Literary Forms* (Princeton, 1985).

instruction and high thoughts. With each temptation and each denial we are further distanced from the familiar landscape, both literal and literary, of the epic mode. Against pomp, state, and regal mystery, against the stylized architecture of heroic poetry and heroic drama, against "palaces adorned, / Porches and theatres, baths, aqueducts, / Statues and trophies, and triumphal arcs" (*PR* 4.35–37), Milton contrasts Christ's "cottage low" (*PR* 2.28), "sheep-cote" (*PR* 2.287), and "private house" (*PR* 4.639). The heroic landscape of this poem is "barren waste," a "pathless desert, dusk with horrid shades" (*PR* 1.354, 296), and the battle of epic attributes is waged between the hero who "reigns within himself" (*PR* 2.466) and a tyrant who would "Subject himself to anarchy within, / Or lawless passions" (*PR* 2.471–72). To identify kingship with sexual luxury and discover the passions lurking in "courts and regal chambers" (*PR* 2.183) is more than to glance at the fabled sexual indulgence of Charles II's Court – a subject brilliantly and indelibly etched in the satires of the mid-1660s – but the broad references to abstinence and constancy, to the regulation of the will and the passions, also have a literary target, for Milton's hero counterpoints both the historical figure and the literary representation of outlandish passions.

The aesthetic challenge is posed by such allusions and applications, by Milton's shaping of the satanic colloquies, and directly by that last and most controversial of the temptations, the arts and eloquence of classical antiquity. The final temptation frames Milton's poignant address to literary culture; it also enfolds a review of literary types that suggests the generic dilemma Milton faced and solved with *Paradise Regained*.

The formal structure of the last temptation is announced at its opening: "Look once more... / behold... / Athens the eye of Greece" (*PR* 4.236–37, 240). The vision that follows is divided between the aesthetic and the rhetorical modes; the rationale for the temptation to rhetorical skill is obvious enough, and Satan provides the necessary links between rhetoric and politics:

> And with the Gentiles much thou must converse,
> Ruling them by persuasion as thou mean'st,
> Without their learning how wilt thou with them,
> Or they with thee hold conversation meet?
> How wilt thou reason with them, how refute
> Their idolisms, traditions, paradoxes?

> Error by his own arms is best evinced.
> Look once more ere we leave this specular mount
> Westward, much nearer by south-west, behold
> Where on the Aegean shore a city stands
> Built nobly, pure the air, and light the soil,
> Athens the eye of Greece, mother of arts
> And eloquence. $(PR$ 4. 229–41$)$

Though the temptation to the powers of oratory does not belong to the Gospel, the idea that rhetoric, and more particularly political rhetoric, should constitute half of the final temptation is an obvious expression of Milton's long engagement with the role of rhetoric in the constitution of the just state. The temptation to rhetorical power is, moreover, anticipated by the opening lines of Book 4, where Satan waxes nostalgic over the powers of "persuasive rhetoric / That sleeked his tongue, and won so much on Eve" $(PR$ 4.4–5$)$; the defeat of Satan reprises the Fall in detail. Nor is the culminating position of rhetoric in these temptations hard to decipher in formal and aesthetic terms, for rhetorical skill and philosophical authority are the most abstracted of temptations. The line of ascent from the feast in the wilderness to Demosthenes and Pericles, Socrates and Plato, is clear enough.

What is not quite so clear, though it occupies a crucial and climactic place in Satan's temptations, as in Milton's poem, is the role of the literary genres in such an argument:

> ... within the walls then view
> The schools of ancient sages; his who bred
> Great Alexander to subdue the world,
> Lyceum there, and painted Stoa next:
> There thou shalt hear and learn the secret power
> Of harmony in tones and numbers hit
> By voice or hand, and various-measured verse,
> Aeolian charms and Dorian lyric odes,
> And his who gave them breath, but higher sung,
> Blind Melesigenes thence Homer called,
> Whose poem Phoebus challenged for his own.
> Thence what the lofty grave tragedians taught
> In chorus or iambic, teachers best
> Of moral prudence, with delight received
> In brief sententious precepts, while they treat
> Of fate, and chance, and change in human life;
> High actions, and high passions best describing.
> $(PR$ 4. 250–66$)$

The temptation of classical eloquence is linked to the schooling of Alexander the Great, Milton's acknowledgment of the relations between arts and empire; as one critic has suggested, eloquence is here "dignified with an access of power."[27] The passage that follows from Milton's invocation of that "secret power / Of harmony in tones and numbers" seems like freestanding praise of Attic literary modes. Nor is such panegyric surprising from the greatest literary classicist of the English Renaissance. What is surprising is that the panegyric is delivered not by the narrator but by the tempter, that it is Satan who sings the praises of classical literary culture. Needless to say, the temptation to eloquence is not part of the Gospel account; moreover, it is difficult to see how exactly to accommodate literary eloquence, Attic or modern, to Satan's other schemes.

That this temptation must therefore be accommodated to Milton's biography is obvious, but the ways in which it is autobiographical are not. Rather than dismiss the models of classical antiquity, Milton had long admired and practiced them. And while the rejection of gentile wisdom is not difficult to grasp when we have allowed the consoling intervention of theology, the rejection of classical antiquity as a cultural model is not so neatly adjudicated by theology. Finally, the arrangement of genres – love poetry, lyric, ode, epic, and tragedy – is slightly unusual in the setting of this poem, for epic here is superseded by tragedy. And the allusion to tragedy, by comparison with Milton's treatment of the other genres, is surprisingly full. Moreover, in Christ's counterpointing of Greek by Hebrew literary genres – hymns and psalms, "Hebrew songs and harps" (*PR* 4.336), for "various-measured verse" and "Dorian lyric odes" – he offers nothing from scripture with which to answer the claims of drama. Earlier we hear of "celestial measures," of "odes and vigils tuned" (*PR* 1.170, 182); perhaps these are the divine counterpart to "Sion's songs" (*PR* 4.347). Christ's dismissive reference to "swelling epithets thick laid / As varnish on a harlot's cheek" (*PR* 4.343–44) surely glosses Greek epic; but what is summoned to answer the lofty tragedians? If Milton is replaying, in Christ's answer to the arts and eloquence of Greece, his own confrontation with and triumph over classical genres, from pastoral elegy through Homeric epic, it was not until publication of *Paradise Regained and Samson Agonistes* that he could have felt the colloquy with classical antiquity complete. *Samson*

---

[27] Arnold Stein, *Heroic Knowledge* (Minneapolis, 1957), p. 96.

Agonistes is part of the answer – so much is obvious – and its choric method and echoes of Greek tragedy juxtapose the Hebraic spirit with and perfect the Attic model. *Paradise Regained* is the second part of Milton's response to the challenge posed by tragedy; but here the model of Greek drama is extended, not to say distorted, by the latest innovation of the Restoration stage, the heroic drama.

Rewriting classical tragedy had been made a task especially urgent through the triumph of the heroic drama: its swooning excesses, its rhetoric and its rhymes, and not least its exaltation of a Court whose acts and ethos were celebrated in the guise of exotic emperors and queens, and whose military adventurism had been puffed by a newly dignified laureate who dominated the Restoration theater, using its forms to shadow under such names as Achilles and Almanzor the debauched principals of that Court and to replay, in the most exaggerated of manner, its corruption, its moral squalor, its manners, arms, and arts. Satan's offer of classical literary eloquence reprises Milton's recovery of and triumph over the forms of classical literary antiquity; but in the case of tragedy, a form he had not attempted until the composition of *Samson Agonistes*, Milton faced a particularly vexing challenge, for he needed not only to outgo the classical model but to triumph over and correct the contemporary enactment of that mode. The radical answer he now proposed was a poem challenging the heart of the drama not by accepting the outward form, but by mimicking and inverting its devices, at once acknowledging the gauntlet laid down by ancient and modern drama and rejecting utterly its premises and central modes of expression.

That Milton did not shy from competition is clear from the obvious and forthright challenges he issued in the highly exposed invocations to *Paradise Lost*; it is evident as well in the allusions to and adumbrations of Homer and Virgil, Ovid and Horace, his Italian predecessors, and his near contemporaries Spenser, Shakespeare, and Jonson. But when we come closer to the home Milton had to make after 1660 in a literary London that could hardly have been to his taste, it is not difficult to imagine the ambiguities folded within his sense of literary competition, or to think that Milton may have been reluctant to acknowledge the promise, the fluency, the literary sophistication of his younger contemporaries, or the considerable challenge offered by the most fluent and the most sophisticated of those contemporaries, John Dryden. So much is to cross familiar territory.

The argument that I have tried to make concerning Milton's contestation of the heroic drama not only allows the poet's competition but suggests, I hope, some of its aesthetic consequences. Milton created an exacting, a severe, and a beautifully controlled poem, in response not only to his own sense of canon and career but as well to that most extravagant of contemporary literary forms. Nor does it matter how many of those among Milton's audience would have understood that *Paradise Regained* was shaped by Milton's argument, in the most and least exalted senses of that word, with texts calling themselves *The Siege of Rhodes, Mustapha, The Conquest of Granada*, or *The Indian Emperor* and *The Indian Queen*. Nor was Milton concerned to address himself to one such production in particular; he surely could not have thought them individually worth the dignity of *Paradise Regained*. But to save the idiom, to refurbish the epic drama, such an ideal was worthy of his address. And to that ideal he gave himself in a book called *Paradise Regained and Samson Agonistes*.

But to attribute those competitive impulses to Milton alone, to adjust the story of literary relations between the two greatest poets of the later seventeenth century by suggesting that only Milton combined the higher kinds of literary ambition with less sublime forms of competition and contestation is perhaps to apply a corrective that renders the relations of Milton and Dryden difficult to recognize. And I want to close by allowing the circumstances and aspects of *The State of Innocence* that comprehend both the higher and lower forms of the question about literary relations with which we began.

IV

Perhaps Dryden had made Milton's acquaintance during the 1650s; we know that both, together with Andrew Marvell (who turns up later, triangulating the relations between Milton and Dryden), walked in the funeral cortège for Cromwell;[28] and we know, by anecdote, of Dryden's response to the copy of *Paradise Lost* which Dorset had sent him in 1669. But Dryden's first extended meditation on Milton's poetry came with his adaptation of *Paradise Lost*. Again, by anecdote, we know of Dryden's visit to Milton. The results were mixed. It is impossible to know what Dryden thought he was doing

---

[28] Macdonald, *Dryden*, p. 4 n. 6.

in choosing to render the epic as opera, but we can sense some defensiveness about the results. At first, the text of *The State of Innocence* was not published; perhaps it was intended only for performance at the Duke of York's marriage to Mary of Modena (21 November 1673).[29] When it was published, Dryden fixed to his text an "Author's Apology for Heroic Poetry and Poetic Licence" and a *Dedication* to the new Duchess of York, one that outgoes the panegyric idiom of all his dedicatory prose. As we have come to expect from materials with which Dryden surrounds his poems and plays, these texts make a surprising and fascinating context for and commentary on the works themselves.

First, the more conventional of the pieces, the "Apology," in which Dryden celebrates the nobility and profusion of heroic drama. He aligns it with Greek tragedy and defends what have, by this date, become standard targets: its boldness of language, its excessive figures, its "interrogations, exclamations, hyperbata, or a disordered connection of discourse."[30] Yet more intriguing is Dryden's defense of *Paradise Lost* against these charges, his denial that Milton's poem is guilty of those lapses of taste, "strained ... all fustian, and mere nonsense."[31] If Dryden had seen Milton's prefatory notes to *Paradise Lost* and to *Samson Agonistes*, he may be indulging, by means of defending *Paradise Lost*, a taste for revenge here: not directly answering Milton's accusations, but rather aligning Milton with and indeed praising him for the very excesses he had deplored.

But Dryden also suggests some uneasiness over the text of *The State of Innocence*; he claims that he has been forced to publish the work because so many pirated and false copies have been put in circulation:

I was also induced to it [publication] in my own defence; many hundred copies of it being dispersed abroad without my knowledge, or consent: so that every one gathering new faults, it became at length a libel against me; and I saw, with some disdain, more nonsense than either I, or as bad a poet, could have crammed into it, at a month's warning; in which time it was wholly written, and not since revised. After this, I cannot, without injury to the deceased author of "Paradise Lost," but acknowledge, that this poem has received its entire foundation, part of the design, and many of the ornaments, from him. What I have borrowed will be so easily discerned from my mean productions, that I shall not need to point the reader to the places: And truly I should be sorry, for my own sake, that any one should take the

---

[29] Macdonald, *Dryden*, p. 115 and n. 5; cf. Demaray, *Milton's Theatrical Epic*, p. 17.
[30] *The Works of John Dryden*, ed. Sir Walter Scott, rev. George Saintsbury, 18 vols. (Edinburgh, 1882–1893), 5: 119.   [31] *Ibid.*, 5: 116.

pains to compare them together; the original being undoubtedly one of the greatest, most noble, and most sublime poems which either this age or nation has produced.[32]

We need not doubt Dryden's admiration any more than we should have difficulty glossing the lovely self-deprecation; just as certainly, some of the anxiety that Dryden expresses about false copies of his text represents a genuine nervousness about fitting Milton's epic into the confines of his opera. But my suspicion is that we have still not unfolded all the work here, that Dryden's anxiety was driven not only by the sublimity of Milton's poem but also by his hostility to *Paradise Lost*, perhaps even by his fear that the hostility was all too obvious in the adaptation he had made. *The State of Innocence* may not have been adequate to the job as we would wish he had understood it, but it may have been quite adequate to the job that Dryden wanted to do on *Paradise Lost*. Moreover, it is difficult to believe that if we find Dryden's text trivializing, domesticating, even ridiculous or comic, the poet himself could have been wholly insensitive to those possibilities. Perhaps Dryden's remark that the circulating copies had become "a libel" on him betrays a sensitivity to textual corruption, but it may also reveal the poet's admission that he had been only too well understood, that he was content to have managed this comic diminution.

And what are we to make of Dryden's *Dedication*? Having chosen to render the greatest work of this most sublime poet in operatic form, having taken this theologically dense argument of Protestant radicalism, this poetic statement of republican utopianism, and having eradicated both its politics and theology, Dryden then proceeded to lay his opera at the feet of a fifteen-year-old Roman Catholic, princess of the House of Este, niece of Louis XIV, bride of the Duke of York – in 1674 the most famous and the most feared Roman Catholic in England.[33] If this were not enough, the *Dedication* is a continuous rapture over the beauty and virtue of this Catholic princess, a panegyric that indulges not simply the conventional excesses of courtly praise but conjures the language of Roman

---

[32] *Ibid.*, 5: 111–12.

[33] Hutton writes: "During the previous two years, James had courted another Catholic princess, of Austria, without arousing any disapproval in England. Nor had the faith of Catherine of Braganza provoked any, ten years before. But again, James's conversion changed everything and the new match was regarded as another stage in England's betrayal to Rome;" Hutton, *Charles the Second*, p. 309.

Catholic baroque;[34] Dryden exalts the mystery and glory of her beauty and virtue in an idiom which he adopts pointedly from the writings of St. Theresa.[35] Mary's beauty is a sacred revelation, a "mystery left behind" to express God's perfection: "I confess myself too weak for the inspiration: the priest was always unequal to the oracle: the god within him was too mighty for his breast: he laboured with the sacred revelation, and there was more of the mystery left behind than the divinity itself could enable him to express. I can but discover a part of your excellences to the world ... Like those who have surveyed the moon by glasses, I can only tell of a new and shining world above us, but not relate the riches and glories of the place."[36] The temptation when faced with such language is always to quote Jonson's quip on the *Anniversaries*: "If it had been written of the Virgin Mary it had been something."[37] If this were not quite enough, Dryden next turns to the Duke, "a prince who only could deserve you; whose conduct, courage, and success in war; whose fidelity to his royal brother, whose love for his country, whose constancy to his friends, whose bounty to his servants, whose justice to merit, whose inviolable truth, and whose magnanimity in all his actions, seem to have been rewarded by Heaven by the gift of you."[38] And if this were not quite enough, Dryden toys with the familiar idioms of popish politics: "You render mankind insensible to other beauties, and have destroyed the empire of love in a court which was the seat of his dominion. You have subverted (may I dare to accuse you of it?) even our fundamental laws; and reign absolute over the hearts of a stubborn and freeborn people, tenacious almost to madness of their liberty."[39]

This may remind us of Milton's application of the language of bondage and liberty to heroic verse in the prefatory note to *Paradise Lost*. But we need not hear that echo in order to find Dryden's *Dedication* an astonishing way in which to pay court to the new princess. Dryden's language is of course at once daring and wry; but even if the wonderful exaggeration of the passage is understood as part of the complimentary manner, the choice of political idioms is certainly not. And there are two kinds of work that the passage

---

[34] Cf. James Anderson Winn, *John Dryden and His World* (New Haven, 1987), pp. 294–96.

[35] See the commentary by Montague Summers in his edition, *Dryden: The Dramatic Works*, 6 vols. (1931–1932), 3: 580.   [36] Dryden, *Works*, ed. Scott and Saintsbury, 5: 103.

[37] Ben Jonson, *The Complete Poems*, ed. George Parfitt (Harmondsworth, 1975), p. 462.

[38] Dryden, *Works*, ed. Scott and Saintsbury, 5: 104.   [39] *Ibid.*, 5: 105–6.

performs, one related to Dryden's patronage relationship with this particular branch of the Stuart Court,[40] the other bearing on the more intimate matter of Dryden's relation to Milton. Perhaps in working through the idioms of patronage and praise Dryden was indulging in a bit of scandalous political flirtation; he all but dares his audience to apply the praise of Mary's beauty to the danger of a Roman Catholic succession, a succession quite clear by 1674 both in the obvious barrenness of Charles II's marriage and in the now public Roman Catholicism of the Duke of York and his bride.[41] The idioms of popery and absolutism would be violently stirred a few years later during Exclusion, but even in 1674 the language is daring, the tone – hovering between amusement and contempt for public fears – difficult exactly to fix. This, then, is a piece of service. But there is another kind of service that Dryden indulges in relation to the poet whose work he had adapted. To dedicate Milton's work to James and Mary, to exalt the virtue and honor of this particular Catholic prince and his new bride, is to subject *Paradise Lost* to an astonishing application and to subjugate Milton's Protestant poetry and poetics in a most humiliating way. For Dryden to prepare an adaptation of Milton's epic for the marriage festivities of the Duke of York and then to preface the printed text with such a dedication is not simply to neglect the ideology of his great original or to indulge in a recondite form of ridicule; it is utterly to deny its spiritual and ideological authority.

Of course Dryden's relations with Milton went beyond the literary events of 1673–74, and he returns to Milton's poetry at different times and in quite different moods. The comments on *Paradise Lost* in the *Preface* to *Sylvae* (1685) still display a sharp defensiveness; Dryden acknowledges Milton's importance but resists the pressure of the sublime: "*Paradise Lost* is admirable; but am I therefore bound to maintain, that there are no flats amongst his elevations, when 'tis evident he creeps along sometimes for above an hundred lines together?"[42] But a less defensive response begins to unfold after Dryden's conversion; Milton's presence can often be felt in *The Hind and the Panther*; the "Lines on Milton" date from the year of the

---

[40] On Dryden and his patronage relationship with the Duke of York, see George McFadden, *Dryden the Public Writer, 1660–1685* (Princeton, 1978), pp. 88–94.

[41] Winn suggests that the *Dedication* was an effort by the poet to identify his position in the crises brewing between the king and Parliament in February 1677; he finds the language "humorously exaggerated," though humor does not seem quite the effect of the *Dedication*; Winn, *John Dryden*, p. 296.   [42] Dryden, *Essays*, 1: 268.

Revolution; and echoes of *Paradise Lost* color a number of lines in the Virgil translations.[43] And in *A Discourse Concerning the Original and Progress of Satire* (1693) Dryden balances resistance with affection:

As for Mr. Milton, whom we all admire with so much justice, his subject is not that of an Heroic Poem, properly so called. His design is the losing of our happiness... But I will not take Mr. Rymer's work out of his hands. He has promised the world a critique on that author; wherein, though he will not allow his poem for heroic, I hope he will grant us, that his thoughts are elevated, his words sounding, and that no man has so happily copied the manner of Homer, or so copiously translated his Grecisms, and the Latin elegancies of Virgil. 'Tis true, he runs into a flat of thought, sometimes for a hundred lines together, but it is when he is got into a track of Scripture... Neither will I justify Milton for his blank verse, though I may excuse him, by the example of Hannibal Caro, and other Italians, who have used it; for whatever causes he alleges for the abolishing of rhyme, (which I have not now the leisure to examine,) his own particular reason is plainly this, that rhyme was not his talent; he had neither the ease of doing it, nor the graces of it.[44]

Perhaps it is surprising that after so many years Dryden still wants the last word on rhyme, but this poet had a long memory,[45] and we must allow that memory served him in a number of ways. It took Dryden a long time to make his peace with Milton.

Yet what is most interesting about the curve of Dryden's relation to Milton is the increasing ease with which he turned to his poetry after the conversion to Catholicism, and then after the Revolution. Dryden was able to reread Milton with greater sympathy once he had come to embrace, and then been forced to accept, a minority position in his own culture. Part of the openness must have been sympathy for the marginal; so much is obvious. But there is also a sense that the strong ambitions and bitter partisanship of Dryden's laureate years have given way to broader literary sympathies, to a sense of kinship within an extended family of poets:[46] Homer and Virgil, Horace and Ovid, of course, but as well Chaucer and Spenser, Jonson, Waller, and now Milton. "Milton was the poetical son of Spenser, and Mr. Waller of Fairfax; for we have our lineal descents

---

[43] See the commentary and annotation in vol. 3, edited by Earl Miner, and vol. 6, edited by William Frost, in the California edition, *The Works of John Dryden*, ed. E. N. Hooker and H. T. Swedenberg, Jr., *et al.* (Berkeley, 1956–).   [44] Dryden, *Essays*, 2: 29–30.

[45] See Dryden writing of Virgil and himself in *The Dedication of the Aeneis* (1696): "But one Poet may judge of another by himself. The Vengeance we defer, is not forgotten"; Dryden, *Poems*, 3: 1016.

[46] On this theme, see David Bywaters, *Dryden in Revolutionary England* (Berkeley, 1991), chapter 4, "The Poet, Not the Man: Poetry and Prose, 1692–1700."

and clans, as well as other families. Spenser more than once insinuates, that the soul of Chaucer was transfused into his body; and that he was begotten by him two hundred years after his decease. Milton has acknowledged to me, that Spenser was his original; and many besides myself have heard our famous Waller own, that he derived the harmony of his numbers from Godfrey of Bulloign, which was turned into English by Mr. Fairfax."[47] Are we wrong to hear in this language a new intimacy with Milton, the affection of one poet for another, a glimpse of that Parnassus where poets speak across the years, Dante to Virgil, Spenser to Chaucer, Dryden to Milton? There is something quite touching about the sentence that begins, "Milton has acknowledged to me, that Spenser was his original..."; Dryden allows us to overhear a moment of shoptalk when affinities can be affirmed without competition. It took Dryden a long time to arrive at this sentence, but it would be nice to think that the last sentence Dryden wrote about Milton tells us something important about both competition and admiration, about the journey and the arrival.

---

[47] Dryden, *Preface to Fables, Essays*, 2: 247.

CHAPTER 8

"Is he like other men?" The meaning of the Principia Mathematica, and the author as idol

Robert Iliffe

[Leibniz] falls foul upon my Philosophy as if I (and by consequence the ancient Phenicians & Greeks) introduced Miracles and occult qualities... notwithstanding all this, he glories in the number of disciples, you know what his disciples are in England & that he has spent his life in keeping a general correspondence for making disciples, whilst I leave truth to sift for it self.

Isaac Newton[1]

We always took care on Sunday to place ourselves before him, as he sat with the heads of the Colleges; we gaz'd on him, never enough satisfy'd, as on somewhat divine... drawn forth into light before, as to his person, from his beloved privacy in the walls of a college.

William Stukeley[2]

This paper links one aspect of the genealogy of Newton's *Principia* to the processes of self-fashioning which its author adopted. I examine how Newton prepared the *Principia* for publication during the mid-1680s in the light of his belief that the Ancients had once possessed the true religion and philosophy, and then lost it because of idolatrous tendencies. I demonstrate how he controlled accounts of the meaning of the *Principia* by selectively allowing access to himself and to his private notes.

I THE AUTHOR OF THE *PRINCIPIA*

From Newton's methodological claims that he did not wish to invent hypotheses, or that he only published at the request of others, commentators have constructed a psychological account of Newton

[1] Newton to Conti, draft letter of 26 February 1716, Cambridge University Library (hereafter "CUL"), Add. MS fos. 591 and 589.

[2] William Stukeley, *Memoirs of Sir Isaac Newton's Life*, ed. A. Hastings White (1936), p. 10, referring to a period around April 1705.

as a private and shy workaholic. In 1734, for example, J. T. Desaguliers wrote that the "Queries" which Newton placed at the end of his *Opticks* in 1704 "contain a vast fund of Philosophy; which (tho' he has modestly delivered under the names of Queries, as if they were only conjectures) daily experiments and observations confirm."[3] Since then, historians have argued that, from his first public appearances, their hero was misunderstood by contemporaries. Being misinterpreted occasionally caused him to become heated in debate against obstinately defended positions, but the final portrait tends to remain that of a moral and virtuous person locked in his own titanic struggle with truth. Psychological profiling has enabled historians to guess at Newton's intentions when releasing work to, or withholding it from, the public, and to judge whether his most private, or his most public writings are what he *really* meant, thought, and believed. But there tend to be as many psychological portraits as historians, and explanations of his specific decisions to suppress or publish elements of his natural philosophy vary as much as accounts of his personality. In this section, I examine some evidence of Newton's self-fashioning by focusing on his general strategies rather than on a supposed psychological profile.

From the very start of his career, Newton told correspondents that he was wary of the public forum as a suitable site for discussion and evaluation of his work. From 1670, his major contact was John Collins, who, though not considered a major contemporary mathematician, had helped a number of mathematical works toward publication. On 27 September 1670, Newton told Collins that he did not intend to add to what he had sent him regarding his annotations to Kinckhuysen's *Algebra*, because "there being severall Introductions to Algebra already published I might thereby gain ye esteeme of one ambitious among ye croud to have any scribble printed." On 20 July of the following year, when Collins asked him for a new "discours of infinite series," Newton lamented that he had not "yet had leisure to return to those thoughts ... being suddainly diverted by some buisinesse in the Country." Four days after he had contributed his "poore & solitary endeavours" on the constitution of

[3] Desaguliers, *A Course of Experimental Philosophy*, 2 vols. (1734–44), 1: sig. cl. R. S. Westfall, *Never at Rest* (Cambridge, 1980), comments that the "demand for picturability" of the mechanical philosophy "obstructed [Huygen's] understanding of Newton's discovery that light is heterogeneous" (p. 249). There is also a seductive psychoanalytical account of Newton in F. E. Manuel, *A Portrait of Isaac Newton* (1968).

light and colors to the Royal Society (on 6 February 1672), he thanked its Secretary, Henry Oldenburg, for the Society's kind reception of the paper and told him of his fear of "exposing discourses to a prejudic't & censorious multitude (by wch means many truths have been bafled and lost)." Meanwhile, Collins was surprised to learn that Newton designed his instruments and made them with his own hands; at his earliest encounter with the newly appointed Lucasian Professor of Mathematics, he was told by Newton in person that he was "himselfe a practicall grinder of glasses."[4]

Newton's small public soon learned that he built his own telescopes and that his work was to be composed in his leisure, to be received only by a restricted but learned audience. This conflicted with the more open accounts of the legitimation of natural knowledge that were promoted by contemporaries such as Robert Boyle, and Newton referred in his correspondence to a stock of private treatises and mathematical discoveries rather than to any credible gentlemen who might be able to vouch for his claims. He attempted on a number of occasions in the following months to withdraw from the Royal Society and from the public debate that attended publication of his work.[5] He complained that he would "not enjoy [his] former serene liberty till [he had] done" with the Press, and that he had been "cut short of that fredome of communication wch [he] hoped to enjoy." In early 1673, he drew attention to the massive geographical gulf between Cambridge and the Royal Society in London, informing Oldenburg, "I shall neither profit them, nor (by reason of this distance) can partake of the advantage of their Assemblies."[6]

This excuse perplexed Oldenburg, who noted on the back of the letter that he "represented to him my being surprized at his resigning for no other cause, than his distance, wch he knew as well at the time of his election." Such moves to emphasize the lack of proximity between Newton and London continued throughout the 1670s, despite Oldenburg's efforts to reassure Newton of the Society's friendly bearing toward him – reinforced by testimony of members such as Boyle, who "desired" Oldenburg to send Newton his book on

[4] *The Correspondence of Isaac Newton,*ed. H. W. Trunbull, L. Tilling, and A. R. Hall, 7 vols. (Cambridge, 1959–77), 1: 44, 68, 79–80, 108–09, 53.

[5] *Ibid.*, 1: 282, 294–95, 328. On the rhetoric of withdrawal from public life, see Brian Vickers's Introduction to *Arbeit, Musse, Meditation: Betrachtungen zur Vita Activa und Vita Contemplativa* (Zurich, 1985), pp. 1–19, and S. Shapin, "'The Mind is its Own Place': Science and Solitude in Seventeenth-Century England," *Science in Context* 4 (1991): 191–218.

[6] *Correspondence* 1: 161, 262–63.

"Effluviums" in Boyle's name, "wth his very affectionate service, and assurance of ye esteem he hath of your vertue and knowledge."[7]

Newton released more examples of his private work in late 1675 to quell criticism of his work on light and colors, but this tactic did not stifle criticism of his major claims concerning the nature of light or of his honesty in reporting his own experiments. At one point Newton planned publishing a more substantial tome. Collins heard in March 1677 that Newton's picture was to be affixed to a book on light and colors: "Mr Loggan informs me he hath drawn your effigies in order to a sculpture thereof to be prefixed to a book of Light Colours Dioptricks which you intend to publish,"[8] but this work never appeared. After skirmishes with his Jesuit critics, Newton retired from public debate on the pages of the *Philosophical Transactions*, concentrating instead on theology and his "Chimicall Studies on practises."[9] Consequently when Hooke, the chief critic of Newton's theory of light and colors, attempted to engage him in the affairs of the Royal Society once more at the end of 1679, he encountered a scholar who had created an almost entirely private forum for his studies. Commenting on his withdrawal, Newton's remarks warn against facile psychologizing about his reasons. He told Hooke: "I had for some years past been endeavouring to bend my self from Philosophy to other studies in so much yt I have long grutched the time spent in yt study unless it be perhaps at idle hours sometimes for a diversion." He had as little concern for "Philosophy" as one tradesman had "for another man's trade," or "a country man about learning"; it was "not out of any shyness reservedness or distrust yt I have of late & still do decline Philosophicall commerce but only out of my applying my self to other things." He added: "and possibly if any thing usefull to mankind occurs to me I may sometimes impart it to you by letter."[10]

By the early 1680s, Newton had failed to convince his adversaries about the heterogeneous character of white light, a fact which largely related to his failure to provide any witness to the relevant experiments. With only a modicum of support for his work in natural philosophy (mathematicians were well aware of his mathematical prowess), Newton assumed the role of the retiring scholar. Whatever profiles of his personality we might construct, Newton's reputation was a deliberately cultivated one, a public pose carefully fashioned to

[7] *Ibid.*, 1: 305.   [8] *Ibid.*, 2: 200.   [9] *Ibid.*, 1: 356.   [10] *Ibid.*, 2: 300–2.

suit his own interests. Adopting the persona of the withdrawn don allowed him to pursue such studies as alchemy and scriptural hermeneutics, which were neither suited to nor acceptable in a public sphere. The implications of these pursuits were extremely radical, and were known only to a circle even smaller than that of his mathematical audience. Indeed, he had held to an Arian variant of anti-Trinitarianism since the early 1670s, a belief which was hardly acceptable in the confines of Trinity College. Given that Newton considered "Philosophy" to be "such an impertinently litigious Lady that a man had as good be engaged in Law suits as have to do with her," the publication of the *Principia* in 1687 represented a significant transformation of this authorial strategy.[11]

II THE DESIGN OF THE *PRINCIPIA*

Halley's visit to Newton in August 1684 plays a central role in the folklore surrounding the *Principia*'s genesis. Newton recalled Halley asking what planetary path would result from a force directed toward the Sun that varied inversely according to the square of the distance. Newton replied that this would be an ellipse; although he was unable to proffer a "demonstration" of this immediately, he claimed that he did have such a proof. In November he supplied Halley with a relevant nine-page manuscript entitled "De motu corporum in gyrum." By autumn of the following year, an early version of *Principia* was nearing completion. It was to be composed of two books, both provisionally entitled "On the Motion of Bodies" ("De motu corporum, liber primus" and "De motu corporum, liber secundus"). Nevertheless, at some point in late 1685, this project was jettisoned: the first book was expanded, then split into two, and the second part (ultimately Book Two of the *Principia*) attacked the Cartesian doctrine of vortices by analyzing the motion of bodies in resisting media. The original "liber secundus" was rewritten into a bravura technical account of how to ascertain the correct elliptical orbit of comets, an analysis contained within a general application of Newton's definitions and laws to the real physical world. Eventually this became Book Three, "De Mundi Systemate Liber Tertius," of the published *Principia*.[12]

---

[11] *Ibid.*, 2: 437.
[12] For accounts of the genesis of the 1687 edition of the *Principia*, see I. B. Cohen, *Introduction to Newton's Principia* (Cambridge, 1978), pp. 47–129; J. Herivel, *The Background to Newton's*

What early plans did Newton devise for the *Principia*? What was he trying to do by publishing it? In answer, historians have naturally located the work in the early history of physics and rational mechanics. The book laid down modern notions of force and inertia, and announced the concept of universal gravitation, while its author used its techniques to show that comets were periodic phenomena. Although this story is largely incontrovertible, the work had a more complex history than this account would suggest; Newton tinkered with its format right up to the third edition of 1726.[13] To grasp the breadth of Newton's interests while he was planning the *Principia*, one must return to the suppressed "liber secundus" of autumn 1685. This text offers definitive evidence that Newton was at one stage going to publish his belief that the Ancients had once possessed the true (Copernican-Newtonian) philosophy, but that this had become lost through corruption of its meaning.[14]

The structure of the "liber secundus" reveals that Newton initially envisaged a treatise quite different from the *Principia* as it eventually appeared, while his working notes from 1684–85 display the extent to which he was steeped both in the texts of the Ancients and in the tradition of scholarly commentaries contained in compilations of their writings. Did Newton abandon the early form of the *Principia* because he decided these interests did not properly constitute natural philosophy? Or was it because he decided they were insufficiently serious, being mere glosses to the main text? Some years later, in 1691, when it looked as if a new edition of the text was shortly to appear, he began to work anew on the learning of the Ancients and released the gist of his findings to his closest disciples. Newton's apparent belief in the so-called *prisca sapientia* quickly came to the notice of Christiaan Huygens in early 1692 via Fatio de Duillier, who told him that Newton believed that if one put various fragments of these ancient texts together, "effectively [the Ancients] had the same

'*Principia.*' *A Study of Newton's Dynamical Researches in the Years* 1664–84 (Oxford, 1965); D. T. Whiteside, "The Prehistory of the *Principia* from 1664–1686," *Notes and Records of the Royal Society* 45 (1991): 11–61, and Westfall, *Never at Rest*, pp. 402–68. On the links between Newton's cosmetography and other interests, see Simon Schaffer, "Newton's Comets and the Transformation of Astrology," in P. Curry, ed., *Astrology, Science and Society* (Suffolk, 1987), pp. 219–43.

[13] Newton's *Philosophiae Naturalis Principia Mathematica* was first published in London in 1687, followed by a second edition published in Cambridge in 1713, and a third edition in 1726.

[14] The MS of the "liber secundus" is CUL Add. MS 3990. Add. MS Dd. 4.18 is a copy of the first part of it. Both are in the hand of Newton's amanuensis, Humphrey Newton (no relation), who arrived at some time in the beginning of 1684.

ideas as those laid out in the *Principia.*"[15] Of this later set of researches, McGuire and Rattansi argue that "it should be quite clear that Newton's textual analysis of ancient natural philosophy was not consciously based on *post hoc* procedure."[16] In this section I support their view by looking at the unpublished material on natural philosophy and religion from which the beginning of the "liber secundus" was drawn. With this evidence, it is hard to believe that these researches were merely supposed to decorate the serious scientific text, while Newton himself claimed that he was merely "rediscovering" a lost knowledge.[17]

In the rejected "liber secundus," Newton argued that the Ancients had worshipped in orbital temples around perpetual fires, or "prytanea." The Egyptians were the first astronomers and they spread their knowledge abroad to people like the Greeks, "a people more addicted to the study of philology than of nature."[18] However, this learning became perverted during its transmission, leading to the corrupt Aristotelian and scholastic doctrine of solid planetary orbs. In draft notes, he prepared a long story which forms part of a text he called "Theologiae Gentilis Origines Philosophicae" ("The Philosophical Origins of the Gentile Theology"). Newton claimed that the true Egyptian learning, taken in by men such as Orpheus and Pythagoras who sailed to Africa to acquire the relevant skills, consisted of

a dual philosophy both sacred and vulgar... The Philosophers handed down [this] sacred philosophy by means of types and enigmas, while the speakers wrote down the vulgar version openly and in a popular style... [this] philosophy flourished greatly in Egypt and was founded upon the knowledge of the stars. This is clear from the annual procession of the

---

[15] *Correspondence* 3: 193.

[16] J. E. McGuire and P. M. Rattansi, "Newton and the Pipes of Pan," *Notes and Records of the Royal Society* 21 (1966): 108–43, this passage p. 137.

[17] For Newton's later work in this area, see F. Manuel, *Isaac Newton, Historian* (Cambridge, 1963). The pre-*Principia* notes are examined in Westfall, *Never at Rest*, and the same author's "Isaac Newton's *Theologiae Gentilis Origines Philosophicae*," in W. Warren Wager, ed., *The Secular Mind: Transformations of Faith in Modern Europe* (1982), pp. 15–34. For the proposed "Classical Scholia" of the early 1690s, see P. Casini, "Newton: the Classical Scholia," *History of Science* 22 (1984): 1–59. Casini makes no mention of what I take to be the notes for the "liber secundus" now held at the Jewish National Library, Jerusalem in Yahuda MSS 13.3, 16.2, and 17.3, material which was not generally available until the early 1970s.

[18] The "liber secundus" was translated by Andrew Motte and published as an addition to his translation of the *Principia* in 1729 as "Newton's System of the World." References are to F. Cajori, ed., *Sir Isaac Newton's Mathematical Principles of Natural Philosophy and his System of the World*, 2 vols. (1962): 2: 549–50.

Priesthood which was instituted in honour of this knowledge... The procession was formally closed by the Chief Priest and Overseer of sacred things, well versed in theology and religious ceremonies. By linking their knowledge of the stars and the world to theology, and giving precedence to that knowledge, they were hinting that their theology gestured towards the stars.[19]

Drawing from Ralph Cudworth's *True Intellectual System* and other similar modern works, he developed a story of this philosophy of Orpheus and Pythagoras. From the Egyptians, "who concealed mysteries which were above the capacity of the common herd under the veil of religious rituals and hieroglyphic symbols," Orpheus learned of the true theology and mythology, while Pythagoras learned the "significance of the symbols and numbers which derived from the occult philosophy." Like Orpheus, Pythagoras learned "the art of mystical discourse, and of speaking allegorically in numbers and symbols." Amongst his own disciples he "propagated the Copernican astronomy by explaining the meaning of his allegories," and Numa Pompilius did the same.[20] This knowledge was an amalgam of all that was true in astrology, alchemy, astronomy, and natural philosophy. Above all, the Egyptians and their Greek and Roman disciples correctly understood the heliocentric nature of the cosmos and the correct order of the planets. In astrology, they derived the names of their gods from this planetary order. Such was the importance of this natural knowledge, that Pythagoras enjoined his pupils to absolute secrecy lest the allegorical meaning of the priestly discourse should decay into a vulgar one. However, too many sailors encountered these Egyptian ceremonies in ignorance, and in Greece "because the schools of the mystical philosophers were not erudite, the true meaning of the mystical discourse came to be incorrectly understood and the philosophers fell into conflicting opinions."[21]

In the early 1690s, Newton developed further his account of the ancient religion of the prytanea or Vestal fires which he had nearly published in the mid-1680s. "The Original of Religions," tells a long tale concerning this religion and its dissemination. The Vestal religion was the oldest of all, having left its traces in the records of all

[19] Yahuda MS 16.2 fos. 1r-v, 2r, and 17.3 fo. 20r.
[20] Cajori, *Newton's Mathematical Principles*, 2: 549.
[21] Yahuda MS 17.2 fo. 18r-19r. Newton's notes on Cudworth, "Out of Cudworth," the basis for much of his interpretation, are now held by the William Andrews Clark Library at UCLA.

known civilizations. Abraham took prytanea with him or built new ones wherever he went, and the Vestal fires burned in the cities of Canaan and Syria "before the days of Moses." In scripture they were called "high places" because these nations worshiped on the top of mountains:

So when we find several altars in Israel as in Samuels days when there was one at Mizpeh, another at Gilgal another at Bethlehem, another at Ramah, wch was built by Samuel, another in Gibsah, wch was built by Saul ["[in] Solomon's reign & is called a great high place" added]: it is to be understood that these altars so long as a fire was kept burning on them ["(wch seems to have been till the captivity of the ten tribes)" added] were of ye same nature wth Prytanea of other nations.[22]

Such places of worship were also to be found in Denmark, Ireland, China, India, and "in England neare Salisbury" where there was "a piece of antiquity called Stonehenge," a feature "wch seems to be an ancient Prytaneum." Such was the religion of Noah and his sons, who settled in Egypt some time after the Flood. He cites his friend John Spencer's controversial *De Legibus Hebraeorum* and argues that Moses had merely retained the authentic remnants of the Old Egyptian religion – "the Sun Planets & Elements, Jupiter Hammon, Osyris [sic], Isis, Orus and ye rest" – and he claims that this was the same religion as the Jewish and Noachid. Above all, Newton emphasized the role of the priest because "it was ye Priests anciently [who] were above other men skilled in ye knowledge of ye true frame of Nature & accounted it a great part of their Theology." Returning to the thesis of the "Philosophical Origins," Newton suggests that this intimate connection between theology, natural philosophy, and astronomy was no coincidence, as the religion was instituted in the first place because men were supposed to worship their God "by the Study of the frame of the world." All over the learned world, worship was organized by the local equivalent of the priest. For example, the learning of the Indians

lay in ye Brachmans who were their Priests, that of ye Persians in ye Magi who were their Priests, that of ye Babylonians in ye Chaldaeans who were their Priests. And when ye Greeks travelled into Egypt to learn astronomy & philosophy they went to ye Priests. And what there was of ye true knowledge ["of nature" added] amongst ye Greeks lay chiefly in ye brest of some of their Priests ... So then the first religion was the most rational of all

---

[22] Yahuda MS 41 fo. 1. This text is closely related to Keynes MS 146 (" The Original of Monarchies"), reprinted in Manuel, *Newton*, pp. 198–221.

others ["till the nations corrupted" added]. ffor there is no way [" (wthout revelation)" added] to come to the knowledge of a Deity but by the frame of nature.[23]

For Newton, the importance of this history for modern science was the connection between corrupt natural philosophy and idolatry. David Gregory, meeting with Newton in May 1694, remarked that Newton held that "Moses began a reformation but retained the indifferent elements of the Egyptians (it was the Egyptians who most of all debased religion with superstition and from them it spread to other peoples)." In the "Original of Religions" (almost certainly the text from which Gregory took notes), Newton detailed the progress of idolatry from its origin in the worship of heavenly bodies. Mankind soon fell to worshiping these bodies and the heavenly elements; "[it] being more plausible than [the worship] of dead men and statues, mankind was more prone to it and hence it spread further."[24] Yet the less plausible idolatry was the more pernicious, and men soon came to worship their ancestors by attaching their names to heavenly bodies, just as the Roman Catholic Galileo did in the seventeenth century. So they

represented them by various hieglyphical [sic] figures wings like angels to denote ye motions of ye stars... & by this means their names being preserved, grew into more & more veneration. At length they feigned their Souls or Spirits ["wth their qualities" added then deleted] to be translated into ye stars & by these spirits & intelligences ye stars were animated & shone & moved in their courses & understood all things below... to make this hypothesis the more plausible they feigned that ye stars by virtue of these souls were endued wth the qualities of ye men ["& according to those qualities governed the world... " added]. And by means of these fictions ye soules of ye dead men grew into veneration wth ye stars and by as many as received this kind of theology were taken for ye Gods wch governed the world.[25]

Almost a decade earlier in the "The Philosophical Origins," Newton had attacked the corrupt priesthood which had manipulated mankind's tendency to idolatry for it own ends. Specifically, it had promoted the lie that the souls of the dead transmigrated into the stars, and even into "cows, oxen, and other animals, and into plants and unformed stones, and finally into statues and sculptures of all

---

[23] Yahuda MS 41 fos. 3r-v, 5r (based on earlier drafts at Yahuda 17.3 fos. 11r-v and 12r), and 7r (from Yahuda MS 17.3 fo. 9v).   [24] Yahuda MS 41 fo. 9v.
[25] Yahuda MS 41 fo. 9v.

kinds." From this fiction they claimed the right to interpret heavenly signs and derived the means of controlling the lives of ordinary people:

And so Astrology and the Gentile Theology were introduced by cunning Priests to promote the study of the stars and the growth of the Priesthood, and at length they were propagated across the world. Indeed, other Peoples received the names of the Gods from the Egyptians and applied them to their own important ancestors, and hence there were many Saturns, Joves, and Hercules, and many other Gods.

He noted that it was a short step from this corruption to the origins of the great idolatry of Roman Catholicism, for this power-seeking group next "instituted the veneration of sacred animals and plants and the cult of Bethels and columns and statues, as well as various prophetic and magic and necromantic incantations."[26]

So this was how Newton – writing in a period when the king of England was a practicing member of the Church he identified with the Beasts of Revelation – explained the deep links between religion and philosophy and the manner of their corruption. He drew from his notes on Cudworth to show how misinterpretation of the true meaning of ceremonies, such as that surrounding the use of prytanea, could lead to bad natural philosophy. In his correspondence he insisted that misunderstandings and disputes resulted either from willful ignorance, or from shunting into the public sphere materials which properly belonged in a more restricted setting. This was why he frequently spoke of the peace and solitude of Cambridge, and why he always claimed to wish to avoid any disputes. Interpretation and debate belonged to the private domain, to be carried on by qualified individuals; he told his inveterate antagonist Robert Hooke that "what's done before many witnesses is seldome without some further concern then that for truth," but on the other hand, "what passes between friends in private usually deserves ye name of consultation rather then contest."[27] Exposed to the now public (and hence vulgarized) sacred mysteries, the "ignorant vulgar" were apt to read the symbols literally not mystically, and were prone to interpret the Vestal fires as depicting "some invisible and fictitious I know not what ["nescio quid"] in the centre of the Earth" rather than the

---

[26] Yahuda MS 17.3 fos. 14r-v, 15r, and 8r (see also fo. 5v). On fo. 14r, Newton cites Spencer and notes a quotation from Plotinus in Cudworth's *True Intellectual System*. He has then attempted to erase evidence of this debt.   [27] *Correspondence* 1: 416–17.

Sun. In addition to this, ignorance of the true meaning of the harmony of the spheres led to the doctrine of solid orbs, and without the guidance of a priesthood trained in the true philosophy, they "fell into disputing with each other." Empty disputing along these lines also awaited seventeenth-century scholars who did not follow the methodology specified in the *Principia*.[28]

III REWORKING THE *PRINCIPIA*

By autumn 1687, Newton's masterpiece was public. As far as we can tell, the account of the Vestal ceremonies and his analysis of idolatry remained an entirely private interest, though his disdain for Roman Catholicism became known outside Cambridge when – in April and May 1687 before Judge Jeffreys – he represented the University in efforts to prevent James II imposing a Benedictine Monk as MA in Sidney Sussex College.[29] Apart from this, Newton had revived his alchemical and scriptural studies, and found time to become a Member of Parliament for Cambridge University in 1689. Nevertheless, he was also planning both an edition of his optical work, and a second edition of the *Principia*. To this end, he set about collecting accounts of various errors in the 1687 text, and worked in harness with a number of selected acolytes. Amongst these, the Swiss mathematician Fatio de Duillier soon became a favorite. In April 1690, Fatio went to Holland with a list of corrections and additions, a copy of which he left with Huygens. As a confidant of Newton, Fatio was well situated to function as a conduit for the views of Huygens and Leibniz, and he wasted little time in reporting Newton's private beliefs to these scholars.[30]

From February 1690, Fatio let it be known that Newton wanted to entrust him with the proposed second edition, but Newton was still stalling at the end of 1691. Yet the project looked like being realized in early 1692, when Fatio informed Huygens that Newton believed in the "Newtonian" *prisca*; that October Newton supplied him with a new list of errata and addenda. Fatio had designs of his own, and still claimed to Leibniz in 1694 that Newton believed his own theory of gravity was the one he favored over all other "mechanical" accounts. However, David Gregory had noted as far back as December 1691

---

[28] Yahuda MS 17.3 fos. 11v-12r.   [29] Westfall, *Never at Rest*, pp. 478–79.
[30] Cohen, *Introduction*, pp. 177–78.

that "Mr. Newton and Mr. Hally laugh at Mr. Fatio's manner of explaining gravity."[31] Gregory was an avid disciple of the author of the *Principia* from an early stage, and was amply rewarded when Newton's backing helped him beat Halley to obtain the Savilian Chair of Astronomy at Oxford in 1691. In May 1694, Newton let him see "The Original of Religions" as well as a number of textual changes which Gregory was told would be incorporated in some way into the second edition.

The range of Newton's use of the ancient snippets was vast. He was to show that his mathematical tools were known to the Ancients, and told Gregory that "the[ir] resolved locus [was] a Treasury of Analysis," and much of the work centered around restoring lost books such as Euclid's *Porismata* (dealt with in Book VII in the work of Pappus). Other remarks recorded Newton's claim that "a continual miracle is needed to prevent the Sun and the fixed stars from coming together through gravity," and that "the great eccentricity in Comets in directions both different from and contrary to the planets indicates a divine hand: and implies that the Comets are destined for a use other than that of planets." Jupiter's and Saturn's satellites could take the place of other planets (such as Earth), "and be held in reserve for a new Creation."[32]

All this agreed very well with the doctrines of the Ancients, and especially Thales. More radically, Newton now argued that "the philosophy of Epicurus and Lucretius is true and old, but was wrongly interpreted by the Ancients as atheism." In July, Gregory confirmed that Book Three of the *Principia* would show that the Egyptians taught the Copernican system, and that a text explaining "the authentic design of the Ancients" would be appended to the entire work, in which "the errors of the moderns about the mind of the Ancients are detected." Gregory was now confident that his "Notes on the Newtonian Philosophy" would be published, as he had proposed to Newton after their meeting in May. In any case, Newton himself had the new Classical Scholia ready for publication. As Gregory's notes reveal, Newton had shifted his attention to the ancient atomists, while still incorporating significant pieces from Macrobius's *Somnium Scipio* concerning the mysteries of the Pythagorean philosophy. Newton's style in these Classical Scholia did not suggest that they were speculations, and he forcefully asserted that

[31] *Ibid.*, pp. 178, 184; *Correspondence* 3: 193, 309; and see 3: 191.
[32] *Ibid.*, 3: 332, 336, 338; see Westfall, *Never at Rest*, p. 542 n.143.

the Ancients "were aware of" and "believed in" the true physical system of the world.[33]

This was a complex display of hermeneutic analysis. Newton claimed to decipher what the Ancients meant when they spoke in code, because he had rediscovered the truths underlying their mysteries. His treatment of the Ancients' work also allowed Newton to state publicly his views on issues which otherwise would lead to unnecessary disputes. So to Proposition Nine, he proposed a new scholium which described the cause of gravity, by explaining what the Ancients taught about the new phenomenon:

Thus far I have explained the properties of gravity. But by no means do I consider its cause. However I will say in what sense the Ancients theorized about it. Thales held that all bodies were animate, inferring this from magnetic and electrical attractions ... He taught that everything was full of Gods, and by Gods he meant animate bodies.[34]

Likewise, Newton agreed with Cudworth that the Ancients had designated atoms "hieroglyphically" as "monads," referring to physical and not mathematical indivisibles.[35] If this *prisca sapientia* in its prelapsarian pristinity was what the Ancients had believed, then the *Principia* was also true, and one needed the great work to understand the Classical remains. But how was the ordinary mortal to understand the *Principia*?[36]

IV UNDERSTANDING THE *PRINCIPIA*

While releasing evidence of his private interests to people like Fatio and Gregory, Newton was also issuing instructions on how to approach the public text. These linked strategies enabled him to exercise imperious control over the way the book was to be read and understood. Authority came from his status as its author, and rival

---

[33] *Correspondence* 3: 338, 384–86. The Classical Scholia are conveniently reprinted at the back of Casini, "Newton." The main sources for these researches are Royal Society Gregory MS 247 fos. 6r–14v; CUL Add. MS 3965 fos. 270r–72r; CUL Adv.b.39.1.

[34] Gregory MS fo. 13; see also CUL Add. MS 3965 fos. 271–72.

[35] Newton, "Out of Cudworth," fo. 1.

[36] Gregory MS 247 fo. 13r; CUL Add. MS 3965 fos. 271r–272r; CUL Adv.b.39.1 fos. 2r–4r (folded within pp. 412–13 of Newton's copy of the 1687 *Principia*); Newton, "Out of Cudworth," fol. 1. Compare with the much later Gregory Memorandum of December 1705, in which Newton thought of explaining his views on the cause of gravity by citing the belief of the Ancients, that "they reckoned God the Cause of it, nothing els... " in W. Hiscock, ed., *David Gregory, Isaac Newton and his Circle: Extracts from Gregory's Memoranda, 1677–1708* (Oxford, 1937), p. 30.

accounts of its meaning had better beware in case Newton or his allies ruled that these were misunderstandings. Such proprietorial concerns had nearly forced him to shelve the whole project as early as 1686 when he was told that Hooke was claiming priority both for the discovery of universal gravitation and of proof that planets in elliptical orbits followed the inverse-square force law. In June and July, Newton went back over the correspondence that had passed between them at the end of 1679, informing Halley that Hooke's claims were tantamount to saying that Newton did not understand the implications of his own doctrines. In a letter of 27 July 1686, he told Halley that he had by chance alighted upon an old letter to Huygens in the hand of his roommate John Wickins, "& so it is authentick." Although Newton did not "express" the inverse square relationship in the letter, if it were compared to passages in his "Hypothesis" (sent to the Royal Society in late 1675), "you will see yt I then understood it." Understanding the doctrines of the *Principia* was to be crucial for gaining authority to speak about and use the book.[37]

Correspondents with Newton and reports of the contents of the book remarked on the total otherness of the text and its author, and Newton did not discourage these impressions. Halley referred to his "divine Treatise," and in a review of its contents for the *Philosophical Transactions* concluded that "it may justly be said, that so many and so Valuable Philosophical Truths, as are herein discovered and put past Dispute, were never yet owing to the Capacity and Industry of any one man." [38] Gregory speedily thanked him for "having been at the pains to teach the world that which I never expected any man should have knowne." Those interested in coming to terms with the contents of the book told Newton that they hoped they might "understand" only a few of its sections, while Newton sent his amanuensis to give copies to some twenty or so acquaintances and heads of Cambridge colleges, and "some of wch (particularly Dr. Babington of Trinity) said that they might study seven years, before they understood anything of it."[39] John Locke got the gist of the work from Huygens and was reassured that the mathematics and mechanics were sound, and he confessed that there were "very few that [had] Mathematicks enough to understand his Demonstrations."

[37] See *Correspondence* 2: 431–73, passages cited 2: 446–47.
[38] *Ibid.* 2: 473; *Philosophical Transactions* 16 (1686–87): 291–97, passages cited 291–92, 297.
[39] *Correspondence* 2: 484; Westfall, *Never at Rest*, p. 468.

Locke was correct, and a student attained immortality amongst Newton scholars by supposedly remarking as the Lucasian Professor passed by "there goes a man hath writt a book that neither he nor any body else understands." Canonized along with his text, Newton had moved far from the domain of mere mortals long before Pope pointed to his divine beginnings.[40]

If Newton's superhuman genius and restless industry had led to the book's creation, then potential disciples had better work just as hard to believe in and master its contents. John Craig told Colin Campbell at the end of 1687 that he thought Newton would "take [Campbell] up the first month [he] had him," but over a year later he wrote sympathizing with him for having been "at so much pains with Mr. Newtons book."[41] Fatio stressed to Huygens that he was the only person equipped to tackle the second edition, and that he did not think there was anyone who deeply comprehended as much of the book as himself, "thanks to the pains I have taken and the time I have taken up to surmount its obscurity." In any case, he could "easily make a trip to Cambridge" and get from Newton an explanation of anything he had been unable to understand.[42] In February 1692 he told Huygens that Newton had traveled "infinitely further" in mathematics than either Leibniz or Huygens, while in a different vein, Abraham de Moivre displayed his faith by tearing out the pages of the "divine Treatise" "in order to carry them in his pocket and to study them during his free time."[43] Craig gave William Wotton an extraordinarily long list of works to read before embarking upon the book's contents. Richard Bentley, put out by this list and anxious to join the ranks of Newton's inner circle, approached the Master directly and was given a less demanding set of readings. In preparation for his forthcoming Boyle lectures, Bentley was also told that he should not "ascribe the notion" that gravity was "essential and inherent to matter" to Newton, since this cause was "what [he] did not pretend to know," and he learned that Newton composed the *Principia* with "an eye upon such Principles as might work wth considering men for the beliefe of a Deity." Newton also tantalized him with the comment that he had another "strong" argument for proof of God's existence, "but till ye principles on wch it is grounded be better received," he thought it "more advisable to let it sleep."[44]

[40] *Ibid.*, p. 470.   [41] *Correspondence* 2: 501 n.2; 3: 7.   [42] *Ibid.*, 3: 186–87.
[43] *Ibid.*, 3: 194; Westfall, *Never at Rest*, p. 471.
[44] *Correspondence* 3: 150–51, 152, 155–56, 233–34, 236, 240.

The *Principia* gained in stature amongst a wider but still restricted audience as Newton consolidated links with various allies and moulded himself into a public figure, becoming Warden and then Master of the Mint in the late 1690s. But it was his private life which attracted the interest of other scholars. Droves of foreign visitors began to visit. The Marquis de l'Hôpital asked John Arbuthnot in 1696 "does he eat & drink & sleep? Is he like other men?"; he was "surprized when the Dr. told him he conversed chearfully with his friends, assumed nothing & put himself upon a level with all mankind."[45] Yet Newton suggested at various times that his aim in writing was to satisfy only a select band of scholars. This elite readership was always the mathematically literate, and in the early 1690s he composed a draft conclusion to a proposed edition of the *Opticks* suggesting that he had not been able to publish in the *Principia* his belief that Nature "observes the same method in regulating the motions of smaller bodies wch she doth in regulating those of the greater" because

This principle of nature being very remote from the conceptions of Philosophers I forbore to describe it in that Book leas[t It] should be accounted an extravagant freak & so prejudice my Readers against all those things wch were ye main designe of the Book: & yet I hinted both in the Preface & in ye book it self... but the design of yt book being secured by the approbation of Mathematicians, [I have] not scrupled to propose this Principle in plane words.[46]

He also let others know of this attitude, telling William Derham that he "abhorred all contests" and "mainly to avoid being baited by little Smatterers in Mathematicks," he had "designedly made his *Principia* abstruse; but yet so as to be understood by able Mathematicians, who he imagined, by comprehending his demonstrations, would concurr with him in his Theory."[47] Soon after the publication of the second edition of the *Principia*, and in defense of his priority for the invention of the calculus, Newton explained that he had suppressed references to his knowledge of the calculus and so to the book's true "analytic" genesis, because "the Ancients for making things certain admitted nothing in Geometry before it was demonstrated synthetically." This made it hard for "unskilful men to see the Analysis by which these Propositions were found out." While the propositions undoubtedly owed their origin to his development of the calculus, no versions of these proofs in a different form from the

---

[45] Westfall, *Never at Rest*, p. 473.   [46] *Ibid.*, pp. 521–22.   [47] Keynes MS 133.10.

published account have been found and, in the words of one historian, the book's style was "a façade of classical geometry."[48]

The post-*Principia* Newton moulded himself into a *fin de siècle* priest of nature, although the extensive religious significance of the text remained generally unknown to the public until the "General Scholium" and its footnotes on idolatry were published in the second edition of 1713. His treatment of the *Principia*, and his management of the dissemination of its truths among the mathematically illiterate, imitated what he had discovered was practiced amongst the learned Ancients. Newton's private life remained necessarily elusive, for his publishing and self-fashioning strategies required that he and his disciples appeal to this morally unpolluted sanctum for authoritative accounts of both his and the *Principia*'s true meaning. Rather than assuming (along with contemporaries) that achieving direct access to Newton was also to gain entry to some real or privileged meaning of the text through the mind of "genius," historians should perhaps view the deployment in any given setting of discourses invoking privacy as strategies to speak authoritatively about truth and meaning. Newton could remark to Bentley obscurely about "another argument for the Deity" which he had to hand, and he could write publicly in the *Principia* and the *Opticks* about the theological functions of comets and of the fixed stars. His young relative, John Conduitt, went to some lengths to gather material for a biography of his hero and noted – in terms whose theological resonances would surely have irked his idol – that Newton's "virtues proved him a Saint & his discoveries might well pass for miracles." In one audience with Newton, he was told that the author of the *Principia* did "not deal in conjectures," but Conduitt pointed out to him conjectural passages in the *Principia* and asked him "why he would not own as freely what he thought of the Sun as what he thought of the fixed stars." The Great Man, not usually given to humour, told Conduitt that his question "concerned us more, and laughing added he had said enough for people to know his meaning."[49]

---

[48] "An Account of the Book entitled *Commercium Epistolicum*," *Philosophical Transactions* 29 (1714–16), p. 206; Westfall, *Never at Rest*, pp. 423–24. Note Newton's argument in a letter to Thomas Burnett of January 1681 that Moses had "adapt[ed] a description of ye creation as handsomly as he could to ye sense & capacity of ye vulgar ... as if he had then lived & were now describing what he saw," and that this was neither "Philosophical [n]or feigned" but true; a more "distinct" account would "have made ye narrative tedious and confused, amused ye vulgar & become a Philosopher more then a Prophet," *Correspondence* 2: 331–33.
[49] Discussions with Conduitt, March 1725, Keynes MS 130.11.

PART III

Women and writing

CHAPTER 9

A woman's best setting out is silence: the writings of Hannah Wolley

Elaine Hobby

Hannah Wolley (or Woolley) has been much celebrated in twentieth-century accounts of Restoration women, and stories about her life have been repeated frequently. It seems she was the first British woman to publish cookery books, her career beginning with *The Ladies Directory* (1661, 1662) and progressing, it is usually thought, through eight different titles by 1675, some of these works coming out in several editions and two of them, *The Queen-Like Closet* (1670) and *The Ladies Delight* (1672), being translated into German.[1] She is found to be of particular interest because her later books contain not just recipes and medical remedies, but also more general advice on the proper running of a household, guidance on letter-writing, some lengthy autobiographical passages, and trenchant opinions on the restrictions imposed upon the female sex in Restoration England. It is not surprising, then, that this century's tradition of feminist or woman-centered scholarship has taken an interest in Wolley: she was referred to warmly by Myra Reynolds in *The Learned Lady in England 1650–1760* in 1920, and by Ada Wallas in *Before the Bluestockings* in 1929, and their accounts served as the basis for those appearing in works by Kate Hurd-Mead, Doris Stenton, Hilda Smith, Patricia Crawford, and Antonia Fraser, to name only the

---

[1] The works usually attributed to Wolley are: *The Accomplished Ladies Delight* (1675, rpt. 1677, 1683, 1684, 1685, 1686, 1696); *The Compleat Servant-Maid* (1677, rpt. 1682, 1683, 1685, 1691, 1700); *The Cooks Guide* (1664); *The Gentlewomans Companion* (1673, rpt. 1675, 1682), reprinted as *The Compleat Gentlewoman* (1711); *The Ladies Delight* (1672); *The Ladies Directory* (1661, rpt. 1662); *The Queen-like Closet* (1670, rpt. 1672, 1675, 1681, 1684, 1685); *A Supplement To The Queen-Like Closet* (1674, rpt. 1680, 1684). Although both *The Accomplished Ladies Delight* and *The Compleat Servant-Maid* borrow from Wolley's books, they were not attributed to her during her lifetime, and do not appear to be substantively by her. Wolley frequently borrows from her own earlier writings when publishing a new book, and both *The Queen-like Closet* and *The Ladies Delight* are substantially based on the earlier *The Ladies Directory* and *The Cooks Guide*. References to *The Gentlewomans Companion* (1673), and *A Supplement To The Queen-Like Closet* (1674) are given parenthetically in the text, marked *GC* and *S* respectively.

most prominent.[2] She was also the subject of correspondence in *Notes and Queries* during 1852, 1912, and 1926; is one of the few seventeenth-century women to have an entry in the *DNB*; has been cited by Lawrence Stone, Roger Thompson, and David Roberts;[3] and Matthew Hamlyn's *The Recipes of Hannah Woolley* (1988) goes so far as to assert in its dust-jacket blurb that "much of this book's attraction lies in the character of Hannah Woolley herself." The passage on which these assessments are commonly based is also often quoted:

The right Education of the Female Sex, as it is in a manner everywhere neglected, so it ought to be generally lamented. Most in this depraved later Age think a Woman learned and wise enough if she can distinguish her Husbands Bed from anothers. Certainly Mans Soul cannot boast of a more sublime Original than ours, they had equally their efflux from the same eternal Immensity, and therefore capable of the same improvement, by good Education. Vain man is apt to think we were meerly intended for the Worlds propagation, and to keep its humane inhabitants sweet and clean; but, by their leaves, had we the same Literature, he would find our brains as fruitful as our bodies. Hence I am induced to believe, we are debar'd from the knowledg of humane learning, lest our pregnant Wits should rival the towring conceits of our insulting Lords and Masters.

Pardon the Severity of this expression, since I intend not thereby to infuse bitter rebellion into the sweet blood of Females; for know, I would have all such as are enter'd into the honourable state of Matrimony, to be loyal and loving Subjects to their lawful (though lording) Husbands. I cannot but complain of, and must condemn the negligence of Parents, in letting the fertile ground of their Daughters lie fallow, yet send the barren Noddles of their Sons to the University, where they stay for no other purpose than to fill their empty Sconces with idle notions to make a noise in the Country. (*GC*, pp. 1–2)

Since the book continues with an account of this woman's straitened origins, her service in the houses of two aristocrats, her learning of

---

[2] See Myra Reynolds, *The Learned Lady in England 1650–1760* (1920), pp. 91, 434; Ada Wallas, *Before the Bluestockings* (1929), pp. 19–51; Kate Hurd-Mead, *A History of Women in Medicine from the Earliest Times to the Beginning of the Nineteenth Century* (New York, 1938), p. 402; Doris Stenton, *The English Woman in History* (1957), p. 193; Hilda Smith, *Reason's Disciples: Seventeenth-Century English Feminists* (Urbana, 1982), pp. 105–09 and *passim*; Patricia Crawford, "Women's Published Writings 1600–1700," in Mary Prior, ed. *Women in English Society 1500–1800* (1985), p. 227; Antonia Fraser, *The Weaker Vessel: Woman's Lot in Seventeenth-Century England* (1975), pp. 41, 309.

[3] See Stone, *Family*, pp. 344–45; Roger Thompson, *Women in Stuart England and America: A Comparative Study* (1976), pp. 194–206; and David Roberts, *The Ladies: Female Patronage of Restoration Drama* (Oxford, 1989).

medicine, French, Italian, her delight in dancing and music, and her abandoning of that life upon falling helplessly in love, it is a dream of a text: a secular autobiography by a woman of middling status, who speaks with the fire of the witty heroine of Restoration comedies.

What is interesting is that this much-quoted work is not by Hannah Wolley at all, nor by any woman, but instead is the product of a male hack writer. Part of why this is significant is that the text's authorship is not a new discovery: the earliest commentators, including Wallas and the *Notes and Queries* correspondents, made extensive use of the "autobiographical" and "personal" sections of *The Gentlewomans Companion* despite having themselves referred to Wolley's anger at her name being falsely used on its title page. In *A Supplement To The Queen-Like Closet*, Wolley explained that *The Gentlewomans Companion*, though based in part on her *The Ladies Guide*, was the work of a writer hired by the bookseller Dorman Newman. She said that the hack had "so transformed the Book, that it is nothing like what I had written," and that it contained material that she perceived as "scandalous, ridiculous and impertinent" (*S*, pp. 131, 132). She also objected to the expense of the book, which was on sale for two shillings and sixpence, when her own books cost between one shilling (*Ladies Guide*) and two shillings (*Queen-Like Closet*). It is curious, then, that historians and literary critics have continued to cite this book as if it were autobiographical, and even as if it were therefore proof, to quote Crawford, that "the female perspective was different" from men's.[4]

Since the works making use of *The Gentlewomans Companion* span more than a century, belong to various academic disciplines and are written from widely varying political perspectives, there is no simple explanation of the self-contradictory ways in which this book has been represented. An assortment of powerful desires must have operated to maintain its centrality: its espousal of education as the route to female freedom, for instance, finds many echoes in twentieth-century feminism, whilst the embracing of romantic love that follows this is useful to those seeking a "female perspective" on courtship and marriage. The instructions that the book contains on the proper relations between a mistress and her servants, and the cookery recipes

---

[4] Crawford, "Women's Writings," p. 227. In this same essay Crawford also cites the satirical *The Womans Almanack* (1659), published under the name "Sarah Ginnor" to mock the almanac-maker Sarah Jinner, as if it were authentically the work of a woman. For a discussion of the Jinner-Ginnor relationship, see Hobby, *Virtue of Necessity*, pp. 180–82.

and medical remedies, might also seem to offer a female equivalent to the kind of domestic detail given in Pepys's *Diary*. *The Gentlewomans Companion* loses its value if is it not by a woman of the middling sort, so by a woman of the middling sort it must be. My purpose in this essay is to suggest that more can be added to our understanding of the Restoration period by analyzing the differences between the works claimed by Hannah Wolley as her own and the one she repudiated, than is gained by promoting the myth that *The Gentlewomans Companion* gives us access to a female, or even feminist view.

Hannah Wolley was born in about 1622, and she reports, in *A Supplement To The Queen-Like Closet* (pp. 10–11), that, having been raised in a household where her mother and elder sisters were medically skilled, she was a servant to a noblewoman between the ages of seventeen and twenty-four. After her marriage in about 1646 to the plebeian Jeremy Wolley,[5] the master of the Newport Free Grammar School, Essex, her work centered on caring for the school's sixty boarders. Her husband was probably at least ten years older than she, since he was awarded his BA at Queen's College, Cambridge in 1632, his MA in 1635, and had worked at the school before becoming its master in 1637.[6] In about 1653 they moved to Hackney, then a village north of London, where they kept another school until Jeremy's death in August 1661.[7] In that same year, she published her first book, *The Ladies Directory* (first advertised in the *Term Catalogues* a month before her widowhood), following it in 1664 with *The Cooks Guide*. By 1666 she had moved to Westminster, and in April that year she married a forty-five-year old widower and gentleman, Francis Challiner, at St. Margaret's, Westminster.[8] It would seem that he did not long survive the marriage, since in the will she made in February 1669 she was again using the name Wolley, and describing herself as a widow living in Manuden, Essex.

The evidence of this will also suggests that despite her second marriage having taken place in an Anglican church (St. Margaret's was, indeed, the parish church of the Houses of Parliament), Wolley

[5] Jeremy (or Jerome) Wolley is misnamed as Benjamin in William Page, ed., *The Victoria History of the Counties of England: Essex* (1907), and this error has been repeated by many, including myself. His name and details of his work at Newport Grammar School appear in Fred Thompson, *Newport Free Grammar School: A Brief history* (1987), p. 29.

[6] See John Venn and J. A. Venn, *Alumni Cantabrigienses. Pt. 1, From the Earliest Times to 1751*, 4 vols. (Cambridge, 1922–24; rpt. Nendeln, Liechtenstein, 1974), 1:445 and Thompson, *Newport*, p. 29.   [7] Page, ed., *Victoria History*, 2:399.

[8] Wallas, *Before the Bluestockings*, p. 28.

had nonconformist sympathies: she affirms her confidence that she will share in "that Eternall & immortal Kingdom which is prepared for the Elect."[9] In 1670 she published her most successful book, *The Queen-Like Closet*, which went through eleven editions before the end of the century. By 1674 when she published *A Supplement To The Queen-Like Closet*, the book which contains her repudiation of *The Gentlewomans Companion*, she was living in the City of London at the house of one of her sons, Richard, a graduate like his father from Queen's College, Cambridge, Reader at St. Martin's, Ludgate, who had been awarded his MA in 1671.[10] She appears to have had at least five other children, three sons and two daughters.[11] The date of her death is not known, but it might well have been around 1675, since she made no public protest about *The Ladies Delight* being pirated and remade into *The Accomplished Ladies Delight* (1675), or about the fact that the edition of it published in 1684 and 1685 also contained William Faithorne's portrait of Sarah Gilly wrongly presented as a picture of her; it had earlier served as the frontispiece of the book she so hated, *The Gentlewomans Companion*.[12]

A number of elements of this outline of her life indicate that she could be an interesting source for the "collective biography"[13] of Restoration Englishwomen of her rank. She was a woman of middling status, who had worked as a household servant in a period when "the

[9] This will is held in the Essex County Record Office, Chelmsford. It is also possible that her son, Richard, had nonconformist sympathies, since in the 1690s he was employed by the Whig bookseller John Dunton. It is ironic, in the light of Hannah Wolley's irritations at the hack writer who compiled *The Gentlewomans Companion*, that Richard Wolley came to earn his living in such a fashion. He was the "London Divine" employed by Dunton to write the periodical *The Compleat Library* from May 1692 to June 1694; see Stephen Parks, *John Dunton and the English Book Trade: A Study of His Career with a Checklist of His Publications* (1976), p. 70.

[10] Richard Wolley is listed in *Alumni Cantabrigienses* as having been admitted as a sizar (poor scholar) on 6 December 1663, matriculating in 1664, receiving his BA in 1668 and his MA in 1671. Matriculation was normally at the age of 17, according to J. A. Sharp in *Early Modern England: A Social History 1550–1760* (1987), p. 258. This would indicate that Richard was born around 1647. He was therefore probably the Wolleys' eldest child. *A Supplement To The Queen-Like Closet* gives his address as Old Bailey, Golden Cup Court, and asserts his association with St. Martin's, Ludgate. This is puzzling since Ludgate was badly damaged in the fire of 1666 and the rebuilding of St. Martin's was not undertaken until 1677–84; see Basil Clarke, *Parish Churches of London* (1966), p. 36. Perhaps there was a congregation which met elsewhere at this time, Wolley serving as reader or curate.

[11] *Supplement*, p. 140, says she has four sons living. Her will names one of these as her co-heir, Robert, and also names two daughters, Hannah King and Ann Fisher.

[12] The portrait is identified as Sarah Gilly's in A. W. Oxford, *Notes from a Collector's Catalogue. With a Bibliography of English Cookery Books* (1909), p. 82.

[13] Louise A. Tilly's phrase, in the preface to her edition of Doris Stenton's *The English Woman in History* (rpt. New York, 1977), p. ix.

majority of women worked as servants for wages and board before they married."[14] She was a remarrying widow, increasing her social status through marrying first a plebeian, then a gentleman. If an improvement in her status was a factor in her decision to remarry – and her having an eye to such considerations would be consistent with the priorities espoused in her writings, as I shall show – her trajectory differs from that of the majority of Abingdon widows analyzed by Barbara J. Todd.[15] She was a mother, and also a woman with an independent income from her writing, predating Aphra Behn, so often cited as the first professional woman writer, by a decade.[16] Her books deal with the practicalities of running a household in a period when this work was not just associated with consumption and final-stage production, and they give recipes not only for food but also for medical remedies, which has led Doreen Nagy to suggest that one fruitful place to look to discover more examples of women who worked as healers might be the wives of schoolmasters.[17] If only she were to write as expansively on these topics as the author of *The Gentlewomans Companion* does about education and love, she would be a rich source indeed.

Not only the opening paragraphs of *The Gentlewomans Companion*, but also the conventions of the "advice-book" genre within which the cookery book falls, might suggest that Wolley's works would indeed give such insights. Suzanne Hull has demonstrated that the majority of male-authored books explicitly addressed to women during the period 1475–1640, whilst presenting themselves as "practical, how-to-do-it guides," contained material which was "frequently general and philosophical. They gave counsel or instructions on how to educate young girls, how to live as a wife, as a widow, or as a nun, how to give birth ... how to behave to servants, how to write letters, garden, cook."[18] If men addressing women

---

[14] Crawford, "Women's Writings," p. 54. See also Christina Hole, *The English Housewife in the Seventeenth Century* (1953), p. 119; Roberts, *Ladies*, p. 127; Ivy Pinchbeck and Margaret Hewitt, *Children in English Society. Volume I: From Tudor Times to the Eighteenth Century* (1969); and Dorothy Gardiner, *English Girlhood at School. A Study of Women's Education through Twelve Centuries* (Oxford, 1929).

[15] Barbara J. Todd, "The Remarrying Widow: a Stereotype Reconsidered," in Prior, ed., *Women*, pp. 54–92.

[16] Wolley was herself predated as a professional writer by the almanac-maker Sarah Jinner; see Hobby, *Virtue of Necessity*, pp. 180–82.

[17] See Doreen Nagy, *Popular Medicine in Seventeenth-Century England* (Bowling Green, Ohio, 1988), p. 61.

[18] Suzanne Hull, *Chaste, Silent and Obedient, English Books for Women 1475–1640* (San Marino, Calif., 1982), p. 31.

could write so freely on these matters, might not a woman adding to the list of such books include similar disquisitions?

If *The Gentlewomans Companion* were really by a woman, the answer to that question might at first sight seem to be yes. It opens with more than 100 pages of "autobiography," advice, and guidance, with instructions concerning such matters as "*What qualifications best become and are most suitable to a Gentlewoman,*" "*the guidance of a Ladies love and fancy,*" and "*Womens Behaviour to their Servants, and what is to be required of them in the house or what thereunto appertains*" (*GC*, pp. 29–32, 87–98, 109–13). A closer look at these sections of the book reveals, though, that they are made up of commonplaces. The part entitled "*Of Marriage, and the duty of a Wife to her Husband,*" for instance, explains, "There are these two Essentials in Marriage, Superiority and Inferiority. Undoubtedly the Husband hath power over the Wife, and the Wife ought to be subject to the Husband in all thing [sic]" (*GC*, p. 104). This is not original, but the kind of material everywhere found in conduct and courtesy books. Gertie Noyes has suggested that this part of *The Gentlewomans Companion* is closely based on Anna Maria van Schurman's *The Learned Maid* (1659),[19] and a number of other sources are also evident, both those listed by the author, such as works by Cornelius Agrippa, Nicholas Culpeper, and John Parkinson (*GC*, pp. 29, 183–84), and much-borrowed texts like Richard Brathwait's *The English Gentlewoman* (1631).[20]

The disquisition on female education that opens *The Gentlewomans Companion* – a book described authoritatively in its dedicatory epistle as "a *Universal Companion* and *Guide* to the Female Sex, in all *Relations, Companies, Conditions,* and *states* of *Life,* even from *Child-hood* down to *Old-age*; and from the Lady at the *Court,* to the Cook-maid in the *Country*" (*GC*, sig. A3v) – can indeed best be understood not as the prelude to a woman's autobiography, but as part of a thriving seventeenth-century tradition of male assertions about what could be achieved by women if they were properly trained, or followed appropriate role-models drawn from the Classics. Such books would make an interesting focus of study for what they reveal about the interconnections between women being approved of and female

[19] Gertie Noyes, *Bibliography of Courtesy and Conduct Books in Seventeenth-Century England* (New Haven, Connecticut, 1937), p. 103.

[20] One specific and ironically significant borrowing from Brathwait is the proverbial injunction to female silence, which appears in Brathwait's *English Gentlewoman* (1631), p. 41, and is repeated in *Gentlewomans Companion*, p. 16, almost verbatim.

suffering; Charles Gerbier's *Elogium Heroinum* (1651), for instance, whilst insisting that "Women are capable of the highest improvements, unto which Man may attaine" (p. 11), also catalogues large numbers of "virtuous" women who killed themselves for their men's sakes. Thomas Heywood, disturbingly, appears to take a salacious delight in his detailed descriptions of noble women suffering and dying in *The Generall History of Women* (1657), and the book as a whole seems at least as concerned to display the author's wide-ranging knowledge of Latin and Greek sources as it is to defend women's potential. This is not to deny the pro-women sentiments which also characterize these works, or others at least as well known, such as Poulain de la Barre's *The Woman as Good as the Man*, or Agrippa of Nettesheim's *Female Pre-eminence*, 1670.[21] What is significant in the context of this present analysis is the relationship within such texts between overt defenses of women, and apparent fascination with myths concerning their sufferings or inadequacy. *The Gentlewomans Companion* is no exception in this respect. Its liberal assertions are not confined solely to the call for good female education, but include, for instance, a proposal that children be treated more gently by their parents (*GC*, pp. 4–7). But in the courtesy and conduct sections that follow, there is much material which flatly contradicts the idea that the author is coherently committed to a change in gender roles, or to a positive reinterpretation of women's abilities. The author declares, "The first things I judg most necessary, and do wish, with *Socrates*, were in you Ladies, as he desired in his Pupils, are *Discretion*, *Silence* and *Modesty*"; and he continues, "Silence in a Woman is a moving-rhetorick, winning most, when in words it woeth least. If opportunity give your Sex argument of discourse, let it neither taste of affectation, for that were servile; nor touch upon any wanton relation, for that were uncivil; nor any thing above the Sphere of your proper concern, for that were unequal." It scarcely comes as a surprise, then, to find this book, which declares itself to be by a woman committed to teaching housewifery, insisting, "To govern an House is an excellent and profitable employment; there is nothing more beautiful than an Houshold well and peaceably governed; it is a profession that is not difficult; for she that is not capable of any thing else, may be capable

[21] See Gerald MacLean, ed., François Poullain de la Barre, *The Woman As Good As The Man: Or, The Equality of Both Sexes*, trans. A. L., 1677 (Detroit, 1988) for a good modern edition, the introduction to which gives more information about the tradition of male-authored defenses of women. MacLean's interpretation of the significance of such writings differs from the one given here.

of this" (*GC*, pp. 33, 43, 108). Assertions like these are never quoted by those who wish to see the author of *The Gentlewomans Companion*, supposedly Hannah Wolley, as an early "feminist."

I would guess that if *The Gentlewomans Companion* consisted solely of such plagiarized sentiments it would have been found less appealing by modern scholars, and not been ubiquitously quoted, but the book also contains an "autobiographical" section, proffering details of the heroine's state of mind and emotion, thereby lending to the conduct-book pronouncements a semblance of a different kind of authenticity. A reader familiar with the way in which other Restoration women wrote about personal matters might none the less conclude that the story told here more closely resembles the conventions of romance than those of autobiography. For instance, the supposed author's decision to marry Jeremy Wolley is explained as being a result of having "gained so great an esteem among the Nobility and Gentry of two Counties, that I was necessitated to yield to the importunity of one I dearly lov'd, that I might free my self from the tedious caresses of a many more" (*GC*, p. 13). Love is indeed central to the life of this "lady," who affirms:

How incident and prone our whole Sex is to love, especially when young, my blushes will acknowledg without the assistance of my tongue; now since our inclination [sic] so generally tend to love and fancy, and knowing withal how much the last good or evil of our whole lives depend thereon, give me leave to trace them in all or most part of their *Meanders*, wherein you will find such suitable instructions as will give you for the future safe and sound direction. (*GC*, pp. 87–88)

The appeal to "my blushes," and the personal history which opens the book, serve to present this as a genuine female perspective on life's priorities. When read alongside the large numbers of autobiographical accounts written by other women of the period, however, or books claimed by Wolley as her own, the viewpoint comes to appear peculiarly male, and in itself questions the attribution of *The Gentlewomans Companion* to a woman.[22]

Of the insistence that women "generally tend to love and fancy," Hannah Wolley might have joined with Virginia Woolf in remarking

---

[22] This avoidance of explicit discussion of emotional and sexual matters is even true of *The Memoirs of Lady Anne Halkett* which are renowned for their centering on her treatment of a pre-marital affair, and *A Vindication of Anne Wentworth* (1679), which justifies the author's decision to leave her violent husband. See *The Memoires of Anne, Lady Halkett and Ann, Lady Fanshawe*, ed. John Loftis (Oxford, 1979), and Wentworth in Elspeth Graham, *et al.*, eds., *Her Own Life: Autobiographical Writings by Seventeenth-Century Englishwomen* (1989), pp. 180–96.

that, in works by men, women are "seen only in relation to the other sex. And how small a part of a woman's life is that."[23] A similar satirical slant is displayed in Aphra Behn's novels *The Fair Jilt* (1688) and *The History of the Nun* (1689).[24] Despite Cynthia Pomerleau's assertion that seventeenth-century women's secular autobiography demonstrates that "love was inherently more important to women than it was to men ... it was crucial to the way women saw themselves,"[25] Wolley's own works, like those of her female contemporaries, have quite different priorities. This is shown in part in the ways in which men, courtship, and love make their appearance in *A Supplement To The Queen-Like Closet*. In the sample letters Wolley includes to instruct women in letter-writing, for instance, many of the men are profligate, absent, or dead. One, "*From a Widow to her Friend, desiring her Assistance,*" has as its impetus the problem that the recently deceased husband has left his widow destitute; it is to a female friend that she turns for financial assistance to set herself up in trade (*S*, pp. 163–64), as do the imagined authors of letters concerning the situation of a woman debtor imprisoned after her husband's desertion of her (*S*, p. 165), and arranging for the effective adoption of a dead sister's child (*S*, p. 161). Another sample letter discusses the likely plight of a woman whose husband, having courted her for money, discovers she is not wealthy (*S*, pp. 178–80), and there are sufficient parallels between the circumstances outlined in this fiction and the real-life experiences of Mary Carleton, "the German Princess," to raise the question whether Wolley might have had her specific history in mind. Carleton, having failed to find an honest way to make a living after being disowned by her husband, was hanged for theft in 1673, her case receiving much attention in contemporary ballads and pamphlets.[26]

Where Wolley's model letters eschew a focus on male-female relationships, the author of *The Gentlewomans Companion* followed a well-established seventeenth-century pattern of letter-book writing. Jean Robertson and H. S. Bennett have shown that many of the

[23] Virginia Woolf, *A Room of One's Own* (1977; first published in 1929), p. 79.

[24] The novels wittily demonstrate that women are, and must be, more concerned with economics than love, despite the ironic opening sentence of *The Fair Jilt*: "As Love is the most noble and divine passion of the soul, so it is that to which we may justly attribute all the real Satisfactions of Life."

[25] Cynthia Pomerleau, "The Emergence of Women's Autobiography in England," in Estelle C. Jelinek, ed., *Women's Autobiography: Essays in Criticism* (1980), pp. 21–38, this passage p. 25.

[26] See Hobby, *Virtue of Necessity*, pp. 92–96; Graham, *et al.*, eds., *Her Own Life*, pp. 131–46.

form-letters appearing in such texts are modeled on Nicholas Bretton's *A Poste with a Packet of Madde Letters* (1602),[27] and that *The Gentlewomans Companion* sits comfortably within this tradition of imitation and plagiarism in its inclusion, for instance, of a number of letters focusing on female appearance – "*To a Kinswoman discoursing about Fashions,*" "*A Letter from one Lady to another, condemning Artificial-beauty,*" "*The Answer of an ingenious Lady,*" "*A Lady to her Daughter, perswading her from wearing Spots and Black-patches in her face,*" "*The Answer of a dutiful Daughter*" – and its series of interlinked dialogues which develop a long story (*GC*, pp. 236–45, 248–62). Wolley's use of the form in *A Supplement To The Queen-Like Closet* is peculiar in its rejection of such priorities. The clearest example of this is the way the book closes. Her final form-letter is one entitled "*Another Letter from a Gentlewoman, to one who Courted her for his Mistress*" (*S*, p. 181), in which the woman character dismisses his advances and insists he makes a public apology for his behavior in order to restore her chaste reputation. The book does not end there, however. Wolley continues by informing her reader that she "did here intend to have finished my Book, but being unwilling to keep any thing from you, I here present you with a good Receipt, how to make Wax-work" (*S*, p. 182). Neither romance nor anything to do with it has the last word in her book.[28]

I am suggesting, then, that it is not tenable to read *The Gentlewomans Companion* as if it were the authentic voice of a Restoration woman of middle-rank. This is not to say that the text is not worth thinking about: placed within the tradition of male-authored advice and courtesy books in which it belongs, it is as revealing as they are of contemporary expectations of correct female behavior. I also find its interest increased by the use of Wolley's name on the title page, which suggests that her works in particular were seen as a saleable

[27] Jean Robertson, *The Art of Letter Writing: An Essay on The Handbooks Published in England during the Sixteenth and Seventeenth Centuries* (1942), and H. S. Bennett, *English Books and Readers 1603 to 1640, Being a Study in the History of the Book Trade in the Reigns of James I and Charles I* (Cambridge, 1970).

[28] Robertson, in *Letter Writing*, indicates four standard types of letters: "the begging letter, the misogynistic letter dissuading a friend from marrying, the railing letter, and the letter of the rustic wooer, which was intended more for the amusement of the sophisticated reader than for the use of country people" (p. 26). Wolley's refusal of these conventions is itself significant: her begging letters appeal to female networks of support; there is no misogynistic letter, though marriage is not much encouraged by the examples she gives in passing of male unreliability; the "rustic" letter is not concerned with romance, but is offered as an example of how not to write, and is addressed from a young servant to her parents.

commodity; and I think that an analysis of *The Gentlewomans Companion*'s construction through borrowings from other popular works can add to our understanding of the processes of hack writing in this period before the invention of authorial copyright. Readers with other interests could add to this list. But evidence of "fighting … a losing battle in that unenlightened age for the recognition of female intelligence" it is not.[29]

I have already suggested that works claimed by Wolley as her own follow less closely the advice-book conventions than does *The Gentlewomans Companion*. Her consistent concern, it seems, is rather to educate her upwardly-aspirant woman reader in how to present herself, and her home, as richer and more fashionable than they really are. The instructions for letter-writing are just one part of this endeavor, examples of which are legion. Her directions to servants in *The Queen-Like Closet*, for instance, add to the expected injunction to moral behavior the promise of upward mobility: "such an one that will take the Counsel I have seriously given, will not only make her Superiors happy in a good Servant, but she will make her self happy also; for by her Industry she may come one day to be a Mistress over others" (*Queen-Like Closet*, p. 372). In *A Supplement To the Queen-Like Closet* she makes an observation of a similar nature about the value of embroidery: instructions that begin like the standard condemnation of the immorality of women using artificial beauty aids, such as are discussed at great length in *The Gentlewomans Companion*, become a promise that any woman can have access to finery, as long as she is prepared to pay Wolley the cost of teaching her how to make it herself:

The World is grown very fine of late years, but it is with so much charge (together with so ill a phansie some have in choosing things) that they look more like Stage-players than fit to come into any Church, or Civil places: Some wil plead Ignorance, not knowing how to do these things, but that's a bare Excuse; for if they know not already, they may learn: In a Weeks time I dare undertake to teach any Ingenious Person to Embroider any of these things. (*S*, p. 82)

Wolley's financial endeavor of turning herself into a writer – her first book was apparently published at her own expense, since the title page says it is printed "by Tho. Milbourn for the authoress" – is one that fits her to equip her woman reader with economical and

[29] John Butt, *Pope, Dickens and Others: Essays and Addresses* (Edinburgh, 1969), p. 69.

practical advice. Her promise to her reader is that following the guidelines she gives on letter-writing will make her correspondence "effectual in what you shall desire, and also acceptable to those you write to" (*S*, p. 151): these are books written by a woman who has to be "acceptable," and who, if she is "effectual," will be able to make a living as a writer/teacher. What is on offer for the reader is a comparable effectiveness and financial care. This echoing of Wolley's own position in her assumptions about that of her readers is what characterizes all of her books, and differentiates them from the male advice-book tradition they emerge from. Where that tradition concerns itself with maintaining and defining the *status quo*, she guides women in climbing the social ladder and attaining a modicum of independence.[30]

To say that Wolley's works are less confined than *The Gentlewomans Companion* is by the conventions of the advice-book tradition is not to suggest that she offers us a neatly packaged alternative to that work's highly quotable explicit defense of women's intellectual potential. There is no equivalent extended discussion of women's position in Wolley's own writings. Instead, where *The Gentlewomans Companion* deals first with questions of conduct and courtesy, only then moving on to practical instructions concerning cooking and healing (as if these aspects of a woman's life were not inextricably interlinked), Wolley addresses problems of social values, behavior, and morality amongst her discussions of running a home. It is impossible to predict when an issue of moral or political significance might surface in her text, to know when it will be moved on from, or to decide whether this interspersal of practicality and ethics is the result of authorial strategy. The result, which comes increasingly to characterize Wolley's later books, is that readers find themselves encountering observations about gender division, or about poverty, or about the meanings of language, or about the lives of women and of the author in particular, in between or in the midst of instructions about the proper running of home and family. The most striking example of this is the fact that the extended autobiographical passage in *A Supplement To The Queen-Like Closet* which serves explicitly to rebut the claims made about Wolley in *The Gentlewomans Companion*, appears in a section of the book entitled " *To keep the Teeth clean and sound*," and

[30] Wolley's eye to practicalities makes an amusing contrast to the political concerns of Waller and Cowley in their poems concerning Henrietta Maria's refurbishing of Somerset House in 1665.

follows on from a number of directions for cleaning and washing. Wolley's writing practice is most clearly represented by a simple transcription of this page:

To keep the Teeth clean and sound.

Take common white Salt one ounce, as much of Cuttle-bone beat, [sic] them together, and rub your Teeth with it every Morning, and then wash them with fair water.

I have spoken enough concerning your Cloaths, and Face and Hands; now I will give you direction for to be your own Chirurgions and Physicians, unless the case be desperate: but before I begin to teach, be pleased to take notice of what Cures I have done, that you may be assured of my ability.

First, Take notice that my Mother and my Elder Sisters were very well skilled in Physick and Chirurgery, from whom I learned a little, and at the age of seventeen I had the fortune to belong to a Noble Lady in this Kingdom, till I Married, which was at twenty four years (those seven years I was with her) she finding my genius, and being of a Charitable temper to do good amongst her poor Neighbours, I had her purse at command to buy what Ingredients might be required. (*S*, p. 10)

Interconnected are the details of how to make toothpaste, the possibility of the reader being a largely self-sufficient medical practitioner, Wolley's qualifications to teach about these matters, and the role of women – both family members and employer – in fitting her to be such an instructor.

Wolley's allusions to social issues are similarly concealed in the midst of other more overt concerns, as the details she gives of her experience as a healer show. Many of the curses she chooses to cite evidence the importance, in a period when the wealthy College of Physicians was trying to bring medicine under its own control, of keeping healing in the hands of practitioners like herself.[31] Her examples also implicitly demonstrate the disregard with which people were treated by those in positions of power over them. She does not, however, overtly discuss such matters. Instead, she insists that her own skill is proven by her curing of a woman who had been "kicked by a Churlish Husband on her Leg, so that a Vein was burst, whereby she lost at the least a pottle [four pints] of Blood" (*S*, p. 12), and that

I Cured a Bricklayer who had a sore leg by the fall of Timber, and because he was poor his Chirurgion gave it over.

---

[31] Charles Webster, *The Great Instauration: Science, Medicine and Reform 1626–1660* (1975), pp. 250–51.

I Cured a Shoe-maker of a sore Leg, who had spent three pounds on it before he came to me.

I Cured a poor Woman of a sore Leg, who was advised by a Chirurgion to have it cut off. (*S*, p. 16)

No specific challenge to the ethics and practices of male professionals is made, but such a catalogue certainly invites moral judgments from the reader. It is consistent with this that whilst Wolley does not confrontationally claim cookery as a valid job for a woman, her description of what is involved opens with the words "The Cook, whether Man or Woman, ought to be very well skilled."[32] Her most popular male contemporary, by contrast, is clear that this "new Faculty or Science" of cooking is male territory, comparable to men's other professions.[33] Robert May addresses his book "To all honest well intending Men of our Profession, or others," and asserts that it requires "new *Terms of Art*."[34] Wolley's defense of women, and in particular of their economic circumstances, is everywhere implied.

This method of writing allusively about social issues through a series of practical examples is, I would argue, far more common amongst women writers of the period than any candid intervention into intellectual debate. Just as the women activists of the Commonwealth and Restoration period appear not to have engaged in debates about suffrage, but instead used their activities to demonstrate women's right to an active part in the political world,[35] so Wolley makes her analyses implicit. It is no coincidence that the only texts written by women to engage outspokenly in the education debate were by a Dutchwoman living in Holland, Anna Maria van Schurman;[36] an aristocrat, Margaret Cavendish the Duchess of Newcastle (whose works also include grim dismissals of women's intellectual capacity);[37] and a woman (and one-time tutor to the royal family) writing under the guise of male authorship to advertise a school she was running, Bathsua Makin.[38] Women were constrained

---

[32] *Queen-Like Closet*, p. 370.

[33] Robert May, *The Accomplisht Cook, Or the Art and Mystery of Cookery* (1660), sig A5.

[34] *Ibid.*, sigs. A4, A5.   [35] See Hobby, *Virtue of Necessity*, pp. 26–53.

[36] Anna Maria van Schurman, *The Learned Maid* (1659), and see Joyce L. Irwin, "Anna Maria van Schurman: The Star of Utrecht (Dutch, 1607–1678)," in J. R. Brink, ed., *Female Scholars: A Tradition of Learned Women Before 1800* (Montreal, 1980), pp. 68–85.

[37] Hobby, *Virtue of Necessity*, pp. 17–21.

[38] Bathsua Makin, *An Essay to Revive the Antient Education of Gentlewomen* (1673). And see Hobby, *Virtue of Necessity*, pp. 199–203; Vivian Salmon, "Bathsua Makin: A Pioneer Linguist and Feminist in Seventeenth-Century England," in Brigitte Asbach-Schnitker and Johannes

by the requirement that they maintain a modest reputation; rallying forth with arguments about female excellence, or even female potential, was dangerous and perhaps for most women unthinkable.[39]

The opinions expressed within *The Gentlewomans Companion* are not, therefore, what differentiate it most strikingly from books claimed by Wolley as her own. The way in which judgments are conveyed differs, as does the use of language. These are contrasts which probably indicate the distinction between the vocabulary and syntax of a grammar-school educated man, and those of a woman of similar class status living in a society where such schooling "was virtually a male monopoly."[40] The passages quoted above from *The Gentlewomans Companion* are typical of this hack writer's work: the vocabulary is frequently Latinate (sublime, efflux, propagation, literature, pregnant), and there is ample evidence of the use of such rhetorical devices as alliteration, metaphor, and synecdoche.[41] Wolley's writing in *The Queen-Like Closet* and *A Supplement To The Queen-Like Closet*, by contrast, shows no evidence of such training, and indeed she prides herself on "not confounding the Brains with multitudes of Words to little or no purpose, or vain Expressions of things which are altogether unknown to the Learned as well as the Ignorant."[42] There is a significant irony here, given that Wolley spent a substantial portion of her working life running grammar schools. Her role, however, was not to teach the Latin-centered curriculum, but to see to the boys' well-being. When her schoolmaster husband died and she turned to making a living from the educational

Roggenhofer, eds., *Neuere Forschungen zur Wortbildung und Historiographie der Linguistik: Festgabe für Herbert E. Brekle* (Tübingen, 1987), pp. 303–18.

[39] As late as 1694, Mary Astell's *A Serious Proposal to the Ladies for the Advancement of their True and Greatest Interest* justifies women's education largely in terms of women's resultant spiritual improvement and consequent contribution to social stability.

[40] W. A. L. Vincent, *The Grammar Schools. Their Continuing Tradition 1660–1714* (1969), p. 46.

[41] I am grateful to the Feminist Research Group of the English and Drama Department, Loughborough University, and in particular to Gill Spraggs, for their extensive help in analyzing the differences in style noted here.

[42] *Queen-like Closet*, p. 181. *Supplement* has a prefatory poem whose language and mode of address is quite different from the prose sections of her books, addressing the woman reader in terms borrowed from romance: "Servant to Ingenuity I'le be, / Such Ladies shall command all Arts from me. / Nothing from them I'le hide, that's in my heart, / To wait on them I think it is my part." The Feminist Research Group at Loughborough suggested that this poem might have been contributed by a "jobbing poet," and references to use of hacks to write poems is indeed not uncommon in seventeenth-century works. The need to raise such questions draws attention to the impossibility of assigning certain authorship to any part of a book of this kind in a period when borrowings from other texts and multiple authorship were common.

use of her own skills, the available alternative was to write books concerning cookery and household management. She was so successful at this, it would seem, that a publisher believed it worth his while to make use of her name on the title page of a book indeed based partly on her work.

To a woman, the choice of school-teaching might in any case have seemed a poor alternative to the profession of independent enterprise which Wolley carved out for herself. Josephine Kamm indicates that the curriculum in girls' schools consisted largely of "music and dancing as well as languages [and] a variety of handicrafts of an intricate and useless variety."[43] A number of contemporary writers, including Richard Brathwait and Bathsua Makin, were dismissive of the value of the training offered at these establishments.[44] In 1671 Edward Chamberlayne saw fit to make the very idea of female education an object of satire in his mock advertisement *An Academy Or Colledge: Wherein Young Ladies and Gentlewomen May at a Very Moderate Expence be duly instructed*. There is also ample evidence of Restoration women being unimpressed by the intellectual content of the academic training offered in the traditional male system, for all its greater prestige. *The Gentlewomans Companion* itself, like a number of contemporary works addressing the issue of women's education, has as one of its objects of attention the superficiality of traditional grammar-school drilling, and suggests that young gentlewomen should learn Latin to prevent their being bamboozled by "Fops of Rhetoric, spawns of non-intelligency" (*GC*, p. 31). These appeals, being made in language which conforms to the grammar-school rules of rhetorical construction, are more self-contradictory than the rejections of the conventions of male learned language that appear frequently in early Restoration women's writing, most delightfully in Behn's Preface to *The Dutch Lover* (1673):

I have heard that most of that which bears the name of Learning, and which has abused such quantities of Ink and Paper, and continually employs so many ignorant, unhappy souls for ten, twelve, twenty years in the University (who yet poor wretches think they are doing something all the while) as Logick etc. and several other things (that shall be nameless lest I misspel them) are much more absolutely nothing than the errantest Play that e'er was writ... For waving the examination, why women having equal education with men, were not as capable of knowledge, of whatsoever sort

[43] Josephine Kamm, *Hope Deferred: Girls' Education in English History* (1965), pp. 68–69.
[44] Brathwait, *Gentlewoman*, p. 74; Makin, *Essay*, pp. 4, 22.

as well as they: I'l only say as I have touch'd before, that Plays have no great room for that which is mens great advantage over women, that is Learning. (sigs. A2-a1)

Like Behn, Wolley refuses to be overawed by the assumption that writing of worth can only be achieved by those educated according to male traditions. Her resultant books are less discursive than the male equivalents, and, in general, less carefully organized.[45] They none the less appear to have been acceptable enough to the reading public for it to have been possible for her to make a living.[46]

Wolley's books do not, of course, give us an unmediated access to the "truth" of a woman's life. To say that they are not delimited in the same ways that *The Gentlewomans Companion* is by the truisms of the conduct-book traditions is not to argue that they simply reflect female reality. The clearest evidence of this are the disjunctions between what *A Supplement To The Queen-Like Closet* says about Wolley's family, and what her 1669 will reveals.[47] Where *A Supplement To The Queen-Like Closet* lists as her blessings her two good husbands and four sons, her will not only leaves property to one of those sons but also to two daughters and a granddaughter, and names her widowed daughter, Ann Fisher, as sole executor. I am not suggesting that the "falsehoods" of *The Gentlewomans Companion* can be replaced by the "veracity" of Wolley's works, but that different constraints of both gender and genre are at play in determining what these writings say and how they say it. They provide, too, a source for those interested in the Restoration quite different from that present in the conduct-book tradition of *The Gentlewomans Companion*.[48]

[45] Hobby, *Virtue of Necessity*, pp. 167–68, 175.

[46] Other examples can be found in Behn's *The Lucky Chance* (1687), Jane Sharp, *The Midwives Book* (1671), Margaret Cavendish, Duchess of Newcastle, *The Worlds Olio* (1655; rpt. 1671), and see Hobby, *Virtue of Necessity*, pp. 190–210. For schemes during the Commonwealth and Protectorate to produce a new, nation-wide education for both girls and boys, see W. A. L. Vincent, *The State and School Education, 1640–1660 in England and Wales. A Survey based on Printed Sources* (1950), and Charles Webster, ed., *Samuel Hartlib and the Advancement of Learning* (1970).

[47] This division of Wolley's property should not be read as evidence that her other children were in disfavor. Susan Amussen points out that married children will often have already received their share of parental property: *An Ordered Society: Gender and Class in Early Modern England* (Oxford, 1980). And H. C. F. Lansberry indicates that "Because their sons and grandsons had usually inherited under their husbands' wills, the majority of their [widows'] bequests then to be to women relatives and friends," *Sevenoaks Wills and Inventories in the Reign of Charles II* (Kent Archaeological Society, 1988), p. xxviii. Wills, then, also have their own generic features.

[48] David Roberts, assuming *The Gentlewomans Companion* to be by Wolley, uses it as evidence that "conspicuous leisure remained a predominant feature in the lives of many Restoration women; however diversely it could be employed it accounted for much of the low value

There are a number of ways in which the kind of material Wolley published remains interesting today. First, it may be that cookery books published in the mid-seventeenth century will prove to be a useful index of ways in which political positions could be signalled. During the Protectorate, some authors and booksellers used cookery books as a means of continuing to publicize royalist sentiments. The most obvious example of this is *The Queens Closet Opened* (1655), which advertised itself as "True Copies of her Majesties own Receipt Books," and contained a frontispiece portrait of Henrietta Maria. Robert May's *The Accomplisht Cook* was actually more confrontational, its introduction to the reader, dated January 1660, harking back to a perfect time of social harmony in the days before the revolution:

> then were those golden dayes wherein were practised *the Triumphs and Trophies of Cookery*, then was Hospitality esteemed, Neighbourhood preserved, the Poor cherished, and God honoured; then was Religion less talk'd on and more practis'd, then was Atheism and Schisme less in fashion, and then did men strive to be good rather then to seem so.[49]

May's book was republished many times after the Restoration, and comparable affirmations of loyalty to the Crown continued to appear in Restoration cookery books, most notably *The Court & Kitchen of Elizabeth, Commonly called Joan Cromwel, The Wife of the late Usurper, Truly Described and Represented* (1664), which contains not only recipes, but also, as its satirical title implies, a prefatory attack on Cromwell's period of power.[50] Such connections between these books and political sentiment are less surprising than might at first appear: they found their market, in part, through offering recipes for dishes that no household of middling status would seriously contemplate eating.[51] With their heavy use of names of aristocrats as the supposed

---

placed upon women at the time," *Ladies*, p. 12. The argument is both wrong in matter of fact (the book is not Wolley's, and the leisure he attributes to women is not indicated by more reliable sources); and upside down: misogynistic attitudes, such as those informing *The Gentlewomans Companion*, led to women's work being presented by men as trivial and their lives seen as leisurely.

[49] May, *Accomplisht Cook*, sig. A6v. In *Ideas of the Restoration*, p. 47, Jose analyses the use of such nostalgic appeals to a Golden Age in the establishment of Restoration mainstream culture in the 1660s. May is interesting as evidence of this tendency predating the Restoration itself.

[50] A. W. Oxford, in *English Cookery Books to the Year 1850* (Oxford, 1913), gives details of other cookery books of the 1650s and 1660s which could be consulted to expand this analysis.

[51] See Lorna Weatherill, *Consumer Behavior and Material Culture in Britain 1660–1760* (Cambridge, 1988), p. 146.

authors of individual recipes, and their specifying of expensive
ingredients, they could serve as seventeenth-century equivalents of
the modern coffee-table book, as much a source of dreams of wealth
as manuals of practical instruction.[52]

Wolley's books seem on first acquaintance to fit unproblematically
into these conventions, with the claim on the title page of *The Ladies
Delight* (1672), for instance, that Wolley has herself cooked many of
the grander dishes she describes "for the Entertainment of His Late
Majesty, as well as for the Nobility." At least in part this would seem
to have been a marketing ploy: her gloss to the title of *The Queen-Like
Closet* makes it clear the book should be considered worthy of its title
not for its position in relation to matters of state politics, but because
it is designed to enable the reader to be a "queen" in another sense
– someone having preeminence or authority in a specified sphere
(*OED* sense 5d), who through reading Wolley's instructions has
become "perfect in [her] Practices." Wolley is also insistent that her
fancy recipes and other directions are not given just as an object of
admiration. Of her three-page recipe " *To make a Rock in Sweet-Meats*"
she remarks, "Do not take this for a simple Fancy, for I assure you,
it is the very same that I taught to a young Gentlewoman to give for
a Present to a Person of Quality" (*Queen-Like Closet*, pp. 345–47). She
wants her directions to be seen as useful in gaining social influence or
acceptance; in providing women with a parallel route to success
promised to boys through a grammar-school education. Indeed, she
urges her reader to recognize how following these directions can
enable her either to pass as wealthier than she is – "It will look like
a Frame of great price, but it will not cost any great matter"; "Thus
you may go fine, and with less cost than if you bought good Lace";
– or make it possible for her to sell her wares for money – "For these
kind of Feathers I have taken many a pound" (*S*, pp. 70, 81, 76).
Such books are a source, then, to question and supplement the
conclusions drawn by historians using archival materials, who have
suggested that whilst cookery was seen as a high-status activity,
washing and cleaning would be left, if possible, to the servants,[53] and
have indicated the difficulty of calculating how rapidly the market

---

[52] Cookery books were also sometimes used by their owners to record key family events such
as births, deaths, marriages, and to pass on specific advice, perhaps from mother to
daughter. I have seen evidence of such jottings in many cookery books, including the copy
of the 1675 edition of Wolley's *Queen-Like Closet* held at the Library of Congress (shelfmark
TX705.W6 1674 Pennell Collection), and the copy of the same book in the British Library
(shelfmark 1037.a.38).   [53] Weatherill, *Consumer Behaviour*, p. 149.

for manufactured household goods increased, because the records of activities of chapmen, trowmen, higglers, and the like are scarce.[54] Wolley shows us how "low-status" activities could be perceived as ways of saving money and thereby buying status, and her instructing women in how to make for themselves the new manufactured goods might indicate that the increased appearance of such items in Restoration inventories does not necessarily reveal a commensurate rise in their purchase.[55]

The question arises, then, whether a more extended consideration of the activities these books reveal to be involved in maintaining a household might not complicate some of the common assumptions about the development of a public/private divide in the period. From the perspective of the male historian the household has largely been analyzed as a place of refuge from the demands of male work outside the home, and the locus of emotion and family structure.[56] From the female viewpoint it was a workplace, where wages were paid to servants, money made by housewives through excess production "saved" through mimicking of fashionable goods in a world where "goods of high quality were beginning crudely to correlate with and buy status."[57]

Wolley's version of the middle-class woman's life also challenges the stereotypes offered through Restoration comedies such as Etherege's *The Man of Mode* (1676), Behn's *The Lucky Chance* (1686), and Susanna Centlivre's *The Basset Table* (1705). Perhaps *The Gentlewomans Companion* goes on being used, finally, because it confirms the illusions about middle-class women promoted in such works. "The idea of the Restoration conjures up lively images of sultry buxom women in deshabille, or heavy-lidded Rochesterian rakes... Our sense of the period historically is always mediated by our literary

[54] Joan Thirsk, *Economic Policy and Projects. The Development of a Consumer Society in Early Modern England* (Oxford, 1978), p. 3.   [55] Weatherill, *Consumer Behaviour*, p. 8.
[56] See Stone, *Family*.
[57] Jose, *Ideas of the Restoration*, p. 19. Stevi Jackson, in "Towards a Historical Sociology of Housework: A Materialist Feminist Analysis," *Women's Studies International Forum* 15: 2 (1992): 153–72, offers an important discussion of the theoretical and political issues at stake in writing a history of housewifery. Alice Clark's *The Working Life of Women in the Seventeenth Century* (1919) is still the crucial point of reference for historical work on seventeenth-century women's work. For indications of some shortcomings in her analytical categories, see Amussen, *Ordered Society*, Chris Middleton, "Patriarchal Exploitation and the Rise of English Capitalism," in Eva Gamarnikow *et al.*, eds., *Gender, Class and Work* (1973), pp. 11–27, and Middleton's later study, "Women's Labour and the Transition to Pre-Industrial Capitalism," in Lindsey Charles and Lorna Duffin, eds., *Women and Work in Pre-Industrial England* (1985), pp. 181–206.

experience of it."[58] This might suggest that the study and teaching of Restoration women would be well served by dislodging the place of *The Country Wife*, and even *The Gentlewomans Companion*, and by reading and teaching *A Supplement To The Queen-Like Closet*.

---

[58] Jose, *Ideas of the Restoration*, p. xiv.

CHAPTER 10

Obedient subjects? The loyal self in some later seventeenth-century Royalist women's memoirs

N. H. Keeble

In April 1644 William Cavendish, Marquis (and afterwards Duke) of Newcastle, received from Charles I a letter in which the king, seeking to secure the continuing service of his Captain-General in the north of England, exhorted Newcastle not to be discouraged by the hostile criticism his military failures were attracting. "Remember," he wrote, "all courage is not in fighting, constancy in a good cause being the chief... ingredient."[1] To prevent Newcastle's disaffection Charles appealed to the definitive value in loyalist ideology. Their constancy in adversity and steadfast allegiance despite all temptations to desert would be the self-justifying and self-defining themes of many a Royalist memoir written after the Restoration to promote the proper claims of their authors both upon royal gratitude and upon the respect of posterity.

This commitment to the unswerving obedience of subjects was articulated as wholeheartedly by female as by male chroniclers. It was precisely as the "short history... of the actions and sufferings of your most loyal subject"[2] that the Duchess of Newcastle recommended to Charles II her *Life* of the Duke, and "the truth of your loyal actions and endeavors, for the service of your King and

---

[1] *The Letters, Speeches and Proclamations of King Charles I*, ed. Charles Petrie (1968), p. 143.

[2] Margaret [Cavendish], Duchess of Newcastle, *The Life of William Cavendish Duke of Newcastle to which is added the True Relation of my Birth Breeding and Life*, ed. C. H. Firth (1906), p. xxxiv. Subsequent parenthetical references in the text prefixed by *C* are to this edition. For the Duchess of Newcastle (1623–73) see, in brief, *DNB* and Janet Todd, ed., *A Dictionary of British and American Women Writers 1660–1800* (1987), pp. 231–33, and, more at large, Douglas Grant, *Margaret the First: a Biography of Margaret Cavendish, Duchess of Newcastle* (1957); Kathleen Jones, *A Glorious Fame: The Life of Margaret Cavendish* (1988). The *Life of William Cavendish*, "the first biography of a husband to be published by an Englishwoman" (Todd, ed., *Dictionary*, p. 232), appeared in 1667; the "True Relation," the "first autobiography published by a woman in England" (*ibid.*, p. 232), was printed in *Natures Pictures Drawn by Fancies Pencil to the Life* (1656). Sara Heller Mendelson, *The Mental World of Three Stuart Women* (Brighton, 1987), p. 61, holds that both texts inspired, and provided models for, other women writers, including Halkett and Fanshawe.

country" which, in her dedicatory epistle to her husband, she proposed "to set forth and declare to after ages" (*C*, p. xxxv). "Loyalty being the principle" which motivated Anne, Lady Halkett throughout the 1640s and 1650s, "itt is not to bee doupted" that the "earnest desire I had to serve the King made mee omitt noe opertunity wherein I could bee usefull," even when "the zeale I had for His Majesty made mee not see what inconveniencys I exposed my selfe to" through the frequent private visits to the Royalist agent Colonel Joseph Bampfield which earned her an ill reputation.[3] Recounting details of his "nearest relations by your father" for the benefit of her one surviving son, Richard, 2nd Baronet, who had been only ten months old when his father died in 1666, Ann, Lady Fanshawe assures him that "without vanity none exceeded them in their loyalty, which cost them dear" (*F*, p. 108).[4]

It was to failure in such loyalty that this ideological commitment pointed in the 1660s to interpret the otherwise incomprehensible events of the 1640s and 1650s. The Civil War and Interregnum were seen as divine judgment upon the merely conditional and partial obedience which subjects had granted to their sovereign. Nothing less than complete and unqualified submission to patriarchal authority would serve. Anne Halkett recalled how the Royalists were admonished by the "unexpected defeat which the King's army had att Dunbar" in 1650 to "see how litle confidence should bee placed in anything butt God, who in his justice thought fitt to punish this kingdome and bring itt under a subjection to an usurper, *because they paid nott that subjection that was due to theire lawfull King*" (*H*, p. 54, emphasis added). Like the apostatizing children of Israel, Royalists are to learn true obedience through suffering. The Interregnum is configured as an Old Testament wilderness through which the loyal remnant toil regardless of hardship, and, being found faithful, enter into their promised land in 1660: "as faith is the evidence of things not seen," writes Ann Fanshawe, quoting Hebrews 11:1, "so we

---

[3] *The Memoirs of Anne, Lady Halkett and Ann, Lady Fanshawe*, ed. John Loftis (Oxford, 1979), pp. 26–27. Subsequent parenthetical references in the text prefixed by *H* and *F* are respectively to the Halkett and Fanshawe texts in this edition. For Lady Halkett (1622–99) see *DNB* and Todd, ed., *Dictionary*, pp. 146–47. Her *Memoir* was written 1677–78, the year after her husband's death; it was first printed as *The Autobiography of Anne Lady Halkett*, ed. John Gough Nichols, Camden Society, ns xiii (1875).

[4] For Lady Fanshawe (1625–80) see: *DNB*; Todd, ed., *Dictionary*, pp. 119–20; and the very extensive annotation to *The Memoirs of Ann Lady Fanshawe*, ed. H. C. Fanshawe (1907). Addressed to her son, Richard 2nd Baronet, her *Memoir* was written (or transcribed) in 1676; it was first printed in 1829.

upon so righteous a cause cheerfully resolved to suffer what that would drive us to" (*F*, p. 113). The 1650s were an Egyptian bondage to which there was "noe remedy butt to submitt till the Lord thought fitt to give them deliverance" (*H*, p. 61). Adversity was to be embraced "with a martyrlike cheerfulness" in the knowledge that the unsettled and nomadic life led by embattled and exiled Royalists recalled that of Abraham (*F*, p. 186). Through trial, "true loyalty is both manifest and refined: patience hath armed, and misery hath tried us," writes the Duchess of Newcastle (*C*, p. 171). And, of course, the greater the trial, the greater the fortitude demonstrated.

The rhetorical strategy of Royalist memoirs consequently insists upon the destructive civil anarchy and the monstrously unnatural license through which the loyal subject had to maintain faith during the Interregnum. It is to the imagery of irresistible destructiveness – the "unnatural war came like a whirlwind, which felled down [the] houses" of the relations of the Duchess of Newcastle (*C*, p. 160) – of disease – the "plague" of the Scots "infected the whole nation" (*F*, p. 111) – and of storm and shipwreck (*F*, p. 115), that they turn to convey "the greatest troubles our nation hath ever seen" (*F*, p. 186).

Most commonly, it is through detailed demonstration of the material deprivations to which Royalists were subjected that their trial is rendered. Both "the family I am linked to" by marriage and "the family from which I sprung" are "ruined ... by these unhappy wars" asserts Margaret Cavendish (*C*, p. 163). Her husband's loyalty is proved "by his often hazarding of his life, by the loss of his estate, and the banishment of his person, by his necessitated condition, and his constant and patient suffering" (*C*, p. 171). She devotes many pages to precise itemization of these losses (*C*, pp. 68–81), in fact, distorting and exaggerating their extent,[5] and still more pages to outlining his "Misfortunes, Obstructions and Sufferings" (*C*, pp. 89–97), to conclude that he "hath lost and suffered most of any subject ... except those that lost their lives" (*C*, p. 93). Despite this, she writes: "I have heard him say out of passionate zeal and loyalty, that he would willingly sacrifice himself and all his posterity, for the sake of his Majesty and the royal race" (*C*, p. 64).

Ann Fanshawe's family similarly experienced impoverishment. In 1643 the London house of her father, Sir John Harrison, was plundered, and, upon his joining the Court at Oxford, his estate was

---

[5] Mendelson, *Mental World*, pp. 49–50.

sequestrated. When his daughters joined him there it was to find their stable lives rudely disrupted and their circumstances greatly straitened:

> we, that had till that hour lived in great plenty and great order, found ourselves like fishes out of the water and the sene so changed that we knew not at all how to act any part but obedience; for from as good houses as any gentleman of England had we come to a baker's house in an obscure street, and from roomes well furnished to lye in a very bad bed in a garret, to one dish of meat and that not the best ordered; no mony, for we were as poor as Job, nor clothes more than a man or two brought in their cloak bags. We had the perpetuall discourse of losing and gaining of towns and men; at the windows the sad spectacle of war, sometimes plague, sometimes sicknesses of other kind, by reason of so many people being packt together, as I believe there never was before of that quality; alwaies want … (F, p. 111)

Disorientated and bewildered by the revolutionary times ("like fishes out of the water") they have only their loyalty to traditional hierarchical order to cling to ("we knew not how to act any part but obedience"). If the allusion to Job holds out the promise that such steadfast allegiance to the Court in its displacement (and, later, exile) will be rewarded, it is a reward hard earned. In 1646, for example, when Ann Fanshawe and her husband Sir Richard, a member of the Council of the prince of Wales, followed the prince to the Scilly Isles, goods remaining on the shore were stolen by the man in whose care they were left while those carried on board ship were plundered by the seamen; nor was the prince's entourage in better plight: "we were destitute of clothes, and meat or fewell for half the court, to serve them a month, was not to be had in the whole iland. And truly we begg'd our dayly bread of God, for we thought every meal our last" (F, p. 118).

Such hardships are the common burden of Royalist memoirs and apologias, but when their author is a woman there is often a further, and greater, deprivation to be endured: enforced separation from the husband. The domestic life which is her proper sphere is disturbed not only by the theft of goods and, often, loss of the house itself, but also by the breakup of the family, with the husband and father leaving the wife and mother to care as best she can for the children while he pursues military and political matters elsewhere. In March 1645, ten months after his wedding to Ann, Sir Richard Fanshawe "went to Bristol with his new master," the prince, "I then lying in of my first son Harrison Fanshaw, who was borne on the 22nd of

February last ... the sence of leaving me with a dying child, which did dye 2 days after, in a garrison town, extream weake and very poor, were such circumstances as he could not beare with, onely the argument of necescity. And for my own part, it cost me so dear that I was 10 weeks before I could goe alone" (*F*, p. 114). This isolation and consequent vulnerability is repeatedly underscored. After visiting Charles II in Scotland in 1650, Sir Richard left for Holland and "wrote to me to arm myself with patience in his absence," adding that because of the need for secrecy his wife should not expect many letters henceforth: "God knows how great a surprise this was to me, being great with child, and two children with me, not in the best condition to maintain them; and in dayly fear of your father's life" (*F*, p. 133). With both her familial and her national head effectively banished, she is deprived of security in the home as in the state: "I stay'd in this lodging almost seven months, and in that time I did not goe abroad 7 times, but spent my time in prayers to God for the deliverance of the king and my husband" (*F*, p. 133).

This is a vignette of immobility and incapacity, of the weakness of woman bereft of patriarchal stay in private as in public life. The cultural terms in which it epitomizes the experience of Royalist women during the Interregnum are orthodox and unexceptionable. We would expect Royalist memoirs written after "the happiest May-day that hath been many a year in England,"[6] on which Parliament voted the restoration of monarchy, to emphasize both what was formerly endured and the blessing of what is now enjoyed by painting an overwhelmingly bleak picture of what befell the nation until "his Majesty was invited by his subjects, who were not able longer to endure those great confusions and encumbrances they had sustained hitherto, to take possession of his hereditary rights" (*C*, p. 65). However, there is in these politically and socially conservative women's constructions of the past another, unexpected, and even radical, element. The prospect of female vulnerability and wifely helplessness is far from being the dominant image of their memoirs: there is also, and perhaps for the first time in narrative texts, the prospect of female indomitability, of women who can act on the public stage independently of men. Something, it seems, was lost, as well as gained, with the return of subjects to their true obedience, of wives to their husbands. These memoirs are not, of course, nostalgic

---

[6] Pepys, 2 May 1660.

for the revolutionary past. Nevertheless, national anarchy has an animating rather than an enervating effect upon their narratives; domestic instability proves to be enabling rather than paralyzing. To this extent, these testimonies of loyalty and obedience to prince and to husband are politically and culturally disobedient. They are plotted as a series of challenging adventures, casting their authors in the role of dynamic and initiating protagonists, rather than repining and lonely wives. They call upon them to forgo the passivity supposed to be naturally womanly and to assume in its place the audacity and courageousness supposed to be the privilege of the men.[7]

For a telling example of this we may turn to Ann Fanshawe's narrative. In October 1649, injured by a fall from her horse and pregnant, she found herself alone in Cork when the garrison revolted and transferred its allegiance to the Commonwealth. Having packed up what was portable, "about 3 a clock in the morning, by the light of a tapour and in that pain I was in," she sought out the garrison commander and persuaded him to write her a pass, with which "I came through thousands of naked swords" to Kinsale where she found her husband "the most disconsolate man in the world, for fear of his family, which he had no possibility to assist" (F, pp. 123–24). This episode tellingly reverses gender roles: it is *she* who takes the initiative, *he* who sits helplessly and impotently by. While he is unable to fulfill his responsibilities as protector she, even though the weakness supposed natural to her sex is aggravated by injury and pregnancy, is able effectively to disarm masculine aggressiveness and to immobilize those phallocratic emblems, the "naked swords." She furthermore shows herself quick-witted and politically adept by bringing with her Sir Richard's papers. In so doing she frustrated the desires of no lesser a person than Cromwell himself, whom she reports as saying that "'It was as much worth to have seised his papers as the town; for I did make account of them to have known what these parts of the country were worth'" (F, p. 124).

This reversal of gender roles is most evident in the expedient of disguise which was so frequently adopted by Royalist spies and informers and upon which many a Royalist plot depended. Loyalty to patriarchal order, it appears, frequently demands cross-dressing. Men who wish to pass unnoticed dress themselves as women, while the active and dynamic role the Civil War required of women

---

[7] For historical examples of such female responses to the challenge of Civil War see Antonia Fraser, *The Weaker Vessel: Woman's Lot in Seventeenth-century England* (1984), pp. 163–221.

separated from their husbands demands masculine attire. Through her association with the Royalist spy, Colonel Bampfield, Anne Halkett was in 1648 involved, with the approval of Charles I, in the plot "to contrive the Duke of Yorke's escape outt of St James' [House]" (*H*, p. 23) where he lived under the charge of Algernon Percy, 10th Earl of Northumberland. This she effected by providing the duke with a "wemen's habitt." Though her tailor, ignorant of the plot, exclaimed that "hee had never seene any women of so low a stature have so big a wast" as was indicated by the duke's measurements, yet, she adds, he "was very pretty in itt" (*H*, pp. 24–25). The contrary case appears when, sailing from Galway to Malaga in February 1650, Ann Fanshawe and her husband were pursued by a Turkish galley. Women and children were cleared from the deck but, in return for half-a-crown, Ann Fanshawe persuaded her cabin boy "to give me his blew throm cap he wore and his tarred coat," and, so dressed, she returned to the deck and "stood ... by my husband's side as free from sickness and fear as, I confess, from discretion; but it was the effect of that passion which I could never master" (*F*, p. 128).

The narrative voice there is unmistakably reproving. Ann Fanshawe the narrator finds it impossible to condone the action of the Ann Fanshawe who is her subject. The protagonist is measured against a standard of restrained behavior becoming in a woman, and is found wanting.[8] That standard controls her eulogy of her mother: a woman "of excellent beauty and good understanding, a loving wife and most tender mother, very pious and charitable" (*F*, p. 109). Though a positive image, biblically founded and endorsed by every handbook and guide to godliness of the age, this formulation renders Margaret Harrison not as an individual but as an exemplary fulfillment of the feminine gender role (which certainly did not involve dressing like a man). It is a role which the daughter herself apparently endorses. With no word of demur or regret from the narrator, Ann Fanshawe's education is presented as the proper taming of individuality and of unruly female passion:

---

[8] For this standard see the selection of primary materials in N. H. Keeble, ed., *The Cultural Identity of Seventeenth-Century Woman: A Reader* (1994), esp. pp. 96–109, 143–68, and, though taken from a slightly later period, in Bridget Hill, ed., *Eighteenth Century Women: An Anthology* (1987), esp. pp. 18–68, and Vivien Jones, ed., *Women in the Eighteenth Century: Constructions of Femininity* (1990), esp. pp. 17–139. Estelle C. Jelinek, *The Tradition of Women's Autobiography* (Boston, 1986), p. 26, comments on the contrasting and "extraordinary courage and spunk" demonstrated in Fanshawe's text.

my mother's education of me...was with all the advantages that time
afforded, both for working all sorts of fine works with my needle, and
learning French, singing, lute, virginalls, and dancing; and, not with-
standing I learned as well as most did, yet was I wild to that degree that the
houres of my beloved recreation took up too much of my time, for I loved
riding in the first place, and running, and all acteive pastimes; and in fine
I was that which we graver people call a hoyting girle. (*F*, p. 110)

The narrator is avowedly one of those "graver people" who find such
activities reprehensible not intrinsically but when performed by a
girl; they are gender-specific.

In this, Ann Fanshawe is typical. The narrators of these memoirs
generally keep a pretty strict eye on any untoward tendencies in the
sexual politics of their narratives. As befits a girl, Anne Halkett was
taught "to writte, speake French, play [on the] lute and virginalls,
and dance...all kinds of needleworke." This, she claims, "shews I
was nott brought up in an idle life" (*H*, p. 10), but it was active only
within narrowly circumscribed limits. As narrator, Anne Halkett is as
convinced as Ann Fanshawe that a woman's proper bearing is
submissive, dutiful and retiring.

The Duchess of Newcastle is yet more vociferously dismissive of the
emancipation granted by war to women and contemptuous of
women's engagement in public affairs, especially in their husbands'
interests. She was herself a suitor to the Committee for Compounding
with Delinquents for some allowance from her husband's sequestrated estates, but she disdains the role:

the customs of England being changed as well as the laws, where women
become pleaders, attornies, petitioners, and the like, running about with
their several causes, complaining of their several grievances, exclaiming
against their several enemies, bragging of their several favours they receive
from the powerful, thus trafficking with idle words bring in false reports and
vain discourse. For the truth is, our sex doth nothing but jostle for the pre-
eminence of words (I mean not for speaking well, but speaking much) as
they do for the pre-eminence of place... But if our sex would but well
consider and rationally ponder, they will perceive and find, that it is neither
words nor place that can advance them, but worth and merit. Nor can
words or place disgrace them, but inconstancy and boldness: for an honest
heart, a noble soul, a chaste life, and a true speaking tongue, is the throne,
sceptre, crown, and footstool that advances them to an honourable renown.
(*C*, pp. 167–68)[9]

[9] Quoted in Hobby, *Virtue of Necessity*, pp. 83–84, in the course of a discussion of the "highly
repressive image of her own femininity" to be found in Cavendish.

This is to reprehend the immodesty of boldness and the shame of what Richard Baxter called "a laxative running tongue"[10] as categorically as any misogynistic homily. In a similar identification of the feminine with the reticent and the timid, she presents herself as wholly incapable when, separated from her family, she served as a maid of honour to Henrietta Maria at Oxford:

I was so bashful when I was out of my mother's, brothers', and sisters' sight, whose presence used to give me confidence... that when I was gone from them, I was like one that had no foundation to stand, or guide to direct me ... and though I might have learnt more wit, and advanced my understanding by living in a Court, yet being dull, fearful, and bashful, I neither heeded what was said or practised, but just what belonged to my loyal duty. (*C*, p. 161)

And, as she tells it, it was precisely this demure and docile nature which recommended her to the marquis, who "did approve of those bashful fears" since he "would choose such a wife as he might bring to his own humours, and not such a one as was wedded to self-conceit" (*C*, p. 162). Biddable, submissive, obedient subjects: these each of our narrators would have their readers believe they were, as, they insist, all women should be.

And yet, as in the case of the Turkish galley just cited, the exhilaration of independence repeatedly subverts such protestations. Ann Fanshawe's comment that on that occasion she was "as free from sickness and fear, as ... from discretion" is ambivalent. While it explicitly acknowledges and implicitly reproves the indiscretion and unwonted license with which she acted, it also recognizes that this freedom from discretion liberated her from the customary constraints of feminine weakness. She reprehends her insubordination as "the effect of that passion which I could never master," as she ought; and yet it is precisely that passion which many times saves her and her children when proper womanly incapacity would have lost all. Furthermore, it saves her husband. When Sir Richard was taken prisoner in 1651 following the battle of Worcester, it was Ann Fanshawe who was a successful petitioner to Cromwell for his release (*F*, p. 135). More generally, he depended upon her for financial solvency. The moment in 1647 when she assumed this new, and independent, role is registered in the text with some satisfaction:

---

[10] Richard Baxter, *A Christian Directory* (1673), p. 532, para. 10.

"This was the first time that I had undertaken any journy without your father, and the first manage of business he ever put into my hand, in which I thank God I had good success" (*F*, p. 119).

Such "good successes" on her part threaten to jeopardize narrative decorum for they betray a text more taken with a woman's exercise of independent authority than with her fulfillment of her subordinate wifely role; the narrative is at odds with the feminine propriety of its narrator's persona. In its detailed account of the way in which in 1659 she acquired a pass to Paris by assuming a disguise and then forging her own name on the document (*F*, pp. 138–39), Ann Fanshawe's memoir is less interested in the reunion with her husband in France than it is in the means she adopted to achieve that end. The initiative and dexterity (literally, as each altered letter of the name is spelled out) are *hers*; *he* is marginalized, indeed, excluded. Ann Fanshawe is rewriting more than her pass: she is transforming narrative conventions to create a gynocentric text chronicling a woman's frustration and evasion of patriarchal power. Her memoir is, of course, clear that such forward behavior is occasioned and legitimized only by the exceptional and pressing needs of king and husband, but it is nevertheless the impotence of masculine authority which is insistently revealed. As traditional chivalric romance depended upon feminine fragility and passivity, so masculine passivity, the absence of king and husband, permits a transgressively bold female protagonist. During her husband's imprisonment in Whitehall, Ann Fanshawe "failed not constantly to goe, when the clock struck 4 in the morning, with a dark lanterne in my hand, all alone and on foot, from my lodging" to "goe under his window and softly call him"; "thus we talked together" (*F*, pp. 134–35). "All alone and on foot" here signifies not feminine vulnerability but an enabling courage and resourcefulness. This time, it is the prince in the tower who stands in need of rescue, which she effects through her address to Cromwell. And as in the old romances the reader rode out with the knight, leaving the wife at home, so now, when "the necessity both of the publick and your father's private affairs obliged us often to yield to the trouble of absence" (*F*, p. 122), it is with her, not with him, that the narrative remains. Indeed, the first-person singular pronoun can supplant the first plural even when wife and husband are *not* separated: "we" embark for the Isle of Scilly in 1646 but, "extreamly sick, and bigg with child, I was set ashore almost dead," and "I went immediatly to bed" on arrival, awaking "so cold I knew not what to doe" to discover "our bed was neer swimming with the sea;" of what *he* thought of the night's lodging the text is silent (*F*, p. 118).

This newly-centered "I" thus assumes to herself the prerogatives of the old heroes. The appeal to such a model is explicit in the Duchess of Newcastle's account of the bearing of her mother, Elizabeth, Lady Lucas, when the family home at Colchester was sacked in 1642. In her widowhood she had "made her house her cloister, inclosing herself, as it were, therein," but "these unhappy wars fourced her out, by reason she and her children were loyal to the King; for which they plundered her and my brothers all their goods":

> in such misfortunes my mother was of an heroic spirit, in suffering patiently where there is no remedy, or to be industrious where she thought she could help. She was of a grave behaviour, and had such a majestic grandeur, as it were continually hung about her, that it would strike a kind of an awe to the beholders. (*C*, p. 163)

Heroic fortitude and majestic stoicism invest this woman with a dignity and a stature denied to such disconsolately helpless husbands as Sir Richard Fanshawe.

In Anne Halkett's self-construction there is something more vital and canny but hardly less indomitable. The exigencies of war, the desire to serve her prince, and the need to secure the inheritance which her reputation as a malignant withheld from her in legal wrangling compel her to journey throughout her memoir, but her narrative is also a story of courtship and of crosses in love. Hers is a quest for security, but though that security is patriarchally imaged in the rightful headship of the king and of a future husband, it is the challenge of seeking them rather than the satisfaction of securing them which drives the text. The course of each of her three relationships with suitors is no less bound up with the circumstances of war than is her service of her prince, and in recounting them, no less than in recounting her Royalist plottings, it is the resilience with which she engages a hostile world and the ingenuity by which she surmounts sudden hazards in which the narrative delights. She claims that "my owne hart cannott challenge mee with any imodesty, either in thought or behavier, or an act of disobedience to my mother" (*H*, p. 11), and yet the same paragraph tells how she contrived to attend plays without gaining a reputation for moral laxity by going in the company of her sisters, "giving the mony to the footman who waited on us, and hee gave itt in the play-howse"; and in the next paragraph she records her disobedience in accepting the addresses of a man forbidden by her mother. It is, indeed, frequently her wit and deviousness which impress more than her modesty. When her mother threatened to turn her out of doors should she again see her suitor, Thomas Howard, Anne Halkett returned the equivocal reply, "itt should be against my will if ever shee heard of itt" (*H*, p. 15). In the event she contrived to bid him farewell without seeing him by receiving him blindfolded (*H*, p. 18). It is the casuistically deft contrivance of disobedience under the guise of scrupulous obedience which the narrative here celebrates, and the ingenious stratagems with which she meets both personal reverses and political demands will continue to carry her memoir. Even as a young woman she was sufficiently assertive to insist that "though duty did oblieege mee nott to marry any withoutt my mother's consent, yett it would nott tye mee to marry any without my owne" (*H*, p. 15). And indeed, it is not long before the mother vanishes from the text, and Anne Halkett operates as an unconstrained and free agent, a single woman but yet an equal schemer for the Royalist cause with Bampfield and with her future husband, Sir James Halkett. The Edinburgh house of John Hay, 2nd Earl (afterwards Marquis) of Tweeddale, where she lodged in the 1650s (*H*, p. 64), "was the rendevous of the best and most loyall when they came to towne" (*H*, p. 67), and she is not excluded from this cabal or its deliberations.

The radical implications of this political involvement are apparent in Anne Halkett's account of her meeting in 1651 with the Fifth Monarchist, Robert Overton, then a Parliamentarian commander in Scotland.[11] When, during their conversation at Fyvie Castle, Aberdeenshire, where Anne Halkett was staying with Mary Seton, Countess of Dunfermline, Overton opined that "God had wonderfully evidenced his power in the great things hee had done," he received the pointed retort, "noe doupt butt God would evidence his power still in the great things hee designed to doe" (*H*, p. 60). The irony was not lost on Overton, with whom, upon the assurance that it would not be used "'to the prejudice of the noble family I live in, for I can hold my toung,'" she engaged in an impassioned discussion of contemporary affairs, answering as his intellectual and political

[11] For Robert Overton (flourished 1640–88) see *DNB*, and, for this episode, Loftis, ed., *Memoirs*, p. 201.

equal, his republicanism with her loyalism. When he appealed to Daniel to justify "the distruction of monarky," she, wondering why no subsequent settlement of the constitution had yet satisfied the army, conjectured, "'so you will ever find reason to change what ever governmentt you try till you come to beg of the King to come home and governe you againe'." "'Well,' (says hee), 'if this should come to pass, I will say you are a prophetess'" (*H*, p. 61). Not only does it appear that when she is silent she holds her tongue out of deference not to womanly modesty but to political expediency – the times require secrecy and anonymity, she observes elsewhere (*H*, p. 80) – and that she can speak on state affairs as pointedly as any man when she chooses, but also that she is prepared to accept a Puritan's bestowal upon her of the most radical of the roles the English Revolution made available to women.[12]

The geographical journeys undertaken by these heroines are a measure of their cultural journey: as they come out of their houses, so they come out of their housewifely roles. *He* may be her "North Starr," as Ann Fanshawe says of her husband, "that only had the power to fix me" (*F*, p. 122), but the North Star is navigationally useful only to those on the move. Margaret Cavendish may insist that hers has been "a strict and retired life," but she admits that "I have been a traveller both before and after I was married" (*C*, p. xxxvii). It is, indeed, remarkable how little time in these memoirs is passed in retirement, how much in activity, how seldom we are within doors, how often without, how rarely we engage in domestic business, how often in political. We are usually either on the road or on shipboard. These authors would not be pleased to be associated with Chaucer's Wife of Bath, who "koude muchel of wandrynge by the weye,"[13] but there is something of the same quality of moral and intellectual venturing in their traveling; the audacity of travel physically is matched by an imaginative, political, and intellectual audacity. The latter part of Ann Fanshawe's memoir becomes, in fact, a kind of travelog, curious about and fascinated by unfamiliar foreign sights and sounds. Her biographical record of her husband's life is very largely an account of "all *my* travells" (*F*, p. 132, emphasis added), for, while her "North Starr" is confined in ambassadorial negoti-

---

[12] For female prophets in the English revolution, see Hobby, *Virtue of Necessity*, pp. 26–53, and Nigel Smith, *Perfection Proclaimed: Language and Literature in English Radical Religion 1640–1660* (Oxford, 1989), index.

[13] Geoffrey Chaucer, *The Canterbury Tales*, "General Prologue," l. 467, in *The Complete Works*, ed. F. N. Robinson, 2nd edn. (1957), p. 21.

ations, she is abroad, looking about her. This is most sustainedly so on the occasion of her husband's appointment as ambassador to Spain. The journey from London to Madrid in 1664 is given in considerable detail (*F*, pp. 152–63), culminating in an audience before Philip IV (*F*, pp. 163–65) and an account of the customs and manners of "the best established court but our own in the Christian world that ever I saw, and I have had the honour to live in seven" (*F*, p. 172).[14]

Occasionally, amidst reiterated approvals of excellent wives, there are indications of admiration for the boldness of women who so venture. When Ann Fanshawe remarks of her sister-in-law, Elizabeth, second wife of Thomas, 1st Viscount Fanshawe, that "She was a very good wife, but not else qualified extraordinary in anything" (*F*, p. 106), the possibility – even, desirability – of extraordinary female achievement of another kind is conceded. It is recognized in her mother-in-law, Elizabeth, Lady Fanshawe, whom she admires less because, "being left a widow at 39 years of age, handsom, with a full fortune," she "kept her self a widow," than for the skillful financial management which enabled her to increase her children's legacies and dowries (*F*, pp. 107–08). More striking still, during Sir Richard's embassy to Portugal, she "severall times waited on the Qween Mother," Luisa de Guzman, who was "magnificent in her discourse and nature, but in the prudentest manner. She was ambitious, but not vain. She loved government, and I doe believe the quitting of it did shorten her life" (*F*, p. 146). Those adversative conjunctions, conceding what is due to feminine modesty, cannot disguise the excited awe with which she contemplates the magnificence of political power in the hands of a woman; for the sentence neglects to add, as it ought, that the queen's life was *justly* shortened for this usurpation of masculine authority. On the contrary, the queen's disappointment appears to be sympathetically understood.[15]

---

[14] Dale Spender, *Mothers of the Novel* (1986), p. 34, comments upon Ann Fanshawe's responsiveness to foreign culture and her "talent" for rendering it in realistic detail. See also Sandra Findley and Elaine Hobby, "Seventeenth-Century Women's Autobiography," in Francis Barker *et al.*, eds., *1642: Literature and Power in the Seventeenth Century* (Colchester, 1981), p. 33, which discerns in Fanshawe anticipations of the manner of Defoe. Jelinek, *Women's Autobiography*, pp. 29–30, recognizes a similar "novelistic skill" in Halkett.

[15] With Ann Fanshawe's sentiment one might contrast the conventional contemporary view of Lucy Hutchinson that "never is … any place happie where the hands that are made for distaffes affect the management of Sceptres," *Memoirs of the Life of Colonel Hutchinson*, ed. James Sutherland (Oxford, 1973), p. 48. Lucy Hutchinson's Puritan *Memoirs* reveal tensions similar to those here analyzed in Royalist memoirs: see my "'The Colonel's Shadow': Lucy Hutchinson, Women's Writing and the Civil War," in Thomas Healy and Jonathan Sawday, eds., *Literature and the English Civil War* (Cambridge, 1990), pp. 227–47.

These memoirs are thus in the way to fashion a female self who is anything but an obedient feminine subject.[16] Some pretty strenuous apologetic strategies are needed to legitimize such an enterprise. Of these, the most obvious is to propose to tell not the woman's improper story but the man's proper one. This is the expedient of Margaret Cavendish, as of Ann Fanshawe, and yet it is not any easy one to manage, precisely because the narrator is excluded from her chosen narrative. Early in her memoir, Ann Fanshawe tells the exemplary story of her education into her wifely role. Misled by Elizabeth Savage, Countess Rivers, "a brave woman, and one that had suffered very many thousands pounds loss for the King, and that I had a great reverence for" into supposing that "it being a fashionable thing [it] would make me more beloved of my husband" to show an interest in state affairs, she questioned him repeatedly concerning Court business, only to be told:

"...when you asked of me my business, it was wholy out of my power to satisfy thee. For my life and fortune shall be thine, and every thought of my heart, in which the trust I am in may not be revealed; but my honour is my own, which I can not preserve if I communicate the Prince's affaires, and pray thee with this answer rest satisfyed." So great was his reason and goodness, that upon consideration it made my folly appear to be so vile, that from that day untill the day of his death I never thought fit to aske him any business, but that he communicated freely to me, in order to his estate or family. (*F*, pp. 115–16)

Ann Fanshawe has learned the folly of inquiring into men's affairs; she has been properly rebuked and has learned that hers is the private, not the public, sphere. "Man is made to govern Common-Wealths and women their private Families," as Margaret Cavendish put it.[17] Thus excluded, she cannot, as a narrator, treat of a world of which she has no knowledge; nor, of course, would decorum permit her to treat of domestic or familial affairs, still less of the intimacies of her relationship with her husband. Consequently, she wants material even for the eulogizing and memorializing of her husband which, as a woman, can be her only legitimate literary business. Like *The Life of William Cavendish*, whose author concedes that she was "neither actor nor spectator" of much of her husband's life (*C*, p. 1), Ann

---

[16] For tensions within Cavendish's self-construction and her determined self-centering and self-exaltation, see Janet Todd, *The Sign of Angellica: Women, Writing and Fiction, 1660–1800* (1989), pp. 55–68, the most persuasive account we have of the duchess's work.

[17] Cavendish, *Natures Pictures*, pp. 112–13, quoted in Todd, *Sign of Angellica*, p. 65.

Fanshawe's is a text in search of a subject. Under the guise of homage from the feminine to the masculine (it is her *husband*'s life) it in fact has altogether less deferential business on hand.

These autobiographical texts hence come to ironize their narrators' patriarchal commitment. Explicitly dedicated to the vindication and commemoration of loyalty, memorializing husbands, addressed to sons, and written under the confident aegis of a restored patriarchal order, they nevertheless create from the exceptional experiences of the Interregnum years wayward heroines whose transgression of the bounds of the "naturally" womanly, though in the loyal service of patriarchy, contradicts its sustaining ideology. They begin to create a discourse which not even their narrators can approve, or, perhaps, recognize. Apparently devoted to the true centers of their political and private worlds – king and husband – they are in fact centering what should be marginal, granting a voice to what should be silent, affording a story to what should be uneventful. Consequent tensions between the tendency of these texts and their dutiful narrators are most signally present in Margaret Cavendish's convoluted justification of her own autobiographical essay: "some censuring readers will scornfully say, why hath this Lady writ her own life? since none cares to know whose daughter she was or whose wife she is, or how she was bred, or what fortune she had, or how she lived, or what humour or disposition she was of." In reply, she appeals to tradition – "there have been many that have done the like, as Caesar, Ovid, and many more, both men and women" – but the inappropriateness of the precedents (Caesar? Ovid?), and the slightly desperate "men and women" subvert the claim. There is no sustaining tradition, and she can finally only protest to her readers: "I write it for my own sake, not theirs" (*C*, p. 178). This is a moment of undisguised self-assertiveness, perhaps the assertiveness of exasperation, but, more revealingly, it is also a tense moment of incongruity in the text. This outburst is immediately covered by a final explanation, that the "True Relation" is written to prevent posterity's confusing Margaret, the duke's second wife, with his first (*C*, p. 178).[18] The

---

[18] In a recent review Donald Davie, quoting this passage, wonders whether it is deliberately parodic: "did she not know what the rhetoricians required of a peroration, or did she know, whether by luck or good management, how to design a peroration that breaks the rules and is the better for it?," *TLS* 4630 (27 December 1991), p. 6. Supposing that the "True Relation" ends "rather oddly and pathetically for a modern reader," Todd suggests that the duchess's desire to distinguish herself may be taken as "self-assertion, the pushing forward of an individual woman," *Sign of Angellica*, p. 60.

awkwardness and absurdity of this, often mocked, is a measure of how far the text flouts received canons of literary propriety. Without an authorizing precedent, without a proper subject, and without a suitable deferential tone, Margaret Cavendish, writer, must take refuge behind Margaret Cavendish, wife. The text's creatively assertive individuality is brought to dutiful heel by this declaration that the "I" for whom the "True Relation" is written is the latter, not the former.[19]

And so it must be, since there was no recognized role for a woman writer, or none other than as, at best, a bold and immodest self-publicist, at worst, a whore.[20] It is an implicit recognition of this which lies behind Margaret Cavendish's reiterated insistence upon her quietude and quiescence, and, especially her dismissal of her compositions in comparison with her husband's: he "creates himself with his pen, writing what his wit dictates to him, but I pass my time rather with scribbling than writing, with words than wit" (*C*, p. 172). Such self-effacement is proper and becoming, and is a common strategy in women's writing of this period, but it sorts ill with the text's self-assertiveness. This reprover of bold loquacity in women, who, when her husband is present, would "rather attentively listen to what he says, than impertinently speak," claims to be "addicted to contemplation" (*C*, p. 172). Her contemplativeness, however, proves to be not a meditative passivity but the occasion for an active creativity not possible to her (or not admitted by her) in any recognized woman's role. In her statement that she was "addicted from my childhood to contemplation rather than conversation, to solitariness rather than society, to melancholy rather than mirth, to write with the pen than to work with a needle, passing my time with harmless fancies, their company being pleasing, their conversation innocent" (*C*, p. 172) the parallelism which establishes her retiring nature ("contemplation *rather than* conversation," "solitariness *rather than* society") apparently presents writing as an equivalent, and equally feminine, characteristic of her behavior ("to write with the pen [*rather*] *than* to work with a needle"), but there is duplicity here:

[19] For a contrary reading of this passage as an attempt to establish Cavendish's "individuality and identity separately from the husband whose name she bears," see Hobby, *Virtue of Necessity*, p. 82.

[20] For contemporary views on the impropriety of women writing see the extracts in Jones, *Glorious Fame*, pp. 140–91, and the discussions in Jane Spencer, *The Rise of the Woman Novelist: from Aphra Behn to Jane Austen* (Oxford, 1986) pp. 3–6, 24–25, 28–29; Todd, *Sign of Angellica*, pp. 33–35; and Mendelson, *Mental World*, pp. 34–36.

the terms have been reversed. The opposition is now between a metonym for wifely domesticity ("needle") and for masculine creativity ("pen"), but it is the latter, not the former, which occupies the rhetorical position of the acceptably feminine within the structure of the sentence. There is an implicit awareness of this in the sentence's immediate attempt to mollify and justify – these are only harmless, pleasing, innocent (*women's*) fancies – but the admission has been made: the pen is preferred to the needle.[21] Furthermore, her "contemplation" enables her to converse very well without having to wait upon an interlocutor; to indulge in fancies inadmissible in polite social discourse; to follow her own will, rather than another's. The entire passage, couched in terms of womanly withdrawal, is a strategy to secure the liberty to create and to publish her own autonomous subject. And, as tends to be the way with texts, this subject proves to be far from culturally obedient.

---

[21] For discussion of the justification of writing in relation to housewifely duties elsewhere in the duchess's work, see Todd, *Sign of Angellica*, pp. 61–62.

PART IV

Empire and aftermaths

Seventeenth-century Quaker women: displacement, colonialism, and anti-slavery discourse

Moira Ferguson

I SPIRITUAL EQUALITY, THE RETREAT FROM MILITARISM, AND THE POLITICS OF COMPENSATION

The polemic on freedom as a human right delivered by Aphra Behn's eponymous hero in *Oroonoko; or, The History of the Royal Slave* (1688), anticipated future anti-slavery demands and sounded a void in the first century of white British women's commentaries on slavery.[1] By contrast, religious equality still surpassed emancipation as a more consistently discussed topic during these hundred years. Among its vital early proponents were women in the Society of Friends whose spiritual beliefs and refashioned political direction explain their unorthodoxy.[2] Like Behn's writings, their commentaries derived from first-hand personal experience, but they largely confined themselves to discussions of spiritual access and compensation. Demands for full-scale emancipation within the Society, early by the standards of society in general, were a hundred years away.

Quaker women had militated vigorously during the Civil War but had quickly lost any power and influence they had garnered at the Restoration. By 1661–62 Quaker men and women experienced

---

[1] Aphra Behn, *Oroonoko, or The History of the Royal Slave* (1688), ed. K. A. Sey (Tema, Ghana, 1977), p. 56.

[2] Among many good accounts of Quaker involvement in the anti-slavery struggle, see Auguste Jorns, *The Quakers as Pioneers in Social Work*, trans. Thomas Kite Brown, Jr. (New York, 1931), and Richard Vann, *The Social Development of English Quakerism, 1655–1755* (Cambridge, Mass., 1969). Although William Braithwaite in *The Second Period of Quakerism* (1919) confines himself to the seventeenth century, he mentions some aspects of early anti-slavery thought among Friends and provides for an understanding of the Society's later, more forward-looking tendencies; see especially pp. 415, 436, 596, 618, and 621. George Fox's *Epistles* contain the fullest information about the developing view of slavery in the Society of Friends: *A Collection of Many Select and Christian Epistles, Letters and Testimonies, Written on Sundry Occasions by that Ancient Eminent, Faithful Friend and Minister of Christ and Jesus, George Fox*, with preface by George Whitehead, 2 vols. (1698). See also David Brion Davis, *The Problem of Slavery in Western Culture* (Ithaca, New York, 1966).

severe repercussions for opposing the *status quo* – so much so that, as
Barry Reay compellingly argues, the Society of Friends at the point
of its threatened dissolution began to conceal prior militarism to
avoid persecutions:

Before [1661] it is impossible to talk, as it is later, of the Quakers as a
predominantly pacifist group. Self-preservation after the restoration of the
monarchy in 1660, disillusionment with the effectiveness of political action,
encouraged them to project their pacifism backwards. "Pacifism was not
characteristic of the early Quakers: it was forced upon them by the hostility
of the outside world."[3]

The Quaker Act of 1662 that forbade religious assemblies of over five
members incited soldiers to invade Friends' meetings, "beating and
kicking and hurling the people on heaps and pushing them with the
ends of their muskets and weapons."[4] In the face of this gratuitous
dragooning, Quakers retreated tacitly from overt activism. However, a few among them – Dewars Moray, Dorothy White, and
Hester Biddle – did continue to agitate for activism.[5] Not until two
years after the Great Fire of London (1666) did such violence
substantially diminish, and then only temporarily.[6] By that time
moves were afoot to reorganize and streamline the Society in
accordance with their strategic and understandably self-preserving
withdrawal from vanguardist hostilities.

During these decades of policy transformation, George Fox's
epistolary exhortations to Friends in the Caribbean persisted and
even escalated.[7] By 1657 in an Epistle addressed to "Friends beyond
Sea, that have Black and Indian Slaves," he was urging uncon-
ditioned access to the Gospel.[8] In 1671 he entreated planters to

---

[3] Barry Reay, "Quakerism and Society," in J. F. McGregor and B. Reay, eds., *Radical Religion in the English Revolution* (Oxford, 1984), pp. 141–64, this passage p. 153, quoting A. Cole, "The Quakers and Politics, 1652–1660" (University of Cambridge Ph.D thesis, 1955), p. 284; and see Reay's "The Quakers, 1659, and the Restoration of the Monarchy," *History* 63: 208 (June 1978): 193–213.   [4] Braithwaite, *Second Period*, p. 24.

[5] Private correspondence from Elaine Hobby to Moira Ferguson, January 1991.

[6] In 1672 the Declaration of Indulgence suspended the Penal Laws against Nonconformists, who could meet from that point on. At the Great Pardon of 1672 many Quakers were released. Over the next two years, discriminatory laws were reinstituted. Fox instigated segregated sex-differentiated meetings after this renewal of persecution.

[7] Out of 420 epistles written by Fox, nineteen concern slavery, including two that focus on captives in Algiers. Several specifically address the inhabitants of Barbados.

[8] Herbert Aptheker, "The Quakers and Negro Slavery," *The Journal of Negro History* 25 (1940): 331–62.

"endeavor to train [slaves] up in the Fear of God...[and] after certain years of servitude...make them free."[9] Fox's language in regard to possessing and training slaves underscores predetermined relations of power between Friends and their slaves and upholds the colonial bureaucracy while urging the importance of spiritual practice. In 1674 he was encouraging Friends to step up their counseling of the reluctant or the faithless: "and all that are not Faithful, let them be admonished to Faithfulness, that so they may come into the Light, and Life, and service of God and Christ."[10] Caribbean administrators abhorred this concern for slaves' spiritual welfare and subsequently accused Friends of provoking insurrection. In 1675 slaves in Barbados were planning the first known major rebellion, a "Coromantee plot led by Tony and Cufee,"[11] which was exposed after an informer, Anna, alias Fortuna, tipped off her master, Judge Gyles Hall. White governors brutally avenged the leaders. William Edmundson, another Friend who traveled with Fox to Barbados in the 1670s and argued before the governor that all souls were born with an "eternal destiny," no exceptions, was accused of incitement, since the racist governor scoffed at the very idea of slaves unilaterally executing a rebellion.[12] Unlike Fox, Edmundson outspokenly challenged slavery and earmarked himself as a plantocratic target, an upstart, oppositional outsider. Anti-Quaker laws were subsequently enacted to undermine potential support for armed rebellion.[13]

To make matters more difficult, Quakers themselves were being subjected to persecution in Barbados.

[9] *The Journal of George Fox, Revised by Norman Penney* (1924), p. 277.
[10] The epistle of 1674 is entitled "For the Men and Womens Meetings – Barbados," Fox, *Epistles*, epistle 314, p. 343. In epistle 315 of 1675, "to Friends in Barbados," Fox discusses intensified persecution in England and the supportive letters received from Friends abroad; Fox, *Epistles*, p. 353.
[11] Michael Craton, *Testing the Chains: Resistance to Slavery in the British West Indies* (Ithaca, New York, 1982), pp. 105–14, 335.
[12] Aptheker, "Quakers," p. 333. See also *Early Quaker Writings* ed. Hugh Barbour and Arthur O. Roberts (Grand Rapids, Michigan, 1973), p. 591. Note too that protesters existed outside the Society of Friends: among the few were Morgan Godwyn, *The Negro's and Indian's Advocate, Suing for their Admission into the Church* (1680), and Richard Baxter, *Chapters from a Christian Director, or a Summ of Practical Theology and Cases of Conscience* (1664–65), rpt. ed. Jeanne H. Tawney (1925). In *Christian Directory* (1637), the celebrated nonconformist, Richard Baxter, condemned slave-hunters as "the common enemies of mankind," although he condoned slavery as long as it were well-regulated; see Sir Reginald Coupland, *The British Anti-Slavery Movement* (1933), p. 40. For more information, see Davis, *Problem of Slavery*, pp. 204–06, 338–41.   [13] Aptheker, "Quakers," p. 334.

[Since] Barbados was the first island of the West Indies to come into English Possession[,] Quakers had been banished to this island and to Jamaica; and Fox visited them on his missionary journey.[14]

In the 1650s, when Lieutenant-Colonel Rous, an affluent plantation-owning friend of the governor, had joined the Society, their Barbadian membership grew rapidly and the island became a missionary headquarters.[15] But by October 1677 William Penn and Thomas Corbett examined "the laws and charter of Barbados" with a view to addressing the king and Council of the House of Commons on behalf of Quaker "sufferers" there. Fox was well aware of the possibility of responses like the "savage floggings, brandings, and imprisonments" that occurred in the New England colonies.[16]

In 1678 Fox bowed to pressure, pleading his case before the Barbadian governor against an accusation that Friends were pro-voking slaves to resist. Far from confessing that he sided with the rebels, Fox denounced uprising as "a thing we utterly abhor in our hearts" and counseled slaves "to love their masters and mistresses, to be faithful and diligent [so they will receive "kind and gentle" treatment] ... nor commit adultery, nor fornication nor curse, swear, nor lie."[17] Since anti-establishment activities in Britain, together with Friends' aid supplied earlier to African-Caribbean slave insurrectionaries, had threatened their sectarian existence, Fox opted for the more self-preserving tactic of non-resistance. There are clear parallels here with Quakers resorting to class order and urging servants to be obedient, positions being adopted as official policy by Meetings at the time. Just as much or perhaps more to the point, a substantial number of Friends still owned slaves, the result of "filthy covetousness," and persisted in doing so until well into the eighteenth century.[18] Nor were Friends exempt from the double standard of society at large. Complicitous with African-Caribbean slavery, Friends also made plans to redeem any of their members who were:

... taken captive by the Barbary pirates. The first appeal for funds, issued in 1679, brought in more than eleven hundred pounds and at no time did the

---

[14] Jorns, *Quakers*, p. 198.
[15] John Rous, son of the Lieutenant Governor, who was a rich planter, married a daughter of Margaret Fell Fox by her first marriage to Judge Fell. See Braithwaite, *Second Period*, p. 618.
[16] William Braithwaite, *The Beginnings of Quakerism* (1912), p. 403.
[17] *Memoirs of the Life of George Fox. The Friends Library: Comprising Journals, Doctrinal Treatises, and Other Writings of Members of the Religious Society of Friends*, vol. 1, ed. William Evans and Thomas Evans (Philadelphia, 1838), p. 81.
[18] Eric Williams, *Capitalism and Slavery* (New York, 1944), pp. 43–44; Jorns, *Quakers*, p. 207.

balance fall below four hundred pounds... The earliest reference so far found in the Quaker records to the redemption of captives is a note of a gift of ten pounds of 1674 to help two Friends in Turkey, and the great majority of the entries occur between 1679 and 1688.[19]

The historical contradiction between helping kidnapped Europeans and upholding colonial slavery remained. Despite compromises with the plantocracy, however, there were elements in the Friends community that opposed slavery. In 1688, in colonial America, Francis Daniel Pastorius mounted the first public anti-slavery protest in Germantown, Pennsylvania, which inaugurated an unsystematic series of protests in the late seventeenth and eighteenth century until emancipation became Friends' official policy in 1761.[20]

II THE EFFECT OF PACIFISM ON FEMALE FRIENDS

Quietist ideology seriously circumscribed the lives of Quaker women because, unlike women in British society at large, female Friends had wielded substantial power within the Society of Friends. Not to mince matters, the pacifist retreat resulted in such restrictive roles for Quaker women that the Society's view of women became virtually indistinguishable from the view held in British society as a whole.[21] None the less, Quaker women fought to hold their own and at least a celebrated handful refused to be bound by the new conservative politics.

The first person to join George Fox in the Society of Friends, and a single-minded, open-hearted radical by the time she met him, Elizabeth Hooton inspired men and women alike; probably she motivated Fox's first defense of a woman preacher.[22] In fact, the

---

[19] Arnold Lloyd, *Quaker Social History 1669–1738* (1950), Introduction by Herbert G. Wood, p. 38. [20] Jorns, *Quakers*, pp. 202–20; and Aptheker, "Quakers," pp. 335–36.

[21] For an extensive view of the role of Quaker women in the Society of Friends, see Hobby, *Virtue of Necessity*. This essay is indebted to Elaine Hobby's extensive research. See also Phyllis Mack's compelling article, "Women as Prophets During the English Civil War," *Feminist Studies* 8: 1 (1982): 19–45, and Mabel Richmond Brailsford, *Quaker Women*, *1650–1690* (1915). For a conventional view of women's role increasingly being challenged, see Braithwaite, *Second Period*, p. 341. See also Reay, "Quakerism," pp. 143–46. For the role of women in Civil War sects, consult K. V. Thomas, "Women and the Civil War Sects," *Past and Present* 13 (1958): 42–63; Ellen McArthur, "Women Petitioners and the Long Parliament," *EHR* 24 (1909): 698–709; and E. M. Williams, "Women Preachers in the Civil War," *Journal of Modern History* 1 (1929): 561–69; and see Hobby, *Virtue of Necessity*, pp. 47–49.

[22] Elaine Hobby drew my attention to the fact that Hooton was "already an established preacher" before joining the Society of Friends. See Hobby, *Virtue of Necessity*, pp. 36–37, and Brailsford, *Quaker Women*, p. 17. See also Emily Manners, *Elizabeth Hooton: First Quaker*

received view of the early Fox as the Society's original proponent of women's rights disregards the fact that women's robust activism predates participation. In Elaine Hobby's words,

Women had played important parts in the development of the Familists and Anabaptists earlier in the century ... [and] while it is true that Fox supported a woman's right to speak in church, the initiative in the much-cited case was taken by the woman who asked the question.[23]

Edward Burrough mentions "the very first occasion of the first setting up [of] that meeting of women, to visit the sick and to search out the necessities of the poor, weak, widow, and aged." At one point, Fox rejected out of hand John Bunyan's view that women were "that simple and weak sex."[24] A certain sentence from the Bible that Fox frequently quoted more aptly expressed his views: "Christ renews man and woman up into the image of God as they were in before they fell."[25] But times changed, although the association of women with benevolence and healing did not.

Monthly and quarterly meetings were established in 1667 and 1668 to organize the Society more systematically. Formal meetings, including meetings of women alone, were established "in some though not all areas about a decade later," justified by the fact that, in Fox's words, "many things... [are] proper for the women to look into ... which is not so proper for the men."[26] Gender-segregated meetings signified a new direction for the Society, a recognition of female power and (we could speculate) an attempt to suppress it through marginalization. Before marriages between Friends could take place, women's meetings had to grant permission; as people "in the know," more specifically home-oriented than their male counterparts, women could head off domestic strife. In response, men who objected to women's meetings and felt "subjected to the power of women" formed separatist groups.[27] They ran afoul of young and old alike.[28] Some of the most powerful women in these women's meetings were quite elderly – Margaret Fell herself and Theophilia Townsend,

Woman Preacher (1660–1672) in *The Journal of Friends Historical Society*, ed. Norman Penney, Supp. 12 (1914).

[23] Hobby, *Virtue of Necessity*, p. 36; and see Lloyd, *Quaker Social History*, pp. 107ff. For the controversy about women, see also Vann, *Social Development*, pp. 103–04.

[24] Lloyd, *Quaker Social History*, pp. 109, 107. For specific ideological differences between B·rrough and Bunyan, see Braithwaite, *Beginnings*, pp. 285–88.

[25] Lloyd, *Quaker Social History*, p. 108.   [26] *Ibid.*, p. 110.

[27] Vann, *Social Development*, p. 103 and note 25.

[28] I thank Elaine Hobby for this and other insights.

for example. They had been around and even active during the 1650s, as Civil War activists. In fact, as Hobby puts it, one of the more distressing things about the women's meetings policy statements is that they include statements by older women counseling younger women on being good and dutiful wives and mothers.

The transformative Restoration vision of ideal womanhood, spelled out by the anonymous author of *The Ladies Calling* (1673), included modesty, meekness, affability, and piety. Precisely this vision had rendered the poet Katherine Philips "matchless" in the eyes of many contemporaries, and stamped the earthier Aphra Behn as beyond the pale. In the preface to *The Ladies Calling*, the anonymous author sited women's intellects "below" those of men: "Yet sure in the sublimest part of humanity, they are their equals. They have souls of as divine an Original, as endless as Duration, and as capable as infinite Beautitude." The author went on to say that women "will forge that more intrinsic part of their being, lie as if they were all body, reject the Manna, and rave after the Quails, that destruction ... they must own to spring from themselves."[29]

Becoming a female traveling missionary in the Society of Friends may not have been what the author of *The Ladies Calling* meant by raving after quails, but in that age of patriarchal mandate and restipulation of women's roles, missionary work presented an acceptable way out of the impasse in power relations, its popularity attested to by the number of females who offered their services.[30] In the 1650s, having envisioned Friends as people with a sacred "Universal mission [to carry] their message beyond seas," Fox organized groups to implement that mission. The qualification for "the ministration of the Gospel was anointing or being inspired to speak at a meeting after a very serious self-examination."[31] According to David Brion Davis, Friends were the first English Protestant evangelizers of African-Caribbean slaves and provided an oper-

[29] *The Ladies Calling. In Two Parts. The Second Impression* (Oxford, 1673). Angeline Goreau in *The Whole Duty of Woman: Female Writers in Seventeenth-Century England* (New York, 1985), p. 12, speculates that the author may have been Richard Allestree, and discusses contemporary women's rights.

[30] The institution of the traveling missionary was apparently disintegrating during the period. Richard Vann cites this disintegration as "one of the first effects of persecution," *Social Development*, p. 96. However, the women in question refused to abandon the hard-won freedoms of the 1640s, 1650s, and early 1660s. As Phyllis Mack argues, they may well have seen themselves as akin to Old Testament prophets. For hardships suffered by female traveling missionaries, see Joseph Besse, *Collection of the Sufferings of People Called Quakers* (1753). [31] Vann, *Social Development*, pp. 99–100.

ational model. Uneasy about slavery, Morgan Goodwyn had vigorously denounced Friends, but he had also witnessed the activities of George Fox in Barbados, presumably softening his opinion.[32] As Joyce Irwin comments, "in accordance with the generally prominent role of women in the Society," a strikingly high percentage of the missionaries were women.[33] In 1655 Mary Fisher and Anne Austin were first in the Caribbean, Fisher having determined on "a moshon to Barbados."[34] Many women who joined the Society, moreover, had formerly been itinerant preachers and simply continued that practice in a new guise.

By the 1660s and 1670s, missionary networks radiated far afield. When Anne Whithead wrote from England to women's meetings in Barbados asking for money to be distributed among local sufferers, she received a reply from 187 women.[35] Ignoring orthodox rules of behavior, some Quaker women ventured to ameliorate the situation of slaves, remaining silent as to any contradiction between a commitment to spiritual equality and the condoned insti-tutionalization of human bondage. Of course, any agitation on behalf of slaves would automatically place Europeans on the border territory of their community. Having said that, I want to turn now to the case of Alice Curwen, who bypassed some of Fox's pro-slavery accommodations, subtly and discursively, querying the institution's legitimacy.

III ALICE CURWEN

In the 1670s Alice Curwen insisted not only on the right of slaves to inner light and spiritual salvation but, more crucially, she anticipated an emancipationist outlook in her refusal to treat African-Caribbeans as commodities. Her personal circumstances explain her novel ideas and praxis.

When Alice Curwen and Thomas Curwen, Friends from Lanca-shire, visited Barbados about 1675, renewed persecution was driving many Quakers from the island. Long eager to proselytize despite her husband's reluctance, Alice Curwen was singularly undeterred. Besides, she was intent on evading the brutal harassment of Quakers

---

[32] Davis, *Problem of Slavery*, p. 214; see footnote 12.

[33] Joyce L. Irwin, *Womanhood in Radical Protestantism 1525–1675* (New York and Toronto, 1979), p. 235.   [34] Brailsford, *Quaker Women*, p. 38.

[35] Lloyd, *Quaker Social History*, p. 115. Elaine Hobby has shown that some Quakers in London had been organizing women's meetings "since about 1657;" Hobby, *Virtue of Necessity*, p. 47.

in Britain and the specific intimidation of her own family. In the opening of *A Relation of the Labour, Travail and Suffering of Alice Curwen*, she explains how she was spiritually motivated to record her experiences.[36] She cannot ignore the sequential directive of her double-voiced discourse – the name of the father spoken through his ambassador for the civilizing mission:

The 10th day of the 11th month, 1677. When I was retired in my Mind waiting upon the Lord, it was opened in my Heart by the invisible Power of the living God, the vertue of which I felt, and the Springs of Life being witnessed, I was moved to write of the Dealings of the Lord with me, and of my Travels and of my Testimony in writing, since I went from my outward Being; and what I had received from Friends in writing, of the good Success, and Blessing, and Presence of the invisible God ... of my Heart, What thou hast kept, write: but I fearing said within myself, Why should it be known? and the answer was, For the Encouragement of them that thereafter may put their Truth in the Lord; and then I was made willing to write as followeth. (p. 2)

Curwen then deplores the "great tribulations" suffered by "servants of the Lord" in Boston, Massachusetts, mentioning "cruel whippings ... bonds and imprisonments" (p. 2). She and her husband journeyed to several towns on the east coast, but, unlike her husband, Curwen remained apprehensive about visiting Barbados. Eventually, as she tells it, her obedience to the law of the father, coded as her faith, infused her with necessary courage. During their seven-month Barbadian visit from March to October 1677, the couple inspired several "convincements" – "we had good service both amongst Whites and Blacks" – which they attributed to their facility for radiating "everlasting praises." They aimed to save one and all "in every nation" (p. 6). In this sense of mission Alice Curwen echoed the reasons for traveling of Friend Sarah Cheever who had set off with Katherine Evans in 1568 for Alexandria and had traveled widely abroad:

[36] Alice Curwen, *A Relation of the Labour, Travail and Suffering of that Faithful Servant of the Lord Alice Curwen. Who departed this Life the 7th Day of the 6th Moneth, 1679, and resteth in Peace with the Lord. Here is the patience of the Saints, here are they that keep the Commandments of God, and the Faith of Jesus, Rev. 14.12. The Souls of the Righteous are precious in the Eyes of the Lord, and they shall be had in Everlasting Remembrance. Printed in the year 1680. Some of Alice Curwen's Testimony. Such did he upon her to declare some few dayes before she departed out of the Body; she spoke for one to come and write, and there was one that did come, and did propose to write, but the Lord's power and presence was so with her, that the Friends that were with her were so broken into Tenderness that there could do nothing to be written, but there was one Friend which was present with her at the time which did remember something of what she did speak as followeth, whose name is Ann Martindall*, Huntington Library, Box 131.

He hath chosen me, who am the least of all: but God, who is rich in mercy, for his own name's sake hath passed by mine offences, and hath counted me worthy to bear testimony to his holy name, before the mighty men of the earth. Oh the love of the Lord to my soul! My tongue cannot express, neither hath it entered into the heart of man, to conceive of the things that God hath laid up for them that fear him ... What profit is there, to gain the whole world, and lose your own souls? Seek first the kingdom of god and the righteousness thereof, and all other things shall be added to you.[37]

The Curwens' visit coincided with the inception of separate Friends' meetings in Britain and the concomitant diminution in women's power. Race-segregated meetings in Barbados were initiated over the next five years. Although the island had been formerly viewed by Quakers, in George Rofe's phrase, as "the nursery of the truth," a place where Friends could freely discuss and propagate their belief, they now felt obliged to accede to government pressure and relinquish their former more liberal practices.[38]

One remarkable incident recounted in her *Relation* denotes Alice Curwen's egregiously independent mind and spirit. She tells of chiding a widow for making spiritual decisions on behalf of slaves: "For in love we came to visit thee" (p. 18). This account, printed in 1680, the year following her death, pinpoints her concern for spiritual compensation or religious conversion for slaves. She heard of a widow in Barbados named Martha Tavernor, who had "Negro's to her Servants, who were convinced of God's Eternal Truth" (p. 18). Whether Curwen heard this from a missionary or slaves is unclear but most likely she received her information from a missionary who in turn Eurocentrically voiced the opinions of slaves. Curwen goes on to describe how she "was moved to go speak to the Woman for their coming to our Meetings" (p. 18). Curwen's reference to "their coming to our Meetings" exemplifies a familiar discourse about slaves. What Mary Louise Pratt calls a "familiar, widespread, and stable form of othering" is spoken by a European subject or narrator in the stance of an observer. These totalized others, Pratt goes on to say, are:

distilled even further into an iconic "he" (the standardized adult male specimen). This abstracted "he"/"they" is the subject of verbs in a timeless present tense, which characterizes anything "he" is or does not as a particular historical event but as an instance of a pregiven custom or trait

[37] Cited in Irwin, *Womanhood*, pp. 236–37.
[38] George Rofe, *The Righteousness of man, Wherein he was created: ... With a True Declaration how I lived before I knew the truth, and How I came to know the truth, and overcame deceit* (1656), p. 244.

... Through this discourse, encounters with an Other can be textualized or processed as enumerations of such traits.[39]

In a dialogical sense, the text yields other possibilities. In at least containing within her remark the possibility that slaves might have initiated the request to attend prayer-meetings, Curwen indirectly gives voice to unheard but physically present speakers, and refers to earlier dialogues that restore some humanity to now faceless and speechless "Negroes." It is not simply Widow Tavernor as the "concrete listener" who enters in but slaves too, who could be making requests on their own spiritual behalf, though always indirectly and through the Quaker protagonist.[40]

Moreover, if Curwen unilaterally assumes that "Negroes" would welcome, benefit from, or seek membership, then she effectively brushes aside the slaves' own spiritual practices. African religious and ontological beliefs, tied in the Eurocentric mind to fetishisms, devils, superstition, idolatry, and savagery, are thus rendered invisible. And this invisibility and denial of African reality is reconfirmed by the fact that speechless slaves do not appear to have a (thinking) consciousness. They are not subjects but objects, occupying no space in the discourse outside of the observer's indirect statements.

When Tavernor refused Curwen's request, the latter explained her spiritual purpose in a letter: she could not "pass by, but in Love write to thee, for in love we came to visit thee, and to invite thee and thy Family [i.e., household] to the Meeting [of Friends]" (p. 18). Curwen extends the Friends' all-embracing spirit to Tavernor and Tavernor's household. She compares Tavernor to "him that was invited to work in the Vineyard, and went not," a reference to the parable of the two sons whose father invited them to work, whereupon the first declined "but afterward he repented, and went," (p. 18) while the second responded affirmatively and then did not go.[41] Just as Jesus warns that scoffing chief priests and scribes will not attain the kingdom of heaven, in contrast to repentant tax collectors and prostitutes, so Curwen suggests that Tavernor, who affects to believe but is scared like Peter, denies, and turns away, similarly jeopardizes her own chance of salvation. Having summarily delivered a spiritual

---

[39] Mary Louise Pratt, "Scratches on the Face of the Country; or, What Mr. Barrow Saw in the Land of the Bushmen," in Henry Louis Gates, Jr., ed., *Race, Writing, and Difference* (Chicago, 1985), pp. 138–62, this passage p. 139.

[40] See M. M. Bakhtin, "Discourse in the Novel," in *The Dialogic Imagination*, ed. Michael Holquist, trans. Caryl Emerson and Michael Holquist, (Austin, Texas, 1981), p. 277.

[41] St. Matthew 21: 28–31.

threat, Curwen then refers to "thy servants, *whom thou callest thy slaves*" [emphasis added]. She reprimands Tavernor for trying to "reign over" the conscience of "others" in "Matters of Worship of the Living God," reminding her that "thou thyself confessedst, that they had Souls to save as well as we." Curwen's self-conscious and sarcastically rendered rejection of the word *slaves* and her deliberate substitution of the word *servants* marks a forthright and critical rupture in the text. Curwen speaks through Tavernor to her readers and simultaneously speaks in her own voice, asking them to decide between her opinion and the law's opinion, represented by Tavernor. A few lines later, Curwen reiterates her objection to Tavernor's terminology: "For I am persuaded that if they whom thou callest thy slaves, be Upright-hearted to God, the Lord God Almighty will set Free but in Christ Jesus, for all other Freedom will prove but a Bondage." Curwen's refusal to use the term *slaves* to describe West African peoples signifies an anomalous refusal for her epoch and underscores her personal strength, political conviction, and sense of herself as spiritual model. Implicitly, her moral terminology amounts to an absolute repudiation of popular ideas about women's silence, conformity, and mental inferiority in conventional society. Quakers had stood so long at the receiving end of superior attitudes toward "others" that Curwen perceived *Quakers* and *slaves* as synonymous and interchangeable terms in that one sense. To attack Tavernor's prejudicial household rules was part and parcel of taking up cudgels outside colonial law yet engaging with a representative of that symbolic order. Even within Quaker circles her knife-edged responses cut at the *status quo*. Alice Curwen disparages Tavernor's labelling of people as "slaves" (p. 18) that denies their sacred worth. On the other hand, Curwen also fudges an issue here. She offers "Christ Jesus" as "Freedom," ignoring, refusing, and silencing the real "Bondage" that the slaves must still suffer, whatever they are called. Perhaps contemporary Quaker exhortations to *servants* to be of good behavior and morality are relevant to an understanding of the possible limits to Curwen's radicalism.

Certain historical events that occurred in the 1670s explain Curwen's staunch temerity. In the first place, she journeyed to Barbados when controversy was rife about how to describe Africans in captivity. In the 1660s the Royal African Company still used fictional terminology to comply with requirements about what constituted legal cargo: shipped Africans were "Negro-Servants."

By 1677, after considerable discursive posturing, the Solicitor-General pronounced that "negroes ought to be esteemed goods and commodities."[42] Curwen unequivocally rejects the Solicitor-General's twofold denial of African humanity, being acutely and experientially aware of the devices used by the powerful to run those perceived as outsiders aground. The testimony of countless Friends (and they testified in peril of their lives during the Civil War) deplored all infringements of individual liberties and physical punishment of any individual. Curwen's husband's four-year imprisonment for writing a document denouncing a Friends' political enemy, the zealous jailing of Quakers in general, and even the very name Quaker – implying ecstasy and hence incurring ridicule – kept her close to the consequences of persecution.[43] Resolutely and frontally, she asserts a universal human right to "inner light" by actively repudiating the language of bondage as illegitimate. Taking care of slaves was taking care of Friends.

In attempting to undermine Tavernor's individual form of religious persecution, Curwen also ironically (but unconsciously?) exposed contradictions between Quaker ideas about spiritual equality and Quaker practice in maintaining slaves and tacitly condoning the institution. Curwen's demurral at the terminology of slavery that perhaps intentionally echoed Edmundson's earlier objections placed her in a very small but distinct group of Friends who never fully embraced slavery's legitimacy. These early manumission-inclined Friends ideologically foreshadowed eighteenth-century abolitionists who privileged the material rather than the spiritual condition of slaves in their advocacy of abolition and emancipation.

On the other hand, Curwen's argument about the right of slaves to free spiritual expression was based on a European belief that all individuals potentially constituted God's world-wide Christian family. Her text assumes that no one would *want* to be excluded, that slaves would desire and cherish these values, would want to emulate Europeans.

[42] For this linguistic shift, see James Walvin, *Black and White: The Negro and English Society, 1555–1945* (1973), pp. 37–43. For background and further details, see Peter Fryer, *Staying Power: The History of Black People in Britain* (1984), pp. 1–32.

[43] Thomas Curwen, *This is An Answer to John Wiggans Book, Spread up and down in Lancashire, Cheshire and Wales, who is a Baptist and a Monarch-man. Wherein may be seen how he exalts Himself, against Christ the Light, that doth enlighten every Man ... From the Prisoners at Lancaster, where he then opposed being then a Prisoner, Thomas Curwen, William Houlden, Henry Wood, William Wilson* (1665). Preface "To The Reader" is dated the 2nd of the 5th Month 1664.

And second, as a self-appointed spokeswoman for slaves, Curwen denies both the voice and name of slave with a "convincement." Troped as the epitome of victimization, Africa and slaves "speak through and by virtue of the European imagination ... Not so much a pen writing as a voice pronouncing."[44] But we cannot discount the possibility – often mentioned covertly in slave narratives – that African-Caribbean slaves in Tavernor's household realized the advantage of accommodating themselves to organized Christian proselytizers. The stigma of immorality and innate benightedness disappear at one blow. To mimic the Quakers, in this case, would be to divide the whites and be attached to a group that, theoretically at least, was committed to humane treatment, given the temporal reality of slavery. In mimicking, too, black people make subjects of themselves, a fact that is quietly understood in Curwen's text.[45] That slave-owners so violently opposed conversion lends credence to the idea that slaves discerned its benefits; that the slaves' presence graphically invoked by Curwen, although she technically silences and promiscuously collectivizes them, ruptures her discourse and signifies her internalized political conflicts.

Alice Curwen's *Relation* denotes an early transitional phase in female anti-slavery discourse. As Friends sought to establish a working relationship with the plantocracy, Curwen exposed a fundamental fissure between Friends' religious ideas and cultural practice. She unearthed an occasionally glimpsed cleft in Friends' response to slavery that kept widening. By the 1760s, Friends no longer could reconcile or ignore contradictions between their philosophy and practice, and the London Yearly Meeting in 1761 outlawed slavery among its members.[46]

IV ELIZABETH HOOTON

Elizabeth Hooton preceded Alice Curwen as a missionary drawn to emancipation, her refusal to imbibe orthodox attitudes impressively evident in her encounter with Indians in colonialist America. Like Curwen, in voicing and speaking for "others" as well as herself, she depicts Indians as "barbarous savage people, which neither know God nor Christ; [they] have been willing to receive us into their

---

[44] Edward Said, *Orientalism* (New York, 1979), pp. 56, 125.
[45] See Jacques Lacan, *The Four Fundamental Concepts of Psycho-Analysis*, trans. Alan Sheridan (1977), pp. 98–100.   [46] Davis, *Problem of Slavery*, pp. 330–32.

wigwams, or houses, when these professors [of the Truth (a reference to Anti-Quaker Christians)] would murther us."[47] Hooton refutes claims of Indian savagery in her own ironic voice while indirectly denoting the indigenous people as warm and generous people who offer hospitality to another group of persecuted others. Her experiences moved her to ally with Indians and their sufferings rather than with truth assassins: "The love I bear to the Souls of men makes me willing to undergo whatsoever can be inflicted on me."[48]

On another occasion, Hooton's commitment to a more harmonious European-conceived global community based on love elicited empathy for the underprivileged. Unconventionally, she blames those who provoke starving men into robbery through privation rather than blaming the black robbers themselves:

There is great Cry of the Poore being Robbed by Rich mens Negroes ... Now it is the Duty of Every Man to take care and see these family have sufficient food and any thing else they stand in need of.[49]

When Hooton visited Barbados with Fox in 1671 as an official Friends' missionary, she knew that Fox had proposed limiting the terms of a slave's servitude and had advocated that the master-slave relationships be "informed by love." Just before she died, she invoked this principle when, at seventy years old, she wrote to an island governor, echoing both Fox's and Curwen's language of love and salvation in her injunction: "Soe Returne to the Light in thy Conscience," she instructs him, "which will not let thee doe any Wrong to any if thou be obedient to It."[50]

By assailing the cruelty of non-Quaker whites toward Friends, Elizabeth Hooton declined to accept anything at face value. In blaming European exploiters ("Rich men") for food-stealing by "Rich mens Negroes," she similarly questioned common seventeenth-century assumptions about the sacred order of things. "Rich mens Negroes" embeds a question as well as a statement. Why should rich men "possess" any Africans? Once again, the material conditions of Friends' lives, the physical punishments they endured, the constant psychological persecution and political subjection, their heightened awareness about the necessity to retaliate in some way or

[47] Manners, *Elizabeth Hooton*, p. 45. [48] Brailsford, *Quaker Women*, p. 34.
[49] Manners, *Elizabeth Hooton*, p. 71.
[50] *Ibid.*, p. 72. Her final end in the Caribbean reflects her lifelong mission to build spiritual equality. She died in Jamaica in the early months of 1762. Fox reported tersely, "Wee buried Els: Hutton in Jamaica about a week after wee landed ther;" Brailsford, *Quaker Women*, pp. 38–39.

other, and their belief in individual spiritual access without reserve
made them more likely than, or at the very least as likely as any other
European, to interrogate and contest the institution of slavery.

V JOAN VOKINS

Another celebrated Quaker and traveling missionary, Joan Vokins,
recited comparable responses when she met slaves in 1681: "I met
with many Friends at Bridgtown ... and most Days I had two or three
meetings a Day, both among the Blacks, and also among the White
People. And the power manifested, so that my soul was often melted
therewith, even in the Meetings of the Negro's or Black, as well as
among Friends."[51] The segregation of British people from African-
Caribbeans at certain meetings, though the causes differed, par-
alleled the recently mandated segregation of men and women at
Friends' meetings in Britain and the Caribbean.[52] Such separations
depended on an unspoken view of white men as natural leaders, of
slaves as lesser beings, and of white women as people who should
concern themselves with domestic and family affairs. Vokins's near
surprise and boasting delight at commensurate religious power being
manifested "even" at Blacks' meetings rearticulates a Eurocentric
discourse that definitively constructs slaves as naturally inferior
colonial others; her surprise emphasizes the rarity of any form of
institutionalized equality in any form.

On the island of Nevis eight months later, Vokins's report on a
potential catastrophe at sea reaffirmed the segregation of prayer
meetings while recapitulating Hooton's feelings of love:

I have been most of this Winter upon the roaring Sea, Two Months at a time,
and saw no Land, and my Clothes were not off Two Nights all that time, so
far as I can remember, and there was no conveniency for my weak Body;
There were French, and Dutch, and Irish, and Barbarians, and English, and

---

[51] Joan Vokins, *God's Mighty Power magnified: As Manifested and Revealed in her Faithful Handmaid
Joan Vokins, who departed this life the 22d of the 5th month, 1690, Having finished her course, and kept
the Faith. Also some account of her Exercises, Works of Faith, Labour, Love, and great travels in the
Work of the Ministry, for the good of souls* (1691), pp. 42–43; British Library shelfmark 1419a28.
The passage quoted concludes: "Written aboard the ship coming from Barbados, in the
third month, 1681," p. 77. Several other Quaker missionaries in Barbados, such as Jane
Hoskins, made no reference to the black population in their writings; see *The Life of the
Faithful Servant of Christians, Jane Hoskins, The Friends Library: Comprising Journals, Doctrinal
Treatises, and Other Writings of Members of the Religious Society of Friends*, vol. 1, eds. William
Evans and Thomas Evans (Philadelphia, 1846), pp. 469–71.

[52] Vokins returned home hastily about 1680 when she thought "we were likely to have lost our
Women's Meetings," quoted in Hobby, *Virtue of Necessity*, p. 49.

I had sore Exercises amongst them, both inwardly and outwardly; but yet I had good service also amongst them, and they did confess to the Power of my God. And although they were most of them very wicked, yet they were chained by it, and the Passengers were kind to me for the Truth's sake; and when it pleased the Lord to bring us to Land, we arrived at the Island of Antegoi [Antigua] in the West Indies, and there I found a precious People, and had Two Meetings a Day for a Week, with White People and Blacks; and on the 7th Day is their Childrens Meetings, and they have also Mens and Women's Meetings, and the Gospel order is established and establishing in those remote islands, Glory to God for ever. (*God's Mighty Power*, pp. 60–61).

VI CONCLUSION

The three Quakers – Curwen, Hooton, and Vokins – collectively responded to African-Caribbean slaves as men and women entitled to certain human rights. These they defined as the right to love God and the right to worship, early steps in the slow movement toward general emancipation. Their perspective also highlighted what Europeans' discourse consistently lacked: any conceptualization of the rich diverse humanity of slaves, any notion of their status as the full equals of European men and women. But Friends' circumscribed historical consciousness – understandably – is always evident too. Whereas they agitated for their own civil, social, and political as well as religious rights as female Friends, for slaves they argued for spiritual equality within the family of God. Curwen's apparently unique call for a change in nomenclature was the only exception.

Within limitations imposed by their epoch, Friends functioned as religious apostles of British-Christian values in colonized lands. Although they sincerely meant to share spiritual abundance, their ventures added to the construct of what Howard Temperley defines as cultural imperialism.[53] With Christian conversion at stake, African people's distinct cultures and religion scarcely counted or registered. Nor was slave membership in the Society controversial at this time (as far as I know), though a century later discussions about and rejections of "negro membership" began in earnest.[54]

[53] Note Howard Temperley's persuasive argument in "The Ideology of Antislavery," in *David Eltis and James Walvin, eds., The Abolition of the Atlantic Slave Trade: Origins and Effects in Europe, Africa, and the Americas* (Madison, 1981), pp. 20–37, that "the attack on slavery [as well as the imposition of slavery] can be seen as an attempt by a dominant metropolitan ideology to impose its values on the societies of the economic periphery," p. 29.

[54] Henry J. Cadbury, "Negro Membership in the Society of Friends," *The Journal of Negro History* 21 (1936): 151–213, especially pp. 172–76 for the case of Cynthia Myers, "a Mulatto woman."

Nor, to expand the argument well beyond Martha Tavernor's household, does any corroborating evidence exist that African-Caribbeans sought convincement –"coming to our meetings" in Alice Curwen's phrase – in order to join a white Christian family unit that would substitute for their already existing communities. What in fact was enacted by the slaves was widespread physical resistance; petitioning for convincement added to that oppositional movement. Michael Craton observes that:

Few voyages [from West Africa to the Caribbean] were ever completed without the discovery or threat of slavery conspiracy ... The sheer ignorance of all whites about internal African conditions, the complexity of African cultures, and the general psychology of slave resistance compounded the problem ... The one growing certainty was there was no such creature as a genuinely docile slave.[55]

These facts were borne out by numerous incidents before 1700: four plots and one revolt in Barbados, two plots in Bermuda, six incidents of revolt, resistance, and escape in Jamaica, massive escapes and "maroon activity in Antigua; and an uprising in St. Kitts."[56] Forging alliances with spiritually radical whites, themselves on society's rim and subject to persecution, helped to identify if not unify opposition to the plantocracy. The number of slaves who converted to Christianity in the eighteenth and early nineteenth centuries intimates that such alliances were a form of conscious or unconscious political strategy – as well as a form of spiritual release – in response to a ruling elite who harshly suppressed all forms of belligerence, active or passive.

Revered in their own circles, Alice Curwen, Elizabeth Hooton, and Joan Vokins exemplified a living Christian-like altruism in their own terms. In many senses they act as role models for other women. Elaine Hobby writes:

Joan Vokins, for example, returned home to investigate the new departure of separate meetings for men and women, even though such meetings arguably spelled the apparent downgrading of female Friends. Vokins left husband and family behind in England during her voyages. What *is* silenced among them is an explicit defense and interrogation of women's role in their work. But they do not ally themselves with the new conservative tendency either: they are simply silent on the issue and, perhaps, allow their recorded

---

[55] Craton, *Testing the Chains*, pp. 24–25.   [56] *Ibid.*, pp. 335–37.

actions to speak for them. Their near-silence in this and their near-silence on questions of race and slavery might be linked; certainly they constitute two related absent centers in their texts.[57]

They rechannel or displace their energies, in one sense self-denyingly, into battling for others who are the victims of different and particularly atrocious forms of persecution. But even more tellingly, working as traveling missionaries implied an act of will and of attentiveness to others that belonged to a self-determining process. The fact that these philanthropic "feminine" attributes were sometimes pressed into the service of questioning slavery marks a gendering of anti-slavery discourse. In a society uneasy about female independence, women writers, and radical sectarians, the adventurous global undertakings of Hooton, Vokins, and Curwen signified a widespread female presence. Women spearheaded the missionary effort in Barbados as they had pioneered missionary work somewhat earlier in southern England. According to the most recent data, if a Quaker author were officially approved by Fox, their publications would have been nationally targeted, even if their views were not; in terms of influence, counting distributions abroad, as many as two thousand copies *could* have been printed of each account.[58] In Joan Kelly's phrase, the missionary work was "a feminism of practice," a public and published display of female intrepidity, a displaced way of exercising the right to moral and political decision-making.[59] Eschewing prescribed separate spheres in society and within the Society, they championed the rights of outsiders. Striking at the roots of convention, Curwen emerged as a Janus (jana)-like figure, a spiritual and political daughter of Civil War female agitators; one of the earliest pioneers of white proto-abolitionist ideology who discountenanced the very language that accredited slavery.

As Quaker female missionaries advocated spiritual equality, they collectively empowered themselves and deplored their own denied status. Self-consciously religious propagandists and avowed spiritual equals of slaves, with the most positive but historically received Eurocentric intentions, they also assumed the right to speak for and

---

[57] Private correspondence to Moira Ferguson.
[58] This information was supplied in private correspondence from Maureen Bell, whom I thank for her promptness and generosity. See Tom O'Malley, "Defying the powers and tempering the spirit," a review of Quaker control over their publications in *Journal of Ecclesiastical History* 33: 2 (January 1982): 72–88.
[59] Joan Kelly, "Early Feminist Theory and the *Querelle des Femmes*," in *Women, History and Theory: The Essays of Joan Kelly* (Chicago, 1984), p. 68.

decide what was best for enslaved African-Caribbeans; in the manner of Jesus Christ they were defending the vulnerable and unprotected. No tension existed for them between their commitment to spiritual equality and their implicit denial of self-determination to Africans.

Over the next fifty years, the Quaker position on slavery changed qualitatively as they became the first unified group of British men and women to demand abolition and emancipation. In the Restoration, those female Friends who initiated a moral discourse about slavery and the marginalized status of slaves also spoke to their own desire for social reintegration. In supporting the right of slaves in historically constrained ways, they asserted their own right (consciously or not) to a discourse on and of freedom and a public-political identity. Given the mandated roles for white British females, they tested far-reachingly the theoretical and practical possibilities of those structures. Moreover, in advocating one form of spiritual equality they paved the way for others and helped inaugurate women's rights to the highly politicized discourse on freedom. Importantly too, given the reluctance of most women to speak in public, they validated not only protest itself but an overt, vocal alliance against the morally corrupt. In this process of pioneering spiritual negotiations on behalf of slaves, however, they simultaneously helped to consolidate an ethnocentric discourse that was to characterize anti-slavery prose and poems well beyond the successful passage of the Emancipation Bill in 1834.

CHAPTER 12

Republicanism, absolutism and universal monarchy: English popular sentiment during the third Dutch war

Steven C. A. Pincus

I

"No one is able to explain why the people of England detest the French alliance so violently or why they wish for peace with Holland at any cost," complained the Venetian secretary in England, Girolamo Alberti, in the autumn of 1673.[1] Especially perplexing for contemporary observers was the sudden shift in English opinion from general support of the third Anglo-Dutch war (1672–1674) to virtually unanimous condemnation.

Modern historians, while acknowledging the importance of this shift in popular opinion, have been no less uncertain of its causes. K. H. D. Haley offered an intriguing and persuasive explanation. Before the summer of 1673, Haley argued, public opinion and the House of Commons were "quite unmoved by foreign considerations."[2] It was at this point that William of Orange, and his propagandist *par excellence*, Pierre Du Moulin, intervened decisively on the English political scene. Haley carefully described, with language redolent of Cold War spy thrillers, how Du Moulin wrote and disseminated his classic pamphlet, *England's Appeal from the Private Cabal at Whitehall to the Great Council of the Nation* of 1673. "It was this famous pamphlet," Haley contended, "which did more than anything else to identify the French alliance in foreign affairs with the danger of Popery at home, and consequently to lead public opinion and the Country Party in Parliament to turn against the war." In so doing Du Moulin, and the rest of

---

I am grateful to Toby Barnard, Margot Finn, Tim Harris, Nelly Oliensis, Jenny Paxton, John Robertson, Jennifer Poulos, and Blair Worden for criticizing this essay.

[1] Alberti to Doge and Senate, 31 October/10 November 1673, *CSPV*, p. 170.

[2] K. H. D. Haley, *William of Orange and the English Opposition 1672–4* (Oxford, 1953), p. 90.

William's agents, had begun "a process which culminated in 1688–89."[3]

Recently Haley's thesis has come under attack by revisionist historians. The English throughout the early modern period, these historians claim, were far more interested in local, county and domestic events than in international politics. Members of Parliament might be "men of considerable local standing and influence" but they had "often limited their mental and political horizons."[4] The restored monarchy, Ronald Hutton insisted, aimed to promote a "lack of interest in public affairs," and it largely succeeded.[5] According to the revisionists, this outlook was typical of the makers of policy as well as of the public at large. The historian of the Cabal has argued that Charles II and his chief ministers were "insular" in outlook, always determining their foreign policies "by the exigencies of [Charles's] position at home."[6]

From this perspective, then, the effect of European affairs in shifting popular sentiment should have been small indeed. "The war," J. R. Jones has suggested, "affected relatively few men directly." Given English political insularity the only reason that Du Moulin's pamphlet had any impact was that it concentrated "on the king's domestic policies, rather than on the war itself."[7] The decisive domestic event, "the one event [that] changed everything," Hutton has concluded, was "James's public profession of his faith."[8] Fears for the Protestant religion, not concern for the European balance of power, convinced the English political nation to turn against the war.[9]

In this essay, by contrast, I will claim that there was a native and lively popular discussion about European affairs in England through-

---

[3] Haley, *William of Orange*, pp. 97–98, 220. John Miller has also recently claimed that the 1670s marked a watershed in the public awareness of foreign political developments; see his *Charles II* (1991), p. 221.

[4] J. R. Jones, *Britain and the World 1649–1815* (Glasgow, 1980), p. 12.

[5] Hutton, *Restoration*, p. 157 and *passim*.

[6] Maurice Lee, *The Cabal* (Urbana, 1965), p. 79 (Arlington), p. 96 (Charles II), p. 213 (Shaftesbury).   [7] J. R. Jones, *Charles II: Royal Politican* (1987), pp. 97, 112.

[8] Hutton, *Charles the Second*, pp 308–317. Lee also makes this point, *Cabal*, p. 226.

[9] Recently a new group of historians has argued that the English were concerned with international developments, but that they understood them in exclusively confessional terms. See Conal Condren, "Andrew Marvell as Polemicist: his Account of the Growth of Popery and Arbitrary Government," in Conal Condren and A. D. Cousins, eds., *The Political Identity of Andrew Marvell* (Aldershot, 1990): 157–87; and Scott, *Sidney*. However, these scholars have not yet pushed their interpretation back into the early 1670s.

out the later seventeenth century,[10] and that this discussion had always connected domestic and foreign concerns. In England, as in the rest of Europe, this debate turned on the proper identification of the universal monarch. The third Anglo-Dutch war proved to be a time in which two rival interpretations – the one claiming that the republican Dutch, the other that the absolutist French, were seeking universal monarchy – could be tested. While *England's Appeal* did play a large role in persuading the English to demand peace with the Dutch and war with the French, it could only do so because it dovetailed nicely with earlier English polemic. Far more important than the publication of Du Moulin's pamphlet – the central event of Haley's story – were the political developments of 1672, which invalidated claims that the Dutch were seeking universal dominion while strengthening the belief that Louis XIV coveted the throne of Charlemagne.

II

Far from exhibiting an indifference to European events, the English during the Restoration eagerly sought out, collected, and commented upon the tiniest tidbits of information about continental affairs. Newspapers and newsletters were dominated by summaries from foreign correspondents. Patrons of coffee-houses, alehouses, and clubs chattered incessantly about the most recent reports from abroad. The streets of London and provincial towns were littered with pamphlets, broadsides, and poems offering glosses on and witticisms about the most recent doings of European dignitaries. Oxford and Cambridge society was enlivened with conflicting comparisons between contemporary events and the heroic deeds of the ancient Greeks and Romans. Anglican churches and dissenting meeting houses thundered with sermons inciting congregations to take an interest in momentous developments across the English channel.

---

[10] For the purposes of brevity I am restricting this article, on the whole, to material from the 1670s. For the 1660s see my "Popery, Trade and Universal Monarchy: The Ideological Context of the Outbreak of the Second Anglo-Dutch War," *EHR* 422 (1992): 1–29, and *Protestantism and Patriotism: Ideology and the Making of English Foreign Policy 1650–1686* (Cambridge, forthcoming). C. R. Boxer has also argued that the English "reading public" was "reasonably well informed" about the United Provinces, though he has not made clear how the English understood the totality of European power politics, or when the English became well informed. See his "Some Second Thoughts on the Third Anglo-Dutch War, 1672–1674," *Transactions of the Royal Historical Society*, fifth series, 19 (1969): 67–94, this passage p. 94.

Frequently, the English placed their interpretations of international events within the framework of a discussion about universal monarchy. The English knew that their forebears had successfully obstructed the Habsburgs' quest for universal monarchy, a quest which definitively ended when the Spanish were compelled to acquiesce to the ignominious Treaty of the Pyrenees. They also knew that in the previous decade they had fought a war to prevent the Dutch Republic from achieving universal dominion and that they had been party to a treaty designed to prevent Louis XIV from conquering the Spanish Low Countries, an area long seen as the key to European domination.

Unlike their forebears, however, Restoration Britons knew that commerce – especially long-distance maritime commerce – and not mere population forged the sinews of power. Since the establishment of the lucrative East Indian spice trade and the exploitation of the South American silver mines, the nature of European warfare had changed: supplying armies for long periods of time determined victory or defeat more often than battlefield prowess. The aspiring universal monarch, therefore, needed to achieve control of the sea. The Earl of Orrery made the point in the epilogue to his play *The Black Prince*: "And when the universe was to be made / The vast design was on the waters laid."[11] John Evelyn summed up current political thinking when he insisted that "to pretend to Universal Monarchy without fleets was long since looked on as a politick chimera."[12]

This new emphasis on trade made claims that the Dutch were seeking universal monarchy, voiced frequently by the supporters of the Restoration regime, appear credible. While the Dutch Republic was made up of a small cluster of watery provinces in Europe, its merchants dominated trade in the East Indies, the West Coast of Africa, the Caribbean, and the Mediterranean. "The sole design of the Hollanders," averred the aptly named William De Britaine, "is to get the riches, trade, and dominion of the whole Indies into their own power."[13]

English observers claimed that the Dutch had not achieved their

[11] Roger Boyle, Earl of Orrery, *The Black Prince*, in *The Dramatic Works of Roger Boyle Earl of Orrery*, ed. William Smith Clark, 2 vols. (Cambridge, Mass., 1937), 1: 372.

[12] John Evelyn, *Navigation and Commerce* (1674), p. 16.

[13] William De Britaine, *The Dutch Usurpation* (1672), p. 18. The same point was made by the Venetian observer Pietro Mocenigo in his "Account of England," 30 May/9 June 1671, *CSPV*, p. 59.

economic domination through virtue and industry, but through unfair trading practices. "The Netherlanders from the beginning of their trade in the Indies, not contented with the ordinary course of a fair and free commerce, invaded diverse islands, took some forts, built others; and labored nothing more than the conquests of countries, and the acquiring of new dominion."[14] The tragedy of Amboyna – an event memorialized in plays, skits, poems, and squibs in the early 1670s – made certain that every social stratum of English society was aware that the basis of Dutch prosperity was the "bloody and inhumane butcheries committed by them against us."[15] It was clear that "the artifice and undue practices of the Hollanders," their "lies and cheats," aimed only "to supplant all our foreign trade."[16]

All of these actions by their neighbors convinced supporters of the restored monarchy that the Dutch Republic was indeed seeking universal dominion. "What straits, gulfs, trading bays, spare they to pierce / By water to take in the Universe?" queried the author of a poetic rendering of one of Aesop's fables. "Are they with force not able to invade? / No matter; they'll undo the world by trade."[17] Charles II's chaplain, Francis Gregory, insisted that the question now was "whether rebels shall lord it over sovereigns? whether the Texel shall rule the ocean? Or, which is all one, whether Amsterdam shall give check to London, and law to the World?"[18] With such lectures from his divines, it was hardly surprising that Charles II was

---

[14] *The Emblem of Ingratitude; A True Relation of the Unjust, Cruel and Barbarous Proceedings against the English at Amboyna* (1672), sig. A7. See also *A Discourse Written by Sir George Downing* (1672), pp. 44–45.

[15] *Poor Robins Character of a Dutch-Man* (1672), p. 2; William Lilly, *The Dangerous Condition of the United Provinces* (1672), p. 4; *Discourse Written by Sir George Downing*, pp. 3–4; John Dryden, *Amboyna: A Tragedy* (1673); Theophilus Philalethes, *Great Britains Glory* (1672), p. 9; De Britaine, *The Dutch Usurpation*, pp. 14–15; *A Prophecie Lately Transcribed From an Old Manuscript of Dr. Barnaby Googe* (1672), p. 3; *A Familiar Discourse, Between George, a True-Hearted English Gentleman: and Hans a Dutch Merchant* (1672), pp. 8–9; Mrs. E. P., *On His Royal Highness His Expedition Against the Dutch* (1672) broadside; among Joseph Williamson's papers, dated 11 November 1672, appears an "Announcement of a representation, from 2 to 4 p.m., of the Dutch cruelties at Amboyna," *CSPD*, p. 148.

[16] William De Britaine, *The Interest of England in the Present War with Holland* (1672), p. 1; *Familiar Discourse*, p. 28.

[17] *The Frog, or The Low-Countrey Nightingale, Sweet Singer of Amsterdam* (?1672), pp. 1–2 (a broadside version of this poem appeared in 1672); John Ogilby, *The Holland Nightingale or The Sweet Singers of Amsterdam* (1672). Another poetic fabulist made a similar point: see *The Fable of the Sun and the Frogs* (1672), p. 8.

[18] Francis Gregory, Rector of Hambleton, *The Right Way to Victory* (1673), sig. A3v. Identical arguments were made in poems and plays as well. See Dryden, *Amboyna*, prologue, sig. ar; T. S. (of Gray's Inn), *Upon His Majesties Late Declaration for Toleration, And Publication of War Against the Hollander* (1672), p. 2.

"convinced that the Dutch republic, at its present pace, would monopolize all trade and crush neighboring powers."[19] This perception was clearly not limited to courtly circles. When a Dutch man in a country tavern demanded to know "why the English called his country less men butterboxes," he was reputedly told "because they find you are so apt to spread every where, and for your sauciness, must be melted down."[20]

Why had the Dutch, who were so recently England's allies against Habsburg imperialism, suddenly become aspirants to universal dominion? For enthusiastic supporters of the restored monarchy, for men and women who had loathed and feared the English Commonwealth, the answer was not far to seek. The Dutch truly had been a virtuous and liberty-loving people when led in war and peace by a member of the House of Orange. However, since the death of William II in 1650, and the subsequent political revolution, the Dutch people had been deluded and deceived by a corrupt republican government.

The Dutch republicans, the Loevestein party, had turned the United Provinces into an "academy of revolting."[21] "A republic is nothing but an engine (erected by sedition and treachery to subvert monarchy)," sneered William De Britaine, "and we see that Holland hath been a retreat for all rebels, and a sanctuary to the worst of men. All heresies, schisms, and anti-monarchical principles have been there hatch'd, and then fly into the dominions of Kings and Princes, and on their way carry nothing but poison and contagion to infect their subjects."[22] No wonder that one fabulist asserted that the frogs, as the Dutch were frequently called, had become "a plague to princes."[23] Dutch republicanism was not merely a theoretical problem for English Royalists. "In print and pulpit," "in their abusive pictures," and in "their satirical effusions," the Dutch themselves did all they could do to "excite rebellion against the King of England."[24] From an English perspective, the Dutch republic

---

[19] As reported by Alberti to Doge and Senate, 19/29 April 1672, *CSPV*, p. 203. James, Duke of York, was reputed to hold similar views: Alberti to Doge and Senate, 5/15 January 1672, *CSPV*, p. 145.   [20] *The Complaisant Companion* (1674), Part 2, p. 32.

[21] *Hogan-Moganides: Or, The Dutch Hudibras* (1674), pp. 7–8.

[22] De Britaine, *Interest of England*, p. 14.

[23] *Fable of the Sun and the Frogs*, p. 7. The Venetian ambassador explained this as the main cause of the war: Alberti to Doge and Senate, 24 May/3 June 1672, *CSPV*, p. 221.

[24] Theophilus Philalethes, *Great Britains Glory*, p. 8; *Discourse Written by Sir George Downing*, p. 30; Alberti to Doge and Senate, 24 May/3 June 1672, *CSPV*, p. 221; *Annus Prodigiosus* (1672), p. 4.

represented the epitome of ingratitude. The Dutch state treated England much as Brutus had treated Caesar, stabbing the source of the very favors which had made possible its rise.[25]

The Dutch Loevestein party, much like the earlier Roman republicans, was expansionist in its aims.[26] The Dutch had "built their State on other's ruin, / And therefore always sought by warring / To keep their neighbors still a jarring." Since the merchant republic was able to grow "fat upon the prey" of warring European states, "she hath been the common incendiary, directly or collaterally, of all the combustions that have happened this side of the line, ever since [the] revolt from Spain."[27] Another observer thought the Dutch the "scourge of Europe" who have "made greater distempers and confusions, and caused more effusion of blood, and expense of treasure in Europe, than the Great Turk hath done for these 500 years."[28] The only hope for Europe, the only chance to "establish peace in Christendom," was "to reduce them under the obedience of a good prince" – a Prince of Orange.[29]

Republicanism led ineluctably to grasping imperialism, English Royalists argued, because the very essence of a commonwealth necessitated the evisceration of virtue. "Interest's the God they worship in their State," thought John Dryden while pointing out that "Monarchies may own religion's name, / But States are atheists in their very frame."[30] Sir John Birkenhead agreed, telling the House of Commons that "religion in Holland is subservient to trade."[31] In fact, in the United Provinces religion itself "was but a trade ... Where saint and devil link together, / Turk, Jew; and makes no matter whether, / As far as for their ends they make / Not conscience, but for commerce-sake."[32] The point was that the Dutch in grasping for glory had sacrificed all to satisfy their own ambition. The Dutch, like all "those which study to be great by any means," did "by all means forget to be good."[33]

John Crowne staged all of these themes for London audiences in his

---

[25] *Discourse Written by Sir George Downing*, pp. 2–3.

[26] This, the Venetian secretary thought, was the perception of the English Privy Council. Alberti to Doge and Senate, 19/29 January 1672, *CSPV*, p. 156. The Loevestein party – named after the Dutch prison where its leaders were incarcerated by Prince Maurice – were the Dutch republican and Remonstrant grouping, led in the period 1650–71 by the Pensionary of Holland, John De Witt.   [27] *Hogan-Moganides*, pp. 26, 51–52, 113–14.

[28] De Britaine, *Dutch Usurpation*, pp. 23, 33–34.

[29] De Britaine, *Interest of England*, pp. 15–16.   [30] Dryden, *Amboyna*, prologue, sig. av.

[31] Sir John Birkenhead, 11 March 1668, Grey, *Debates*, 1: 113.

[32] *Hogan-Moganides*, pp. 97–99.   [33] De Britaine, *Dutch Usurpation*, p. 19.

1672 play *The History of Charles VIII of France*. The play opens as the
French king's armies are descending upon the Aragonese state of
Naples in an apparent display of imperialist aggression. The fear
generated by the approach of the massive French armies allows the
discontented Prince of Salarne to lead a popular rebellion against the
new Neapolitan king, Ferdinand. Instead of taking advantage of the
situation, however, Charles VIII agrees to help Ferdinand to quash
the rebellion, proclaiming that

> the rebels are my enemies,
> And every king's concern as well as his.
> Rebellion is a monster would devour
> The kingly dignity, and Sovereign power,
> A sort of atheism, that doth crown blaspheme,
> And styles the sacred power of kings a dream.[34]

Through this temporary alliance Charles and Ferdinand become
close friends, discovering both mutual interests and complementary
loves. Charles VIII – like his descendant Louis XIV, Crowne implies
– is wrongly accused of seeking universal monarchy. "Rome,
Millane, Venice, Germany, and Spain, / With all the little Princes
they can gain" have forged an alliance "To check, as they pretend
my growing pride, / That must now make war on half mankind, /
And gain that Empire which I ne'er designed."[35] Gradually Crowne
reveals that Charles VIII entered Italy not in quest of universal
dominion, but at the self-interested behest of the Milanese usurper.
Meanwhile the Venetian republic, "an envious and mechanic State,
/ Whose nature is crown'd heads to fear and hate," builds up a
league against France and mortgages the power of Ferdinand's
beloved, the good Queen Cornelia of Cyprus.[36] The real dangers to
Italian, and Crowne hints to European, peace are the activities of
rebels and republics. The play concludes with the demise of the rebels
and the restoration of Ferdinand to his throne. Crowne's drama, like
the Anglo-Dutch war, did "Kings and Monarchy advance, / ...
guarded with the names of Charles and France."[37]

---

[34] *The History of Charles VIII*, in Crowne, *Works*, 1 : 144–45.   [35] *Ibid.*, 1 : 180.
[36] *Ibid.*, 1 : 180.
[37] *Ibid.*, 1 : 217. Dryden's play *Amboyna: A Tragedy* also quite openly urged his audience to war
against the Dutch: "So wou'd our poet lead you on this day: / Showing your tortur'd
Fathers in his play" (Epilogue, sig. KV). Restoration playwrights commonly sought to
engage in contemporary political debate. See also Elkanah Settle, *Cambyses King of Persia*:

Supporters of the restored monarchy, then, wanted war against the Dutch because they thought the Dutch republican leaders were seeking universal dominion. The point was not to seize Dutch trade routes – most merchants knew that "trade will suffer" during a maritime war – but to prevent the Dutch from monopolizing all the wealth of the Indies.[38] This war was not fought to eviscerate the Dutch people, but rather to liberate them from "the tyranny and oppression of those insolent States."[39] After all, as Dryden pointed out, "their new Common-wealth has set 'em free, / Only from honour and civility."[40] War against the Dutch, it was asserted, was necessary because their republicanism was a cancer which ate away at all monarchies, a cancer which would not stop spreading until it had achieved universal dominion.

English political and religious radicals, by contrast, maintained that it was rather the absolutist French King Louis XIV who was attempting to establish a new universal monarchy. Far from accepting the claim that the Dutch were morally depraved and devoid of political virtue, the English radicals praised the Dutch for their historical role in defending European liberty. The Dutch, argued the republican Slingsby Bethel, were the "principle instruments in preventing the House of Austria in their grand design for the Universal Monarchy." "Having traveled their countries, observed their manners, and read disputes with other nations," he insisted, "I think it but an act of justice to acknowledge that in the generality of their morals, they are a reproach to some nations."[41]

Not surprisingly such a virtuous nation had not become wealthy by illegitimate means. Rather the success of Dutch commerce was "alone the effects of industry and ingenuity."[42] The celebrated massacre at Amboyna was, even Bethel confessed, "to be had by all in abhorrence," but it "was acted but by a few, and disowned" and could be overlooked since "the Popish Nations have (in all ages down to our times) driven in massacres, and cruel torturings."[43]

A Tragedy (1671), p. 87; Thomas Shadwell, *The Humorists* (1671), in *The Complete Works of Thomas Shadwell*, ed. Montague Summers, 5 vols. (1927), 1: 183–84; *The Royal Shepherdess* (1669), in *Works*, 1: 172; and *Epson-Wells* (1673), in *Works*, 2: 111.

[38] Dr. William Denton to Sir Ralph Verney, 28 September 1671, Princeton University Firestone Library, Verney MSS (microfilm), Reel 124 (unfoliated); Alberti to Doge and Senate, 10/20 November 1671, *CSPV*, p. 121.

[39] De Britaine, *Dutch Usurpation*, pp. 11, 33.   [40] Dryden, *Amboyna*, Epilogue, sig. KV.

[41] Slingsby Bethel, *The Present Interest of England Stated* (1671), pp. 30–31.

[42] *Ibid.*, p. 31; the same point was made by Thomas Culpepper, *Plain English* (1673), p. 15.

[43] Slingsby Bethel, *Observations on the Letter Written to Sir Thomas Osborne* (1673), p. 4.

From this ideological perspective, wars against the Dutch made no economic sense. The Nonconformist divine Joseph Hill derided "the senseless clamor of men" for war, crying "We are competitors for trade! It's our interest! Our interest! Down with the Dutch! Down with the English!" because it was manifestly clear that "the world is wide enough, and the sea large enough for both nations to exercise their skill and industry."[44] War, especially naval wars, are disastrous for the economic health of trading nations. It was clear to the author of *A Free Conference Touching the Present State of England* that "for merchant-men's fleets to be changed into naval armies, and the substance of the people melted into magazines unusefully, which might more profitably be employed in rich and gainful navigations, cannot be the proper interest of England."[45]

Instead of advancing the aims of either the English or the Dutch, the Anglo-Dutch wars only made France into a great maritime trading power. "The English and Dutch have of late by a furious war contended who should enjoy" the world's trade, agreed the merchant Roger Coke, "but whilst these covetous combatants contend so fiercely for her, the French King by all the modes of France courts her for himself."[46] While the two great Protestant maritime powers are "ruining themselves," Algernon Sidney fumed, "the King of France will gain all the traffic, and increase his power at sea, as fast as either of ours can diminish," putting him in a position to "give law to them all."[47]

English radicals proclaimed with a united voice that universal monarchy was in fact the sole aim and purpose of French policy. They, like the rest of Europe, were aware of "the great design of France, who seemeth no less now to endeavor and affect the same design of an Universal Monarchy & direction of affairs as Spain was once doing."[48] "It is agreed to all hands," insisted Slingsby Bethel in

---

[44] Joseph Hill, *The Interest of these United Provinces* (Amsterdam, 1673), sig. G2.

[45] *A Free Conference Touching the Present State of England Both at Home and Abroad: In Order to the Designs of France* (1668), reprinted in 1673, pp. 12–13.

[46] Roger Coke, *A Discourse of Trade* (1670), sig. Blv. The same point is also made in *A Free Conference*, pp. 48–49; and Ludlow, "Voyce," p. 1052.

[47] Algernon Sidney, "Court Maxims, Discussed and Refelled," Warwickshire County Record Office, p. 177. The Venetian observer Pietro Mocenigo also noted "the spleen of the nation" as the English viewed French commercial and naval expansion "with resentment;" "Account of England," 30 May/9 June 1671, *CSPV*, p. 69.

[48] M. Appelbome to Chancellor of Spain, 6/16 October 1665, Bodleian Library, Clarendon MSS 83, fo. 251r. This point was, of course, classically made by the Baron de Lisola in his *The Buckler of State and Justice* (1667).

pamphlet after pamphlet, "that the French set up for an Universal Monarchy." The implication was that "the interest of the European princes is changed from that of being against the House of Austria, and for France, to that of being for it, and against France, the latter being at present, under more than suspicion, that having now got the advantage of Spain, they intend to improve it to an Universal Monarchy, as Spain formerly designed."[49]

After the French invasion of the Spanish Netherlands in 1667, this line of argument appealed to an increasingly broad segment of the English political nation. "Here hath been great talk of the French," Dr. William Denton reported from London in 1671.[50] "The French indeed [are] generally hated to the devil by all the English except the King in the first place & the gentry or noblesse who had seen the world and traveled abroad," explained the English envoy John Doddington to a French traveler in a Savoyard inn.[51]

Before the outbreak of the third Anglo-Dutch war it was possible to accept some aspects of both of these interpretations. It was possible to believe – and many did – that the Dutch Republic was trying to achieve universal dominion by monopolizing commerce, while Louis XIV sought universal monarchy through brute force. But when England, in concert with France, declared war against the United Provinces in spring 1672 the English political nation was forced to decide which was the greater threat. Most moderates trusted the government's assessment and supported the war.[52] Seamen volunteered to serve in the fleet in droves, provoking one observer to exclaim that "never so great a cheerfulness [was] known in the seamen to enter into that service as now; everyone freely offering

---

[49] Bethel, *Present Interest*, sigs. A2-A3 (although the pamphlet is anonymous, the repetition of phrases from it verbatim in Bethel's later pamphlets convinces me of the identification); Bethel, *Present State of Christendome and the Interest of England* (1677), pp. 11, 15; Bethel, *An Account of the French Usurpation upon the Trade of England* (1679), pp. 1–2; Bethel, *Interest of Princes and States* (1680), sigs. A3-A4, A6.

[50] Denton to Verney, 20 April 1671, Verney MSS, Reel 24 (unfoliated).

[51] John Doddington to Joseph Williamson, 27 June 1670, Huntington Library, MSS STT 625.

[52] Verney was one such moderate who was extremely fearful of the French in the later 1660s and early 1670s, but supported the war. His ideological progression is discussed in the next section. Thomas Papillon, whom Margaret Priestley has described as violently Francophobic in the later 1670s, clearly appreciated the threat from the United Provinces in this period. As a negotiator at Breda in 1667 he had castigated the Dutch for their economic greed. Throughout the third Dutch war he served as a victualer of the navy. See Priestley, "London Merchants and Opposition Politics in Charles II's Reign," *Bulletin of the Institute of Historical Research* 29 (1956): 205–19; and Papillon's "Account of the Negotiations at Breda," (*c.* 1667) Centre for Kentish Studies, MSS U1015/F16/1.

themselves to it & pressing who shall get in first."[53] "It cannot be denied," insisted the Earl of Arlington to Henry Coventry, "but the world is now generally convinced that the provocations his Majesty hath exposed in his declaration to have received from the Dutch do sufficiently justify the war he is making upon them."[54] "War against Holland was proclaimed yesterday at all the usual places in London," the Venetian secretary Alberti reported to the Doge and Senate, "there were crowds of people who being aware of the causes, through the declaration reported, approved of the step, blessing his Majesty with one accord and willingly sacrificing all commercial consider- ations for the sake of the honor and glory of the country."[55] While John Miller is probably right to claim that "the government was going into a war with far less support than in 1665," the government was clearly able to persuade most people that war against the grasping and insolent Dutch Republic was necessary.[56]

III

Yet even as news reached England of the spectacular early successes of the allied forces in the very first campaign, English popular opinion turned against the war. Political moderates, those who had been willing to accept the government's argument that the Dutch Republic represented a more immediate and dangerous threat than the French monarchy, revised their assessment. Sir Thomas Clarges was sure there was a "universal hatred against this French alliance."[57] Reports of French military defeats were received "by the

[53] Newsletter from London, 6 February 1672, Library of Congress, MSS 18124, vol. 3, fo. 148r. See also Newsletter from London, 10 February 1672, Library of Congress, MSS 18124, vol. 3, fo. 150r. for a similar report from the West Country. This account of naval recruitment in the early phases of the war is substantiated by the most recent and authoritative historian of the Restoration navy. See J. D. Davies, *Gentlemen and Tarpaulins: The Officers and Men of the Restoration Navy* (Oxford, 1991), pp. 160–63.

[54] Arlington to Henry Coventry, 29 March 1672, Longleat Coventry MSS LXV, fo. 155r. The letter also emphasizes the enthusiastic support for the fast declared to implore divine support in the war.

[55] Alberti to Doge and Senate, 20 March/8 April 1672, *CSPV*, p. 195. See also Alberti to Doge and Senate, 3/13 November 1671, *CSPV*, p. 119.

[56] Miller, *Charles II*, p. 188. C. R. Boxer has also claimed that there was no popular support for the war at its beginning, but his argument is based exclusively on Dutch newspaper reports, reports concerned above all in demonstrating that the English could not sustain the war; see Boxer, "Second Thoughts," pp. 74–75. Ronald Hutton agrees with my position; see Hutton, *Charles the Second*, p. 297.

[57] Sir Thomas Clarges, 12 January 1674, Grey, *Debates*, 2: 232. See also Major T. Fairfax to Joseph Williamson, 7 November 1673, *CSPD*, p. 10.

generality of the people as good news."[58] The Venetian secretary thought "that the country would subscribe any sum for an open war with France."[59]

There could be no doubting Parliament's antipathy for the French alliance in the autumn session of 1673. On one morning the speaker discovered a wooden shoe on his chair with the arms of the king of France on one side and those of Charles II on the other, and the note "of one of the two."[60] In January a memorandum entitled *Verbum Sapienti* was circulating among MPs proclaiming that "all the mischiefs we have felt or may hereafter fear from the Hollanders, though ten times greater than what are falsely pretended, cannot possibly be of half that dangerous consequence to us, as the advantages now given to the growth of French power, by this pernicious league," advantages which had allowed Louis XIV to "overcome the greatest difficulty in his way to that universal monarchy to which he has so long aspired."[61] These were not the works of cranks and radicals. Sir John Hobart reported that "the House were clear and unanimous in their dislike of the war with the Dutch & friendship with the French."[62] Sir Christopher Musgrave agreed that "as much sharpness was expressed against the war with Holland and the alliance of France as the spirits of our corner could conceive."[63]

In the streets and shops of London, and around the country, similar sentiments were expressed. In London coffee-houses "the people continue their too open hate to the French, and discourse of them with the greatest contempt imaginable."[64] "From peace with the French and war with the Dutch, / From a new mouth which will cost us as much, / And from councils of wits which advise us too much, / Libera Nos Domine," ran a litany found in a Lincoln's Inn boghouse in 1672.[65] "The dissatisfaction is so great at this conjunction with the French," Robert Yard wrote to Joseph Williamson, "that the general speech in the City and that amongst the soberest and

[58] Henry Ball to Williamson, 19 September 1673, in W. D. Christie, ed., *Letters Addressed from London to Sir Joseph Williamson*, 2 vols. (1874), 2: 20.
[59] Alberti to Doge and Senate, 24 October/3 November 1673, *CSPV*, p. 163.
[60] Alberti to the Doge and Senate, 31 October/10 November 1673, *CSPV*, p. 168.
[61] *Verbum Sapienti*, January 1674, *CSPD*, pp. 128–29.
[62] Sir John Hobart to Mr. John Hobart, 1 November 1673, Bodleian Library, Tanner MSS 42, fo. 56r.
[63] Sir Christopher Musgrave to Williamson, 3 November 1673, Christie, ed., *Letters*, 2: 59.
[64] Henry Ball to Williamson, 1 September 1673, Christie, ed., *Letters*, 2: 1; see also Henry Ball to Williamson, 29 August 1673 in *ibid.*, 1: 194.   [65] "A Litany," in *POAS*, 1: 190.

chiefest persons is that unless this alliance with France be broken the nation will be ruined."[66]

The same pattern of Francophobia was manifest throughout the country. "Our country talk is of no war but, if any, with France," reported Allan Wharton from Whitby in North Yorkshire.[67] Richard Bower, Williamson's Yarmouth correspondent, lamented that "we are so Dutchified here that a Dutch man cannot be more dejected than our people are generally for the sad condition we understand the Hollander to be in."[68] In Dartmouth "the agitation for peace was very welcome, and we pray the hastening of it."[69]

Those who were fighting the war, the same men who had rushed in droves to volunteer, quickly turned against it. Seamen complained constantly of the practices of the French navy. Reports of French naval performance played a large role in turning opinion against the war. One reported from Weymouth that the French sailors "bragged that after they had Holland, they hoped to have England."[70] By the summer of 1673, the naval officer Sir Charles Lyttleton prayed that "God send his Majesty a good peace," which he assured Arlington was "as well the prayer of almost all I have spoken with of that matter."[71] That same summer the English land forces "were ready to mutiny at their decamping at Blackheath, only upon a report of their uniting with the French army."[72] This sort of behavior was hardly surprising, Edmund Verney explained to his father Sir Ralph, "because it is a very hard thing to force men to hazard their lives and fight for those whom they hate."[73]

Many moderate Royalists of all social strata now joined their more radical brethren in denouncing the French alliance and the war with the United Provinces. The Presbyterian Royalist Anthony Ashley Cooper, Earl of Shaftesbury, was merely the most flamboyant of those who shifted from an anti-Dutch to an anti-French alignment in

---

[66] Robert Yard to Williamson, 29 August 1673, Christie, ed., Letters, 1: 194–95. See also William Bridgeman to Williamson, 16 January 1674 in ibid., 2: 112; and Sir Francis Chaplin to Williamson, 14 July 1673, CSPD, p. 437.

[67] Allan Wharton to James Hickes, 11 July 1672, CSPD, p. 330.

[68] Richard Bower to Williamson, 24 June 1672, CSPD, p. 272. See also Captain T. Guy (Yarmouth) to Williamson, 30 September 1672, CSPD, p. 671.

[69] William Hurt to James Hickes, 5 November 1672, CSPD, p. 127.

[70] Nathaniel Osborne to James Hickes, 10 August 1672, CSPD, pp. 470–71.

[71] Charles Lyttleton to Arlington, 23 July 1673, CSPD, p. 455.

[72] Henry Ball to Williamson, 18 July 1673, Christie, ed., Letters, 1: 116.

[73] Edmund Verney to Sir Ralph Verney, 20 November 1673, Verney MSS, Reel 27 (unfoliated) (my translation).

the early 1670s. As Lord Chancellor, and member of the infamous Cabal, Shaftesbury had delivered the single most celebrated piece of Restoration oratory. Comparing England to Rome, the United Provinces to Carthage and himself to Cato, he had exclaimed, "*Delenda est Carthago.*"[74] "Let this be remembered," Shaftesbury thundered, "the States of Holland are England's eternal enemy both by interest and inclination." This, he explained, was because they were "the common enemies to all monarchies, and I may say especially to ours, their only competitors for trade and power at sea, and who only stand in their way to an universal empire, as great as Rome."[75] Although this speech has usually been interpreted as a spectacular piece of Hollandophobic rhetoric, Shaftesbury was at pains to make clear that he attributed Dutch policy not to the nation as a whole but to the republican faction. England declared war against the Dutch Republic, Shaftesbury made clear in the autumn of 1673, because "the king was obliged for the security of a lasting peace, as also by the laws of gratitude and relation, to see the House of Orange settled, and the Loevestein, that Carthaginian party brought down."[76]

Shaftesbury was not being inconsistent, nor displaying pique for having been dismissed from the Privy Council,[77] when in 1675 he warned that the king of France "is grown the most potent of us all at sea." "It is incredible the money that he hath bestowed in making harbors, he makes nature itself give way to the vastness of his expenses," marveled Shaftesbury, "and after all this, shall a Prince so wise, so intent upon his affairs, be thought to make all these preparations to sail over land and fall up on the back of Hungary, and batter the walls of Kaminitz, or is it possible he should oversee his interest in seizing Ireland, a thing so feasible to him. If he be master

---

[74] 5 February 1673, Grey, *Debates*, 2: 2.
[75] Anthony Ashley Cooper, "Delenda Carthago, or the true Interest of England in relation to France and Holland," printed in Sir Walter Scott, ed., *A Collection of Scarce and Valuable Tracts ... Particularly that of the Late Lord Somers* (1812), 7: 37–39; *LJ*, 5 February 1673, 12: 525–26. The comparison between the Anglo-Dutch rivalry and that between Carthage and Rome was a common trope in Restoration literature. Both were seen as naval conflicts in which "the Empire of the Universe" was at stake; e.g. Thomas Ross, (Keeper of His Majesties Libraries & Groom of the Privy Chamber), *The Second Punick War ... from the Latine of Silius Italicus* (1672), sig. B2r. See also Dryden, *Amboyna*, sig. KV; Roger Palmer, *A Short and True Account of the Material Passages in the First War Between the English and the Dutch Since His Majesties Restauration*, second edition, (1672), pp. 103, 108–109; *The Roman History of Lucius J. Florus* (1669), pp. 53, 60, 71–72. [76] *LJ*, 27 October 1673, 12: 589.
[77] Indeed Hutton has claimed that Shaftesbury was dismissed from office because Charles thought he had turned against the war; see Hutton, *Charles the Second*, p. 308.

of the seas, as he certainly now is, and which when attained gives him all the Mediterranean, East and West India trade and renders him both (by situation and excellent harbors) perpetual Master of the Seas without dispute." The only hope for "disengagement from the French interest," Shaftesbury insisted, lay in the "House differing from the sense and opinion of Whitehall."[78]

Sir William Coventry, who despite his impeccable Royalist pedigree had lived quietly under the Protectorate and apparently adopted that regime's support for religious liberty,[79] was one of the most prominent opponents of the third Anglo-Dutch war. "It is vain to think that the European trade can be maintained by us by a war," he argued, asking incredulously, "what probability is there, if we beat the Hollander, that we shall get all trade?"[80] Indeed, Coventry thought it "strange that we and Holland should be divided by one whose interest is destructive to us both."[81] The real danger to Europe was that "France is too big." The true "interest of the King of England," he reminded the House of Commons, "is to keep France from being too great on the continent." Endless procrastination, debate, and negotiation simply would not do. "If you stay till all Flanders be gone," he urged the historically minded, "you will do as King James did in the Palatinate War, treat, and treat, till all was gone, and nobody to treat with him."[82] Although Louis XIV was certainly responsible for spoiling English markets, he did not intend to stop there, "the end and purpose of France's conquests is not for trade."[83] "The main stress of our matter is to hinder the French from universal trade, all the world over," Coventry reasoned, not because trade was an end in itself, but because the French were "an enemy to us and all Christendom." If France was not stopped in the United Provinces "he may the sooner fall upon us" since "this swelling monarchy of France is founded on maxims of greatness and action."[84]

[78] Shaftesbury's speech of 20 October 1675 in *Two Speeches* (Amsterdam, 1675), pp. 8–9.

[79] William Coventry to Thomas Thynne, 23 November 1672, Longleat Thynne MSS 16, fo. 24r.; Coventry to Thynne, 1 January 1673, Thynne MSS 16, fo. 53r.

[80] Coventry, 31 October 1673, Grey, *Debates*, 2: 203. For Coventry's opposition to the earlier war, see my *Protestantism and Patriotism*, sections 3–4, *passim*.

[81] Coventry, 31 October 1673, Grey, *Debates*, 2: 204.

[82] Coventry, 31 October 1673, *ibid.*, 2: 213; 22 February 1677, *ibid.*, 4: 133; and 11 May 1678, *ibid.*, 5: 387. He expressed similar views – calling Louis XIV "a Match for all Europe" – in a letter to Thomas Thynne, 4 January 1675, Thynne MSS 16, fo. 212r.

[83] 6 March 1677, Grey, *Debates*, 4: 188–89. On France's pernicious economic policies see Coventry, 27 February 1668, *ibid.*, 1: 97; and 10 May 1675, *ibid.*, 3: 125.

[84] Coventry, 29 January 1678, *ibid.*, 5: 18–20.

Sir Thomas Littleton, who had been an ardent Royalist in the 1640s, blamed England's economic decline on the twin evils of religious persecution and "the trade we have with the French nation." Though he frequently spoke in favor of the third Anglo-Dutch war at its outset, by the later 1670s he spoke just as strongly in favor of an Anglo-Dutch alliance to fight the "great tyrant" Louis XIV. "We have run into the error manifestly of assisting the King of France," he complained, "in the Palatinate business Spain then stood in the room of France, and was then as formidable as the French are now, ready to swallow up the world."[85]

Even those, like Sir Philip Warwick, who had loyally served the Caroline Court and who had castigated the Dutch for pursuing the "Sea-Monarchy as eagerly as Charles the Fourth or Francis the First did the Land-Monarchy," found French power simply too threatening to ignore. "I believe, he had never affected to have been an East and West Indian merchant, but as he foresaw with Old Rome, in vain it was to affect the Universal European Land Monarchy without he became considerable at sea," wrote Warwick of Louis XIV, "nor had he become considerable but as the jealousies of Holland toward us shrouded him till he thrust forth a top, that will shade us both, unless we hold a stricter correspondence & confidence in each other than hitherto we have done."[86] After hearing the news of the spectacular French victories, the Bishop of Lincoln – hardly a radical critic of the Court – worried that while "Holland deservedly suffers all the miseries it now lies under...if it submits to France, where are we? I am persuaded France will treat and conquer on, till there be little left to treat for."[87]

Although different people perceived the danger from France at different times, and expressed their concerns with varying degrees of sophistication, the events of the third Anglo-Dutch war convinced most moderates that the most serious aspirant to the universal monarchy, and the greatest threat to English political culture, was

[85] Sir Thomas Littleton, 26 January 1674, *ibid.*, 2: 346; 19 April 1675, *ibid.*, 3: 3; 10 November 1675, *ibid.*, 3: 445; 29 January 1678, *ibid.*, 5: 25; 31 January 1678, *ibid.*, 5: 44.

[86] Sir Philip Warwick, "Of Government," 28 August 1679, Huntington MSS HM 41956, p. 182. See also Warwick, 14 March 1678, Grey, *Debates*, 5: 230. Despite having harbored the great Anglican theologian, Henry Hammond, during the Interregnum, Warwick had come to support "some indulgence" for Dissenters: 11 March 1668, *ibid.*, 1: 111. This was a position not dissimilar from that of his patron the Earl of Southampton. For more on Warwick, see Basil Duke Henning, ed., *The House of Commons 1660–1690*, 3 vols. (1983), 3: 674–77. I owe this reference to the kindness of Blair Worden.

[87] William, Bishop of Lincoln, to Williamson, 22 June 1672, *CSPD*, p. 264.

Louis XIV. People were not disillusioned with the war because it was a military disaster; they felt rather that it was manifestly contrary to England's interest. The English people not only called for the end of an economically disruptive war, but also for a diplomatic and ideological realignment.

IV

Why did moderate English opinion shift from an Hollandophobic to a Francophobic orientation over the course of the third Anglo-Dutch war? Why had the English ceased to fear the grasping ambition of the Dutch? Why did they insist that their government withdraw from a war when they had every reason to believe that the Dutch could be forced to an ignominious peace?

Some have claimed that the revelations in the summer of 1673 that the Duke of York and Lord Treasurer Clifford were Roman Catholics explains this shift in popular sentiment. Fear of Catholicism, and consequently Catholic France, was revived in 1673 – the same fear which would be rekindled in 1678 and again in 1688. Religion rather than altered perceptions of European developments, then, accounts for the demands for peace with the Protestant Dutch and war against Catholic France.

There are, however, many reasons for questioning this claim. For example, the shift in public opinion began in the summer of 1672, well before anyone could be certain of the religious proclivities of James or Sir Thomas Clifford. Nor were fears of popery exclusively religious fears. By the late seventeenth century most English people understood popery as a means of instituting arbitrary government. Popery was the religion of seventeenth-century baroque monarchies. Charles and James – men known more for the amount of time they spent with their mistresses than with their spiritual advisers – were thought to be sympathetic to the Catholic religion because it was "the only one which keeps subject to their allegiance."[88]

The panic about popery grew out of fears of a French universal monarchy, rather than the other way around. "The Papists [are] not considerable here," Henry Powle pointed out, they would hardly be a danger "unless they had encouragement at home, or dependence on some foreign prince," some "great prince aspiring to the Western

[88] Alberti to Doge and Senate, 31 May/10 June 1672, *CSPV*, p. 225.

Monarchy.''[89] ''Our jealousies of Popery, or an arbitrary government, are not from a few inconsiderable Papists here,'' concurred the moderate Sir Thomas Meres, ''but from the ill example we have from France.''[90] Louis XIV sought universal monarchy purely to satisfy his lust for power; he was not thought to be promoting a religious crusade. It was true that he persecuted his Protestant subjects, but, Sir William Coventry was quick to point out, ''the rigors in religion in states, arise from interest rather than religion; formerly Spain was more rigorous in religion, and now France.''[91] There is therefore little reason to doubt the Spanish ambassador's assessment that ''the Duke of York was too partial to France, and that was the reason, not his marriage to a Catholic'' – not his religious proclivities – ''why he suffers so much persecution at the moment.''[92]

The heated popular debate about the Duke of York's marriage makes it clear that the English feared French domination more than they feared Roman Catholicism. Soon after the death of Anne Hyde, the English government began negotiating for a new bride for the Duke of York. The first nominee was the Archduchess of Innsbruck, a Catholic member of the House of Habsburg.[93] Far from eliciting cries of ''No Popery,'' it was ''publicly hoped that the marriage'' would soon be concluded.[94] The moderate Edmund Verney wrote to his father full of enthusiasm for the prospect.[95] Nor did Parliament disapprove. The negotiations for the Innsbruck marriage were well known, Gilbert Burnet later marveled, ''and yet no address was made to the king to hinder [the duke's] marrying a papist.''[96] It was only after the negotiations for the Innsbruck marriage fell through – the archduchess chose to marry the Holy Roman Emperor instead – that the Duke of York selected the Duchess of Modena. The marriage was immediately unpopular. ''The generality of the people ... cannot

[89] Henry Powle, 23 October 1675, Grey, *Debates*, 3: 334. Powle, significantly, was one of the leaders of the opposition to the Modena marriage; see Bridgeman to Williamson, 20 October 1673, Christie, ed., *Letters*, 2: 49.

[90] Sir Thomas Meres, 11 May 1675, Grey, *Debates*, 3: 136. For his moderation see Henning, ed., *House of Commons*, 3: 48–59. Similar views were expressed in *Verbum Sapienti*, January 1674, *CSPD*, p. 131.   [91] Coventry, 31 October 1673, Grey, *Debates*, 2: 203.

[92] Alberti to Doge and Senate, 28 November/8 December 1673, *CSPV*, p. 182.

[93] Alberti to Doge and Senate, 17 April 1671, *CSPV*, p. 38, and 19/29 April 1672, *CSPV*, p. 203.   [94] Alberti to Doge and Senate, 17/27 October 1672, *CSPV*, p. 306.

[95] Edmund Verney to Sir Ralph Verney, 10 February 1673, Verney MSS, Reel 25 (unfoliated).

[96] Burnet, *History*, 2: 30. Henry Coventry made a similar point in Parliament: Alberti to Doge and Senate, 31 October/10 November 1673, *CSPV*, p. 169. Sir Heneage Finch also pointed out that the Innsbruck marriage elicited no religious opposition: speech by Finch, 30 October 1673, Leicestershire Record Office, D. G. 7/Box 4957/ p. 33.

now be pleased," Robert Yard wrote to Williamson.[97] Edmund Verney, writing from Buckinghamshire, thought that "very few of his Majesty's subjects... celebrated [the marriage] from their hearts or with their mouths."[98] The explanation for this popular antipathy was ubiquitous. Marriage with the Duchess of Modena was a wedding with "an adopted daughter of France," a "marriage by the French interest," a marriage "of French contriving."[99] The people were said to "wish there may be [no marriages] of the French making."[100] The English were terrified that the Italian princess would act as a French agent at the English Court. In fact, as the Duchess of Modena and her mother made their way through France toward England, it was rumored that "the French King goes himself to meet the old lady, and to instruct her how to work his interest here."[101] The Venetian secretary merely emphasized the obvious when he informed his government that "the opposition to the Modenese marriage proceeded from the princess being the nominee of France and not of Spain, like the Archduchess of Innsbruck."[102]

The English political nation was far more concerned with putting a halt to French expansionism than with reviving a Protestant confessional alliance. Rumors that Spain or the Empire would take the field against the French were greeted with unbridled enthusiasm. In his outline of the desired ends of English foreign policy, the country MP Sir Richard Temple made it clear that "foreign alliances" are to be secured "with respect to the balance of monarchy

---

[97] Robert Yard to Williamson, 17 October 1673, Christie, ed., *Letters*, 2: 48; and see Miller, *Charles II*, p. 210. Effigies of popes were burned as soon as she set foot on English soil: see Thomas Derham to Williamson, 5 December 1673, *CSPD*, p. 44, and Walter Overbury to Williamson, 1 December 1673, *CSPD*, p. 40.

[98] Edmund Verney to Sir Ralph Verney, 27 November 1673, Verney MSS, Reel 27 (unfoliated).

[99] *A Relation of the Most Material Matters in Parliament Relating to Religion, Property, and the Liberty of the Subject* (1673), pp. 19–20; Ralph Josselin, 11 February 1674, *The Diary of Ralph Josselin 1616–1683*, ed. Alan MacFarlane (1976), p. 573; Alberti to Doge and Senate, 1/11 August 1673, *CSPV*, p. 85. See also Henry Ball to Williamson, 31 July 1673, Christie, ed., *Letters*, 1: 137–38; Robert Yard to Williamson, 4 August 1673, *ibid.*, 1: 142–43; Henry Ball to Williamson, 4 August 1673, *ibid.*, 1: 144. This was how the marriage was recalled in popular verse: see "The Duke of York's Farewell Speech to his Friends," (*c.* 1680), Folger Library, MSS G. c. 2.

[100] Robert Yard to Williamson, 22 August 1673, Christie, ed., *Letters*, 1: 182.

[101] Henry Ball to Williamson, 10 October 1673, *ibid.*, 2: 36. It was long known that Louis XIV hoped to gain political influence through the Duke of York's bride: Alberti to Doge and Senate, 7/17 April 1671, *CSPV*, p. 38; Alberti to Doge and Senate 16/26 May 1673, *CSPV*, p. 52. Charles II was said to support the match for precisely those reasons: Alberti to Doge and Senate, 8/18 August 1673, *CSPV*, p. 91.

[102] Alberti to Doge and Senate, 7/17 November 1673, *CSPV*, p. 174.

& obviating that design [for universal monarchy]." Therefore, Temple concluded, "not only Protestants but all who are on a distinct foot as Portugal, the Catholic Princes of Germany, Dutch, Italian Princes not dependent on Spain, nay the Pope himself, *qua* Prince are to be united in this common bottom."[103]

The argument that the Dutch propaganda campaign successfully transformed English popular sentiment is a great deal more plausible. There can be no doubt that the Dutch successfully smuggled large numbers of pamphlets into England during the war.[104] Nor can it be questioned that the English government was extremely fearful of the efficacy of the Dutch polemics.[105] But no work of propaganda, not even one by so skilled a polemicist as Pierre Du Moulin, can persuade its target audience if its assumptions are not credible. *England's Appeal* worked precisely because it fitted in so well with English experience and English perceptions of European power politics. Du Moulin emphasized, as English defenders of the Triple Alliance had done in the late 1660s, "the ambitious designs of France," pointing out that Louis XIV was already acting like "an Universal Monarch" by pretending "to a right of displacing Princes, and disposing both of their lives and of their territories."[106] More importantly, he conceded that the Dutch republican regime had been pernicious. Now, Du Moulin insisted, everything had changed since "the Prince of Orange was miraculously restored to the dignity and authority of his ancestors."[107] In these new circumstances continuing the Anglo-Dutch war would only enable Louis XIV "to invade all Christendom & to extend his Empire without bounds."[108] The pamphlet was read as a contribution to an English debate, not as a foreign intervention on the English political scene. So familiar were the arguments of *England's Appeal* that at least one contemporary attributed the anonymous pamphlet to the former Privy Councilor Sir William Coventry.[109]

Why had these Francophobic arguments become so persuasive?

---

[103] Sir Richard Temple, "An Essay Upon Government" (1667?), Bodleian MSS Eng. Hist. c. 201, fo. 13r.

[104] Alberti to Doge and Senate, 25 March/4 April 1672, *CSPV*, p. 189; Arlington to Sir William Thompson, 21 May 1672, *CSPD*, p. 30; Silas Taylor to Williamson, 18 March 1673, *CSPD*, pp. 58–59; Examination of George Verleken, 19 March 1673, *CSPD*, p. 66; Examination of Nicholas Van Hull, 22 March 1673, *CSPD*, p. 74; W. Bridgeman to Williamson, 26 December 1673, *CSPD*, p. 69.

[105] Anon. to Marquess of Baden Hochberg, 3 April 1673, *CSPD*, p. 127; Privy Council Minute, 18 June 1673, *CSPD*, p. 380.   [106] *England's Appeal*, p. 34.   [107] *Ibid.*, p. 21.

[108] *Ibid.*, pp. 1–2.   [109] See Bodleian Library, G Pamph. 1125.

Why were moderates now willing to accept the political analysis that the radicals had long offered? Three decisive developments during the war had served to heighten fears of French universalist aspirations, and to invalidate arguments that the Dutch aimed at universal dominion.

First, the French land offensive of 1672 was far more successful than anyone had expected. Throughout the spring and early summer each packet boat arriving in England brought news of another French military victory. By June, the once mighty Dutch Republic had been largely reduced to the province of Holland. In desperation the citizens of Amsterdam and The Hague flooded their suburbs to slow the onslaught of the seemingly invincible French troops. It was very hard to imagine a Dutch universal dominion while so much of what was left of the United Provinces lay under water. "We discourse of nothing but sea [affairs] and Holland," Henry Coventry wrote in the late summer, "and most of the latter we hear is water."[110] The Dutch had clearly been humbled; the time had come, many thought, to negotiate a satisfactory peace.[111]

The French invasion not only made claims that the Dutch were seeking universal monarchy appear ridiculous, but it also gave rise to a political revolution in the United Provinces. The English moderates had supported war against the Dutch because the Dutch republican party, led by John De Witt, had been committed to the overthrow of the English monarchy.[112] This republican faction, not their domestic enemies the Orangists, had fallen from virtue, replacing godly worship with a base materialism. All of the Dutch infringements on the English fishing trade, the atrocities perpetrated in the East Indies, the casuistical application of treaties, even the ideological justification for Dutch mercantile policy, Grotius's *Mare Liberum*, indeed "all the mischief which hath befallen this nation, hath ever been occasioned, or fomented by that [republican] party."[113] The English moderates

---

[110] Coventry to Sir Edward Wood, 2 August 1672, Coventry MSS LXXXII, fo. 28r.; Stephen Temple to Sir Richard Temple, 4 March 1672, Huntington MSS STT 2200; Newsletter, 9 June 1672, *CSPD*, p. 185; Arlington to the Earl of Sunderland, 17 June 1672, in T. Bebington, ed., *Arlington's Letters to Sir W. Temple* 2 vols. (1701), 2: 374; Sir Ralph Verney to Edmund Verney, 18 June 1672, Verney MSS, Reel 125 (unfoliated).

[111] Edmund Verney to Sir Ralph Verney, 17 June 1672, Verney MSS, Reel 25 (unfoliated).

[112] Henry Coventry to Duke of York, 17 July 1672, Coventry MSS LXXXII, fo. 11r.; Stephen Temple to Sir Richard Temple, 4 March 1672, Huntington MSS STT 2200; Alberti to Doge and Senate, 23 August/2 September 1672, *CSPV*, p. 274; Sir Ralph Verney to Edmund Verney, 22 February 1672, Verney MSS, Reel 25 (unfoliated).

[113] Stubbe, *A Further Justification of the Present War Against the United Netherlands* (1673) sig. C1.

eagerly awaited the day when the republican party would be overthrown, and the Prince of Orange would restore the traditional Anglo-Dutch amity. The moderates "never aimed at the destruction of the Dutch republic," they never hoped to eviscerate the United Provinces, they "merely sought to humble it."[114]

The English could not have been happier when news arrived in August 1672 that "the people of The Hague have in a great fury... cut, mangled, killed pensionary De Witt and then his elder brother Ruwaert Van Putten."[115] Even more reassuring were the reports that "in all places they have made a reformation of the magistracy," reports that suggested the Dutch people now relied upon the Prince of Orange to "redeem them from the misery, the treachery, and the folly their governors have reduced them to."[116] When the first false rumors reached East Claydon that De Witt had been stabbed to death, Edmund Verney enthused that "he had received his just recompense, having been along with his accomplices the cause... of all the ills of his compatriots."[117] Henry Coventry found it difficult to feel sorry for the De Witts, because of their "malice and several foul attempts and indeed scorns against the family Royal (and very likely by consequence the occasion of much blood already and more that may be spent in Europe)."[118] The implications of the political revolution were soon obvious to English observers. The demise of the De Witts, Arlington informed the Earl of Sunderland, "will have pretty well cured [the Dutch] of their ambition."[119] "Since the depression of the Loevestein faction," noted the author of *Verbum Sapienti*, the Dutch "have not only offered us full satisfaction as to our right of the flag, but have also made much fair and honorable proposals as might have been a good foundation of a firm and lasting

---

[114] Alberti to Doge and Senate, 6/16 September 1672, *CSPV*, p. 281. See also Alberti to Doge and Senate, 30 August/9 September 1672, *CSPV*, p. 278; John Trevor to Henry Coventry, 12 December 1671, Coventry MSS LXV, fos. 69v.-70r.; John Trevor to Henry Coventry, 5 January 1672, Coventry MSS LXV, fo. 93. This was the hope expressed in much of the English propaganda. See, for example, *A Letter out of Holland*, (20/30 April 1672), pp. 1–2, 4–5.

[115] Dr. William Denton to Sir Ralph Verney, 22 August 1672, Verney MSS Reel 25 (unfoliated); Newsletter from London, 17 August 1672, Library of Congress MSS 18124, 3: fo. 230r.; Silas Taylor to Navy Commissioners, 17 August 1672, *CSPD*, pp. 499–500; Henry Coventry to Earl of Essex, 29 August 1672, Coventry MSS LXXXII, fo. 51.

[116] Newsletter from London, 11 July 1672, Library of Congress MSS 18124, 3: fo. 2114r.; Newsletter from London, 22 August 1672, Library of Congress MSS 18124, 3: fo. 232r.

[117] Edmund Verney to Sir Ralph Verney, 24 June 1672, Verney MSS, Reel 25 (unfoliated). My translation.

[118] Coventry to Sir Edward Wood, 19 August 1672, Coventry MSS LXXXII, fos. 46–47.

[119] Arlington to Sunderland, 29 August 1672, Bebington, ed., *Arlington's Letters*, 2: 386.

peace betwixt us and them for many generations."[120] Moderates could now place all their hopes in a new Anglo-Dutch alliance, an alliance which would prevent the French from achieving universal dominion. Stephen Temple reported to his uncle Sir Richard that now that the Prince of Orange had been elevated to his hereditary offices "great and rational hopes are builded here upon a league with the House of Austria and some Princes of Germany, who fear the French King's design towards the Universal Monarchy of Christendom."[121] William Coventry concurred that the Prince of Orange was "now at the head of all the business of Christendom."[122]

While both of these political developments in the United Provinces significantly altered the calculations of the English moderates, the conduct of the French fleet in the two naval campaigns of the war convinced all but the greatest Francophiles that Louis XIV had some deep and dark designs. In the opening battle of the war the French fought so poorly that people everywhere cried "we are betrayed." "The populace say that the French have not served England better than they did Holland the last time they succored her," the Venetian secretary informed his government.[123] French performance in the following year's campaign was worse, provoking ubiquitous popular outrage. Despite official attempts to censor accounts of the naval encounters, anti-French descriptions of the battles were widely circulated.[124] These were supplemented by letters and personal accounts by seamen. "'Tis beyond my skill to describe the disorder the people were in here upon the not fighting of the French in the last

---

[120] *Verbum Sapienti*, January 1674, *CSPD*, p. 129. See also the comment in Williamson's Newsletter, 3 February 1674, Folger MSS L.c. 11; and the 1670 poem in Huntington MSS EL 8826.

[121] Stephen Temple to Sir Richard Temple, 11/21 October 1672, Huntington MSS STT 2201.

[122] Coventry to Thomas Thynne, 11 November 1674, Thynne MSS 16, fo. 202.

[123] Sir Thomas Player to Williamson, 6 June 1672, *CSPD*, p. 160; Alberti to Doge and Senate, 14/24 June 1672, *CSPV*, p. 233. See also the similar reports in Richard Bower (Yarmouth) to Williamson, 10 June 1672, *CSPD*, p. 190; Edmund Verney to Sir Ralph Verney, 6 May 1672, Verney MSS, Reel 25 (unfoliated); Sir Thomas Player to Williamson, 4 June 1672, *CSPD*, p, 149; Alberti to Doge and Senate, 21 June/1 July 1672, *CSPV*, p. 235; Burnet, *History*, 1: 613–14.

[124] For government censorship see Sir Ralph Verney to Edmund Verney, 6 June 1672, Verney MSS, Reel 25 (unfoliated); Henry Coventry to Sir William Curtius, 29 August 1673, Coventry MSS LXXXII, fo. 130v.; Henry Ball to Williamson, 5 September 1673, Christie, ed., *Letters*, 2: 13; Sir William Temple to the Earl of Essex, 10 September 1673, in Osmund Airy, ed., *The Essex Papers*, 2 vols. (1890), 1: 121. For some anti-French accounts see *An Exact Relation of the Several Engagements and Actions of his Majesties Fleet* (1673); "A Relation of the Battle," 11 August 1673, Tanner MSS 42, fos. 21–22. On all of these see Davies, *Gentlemen and Tarpaulins*, pp. 172–74.

battle," exclaimed Sir Thomas Player, "the citizens of London looked more disconsolate than when their city lay in ashes."[125] Many celebrated Guy Fawkes Day by shooting a Frenchman in effigy "because they accuse the French of having shirked in the sea fights."[126] English crews refused to salute their French allies.[127] At Sheerness French soldiers had to be protected from "the people's fury." On city streets "every apple-woman makes it a proverb, will you fight like the French?"[128] The English Admiral, Prince Rupert, while carefully avoiding any direct criticism of the French, let it be known that he was furious at their perfidy.[129] Almost overnight he became a popular hero. He and his close friend Shaftesbury – who was already known to be a great Francophobe – were popularly "looked upon to be the great Parliament men, and for the interest of Old England."[130] For the English the failure of the French fleet to engage meant a great deal more than a mere breach of contract. It confirmed that France's real intent was for the English and Dutch fleets to destroy each other by attrition, "that the game of France is to depress all powers which are capable of obstructing the torrent of their enterprises."[131] After the 1673 campaign "all men cried out," Burnet later recalled, "and said, we were engaged in a war by the French, that they might have the pleasure to see the Dutch and us destroy one another, while they knew our seas and ports, and learned all our methods, but took care to preserve themselves."[132] The third Anglo-Dutch war was understood as part of the French grand strategy to achieve control of the sea.

---

[125] Player to Williamson, 9 September 1673, Christie, ed., *Letters*, 2: 16.

[126] Alberti to Doge and Senate, 7/17 November 1673, *CSPV*, pp. 173–74.

[127] William Temple to Essex, 10 September 1673, Airy, ed., *Essex Papers*, 1: 121.

[128] Henry Ball to Williamson, 1 September 1673, Christie, ed., *Letters*, 2: 2–3. For popular sentiment more generally see: William Bridgeman to Williamson, 15 August 1673, *CSPD*, p. 495; J. Richards to Williamson, 18 August 1673, *CSPD*, p. 499; Henry Ball to Williamson, 18 August 1673, Christie, ed., *Letters*, 1: 170; Robert Yard to Williamson, 25 August 1673, *ibid.*, 1: 186, Sir Robert Southwell to Williamson, 31 August 1673, *ibid.*, 1: 197; Sir John Monson, 31 October 1673, Grey, *Debates*, 2: 198–99.

[129] Rupert to Charles II, 17 August 1673, *CSPD*, p. 498; Rupert to Arlington, 23 August 1673, *CSPD*, p. 509; Alberti to Doge and Senate, 22 August/1 September 1673, *CSPV*, p. 100; Alberti to Doge and Senate, 12/22 December 1673, *CSPV*, p. 187.

[130] Henry Ball to Williamson, 19 September 1673, Christie, ed., *Letters*, 2: 21–22; William Coventry to Thomas Thynne, 18 June 1673, Thynne MSS 16, fo. 136r.; Yard to Williamson, 18 August 1673, Christie, ed., *Letters*, 1: 174; Yard to Williamson, 29 August 1673, ibid., 1: 195; Ball to Williamson, 1 September 1673, ibid., 2: 2; Miller *Charles II*, p. 210; Leslie Chree O'Malley, "The Whig Prince: Prince Rupert and the Court Vs. Country Factions During the Reign of Charles II," *Albion* 8 (1976): 338–42.

[131] Lisola, *Buckler of State*, p. 13.   [132] Burnet, *History*, 2: 15.

CHAPTER 13

Reinterpreting the "Glorious Revolution": Catharine Macaulay and radical response

Bridget Hill

As a republican historian who deliberately focused on the seventeenth century because of what she saw as its relevance to her time, Catharine Macaulay (1731–91) provides a link between the seventeenth and eighteenth centuries. Her interpretations of the events of the 1640s and 1650s, the Restoration and the Revolution of 1688–89, not only influenced English radicalism profoundly but also contributed substantially to American and French revolutionary ideology. Above all her rejection of earlier interpretations of the "Glorious Revolution" was crucial to the reshaping of eighteenth-century radicalism. Caroline Robbins distinguished three generations of Commonwealthmen or Real Whigs from the Revolution of 1688 to the end of the eighteenth century. Only the last, "the third generation of the age of the American Revolution," was she prepared to call "early radicals."[1] It is with this group that Macaulay most closely identified and it is with her response to the "Glorious Revolution" that I am mainly concerned. Throughout the century the Revolution remained crucial to all political discussion. "No major debate involving any discussion of fundamental political principles took place," writes H. T. Dickinson, "without the events of 1688–89 being used as a source of inspiration and guidance."[2] It had a shaping influence on all eighteenth-century politics.

The debate over whether the Revolution of 1688–89 was of more long-term significance than that of the 1640s is not one I intend to enter.[3] The claim recently made by a group of historians that views of the Revolution as almost a non-revolution, changing little, are wrong and that the Revolution was far more radical than has been

---

[1] Caroline Robbins, *The Eighteenth-Century Commonwealthman* (Cambridge, Mass., 1959), p. 57.

[2] H. T. Dickinson, "The Eighteenth-Century Debate on the Glorious Revolution," *History* 6 (1976): 28–45, this passage p. 29.

[3] For instance Angus McInnes, "When was the English Revolution?," *History* 67 (1982): 377–92.

thought, deserves attention, but it is not the concern of this essay.[4] Richard Ashcraft's persuasive claims for Locke's radicalism may be valid but do not alter the fact that Lockean arguments played little part in the debate over the Revolution until late in the eighteenth century, more particularly after the American Revolution. The reasons why Whigs defending the Revolution of 1688 appealed rather to the ancient constitution than to any contract theory, was that the implications of that theory, as indeed any mention of the sovereignty of the people, were dangerously reminiscent of the events of the 1640s. "Whig supporters of William III" as Pocock has argued, "could not afford to be identified with this crew of regicides and enthusiasts."[5] Their hysterical reaction to the news of Ludlow's return from exile was representative of their extreme caution. As Macaulay noted, while "a bill to attaint the blood and forfeit the estates of the execrable Jeffries" was unsuccessful, "the brave, the virtuous, the patriotic Ludlow, was refused the satisfaction of spending the short remainder of life in his own country."[6]

If there is evidence of some continuity of radical protest between 1688 and the 1760s, there is also no doubt that the nature of radicalism changed. Criticism of the Revolution of 1688 began from its inception and was continuous thereafter, into and throughout the eighteenth century, but only in the 1760s and 1770s did it lead to a rejection of what was seen as the myth of the "Glorious Revolution" and, in consequence, the adoption of new aims and new methods of political action by the organized extra-parliamentary opposition. Robert Zaller has underlined the point when he writes that "far from picking up where their predecessors had left off" radicals of the 1760s "appeared to reject precisely those Revolution principles – the sanctity of the Glorious Revolution, the legislative independence of the House of Commons – which the last pre-Walpole radicals had espoused."[7] What separates Tory radicalism from that which

[4] Richard Ashcraft, *Revolutionary Politics and Locke's "Two Treatises of Government"* (Princeton, 1987); Lois G. Schwoerer, *The Declaration of Rights, 1689* (Baltimore, 1981); Mark Goldie, "The Revolution of 1689 and the Structure of Political Argument," *Bulletin of Research in the Humanities* 83 (1980): 473–564; H. T. Dickinson, "The Glorious Revolution of 1688–89: A Revolution Made or One Prevented?," *The Clark Newsletter* 15 (1988): 1–3.

[5] J. G. A. Pocock, "Radical Criticism of the Whig Order in the Age between the Revolutions," in Margaret Jacob and James Jacob, eds., *Origins of Anglo-American Radicalism* (1984), p. 36.

[6] Catharine Macaulay, *History of England from the Revolution to the Present Time in a Series of Letters to a Friend* (Bath, 1778), pp. 11–12.

[7] Robert Zaller, "The Continuity of British Radicalism in the Seventeenth and Eighteenth Centuries," *Eighteenth-Century Life* 6 (1981): 17–38, this passage p. 26.

emerged in the 1760s is that the former, although agreed that corruption was preventing the constitution operating as it should, on the whole accepted the Revolutionary settlement. The radicals of the 1760s moved steadily toward its rejection and therefore the need for a fundamental reform of the whole system of representation. As Jack Pole has written, it is "in their attitudes to English history" that the moderate reformers are to be distinguished from the radicals.[8]

In the middle of the eighteenth century, John Brewer reminds us, "a patriot was one who affirmed the ideology of England's Glorious Revolution ... His political purpose was to preserve the constitutional balance of mixed government that was said to have been achieved in 1688 which every politician ought selflessly to pursue." "Nearly everyone" he adds, "agreed the Revolution of 1688 had seen the embodiment of the true principle of the constitution."[9] "*Nearly* everyone" – but there were exceptions and Macaulay was one of them. If Gerald Straka's claim that "not until 1832 was the radical mind to be thoroughly disillusioned with the Revolution principles" has any validity, the roots of that disillusionment lie back in the sixties of the previous century.[10]

Macaulay's criticisms of the "Glorious Revolution" extend over a period of twenty years, from 1770 to 1790. Both the first and the last of her writings on the subject were provoked by Edmund Burke; the first, her *Observations on a Pamphlet entitled, Thoughts on the Cause of the Present Discontents of 1770*, the last her response to his *Reflections on the Revolution in France* of 1790. In between, in two volumes of history, she returns to the theme; in 1778 in the first – and only completed – volume of her *History of England from the Revolution to the Present Time in a Series of Letters to a Friend*, and in 1783 in the final volume of her *History of England from the Accession of James I to that of the Brunswick Line*.[11] Over this period her basic criticisms of the Revolution remain much the same but her emphasis changes in response to con-

---

[8] J. R. Pole, *Political Representation in England and the Origins of the American Republic* (1966), p. 427.

[9] John Brewer, *Party Ideology and Popular Politics at the Accession of George III* (Cambridge, 1976), pp. 98, 261–62.

[10] Gerald M. Straka, "Sixteen Eighty-eight as the Year One: Eighteenth-Century Attitudes towards the Glorious Revolution," *Studies in Eighteenth-Century Culture* 1 (1971): 143–67, this passage p. 164.

[11] Catharine Macaulay, *Observations on a Pamphlet entitled Thoughts on the Cause of the Present Discontents* (1770); *Observations on the Reflections of the Rt. Hon. Edmund Burke on the Revolution in France* (1790); *History of England from the Revolution*; and *History of England from the Accession of James I to that of the Brunswick Line*, 8 vols. (1763–83).

temporary events and her immediate political concerns. This essay looks at how her reinterpretation of the Revolution influenced English radical ideas in the 1760s and 1770s, effectively providing a theoretical basis for the demands of the Wilkites and members of the Society of the Supporters of the Bill of Rights; how her interpretation also contributed toward the rationale for the final severance of all ties of loyalty between the American colonists and the mother country, and thereby propelled America toward war and independence. And finally, after the outbreak of the French Revolution, how her ideas played a role not merely in answering Burke's claim that unlike 1688–89 the Revolution in France was unjustified and unnecessary, but in combating the counter-revolutionary influences in France of David Hume's history.

Macaulay's answer to Burke's *Thoughts on the Cause of the Present Discontents* (1770) came when the Wilkite campaign was at its peak. The campaign highlighted what was wrong with political life and the constitution inherited from the Glorious Revolution, and raised again the question of where exactly sovereignty lay. For a brief period the campaign united the opposition, temporarily disguising the fundamental disagreement between City Radicals and the Rockingham Whigs not only as to the solution of the problems confronting the country – the use of petitions to the king for example, and the comprehensiveness of the attack on government policies – but also the analysis of the roots of those problems, and in particular the attitude to the Revolution of 1688–89. Feeling that the leadership of the opposition was being wrested from their control, the Rockingham Whigs were in need of a propagandist and publicist who would argue convincingly against the City Radicals. They wanted to resume leadership of the opposition but above all, as Macaulay saw, they yearned to be in power. Their only grievance, she wrote, was "the loss of their power," their concern "to guard against the possible consequences of an effectual reformation in the vitiated parts of our constitution and government."[12] The choice of spokesman for the Rockingham Whigs was Edmund Burke.

From her first criticism in May 1770, interpretations of the Revolution are viewed as of immediate relevance to contemporary politics. She recognized that with its "great eloquence, acuteness, and art," Burke's pamphlet was persuasive but it carried within it "a

[12] Macaulay, *Observations on a Pamphlet*, pp. 13, 6.

poison sufficient to destroy all the little virtue and understanding of sound policy which is left in the nation." It was important that the "causes of political evils" be "traced up to their sources." What were seen as the "offences" of George III and the "grievances attending his government" were, she wrote, but "the fruits of seeds sown by his ancestors." The Revolution Settlement had been fatally flawed from the start. It had opened the door for "private interest to exclude public good," and allowed the growth of the "undermining and irresistible hydra, court influence, in the room of the more terrifying, yet less formidable monster, prerogative." "A system of corruption" had begun at the Revolution, had grown and had "been the policy of every succeeding administration." In consequence, she argued, "parliaments, the great barriers of our much boasted constitution, while they preserved its forms, annihilated its spirit; and from a countrouling power over the executive parts of government" had become "a mere instrument of regal administration." Among the evils consequent on the Revolution she listed "the destructive grievance of a debt of one hundred and forty millions," "a strong military standing force, contrary to the very existence of real liberty; an army of placemen and pensioners," "septennial parliaments, in violation of the firmest principle in the constitution," and "heavy taxes imposed for the single advantage and emolument of individuals, a grievance" she added, "never submitted to by any people, not essentially enslaved."[13]

Already there is in her pamphlet the bare outlines of the policy of parliamentary reform later to be adopted by Wilkites: "a more extended and equal power of election, a very important spring in the machinery of political liberty," joined to the traditional Country party demands for more frequent elections ("if triennial parliaments will not serve the turn, change the half, or the whole of your parliament yearly"), increased representation of the counties, a Place Bill, and the application of the principle of rotation.[14] In 1783 she was to advocate "a revival of the statute of Edward III for annual parliaments" and, to prevent further "the abuses of corruption," vote by ballot.[15] Burke had rejected more frequent parliaments "on the shallow pretence of the horrible disorders attending frequent elections, and the committing every three years the Independent gentlemen of the counties into a contest with the treasury." Burke

---

[13] *Ibid.*, pp. 6–7, 9–11.   [14] *Ibid.*, pp. 17–19.
[15] Macaulay, *History of England from the Accession*, 8: 330.

was against the principle of rotation, and thought a Place Bill "would set the executive power at variance with the legislative" and undermine "our excellent constitution." The people, Burke held, were "not to be trusted with any additional ... powers" and he gave no consideration to any reform of the system of parliamentary representation.[16]

By the 1760s, quite apart from Macaulay, there were many – mainly Real Whigs – who saw little difference between Stuarts and Hanoverians. In 1767, Sylas Neville recorded in his diary how "the House of Hanover are now the same to Mr. Hollis [Timothy Hollis] as the House of Stuart, and he agrees with me that they are rather worse, as they spend more of our money, and that this George is of as arbitrary principles as those of the House of Stuart."[17] Two years later Junius sent a letter to the printer of the *Public Advertiser*, the printing of which caused him to be prosecuted for seditious libel. Addressed to the king, the letter concluded:

The people of England are loyal to the House of Hanover, not from a vain preference of one family to another, but from a conviction that the establishment of that family was necessary to the support of their civil and religious liberties. This, Sir, is a principle of allegiance equally solid and rational; – fit for Englishmen to adopt, and well worthy of your Majesty's encouragement. We cannot long be deluded by nominal distinctions. The name of Stuart, of itself, is only contemptible; – armed with the Sovereign authority, their principles are formidable. The Prince, who imitates their conduct, should be warned by their example; and, while he plumes himself upon the security of his title to the crown should remember that, as it was acquired by one revolution it may be lost by another.[18]

As early as 1768 Thomas Hollis feared that "the cause of the Revolution and Whiggism" were "now everywhere ruining." "To my sense," he was to add, "all things here tend worse and worse, and to confusion."[19]

It was not perhaps entirely coincidental that in July 1769, not long before Macaulay's answer to Burke was published, the Society of the Supporters of the Bill of Rights was formed. But if its name was derived from the Bill of 1689 its intentions went far beyond it. Its

---

[16] Macaulay, *Observations on a Pamphlet*, pp. 15–16, 18.
[17] *The Diary of Sylas Neville 1767–1788*, ed. Basil Cozens-Hardy (1950), p. 23.
[18] *Letters of Junius*, ed. John Cannon (Oxford, 1978), p. 173.
[19] Caroline Robbins, quoting the unpublished diary in "The Strenuous Whig: Thomas Hollis of Lincoln's Fields," *William and Mary Quarterly* 7 (1950): 406–53, this passage p. 410; see also *Memoirs of Thomas Hollis*, ed. Francis Blackburne, 2 vols. (1780), 1: 428.

founder, John Horne Tooke, was "warmly attached to the constitution" and "burned with impatience to support its tottering fabric." He had been brought up "in the principles so warmly advocated by the Whigs, at the time of the Revolution." But those ideas had been "fortified," we are told, "by an acquaintance with the history of the ancient commonwealth, and seconded by an ardent temperament."[20] It was almost certainly Horne Tooke who in July 1771 drew up the instructions "intended to be presented by way of *test*" to all parliamentary candidates. They were required to pledge themselves to work for the shortening of parliaments, the exclusion of placemen and pensioners from parliament, and "a full and equal representation of the people."[21] When later Horne Tooke and a number of members of the Society seceded to form the Constitutional Society, they immediately adopted a program of parliamentary reform. Wilkes and those who remained in the Society of the Supporters of the Bill of Rights followed suit in June 1771. A leading member of the Society was John Sawbridge, Macaulay's brother, who from 1771 to 1786 persevered in his efforts to shorten the duration of parliaments by introducing thirteen motions to bring in a bill for the purpose. It was he more than any other individual who kept alive the issue of shorter parliaments. There were others who were to carry forward the programme of radical parliamentary reform. In 1771 Obadiah Hulme outlined what needed doing "to establish the constitution...upon its old foundations." He listed annual parliaments, vote by ballot and more efficiently run elections, the abolition of rotten boroughs and giving the vote in boroughs to "every resident inhabitant, that pays his shot and bears his lot."[22] Five years later, Major John Cartwright outlined the six points of the programme later adopted by the Chartists.[23]

In the two volumes of history in which she discusses the Glorious Revolution, Macaulay relates the events of 1688–89 in some detail. Critical though she was of the Revolution Settlement she recognized it embodied new and important principles. It had given "a different aspect to the constitution" from that of the Tudors and Stuarts. "Hereditary indefeasible right" had once and for all been renounced. "The Crown was no longer regarded as private property, nor the

[20] Alexander Stephens, *Memoirs of John Horne Tooke*, 2 vols. (1813), 1: 54–55.
[21] *Ibid.*, 1: 165.
[22] Obadiah Hulme, *An Historical Essay on the Constitution* (1771), pp. 151, 153.
[23] John Cartwright, *Take Your Choice* (1775).

right of one family to govern, except by a few political bigots,
respected as sacred and unalienable." "The power of the Crown,"
she wrote in 1778, "was acknowledged to flow from no other fountain
than that of a contract with the people; and allegiance and protection
were declared reciprocal terms." "Instead of being treated as beasts
of burden, and live stock on a farm, transferable from father to son,"
the people "were now looked up to as the only legal source of
sovereign authority." It was precisely because the establishment of
such principles presented "this fair opportunity to cut off all the
prerogatives of the Crown, to which they had justly imputed the
calamities and injuries sustained by the nation, and which had ever
prevented the democratical principles of the constitution from acting
to the security of those liberties and privileges vainly set forth in the
letter of the law" that she was so critical of the Convention
parliament. She recognized that those members "most active in
indulging the wishes of William, in regard to an undivided
sovereignty and undiminished prerogatives" had hoped by winning
his gratitude to earn "all those advantages which they had for the
present sacrificed to the exigence of the occasion, or rather to the
earnest desire of shutting every door of hope to the restoration of the
exiled family."[24] But their estimation of William's character had
proved mistaken.

Macaulay emphasized that in the Declaration of Rights of 1689
later embraced by the Bill of Rights, "there was no one article...
which had not been recognized by former princes." "If the alteration
of the succession deprived the sovereign of that reverence, which
ignorance in all ages hath paid to the hereditary line," she argued,
"the influence arising from the disposal of an immense revenue had
... given more permanence and extension to the power of the Crown
than hereditary princes had derived from the notion of unalienable,
indefeasible right." She claimed that William "by profuse and
extensive bribery... obtained from the Commons what Charles the
Second could never obtain from the wickedest parliament with which
England had ever been cursed, namely, a standing army, and a
landed [sic] debt." Her considered view of the Declaration was that
while "some resolutions... confined merely to the flagrant violations
which had been made in the constitution" were "digested into... the
Declaration of Rights," it had omitted "any of those enlargements of

[24] Macaulay, *History of England from the Revolution*, pp. 3–4, and Macaulay, *History of England from the Accession*, 8: 331.

popular privileges, or limitations of power, which might have prevented future abuse." She observed that William "twice refused his assent to a bill for triennial parliaments and never would give his consent to an act for limiting the number of placemen and pensioners." The Whigs "in the very zenith of their power" had retained so great "a respect for the principles of the Tories as to strike off that part of the Declaration ... which, in default of the princess of Denmark's issue, put the nomination of the successor in the hands of parliament; and in default of such nomination in the house of the prince of Orange."[25] Significantly the Declaration made no mention of an original contract.

The Settlement, she claimed, had left far too much power in the hands of the king. The problem with changing the succession was that the "authors of such a Revolution," through "dread of pains and penalties attendant on a Restoration," were led "to concur in strengthening the power of the reigning sovereign, though at the expense of that constitutional freedom they had run the hazard of their lives and fortunes to obtain." The king retained extensive prerogative. "He was left at liberty to convoke, adjourn, or dissolve" parliaments "at his pleasure." He could "influence elections, and oppress corporations"; he possessed "the right of chusing his own council, of nominating all the great officers of the state, the household, the army, the navy and the church." He had "absolute power over the militia" and "so totally void of any improvement was the Revolution system, that the reliques of the star chamber was retained in the office of the Attorney-General, who in the case of libels" could "lodge a vexatious and even a false information, without being subjected to the penalty of cost or damage." It was "the fear of being left in the lurch by their deliverer," she was to add in 1783, that persuaded the Whigs "to give way to the settlement of the Crown, without adding any new trophies to the altar of liberty, or even of renovating those sound principles in the constitution, which, in the length of time, had fallen a sacrifice to the lusts and the opportunities of power."[26]

Unlike the great majority of the political nation – and most Whigs – she asserted the continuity of events in 1688–89 with those of the

[25] Macaulay, *History of England from the Revolution*, pp. 72–73, 76–77, and Macaulay, *History of England from the Accession*, 8: 312–13.

[26] Macaulay, *History of England from the Revolution*, pp. 5–6, and Macaulay, *History of England from the Accession*, 8: 329.

1640s. Robert Zaller has made the point that she and other Wilkite radicals "had to debunk the received interpretation of the Glorious Revolution before they could challenge the system created on it; they had to overcome 1688 before they could recover 1640."[27] Concerned that never again should there be a repeat of the events of the 1640s, "a misinformed and selfish nobility," she wrote in 1770, "viewed any extension of popular powers ... with a jealous eye." "To diminish the force of new acquired privileges" the power of "the reigning prince was to be strengthened by every diabolical engine which the subtle head and corrupt heart of a statesman could invent." Her most savage condemnation was for "this state faction, who called themselves whigs, but who were in reality as much the destructive, though concealed enemies of public liberty, as were its more generous, because more avowed, antagonists the tories."[28] For the Whigs 1688–89 had been a missed opportunity. Anxious to distance herself and other Whigs sharing her views from such Whiggism she quoted Davenant's character of a modern Whig:

What have we in us that resemble the old whigs? They hated arbitrary government; we have been all along for a standing army: they desired triennial parliaments, and that trials for treason might be better regulated; and it is notorious, that we opposed both these bills; they were for calling corrupt ministers to an account; we have ever countenanced and protected corruption to the utmost of our power: they were frugal for the nation, and careful how they loaded the people with taxes; we have squandered away their money, as if there could be no end of England's treasure.

Had such modern Whigs not "abandoned all their old principles," she wrote, "they might have formed us a lasting establishment." In her opinion the transformation of such Whigs was the most damning aspect of the Revolution. No advantages gained were worth "the subversion of all principle in a body of men, whose virtue and resolution had more than once saved the constitution against the combined powers of church and state."[29]

If in her early writings her references to the ancient constitution are few as compared with other writers, it was not that she did not adhere to the idea of a continuous struggle to restore the lost liberties of Anglo-Saxon times. Like many others she saw proposed amend-

[27] Zaller, "Continuity," p. 35.
[28] Macaulay, *Observations on a Pamphlet*, pp. 11, 12 and *History of England from the Revolution*, p. 11.   [29] *Ibid.*, pp. 74–75, 33.

ments of the constitution not as reformation but restoration. She criticized the Revolution Settlement for being "neither agreeable to the regularity of the Saxon constitution which effectively secured every privilege it bestowed nor did it admit of any of those refinements and improvements, which the experience of mankind had enabled them to make in the science of political security."[30] Contrary to Burke's and others' insistence that with the constitution under William III the equivalent of the ancient constitution had been restored, she argued that "the new system introduced by William" had made "fatal encroachments... in the ancient constitution of England" establishing "an unexampled mode of tyranny" and "a universal depravity of manners."[31]

It would be wrong to suggest that Macaulay was alone – or even the first – among historians in her criticism of the "Glorious Revolution." When Clarendon's *History of the Rebellion* was published by his son in 1702–04 in an undisguised attempt to "support Tory historical orthodoxy," it was "denounced by the Whigs as partisan, Tory history."[32] It provoked a number of partisan Whig replies. One of these was by Gilbert Burnet (1643–1715), Bishop of Salisbury; his *History of His Own Time*, which appeared between 1724 and 1734, was, like Clarendon's history, published by his son. Confidant and adviser of the Prince of Orange immediately before the Revolution, and at the same time closely involved with the revolution party in England, Burnet was with William when he landed at Torbay and played a leading role in the Revolution. Macaulay described him as "deeply engaged in the plots which were carrying on in favor of a revolution."[33] It might be expected his account would be prejudiced. In so far as the actual Revolution and the immediate aftermath is concerned – the period in which his involvement was greatest – this is so. Burnet was reluctant to criticize William, whose "Designs were always great and good." If mistakes were made by him "his heroical courage set things right." For all his errors "he ought still to be reckoned among the greatest Princes that our History, or indeed that of any other, can afford." He was sympathetic to William's dislike of "*those*, who expressed much zeal for him, but who seemed at the same time, to have with it a great mixture of Republican principles." Burnet was not uncritical of the course subsequently taken by the

---

[30] *Ibid.*, p. 5.   [31] Macaulay, *History of England from the Accession*, 8: 334.
[32] Roger Richardson, *The Debate on the English Revolution* (1988), pp. 36, 37.
[33] Macaulay, *History of England from the Accession*, 8: 204.

Revolution. He recognized that corruption "was so generally spread, that it was believed every thing was carried by that method" and when the Triennial Act was passed in 1694 hoped that the "Constitution, in particular that part of it which related to the House of Commons, would again recover its strength and reputation ... now very much sunk." The trouble as he saw it was that the country had "fallen insensibly into a Democracy" but "had not learned the virtues that are necessary for that sort of government."[34]

Macaulay in her *History of England from the Accession* relied on Burnet's work and frequently referred to it, but it was more from want of anything else than agreement with his views. The historian John Oldmixon (1673–1742) in the volume of his history published in 1739 made clear that he wrote in direct response to Clarendon's work and his desire to "set the facts of history in a truer light" (*DNB*). "The Party, Enemies to the Revolution, and to the Governments founded upon it" had produced Clarendon's work, he wrote, "when the Nation was pretty well reconcil'd to the Principles of the Revolution ... and the Doctrine of Passive Obedience and Non-Resistance was become so much a Jest, that it was hardly nam'd but in ridicule." He argued that all the Stuarts "from the Accession of the *First* King *James* ... to the *Abdication* of the *Second*" were alike in their attempts "to subvert the Constitution, and subject this Kingdom to Arbitrary Power, Ecclesiastical and Civil." A committed Whig, he dedicated his history to "all true Englishmen, lovers of our present happy constitution."[35] The Anglicised American and friend of Benjamin Franklin, James Ralph (1705?–1762), in his *History of England during the Reigns of King William, Queen Anne, and King George I*, published in 1744, went much further, concluding that the "national Effort which had been made in concert with the Prince of Orange for the glorious Purpose of rendering the Constitution immortal, seem'd to have worn out every Principle of Strength, Vigour and Virtue, which should have given it the requisite Solidity."[36]

If Macaulay was not the first historian to criticize the "Glorious Revolution," it was still sufficiently uncommon to be a daunting prospect. "To contradict the opinion of his countrymen on this

[34] Gilbert Burnet, *History of His Own Time*, 2 vols., (1724, 1734), 2: 4, 133, 247, 304, 306.

[35] John Oldmixon, *The History of England during the Reigns of the Royal House of Stuart* (1730), pp. iii, vii, 781.

[36] James Ralph, *A History of England during the Reigns of King William, Queen Anne, and King George I*, 2 vols. (1744, 1746), 2: 1024.

important subject," she wrote in 1783, a historian must possess "the enthusiasm of a martyr."[37] Her criticism was regarded at best as a curious quirk. In 1770 the *Political Register* wrote that she "attacks the principles and system of government of the revolution, in so strange and unaccountable a manner that her best friends are astonished at it." Surrounded by those who were effusive in their praises, as John Cannon suggests, reformers were made to appear as those who "stubbornly and wilfully refused to count their blessings."[38] Macaulay's criticisms of William expounded at length in her volumes of 1778 and 1783 succeeded in antagonizing many of her contemporaries – even those she had regarded as her friends. She was seen as betraying the Whig cause. John Wilkes, no longer the radical leader he had been earlier, had a preview of her 1778 history. To his daughter Polly he wrote "I find she has attacked the memory of King William with much acrimony, which will please all the tory wretches of the kingdom. Even Shebbeare and Johnson will quote Mrs. Macaulay against King William."[39] When she returned from France in 1778 she had sent a copy of her *History of England in a Series of Letters to a Friend* to Lord Harcourt, who had been responsible for giving her introductions to many of those she met in Paris. He had just conveyed to her the intention of his friend the Duc de Harcourt (no relation) to translate her *History of England from the Accession* into French. She must have anticipated that her depiction of William might not please his Lordship for she wrote anxiously to him, "I hope you are not 'disgusted' with the freedom I have taken with William our great deliverer as he is called." But he may well have been so "disgusted" for the proposal to translate her *History of England from the Accession* into French did not materialize. She insisted that her views were in no way different from those she had expressed earlier. She found it impossible, she wrote to him, "to treat with approbation" a character who had laid "the foundation of our ruin by a funded debt, and by the act of reducing corruption into a system."[40]

While Macaulay was answering Burke in 1770, relations with the American colonies were rapidly deteriorating to the point where war became unavoidable. In the final volume of her *History of England from*

---

[37] Macaulay, *History of England from the Accession*, 8: 329.
[38] *Political Register*, I (1770), p. 363, cited Brewer, *Party Ideology*, p. 261.
[39] *Letters from the year 1774 to the year 1796 of John Wilkes Esq. addressed to his daughter, the late Miss Wilkes*, 4 vols. (1804), 2: 55.
[40] *The Harcourt Papers*, ed. E. W. Harcourt, 14 vols. (Oxford, 1876–1905), 8: 110.

the Accession, Macaulay referred to "the unhappy catastrophe of the American war" which had "so greatly accelerated the downfall of this empire as to bring on…that ruin which we vainly hoped to escape at the expense of our posterity."[41] During the eighteenth century, and increasingly as the crisis in relations between colonists and the mother country deepened, Americans looked back to the history and writings of seventeenth-century England for guidance. The colonists identified their present problems with those of the earlier period. We know that Macaulay's *History of England from the Accession* was familiar to them. The year 1770, when she first expressed her views on the Revolution of 1688, coincided with a period when there was a remarkable interchange of pamphlets and other writing between English radicals and the colonists. Her views on 1688 must have been well known in America – at least in New England. At first the attitude of the colonists to the "Glorious Revolution" had differed little from that of English Whigs. It was "undoubtedly the most desirable and complete form [of government] that the good fortune of man has hitherto produced or their wit been capable of contriving." It was on the basis of the lack of "tumults and disorder" in 1688 that many of the leaders among the colonists pressed for restraint and the use of "proper and legal measures to obtain redress."[42] The main lesson drawn from the Revolution of 1688–89 was the right of resistance in defense of liberties. As early as 1750 Jonathan Mayhew's sermon "Discourse on Unlimited Submission" was written "to counteract those who make Charles I a martyr, forgetting the right of the people to deal severely with Kings who violate their trust."[43] In general the right to resist was seen as one that should only be used in the last resort after everything else had failed. It was a view that coincided with that of Macaulay in her answer to Burke in 1790, when she wrote that "the right of cashiering or deposing monarchs for misgovernment…ought never to be exercised by a people who are satisfied with their form of government and have spirit enough to correct its abuses."[44] In 1767 the possibility of an American Bill of Rights parallel to that of 1689 in England was discussed. When the *Boston Gazette* decided to reprint the English Bill of Rights, the Governor considered it seditious.[45]

---

[41] Macaulay, *History of England from the Accession*, 8: 337.
[42] As quoted by Pauline Maier, *From Resistance to Revolution* (Cambridge, Mass., 1973), pp. 29, 123.   [43] Cited *ibid.*, pp. 31–32.
[44] Macaulay, *Observations on the Reflections*, p. 18.   [45] Maier, *Resistance*, p. 229.

As criticism of the administration increased it was directed at George III's ministers not at the king himself. "Was not George III of the 'Illustrious House of Hanover' which owed its right to rule to the Glorious Revolution of 1688?"[46] Much earlier when James II appointed Sir Edmund Andros as Governor in Massachusetts and the appointment was followed by what the population regarded as a violation of "the religious susceptibilities of the majority of New Englanders," the New Englanders revolted. Andros had taxed them without their consent and called in their land titles. The leaders later identified their revolt with that of the English in 1688–89. As Edward Rawson claimed, "No man does really approve of the *Revolution in England*, but must justifie that in *New England* also."[47] Such close identification of the grievances of the colonists with those of the English people grew stronger during the 1760s. Samuel Adams in his response to the Stamp Act in 1765, for example, argued that "if the whole People of the [British] Nation had thought their inalienable Rights" had been invaded by an Act of Parliament as the Americans thought the Stamp Act had done, "in such a case, after taking all *legal* Steps to obtain redress *to no Purpose*" they "would have taken the same steps and *justify'd themselves*."[48] In the course of the 1770s the distinction between Hanoverians and Stuarts became blurred and ultimately disappeared. George III was increasingly likened to Charles I. Behind this change there lay a discarding of earlier attitudes to the Revolution of 1688. If the Revolution had limited the power of the king he still retained too much. Such a view had led English radicals to adopt a policy of fundamental reform of the whole system of parliamentary representation. It led the colonists finally to reject the Revolution of 1688 as a model.

More than to any other historian before her it was as a response to David Hume that Macaulay's *History of England from the Accession* was seen. At first the Whigs welcomed her *History* as a timely "Whig" answer to what, rightly or wrongly, was interpreted as Hume's Tory *History*. Unlike Macaulay, Hume was at pains to separate the Revolution of 1688 from the events of the 1640s and earlier. He saw no continuity between the two, and if the events of 1688 could be justified, this did not imply any justification for the earlier action of the Commons against the first two Stuarts. Such a view involved

---

[46] Cited *ibid.*, p. 103.
[47] J. R. Pole, *The Gift of Government* (Athens, Georgia, 1983), pp. 6, 9, 14.
[48] Maier, *Resistance*, p. 65.

rejecting as unhistorical any idea that the administration under the Stuarts represented "one continued encroachment on the *incontestable* rights of the people" and to fail to give "due honour to that great event which not only put a period to their hereditary succession, but made a new settlement of the whole constitution." The Glorious Revolution, he wrote, "forms a new epoch in the constitution; and was attended with consequences much more advantageous to the people than the barely freeing them from a bad administration." It had given "such an ascendant to popular principles" as had "put the nature of the English constitution beyond all controversy." "We all in this island," he claimed, "have ever since enjoyed, if not the best system of government, at least the most entire system of liberty, that ever was known amongst mankind." Of William, he wrote that it would "be difficult to find any person whose actions and conduct contributed more eminently to the general interests of society and mankind."[49] As Macaulay was to comment "Mr. Hume...is assiduously careful not to offend in any point of popular recommendation."[50]

Hume could not accept the notion that James II had broken any original contract any more than that "Charles I had set out to destroy established liberty."[51] James's mistake had been to ignore the lessons of the 1640s and 1650s. It was necessary that obedience be paid to government, Hume argued, "because society could not otherwise subsist."[52] "Authority and stability," he claimed, "were more important than liberty because they guaranteed the existence of civil society."[53] When it was claimed that "all lawful government arises from the consent of the people," Hume wrote, "we certainly do them a great deal more honour than they deserve, or even expect and desire from us." Locke's doctrine of the "original contract" was "erroneous" because it led into opinions "so wide of the general practice of mankind."[54] With those who ventured criticism of the Revolution settlement Hume had little patience. "What a reproach must we become among nations, if disgusted with a settlement so deliberately made, and whose conditions have been so religiously

---

[49] David Hume, *History of Great Britain*, 2 vols. (1754, 1757), 2: 421, 443.
[50] Macaulay, *History of England from the Accession*, 8: 329.
[51] Victor G. Wexler, *David Hume and the History of England* (Philadelphia, 1979), p. 41.
[52] David Hume, "Of the Original Contract," in *Essays Moral, Political and Literary* (1905), p. 468.   [53] Wexler, *David Hume*, p. 43.
[54] Hume, "Of the Original Contract," *Essays*, p. 473.

observed, we should throw every thing again into confusion, and by our levity and rebellious disposition, prove ourselves totally unfit for any state but that of absolute slavery and subjection."[55] How sweet such words must have sounded to conservative ears in France.

In pre-Revolutionary France, as Laurence Bongie has argued, Hume's influence was far greater than that of Burke. Indeed he claims "Burke's cranky pamphlet... caused more amusement than concern among those it was meant to annihilate."[56] Burke was not primarily concerned with the Revolution in France but with "the danger of the infection spreading from France to England."[57] But long before the Revolution, Hume's *History* was familiar to many in France and much more than Burke's *Reflections* became "the manifesto of a counter-revolution."[58] So it was that, in something akin to the role it played in the 1760s, Macaulay's *History* was seen as a response to Hume's counter-revolutionary message. Although already familiar to men like Mirabeau and Brissot as well as many other Frenchmen, it was not to appear in translation until 1791/2 but the debate in 1790 between Brissot de Warville and Clermont-Tonnerre makes clear that it "had begun to play an equally important role in countering its [Hume's *History*'s] conservative effect."[59] Indeed it was to play a part in the whole revolutionary debate. Just as in America in the 1760s and 1770s, events in France were seen as running parallel to those in England in the previous century. But in the lessons to be learned from the seventeenth century in England, the French, unlike Hume, did not separate events of the 1640s from those of 1660 and 1688. They saw their own Revolution going through near identical stages. But during the 1790s if it was not primarily the Revolution of 1688 on which they concentrated, it was because they had not as yet reached that stage. In 1801 the parallels between the revolutions were still being drawn: "The long parliament and the death of Charles I; the convention and the death of Louis XVI; then Cromwell and Bonaparte." Looking ahead, Antoine Rivarol asked, "if there is a restoration, will we have another Charles II dying in his bed and another James II leaving his

[55] Hume, "Of the Protestant Succession," *ibid.*, p. 498.
[56] Laurence L. Bongie, *David Hume* (Oxford, 1965), p. 78.
[57] Conor Cruise O'Brien, Introduction to Edmund Burke, *Reflections on the Revolution in France* (Harmondsworth, 1982), p. 17.
[58] James Mackintosh, *Vindiciae Gallicae* 4th ed. (1792), p. xi.
[59] Bongie, *David Hume*, p. 113.

kingdom, and then a foreign dynasty?" He was to add "it is just as likely as this conjecture."[60]

Macaulay's last comments on the Glorious Revolution came in her answer to Burke in 1790. Burke's *Reflections* were provoked by Richard Price's message of congratulations to the National Assembly on behalf of the Revolution Society and to Price's claim, in his sermon of 4 November 1789 on the anniversary of the "Glorious Revolution," that the "King of Great Britain owes his right to the Crown by the choice of the people." Price had claimed that "by the principles of the Revolution the people of England" had the right "to choose their own governors," "to cashier them for misconduct" and "to frame a government for ourselves." The sermon raised again the issue of popular sovereignty that had long been lurking behind the debate on the Revolution of 1688. Just how closely identified government by popular consent was with the events of the 1640s is revealed by Burke's accusation that the Revolution Society in their claim were not thinking of the Revolution of 1688 but of "a revolution that happened in England about forty years before, and the late French revolution." Any comparisons of the French Revolution with that of 1688, he held, were false. No mention of the rights claimed by the Revolution Society had been made in the "wise, sober, and considerate" Declaration of Rights which, Burke held, was "the cornerstone of our constitution, as reinforced, explained, improved, and in its fundamental principles for ever settled." The makers of the Revolution had been concerned to make it "a parent of settlement, and not a nursery of future revolutions." They therefore had sought to make it "almost impracticable for any future sovereign to compel the states of the kingdom to have again recourse to those violent remedies." It had been a revolution to end revolutions. William's accession to the throne was not the result of any choice, Burke argued, but "an act of *necessity*."[61] So little convinced of that necessity were the "English nation at large," Macaulay retorted, that "without the prince of Orange, and the assistance of his Dutch army, there could have been no Revolution" and no deposing of James. "The liberty that was taken in the year 1688 ... to depose king James ... and to vest the sovereignty of the

---

[60] "Le long parlement et la mort de Charles 1er; la convention et la mort de Louis XVI; et puis Cromwel et puis Bonapart. ... s'il y a une restauration aurons-nous un autre Charles second mourant dans son lit et un autre Jacques second quittant son royaume, et puis une dynastie étrangère? ... c'est une idée tout comme une autre que cette prévision." Cited *ibid.*, p. 167.

[61] Burke, *Reflections*, pp. 99–100, 112–13, 102.

realm in his daughter Mary, and her husband the prince of Orange and the settlement of the succession that followed," she argued, "*might warrant a plain thinking man* in the opinion, that the present reigning family owe their succession to the choice or assent of the people."[62]

What distinguishes Macaulay's analysis of 1688–89 is that she not only recognized the importance of convincing people of her own time of the inadequacies of the Revolution, but saw that something much more fundamental than Place and Pension Bills was required if problems were to be solved. "Now that the feeling sense of our calamities has brought conviction home to the heart of every disinterested citizen," she wrote in 1783, it was "of the utmost importance" that people understood exactly what were "the defects of the Revolution." It was essential to avoid "throwing a veil over" them and thus to "mislead the judgment of the public." The "vulgar part of society" had been "taught to consider the protestant succession in the illustrious house of Hanover as an advantage adequate to all the blessings which flow from good government, and the enjoyment of a well regulated freedom." Such "delusion" must be ended.[63] What was needed was not only stronger means to combat corruption – annual parliaments, a system of rotation, instruction of representatives – but a fundamental reform of the whole system of representation involving not only a more equable distribution of seats, but an extension of the franchise and secret ballot.

---

[62] Macaulay, *Observations on the Reflections*, pp. 9–10.
[63] Macaulay, *History of England from the Accession*, 8: 337.

Index